Famous Italian Cities

Famous Italian Cities

Florence. Rome. Venice

Text by
Reinhard Bentmann and
Elisabeth Herget

translated by
J. Hendry

CHARTWELL BOOKS INC.

Frontispiece:
Venice: View from the Riva della Piazzetta
across the Bacino, the inner harbor-basin,
towards San Giorgio Maggiore. Outstanding
buildings in most other cities are grouped
together in solid squares, with parks, but in
Venice it is water shimmering in ever-changing
light that becomes part of the city scene, so
that islands, canals and buildings together
form an endless unity.

 Louise Nelson
PO Box 69355
Oro Valley, AZ 85737

First published in the United States by Chartwell Books, Inc., 1978
A division of Book Sales, Inc.
110 Enterprise Avenue, Secaucus, New Jersey 07094

ISBN 0 89009 217 6

Printed and bound in Italy by
Officine Grafiche di Arnoldo Mondadori Editore, Verona

Contents

Introduction

'In the beginning was the city'. Any general history of culture could well start off in this way, since the sources of traditional history, based on documentary evidence and excavations, have close links with the rise of city culture. 'City' means a marking-off from the 'country'; a division of labour and, eventually, manufactures and industrial production; specialisation in vital functions; organized trade; organized administration and defence; law as a binding force. It is synonymous, in a comprehensive, modern sense, with politics. To the peasant, livestock-breeder or hunter in antiquity the nearest line of hills, the nearest deep wood or marsh was unattainable and unconquerable, a 'pathless unknown'. To the townsman of early times, however, his 'locale' was the starting-point for other town-like locales, which he tried to reach by caravan or by water.

The basics of city-building lead us us back beyond 5000 B.C. to Ancient China, India (the Indus Valley cultures), Egypt and the Near East. The oldest of such settlements that can be dated, in the area that concerns us, the Mediterranean, are Jericho (9000 B.C.) and Damascus. These still exist to-day.

It was the politics of the city-state that took first place when the national and cultural body-politic, in our sense, was coming into being. Our word 'politics' derives from the word for city, *polis*.

This fact becomes particularly clear in the ancient Mediterranean cultures, Italy above all, which developed from the nucleus of one single city—Rome.

The idea of the city-state assumed concrete form, of global significance, on three occasions in European history: in Ancient Greece, Ancient Rome, and the Italy of the Late Middle Ages and Renaissance. The modern era begins with the transition from the Late Middle Ages to Early Renaissance. 'Modern' implies a specific rationalistic early bourgeois consciousness. That turning-point in history is therefore inconceivable in the absence of an urban way of life, which in Italy became concentrated within the focal area of our triad of cities. Florence, Rome and Venice eclipsed in splendour the peninsula's remaining metropolitan centres and in cultural and political matters, as well as in historical durability, put even such places as Milan, Bologna, Naples and Genoa in the shade.

'Town air makes you free' was a popular saying in the Middle Ages. It was unquestionably the shape that urban society, economy and culture took which provided the basis for any and every form of spiritual and political emancipation. Florence, Rome and Venice are the living proof. The peculiar feature of these three centres was the political, economic and cultural climate characterising them, at times equally, in the areas of freedom, progressive outlook, and intensity of purpose. At the same time the *genius loci* which was non-interchangeable, the political and cultural milieu, differentiated all three cities with equal sharpness as individual personalities, just as happened in Greece, permeated by the idea of the *polis,* in the case of Athens, Sparta, Corinth, Miletus and Ephesus. Jacob Burckhardt has defined the Italian Renaissance as the 'discovery [actually re-discovery] of the world and of Man' and a cultural process therefore with which only the Enlightenment in France and Germany, that pre-revolutionary phase prior to 1789, can be compared.

6

The development of a national Italian style via a return to native sources, the native national or, so to speak, classical culture and history of antiquity, took place chiefly within the Florence, Rome and Venice triad. Thence the movement spread over the Alps to Northern and Western Europe as an accepted European style. This national style is illustrated to a greater extent in architecture, sculpture and painting than in the literature, philosophy and music of the time. All three cities constitute a visible illustration, a 'history book in pictures', of which this book, it is hoped, will provide a significant cross-section.

What differentiated these three cities, and what have they in common? That must be our basic query. Of all three, Florence looks most to the North, Venice to the East, and Rome to the South. For all its Mediterranean character, Florence seems most like home to the traveller from the North, comparable to Verona, on account of its many medieval features. Small wonder that Goethe failed to find 'his' Italy there.

Rome, geographical centre of the peninsula, stands for Southern and Mediterranean Italy. The Roman High Renaissance and Roman Baroque, the Mediterranean contribution to the modern cultural history of Europe, could not have occurred elsewhere in this shape and form. It is no accident that the message of Italian Baroque was carried to France (Paris, the Louvre and Versailles) by the 'most Roman' of all the artists of the period, Bernini, just as a century earlier the Italian Masters Primaticcio, Leonardo da Vinci and Serlio, as guests of François I, had conveyed the new art of the Renaissance to Fontainebleau.

Lastly Venice, as the geographical position of this 'amphibious' creation, between land and water, makes clear, for centuries remained almost completely cut off from the rest of Italy. It turned across the sea to the Adriatic coast opposite, to the Aegean, the Southern and Eastern Mediterranean, the Balkans and the Levant. Throughout the Middle Ages, and even in the fifteenth and early sixteenth centuries, places like Constantinople, Athens, Patras, Rhodes, Crete, Cyprus, Damascus, Alexandria and Cairo lay nearer for Venice than Rome, Florence or Genoa. In orientation, it was old Byzantium that Venice looked to, throughout both the early and mature phases of its history. Up until modern times the city also enjoyed a special 'East Roman' status in the matter of ecclesiastical policy, liturgy and religious art, with a Patriarch, and a rite recalling the Byzantine. The striking architectural grouping of St. Mark's and the free-standing Campanile resembles a large, multi-cupola mosque with its minaret, or a Greek or Russian church, rather than a West European religious structure. Equally, the different geographic setting helps to explain the Gothic interior of Florence cathedral, or the abundance of light and space inside St. Peter's in Rome.

Rome, with the Papal States in central Italy, is an example of a theocratic system, with priestly government and spiritual power, which was compelled to assume the form of political power in order to remain a 'power' at all.

Venice never knew kings or princes, nor a real nobility, and yet it had no real republican system of government either. Instead it had a social order which had been preserved for centuries and never altered: an oligarchy of a few families, qualified for the Senate, which in their turn produced the Doge; in other words, it was a dynastic system, 'by the backdoor'. In Venice economics invariably took precedence over politics, and capital over political theory. In that sense it was the most 'modern' of the three Italian cities with which we are concerned. As a commercial and maritime state, its place lay with Genoa and Pisa, among Italy's most important 'overseas' colonial forces. We might indeed assert that Florence is the *country,* always struggling for access to the sea. Rome is mountain, *river* and port, occupying a central position, with the hilly Papal States as hinterland: it nestles within a great loop of the Tiber, with a distant but easily reached seaport in the region of Ostia. But Venice is the *sea,* and as a city an assembly of 'stone ships', floating palaces and houseboats.

Florence

The history of Florence goes back to the very roots of Italian culture. Originally an important Etruscan town, the place was a flourishing seat even in Roman times, and called 'the Flourishing', *'Fiorentia',* Italianised to *Firenze.* Even to-day a glance at the city-plan will reveal the crossed streets of the old camp *(Castrum).* The centuries have chiselled away at the features of this most individual of Italian cities, along with Rome, Venice, Naples and Milan. Behind the modern industrious image with its elegant human types, swift in intelligence, its columns of cars and streams of tourists, its fashion industry and administrative complexes, there looms the stately face of the Renaissance city and the grave mien of the medieval *commune.* The soul of Florence still has a Northern European quality in many ways and yet is intermingled with the full resonance of Roman life. Thus arose the mixture which in his as yet vague and conventionalised picture of Italy at the beginning of his *Italian Journey* so irritated Goethe that he took leave of Florence after a few hours, on his sentimental excursion to 'his own' Arcadian Italy, which he hoped to find in Rome, with its ancient world of ruins, its artistic and political *Grandezza,* its multi faceted contours, its *Italianità* and 'Roman-ness'. Rome may be more serene, more Mediterranean and more monumental, while in Milan or Turin the pulse of Italian commerce beats faster and Venice is more fairy-like, more exotic, less sober; but to-day, just as in the eighteenth century when that Northern European movement in the

Page 8:

1 Florence: General view, showing the Arno and heart of the old city from the Piazzale Michelangelo. This glimpse of one of the most unforgettable city-scapes in the world takes in approximately the area covered by the Roman 'Florentia', beyond which medieval Florence scarcely expanded. From left to right the following landmarks can be seen: the Tower and battlements of the Palazzo Vecchio, by Arnolfo di Cambio, the marble-bright, tent-shaped roof of the San Giovanni Baptistery, the tower of the Bargello Palace (enclosed in scaffolding when the photo was taken) and, in between, the Campanile of the Santa Maria del Fiore Cathedral, built in 1334 with Giotto's co-operation; lastly, Brunelleschi's celebrated Dome (1434), the 'Roof of Florence' and the beginning of Early Renaissance architecture in Italy.

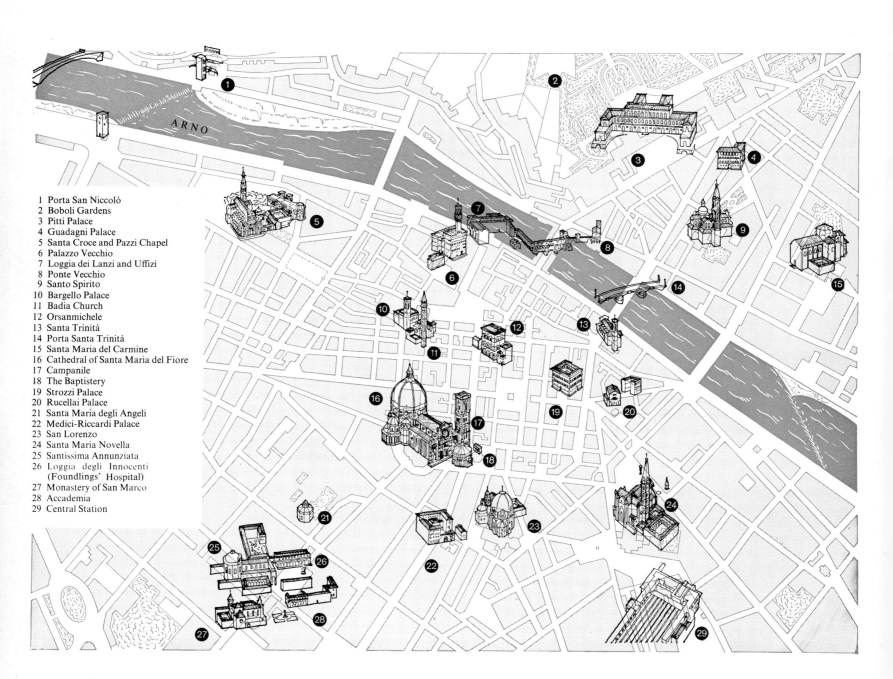

1 Porta San Niccolò
2 Boboli Gardens
3 Pitti Palace
4 Guadagni Palace
5 Santa Croce and Pazzi Chapel
6 Palazzo Vecchio
7 Loggia dei Lanzi and Uffizi
8 Ponte Vecchio
9 Santo Spirito
10 Bargello Palace
11 Badia Church
12 Orsanmichele
13 Santa Trinità
14 Porta Santa Trinità
15 Santa Maria del Carmine
16 Cathedral of Santa Maria del Fiore
17 Campanile
18 The Baptistery
19 Strozzi Palace
20 Rucellai Palace
21 Santa Maria degli Angeli
22 Medici-Riccardi Palace
23 San Lorenzo
24 Santa Maria Novella
25 Santissima Annunziata
26 Loggia degli Innocenti (Foundlings' Hospital)
27 Monastery of San Marco
28 Accademia
29 Central Station

direction of educational tours to Italy began which was to introduce Italian art and culture into England and Germany, Florence still remains one of the capitals in the world of educational tourism, particularly the English, German and Scandinavian varieties, and is the Alpha and Omega of most Italian art tours. A feeling of optimism comes over one on reading the history of the houses at the beginning and end of the venerable Ponte Vecchio (Plate 26) which, though they fit neatly into the overall picture, are immediately recognizable as post-war constructions. The 1944 German retreat before the Allies led through Florence on account of its key position in communications. To halt the rolling advance of U.S. armour, the German general was ordered by the High Command on August 3, 1944 to blow up all the Arno bridges. He hesitated, however, when it came to the Ponte Vecchio. Could one simply blow sky-high a monument of the stature of the Rialto Bridge in Venice, or the Angel Bridge in Rome? The earliest mention of which was in 1177, and which later, in 1570, had been provided by the great Vasari with a corridor connecting with the Uffizi and the Pitti Palace? The lesser evil was chosen. The houses at the bridgeheads were pulled down to form a tank obstacle. The bridge was saved, the houses soon rebuilt, and after the war, the city of Florence paid tribute to its German general with a detailed citation. Similar international concern and similar respect for the spirit of the city and its historical treasures was demonstrated by the world when, following the devastation due to the catastrophic flooding of 1963, money, technical equipment and qualified restorers were summoned from every country in the world in a wave of unparalleled solidarity, to assist in the campaign of salvage.

Let us take a look at the history of Florence.

Classical Antiquity and the Middle Ages

In 9 B.C. the first peasants, fishermen and traders of what is known as the Villanovan culture settled here on the banks of the Arno, the site of modern Florence. This fact has been confirmed by recent discoveries made in the Piazza della Repubblica. The area still had no name and was of no significance, since it stood in the shadow of a flourishing hill settlement in nearby Fiesole, which dates from 500 B.C. and has now been incorporated into the city.

The Roman conquest of Italy, which began in the third century B.C., soon reached the north, and Fiesole. To begin with the hill stronghold was left untouched. A camp was set up at the river-crossing and from there the fortified Etruscan town was eventually starved into surrender. Veterans of Caesar's wars, who had been granted the privilege of creating advance defensive towns by the Settlement Law of 59 B.C. (Gallia Cisalpina—northern Italy and parts of central Italy—was still regarded as colonial territory at that date), founded a colony called 'Florentia' on the right bank of the Arno.

It was laid out in roughly the same way as the usual *Castrum*. Strictly speaking the *castrum*-city proper was supposed to be built on a rectangular plan, but the ground plan of colonial Florence was atypical, since the presence of the marshy river plain resulted in its taking on a trapezoid shape. Yet the layout did still follow the standard system, with its two main axes, the *cardo maximus* and the *decumanus,* intersecting at the central *forum* or main square and ending in four gates with watchtowers set in the city wall. Today the Roman intersection is marked by the Via Strozzi, the Via degli Speziali and the Via del Corso (the *cardo maximus*) and the Via Porta Santa Maria, the Via Calimalia and the Via Roma (the *decumanus*). Archaeologists have also accurately pinpointed the walls and gates of the ancient town, and the shape and site of the old forum can still be picked out in the Piazza della Repubblica.

The city rapidly grew and soon had all the trappings considered obligatory in the Roman Empire. It was indeed modelled on Rome itself, with the gentle line of hills on the banks of the Arno reminiscent of Rome's famous Seven Hills. The forum was surrounded by colonnades and on the artificially banked up Capitol hill stood a large temple dedicated to the official local divinity, Jupiter Optimus Maximus. Near the medieval town hall, the Palazzo Vecchio, the foundations of a classical theatre have been excavated and thermal baths have been found, while outside the walls lay an amphitheatre designed on an oval plan. Near the Baptistery beside the Duomo excavations have shown that the fitments in the dwellings and palaces of Imperial Florence were truly magnificent. Beautiful floor mosaics covering large surfaces and quite unharmed came to light and were seen to equal the finest inlay work in Rome and Pompei. These are important discoveries because in the fifteenth and sixteenth centuries Renaissance art and culture would consciously hark back to the cultural and architectural history of ancient Florentia, with a typically Florentine feeling for tradition, continuity and local pride.

Virtually nothing was left of the ancient ruins, so the situation is very different from Rome, where even today the layout of the palaces, theatres and squares can still be made out, sometimes on several levels.

From early sources we know that as late as about 1300 a classical equestrian statue still stood near the Ponte Vecchio. The great Dante must surely have often walked past it. This gives us some idea of the concept of the grandeur and dignity of classical antiquity that he derived from the chance survival of what was most probably a third-rate example of 'mass-production' in provincial Rome, since he was not familiar with any comparable examples of a higher quality. Following subsequent flooding of the Arno the statue was lost, but it must have seemed important to the people of the 'pre-Renaissance' period, something rather special, or else they would not have handed down the fact of its existence. The same applies to our knowledge of the fact that in about 800 A.D. an equestrian statue dating from classical antiquity stood in front of Charlemagne's palace in Aachen (Aix-la-Chapelle), a visible proof that the Carolingian era saw the birth of the concept of Empire.

This dearth of monuments from their own idealized past in no way troubled the Florentines of the fourteenth and fifteenth centuries, however. Their feeling for history lacked any scientific basis and was refreshingly artless, so that the products of local builders in the Middle Ages were simply declared to be 'classical'. Brunelleschi, like Dante, considered the Florentine Baptistery to be an ancient temple.

City chronicles provide only rare and vague reports concerning the 'dark' transition period. This is true equally of most of Italy's ancient centres. Some account is given of the 250 A.D. martyrdom of San Miniato in the reign of Emperor Decius, a sign of early attempts at Christianization, and strong reaction on the part of the state authorities, as happened all over the Mediterranean territories of the Orbis Romanus. A Florence bishopric is reported from the early fourth century A.D. Then, at the close of the century, in 393 A.D., St. Ambrose, Bishop of Milan, consecrated before the gates of the old town the original structure of San Lorenzo, which, in time if not in importance, ranks alongside the first great 'chief basilicas', in Rome and Milan, of the declining Imperium Romanum.

In the historically 'lost' period, between the fourth and fifth centuries, fluctuating waves of migration passed over Florence, but it remained free of the corpse-robbers of the Roman Empire, owing to its excellent system of communications. Martially-minded, and disliking towns, these migrants left behind no architectural or cultural traces worthy of mention, but did leave heaps of ash. The Goths arrived at the beginning of the fifth century; the Byzantines in 539; and the Longobards about 570. The once brilliant city had shrunk to an insignificant shell, while the decimated population numbered only a few hundred. It was the time of a general return to peasant conditions, which has rightly been called 'the hibernation of the urban social system'. When threatened, the inhabitants all took refuge in the old Roman theatre,

12

2 Unknown artist from the group surrounding Giorgio Vasari: A view of sixteenth-century Florence, with encampment: Palazzo Vecchio. In the late sixteenth century Vasari and his circle painted several rooms in the Palazzo Vecchio, among them the 'Room of the Five Hundred' (Salone dei Cinquecento), the place of assembly for the Standing Conference of Representatives of the People. Large frescoes depict the history of Florence and the Medici, especially the wars against Siena and Pisa. These play an important part in the history of realistic battle-scenes. In content, the picture shown fits into the context of such detailed historical 'snapshots'. It portrays an important moment in history: the siege of Florence by the German mercenaries of Emperor Charles V, after the notorious 'Sacco di Roma', the sack of Rome, in 1527. Florence burrowed into its defences at this time, with the assistance of the fortress engineer Michelangelo, and was able to purchase immunity from plunder on the part of the undisciplined foreign invaders by paying a ransom of 80,000 talers. Otherwise the consequences for Florence's art treasures would have been too terrible to contemplate. The background shows an authentic panorama of Florence with the Arno, the dome Palazzo

2

Vecchio, Badia Church and Bargello Palace. The completely preserved city wall of 1172 with the (earlier) wall surrounding the outlying suburb on the southern bank of the Arno. On the right, in front of the city, the monastery of the Olivetans, with the Church of San Miniato, surrounded by a modern constellation of strongpoints. During the 1527 battles the monastery held a key position as an advanced outpost. It was strongly fortified under Michelangelo, who, in order to protect the half-finished campanile from enemy fire, covered the lower with straw mattresses, one of the earliest examples of wartime protection of cultural property. On one of the hills a fortified German battery can be seen, with large towers made of brushwood fascines and modern gun carriages, conducting an artillery duel with the Florentine battery in San Miniato. The entire city is surrounded by lanes of tents belonging to the investing German forces, and there are genre-like tableaux of camp-life in this period of mercenary troops.

which had been converted into a fortress.

This Florentine 'Theatre Fort' was later given a strong defensive tower, the first indication of a strengthening city identity. There lay the nucleus of the later communal authority, and there, about 1300, arose the Palazzo della Signoria (Palazzo Vecchio), which adopted from the old city fortifications the theme of the proudly erect tower that remains even to-day the city's symbol and landmark (Plate 16).

At the opposite pole to secular rule in the early Middle Ages stood the ecclesiastical district, with the bishop's residence, near the present cathedral of Santa Maria del Fiore.

But all was still on a modest scale. Florentine chronicles begin again with the High Middle Ages. Twelfth and thirteenth century scribes link the city's rebirth with that most illustrious of figures (from their point of view)— Charlemagne. Legend reports, with patriotic exaggeration, on the liberation and re-establishment of Florence from the alleged yoke of the 'barbarians' in the latter part of the eighth century. What is historically accurate is that the city recovered its status as an independent and self-assured commune, but this only in the ninth century, and all we can be sure of is that Charlemagne on his first visit to Rome in 786 attended Christmas Matins, donated generously to the local churches and monasteries, and was later to stay in the city from time to time.

In the tenth century, while the Italian kingdom was weakened by the ambitions of men like Berengar, Adalbert and Arduin of Ivrea, the March of

3

4 Florence: San Miniato al Monte:
Façade. The church lies on a hill outside the
town, on the south bank of the Arno, and was
built to commemorate the city's most eminent
saint, St. Miniatus, who suffered martyrdom
in 250 A.D. in Florence, under Emperor
Decius. The original chapel over the tomb was
probably built on the site of the present
church, Florence's oldest Christian sanctuary.
The church is famed for its façade, in the
finest style of Florentine 'incrustation', with
light and dark marble plaques in strict
geometric pattern, and is a masterpiece of the
Florentine Proto-Renaissance style (1075).
Stylistically the façade is closely related to the
marble incrustation of the Bel San Giovanni,
the Florentine Baptistery (1060).

3 Florence: A view through the battlements
of the 1172 city wall towards the two most
outstanding landmarks, the Palazzo Vecchio
tower, by Arnolfo di Cambio (from 1298),
and Brunelleschi's dome (from 1434).

4 Tuscia, bordered to the south by the 'Patrimonium Petri', 'the Papal State',
and to the north-east by the Romagna-Pentapolis, pushed northwards with a
spur of territory as far as Mantua, and was able to acquire a stable position in
Central Italy as a factor making for political order. Florence was and
remained the centre, and centre also of that great split into two great political
parties, which was to have such a fateful influence on Italy's subsequent
medieval history, and ultimately delay the creation of an Italian nation until
the nineteenth century. These factions were the Ghibellines (so called after the
Hohenstaufen town of Waiblingen) and the Guelphs, or respectively those
who looked to the north and were loyal to the Emperor, and those who
looked to Rome and were faithful to the Pope. This split occurred as early as
the year 1000, and was the result of controversy between the Italian 'national
king', Arduin of Ivrea, and the German Emperor, Henry II. The succeeding
centuries are marked by rapid and, even for the expert historian, almost
inextricable confusion, with first one camp and then the other emerging
victorious throughout the history of Tuscia, or Tuscany. The most prominent
victim of this unhappy quarrel was Florence's greatest son, Dante Alighieri
(1265–1321).

With the Ottonian emperors, the city came under the influence of the
'Empire across the Alps' and so attained its first flowering. The important
Tuscan Margrave Hubert and his son Hugo at the turn of the century
followed a realistic policy as between two great powers, Emperor and Pope.
Their skilful manoeuvring between 'blocks', with some emphasis on the
imperial idea, began to pay off, and the results of Florentine diplomacy were
to be seen in the city's wealth of ecclesiastical and secular monuments, paid
for in part by the foreign powers concerned in the form of gifts. In every
period, including the Early and High Middle Ages, calculation was a
Florentine characteristic, political balance being directly related to the
balance of payments, and political roulette played in the manner of a player
who invariably carries with him a ready-reckoner and a table to show the
potential profits. Jacob Burckhardt, referring to the fourteenth and fifteenth
centuries, has rightly termed Florence and Venice the 'home of statistics'.

The Proto-Renaissance Period

The eleventh century in Florence was characterized by an initial, medieval
'renovatio' in architecture, the Proto-Renaissance style, a particular form of
European Romanesque, and the first international style to succeed the
Graeco-Roman. Examples from this period such as the original San Lorenzo,
San Piero Scheraggio, Santa Felicità, Santa Reparata, and the Badia
Fiorentina, have mostly perished, or been overlaid by newer constructions.
The shape of these spacious basilicas with aisles can however be inferred from
San Miniato al Monte (Plate 4), and the Badia Fiorentina. It was the
Baptistery above all, however, which survived unscathed as brilliant
testimony to Florentine Romanesque. It ranks as one of the finest buildings in
Europe.

The overriding principle of this style is that the surface of the entire
structure, smoothly and artlessly built-up, is given a covering of precious
marble plaques. The thin but valuable panels surround the building like a
skin, and stretch tightly over it, in the membrane-fashion. The decorative and
practical nature of this technique, known also as the incrustation style, is
manifest in some Florentine churches, where the façade, splendidly clad in
light and dark plaques, stands in front of a rough stone basilica which has
remained undressed, thus giving the façade the appearance of some
decorative wall or a magnificent marble panel, thrust, so to speak, like a slab,
in front of the edifice.

Today's traveller to the East is confronted with this same style—in
miniature—as soon as he takes up one of the small inlaid wooden caskets that
are proffered from the Lebanon to Morocco as souvenirs in bazaars. The
smooth surface of the wood is inlaid all over with abstract, geometric designs

Pages 16 and 17:

5   Florence: The Cathedral of Santa Maria del Fiore. Almost all the important Florentine artists of the Late Middle Ages and Early Renaissance took part in the cathedral's construction, which began in 1296: Arnolfo di Cambio (until 1301 Director of the Project); F. Talenti (from 1357 onwards); Giotto (Campanile, from 1334); Andrea Pisano (Campanile, 1336–1348); Orcagna and Brunelleschi (the Dome, 1434–1461). After being frequently brought to a halt, the work was finally completed with the aid of the wealthy and powerful Wool-Weavers Guild (Arte della Lana) as a symbol of civil pride. It became known throughout the world not merely owing to Brunelleschi's outstanding Dome, the 'Roof of Florence', the first piece of Renaissance architecture in Italy, but also on account of the magnificent marble incrustation, along the lines of the Florentine Proto-Renaissance style (Baptistery, San Miniato). The white marble is from Carrara, the green from Prato (verde di Prato) and the red from the Maremma (rosso di Maremma). Originally the church was called Santa Reparata, but about 1300 the municipal authorities changed the name by decree to Santa Maria 'del Fiore', to harmonise with the old name of the city, 'Florentia'. This was a way of announcing that, in accordance with ancient custom, the Blessed Virgin was now the divinity looking after both city and state, or the 'Tyche' (the Greek goddess of Fortune) of Florence.

6   Florence: Cathedral of Santa Maria del Fiore: Campanile (Bell-tower). The history of the bell-tower is closely connected with that of the Cathedral. From 1334 to 1337 Giotto was in charge of the work, and thereafter, until 1348 or 1350, Andrea Pisano. The cupola originally planned to top the structure never in fact materialized, but the tower is generally held to be the loveliest campanile in Italy, its picturesque appearance being due to the happy conjunction of architectural and graphic elements. The strict architectural form combines perfectly with the clear division into storeys and the imaginative treatment of the surface by means of marble incrustations and a series of reliefs. Recent research reveals that the use of free-standing campanili, to be found only in Italy, is connected with a liturgical regulation that bells had to be used in the divine service. This trend occurs, for the first time, in the seventh century, which explains why the early Christian churches of the fourth to sixth centuries (such as Ravenna) had later to be provided with bell-towers. The custom became a tradition in later periods, as the Duomo in Florence illustrates.

6

18

in metal, mother-of-pearl, ivory or fishbone, giving the simple container the character of a treasure-chest or jewel-box, that turns everything in it, even only a few coins, into something valuable. It is therefore most appropriate that the Florentines should have affectionately named 'their' baptistery the 'Treasure-Chest' of the city on the Arno. Dante calls the Baptistery *"il bel San Giovanni",* after its patron, St. John.

Concerning the origins of this style as many contradictory theories abound as there are writers on art. It has no real parallel, either in Italy (Pisa for example) or in the rest of Europe. All we can say is that it seems to be a specifically Florentine invention, which appears suddenly before us, fully-developed, in the eleventh century.

One possible explanation lies in the architectonic legacy left by antiquity. Roman buildings, too, unlike the Greek, had been largely erected in this manner since the first century B.C. At that time shuttering was discovered, and how to face a 'cement' base with conventionally built-up bands of tiles, or ashlar. The technical Roman expression for this was *opus caementicium.* It consisted of a firmly-baked mass of mortar, with other compounds and rubble, or crushed brick. The rough or cement base was then faced with thin marble plaques, and fastened with bronze clamps to form the building's actual façade.

In the High Middle Ages many Roman monuments on Italian soil must have had this marble facing, so that the Florentine incrustation technique was following familiar classical models. This explains why as early as the thirteenth and fourteenth centuries the Baptistery could be mistaken for and idealized as a slightly altered classical building, or a Roman temple to Mars.

The link with Ancient Rome can be brought closer still in the Baptistery, as has already been mentioned. Valuable floor mosaics dating from the Roman period have been discovered recently in the foundations. This mosaic work must have become apparent to the architects of the time, during the excavations in the eleventh century for the new baptistery. That the work was not destroyed by the medieval builders but merely filled in and built over can either be regarded as an early example of conservation or ascribed to the Florentine feeling for tradition, and local sensibility as regards the *'genius loci'.* The Roman mosaics certainly stimulated the imagination of the Masters of the Florentine Baptistery.

What is peculiar about the Baptistery, however, is that here—at the very start of an independent local art—we can already grasp the essential features which subsequently mark the Florentine style up to the fifteenth and sixteenth centuries, i.e. a rational and at times inflexible spirit, which could be called dry and unimaginative were it not a consequence of the Florentine feeling for artistic discipline, mastery of form, economy of shape and shrewd judgement in the application of artistic media. We can imagine the typical Florentine artist of any period as wielding setsquare and ready-reckoner, rather than as some early Bohemian with velvet cap and bow. The people of Florence were apt to reverse the saying: 'Life is earnest and art gay', for to them art and culture were never the décor and background to living, but its very heart and soul.

Roman art with its overwhelming richness of form and imaginative décor, its tendency towards large-scale and often strident effects, plus its grandiose and theatrical or architectonic setting, was as foreign to the Florentine as the graphically delicate nuances of Venetian art, with its golden decorative scheme that sparkled in the half-light, and was as closely wrought as a carpet, conveying the effect of some fresco in a Byzantine church, or of some piece of booty from the gorgeous tent of the Great Khan, exotic, oriental, un-Italian in essence, and broken up by the light diffused across the lagoon into soft nuances free of shadow. The sky above Florence is not as radiant and blue as the sky over Rome, and the air is not as damp and oppressive as in Venice. Thomas Mann's celebrated novel about death could have taken place only in Venice, not in Rome, and certainly not in Florence.

If we compare the important medieval churches in the three cities, St.

Peter's predecessor in Rome, St. Mark's in Venice and the Duomo and Baptistery grouping in Florence, we are at once struck by the marked difference of spirit between them even in medieval times. In the old St. Peter's we have a multipartite complicated organization of architectural masses and great spaces, laid out on long, extensive axes, and all-comprehensive and cosmopolitan in conception; in St. Mark's, a dense shape and colour texture which is difficult to penetrate, consisting of cupolas and bits and pieces, with every surface, even the tiniest corner, full of ornamentation; a creation foreign to the European world which has settled down here like some powerful, mythological creature from the Orient (Plates 93 and 107).

Florence is totally different. The artistic imagination here is tempered, and the formal effect carefully calculated. It must never become a matter of course, overwhelm or get out of control. Formal concepts and morphological inventions are given clear delineation, and react independently on one another. Florentine art knows nothing of the fortuitous, nothing of picturesque effects, or pastoral nooks. Uniquely inspired artistic ideas and spontaneous creations are suspect until they have been confirmed by academic theory, and tested in a long series of practical works. Otherwise the so-called inspiration could have been pure chance.

This is why the Florentines have always proved better at graphic work and design, like the Germans and Northerners. The city has produced magnificent sculpture, in both stone and bronze, characteristically graphic and linear in conception, but has been poor in great painting talent. It was in Florence that (with Donatello) the doctrine of *disegno,* or drawing, was first developed. *Disegno* and draughtsmanship remain constants in Florentine art that override the centuries.

All these features are revealed in the Baptistery. The ground-plan and elevation display a Latin rationality and a kind of Gallic *clarté.* The original structure has the air of a purely Euclidean, geometric body, which states no more in the ground-plan than it does in the formation of the façade; speaks no differently internally than it does externally; and has no ambition to mean any more than it is—an accumulating architectonic crystal, a great prism in the centre of the area covered by the immunity of the Bishop of Florence. In

7

7 *Florence: The Cathedral of Santa Maria del Fiore: Campanile, the bas-reliefs on the rectangular base at the East Side. The original design for these reliefs probably goes back to Giotto and constitutes an ingenious display of the entire doctrine of scholasticism, as relating to society and salvation. The historical and symbolic illustrations call to mind the complicated images decorating the Gothic cathedrals of France. Those shown are the lower reliefs by Andrea Pisano and his School (about 1340). From left to right they represent: 1. Navigation; 2. Hercules with a conquered Giant; 3. Agriculture and 4. Chariot racing.*

its abstraction and at the same time in its deep sensuousness, the building could be described as an architectonic Utopia become a reality, or as an expression in stone of the nature of architecture.

The High Middle Ages

The eleventh century in Florence was characterized in an architectural as well as a political sense by a launching out on to new paths. The town nobles organized on rigid lines and began to gain in influence. They and their economically dependent 'clientèle' formed into solid communities, by street or family, as was a custom in medieval Tuscany, and the powerful defence works in the city, with their high fortified towers, gave significant expression to that fact. Their fascinating town silhouettes are familiar to us from ancient descriptions and pictorial illustrations. The heart of the city, with over eighty such towers, must have presented even in the thirteenth century a significant picture, like a forest of lances, or the skyline of some modern city, with slender towers of skyscrapers. The Palazzo Vecchio (Plate 16) gives some impression of how it all originally looked, as does the centre of San Gimignano in Southern Tuscany, which has been preserved in its medieval form and is one of the most rewarding places in Italy to visit. In Florence nothing of the kind survived, apart from a few remains built into modern structures. Yet in the thirteenth century already the violent party struggles between noble families was beginning to bring down almost entirely that 'forest of towers'. It was in the fifteenth century that by a decree of state the usurping dynasty of the Medici ordained that the towers still standing be torn down. The arrogant claim to power so tangible in these architectural symbols must have proved intolerable to the Medici, who had seized power.

In the twelfth century, Florence's fluctuating course between Pope and Emperor lent such an impulse to the city that the population expanded beyond the confines of the Roman Gastrum Square. The ancient surrounding wall, until then still largely preserved, was taken down, and a larger one put up. The city was also surrounded on three sides by wide moats, while on the fourth the Arno served as a natural defence.

Florence began to develop into an Italian and then a European centre of trade, acquiring an important place in early metropolitan commercial capitalism. Business relations spread across the whole of Europe and also 'overseas', which then meant the Eastern Mediterranean, the Levant, North Africa and the Black Sea. Following the Spanish *Reconquista,* Arab rule in the Central Mediterranean began to collapse from the eleventh century onwards, and the crusades, with their world-wide political and economic repercussions, did likewise. Into the vacuum stepped the Italian commercial cities Genoa, Pisa, Naples, Venice and Florence. Like Venice, the Florence region became one of the first 'industrial landscapes' in Europe, and European and Middle East trade, still largely operating on the basis of barter, was at once the cause and effect of this process. Eastern goods in demand, such as silk, brocades, damask, cotton, camel hair, porcelain, dyes, spices, essences, medicines, pearls, ivory and jewels, reached Europe from Asia and the Levant, via the old caravan routes (the Silk Road) still under Arab control, there to be exchanged for finished goods from Milan, Florence, Upper Germany, Flanders and Brabant. The up-and-coming Italian communes were the governing wheels in this trade exchange in the old world, and among them Florence soon occupied a leading place.

This mercantile expansion, of course, was unlikely to produce a peaceful system of municipal government. On the contrary, it was the cause of internal struggles for power between rival forces in the trading aristocracy. The 'city peace' was forever under threat, and the conflict sharpened once the masked greed of the Florentine commercial overlords discovered that the ideal arena for their squabbles lay in foreign policy. Mutual aversion among a few city families assumed concrete form with their political division into two parties, the Ghibellines and the Guelphs. People joined these parties only partly for

9

8 *Florence: The cathedral of Santa Maria del Fiore, part of the choir. Projecting structures have been placed between the three arms of the choir to take the enormous weight of Brunelleschi's Dome. The photograph on the left shows one of these, at the ends of which Brunelleschi placed semicircular exedras. It also provides a good example of the most attractive interplay of white, red and green marble arranged in geometric patterns on the façade.*

9 *Florence: Santa Maria Novella. The Façade. The front of Florence's most important Dominican church, begun in 1246, constitutes one of the loveliest incrustation façades in the city. it was executed from 1456 to 1470 from plans by the great Leon Battista Alberti (Portal, side pilasters and gable with side volutes). The result is a charming mélange of Medieval and Early Renaissance forms. The gable architrave bears the founder's name in large classical lettering: 'IOHANES. ORICELLARIUS' and the final date 'MCCCCLXX' (1470).*

political reasons, expressed in shouts of: 'The Emperor!' 'The Pope!' The aim was rather to eliminate annoying business competition and get within reach of certain trade privileges and monopolies which the feuding Emperor and Pope were both in a position to distribute. Whenever competitor X deprived competitor Y of the right of pre-emption for a bale of silk or load of pepper, obscenities, directed at a Guelph or Ghibelline patronised by Emperor or Pope, would be hurled from tower to tower under the cover of a shower of arrows; premises would be looted; and nightly brawls take place in the local taverns, among the bodyguards of the various *torri*, who were easily recognisable dressed as they were in the family-colours.

It was this picture of a city rent by internal dissension that writers like Petrarch (1304–1374) and Boccaccio (1313–1375) had before them when they set the ideal of country villas and estates against this distorted and perverted town life, or when, in the style of Roman writers like Cato, Cicero and Columnella, they called on people to return to an utopian pastoral existence. Using expressions such as *brutalità, perversità* e *scandolo* (brutality, perversion and scandal) they lashed out at town life as sum-total of every private and political vice, so that when at last the Black Death, the Plague, entered the narrow streets of the medieval city, no longer a harbour for citizens but only for gloomy secrets, and ruled by spies and murdering

10 *Florence: Santa Croce: General view, West façade and Campanile. Church and Monastery, one of the most powerful Franciscan foundations in Italy, and founded ostensibly by St. Francis himself, were begun in 1295 and completed in 1385. The incrustation façade remained a fragment. It is nineteenth-century work, based on pseudo-Gothic seventeenth-century sketches, and was completed in 1863. The present bell-tower dates from 1842 and derives in a formal sense from the Badia Tower.*

bandits, it seemed as well-merited dispensation of Providence. To Boccaccio the Plague symbolized the political conditions in a city 'sick unto death', and, in actual fact, the party-political quarrel, with its repercussions in the physical, or at least economic destruction of whatever fraction in the thirteenth and early fourteenth century lost power, *did* come to acquire that quality of 'bestialità', or bestiality, treated so movingly by Petrarch and Dante.

After 1250 A.D. the city was politically reorganized by stages, in a democratic sense. These are the glorious days of the so-called 'Primo Popolo', which entered the annals of European constitutional history as one of the first, if not *the* first democratic constitution since the antique world. The Guelph party was not of course acting without a precedent. At the height of the 'Ghibelline era' at the turn of the twelfth and thirteenth centuries the first 'democratic' revolution had occurred, when the guilds, together with the feudal supporters of the Empire, broke the power of great families, the *torri*.

By 1200 the 'New Class' of merchants was hardly distinguishable from the older, established aristocracy, in terms of political weight and economic power, and had partly intermarried with it. Behind it, the guilds were pressing strongly forward, and the two classes inevitably met head-on, as indeed they must, in an early capitalist sense: raw materials and semi-finished products reached the city through the dealers, and were left to the guilds for further processing either through orders, or by them on their own account (First profit stage). After processing, the finished products left town again through the dealers and were disposed of on world markets at a profit (Second profit stage). The upper and lower classes were dependent on each other, so that workers and small businesses could make their demands felt. One prerequisite, of course, was that the classes putting pressure on the 'New Class' should organize themselves. This occurred when the craftsmen formed into seven large guilds in the year 1173, a memorable date in European municipal and class history, and one no less significant in social history than in the history of the cultural superstructure, in other words for Florence's development into one of the first 'art cities'.

The two 'Consuls' at the head of the exclusive Merchants' Corporation had their counterpart in the guilds in the form of freely-elected 'Rectors', who looked after the business interests of their colleagues. Through a tactical coalition with the lower strata the feudal Ghibelline party was enabled temporarily to break the dominant influence of the rich merchants, who were inclined to be anti-Empire and to favour the Guelphs. The 'Emperor's Party' then had to make important political concessions to the plebeians in the form of democratic rights, which were in contradiction to feudal ideology. This was the time when the 'free citizen' came into being, to defend his vital rights henceforth in sturdy and courageous fashion, though neither a noble, nor traditionally wealthy. From 1193 on it could rightly be said in Florence that 'town air makes you free'. Paradoxically enough, the city government was for a brief period both democratic and feudal. The Podestà (Mayor) and his boards were dependent on the guilds. Podestà and City Council were responsible for the administration and military policy, but the guilds had managed to arrange that treaties, the very essence of political activity then as now, could be concluded only with the assent of their 'rectors'.

In 1260 the Ghibelline reaction once again attempted to shatter the painfully acquired peace by means of a putsch, designed to overthrow the constitution of the democratic *'Primo Popolo'*, but failed. The supporters of the Empire had to flee the city, and sought refuge with the people of Siena who invariably looked with distrust on the aspirations of Florence. But the Guelph Party unwisely let itself be lured in pursuit of the conspirators beyond the security of the city wall and suffered a crushing reverse in open country at Montaperti, which has passed into Florentine legend. In addition, denuded of defenders, the city fell into the hands of enemy units operating in the Guelph rear. At the Peace Congress of Empoli, however, the prudent Ghibelline leader, Farinata degli Uberti, succeeded in stressing moderation, thus preventing the total destruction of Florence. Otherwise the present-day visitor would probably find it much poorer, and with great gaps.

Florence then had to continue its painstaking struggle for a position within the circle of Tuscan city-states. Arezzo was finally forced to capitulate, and in 1284, by skilfully woven diplomatic intrigue, the Florentines managed to stoke the fires of conflict between Genoa and Pisa to the point where open hostilities broke out, in which the Genovese decisively defeated the Pisans at the gates of Florence. The city emerged from these conflicts strengthened, and with a consolidated political constitution. Trade and industry flourished, and the coffers of the merchants and armaments manufacturers also filled up, especially in these times of constant minor wars.

In 1293 the famous Florentine 'Ordinances of Justice', put a temporary end

11 Florence: Santa Croce. Cloisters, with Pazzi Chapel. Various elements combine here to form a grouping which is impressive in its effect. First we have the nave of undressed stone, symbol of French simplicity. These spacious preaching churches of the mendicant friars have been called 'prayer-barns'. Then comes the fourteenth century cloisters, among Florence's finest, and finally, the Pazzi Chapel, begun by Brunelleschi in 1430 as a sepulchre for the banking family of the Pazzi, who were opposed to the Medici. The upper floor of the chapel façade remained unfinished, and is topped to-day by an ugly platform roof.

12 Florence: San Lorenzo. The West façade, four-sided cupola and sacristy. San Lorenzo is one of the oldest churches in Florence, or Italy. The first ecclesiastical structure was erected as early as 380, and solemnly consecrated in 393 by St. Ambrose, Bishop of Milan. A new building was put up in 1058, which stood until the fifteenth century. New plans were worked out on the model of Santa Croce about 1418, and between 1420 and 1421 Brunelleschi took charge and set in motion work on Florence's first post-medieval church building. After his death the work was carried on by his pupil, Manetti. Shortly after 1500 Michelangelo began to devote himself to the task. In 1517 he prepared a model in clay for the façade, followed by one in wood with twenty-four wax figures. Between 1518 and 1519 he was in Carrara to break up blocks of marble for the decorative figures on the façade, but Leo X, the Medici Pope, was obliged in the end to cancel the contract, for lack of funds. This renunciation of Michelangelo's plan has been termed the 'tragedy of the façade', and it stands there to-day in raw and fissured condition. The church's importance lies in the Old Sacristy's internal design, Brunelleschi's first work (1419–1428), and particularly in the New Sacristy, by Michelangelo, by means of which the Master was 'compensated' for the failure of the façade project (1520–1523). It is on account of the (incomplete) statuary by Michelangelo for the Medici Tomb (1523–1534) that the New Sacristy must be numbered amongst the world's most important art sites. (c.f. Plates 57–60). This is the reason why it now bears the not quite correct name of 'Cappella Medicea' (Medici Chapel). The Medici family's extraordinary interest in the work is explained by the fact that their ancient seat, the Medici-Riccardi Palace, belonged to the Parish of San Lorenzo. San Lorenzo was thus, so to speak, the original home-parish of the Medicis, even at times when they were supplying Popes and Cardinals.

to the process of self-discovery that had lasted for more than a century, that ceaseless power and class-struggle between guild-members, patricians and nobles, and between producers, distributors and the 'old class' of feudal estate-owners. The 'popolo grosso' (commercial patricians) was finally forbidden by the constitution of 1293 to take part in any political activity. The party intrigues which kept occurring even after 1260 had led as a result at the end of the century to the irretrievable banishment of the 'Whites', the Ghibellines. In 1302 the City Governor, Cante de Gabrielli, had the opposition leaders, who were still in the city, publicly executed. His régime of terror and the cruel physical destruction of his opponents were considered legally justified in the main, in view of the continuing chaotic political conditions operating in the city. Dante, the most prominent victim of this persecution of the 'Whites', was out of the country at the time and so escaped the bloodshed. Italy indeed owes its most outstanding poetry not least to Dante's personal fate and the lament for a lost political identity, i.e. the dream of an ideal national kingdom.

The change in architecture around 1300 was visible evidence of a newly-recovered municipal identity. Architecture thereby became the ultimate medium of political expression. Nobles, guilds and city government entered into fruitful and artistically productive competition, having their own architectural conceptions. A series of monumental palaces illustrates the new style: the Bargello Palace (begun in 1255 and completed in 1346: Plate 19) originally the seat of communal administration departments; the Palazzo dell'Arte della Lana (1308), centre of the eminent Wool Weavers' Guild, which many plastic artists later joined because it was exclusive; the Palazzo di Parte Guelfa (late thirteenth century), headquarters of the Guelph Party, half-way between a trade-union and a political lobby; and lastly, that most splendid creation, the Palazzo Vecchio or Palazzo della Signoria (1298–1314, probably by Arnolfo di Cambio: Plates 16 and 17), seat of city government. These are no longer tower-like fortresses like the seats of the nobles in the High Middle Ages, but 'civil' buildings, constructed like palaces. Personal safety no longer required a fortress-city, capable of bearing arms, but was

12

guaranteed by the wall surrounding the city, and by a system of political treaties, rights and privileges. Nevertheless even the new palaces by no means gave up rampart and battlement, or the tower-overall theme and the powerful, rugged, running walls. Yet these reminders of medieval defensive constructions are now employed symbolically and for effect, since there is nothing more that requires to be physically defended inside the city walls, and the point is merely to represent and preserve abstract political 'titles', positions and privileges.

The Palazzo Vecchio amply demonstrates this. It is difficult to term the building either 'beautiful' or 'ugly', since it is entirely outside aesthetic categories such as these. The extreme concentration of the architecture is nevertheless political and 'representative', down to the smallest detail, a metaphor, in stone, of communal self-awareness. The body, defensive and hermetic as it is on the outside, in its unpolished, squared-off treatment, is yet restrained and well-proportioned. Only the upward straining of the arrogant, thrusting tower, and the duplicated theme of prominent battlement on palace and tower convey a hybrid effect. While the Campanile in Venice (Plate 107) creates the necessary counterpoint to the vast spatial composition of Piazza and Piazzetta, making them into an 'ensemble', and at the same time conferring on them order and articulation like limbs yet without subordinating itself to them, the overpowering tower-motif in Florence

13

breaks through the limited structure of medieval space. The lofty dimensions of tower and palace can scarcely be apprehended by the spectator, or reduced to corporeal terms. It is only from a distance that the Vecchio Tower can be seen in proper perspective as one of the governing features on the city horizon along with the Cathedral. (Plate 1). Mention has been made for this reason of the almost 'rude majesty' of the structure (J. M. Wiesel 1956) and, logically enough, in eighteenth and nineteenth century English architecture reference was made to creations like the Palazzo Vecchio when building assignments came up involving comparable demands in the matter of representation. This illustrative architecture has become a mirror-image of internal and external political positions and claims, and excludes in its apparently North European *robustezza* any interpretation as an expression of Roman or Italian character. By comparison, the Town Halls of the late medieval and the Renaissance periods in Flanders, Brabant or Upper Germany, must occupy a

13 Florence: Santo Spirito. Construction was begun in 1436 under Brunelleschi who died in 1446 a few days before the roof-vaulting started. His successors were unable to reach any unified conception, and the façade remained as it was, to be completed later in its existing rather tedious form. Brunelleschi planned to place pillars at the front, with an opulent four-portal grouping. The flanking gable volutes are a late baroque addition, while the present, smooth plaster-work dates from 1957. The campanile, one of the most elegant in the city, goes back to Brunelleschi but was completed only in 1566.

14 Florence: Santo Spirito, Nave. Brunelleschi's interior, with its strict canonical lines and 'ideal' semi-circular arches over antique columns and high coussinets, is considered a classical development of Early Renaissance architecture.

14

modest secondary position as far as municipal function and representational pretensions are concerned.

Within the wider context of European city life at the end of the Middle Ages the Vecchio Tower, together with the self-effacing Bargello Tower, appears in all its unique political significance. Now that the aristocratic *società degli torri,* with its eighty and more towers, has been destroyed, the city outline stresses the single, dominating tower of the communal palace which deputises for all the other towers, dismantled in the end, and stands as the symbol of a new political era. This applies also to the tower of the Town Hall in Siena (which exceeds Florence's in height, and for reasons of rivalry *had* to surpass it), as well as to other Italian communal palaces.

It was in this final but still medieval guise of aristocratic fortress that the pride of the 'new' middle classes created for itself in Florence a symbol whose undoubted tension and elegance, against the general background, represents

15

new, upward-striving art trends which stand in indissoluble conflict with a serious and pathetic rhetoric, a vocabulary of swallow-tailed and rectangular battlements, tower defences and squared stone bosses which still belongs to the Middle Ages. Jacob Burckhardt summed up the essential features of this structure with laconic precision in his 'Cicerone', using only seventeen words: 'Greatness, memories, stone-colour, and fantastic tower-structure confer on this building a value which far surpasses the artistic.'

Florence's economic, political and cultural upsurge around 1300 can be read of course not only in its secular architecture but particularly in the ecclesiastical buildings. This was the time when the great churches that still grace the city came into being in quick succession. With them the Middle Ages reached its zenith in great and simple form. Santa Maria Novella was begun

16

17 Florence, Palazzo Vecchio: The Courtyard. The late medieval architecture of the courtyard was converted to pre-Rennaissance by Michelozzo in 1453. In 1565 the arcades were decorated by frescoes designed by Giorgio Vasari. The most important features of his design are the 18 views of cities of the Habsburg empire (out of reverence for the Austrian bride of the Archduke Ferdinand, as the courtyard was decorated especially for his wedding). Verrocchio's very attractive "Putto with Fish" stands in the middle of the courtyard, in the centre of the fountain, and is an allegory of the 'Socratic Eros', originally created for the Medici villa in Careggi.

18 Florence, Palazzo Vecchio: Sala dell'Udienza (Audience Chamber). One of the ancient staterooms of the Florentine Republic. The portal was created by Benedetto da Maiano (1529). The frescoes, amongst the finest of Italian Mannirism, are the work of Francesco Salviati (approximately 1550/60) and depict the history of the Roman consular tribune and commander Furius Cammillus, who conquered several Italian tribes and occupied Veji in the 4th century B.C.

18

in 1246 (Plate 9), but it was to take two hundred years before the great Renaissance architect Leon Battista Alberti could complete it. Santa Croce began to expand from 1295 on (Plates 10 and 11) to become one of Italy's greatest and most distinguished Franciscan churches, founded according to legend by St. Francis himself (1181–1226) in 1209, and just six hundred years later (1857–1863) was given a somewhat stiff marble façade, in the form of a pseudo-historical incrustation style, though the façade fits well enough into the city scene and corresponds to the general style. This now stands before the majestically simple Church of the Mendicant Friars, a splendid yet touching tribute by the Florentines of to-day to their medieval past. Tradition has it that Arnolfo di Cambio, Master of the Palazzo Vecchio, was the leading architect here too. He is also accepted as the spirit behind the new structure of the city's largest church, the Cathedral of Santa Maria del Fiore (Plates 5 to 8). This church with its fabulous and costly external garb of incrusted white and dark marble panels forms an unmistakeable and much-praised ensemble together with the Campanile and the Baptistery.

Arnolfo di Cambio did not live to see the completion of his great work, hardly more indeed than part of the brickwork, for he died as early as 1301, just five years after the laying of the foundation-stone. The structure remained as it was and was then carried further in two stages, in 1331 and under Talenti from 1357 on. In the succeeding period it attracted two of the most outstanding artists in Florence: Giotto, who tackled the Campanile from 1334 onwards, and Brunelleschi, who completed the Dome one hundred and fifty years after the beginning of the whole undertaking (1434–1461), this being what we must regard as the beginning of the Renaissance in Italian architectural history. In this case too, the façade met with misfortune. It remained unfinished, was torn down in 1588 as a result of architectural damage, and was not rebuilt until the end of the nineteenth century, with fair historical adaptation to the original facework of choir and nave.

In discussing the contribution made by the city to Italian Gothic, illustrated in this volume by three examples that at the same time represent three different religious architectural requirements—the Parish Church (Santa Maria Novella), the Church of the Mendicant Friars or the Monastery (Santa Croce) and the Cathedral or Bishop's Church (Cathedral of Santa Maria del Fiore)—we touch on a theme which has long been the subject of controversy in the history of art and culture. Jacob Buckhardt, writing in 1855, regarded everything Gothic as a basically foreign and problematic phenomenon on classical Italian soil. 'The intrusion of Gothic architectural forms from the North was fateful for Italian art, a misfortune if you like, but

only for the unskilled, who would not in any case have been in a position to help themselves' *(Cicerone)*. Only the newer way of regarding art made it possible for justice to be done to this style, as a special form, the Italian version of 'Latin Gothic'. In coming to terms with the gothic of French cathedrals some specific Italian features, found throughout Italian art, were developed, such as a pleasing awareness of space, a way of thinking in terms of vast, harmoniously laid out and clearly separated spatial units. This

34

19 Florence: Bargello: The Courtyard. The Bargello, originally the 'Palazzo del Podestà', or seat of the Mayor, was built in 1255 as a token of victory over the aristocracy. The father of Arnolfo di Cambio, builder of the Cathedral, is said to have been the architect. An older family tower, one of the Torri of the noble families, was fitted into the structure, symbolising the aspirations to power of the 'new' middle class. To-day the tower is one of Florence's landmarks. That haughty architecture has witnessed significant scenes in Florentine history. The Pazzi conspirators, for instance, were cruelly tortured to death in the Bargello's dark cells (1478). Previously, on the outer walls, Castagno had portrayed, in mockery and ridicule, the hanging of the Albizzi conspirators. Later on Botticelli carried out a similar commission depicting the Pazzi conspirators on the grim walls. At that time the Palace was the seat of legal authority (Bargello), hence the name to-day. The building now contains one of the most important collections of sculpture, mostly from the Uffizi, which in the nineteenth century was no longer able to house its vast collection of works of art.

characteristic, which was later to leave its imprint even on Renaissance architecture, had already found expression in Italian gothic.

One sociological and political circumstance stands out as even more important than these questions of scholarly assessment and interpretation, which inhibit rather than enrich the visual experience for the untrained visitor. Just as happened with the construction of the Palazzo Vecchio, the rebuilding of the Cathedral was also from the very first a political issue of the greatest importance, and a matter on which every Florentine, from the humblest workman to the lofty Rector of a Guild or a Town Councillor, took sides in the liveliest fashion, not forgetting the polemics. Florence can now be comprehended as an art metropolis *in toto*, one where every significant undertaking is backed by the majority of the citizens, united in their desire for art and creativity, and one in which in certain situations the entire creative strength of the city can concentrate on a single task. Innumerable meetings of City Council and Commission took place on the subject; juries were made up and again dissolved, under protest, as being biased; many people died broken-hearted at the building's failure; old friendships broke up; families fell out for decades because of differences over aesthetic matters, something as unusual and unheard-of then as it would be now.

After Arnolfo di Cambio's early death an open competition was announced, at the third construction stage under Talenti, in which every Florentine could take part, independently of status or profession. This procedure was repeated for every single part and section of the structure. Soon a Talenti and an Orcagna party formed which waged a campaign against each other as venomously as Ghibelline and Guelph had once done. The ground-plan finally accepted in 1366 had been worked out by a committee of no less than thirteen master architects and 11 painters. Eight other master architects signed as responsible for the elevation. The older models were thereupon publicly destroyed. Many of the minutes of the Commission sessions have been preserved, and there seem to have been some pretty hectic scenes as the rival groups around Talenti, Orcagna, Taddeo Gaddi and Neri di Fioravante vied with each other in speaking out of turn.

It remains a miracle and a tribute to the artistic sense and great integrating talent of the Florentine people, in everything pertaining to art and culture, that the work was not spoiled in the end by too many 'cooks' but seems to to-day's observer to have been cast in one mould.

The Age of Giotto and Dante

The creative forces of the city itself were hardly adequate to carry on the manifold artistic tasks facing it: a local School was just beginning to be formed. At the commencement of the great period of Florentine art, therefore, outside artists were 'imported', a procedure that was repeated also in Rome. Later the reverse would be the case and the whole of Italy would for a while become 'Florentine'; the Mediterranean area with France, Spain and even Hungary (Masolino 1427) would talk the language of Florence in matters of art and culture; artists from Northern Europe, German and Flemish in the main, would make a pilgrimage to Florence as if it were Mecca; native artists would become the favoured 'export items' from the city on the Arno. For the moment, however, it was outside forces that were relied upon or, according to the political conception of the day, 'foreigners'. Venetian specialists, trained in the then purely Greek-Byzantine style native to the lagoon city, and familiar with the highly-developed handling there of glass, paste and glass-cutting (Murano), created a considerable part of the roof mosaic on the Baptistery. Arnolfo di Cambio too came from outside, from Colle di Val d'Elsa. Duccio, who painted the famous altar painting in the Rucellai Chapel in Santa Maria Novella (about 1285) was summoned from Siena, to the great annoyance of his fellow-countrymen. Even the great Giotto (1266–1336) was not born within the city walls but in a tiny corner of the country of the Florentine Contado, in Colle di Vespignano. It is not even certain that Cimabue (1240 to after 1302), honoured by Dante as the 'Father of Florentine Painting', was born and brought up in Florence. He is mentioned for the first time in Rome in 1272, was active in Pisa and Assisi, but only in passing in Florence.

With Giotto a new chapter opens in the art history not only of Florence or Italy but of Europe. Giotto is represented in this volume by the celebrated fresco portraying the Death of St. Francis, from the legend of St. Francis in the Capella Bardi in the Franciscan Church of Santa Croce (Plate 27), a moving late work full of classical restraints and lofty spirituality, to which Winckelmann's phrase about 'noble simplicity, silent greatness' applies just as much as to any important important Greek or Roman classic. The argument that the Renaissance began here and not one hundred years later, once the Soft Style, 'international Gothic' *(Gotico internazionale)*, had been superseded, cannot be dismissed out of hand.

Giotto is honoured in a famous Florentine document dating from 1334, as a Master of high *scientia et doctrina,* not simply as a man of vision and a creative artist but as a man of outstanding 'wisdom and learning', though this may only be a standard expression then applied to all important artists. One hundred years later, in his *'Memoirs'* dating from the mid-fifteenth century, Lorenzo Ghiberti ventured a precise art-historical assessment and classification, connecting the revival of art in the modern sense with the names of Cimabue and above all Giotto. He also related the famous story which, via Vasari, has come down to our own day, of how Giotto as a boy was guarding the sheep near his home village of Vespignano and drawing one member of the flock when he was surprised by Cimabue who, coming along the highway from Bologna and struck as if by something miraculous, at once recognized the youth's extraordinary talent.

In choice of subject as well as in presentation Giotto broke completely with the medieval Byzantine style, the *maniera greca,* which before his time had dominated Italian religious painting virtually to the exclusion of other styles. Suddenly we find ourselves looking at living, breathing people; not 'mummified forms' as Jacob Burckhardt so aptly and cuttingly describes them, but people of flesh and blood, with a definable personality and psyche, an earthly material quality and three-dimensionality, people who could literally cast a shadow—this applied even when saints were portrayed. Later this was to become one of Masaccio's main themes, as in his painting of the Lame Man being healed when St. Peter's shadow falls on him (Florence, Church of Santa Maria del Carmine, Brancacci Chapel, after 1423).

Giotto builds up his compositions on the basis of the human figure alone. All his pictorial inventiveness originates in his portrayals of human beings and his entire *oeuvre* concentrates on depicting basic human situations. The formal technique that was so important in the *maniera greca,* such as the hieratic gold priming, the lavish clouds, the stylized architectonic and landscape scenes, which look like stage sets, schemes based on framework and decorations designed to fill the picture surface, plus costly, mannered work on drapery and folds, are reduced with him to a minimum, or become merely a side issue, or are even rejected completely. He felt that they distracted him from the central theme that he followed throughout his life as if possessed—as indeed the only two artists to match him in stature, Masaccio in the fifteenth century and Michelangelo in the sixteenth, were also possessed. He was constantly preoccupied with representing inner processes as expressed in concrete terms in gestures and expressive bearing. These can now be observed for the first time in living people, Tuscan contemporaries, and are not slavishly copied from a long Byzantine pictorial tradition that had now been exhausted.

Giotto's work is invariably clear-cut and great; every new picture is a new discovery; every painting a human drama. And from his total *oeuvre* a new artistic language emerges, in content as well as in form. Above all, Giotto freed painting from the domination of 'Greek' colour, which had originally been strident, even gaudy, but in its decadent phase became increasingly flat

20

20 Florence: Medici-Riccardi Palace. This building, created by Michelozzo from 1444 onwards, is the prelude to Early Renaissance palace architecture in Florence and up until 1540 was the seat of the Head of the Medici family. Later it became the private residence of their wives, widows and children. The former brilliant furnishings, apart from a small remnant (Medici Chapel with the painting by Benozzo Gozzoli), disappeared when Piero de' Medici was banished.

21 Florence: Medici-Riccardi Palace. The Courtyard. The Courtyard, with its refined and well-articulated architecture, deliberately contrasting with the robust, defensive exterior, is one of the most elegant creations of the Early Renaissance in Florence.

and dull. He operates with a few easily distinguished basic colours, which stand out in his frescoes in light and bright transparency, their tonal and lighting values shaded off in ultramarines, and brought into a harmonious unity without any 'forcing', for in Florence feeling for the individual value and character of every colour and every pigment was retained up to the end of the Renaissance. The typical Florentine attitude to colour can be seen already in Giotto. 'The colours stand out with great precision, firm, resonant, bright and effective, ready to enter into combat with one another and become reconciled in a higher unity' (Th. Hetzer: *Giotto*. Frankfurt am Main, n.d.).

Like Dante's work, Giotto's *Oeuvre* was an erratic boulder standing out in its time like a monument impossible to overlook, one that so towered into the era following that no art was possible directly afterwards which did not take it into account or produce successors. Like Dante, he had the effect of creating a large number of schools than ever before and his followers are legion: Stefano Fiorentino, Taddeo Gaddi, Puccio Capanna, Giottino, Bernardo Daddi, Maso da Banco, Andrea da Firenze, to name but a few of the most important of the 'Giottists' in the fourteenth century. Like Dante too, Giotto's fate was to have the art of his followers succumb to mere imitation, exhaust itself in more and more anaemic repetition, until it ran out in the sand and became banal. Just as Dante's linguistic rhythm and music, his ingenious metre and the world of his poetic images ultimately sank among those who plagiarized him to the level of utter travesty, occasional lyrics, political and polemical satire, and propaganda or erotically obscene song-writing, so Giotto's discoveries were carried further into flatter and flatter patterns, to such an extent that by 1400 all that was left in Assisi, Padua or Florence was pale derivatives of Giotto's epoch-making productions.

For this decline, however, Giotto is no more responsible than Dante for his more trivial followers. Little can be added to Burckhardt's judgement that: 'Giotto himself produced a stream of discoveries and new creations. Perhaps no other painter than he has so fully reconstituted art and set it off in a new direction after him' *(Cicerone)*.

To treat of Giotto and Florence is also to treat of Dante. His contribution to Italian national poetry may be considered greater even than Giotto's, Masaccio's, or Michelangelo's to Italian art. Giotto's figures have often been said to be personifications of Dante's. Dante's visions on the other hand could well be scenes for Giotto's figures. Giotto and Dante can only be seen here as a 'unity of opposites'. Temperamentally and spiritually they were fundamentally different, comparable only in their artistic intensity, and yet they were rooted in the same Florentine soil out of which their art grew. In terms of Schiller's categories, Giotto should be classified as 'naive' and Dante as 'sentimental', the one creating out of secure artistic instincts, natural humanity, naive psychology and observation felt rather than considered; and the other always substituting for his poetic features the acuity of Florentine rationalism, and the intellectual approach typical of Florence.

To that extent Dante—as a humanist, man of letters, poetic theorist, political scientist and social Utopian—possessed all the characteristics of the ideal *uomo universale,* the universal genius, as it emerged in Florence one hundred and fifty years later, at the beginning of the Renaissance. As an innovator he challenged a whole cultural epoch: on one side the dry monotony of the decaying world of medieval schools of theology and scholasticism, its teaching become dry as dust through constant repetition, analysis and interpretations of interpretations; and on the other, the world of chivalry and the *Minne,* the lyrics of the Provençal troubadours, frozen into mannerisms.

The political and social scene in Florence around 1250 was opposed to Dante's spirit of renewal. It was an extraordinarily politicised situation, in which all values were being called in question. The aristocracy had played out its historic role and for the first time the 'people', in the form of broad strata of the population, were entering the political arena. The *popolo grasso (grosso),* the guilds and middle class were pressing forward. The constant family feuds

22

38

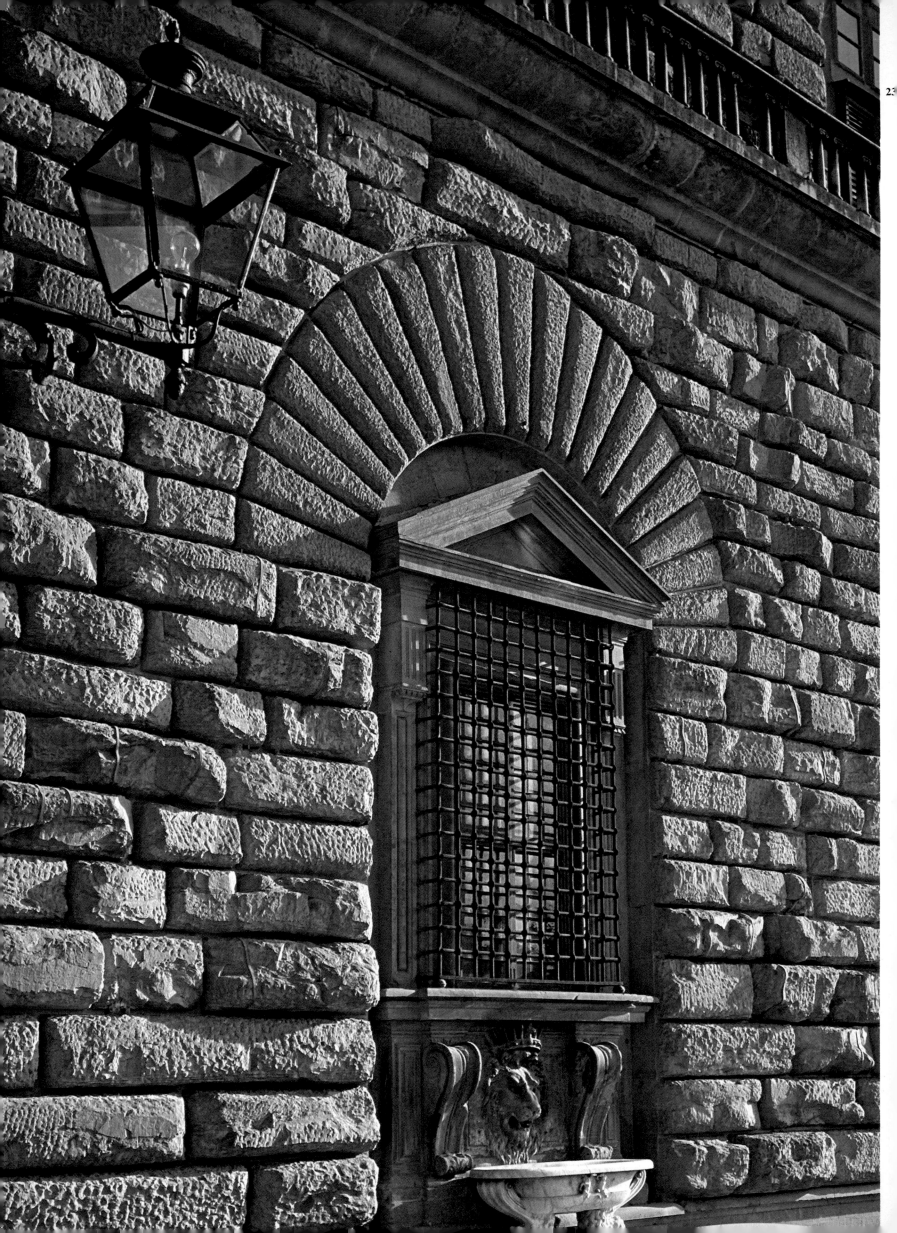

Previous page:
22   Florence: Pitti Palace. The Palace was begun by the Pitti family only a few years after the Medici Palace, and certainly in clearly-stated competition with that of Luca Fancelli (1457–1466). In 1550 it was purchased by the Medici. Up to the eighteenth and nineteenth centuries it was continually being altered and finally was enlarged to gigantic size. When Florence was provisionally Italy's capital (1864–1865), King Victor Emmanuel II had his residence on the upper floor. To-day it is a museum containing many of the main Medici items which even after the building of the Uffizi were privately held by the family.

23   Florence: Pitti Palace. Detail of Façade.

24   Florence: Strozzi Palace. This Palace, begun in 1485 by the Florentine merchant and humanist Filippo di Matteo Strozzi and completed about 1500 with the active assistance of the Medici for local architectural reasons, is the latest in our series and also the loveliest. In it the lofty theme of rustication, with deeply chanelled joints between the masonry blocks, is carried out in the most consistent manner. Enthusiastic expressions of appreciation have been forthcoming about this 'Miracle of rustication.' 'Every stone has the effect of a swelling muscle. The wall rises elastically and full of inner strength, up from the bottom, almost by itself' (G. Kauffmann, 1962).

24

41

and the party struggles between aristocracy, commercially-minded patricians, guilds and lower levels of the population had its counterpart in the cultural field, in the form of great spiritual unrest. The stylized traditions of the old *trouvère* poetry of love lyrics, and the theologians' philosophical problems, ossified in symbolism, no longer sufficed to express this unrest. Both troubadours and theologians did of course deal with the central themes of love, desire, death and pain. But against these Dante set the spiritual power of the 'creative Eros'. New values were thus brought into being. Love for the adored, idealized and therefore distant and unattainable lady was the expression of the new 'nobility of soul', which was demonstrated precisely by the fact that the far-off beloved could only be honoured and sung, not physically desired. To Dante's generation feminine beauty appeared to be a reflection of celestial perfection, and the beloved the personification of heavenly wisdom and of a divine plan of creation manifesting itself in rare cases in the form of a physically and spiritually perfect woman. The adored one became stylized as an angelic intercessor between God and the world. In accord with this angelic aspect, no sooner had Dante's Beatrice and Petrarch's Laura passed from childhood to puberty than they were elevated by the Florentine poets to the rank of sources of inspiration, angelic child-women, untouched and untouchable. The early, far too early death of the childlike beloved (Beatrice, or Laura) was experienced in a mystical sense as a tragic act of purification. She became in the kingdom of poetic imagination the immortal beloved. Her virginity also now acquired a plausible biographical context. Or can we fancy Laura or Beatrice as fulsome matrons, with an indolent Florentine shopkeeper for a husband, and a host of children tugging at their skirts?

The cult of feminine and virginal beauty provided a concrete basis for Aristotle's rediscovered aesthetics and made them Christian. Thus the artistic cult of the Madonna throughout the entire Renaissance and Baroque periods was now philosophically and psychologically prepared. The outward form of this poetic devotion was the *dolce stil nuovo,* the 'new sweet style', a vernacular literature based on the Tuscan-Florentine dialect. The knightly Courts of Love were replaced by metropolitan 'Love Courts'. 'It was a highly-charged, intellectually-lively atmosphere, attracting the fairest women in the city—Dante counted sixty of them in Florence—a divine Court in the centre of which stood Beatrice, Selvaggia, Monna Lagia, Monna Vanna and others. Their outward appearance, dress, passing mood, friendships and family all played a part in their glorification, while the city itself provided the theatre on which was played out the drama of the anguish and joy of love, poetically transfigured (L. Olschki, 1958).

Employing poetic insight, Dante—like Giotto—triumphed over a narrow world that was still basically provincial, and spiritualized a limited earthly reality. His language was the Italian of the people, which he called upon in the struggle against the dry and enervated Latin of the church. It was this language, no longer privileged and identified with certain social strata (only the clergy and a few educated people understood Latin) but understood by everyone, that laid the foundation for a new national literary language and speech which is still to-day the determinant of Italian culture. Dante found in Italy, which had been completely decentralized after the Graeco-Roman period, no less than fourteen established and sometimes very different dialects. In his treatise 'De Vulgari Eloquentia' ('Concerning Popular Rhetoric') he cleverly set out the reasons why it was Florentine that he had selected as the framework of his new literary language. This was because, of all the Italian dialects, it was closest to Latin and—according to Olschki—to the 'solemn majesty of literary Latin' of the Classical Period (not therefore of the Middle and Church Latin decadence).

All classes were seized by enthusiasm for the new vernacular poetry. Worship of Dante began even in his lifetime and persists to-day. There is hardly a single Italian who cannot recite at least a few lines of Dante by heart, and this does not apply only to the so-called educated classes. Visitors to Italy

25 Florence: The Strozzi Palace. The Courtyard architecture of the Strozzi Palace is by Cronaca (after 1497) and matches in quality Michelozzi's courtyard in the Medici-Riccardi Palace. (Plate 21).

Pages 44 and 45:
26 Florence: Ponte Vecchio and view up the river towards the Piazzale Michaelangelo. Florence's oldest bridge, one of the most famous and remarkable in the world, stands on the site of a Roman building on the old Via Cassia, which cut through the Roman Florentia. The first medieval bridge was made of timber. The first stone bridge came in 1080; the second, following a collapse, in 1170; and the third in 1333, after the great 'Flood', the worst in Florence's history, more devastating even than the 1963 catastrophe. The shops on the bridge have been in existence since the thirteenth century and were originally State property, rented out for high sums as one of the best and busiest commercial sites in old Florence. Not until 1495 were these botteghe sold to private individuals. In 1593 Archduke Ferdinando I decreed that henceforth only goldsmiths would be allowed to establish themselves on the bridge. The crowning connecting passage which allowed the Medici to ply speedily between their administration headquarters in the Uffizi and the new family residence in the Pitti Palace unhindered by public traffic dates from the time of Vasari (about 1570). The houses at the bridgeheads on the right and left banks of the Arno are historically skilful adaptations replacing those blown up in August 1944 to form tank barriers, thus saving the Ponte Vecchio itself.

are constantly astonished when the vegetable-seller in Verona's marketplace, or the pizza-baker in Trastevere, suddenly declaims Dante's classical and sonorous verses. There is always some excuse for doing so because Dante's works, like Goethe's, have taken root in the popular mind in the form of a series of quotations. Central to all of Dante's writings is the classical identification of beauty and morality. He thus gave the most resolute expression to an ideal which has never lost its validity, even in the Italy of to-day. Beauty as a virtue in itself has always been one of the fundamental tenets of that essentially aesthetically-minded people, who put it into practice every day in the art of setting the table in the simplest of country inns; in the modest lay-out of the fruit-dealer in the street; or the way in which the azaleas are arranged in stalls on the Spanish Steps in Rome. Such examples combine to make the Italians loved by other Europeans, whose affection is always ensured even though the politics of the day in Italy or the frequently chaotic-seeming business life may not always meet the conception others have of orderly behaviour. When all is said and done, every political action and every demonstration of political will in Italy is observed and judged from the artistic and aesthetic aspect. A politician without the gift of the gab or persuasive rhetoric will never amount to very much here. Socialist and communist parades invariably became aesthetic ventures in this country, with forests of red flags billowing in the breeze, which is how Bertolucci depicted them in his film *1900*. This was the feeling that in perverted form played itself out among the Italian Futurists, as shown in their manifesto on Mussolini's colonial war in Abyssinia, when they demanded 'aesthetic war' and—with Marinetti—lauded the 'fiery orchids of the mitrailleuse' (an ancestor of the machine-gun); the 'new architecture of big tanks; geometric air-squadrons; and spirals of smoke from burning villages.'

The same compulsion to render every aspect of life aesthetic can be seen in the Renaissance theory of the State, which translated the cult of the beautiful into political terms, conceived of the State as a work of art, and compared social reconstruction to a beautiful and perfect piece of architecture.

Thoughts such as these must have been in Dante's mind when in his treatise 'De Monarchia' he dreamt of general peace being the indispensable prerequisite for human welfare in society. A universal ruler of imperial rank with great moral authority seemed to him to be the guarantee of 'eternal peace'. In Dante's view, however, the new morality need not necessarily be based on Christian theology, but could be thought of as grounded in Aristotelian ethics, another anticipation of the Renaissance.

Dante was unable to identify wholly with either Pope or Emperor, since that would have been in contradiction with his Utopian concept of reconciliation. Neither a whole-hearted Ghibelline nor a committed Guelph, he was reckoned by his contemporaries in Florence to be among the 'Whites', i.e. 'Ghibelline' Guelphs. At that time the old parties, Guelphs and 'Imperials', were so mixed up that there was scarcely any difference between 'left' Ghibellines and 'right' Papists. The paradox becomes clear when we discover from Florence's records that Dante, himself of aristocratic lineage, was compelled for party reasons not only to condemn his fellow-poet and social equal the aristocratic Guido Cavalcante, but to take him the verdict in his *Torre* (now part of the modern Villa Bellosguardo). This must have hit Dante particularly hard, since Cavalcante was a friend of his and he had more than once praised his poetic achievement. This contradictory attitude—liberal we might call it to-day—paid off badly for Dante, who always found himself between two stools in the quarrelsome political scene of the time. As a 'white' Guelph he was one of the Priors of Florence in 1300. In 1301 his liberal group lost power to the radical 'black' Guelphs, and Dante had to leave the territory. As we have seen, he was sentenced to death in his absence. Never again did he visit the city. For him it became a part of a poetic super-reality, attainable and tangible only in his poetic imagination, like the early deceased, beloved Beatrice. He consequently declined a humiliating amnesty in 1316 which would have allowed him to return only under conditions that were unacceptable. His ambivalent feelings for his home town found shattering expression in a strongly-worded challenge to Emperor Henry VII, during the latter's visit to Italy for the purpose of reconstituting the Hohenstaufen Empire, to lay Florence low and efface the memory of it from history forever. He had nothing now in common with the city where he had been baptised and where he had hoped, as the crowning-point of his life, to be made 'Poeta laureatus'.

In his restless wanderings through northern Italy he found consolation in studying the ancient writers and ancient philosophy, especially the fatalistic Stoics. He had begun this return to the *sapienta veterum* (Wisdom of the Ancients) in 1292, after the death of Beatrice Portinari. It was an attitude fully in keeping with the spiritual milieu. Free discussion groups were set up everywhere to deal with political and moral problems and were supported by the provincial aristocracy and educated middle class. In these circles of *filosofanti,* as Dante called them, the educational traditions of the ancient world and the intellectual liberalism of the great Emperor Frederick II were carried on, and a foundation laid for fifteenth and sixteenth century Florentine academicism. These were secular forms of the medieval, clerical 'Disputations', and the outcome of the debates between intelligent men affected the entire city as much as the results of the planning competitions for the Cathedral, the Campanile or the Palazzo Vecchio. Florence always had a penchant for settling controversial points of view by talking them over. Dante's *'Vita Nuova'* (begun in 1293), the story of his love, is one result of this training. In the *'Convivio'* (1306–1309) Dante described the history of his intellectual education. The works that followed were always autobiographical in tendency, even the *'Divina Commedia',* which occupied the remainder of his life from 1307 on. This describes the poet's enlightened ascent to God and is a poetical account of the fantastic path which led the poet 'through all heavens and hells', out of the spiritual slavery of the medieval world into a 'Kingdom of Freedom' and the spirit, which is the beginning of the modern world. In the strictest symmetry, constructed, as it were, according to the precise rules of architecture, Dante summed up his view of the world in one hundred songs, including the various stages of purification: Hell *(Inferno),* Purgatory *(Purgatorio)* and Heaven *(Paradiso).* The Utopian content of the poem, with the vestiges of medieval piety and attraction to the future life that it contains, seem out of date now, insignificant and anachronistic. But the 'wealth and power of Dante's poetry' (L. Olschki 1958) have lived on, together with his language and his unmistakably harmonious style, his innovatory metaphors and his universal aspirations. Like Goethe's *Faust* some hundreds of years later, Dante's *Commedia* gives full expression in a profusion of visions and images to the learning of the period, to its collective consciousness, its dreams and disappointments, its hopes and fears, its splendour and its failure, its passions and its capacity for grief.

Like Giotto's work, Dante's poetry was the determining factor, at least as far as form and style are concerned, of the period that followed, the whole of the fourteenth century and the early fifteenth—a period that was once again marked in Florence by harsh social problems and upheavals in the structure of society.

Humanism and the Renaissance
The Emergence of a National Style in Florence

Renaissance—*rinascita*—rebirth, a rebirth of the arts, the birth of a new culture born out of the old. At the very height of this period Giorgio Vasari, its most famous chronicler, who came from Arezzo, had already recognized what the change meant. His *Lives,* the 'Biographies of the most excellent Painters, Sculptors and Architects' of his day, first appeared in 1550 and classifies it accurately on the whole, labelling it as 'classical'. This label is still

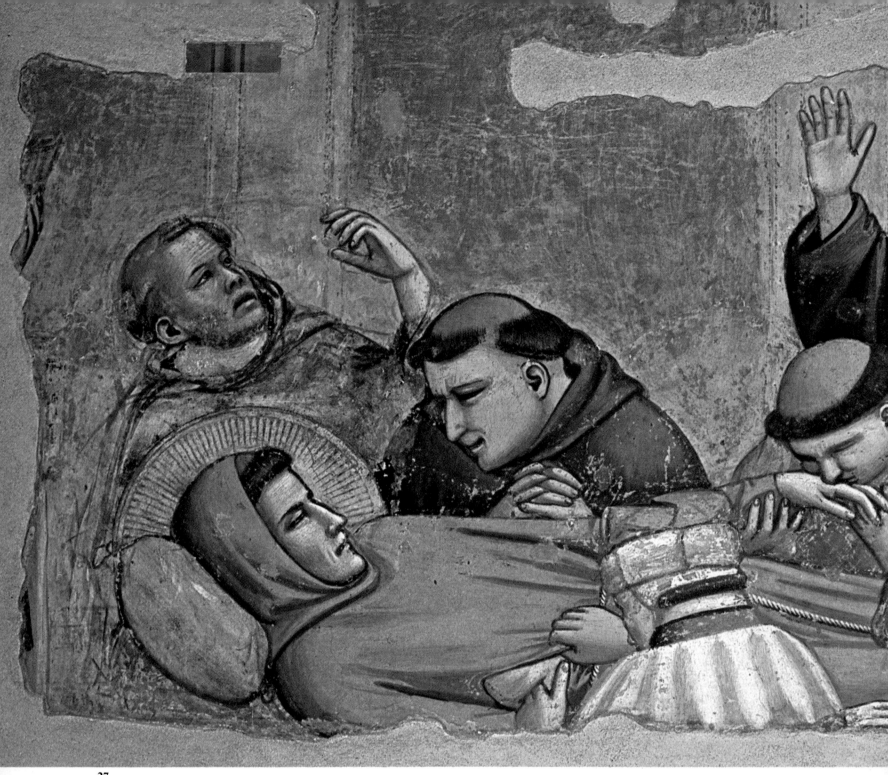

27

27   Giotto: 'The Death of St. Francis', circa
1320. Florence, Santa Croce. The fresco in
the Capella Bardi is one of Giotto's late works
and illustrates the great artistic breakthrough
in Dante's time.

accepted by art historians without question today; Vasari's conception of
history has indeed remained valid over four hundred years of art-historical
research. Since 1850 it has merely been improved and amplified, beginning
with Jacob Burkhardt's basic work on the Italian Renaissance. And the
accepted concept that the entire art and culture of Europe after Christ should
really be seen as a series of Renaissance and resumptions, 'renovations' (even
in the Middle Ages), and that the Renaissance in the fifteenth and sixteenth
centuries in Italy was merely the most consistent and successful and has
operated up to our own time.

In stating above, in connection with Giotto and Dante, that the 'Rebirth of
the arts' and the development of a national Italian style coincide, and that the
turning-point can be fixed as early as 1250, we have the authority of Vasari as
witness. He was the first to divide the art of the known world at the time into
three great eras: the brilliant classical period in Athens and Rome; a 'dark'
transitional period of decline, decay and cultural barbarism (or, in our terms,
the whole of the Middle Ages); and finally the period of 'rebirth', the
'rinascita' of the classical spirit which he places at circa 1250, half a generation

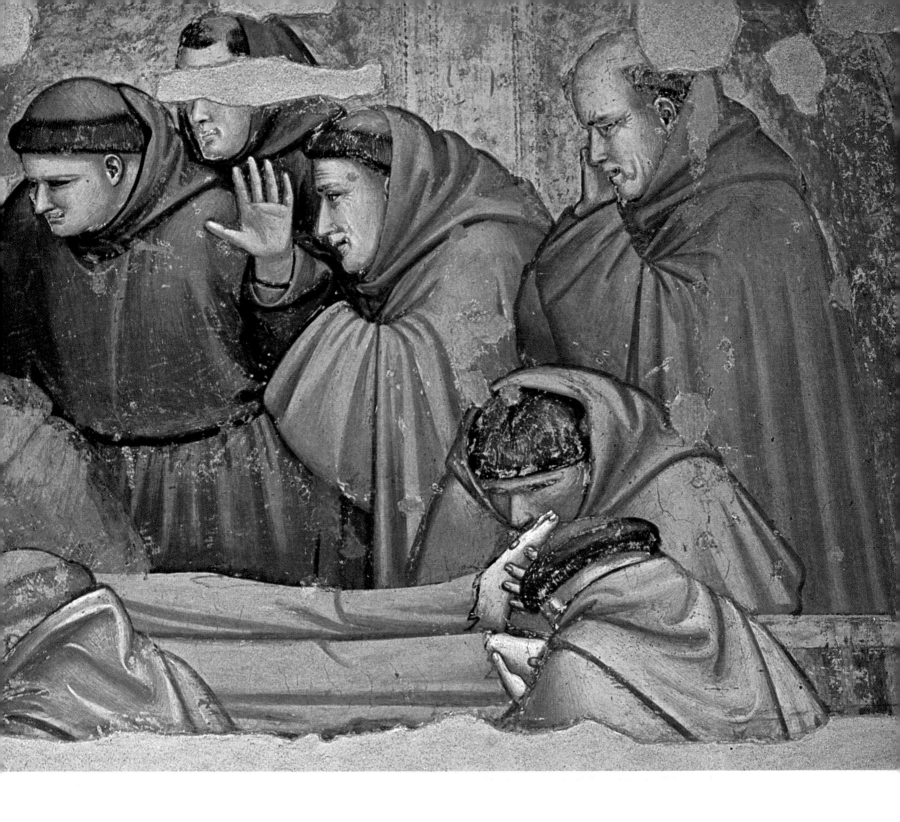

before the birth of Dante and Giotto.

The feeling that a turning-point had been reached must have been in the air in Tuscany. Circa 1280 an important find of ancient shards was made in Arezzo, an old centre of Etruscan-Tuscan and later of Roman culture. This was nothing out of the ordinary on Italian soil, which was full of such discoveries and still is, so much so that almost every deep digging yields such treasures, and indeed uncovered the whole Middle Ages. What was unusual and new was the reaction of cultured circles in Arezzo. A commission was formed, consisting of draughtsmen, sculptors and art-minded citizens, which called for a report on the findings by the historian Ristoro d'Arezzo. This was concluded in 1282. Giotto and Dante were then youths of sixteen or seventeen. Ristoro's report clearly indicates the delight of the 'connoisseurs', who dated the discovery approximately correctly in stating that the fragments had been in the earth for over a thousand years. 'When they saw them, they were beside themselves with delight, reached a pitch of excitement so to speak, raised a loud clamour and remained thunderstruck . . . They were amazed that human nature could show such subtlety and artistic skill . . .

49

[They said] these artists must have been divine, or the vases must have fallen from heaven, for they could not understand how they could have been made so [perfect] in that shape and colour as works of art.' In their time the 1282 discovery and report merely represented an anticipatory procedure and demonstrated nothing but a general trend and willingness. Humanism, and a direct return to the ancient world was still primarily a literary and philosophical phenomenon. Medieval tradition in form and content, and 'International' Court Gothic, were still all-powerful and largely determined the art production of the late thirteenth and the whole of the fourteenth century. Three dates mark the beginning of the 'rebirth', and the triumph of the new trend in art. They define at the same time the period generally referred to as the Early Renaissance. The Platonic Academy was founded in Florence about 1440, within the circle of Cosimo 'the Elder' Medici and at his instigation. Greek scholars such as Manuel Chrysoloras and Bessarion were coming to Italy at the beginning of the century from Byzantium, which was becoming increasingly unsafe as a 'bastion of Europe'. That city had come into direct cultural contact with Italy through the capture of Constantinople in the year 1204, and as early as 1400 émigrés had founded special circles for the study of Classical Greek, and were instituting a Plato renaissance.

The last Christian divine service was held in Hagia Sophia in Constantinople in May 1453, a scene movingly described by Stefan Zweig in his book *The Tide of Fortune*. The city finally fell to the Turks on May 29, 1453 and the church of St. Sophia was turned into a mosque, thus closing a chapter of world history. A second wave of migration thereafter led further Greek-Byzantine scholars to Italy, especially to Florence, and the ancient Greek legacy which had survived in the Byzantine Empire was now looked after in Italy. In the corridors of Hagia Sophia on the other hand the various Greek readings of the New Testament were no longer discussed, nor the question of how far Platonic philosophy had prepared the way for Christian doctrine. Henceforth, in one of Christendom's proudest monuments, it was the Koran which would be read and interpreted.

In 1492, following a sixty-one-day voyage, Columbus landed at Guanahani in what is to-day San Salvador, and afterwards discovered Cuba and Haiti. This was a year that signified a great turning-point in history. Europe's centre of gravity was shifted more and more to the West. A political and cultural front was being built up against the Turkish-Moslem East. The 'Turkish menace' was to be a constant political factor in determining European policy for two hundred and thirty years, until the defeat of the Osman soldiery in 1683, before the gates of Vienna. The sway of Islam over large sections of what had long been known as the 'Old world', and over the whole of the ancient Orient, had its parallel in the Christianization of the 'New World' in the West, first Central America and then the Northern areas of South America. It was then that the 'Europeanization' of the world began, for the world was still 'Eurocentric' by inclination. It was significant that in the same year, 1492, and in close association with Columbus' expedition, the last Arab rump of Empire in Spain, the stronghold of Granada, went ingloriously under. The Moors, literally driven into the sea, had to withdraw to the North African shores of the Barbary Coast, where the chief towns, Melilla and Oran, were also ultimately taken by the Castilians in 1497 and 1509. The end of the Spanish *Reconquista*, or Reconquest, was thus at the same time the beginning of the Spanish and Portuguese Conquest of America. A world had been discovered, and the result was a new feeling about the world, and a new view of the world.

From this aspect, Jacob Burckhardt's formula according to which the Italian Renaissance is the 'discovery of the world and of Man' acquires a universal political background that points far beyond purely cultural history. The source of the new Humanist and Renaissance movement lay in Florence. It was there that the cultural superstructure was created for the political about-turn. Florence's importance in world history lay in the fact that the new style and way of thinking soon acquired an 'international' i.e. an all-

28 Masaccio: 'Trinita' (Trinity), detail: approximately 1425. Florence. Santa Maria Novella. This mural marks the beginning of Early Rennaissance painting. The new 'classical' style is evident in the usage of the discoveries of perspective by the great Brunelleschi, the classic architectural framework, the symmetry and monumentality in the composition and the depiction of individual characters and their inner feelings. This work was of great importance for the young Leonardo and Michelangelo and it was revered and diligently studied during the High-Rennaissance.

30

29, 30 Fra Angelico: the 'Angel of the Annunciation', and 'Mary' (Details). Florence, Monastery of San Marco. These frescoes, created by Brother Fra Angelico for his mother-house in the forties of the fifteenth century, typify the formal language of 'Beato Angelico' and unite him closely with the customary conception of Florentine painting: a mélange of Gothic elegance and inner meaning, and the solid form and management of colour in the Renaissance.

European character, like the mature Romanesque in the twelfth and early thirteenth centuries, or the final court phase of Gothic, early in the fifteenth century. At the outset this artistic and cultural movement could still be regarded as being on a local scale, favoured by a happy constellation of political rulers (the Medici Dynasty), general economic prosperity (Early and Financial Capitalism, plus an organized banking system) and a rich reservoir of creative skills. Within little less than a generation and in astonishingly close succession, the city produced over a dozen artistically gifted individuals, who could all in hindsight claim world stature. To mention only the most outstanding, Brunelleschi was born in 1377; Lorenzo Ghiberti a year later in 1378; Donatello a decade later in 1386; and a year after that Fra Angelico.

Shortly before came the great painter Masolino, in 1383. In another decade there followed Michelozzo (1396) and Paolo Uccello (1397). At brief intervals these were joined by Masaccio (1401), Leon Battista Alberti (1404) and Filippo Lippi (1406). Benozzo Gozzoli in 1420 and Castagno in 1423 brought this important biographical sequence to a close.

Like Dante's *dolce stil nuovo* just one hundred and fifty years previously, the new style soon spread beyond Florence to the whole of Italy and the entire European world. From Brunelleschi onward the world learned to think differently about architecture. Donatello and Ghiberti developed canonical rules for sculpture which apply even up to the present. After Masolino, Masaccio, Lippi and Castagno, painters were forced to look at the world with new eyes, and before Vasari even, the great theorist Alberti laid down rules for a doctrine of art and aesthetics which are still binding to-day. The forces then operating in Florence, with a concentration that was extraordinary, produced one invention after another, the artistic side being only one aspect among others. In the field of economic theory, political science, linguistics and poetics, the exact sciences and medicine, the Arno city was no less productive and was already being compared by contemporaries to Ancient Greece and styled 'The New Athens'. Referring to the painter Pisanello from Verona (1397–1450), who was reconciling Gothic and Renaissance, a contemporary witness has succinctly outlined, in less than a dozen concepts, the artistic programme of these enormously productive decades. Angiolo Galli, writing in 1442 of Pisanello, defined the new 'cult of the beautiful' during the Renaissance as: *'Arte, mesura, aere et desegno, manera, prospectiva et naturale gli ha dato el celo per mirabil dono.'* Literally translated this phrase is flat and almost devoid of meaning: 'The Heavens bestowed on him [Pisanello] a miraculous gift: art, restraint, air and draughtsmanship, manner, perspective and nature.' More fully expressed each one of these concepts has a precise procedural meaning.

Arte signifies artistic skill, perfection in a new, independent sense extending beyond the medieval crafts. *Mesura,* measure or restraint, refers to the wide area encompassing the new doctrine of proportion and composition, the aesthetics of order, based on new mathematical and scientific knowledge, i.e. harmony that can be measured, determining equally the construction of a painted or sculpted human nude; an architectural structure; a piece of music; a poem successful metrically; or the rotation of the stars in their spheres. Here we have art made science, and conversely science made into art, an ideal which was to govern the Renaissance up to the sixteenth century, and art from then on until our own day. *Aere,* air, is to be taken as aerial perspective, i.e. sensitivity to atmospheric phenomena in painting, the grading of colour by perspective in open landscapes, while *desegno,* or *disegno,* the doctrine of the 'correct' anatomical or perspective drawing of a human nude or a figural composition or of architecture and scenery, was of course the Florentine contribution to Italian Renaissance art. This has been mentioned before in connection with the 'graphism' of the Florentine incrustation style. Later on, in the sixteenth century, Italian art theory, as in Vasari, will connect up the doctrine of *disegno* with the concept of the ideal artist, at the same time characterizing the two great centres of Italian art around 1550, 'graphic' Florence and 'painting' Venice, as complementary artistic possibilities. The ideal artist was required to have *il colore di Titiano e il disegno di Michelangelo*—'the colour of [the Venetian] Titian, and the drawing of [the Florentine] Michelangelo'. *Manera,* style, means lightness of touch, the actual technical means, obediently and effortlessly to hand as a matter of course. No one wishing to play late Beethoven sonatas should have to worry about fingering. Any humanist or philologist interpreting Plato must know his vocabulary. No one who, like Pisanello, wants to master large-scale, exceedingly detailed scenes containing many figures can afford to have any problems as regards the technique of pigments, supplies of paint, or choice of the right brush, and the smooth execution of commissions for portraits. Fifty to seventy years later the High Renaissance and Mannerism summed all this

54

up under the concept of the *virtuoso,* a tireless creator who is absolutely sure of his means. Since then virtuosity has become a proof, though not the only one, of artistic quality. *Prospectiva* probably means the newly-discovered linear perspective, based on precise geometric construction. In Early Renaissance paintings in Florence the linear base-points can often be recognized scratched into the background as a construction aid. Dürer has gone into this in detail, basing himself on the preparatory work of Italian theorists like Francesco di Giorgio Martini and Paolo Uccello. The *prospectiva* leads to a new organization of picture space, which now becomes the real space of living experience. No succession of flat, stratified side-scenes remains as in the painting of the entire Middle Ages. *Naturale,* finally, must be translated as meaning truth to nature, nearness to nature, the study of nature, and not as 'naturalism', which was already familiar to Gothic artists.

To sum up, these acquired skills and inherited talents are termed 'gifts from Heaven'. The artist was thereby raised to the status of an exceptional and special phenomenon. His new social rank was decided, beyond the crafts, outside the guilds and beyond normal reproduction of human life. Anyone possessed of Heavenly gifts, so obviously distinguished, stands on a par with the educated and propertied classes, with the patrician who has money and knows Greek, or with the ruler who has political power and soldiers at his command. It is not far from this to the highest distinction which the art critics of the High Renaissance could bestow, namely *'divino',* or 'divine' artist. Michelangelo was so judged, and Raphael and Titian, that constellation of three divine shining lights. This conception of the artist reaches its peak in the story according to which Emperor Charles V, ruler of a kingdom 'on which the sun never set', was sitting for a portrait by Titian and is said to have picked up the painter's brush when in his concentration the latter let it slip. As he did so he bowed, in the gesture of a servant: the Sovereign on Earth kneeling before the Sovereign in the Kingdom of Art.

This relationship of equality, almost of equality of rank, between artists and their eminent patrons was no one-sided affair. It was not only the social position and evaluation of the artist that altered with the Renaissance, or artistic activity that freed itself as something autonomous and special from the 'humiliations' of the medieval crafts. The converse was also true. Learned or rich patrons among the humanist-trained commercial patricians and bearers of political authority also approached the artistic style of existence, became artists themselves, or at least understood a great deal about art. 'Dilettante' was a complimentary term at the time.

Here too it was Florence in the fifteenth century that began it all. The new evaluation of the artist's work and of the artist himself, as having an important role to play in social life, came in the Early Renaissance period from Florence. 'Here, for the first time, the leaders of State recognise the spiritual equality of artists, because they are artists themselves.' (H. Keller, 1960.) We know that Lorenzo 'il Magnifico' Medici made with his own hands an architectural model for the castle of Poggio Reale near Naples. Giovanni de' Medici took part, with his own model, in the final competition in 1587 for the façade of Florence's cathedral. Relations between the Medici and 'their' artists were generally friendly and always on the basis of colleague to colleague.

Michelozzo, the architect and sculptor, accompanied Cosimo de' Medici into temporary exile in Venice in 1434. His sons were brought up in the Medici palace in the city and attained high office as bishop and lawyer. The architectural 'dynasty' of the Sangallos and the Medicis maintained a godfather relationship. Cosimo 'the Elder' Medici and Donatello were demonstrably close friends. The fifteen-year-old, highly-gifted Michelangelo was taken into Lorenzo Medici's household as a *familiaris,* had his own room in the palace and shared the family table. Bertoldo, the sculptor in bronze, also had a touching relationship with Lorenzo Medici. He had his own studio in the palace, in which he slept; often accompanied his princely friend to the mineral baths; was treated by Lorenzo's private doctor, the best

Pages 56 and 57:

31 Fra Angelico: 'The Deposition from the Cross' (cut slightly at the edges). Florence. San Marco Museum. This altarpiece, which was painted from about 1435 to 1440, is a good example of Fra Angelico's style. The Gothic spirit still underlies the elegantly stylized figures, but the draughtsmanship, which is finely conceived in three dimensions, and the sturdy arrangement of the many figures in the composition expresses the Renaissance creative impulse. The landscape in the background—a glimpse of a fortified hill town on the left-hand side and on the right a densely populated valley with a castle on a hilltop—is a typical blend of idealized features and precise observation. The medieval gold background has disappeared and we look out on to the open fifteenth-century landscape as if through a window, with white clouds drifting in the summer sky, trees drawn with botanical accuracy and proper spacing to give perspective. The bright, transparent, resonant colouring, with clearly delineated areas of natural colour and blue and red dominant colours as it were in contrapposto, *is characteristic of Florentine painting.*

in the country; and in one of the Medici's country villas, where he had been taken when mortally ill on account of the good air, died mourned by the princely clan like a close member of the family. Intimate relations such as these between artist and patron were common later throughout sixteenth-century Italy. The close contact in Florence between the power-élite and leading artists is an expression of the public character which art was able to claim in the Late Middle Ages, and of the great public interest aroused among all classes. One sign of this was the Florentine-Tuscan habit of holding competitions for all important public commissions, a novelty in Italian art-history but typical of the cultural scene in Tuscany. The first great competitions for building the Cathedral, at the end of the thirteenth and beginning of the fourteenth centuries, have already been described. This continued in the fifteenth and sixteenth centuries. The lists of commission members in 1490, 1498 and 1504 for the various competitions have been preserved and are interesting and illuminating as to the class-free nature of public opinion. The 1504 competition had been announced on the occasion of setting up Michelangelo's 'David' (Plate 56) in the choir-section of the Cathedral. Later it was the existing site in front of the Palazzo Vecchio that was selected (Plate 16). The lists contain a cross-section of the city's social structure and truly reflect public participation in matters of art. In addition to the most famous of the city's artists, the architects of the Sangallo family and (in the 1504 jury) Leonardo da Vinci, they included, literally, 'butcher, baker and candlestick-maker': several joiners, a few goldsmiths, a mason, a stonemason, a smith, the town-crier and town-piper, plus a few jewellers, a painter of miniatures and a carpet manufacturer.

The artificially charged atmosphere of the city, with the economic climate favouring art and providing splendid opportunities for commissions, not only for 'high' art but for applied art and handicrafts in particular, attracted hordes of major and minor artists from 1450 onwards. The surviving lists of guilds from about 1470 show in the case of Florence seventy butchers and slaughterers, sixty-six grocers and eighty-three silk workers. Parallel with these we find eighty-four craft workshops devoted to wood-carving and inlaid work, fifty-four studios for marble and stone décor and forty-four gold- and silversmiths, an astonishingly equal distribution as regards status. The position is no different among the 'authentically' great artists, except that their story is rather confused, since many of the names of artists that have come down to us cannot be linked to works that have been preserved, and the historical process of selection and destruction has meant that they and their *Oeuvre* have been consigned to oblivion. The St. Luke Guild of *artistes-peintres* numbered in 1472 thirty professional 'figure-painters'. Of these only eight can be historically traced. No fewer than seventeen bearing the name 'Raffaelo' are testified to in Florence from the beginning of the sixteenth century, one of these being the 'divine' Raphael Santi.

Since the artists pouring into the city could no longer organize themselves inside the narrow specialized framework of the appointed guilds of medieval origin, and did not feel themselves to be artisans any more, they chose the guild to which they wanted to belong, freely, on the basis of social prestige and the social achievements of the various 'unions'. This contrasts with the limited freedom of choice offered in the unions of to-day. In 1517 nine plastic artists were accepted into the guild of the *medici e speziali,* Physicians and Apothecaries, probably because the *speziali* were also druggists, and dealt in pigments and other artists' requirements. One of the finest of addresses—best compared with that of an exclusive London club—was that of the Arte della Lana, the Wool-Weavers Guild. Not surprisingly, the names of prominent artists are to be found on their rolls. No little influence was required, as well as recognition of one's work, to achieve entry into this distinguished assembly, which had desirable commissions to distribute or procure. It is no accident that the Arte della Lana was the only guild to describe its headquarters in 1427 as a *palazzo* (palace), equal, therefore, to the Palazzo del Vescovo (the Bishop's residence), the Palazzo della Signoria (City Hall) or the Bargello

58

32 Filippino Lippi 'Resurrection, after fourteen years, of the dead Son of Emperor Theophilus by St. Peter', painted from 1483–1485. Florence. Santa Maria del Carmine: Brancacci Chapel. The painting belongs to the series of frescoes depicting the life of St. Peter which was begun by Masaccio and Masolino and completed by Lippi from approximately 1483 to 1485. Masaccio took part in the work depicted, the figural composition, at least, being traceable to him, though the heads are said to be by Lippi. The Imperial Prince's head is represented by that of a young Florentine noble (Granacci).Masaccio's frescoes in the Brancacci Chapel introduce the new 'classical' Renaissance style based on Greco-Roman models, while the art of Fra Angelico and his colleagues represents a counter-current within Florentine painting in 1440–1450 which is historically minded and Gothic. In this sense the earlier work of Masaccio and his circle can be said to be more 'modern', and it can easily be understood that the young artists of the High Renaissance in Florence, Michelangelo and Leonardo da Vinci in particular, should have had their schooling in the creations of Masaccio and Masolino.

33

(city government), whereas all the other 'union' simply had a *casa* (house). Nor was it an accident that the same guild was given responsibility in 1331 for the most outstanding (and problematic) public construction project in the city, the building of the Cathedral, for people were well aware that only the Rectors of the powerful Wool-Weavers Guild, with its financial and organizing skill and its political authority in the commune, could still rescue the whole enterprise, which was constantly being brought to a standstill. Two hundred years later the Guild did in fact bring the cathedral to completion without further complications. Similar sponsorships were undertaken by other guilds in Florence for other centenary projects, including the Foundlings' Hospital, the San Marco Monastery and so on. That this was by no means a purely Italian phenomenon can be seen from the fact that Strasbourg Cathedral was also completed under guild supervision and the Rathaus and towers in Cologne were similarly completed. All the important guilds in Florence got together in the end to make it possible for Orsanmichele to be garnished with statuary. (Plate 52). No description of the rediscovery of the Graeco-Roman freestanding figure by Donatello, Ghiberti, Michelozzo and Nanni di Banco in the early decades of the fifteenth century, which entered into fertile competition with the draped Gothic style, would be complete without mention in Florentine records of the guilds of stonemasons and joiners, stocking-weavers and butchers, linen-weavers, harness-makers,

33   Filippino Lippi: 'The SS. Peter and Paul before the Proconsul' (detail), circa 1483–85. Florence, Carmine Church, Brancacci Chapel. This frescoe is to be placed in the same context as the previous illustration. Here too, Lippi followed in the footsteps of Masaccio and Massolino. The head of Simon Magus (far left) is probably a portrait of the painter Antonio del Pollaiuole, whereas the young man (above right) could be a self-portrait of Filippino Lippi himself.

34   Filippino Lippi: 'Apparition of the virgin to St. Bernard', circa 1480, Florence, Badia Church. This altarpainting of the vision of St. Bernard is one of Lippi's most outstanding early paintings. The figures have a nearly sculptural plasticity and sharpness of contours. The brilliant portrait of the donor, Domenico del Pugliese (below right), the depiction of the various members of his family and the group of the Madonna with angels are tell-tale examples of the Florentine art of representation. The rugged rock-landscape provides further evidence of the sense of reality, inherent to Florentine painting on the threshold of the High-Rennaissance.

furriers and wool-weavers who here immortalized their patrons and thereby
provided the artists who revived the art of sculpture with an appropriate
basis for their innovatory performance.

The public character of art and, conversely, the public's feeling for art in
fifteenth and sixteenth century Florence, which was both the cause and effect
of the incomparable cultural climate there during the Renaissance, is
illustrated by contemporary anecdotes, which throw a more significant light

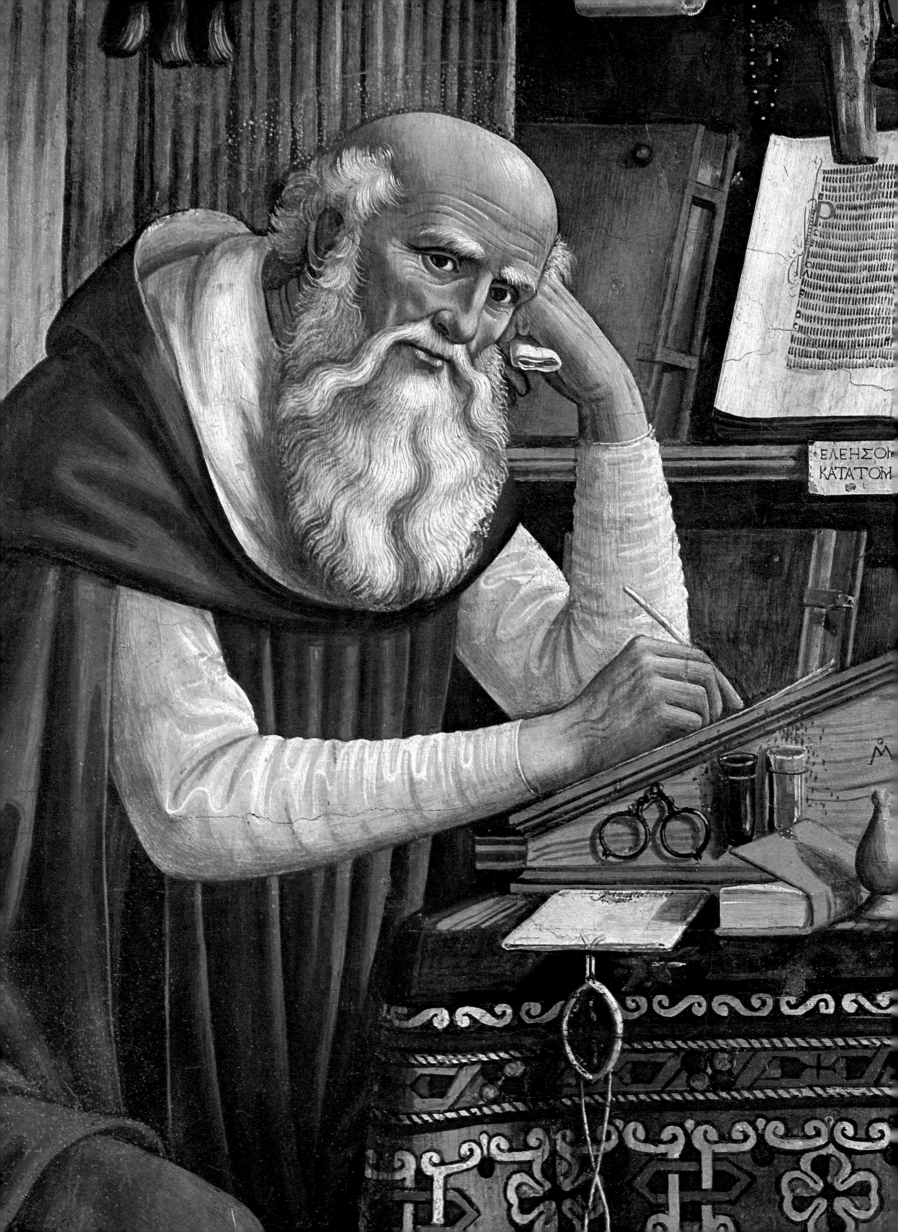

on the scene between 1450 and 1550 than any prolonged analysis. In 1501 Leonardo, as was the custom, publicly exhibited in his studio the cartoon for his celebrated 'St. Anne with Two Others'. Public reaction to this event has been described by Giorgio Vasari, whom we have already had occasion to mention several times: 'It was not only artists who were moved to admire the work. When the cartoon was ready men and women, young and old, could be seen for two whole days making their pilgrimage to the room in order to contemplate Leonardo's marvellous achievement, as if it were all some brilliant festival. The entire population was astonished. 'The same scene was repeated fifty years later with Benvenuto Cellini's famous bronze statue of "Perseus", a masterpiece of mature mannerism, which was completed in 1553–1554 and now graces the Loggia dei Lanzi, by the Palazzo Vecchio and the Uffizi (Plate 66). Shortly before its completion Duke Cosimo Medici suggested to the artist that the work should be exhibited in the studio for a few hours and made the subject of discussion, in order to test public opinion. Cellini did not like the idea but complied with his patron's wish and—lo and behold!—Cellini's fears proved groundless. 'On the day when the Perseus was placed on public exhibition over twenty sonnets were at once affixed to the door. Even when the statue was no longer on show the shower of Greek and Latin verses continued unabated, for the University of Pisa was on holiday at the time, and Florentine students who were staying at home found this demonstration of poetic training a most agreeable way of spending their time. Well-known artists like Pontormo and Bronzino also affixed their adulations in verse to the studio-door.' (H. Keller, 1960.)

After this excursion into Florentine art-sociology let us return to the 'Great Period', between 1420 and 1450.

It is scarcely possible to render a systematic account of these years or of their inventiveness. The best way to master the series of artistic innovations would be to list them in tabular form, like a catalogue, for most of what for us constitutes the artistic, architectural and sculptural inheritance was then new and unusual and had perforce to be regarded as 'invention'.

When Goethe shared the experience of the Feast of the Epiphany in Rome at the beginning of 1787, in the Propaganda Fide with its confusion of tongues, and heard the first sounds in the language of Plato and Euripides, he acknowledged that 'The sound of Greek was like the shining of a star at night.' The Florentines must have felt the same in 1400 when the first of the émigrés arrived from Byzantium and talked to each other in their native tongue. Goethe's enthusiasm is on a par with the delight in life felt by the first Florentine artists to glance into the well of the classical past and discover there their personal and artistic identity—or rediscover it, we have to say, in the Renaissance sense. Vasari clearly reports how Brunelleschi and his friend Donatello the sculptor set out for Rome between 1420 and 1430, armed with stadia rods, measuring-lines and spades; how they very patiently studied the ruins that were still standing; took measurements and made surveys; discussed their purpose and proportions; and probably dug up foundations, half-buried capitals and drum-like columns, which must have scared away the cows and sheep that grazed among the fields of ruins in the heart of Rome and on the Forum, significantly known in the local dialect as the *campo vacchino*. The two friends' mysterious activity and peculiar equipment appeared highly suspicious to the Romans, who took them for conspirators, or—closer to home—treasure-hunters.

The study of nature—and here we recall Angiolo Galli's concept *naturale*—and of the ancient world are the two poles between which art in Florence henceforth moved. It was out of the ancient world and nature that the new style grew and was at once accepted as the national Italian style and as the source of a new national, political identity. Vasari's tirades a century later against the 'barbaric' Gothic of the North now become comprehensible. It was not simply the result of a 'generation gap' between two fundamentally different art eras and styles but also the expression of native identity, which had to be delimited and defended like any other national identity. The

37 Andrea del Sarto: 'St. Filippo Benizzi healing a Woman possessed.' (Detail). 1510. Florence. Santissima Annunziata. Passage in the Outer Court. The painting derives from a series of frescoes dated 1510 and represents the Florentine contribution to High Renaissance painting. Del Sarto's cycle is distinguished particularly by attractive landscape backgrounds, which can be glimpsed through the architectural framework (just visible at the upper edges).

individuality, complexity and originality which the generation of Brunelleschi and Donatello found in the works of the ancients and in the living works of nature now became qualities in artistic creation and characteristics of the artistic individual himself, i.e. of the complex *uomo universale* of the Renaissance.

The 'new style' encompassed equally and uniformly the three most important artistic categories, architecture, painting and sculpture. Contemporaries must already have been aware of this. A favourite game among the Florentine intellectuals, an area, as it were, in which art criticism could be assessed with the weapons of the shrewdest methodology and scientific fantasy, was the *paragone,* comparison of the arts with one another. This involved a question which was passionately debated. To which of the three categories could leading role be given? The plastic arts could, for instance, reproduce the human figure, the central theme of the Renaissance, in palpable three-dimensional form, and the resemblance would be totally convincing. An ancient story would be trotted out as proof according to which a cow painted by Apelles, or cast in bronze by Myron, had been so lifelike that a steer had wanted to mount it. To the 'new' philosophy of fidelity to nature this was an indication of artistic quality. The sculptor, on the other hand, was unable to represent the human ambience and atmospheric phenomena, except in the background of bas-reliefs almost painterly in treatment, and even there only very inadequately. Painting again can convey

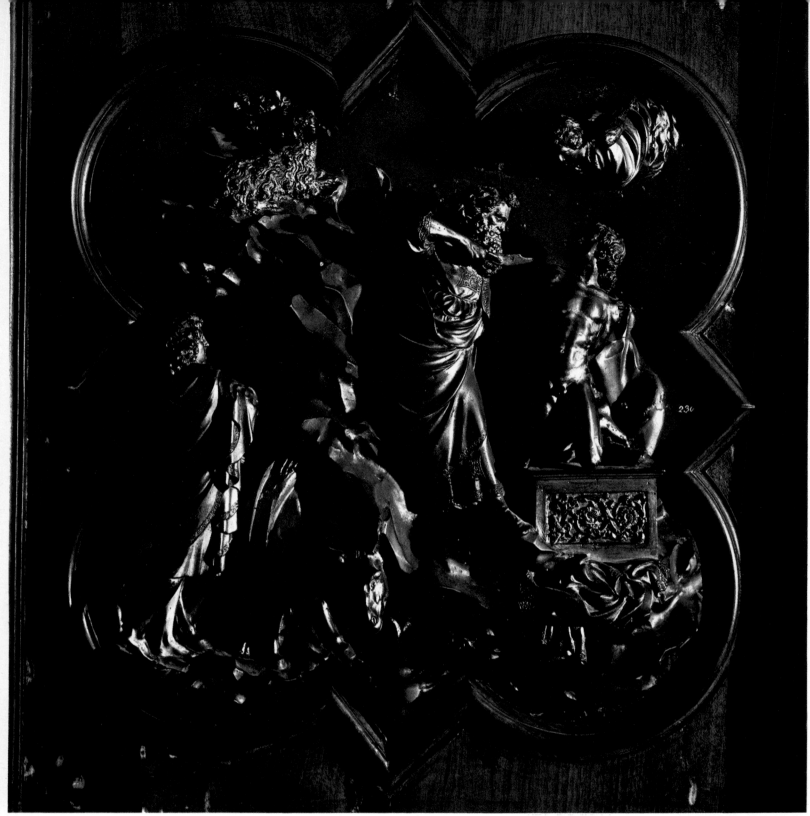

38

any mood in flowing colour washes and atmospheric tones. It can give the illusion of perspective and depth, but is obliged to represent physical volume and plasticity in terms of light and shade, and sometimes the only view of the human body it gives is one that is posed, stiff and as if fixed in whatever stance suits the 'tableau'. It is to the *paragone* idea (typical of the all-embracing principle of rivalry and competition that was the essence of Florentine art) that we are indebted for such profound thinking concerning the nature of art and the arts in general. This friendly argument was never settled. Even Vasari was unable to give a satisfactory answer to a question that was basically insoluble. Each of the three categories posed new problems conditioned by social, religious and political changes. A new language of form was found for these, and new techniques and materials discovered or developed from methods and materials handed down from the Middle Ages.

A leading place was allotted from about 1420 to the great Filippo Brunelleschi and that at a time when in the rest of Europe the Soft Style,

38 *Lorenzo Ghiberti: 'The Sacrifice of Isaac', 1402. Florence. Bargello, National Museum. This bronze relief is one of the gems of the Florentine National Museum. Along with Brunelleschi's 'Sacrifice of Isaac' (illustration following), it was awarded the prize as the best entry in the 1401–1402 competition for the doors of the Florentine San Giovanni Baptistery, but not transferred there, as constituting a 'model example'. This work is the beginning of the breakthrough to the 'new style' in Florence, in reaction to Gothic tradition. Notice the treatment of the upper part of Isaac's body, anatomically accurate and owing everything to classical art; also the dramatic composition, in tense counterpoint.*

39 Filippo Brunelleschi: 'The Sacrifice of Isaac', 1402. Florence, Bargello, National Museum. This sculpture is one of the two 'competition reliefs' for the Florence Baptistery (see previous illustration) that have been preserved. Like Ghiberti's 'Sacrifice of Isaac' it shows mastery of the bronze-casting technique developed from ancient sources, and perfect handling of the central problem of the art of relief, the tension between 'figure' and 'background'.

Court Gothic, still prevailed. As an architect in particular, but also as a sculptor, he produced a new vocabulary of form, starting out from the theoretical and empirical preoccupation with the ancient world (archaeological expeditions to Rome). At that time many more monuments were still standing than there are to-day. Brunelleschi convinced himself and his colleagues that what they had before them was a treasure of inestimable value which had always been available but had escaped attention for centuries owing to the fog produced by 'barbaric' Gothic. 'Brunelleschi was the first clearly to recognise pure gold, so to speak, in this treasure and decided to make out of it a coinage which would drive out of circulation the worn currency of architectural language which had thus far been valid; this seemed to him to have become devalued because of base medieval elements.' (W. Paatz, 1953).

One main result of the Roman studies by Brunelleschi and Donatello was the re-introduction of the four classical orders: 'Doric' (or 'Tuscan');

67

40

40, 41 *Lorenzo Ghiberti: first bronze door on the north side of the Baptistery of San Giovanni in Florence. The door resulted from a competition held in 1401–02 in which Ghiberti's design was chosen in preference to Brunelleschi's. It was executed during the years 1403–1424, with the help of assistants. It follows Graeco-Roman models in the way the three-dimensional decoration has 'crept' from the doorcasing on to the actual door panels. In the temples of classical antiquity, too, artists liked to decorate the portals with figurative decoration.*

'Ionian'; 'Corinthian'; and 'Composite'. These were indisputably to govern the whole of architecture from 1420 up to the advent of functionalism and the Bauhaus in our own time. The Greek and Roman system of load and support, columns, free-standing pillars, wall-panelling and beams or rounded arches now replaced the aspiring Gothic, which was increasingly criticised by the Renaissance theorists as 'contrary to nature'. A series of ideal forms based on Euclidean geometry, such as the cube, sphere, cylinder or hemisphere, was used instead, as the main architectural framework. The central cupola became the monumental *leit-motiv,* built up on the ideal shape of the circle as in Florence's Cathedral, where Brunelleschi's imposing volume was first brought to such a pitch of mastery that the Dome—'the Roof of Florence'— now lies lightly over the city, at once centralizing and protecting (Plates 1 and 5). The return to ideal shapes, 'original forms' we might say, had a metaphysical basis for early Renaissance artists. Architecture was regarded as 'petrified music', a contrived metaphor for the harmony of the spheres. This 'harmonic aesthetic of order', as the art historians who followed this school of thought paraphrased it, implied a major revolution, particularly in ecclesiastical architecture, which continued to be seen as the highest form of

architecture. The Florentine Cathedral Dome (Plate 5), and finally—one of the most perfect, solid and harmonious creations in Florentine architecture—the Pazzi Chapel by Santa Croce (Plate 11), represent the new style. These are all creations of the protean Brunelleschi whose structures did not merely introduce a new chapter in art history but decisively altered Florence's image and left his personal stamp upon it. Following the new Renaissance claims to universality, Brunelleschi invariably thought in terms of wider urban contexts. Thus the harmonious cupolas of Brunelleschi and his successors fit into the Florence profile as a contrast to the sheer towers and façade motifs of the Gothic: the Vecchio Tower, the Bargello and Badia Towers, and the forms assumed by the Cathedral façade, as well as Giotto's free-standing Campanile. Together with these they comprise an unmistakeable unity, pregnant with meaning. (Plate 1).

It was the human figure that provided the key to this architectural composition and proportioning. Leonardo's figure of a man, proportioned-out and with arms and legs outstretched, encircled as in a gyro wheel, is now well-known. The axes of the body divide the circle into four sections. Theorists described the human form, as a proportioned basic figure, in terms of columns. The head then becomes the capital, the trunk the shaft of columns, the greatest projection being in the centre, around the navel; while the feet are the columns' base. Alternatively the human nude was outlined in the basic design of a basilica (Head = apse; breast = crossing; outstretched arms = transepts; legs = nave). These analogies between human and architectural proportions established a direct relationship between the 'microcosm' and the 'macrocosm' and between the earthly and celestial spheres, a typical Renaissance conception. Architecture, the symbol of both heavenly harmony and organic human proportions, thus became the medium for expressing a comprehensive cosmic idea.

This theory of organic and ideal proportions coinciding answered the two decisive ideals of Renaissance aesthetics, firstly the classical, which had made man 'the measure of all things', and secondly the return to the world of nature and the organic, to naturalness (Galli's *naturale*).

In a never-ending attempt to get to grips with classical antiquity and with nature, artists tried to trace the secret laws of proportion by empirical observation and ingenious speculation; to fathom the undoubted beauty of classical ruins, which people were not prepared simply to feel, but wanted also to decipher and imitate scientifically. The ancient basic principles of *contrapposto* and Golden Section were recovered. The principle of the unity of opposites *(contrapposto)* or of harmony between the height and breadth of a wall surface, pictorial area or figural composition (medial Section) were decisive factors in architecture, painting and sculpture.

The ancient ruins, however, not only stimulated the scientific ambitions of the archaeologists and exalted national sentiments in the contemplation of the former greatness of Rome and Italy, but also fostered nostalgic and elegiac feelings, a sense of the former, now irrecoverable spirit of the past and of a 'Golden Age' bound up with Roman times and idealized; an age which in fancy became a long-buried Utopia. Yet there was always an awareness that this kingdom of beauty, dignity, virtue and identity with the *'patria'* could never be recaptured, however much Florence was ennobled, or the Pope in Rome was styled the new 'Imperator Romanorum' in an ecclesiastical empire of Faith and Spirit. Petrarch and Boccaccio both voice feelings such as these. From the fifteenth century onward accounts mount up of learned men of letters visiting Rome's ruins and being transported into a trance-like state by the ancient city; musing on the Colosseum in the sparkling midday heat, or on the Temple of Venus in the luminous evening glow; conversing with the most illustrious spirits of antiquity—Cicero the orator, Cato the moralist, the great Caesar, the Emperor Augustus, or the stoic philosopher Seneca—among the rows of tombs in the Via Appia, shaded by laurel, cypress and plane-tree.

In this atmosphere it caused a world-wide sensation when on April 18 1485, some fifty years after Donatello's and Brunelleschi's alleged stay in Rome, the news ran like wildfire through the city (and soon through the other Italian centres) that Lombard masons looking for treasure on the Via Appia, not far from the celebrated monument to Caecilia Metella, had broken into an ancient tomb. They had at once come upon a marble sarcophagus bearing the inscription: 'Julia, daughter of Claudius'. Taking with them the valuable grave gifts—gold and jewellery—the grave-robbers disappeared, leaving behind quite a different kind of treasure for the rapturous Romans who soon

42 *Donatello (?): 'John the Baptist'. Florence. Bargello, National Museum. The attribution to Donatello of this figure, which combines an attitude that is still Gothic (the motif of the hand) with a fully Renaissance anatomy—scientific and precisely observed (see the collarbone and feet)—is now being disputed all over again. Some experts have even suggested that it is the work of the young Michelangelo, in which case the marble sculpture could be dated to the 1490s at the earliest.*

43 *Donatello: 'David'. 1430–1432. Florence. Bargello, National Museum. This sculpture, carved in 1430–1432, was originally intended for a fountain in the Palazzo Vecchio. Donatello's masterpiece is generally considered to be the most important piece of sculpture dating from this period. (For a complete description see page 79.)*

70

42

43

44 Donatello: Annunciation Relief, 1435. Florence. Santa Croce. This central work by Donatello, standing only a few yards from Michelangelo's tomb, was created as an altar-tabernacle in 1435 under commission from the Cavalcanti family. The two-figured group is wonderfully tender in spiritual expression, revealing the tense relations between the Madonna and the Angel. The architecture of the framework is based on classical models (the aedicula motif), as are the two pink terra cotta putti next to the scrolled pediment at the upper edge of the picture. The two figures (rediscovered only in 1900) imitate classical figurative acroteria, which were also usually of pinkish clay. The original gold paint on the greenish stone was carefully touched up in 1884.

45 Donatello: Bronze pulpit. Florence. San Lorenzo. The two bronze pulpits, only one of which is illustrated here, are in the style of late Classical/Early Christian 'ambos' and thus link up with classical tradition. Donatello did not live to see the completion of the two structures, which were finished by Bertoldo and Bellano between 1460 and 1470. The marble column supports are a mannerist addition. Originally the twin pulpits probably stood on a wooden framework.

discovered the sacrilege. According to contemporary reports the sarcophagus contained the well-preserved corpse of a young woman, almost a child, some fifteen years old, her expression so alive still as to make it seem that she had only just passed away. The limbs were still quite flexible and owing to the finest of embalming materials and fixatives the living colour of the skin, the half-open eyes and the mouth, opened as if to speak, were in a complete state of preservation. The body was solemnly escorted to the palace of the Curator in the Capitol and placed on public exhibition. Then a veritable pilgrimage began of men, women and youths, as if to some masterpiece by Leonardo or Michelangelo, and the stream of sightseers never let up. Even artists came, to take her likeness, for—how could it be otherwise?—the dead girl, reborn so to speak, was as charming in her loveliness as Venus the Goddess of Love herself. In the words of a late fifteenth-century eye-witness she was 'beautiful beyond the power of words or description, and if words or description were possible, no one who had not seen her would believe them.' Pope Innocent VIII felt after a few days that the spectacle had gone on long enough, and put an end to the beauty-cult which for him—despite all his own enthusiasm for classical antiquity—was threatening to assume features that were clearly pagan. He therefore had the body secretly buried without ceremony at an obscure spot in front of the Porta Pinciano. The empty sarcophagus remained in the Palazzo dei Conservatori, and was for a long time still sought out in awe by disciples of beauty fascinated by the ancient world. The memory of that event in 1485 remained so alive that when after the war the comparatively well-preserved body of a woman of the ancient world came to light on the Via Cassia, people believed and insisted on believing that what they had before them was the girl from the Via Appia whom Innocent VIII had put away. *Se non è vero, è ben trovato,* as they say in Italy. Even if it isn't true, it's still a good story, and illustrates the popular mentality at the start of the Renaissance, which hungered after just such myths and legends. It is a matter of indifference whether it really was an aristocratic woman of Ancient Rome who was found, as the Renaissance believed, or whether—as Jacob Burckhardt claims—her fresh appearance was due to a wax mask; or even whether some Egyptian merchant in love had had a little Syrian dancer

artistically embalmed by the methods used in his own country.

The treasures discovered in libraries and archives when looking through ancient writings were of a quite different kind. The yellowed and neglected parchments were just as eagerly hunted down and removed from their dusty tombs as the 'Via Appia beauty', and studied as authentic evidence of the Golden Age of the arts. Every hint in these manuscripts, which were without illustrations, was followed up, and attempts were made to picture the classical forms of decoration and architecture in order to test them out on new buildings. This became particularly evident when a type of building peculiar to the Middle Ages had to be remodelled to conform to the new age: the metropolitan Palazzo, which was the most important assignment in secular architecture, ranking now alongside the ecclesiastical. Transforming the enclosed cube-shaped palace structure by means of cloister-like inner courtyards surrounded by open loggias, which fourteenth century had developed in the Palazzo Vecchio (Plates 16 and 17) or the Bargello (Plate 19), Michelozzo created in Florence in 1444 the prototype in Italy of the Renaissance palace, whose imprint can still be felt in the Roman High Baroque period.

This was the Palazzo Medici (Plates 20 and 21). True, the block-type construction was retained for traditional and representational as well as security reasons (the inner part of the city was still by no means pacified), but it expressed the power and dignity of the politically important families in a way that everyone could understand. The façade, however, was transformed in line with the new principles derived from ruins and the Graeco-Roman theory of art. The mass of the façade henceforth produced the basic architectural problem: statics, support, load, structure of floors from base, main zone and terminal zone. The ground floor, bearer of the greatest load and the link with the ground, displayed its function in a rugged band of large rusticated ashlar left in its rough state at the front. This term comes from the Latin *rusticus*, rustic, country-style, sturdy, smooth. Sturdy, earthy and resistant, like a memory of the defensive constructions of the medieval town-palaces, the pedestal area props up the first floor with finely-formed smoothed

46 Donatello: 'Cantoria', 1433–1439. Florence. Cathedral Museum. Donatello's marble Singing Gallery for the Cathedral in Florence (1433–1439) comes to life in a Bacchic series of putti representing angels dancing and exulting in honour of the Blessed Virgin, Patroness of the Cathedral and protector of the City; and in the ornamental motif, quite in the spirit of the Classical Renaissance.

squared stone, the grooving of which is still clear and separate. On the highest floor the wall becomes a tense membrane, the band of squared stone being apparent only after a second glance at the hair-thin seams. An imposing heavy layer of festooned cornice, counteracting the lightness of the upper storey in *contrapposto*, rounds everything off and traps in deep shadow the force striving upwards. The cornice is built up in the classical manner from classic consoles. The windows stand in regular symmetrical axes and a Renaissance *leit-motiv* appears on the ground floor, caught up by semi-circular blind arches: the aedicula window, with a classical, triangular pediment above classical-looking brackets. With certain deviations—the Palazzo Strozzi, for instance, the latest in our series, begun in 1485 by Benedetto da Maiano (Plate 24), has a classical dentil frieze as floor-division—this type remained the rule for centuries in Florence and throughout Italy, as in the Pitti Palace, which was begun by Luca Fancelli in 1457 from plans by Brunelleschi and not completed until 1650 (Plates 22 and 23).

The inner courts of the Medici and Strozzi Palaces display a calculated, refined contrast to the forbidding authoritarianism of the exterior (Plates 21 and 25). They are friendly and inviting, with light finely-worked arcades, entirely classical in appearance. Ornamental arrangements of columns with classical capitals have 'ideal' elegantly-profiled semi-circular arches and, as decoration, classical round medallions framing the reliefs in the Medici Palace, plus ingenious emblems. We can be sure that the Florentine builders of 1450 to 1480 thought they had recovered in these courtyards the ancient *atrium,* and in the deliberate contrast of inner and outer forms the fundamental principle of the classical Mediterranean house, the *casa degli antichi,* which is valid even to-day. The ponderous dignity and menacing majesty of the rusticated facades, solemnly overshadowed in the accidental light, might then correspond to the *gravitas* and *dignitas* of the town residence of the fine gentlemen of ancient Rome.

Needless to say the noble families residing in such palaces *more romano* tried to trace their origins more or less convincingly to Graeco-Roman roots. The Sienese family of the Piccolomini traced themselves to the ancient Roman Julians; the Barbo from Venice claimed to be descended from the Ahenobarbus; and the Giustiniani, from the Province of Venice, from the late Roman Emperor Justinian. The bourgeois family of Plato from Milan, academics and lawyers, naturally went back to the great Greek philosopher; the new Roman Massimi, to Q. Fabius Maximus; and the Paduan Cornaro—as one might have guessed—to the celebrated Cornelians of classical antiquity.

The Renaissance quest for fame, its personality cult and urge towards classical stylization of the individual found an ideal and flexible medium in painting which, like fifteenth-century architecture and sculpture, produced a whole host of discoveries in form and content, and in the secular sphere particularly expanded the medieval pictorial canon to include a multitude of new themes. 'The discovery of the world and of Man' was a decisive factor in painting also, which now proceeded to incorporate the landscape and architectural scenery, in other words man's material environment, as an autonomous representational content. Contemporary everyday life was portrayed in the 'genre' type of picture, or one dealing with manners and customs. The pictorial cosmos of Humanism opened up in historical painting, allegory and large-scale astrological programming a rich spectrum of newly-acquired cosmological, historical, literary, moral, philosophical and particularly classical mythological material. It was in the portrait, however, which now enjoyed a brilliant flowering, that the Early Renaissance gave of its best.

Like the other art forms painting gradually assumed a quite extraordinary public, political and even ideological function. A good example of this is revealed in 'Negation'. Not only were the splendours and achievements, the virtues and fame of outstanding men honoured and immortalized in

75

DNM IN SCIS EI LAVDATE EVM IN FIRMAMENTO VIRTVTIS EI PAEV IN VIRTVTIBVS EI PAEV SECVNDVM MVLTITVDINEM MAGNITVDINIS EIVS

EVM IN SONO TVBAE LAVDATE EVM IN PSALTERIO ET CYTHARA LAVDATE EVM IN TIMPA

IORO PAEV IN CORDIS EI ORGANO PAEV IN CIMBALIS BENE SONATIBVS PAEV IN CIMBALIS IVBILATIONIS OIS SPS LAVDEI DNM

47

monumental frescoes, but negative propaganda was also conducted in 'scandalous portrayals and caricatures', where the politically defeated, those guilty of high treason and political criminals were condemned to eternal disgrace. The same Castagno who had erected an eternal monument to the mercenary Captain-General Niccolò da Tolentino in a monumental fresco happily accepted a macabre commission by the victorious Medici to exhibit the leaders of the defeated Albizzi party after the Battle of Anghiari (1440) in large tableaux on the walls of the Palace of Justice in Florence, and in the most abusive way: as dishonoured victims of execution, hanging by the feet and swaying in the air. So terrifying was its intentional effect on the townspeople that henceforth the prominent painter bore a name that was surreptitiously whispered from mouth to mouth and did him little credit: 'Andrea the Hangman'. Even the great Leonardo da Vinci undertook a similar irregular commission. He drew the Pisan Cardinal Archbishop Salviati hanged in the Palazzo Vecchio, following his execution on 26 April 1478 for taking part in the anti-Medici Pazzi conspiracy.

Violence and passion, Nature and world, womanly beauty, youthful grace and the fame of the great, esoteric allegory, classical sensuality, the fateful power of Eros—there was no theme that secular Renaissance painting could not deal with, and in each new task it created something great and never seen before.

Yet the Christian art world asserted its supremacy. The church kept on

47, 48 and 49   Luca della Robbia: 'Cantoria' 1433–1438. Florence. Cathedral Museum. This enclosed singing gallery was begun at the same time as and in competition with Donatello's, but was completed a year earlier, in 1438. It also combines older fourteenth-century traditions with the new Early Renaissance spirit. As with Donatello's 'Cantoria', the purpose is not entirely clear. Probably no choir was ever set up here on account of the lack of space. It possibly housed an organ.

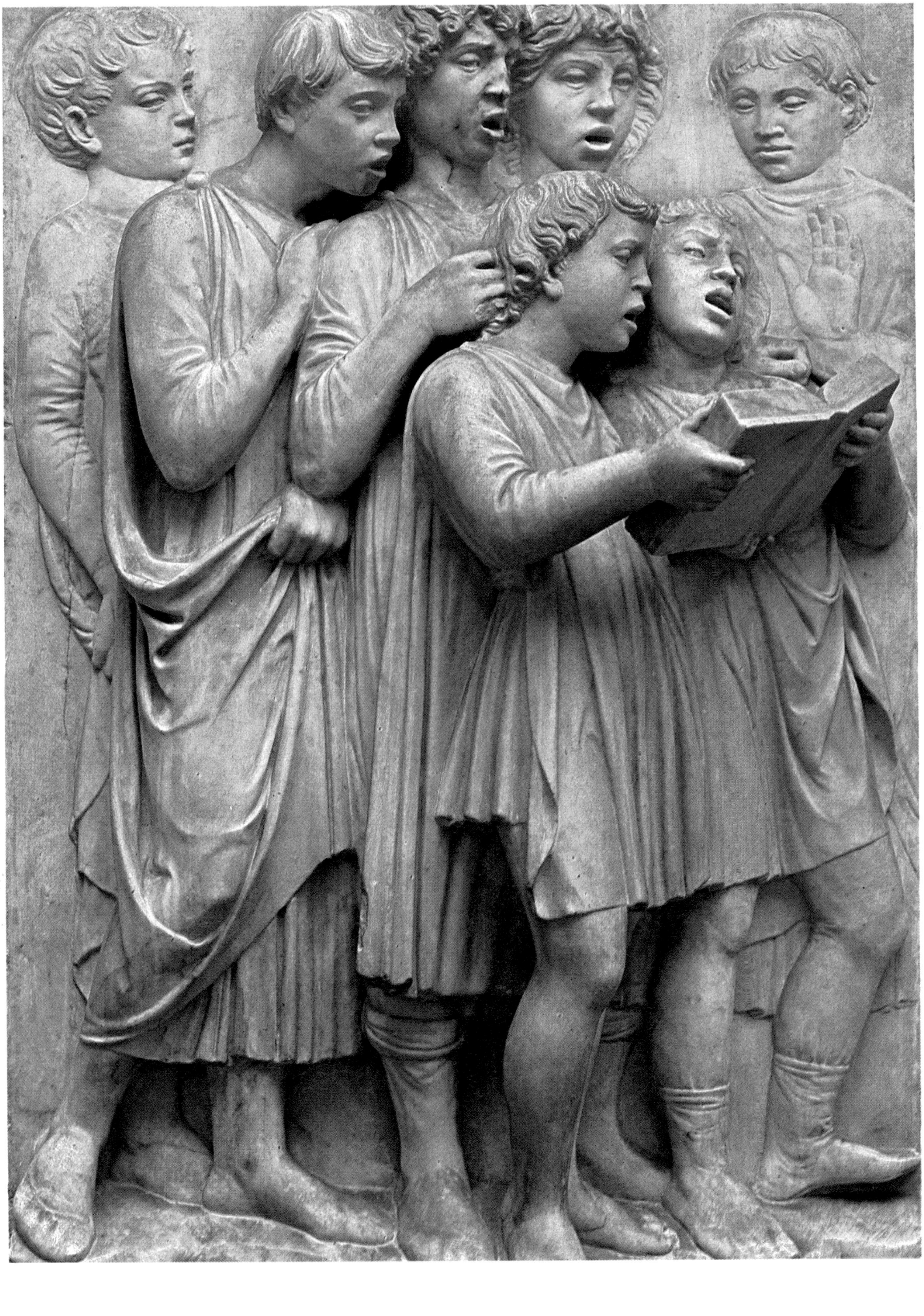

having the most comprehensive, most attractive and best-endowed commissions to distribute, and it was in representing the Christian cosmos that Renaissance painting attained its greatest heights, transforming the basic principles of the Middle Ages in a humanist and classical sense. For this reason, and since we have space for only a limited selection, the Florence section of this volume offers only religious paintings from Florentine churches (Plates 27–37). Giotto's 'Death of St. Francis' in Santa Croce (Plate 27) has already been described in detail (Page 36). The real painting Renaissance in Florence sets in with Masaccio's famous 1425 fresco of the Trinity, in Santa Trinità (Plate 28). This innovatory achievement placed Masaccio, later unreservedly admired by the young Michelangelo and Leonardo, alongside Brunelleschi, who was twenty-four years older, and Donatello (fifteen years older).

In addition to his classically balanced composition, the masterly development of fresco technique, and the nobly sensuous characterization of the holy figures, the tragic greatness of the Blessed Virgin, the prayers of the favourite disciple John, and the majestic suffering of the crucified figure, and of God the Father supporting His Son in loving sympathy, the painting is of world stature because, in the framed and background structure of the group, a niche like a triumphal arch, Masaccio has adapted the knowledge of perspective possessed by his teacher Brunelleschi and employed it to convey a sense of majesty. Nowhere more clearly than here does the formal method of precisely constructed linear perspective appear as a 'symbolical form' (Panofsky). The guiding lines drawn by ruler in the damp finish can still be traced accurately in the picture.

Masaccio created another epoch-making work together with Masolino in the shape of the Brancacci Chapel frescoes in Santa Maria del Carmine, where an extensive series devoted to the life of St. Peter was started between

1423 and 1425 in connection with the performance of plays about the saint, which were traditional in the church. Masaccio was unable to complete the series. It was carried through from 1483 to 1485 by Filippino Lippi (Plates 32 and 33). As was his wont, in these frescoes were concealed portraits of his contemporaries: the young noble Granacci, in the person of the resurrected Imperial Prince (Plate 32); the painter Antonio Pollaiuolo; and himself, in the scene before Herod (Plate 33). So great was Masaccio's impact that the succeeding generation could not escape (nor had any desire to escape) his influence. Castagno, Botticelli and Leonardo regarded the Brancacci Chapel as their textbook in paint. Michelangelo's encounter with the genius of Masaccio left him bearing literal 'stigmata'. It was in a violent quarrel with colleagues about Masaccio that he acquired the severe facial injuries which distorted his face into a tragic mask for the rest of his life.

Quite another figure, taking us back to the fourteenth century and the world of medieval piety and spirituality, greets us in the figure of Giovanni da Fiesole, who after an eventful life found a home in the Florentine Monastery of San Marco. In the forties he created there a whole string of wall-paintings in the cells, corridors and cloisters (Plates 29 and 30). The tender spiritual expression in the faces of the angels and Madonnas, the Gothic elegance of the figures and above all the splendid, harmonious, transparent colouring with accents in light red and blue on a grand scale have made Giovanni, who entered the history of art under the name given to him by his order, Fra Angelico, one of the best-loved of painters, especially among European visitors to Florence.

At the height of this period and its ideal of humanity stand·Botticelli and Ghirlandaio, with the two great companion pictures of the Church Fathers, St. Augustine and St. Jerome in Ognissanti, dating from 1480 (Plates 35 and 36). These utterly personal figures, almost portrait-like in their effect, embody the humanist *uomo universale,* the spiritual man who with passionate understanding breaks through the limits of his previous world and advances into new worlds. St. Augustine (Plate 36) is gazing thoughtfully at a celestial globe. It can be no accident that this painting was the gift of the Vespucci family from which sprang Amerigo Vespucci. Only a little later he did in actual fact open up a 'New World' which was to bear his name: America. The 'cells' of both saints are depicted as the studies of contemporaries, with a pleasure in detail that has a touch of the Netherlands, and is reminiscent of Van Eyck. We seem to be given a glimpse of a fifteenth-century studio, lacking in none of the essentials: inkwell and blotting sand, quill-pen, folios with bookmark, memoranda with notes in Greek, reading desk, spectacles, astronomical and geometrical equipment and a mathematics textbook.

The 'New Style' in Florence probably accomplished its best work in sculpture and the plastic arts. The two celebrated 'Competition Reliefs' by Ghiberti and Brunelleschi for the doors of the Florentine Baptistery (Plates 38 and 39) give a clear picture of the new classical style shortly after the turn of the century. The commission itself, the monumental bronze door with figure decoration, was a conscious link with classical antiquity. In Graeco-Roman temples, too, figurative decoration in the matter of portals had usually been restricted to the door-panels. Ghiberti's two masterpieces, the first bronze door in the 'Bel San Giovanni' from 1403 (Plates 40 and 41) and his world-famous 'Gate of Paradise', 1425, set a standard for the whole of Italy.

A significant new element was the technique of casting bronze. Bronze was quite evidently the favourite material in Renaissance sculpture and from time to time was esteemed more highly than marble in the fifteenth century. Not until Michelangelo's monumental figures, almost all of them wrested out of the 'royal' marble, was this trend reversed in the sixteenth century. Here too history was being repeated, for the writers of the ancient world have reported the importance and high technical level of bronze-casting in their day, as in the case of the Greek sculptor Myron—a legend even to the Ancient Romans—marble copies of whose renowned bronze creations such as the 'Discus Thrower' or 'Athena and Marsyas' had been traded in the Rome of antiquity.

It was certainly no coincidence, then, that probably the most epoch-making production of the period, Donatello's 'David' of 1430 in the Bargello Museum (Plate 43), was executed in this popular medium. With it the divergence of Florentine artists from the European Late Middle Ages was finally settled in favour of the new formal language. Not only is the technique new, but so is practically everything else in this enchanting figure: the formal aspect, guiding idea and spiritual expression. A well-developed, thoroughly-trained youth, still on the threshold of childhood but become a hero and a man through his deed, the vanquishing of Goliath, stands free and self-conscious, in heroic nudity before the onlooker. The rudimentary clothing, the touching straw-hat of the shepherd-boy, decorated with flowers, and the leggings, for protection against thorn-hedges, serve only to emphasize the nudity and high sensuous charm of the bare skin, on which light plays in lively reflections over the polished bronze surface. Pride, something daring and free, but an attractive embarrassment too are contained in the face of the young man, who—if we interpret the biblical story in psychological terms—is gentle and almost girlish in features, as is emphasized by the long locks. The threshold between childhood and manhood is also conveyed in the treatment of the body, which still shows soft, child-like lines, but in the sinewy arms and powerful legs illustrates the biblical figure: the mobile, light-footed shepherd who could handle the sling with unexpected strength and cunning, and who conquered brute force. The figure's erect attitude, the whole weight of the body falling on the right leg, and the free play of the bent and relaxed left leg, with the left arm resting on the hips and the right arm holding the sword as a victory trophy, is at one and the same time full of quiet concentration and nervous tension. This classical weighting according to the principle of ideal *contrapposto,* i.e. tension and relaxation (weight on one leg, none on the other) clearly goes back to Graeco-Roman models. Once this figure is understood, so is the nature of Renaissance sculpture, and Jacob Burckhardt's statement that the Renaissance was the 'discovery of the world and of Man' seems valid. From now on the naked human form, the nude, remains the governing problem in sculpture, like the central structure in Renaissance architecture.

In his two monumental free-standing pulpits on marble pillars for San Lorenzo (Plate 45) Donatello also had reference to the ancient world (or more accurately to the Early Christian-Late Classical-transition period). These are placed opposite each other and allude quite clearly to the practice in classical early Christian churches of employing double pulpits, known as 'ambos', for the separate reading of Gospel and Epistle. The large reliefs relating the story of the Passion can also be traced back to the bronze technique used in classical antiquity and inherit its formal legacy in their accompanying decorative motifs.

Another new sculptural development in Donatello's generation was the free-standing choir-loft. Medieval divine services also had choirs, of course, but the elevated platform then apparently consisted only of perishable material (probably wood), as no example has survived. In the 1430s Donatello and Luca della Robbia tackled this assignment for the Florence Cathedral in monumental fashion (Plates 46 to 49). Both artists selected rare marble as their material and Donatello, in his singing gallery (in Italian, *cantoria*) built between 1433 and 1439, introduced a whole galaxy of classical forms, with double-ringed vases, acanthus leaves, corner palmettes and a dancing row of exulting angels, the effect of which is anything but Christian and reminiscent rather of the Dionysiac transports of putti in some heathen bacchanalia (Plate 46). Luca della Robbia tackled the same assignment in the Cathedral almost at the same time, another demonstration of the Florentine principle of competition. In the group of singing boys and music-making angels (Plates 47 and 48) he combined truthfulness and nature with classical grace. The dress in particular, its transparency permitting like some Greek *peplos* a view of the classically proportioned bodies, is wholly in the classical spirit.

R·P·
BENOTII DEFEDE
RIGIS EPI FESVLANI
QVI VIR INTEGERIMAE
VITAE SVMA CVM LAVD
VIXIT ANNO QVE
M·CCCCL DEFVN
CTVS EST

Luca della Robbia, along with the sculptors Bernardo and Antonio Rossellino and Desiderio da Settignano, also helped to develop a new way of embellishing churches—an imposing wall tomb set in a niche. This sculptural assignment is a particularly clear illustration of the spirit of the time, and of its feeling for antiquity. Whereas medieval man had felt himself a *viator mundi,* a 'wanderer in the world', a modest pilgrim on the way to his heavenly abode, Renaisssance man regarded himself as *fabor mundi,* master, creator and ruler of 'his' world. This now found expression in the tomb-cult. The traditional form of tomb derived from the fourteenth century—a framed niche in the church wall, with the deceased lying on a bier or sarcophagus, a 'perpetuation' of the catafalque so to speak—now underwent a decisive transformation. Two good examples of this style, which evolved in Florence and soon spread all over Italy, are Luca della Robbia's tomb of Bishop B.

Federighi (deceased in 1450) in Santa Trinità (Plate 50) and Antonio Rossellino's tomb of the Titular Cardinal, Jacobus of Lusitania (Portugal) in San Miniato al Monte, dated 1461 (Plate 51). The new version emerges particularly clearly in the Rossellino tomb. The heroic feeling for life possessed by Renaissance man, who was concerned more with life on earth than with the after-life, continued to the very threshold of death. The 'eternal catafalque', occupying its own space and full of self-awareness, stands freely in a large niche, surrounded by a kind of triumphal arch. Little angels flank the corpse. they have the form and cheerfulness of classical putti. Even the remaining celestial figures in attendance scarcely exercise a Christian effect but rather resemble heathen genii. The model for the Madonna in the crowning terra cotta tondo more closely resembles a classical Athena than the Blessed Virgin. The symbol of the cross is not to be found anywhere in the monument, and the foot of the catafalque displays cornucopias, festoons of fruit and fabulous creatures from the humanist treasury. The heaven which this high prince of the church hoped to enter had probably just as much to do with the Olympus of the ancients as with the Christian beyond, and the way thither was indicated by maxims from Greek and Latin philosophy. However that may be, the 'Cardinal of Portugal' undoubtedly saw a reliable pledge of another life and of immortality for his name in his earthly memorial, expressing as it did the period's all-embracing sense of glory and its tendency to immortalize in art a person who was outstanding and render him eternal through art, in a secular kingdom of 'salvation through beauty'. Every Renaissance memorial has this ideal background. from portrait-busts of distinguished people to equestrian statues and monuments to Princes.

Michelangelo: Sculptor in Florence and Rome

It was mere chance that the greatest Florentine artist of all, Michelangelo, was not born in the city in which, apart from Rome, he worked almost exclusively. In the year of his birth, 1475, his father occupied for one year the office of mayor in Caprese (a mountain village north-west of Borgo San Sepolcro) where the *divino* first saw the light on the sixth of March. Michelangelo grew up in Florence and Settignano, where the family possessed a small property. For a brief while only he attended a Latin school and at the youthful age of thirteen was apprenticed to the important Florentine Early Renaissance painter Domenico Ghirlandaio, for three years. After just a year, however, he left the artist's studio to enter a sculptor's, possibly that of Benedetto da Maiano, in 1489. Again only a year later, his academic education and training took a turn very different from that of the usual apprentice. He became a guest in the family palace of Lorenzo the Magnificent. There he familiarized himself with the ideas and philosophy of Neo-Platonism which was studied in the circle around Lorenzo and Politian. In the classical garden of Lorenzo's villa before San Marco he studied and drew the statues and sarcophagi. After Lorenzo's death in 1492, when Michelangelo was seventeen, he returned home and it was at this time that he produced his first two works: the bas-relief of the Madonna of the Steps and the high relief of the 'Battle of the Centaurs' (Plate 54). Though the Madonna of the Steps still betrays a number of uncertain qualities, in the perspective for example (the Christ child's back, the Madonna's foot), the Blessed Virgin is nevertheless splendidly seated in flowing garments, as dignified as a Roman matron. In the 'Battle of the Centaurs' Michelangelo, with the arrogance of youth, appears to have taken delight in his own assurance in handling the chisel. Inspired by the classical sarcophagi displayed in Lorenzo's garden, but also by the pulpits of Niccolò and Giovanni Pisano, he produced the most varied views of the body in different attitudes. Frontal, rear and profile views are displayed almost with enjoyment, and even the problem that had posed difficulties for every sculptor since Phidias, representation of the centaur, i.e. the transition from horse to human, was courageously tackled by skilfully

A partly completed marble block intended to represent a giant, had

been lying in the cathedral's building yard since 1464. Michelangelo was commissioned to complete this in the form of a colossal figure of David (Plate 56), David's victory over Goliath being regarded as the counterpart in the Old Testament of Christ's victory over Lucifer. Even in the Middle Ages it had become a political symbol of bravery and of the freedom won by the victory of the 'weak' over the 'strong'. At the behest of the Cathedral Museum and the Wool-Weavers' Guild a commission was set up in 1504 to decide on a new site. Among the members were Leonardo da Vinci, Botticelli, Filippino Lippi, Giuliano and Antonio da Sangallo. The space in front of the Palazzo Vecchio was selected, for 'just as David defended his people and led and governed with justice, so the protectors of Florence too should defend their city with courage and govern it with justice' (Vasari). Michelangelo's 'David' is the first free-standing sculpture placed on a plinth since the end of the classical era and anyone intelligently observing the 4.10 metre (13') high statue in white marble, contrasting with the Palazzo Vecchio's warm brownish chunks of fairly rough-hewn stone (Plate 16), will willingly admit that the choice of site accorded well with the artist's intentions.

Although he was still barely thirty, Michelangelo was already enjoying the highest form of recognition in Italy, and even in France, where François I later tried in vain to acquire one of his works. That fame was to last until the artist's death and indeed was trumpeted abroad immediately afterwards louder than ever. As early as 1496 an art-dealer had sold a 'Cupid Asleep' by Michelangelo as a piece of Graeco-Roman sculpture. In 1506 the Sultan proposed that he should build a bridge over the Bosphorus, and that at a time when the artist had done little or nothing on the architectural side. When Cardinal Medici was elected Pope in 1513 as Leo X he said of Michelangelo: 'We grew up together.' 'The one who chisels as well as he paints: *Michel più che mortal Angel divin*', (More than a mortal, an Angel Divine), as Ariosto, in the thirty-third song of his *Orlando Furioso*, paraphrased Michelangelo's name in 1516. He who even in his youth had been compared to Phidias would later go so far as to assume the role of Alexander the Great's legendary architect Deinocrates, whose ambition it was to carve a statue of his king out of Mount Athos. In 1505 'Michelangelo planned to fashion a colossus out of a mountain of marble in Carrara which would be a distant landmark for soldiers' (H. Keller 1975). And in 1563, one year before his death, he was elected Head of the Florentine Academy founded by Duke Cosimo, along with the Duke himself. Giorgio Vasari's *Lives of the Most Excellent Painters, Sculptors and Architects* had appeared in Florence in 1550. This account of the lives of Italian artists dealt only with those who were deceased, with one exception: Michelangelo. Three years later came Ascanio Condivi's *Life of Michelangelo Buonarroti*, which was devoted solely to the 'Divino'.

Thanks to Vasari's portrayals, and also to numerous drawings and a lesser number of *Bozzetti* (three-dimensional models of sculptures) we know a lot about Michelangelo's working habits. Drawings were the initial preparation for a work: precisely executed studies of a leg or a head; work-sketches giving the sweeping outline of a complete figure were accompanied by exact details of the measurements, to allow assistants to rough-hew the figure from the marble; and finally full sketches showed figures for a tomb, perhaps along with the architecture, and were probably suitable for showing to patrons. Three-dimensional *bozzetti* were done at the same time, for Michelangelo could only imagine his figures in the round. Beginning with small wax or soft clay figures which were easily worked, he ended up with an original model; the inner core was lattice-work wrapped in oakum, on to which workable plaster of Paris or stucco was finally applied. Two of these original models, river-gods for the Medici Chapel, have been preserved (Florence, Accademia). It was now that the cutting of the marble block began.

Michelangelo supervised and conducted the breaking of the blocks in Carrara and Pietrasanta personally, which was hard work. Streets or even bridges often had to be expressly built for transport, and he complained of this in many a lugubrious letter.

53 *Giovanni della Robbia: 'The Coronation of the Virgin'*, circa 1515. Florence. Ognissanti Church. Façade tympanum. This terra cotta relief constructed about 1515 was transferred from the older façade of the original Church of the Humiliati to the baroque façade of the Franciscan Church of the Order of Friars Minor (completed in 1637), which is why there is some divergence in the arrangement of the individual ceramic surfaces, and why blue tiles have had to be inserted at the edges, as our picture clearly shows. The relief-work on the tympanum is representative of the della Robbia family's abundant output, which is found all over Italy. They specialized in glazed terra cotta. The main area shows the Coronation of the Virgin surrounded by a chorus of angel musicians; and the base the half-figures of the titular saints of Ognissanti (Church of all Saints).

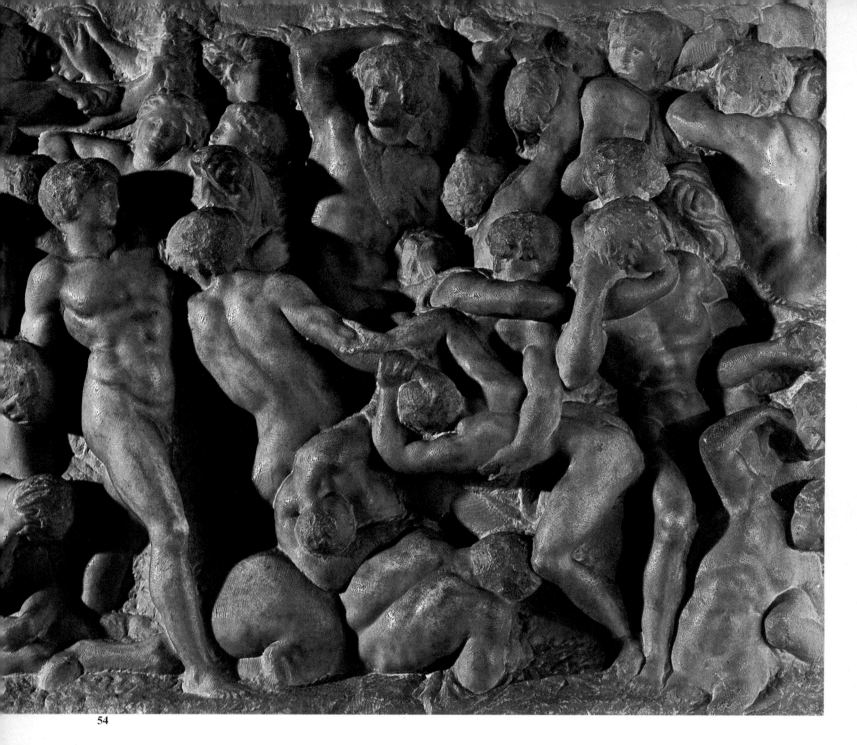

54

For decades he had to devote himself to two major sculpture commissions which, however, remained incomplete: the funeral-chapel of the Medici at San Lorenzo in Florence and the tomb for Pope Julius II della Rovere in Rome.

Negotiations for the Medici Chapel began about 1520. In the same year Michelangelo sent a first draft to Cardinal Giulio Medici (later Pope Clement VII). From then on until 1533, when he finally left Florence for Rome, Michelangelo worked uninterruptedly at this project, which was not however completed. A number of marble figures are missing as well as the whole of the paintwork. As seen by the spectator of to-day, however, it is one of humanity's undying works of art. (Plates 57–60). The figural groupings are linked together in an architectonic framework which is definitely Mannerist in tendency. Into the overlapping and classically architectural structure of fluted pilasters and high tripartite dark stone beams a second much-reduced arrangement is compressed. The figural groupings are sited in front of and within this structure; on the wall to the right of the altar, which is to be thought of as facing the entrance, Lorenzo de' Medici with the figures of 'Dusk' and 'Dawn' (Plates 58 and 59) at his feet; and left, Giuliano de' Medici with 'Day' and 'Night' (Plates 57 and 60). These two Medicis are in no way important members of the family but both had become Dukes: Giuliano, Duke of Nemours, and Lorenzo, Duke of Urbino. The two most outstanding

54 Michelangelo: 'The Battle of the Centaurs', 1492. Florence. Casa Buonarroti. Marble reliefs have a long and worthy tradition in Italy. Ancient triumphal arches and columnar reliefs, as well as hundreds of sarcophagi, had already inspired Italian Gothic sculptors such as Pisani, Arnolfo di Cambio and Maitani. Donatello took up the medium also, so that Michelangelo in this youthful work had a number of great predecessors to look back on. Nevertheless signs of his artistic ideals are plainly visible: joy in portraying the human body from all sides in complicated and contorted attitudes; attraction to the free-standing figure, which seems to break out of the frame; and use of the 'unfinished' technique.

56

Previous page:
55 *Michelangelo: 'Pietà', 1498–1499. Height: 1.71 metres (5' 6") Rome. St. Peter's. This, the earliest of Michelangelo's 'Pietàs', was commissioned by the French Cardinal Jean Bilhères de Lagraulas. The medium-sized group is to-day to be found—rather too high up unfortunately—in the first of the North-East side-chapels, the Cappella della Pietà. The harmony of this genuinely High Renaissance sculpture is revealed not only in the balance and identification of Mother and Son, beyond earthly suffering, but also in the perfect technique employed in the handling of the gleaming white Carrara marble. It is the only work signed by Michelangelo. The ribbon crossing the Madonna's breast is inscribed: 'Michelangelus Buonarotus Florentin[us] faciebat.'*

56 *Michelangelo: 'David', 1501–1504. Florence, Academy. The external measurements alone of this 'Statue to Liberty', which is indeed what it was intended to be, and which one has to imagine in its original setting before the Palazzo Vecchio (c.f. Plate 16), make it a matter of astonishment that this youthful work should have become such a perfect masterpiece. The 'spoiled' block, which nobody dared to work, had a base only 38 centimetres (15") deep and 44 centimetres (17¼") wide, for a height of over 4 metres (13'). Michelangelo therefore had to attempt to give the figure the required expansion through twisting (turning of the longitudinal axis) and extremely skilful design.*

members of the family, Lorenzo Magnifico and his brother Giuliano, murdered in the Pazzi conspiracy, were to rest in two adjacent sarcophagi at the Madonna's feet.

The need to balance the two times of day on the volutes of the high sarcophagi covers would have been reduced by the river-gods lying on the ground; and the vacant intervening space would have been bridged over so that the whole scene approached the classical High Renaissance ideal more closely. The Dukes are clad in the close-fitting leather mail of the Roman general. 'Their theme is inner mobility with exterior calm.' (H. von Einem, 1959). Lorenzo is usually nicknamed *Il Pensieroso* (the Thinker) on account of the fact that his head is resting on his hand, whereas Giuliano is called *La vigilanza* (The Wakeful), his face open and the field-marshal's baton on his knees. Both sedentary motifs express a rest that is everlasting, while the 'inner mobility' appears to break through the architectonic framework. *Dawn* and *Twilight* (Plates 58 and 59) present themselves totally to the visitor. *Twilight* in his looseness of limb seems to be already sunken in expectation of the night. 'Dawn', tense, resilient, and turned towards the work of the day, still has her head veiled in night.

The sacred Pietà theme, an image of the Blessed Virgin with the dead body of Christ in her lap, had been a widespread one in the countries north of the Alps in countless stone, wood or clay figural groupings ever since the fourteenth century. It was left to Michelangelo to introduce it into Italian sculpture with an early work, the 'Pietà of St. Peter's' (Plate 55), and three large late Pietàs, the 'Pietà' in the Cathedral at Florence (Plate 62), the 'Palestrina Pietà' in the Academy, Florence (Plate 63), and the unfinished 'Pietà Rondanini' in the Castello Sforzesco in Milan, on which he was working up to a few days before his death.

Michelangelo received his commission for the 'Pietà of St. Peter's' in 1498 from the French Cardinal Jean Bilhères de Lagraulas, who probably wanted the 'Vesper Figure' for his own tomb, as was the French custom. 'The young sculptor thus found himself facing the task of making a three-dimensional marble group, offering several aspects, out of a Gothic image which had no depth and was on one plane.' (H. Keller 1966). Iconographically, too, Michelangelo took completely new paths. Mary is no longer the careworn mother of a thirty-three-year-old son but a still girlish and beautiful woman—possibly a reference to the Virgin Birth—whose grief is barely perceptible. Nor do the features and body of Our Lord betray anything of the agony that has gone before. The wound in the side and the marks of the nails are scarcely indicated. He rests in all his beauty like a figure from the ancient world, with a sensitive yet well-formed body. The 'Pietà of St. Peter's' is a typical work of the High Renaissance which could on no account permit the degradation of the human being however lofty the end. This group is also the only work signed (on the ribbon over the Madonna's breast) by Michelangelo, as well as the only one polished throughout to a high brilliance.

Of the late Pietà groups the one in the Cathedral at Florence is the earliest, dating probably to a little before 1550 (Plate 62). This group has also been enlarged by the figures of the sorrowing Mary Magdalene and Nicodemus, and is much more vertical in structure. Christ's body is almost upright and dominated by the expressive form of Nicodemus. So deep are the feelings involved that the spiritual meaning can only be guessed at, for example from the way in which the Blessed Virgin presses her cheek ardently against her Son's. The work also remained unfinished because Michelangelo had 'spoiled' it. The left leg of the Christ figure, draped over the Madonna's upper thigh, broke off in the course of the work. Pupils undertook restoration, but not always as Michelangelo wished. The work was intended for the artist's tomb in Rome's Santa Maria Maggiore. For this reason the splendidly-worked features of Nicodemus, controlled in their grief, are thought to be a self-portrait of Michelangelo, an assumption which is totally convincing.

Pope Julius II della Rovere was one of the most outstanding and interesting personalities in the Holy See. With Leo X Medici he was in any case *the*

Renaissance Pope. He commissioned Bramante to rebuild St. Peter's; Raphael to paint the Vatican *Stanze* and Loggias; and Michelangelo to paint the Sistine Chapel ceiling. But even before he undertook these projects he was thinking, like a true man of the Renaissance, of his own posthumous fame. Fifteen months after he had become Supreme Pontiff in March 1505, he summoned Michelangelo to Rome. In the choir of the church to be erected by Bramante he was to build for the Pope a monumental free-standing tomb, conceived in the most 'hybrid' way, with numerous figures. Thereafter the artist spent forty years on the project, the dimensions of which were steadily reduced. He went to Carrara for eight months to excavate marble for the tomb, but only five months after his return misunderstandings and quarrels with the Pope led to Michelangelo's sulky withdrawal to Florence. In the end he and Julius II were reconciled and he was recalled to Rome, this time with a commission to paint the Sistine Chapel. Julius died in 1513 and his executors concluded with Michelangelo a contract for Julius' tomb, which this time would be a wall tomb.

The work, to which Michelangelo had allotted seven weeks, kept undergoing delays. In the decades that followed two Medici, Leo X and Clement VII, became Popes and pressed for the completion of their own funeral-chapels in Florence. The tomb was finally completed in 1545, with the number of figures again reduced, and was installed in San Pietro in Vincoli, where Julius had been Cardinal before becoming Pope. Only the two female figures of 'Leah', representing the *vita activa,* and 'Rachel', as an allegory of the *vita contemplativa,* plus the powerful (2.35 metres (7′ 8″) high) figures of 'Moses' (Plates 64 and 65) with the menacing Old Testament head 'sparkling with inner fire' (H. von Einem 1959), are actually by Michelangelo. A few figures have still survived, however, from the second version, partly unfinished. Among these are the two 'Slaves' in the Louvre, the four unfinished 'Boboli Slaves' (formerly built as Atlantes into the grotto of the Boboli Gardens in Florence and now in the Academy) and finally one of the Virtues trampling Vice into the dust, 'Victory' (Florence, Palazzo Vecchio, Plate 61). This marble group (2.6 metres (8′ 6″) high), has clearly Mannerist tendencies, which is rare in Michelangelo's sculptures. The slender, elongated figure twists and turns so subtly that we are constantly being offered a different viewpoint. The bent right arm and the left leg, which is thrusting the figure of Vice to the ground, are symmetrically arranged so as to balance the figure.

Observing Michelangelo's sculpture we constantly come up against something uncompleted, or sections that have been only roughly treated and 'remain in the raw'. Certainly these can often be written off as unfinished or abandoned, none too surprisingly if we follow the vicissitudes of the great projects for the Medici Chapel and the tomb of Julius. But Michelangelo made deliberate use of this stylistic approach in one of his earliest works, 'the 'Battle of the Centaurs', in order to achieve greater depth in the relief-work. Is it certain that the roughly worked head of 'Day' in the Medici Chapel was really to be given further treatment? Or does its unfinished state not convey precisely that though the body is ready for the daily chores the spirit still lingers in the twilight of night? Should we not rather, in this and many other sculptures, accept a certain 'deliberate style', i.e. the *stilo nonfinito*? There can never be a clear and full explanation, but it is certain that Michelangelo's contemporaries, Vasari above all, wanted it recognized as deliberate, and that his pupils imitated it, especially in Mannerism. *Nonfinito* became a catchphrase in the art-world, even in the High Baroque period, where the approach was widely adopted in architecture.

The genius of even so transcendent an artist as Michelangelo may wait on a favourable opportunity to bear fruit. We may ask ourselves whether creations such as the sarcophagus sculptures of 'Day' and 'Night' in the new Sacristy of San Lorenzo in Florence (Plate 60) would ever have left Michelangelo's studio had not Cardinal Giuliano de' Medici, later to become Pope Clement VII, taken it into his head in 1519 to have a monumental burial chamber

57 Florence: San Lorenzo, Medici Chapel. A view of the entrance side with the Madonna and Medici saints Cosmas and Damian (the group was originally intended to be an architectonic unit) and the figures of Giuliano de' Medici, and Michelangelo's 'Day' and 'Night' (left). The need to balance the sculptures on the cover of the sarcophagus, in the absence of the counterweight provided by the river-gods planned for the floor, is quite evident from this photograph.

57

constructed by the leading artist in the city and of the day, for Lorenzo 'il Magnifico' and other members of the family; or if Michelangelo would ever have had a chance to show his conception of the founder of monotheism had the opportunity not offered itself in the figure of Moses for Pope Julius' Roman tomb. Quite conceivably the world in that case would have lost what is most certainly Michelangelo's most famous work (Plates 64 and 65), whose *terribilità* (terrifying aspect) is attested to even in the sixteenth century, so sublime was the impact of Moses on Michelangelo's contemporaries. The question is a rhetorical one, unanswerable in effect. There can be no doubt that had their *coup d'état* against the Medici in 1440 not been so amateurishly bungled, the Albizzi and the Pazzi too—had the 1478 murder in the Cathedral

93

become a double murder by including Lorenzo the Magnificent—would also have promoted 'their own' artists and had 'their own' monuments erected, thus turning Florence into a hall of fame of their own. And certainly the names of the bankers who at a precise moment in the history of Early Florentine capitalism determined policy, i.e. economic policy, could easily have been changed.

From 1434 onwards, however, the municipal history of Florence is identified with the history of the Medici family, and art-history is obliged to discuss the way in which Florence increasingly became for the Medicis one great 'Hall of Fame'. After the popular movement of the *ciompi,* the

60 Michelangelo: 'Night' and 'Day', 1520–1534. Florence. San Lorenzo: Medici Chapel. The homogeneous character of the two companion figures becomes evident, particularly in their attitudes. To some extent it is a question of a classical contrapposto *design, distributed of course over two figures: a frontal view of 'Night', with right arm outstretched and left leg curved high up; and the same position for 'Day', but as a rear view. The attitude of head and arm in both also corresponds to the principles of* contrapposto.

'proletariat' not organized in guilds, had culminated in a bloody revolt in 1378, one of the last painful consequences of the social conflicts of the Late Middle Ages, and certain formal rights at least had been conceded to the workers, succeeding generations saw more and more power concentrated in the hands of the 'Magnates', or 'Optimates', as the refined humanistically-educated gentlemen called themselves, referring back to Ancient Rome. The Optimates, however, were identical with the great banking houses. A mercantile sense, ruthless communal policy and intelligence then brought the Medicis to the top of an internally-complicated party scene. Cosimo de' Medici (1389–1464), Head of the House and founder of the dynasty, in the end accumulated such power that he was imprisoned as a danger to the Republic and subsequently banished (1433). A year later he was back, abrogated the existing constitution, and changed the republic into a 'Signoria'. Such was the beginning of the Medici autocracy, which was to last until 1737, when the House died out. Among the serious crises were the 1440 Albizzi conspiracy, and the 1478 attempt at a *coup d'état* by the rival Pazzi, and finally the 1494 expulsion of the Medici and the interregnum of Savonarola, the censorious preacher of penitence (1452–1498), a monk whose ambition it was to set up in Florence St. Augustine's 'Kingdom of Heaven on Earth', and to purify the people through strict rules of morality and order. His anger was directed chiefly against the 'devil's work' he saw in art. Only pious imagery was permitted. Before long the most splendid paintings, sculptures and manuscripts were being burnt on great pyres in the city, among them even irreplaceable treasures by Botticelli, which Savonarola regarded as corrupt. But the spectre of this theocratic democracy, a political utopia as unfortunate and anachronistic as it was grandiose, was soon over and Savonarola himself, condemned as a heretic, perished at the stake in 1498.

The colossal upsurge of the arts in Florence around 1500 was indissolubly linked with the rise of the House of Medici, as was its ultimate decline. Following a renewed expulsion of the Medici from the city in 1527, Duke Cosimo I assumed power in 1537, when the government was transformed into a hereditary dynasty and the last democratic rights were extinguished. Art in Florence now became 'Court art' and many artists left the city, alienated by the Medici claim to omnipotence, and attracted by the freer air of Rome. In 1555 Cosimo I finally succeeded in defeating Siena and in extending his nominal sway throughout Tuscany. This was legalized by Pope Pius V, on Cosimo's appointment as Grand Duke.

From then on the history of the arts in Florence, like that of the Medici, is one of an agonizingly slow decline. Its élan grew weaker with the degeneration of the Medici dynasty, so that from 1533 or thereabouts, when Michelangelo finally moved to Rome, Florence's role in art was in the main played out. All that remained was to preserve and record. Significantly, museums were built, like the Uffizi or the Pitti Palace. Florence's contribution to European baroque can be left unmentioned. Jacob Burckhardt rightly accorded it only a few lines. The Uffizi Gallery's name derives from *ufficio*, office. It was originally conceived as an administrative centre for the politics and business affairs of the House of Medici. It included administration of the arts when creative energy subsided towards the end of the sixteenth century. It was no coincidence that the Uffizi was launched in 1560 by Georgio Vasari (1511–1574). Though an indifferent artist, he was a great critic and theorist and therefore one of the leading museum officials. In 1580 the Uffizi was wound up, with the incorporation of the Loggia dei Lanzi. Under Grand Duke Francesco I, son of Cosimo, the upper floor was rebuilt, the rebuilt section housing from the beginning the splendid Medici art collections. At the same time artists' studios and dwellings were installed. The results of this 'organization' of artistic activity into an almost business framework within the Medici bureaucracy were not impressive. The last of the Medicis, Gian Gastone, died in 1737, leaving no descendants. The city became impoverished, churches and monasteries decayed, private collectors had to live by selling off their treasures and Florence became one great antique shop.

In 1801 Napoleon created the synthetic 'Kingdom of Etruria', which in 1809 was once more transformed, with Florence, into a Grand Duchy. At the time of the Risorgimento and national unification, Florence temporarily became the seat of Italian government (1865), but soon had to surrender the function of Italian capital to Rome, which had finally relinquished that rank over three hundred years previously, at about the time when Michelangelo turned his back on it.

61 Michelangelo: 'Victory', 1532–1534. Height: 2.61 metres (8' 5"). Florence. Palazzo Vecchio. This is the only piece of sculpture actually executed from among the six groups of 'Virtues' overthrowing 'Vices', which were planned for the tomb of Julius II. Michelangelo here demonstrates in a most elegant and instructive fashion his supreme skill and mastery in handling human anatomy. Its ability to be viewed from many sides makes 'Victory' a definitely Mannerist work.

64

Page 101:
63 Michelangelo: 'The Palestrina Pieta', circa 1556. Florence. Academy. The third in the series of late Pietà groups by Michelangelo was in Palestrina near Rome until 1939. Chiselled from an ancient block of marble, the remains of an architrave can be recognised on the back. The Palestrina Pietà comes between the two other illustrations. By comparison with the frontally outspread, athletic body of Christ—a 'lame giant'—The Blessed Virgin and the favourite disciple, John, appear as incidental, marginal figures.

Page 100
62 Michelangelo: 'Pietà', circa 1550. Height: 2.26 metres (7' 6"). This Pietà group, extended to include Mary Magdalene and Nicodemus, was begun by Michelangelo about 1550, since it is mentioned in the first edition of Vasari's Lives, but was not completed, as being 'spoiled'. The left leg of the Christ figure broke during the work. The supplementary and restoration work was undertaken by Michelangelo's pupil, Tiberio Calcagni. Originally it had been intended for Michelangelo's own tomb in Santa Maria Maggiore in Rome. Despite its unfinished and badly restored condition it remains a piece of sculpture which attracts the observer by its profound earnestness.

64 Michelangelo and others: 'The Tomb of Julius II'. Installed 1542. Rome. San Pietro in Vincoli. What remained of the prodigious project for the tomb of Julius II was assembled here in 1542. Only the lower figures are by Michelangelo: the calm and introspective figures of Rachel and Leah (vita contemplativa and vita activa) were created only in 1542 and the figure of Moses executed as early as 1513–1516. The architectural framework, at once too rich and too subdivided, dates from 1505 and 1513–1514 (later version here). Moses was originally conceived of as a freely-seated corner figure in the upper row. The frontal view of to-day does not therefore correspond with the figure's composition and is also too low and confined. The upper section contains the Pope, resting on his sarcophagus, with the Madonna above him, and on each side a Sibyl and a prophet, all executed by pupils from Michelangelo's circle.

65 Michelangelo: 'Moses', installed 1542. Rome. San Pietro in Vincoli. Tomb of Julius II. Of the few completed figures for the tomb of Julius II, that of Moses is certainly the most powerful. Here is the menacing leader of his people, just down from Mount Sinai, bringing the Ten Commandments recorded in the Tables of the Law, on which his right hand rests. The figure is full of urgent action, and seems to break out of the niche.

Page 104
66 Benvenuto Cellini: 'Perseus with the Head of the Medusa', 1533. Florence. Loggia dei Lanzi. Cellini's bronze figure of Perseus, dated 1533, is a masterpiece of Florentine Mannerism. It was destined from the outset for installation in the Loggia dei Lanzi, a Hall of Honour and Ceremonial (1374–1381) by the Palazzo Vecchio, which even to-day, as on St. John's Day for example (June 24) is lavishly decorated with carpets and hung with flowers. (The name 'dei Lanzi' comes from Duke Cosimo I's bodyguard, whose lancers (mounted troopers) were quartered here).

65

Rome

After his hurried journey through Italy in the autumn of 1786, eyes bent on the great goal, Goethe noted in his diary on the day he arrived in Rome (1 November): 'Well, at last I have arrived in the capital of the world!' A few days later, when the flood of initial impressions had abated somewhat, he entered the following observations under November 5: 'Traces are to be found of a splendour and a destruction that surpass anything we can conceive of. What the barbarians left has been laid waste by the architects of the new Rome. When you look at a way of life like this, two thousand years old and more, so diverse and fundamentally transformed by the flux of time and yet the identical soil, the identical hill, yes, even the same walls and columns, and hints of the ancient character still in the people, you share in the great decrees of destiny, and so it grows difficult at the very outset for the observer to

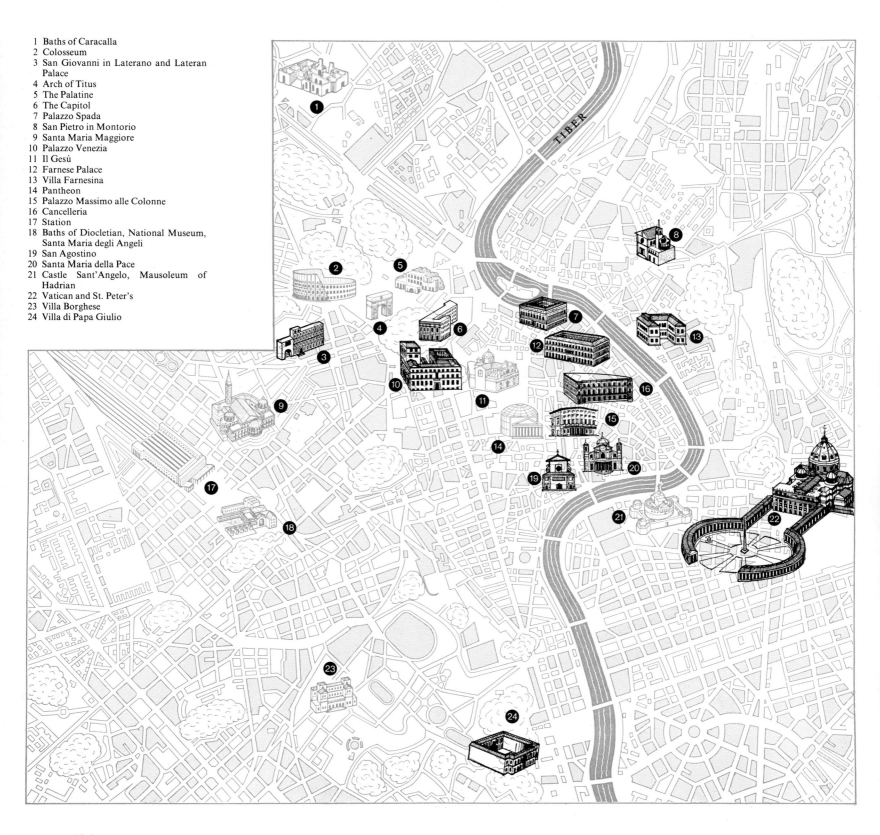

unravel how Rome succeeds Rome, not just how the new succeeds the old, but how the various eras of the old and new themselves succeed one another.'

The classical genius of the city had such an effect on the German poet, whom it had totally transformed, that twenty-eight years later, in May 1814, he could still confide to his friend, Chancellor von Müller, how he longed for Rome. Von Müller reports: 'Suddenly he stopped musingly in front of that picture of Rome and pointed to Ponte Molle which you cross, coming from the North, into the Eternal City. "I don't mind confessing to you," he said, "That I've never had a really happy day since I crossed the Ponte Molle on the way home." '

To-day it is just as hard to abandon the magic of that city landscape, its great historical memories and the eloquent testimony of its monuments as it was in Goethe's time, and the twenty-seven centuries that have passed since the ancient Romans entered history constitute through their remains a challenge to the penetration and capacity to experience and absorb of even the modern art tourist, fully equipped with reliable guide-books and plans of the city. This volume, with its twenty-five or so illustrations coming under the general theme of the Renaissance, can provide only a modest survey covering some two hundred years out of close on three thousand. The earliest monument is the Palazzo Venezia, built in 1451. Its towers and battlements still remind one of the Middle Ages, while its inner courtyard and lay-out signify the coming of Early Renaissance architecture to Rome. (Plate 67). Our series of illustrations ends, in time, with the Bernini-designed St. Peter's Square and the famous St. Peter's Colonnade, which emerged from the building-pit between 1656 and 1667 and introduces a new chapter, the Rome of High Baroque, which falls outside our province.

History

Rome's universal importance was a solid proverbial concept even for those living in the ancient world. 'All roads lead to Rome', the saying went; and *'Roma caput mundi'*, 'Rome is the capital of the world'. Apart from brief interruptions this had always been accepted, ever since the Latin people of shepherds and peasants and its Etruscan kings had set out in historically early times in the Alban and Sabine Hills and in the lower reaches of the Tiber to impress their name upon the world. Rome was the world capital after the defeat of Carthage, and its sway later extended to Greece and the Near East, for the *Orbis Romanus*, the Ancient World, was identical with the *Imperium Romanum*: the Mediterranean Basin *was* the ancient 'world'.

In the High Middle Ages and Renaissance, before Italy was consolidated into a united national state, Rome was capital of the most powerful Italian autocracy, the Patrimonium Petri or Papal State; and in the quarrel between Pope and Emperor during the High Middle Ages the European world looked, as the ancient world once had, to Rome, this time as the centre of Christendom. To-day Rome with its majestic setting pulsates with life as the capital of the (comparatively young) Italian nation; and with the Città del Vaticano, the Vatican City, it is at the same time the 'ideal', spiritual capital of the most far-flung and numerically important religious community in the world, Catholicism, which has seven hundred and ten million believers in Europe, Africa, Asia, America and Australia.

Rome to-day has over two million inhabitants, and is thus the most populous city in the Mediterranean. In the ancient world the *Città eterna,* the Eternal City, was the most populous city in the world: 'the magnetic and creative centre of Mediterranean cultures' (A. Henze, 1962). Ancient Rome's eternal character revealed itself not only in its continued rise within the ancient world over a period of more than seven hundred years, but again when it survived the decline of that epoch, and once more stepped to the forefront of the post-classical Christian era, with the Apostles Peter and Paul. In the High Renaissance, and especially in the Baroque period, Rome finally became the focal point of European art and culture and was to remain so for

67

Italian and classically-minded aesthetes up to the eighteenth century and the period of Goethe. Most of his educated contemporaries in the Late Baroque era must have shared Goethe's views of Rome as the undisputed 'Capital of the World'. How did it all start?

According to modern archaeologists Rome began as a Latin village on the Palatine Hill in the tenth century B.C. The remainder of this hill has been excavated. In the eighth century B.C. settlements of Sabine farmers, shepherds and fishermen were established in defensive positions on the Esquiline and Quirinal. Mythology links the foundation of a township to the story of the twin demi-gods Romulus and Remus, issue of a love-affair between Mars and a queen's daughter named Rhea Silvia, who were abandoned on the Tiber by her great-uncle and suckled by the she-wolf on the Capitoline. Exactly what palace intrigue in which royal court gave rise to this story can no longer be discovered. In any case Romulus's origins seemed aristocratic enough to classical Romans to raise him to the status of city-founder. With their preference for precision, to say nothing of their artless manipulation of history, the Romans named the exact day and year when the

67   Rome: Palazzo Venezia. This palace was begun after 1451 by the Venetian Cardinal Pietro Barbo in the grounds of his titular church, San Marco. However much this, the earliest of Roman Renaissance palaces, with its battlemented cornice and tower, may seem to owe to the defensive palaces of the Middle Ages, the greater number of windows and especially the wide open Loggia point to the beginning of the Renaissance.

68 *Rome: The Franciscan church of San Pietro in Montorio. The Tempietto in the monastery courtyard. Legend has it that the round temple built by Bramante in 1502 marks the spot where St. Peter was crucified. The purely circular central structure expresses the perfect structure of ideal High Renaissance architecture. At the top of three concentric steps sixteen Doric columns surround the central core, which is provided with pilasters corresponding to the columns of the ambulatory. A classical frieze with triglyphs and metopes supports the balustrade, and behind it the upper floor, which is set back, repeats the arrangement of the lower storey. The interior is of no artistic importance, the oustanding feature being the three-dimensional structure of the exterior and the classical proportion of the whole building.*

69 *Rome: Cancelleria. Courtyard. The courtyard of the Cancelleria, which dates from after 1483, was built as a palace for Raffaele Riario, nephew of Sixtus IV, and is associated with the High Renaissance in its purest and clearest form. Two floors with delicate, elegant, beautifully proportioned pillared arcades open on to the courtyard. The same theme is taken up in the enclosed third storey, which has Corinthian pilasters set against the walls, with the windows placed between them. The charm and high architectural quality of this courtyard, which at first sight appears almost over-simple, lie in its harmonious proportions and the extremely fine and elegant treatment of the details.*

city was founded: 21 April 753 B.C. Rome's first kings and the nobles certainly came from the 'Twelve Towns', the federal state of the Etruscans on its northern borders. An ironworking people, they had penetrated into Tuscany, which was rich in metals, from approximately 1000 B.C. on. The famous bronze figure of the Capitoline she-wolf with the twins (added later in the Renaissance) which embodies the founding story is a masterpiece from the period when Etruscan art was in full flower, and 'zoologically' is so close to the well-known bronze 'Chimera' of Arezzo (Florence, Archaeological Museum) that one is tempted to ascribe it to the same school of sculpture. The early Roman triad of gods, Jupiter, Mars and Virinus unmistakably points to Etruscan origins.

Other Etruscan cultural legacies to the young Roman state were the insignia worn by dignitaries, the purple-bordered toga; the official chair with its ivory decoration (*sella curulis*); and the lictors, the ushers, who carried the symbol of power over life and death, the *fasces* or bundle of rods with the axe, which was taken over by the fascists. The decline of the Etruscans was therefore quite obviously not a dramatic, violent and brief process as was

once thought, but the result of prolonged cultural, political and social fusion. 70
The Etruscan character merged throughout with the new Roman culture and
became a constituent part of it, giving evidence of the power of this human
type to adapt and incorporate whatever was strange and came from outside,
and to create a third element out of what was native and what was borrowed.

The Capitoline Hill was the centre of the loosely associated Latin and
Sabine community on the Seven Hills at the bend of the Tiber. A fortress-like
system of defensive works and the supreme popular sanctuary, the Temple of
Jupiter Capitolinus, were to be found here. For over 1790 years the dominant and controlling function of the 'Top Hill' remained undisputed, until
Michelangelo gave Rome back its old centre in a new form around 1540
with the splendid municipal architecture that re-designed the Capitol's square
by providing a Senatorial Palace, a Museum, a Palace of the *Conservatori*
(Councillors), open-air steps and a classical equestrian statue of Emperor
Marcus Aurelius. (Plates 72 and 73). Nor was it purely by chance that the
lovely 'dead girl from the Via Appia', from whose 'rebirth' could be dated the
beginning of the Renaissance in Rome, was conducted in triumphant
procession, with a marked sense for the historical setting, to the Capitol
on 18 April 1485 (almost 2238 years to the day after the legendary foundation
of the city, on April 21st) (c.f. Page 73) to be placed on exhibition.

The Latin-Sabine 'Septimontium', the group of seven hill settlements,
formed an Etruscan royal city, and as such was split up into four *regiones,* or
administrative areas: the Roman Quadrata, with the four most important
hills, the Palatine, Esquiline, Viminal and Quirinal. But this political unit
should not be accorded too much importance, since it did not number more
than a few thousand souls.

Kingly rule and with it the domination of the Etruscan nobles were finally
shaken off, and the first seven kings, Romulus, Numa Pompilius, Tullus
Hostilius, Ancus Marcius, Tarquinius Priscus, Servius Tullius, and
Tarquinius Superbus passed into the cloudy realms of fable. The Roman
Republic was founded. For this too the Imperial Roman historians have
given us the exact date: the year 510 B.C. When the kings had been driven out
the patrician class assumed political power, as well as the control of religion,
which was inseparably bound up with it. The Roman Republic had done away
with feudalism but had its own problems to face in the shape of those who
were prominent and in the limelight and those who remained in the shadows.
Peasants had become large landowners, shepherds uncouth cattle-dealers
(the Roman word for money, *pecunia,* derives from *pecus,* cattle) and simple
manual workers entrepreneurs in the metal-working 'industry'. Society began
to be differentiated into 'employers' and 'employed'. The Republic—*res
publica* in Latin—was torn for centuries by dissension between the 'haves' and
the plebeian 'have-nots', the *terrae filii,* or orphaned 'Sons of the Land'. An
attempt was made to heal this breach by an ever more-complicated and still
unwritten constitution. There were the estates of the realm, the Senate; a
powerful administration (Municipal Council) with judiciary (Praetors); a
Financial Department (Censors); authorities maintaining order and police
(Aediles); and the Higher Financial office (Quaestors). In addition, as
democratic cover, a popular assembly had the privilege of being convened
when the State was in danger and soldiers were required. The conflict
sharpened owing to fraudulent dealings among the privileged classes, which,
as everywhere, preserved their threatened privileges by breaking their word
and multiplied their privileges by the same process. In 450 or thereabouts
something unheard-of took place. Instead of the nobles being banished, it was
the people who went into exile, though not far, to the Aventine. There came
the Law of the Twelve Tables, which was laid down in bronze in the Forum.
Idealist historians summed this up as the 'victory of the idea of the State over
the class-concept'.

External threats—the pressure of neighbouring Latin tribes, and the
city's sack by the Gauls in 390 (*Vae victis!*—'Woe to the Conquered!')—were
met by paying a high ransom and erecting the first Servian Wall around the

70 *Rome: Palazzo Farnese: The Inner
Courtyard. This palace was built, from 1541
on, by Antonio Sangallo the Younger, for
Pope Paul III Farnese. After his death in 1546
the work was carried on by Michelangelo.
Open arcades mark out the ground-floor, with
Doric half-columns set in front of the
pillars—another feature borrowed from
classical Rome. This arrangement is repeated
in the Ionic semi-columns of the centre storey,
while in the upper, Corinthian pilasters
arranged in the orthodox manner complete the
picture.*

71 *Rome: Villa Farnesina. Agostino Chigi,
probably the richest banker in Rome, was
interested in all the fine arts, and had this villa
built between 1508 and 1511 by Baldasarre
Peruzzi. The building was not acquired by the
Farnese until 1580. They fitted it axially and
in terms of artistic composition into their
expanding domain by having it converge with
the Palazzo Farnese, on the other side of the
Tiber. The Farnesina can be regarded as a
contribution to the development of Italian villa
architecture: a two-storeyed summer-palace,
with an open loggia on the ground-floor and
two stepped, projecting wings, it anticipates
the baroque castle-type of building by more
than a hundred and fifty years. The costly
internal decoration by Raphael and his
School of course far exceeds in quality and
significance the external structure (c.f. Plates
91 and 92).*

Seven Hills (387); they thus united the state internally. Roman politics became increasingly aggressive. The Roman policy of security and peace became identical with military policy and was to remain so until the Empire's decline and fall. The surrounding country, Latium, was subjugated as far as the eye could see from the Capitol. Etruria and Central Italy were subjugated as far as the eye could see from the advanced hill-forts. But there was always another threatening hill further off with an unknown stronghold on it. Finally it was the neighbouring sea the Romans looked over, to the coast on the far shore, which also seemed menacing. The Roman Republic had soon extended very much further than the eye could see. Hungry mouths that produced nothing themselves had to be filled: officers, front-line soldiers, government officials, priests, and politicians were expensive but indispensable luxuries that upheld the State. The land surrounding the capital was no longer the only land to feed it. Traders settled in large numbers, and soon included traders from overseas. The Roman farmers and shepherds had metaphorically beaten their ploughshares into swords, and their shepherd's crooks into lances.

A port had been established in the kingdom at Ostia, and saltworks at the mouth of the Tiber to extract salt from seawater, since it was much in demand

72

in the markets of the ancient world. Now the Romans became seafarers as well, though not particularly adept ones, and Roman warehouses began to fill up with 'colonial produce' to fill the hungry bellies of the fast-growing city. The Roman Republic came into conflict with Carthage, its commercial and maritime rival. The first State Treaties of the young Roman Republic, in 510, 348 and 306, still marked the result of negotiations. Certain Carthaginian trade-monopolies were respected by the Romans (the Western Mediterranean and Gibraltar). In return the Carthaginians refrained from interfering with the allies of Rome. Carthage and Sicily became free-trade areas. But Rome was becoming more powerful. By 270 it had secured domination of the coast in Lower Italy, opposite Carthage. The Roman State,

72, 73 Rome: Ascent to Campidogiio and Senatorial Palace, and equestrian statue of Marcus Aurelius. The broad, sloping steps leading up to the Square on the Capitol, the most prestigious of Rome's Seven Hills, were executed from a design by Michelangelo. The equestrian statue of Marcus Aurelius between the two ancient Dioscuri appears a focal point to the visitor, since he sees it set against a background of the Senatorial Palace, erected in the late sixteenth century partly on classical and medieval foundations. (Giacomo della

112

73

Porta, Girolamo Rainaldi). The reverse view (Plate 73) shows how magnificently centred the statue is:

Helios, the sun, in his elliptical starry galaxy, flanked by the trapezoid-shaped arrangement of the Palace of the Conservatori and Capitoline Museum buildings, which lead the eye, guided by the commanding gesture of Marcus Aurelius, over the Square and down once more into the depths of the Piazza Venezia.

subdivided, according to privilege, into citizens of Rome, citizens of communities which had Roman Law and allies, covered an area of 130,000 square kilometres (50,800 square miles) and had 292,000 full Roman citizens capable of bearing arms. What had at first been a trade war at sea, with rich prize ships being seized or fishing villages burned, grew into a life-and-death struggle. The Punic Wars began. They lasted, with interruptions, for over a century (from 264 to 146 B.C.). The Romans now had to learn to fight at sea. They invented the technique of boarding and so were able to translate the rules for land battles into a naval strategy. They adopted the principles of building warships from a five-oared Punic vessel that had been left stranded. Hannibal crossed the Alps in the snow with five hundred elephants. And in

the first battle of annihilation in history, at Cannae, Quintus Fabius Maximus, known as 'the Procrastinator' and military dictator of Rome, sacrificed fifty thousand Romans and the fearful cry of *Hannibal ante portas*! ('Hanibal is at the gates!') ran through the city.

The elderly Cato closed his speeches with the stubborn political slogan 'Ceterum censeo Carthaginem esse delandam': 'Furthermore I consider that Carthage must be destroyed'. In the end Rome was victorious. Scipio, who was later given the title of 'Africanus', sailed over to North Africa and routed the Carthaginians in 202. Rome had undergone critical changes in those hundred years. The inevitable result of the Punic Wars was a highly-developed military and armaments industry. The impoverished peasants

74, 75   Rome: St. Peter's: The Cupola. On Michelangelo's death in 1564 the structure had advanced as far as the tambour. The shell of the cupola was completed by Giacomo della Porta between 1588 and 1590. The cupola rests on the pillars of the crossing, which are 24 metres in diameter (78'). The circular dome tambour opens up in sixteen windows, between protruding double pilasters. Sixteen ribs matching the windows culminate in the tower, again with sixteen windows. The cupola is 42.34 metres in height (137' 7", and 119 metres (386' 8'') to the top. The interstices between the arches of the crossing and the

75

from devastated Lower Italy moved into the city to form an unskilled proletariat. Rome became the leading capitalist and banking centre. Immeasurable wealth was concentrated in a few hands, while a new stratum came into being below the propertyless class, that of the class without rights, the slaves. In 136, ten years after the end of the Third Punic War, they rose *en masse* in Southern Italy. The result was the first mass slaughter known to history. Twenty thousand crucified slaves lined the long, straight military and commercial Roman roads. Rome had now finally changed from an agricultural state into a highly-organized modern state of officers, officials, technocrats and business-men.

Inheriting Attalos' kingdom of Pergamon in Asia, Rome in the year 133

became the undisputed dominating power in the entire Mediterranean. Social disturbances and struggles for power between rival groups henceforth took on the character of inter-Roman civil wars and led to the Republic's downfall: the reform movement of the Gracchi and the Confederate War for greater rights, Sulla, Pompey, the 'Catiline conspiracy' and the inexorable path to power of the great Caesar (murdered in 44 B.C.), which finally, after the days of the Principality, led to the accession of the Pater Patriae, Caesar Augustus, to the leadership of Rome as Pontifex Maximus and life consul (40 B.C.–A.D. 14). Under a series of Caesars, some eminent men, others pitiful figures, some sensitive art-lovers, others uncouth military men or perverse voluptaries—one of them, Caligula, is said to have made his horse a consul—the Roman Empire enjoyed three centuries of unequalled brilliance in both the political and cultural spheres. It can only be compared with Athens in the classical era, the *grand siècle* under Louis XIV, the Hohenstaufen period or Charlemagne's empire, but it lasted longer than any of them. The entire cultural world of Europe, the Near East and North Africa was Roman. The Mediterranean peoples, who in Plato's delightful phrase sat around the sea 'like frogs round a pond', conversed in terms of Roman politics and culture. Rome was the leader of the world and under auspicious emperors such as the cultured, Greek-minded and much-travelled Hadrian (A.D. 117–138) or the 'Emperor of Peace', Antonius Pius (138–161) or Marcus Aurelius (161–180), the 'Philosopher king', the supreme imperial leader was a symbol and figurehead for traders and legionaries in the farthest outposts of the ever-expanding Empire. In the third century the Imperium's greatest expansion was surpassed. Significantly it was now proven soldiers from the border provinces who tried to snatch the imperial Crown (the 'Soldier-Emperors'), supported by the legions loyal to them. It testifies to the vast extent, internationalism and also the tolerance of Rome that it should be the son of an Arab Sheikh, Emperor Philip the Arabian (244–249), who celebrated the thousandth anniversary of the founding of Rome.

What had Rome to bequeath to the post-classical and Christian world after Constantine the Great received Christian baptism on his deathbed (337), and after Christianity became the official state religion (391) and all pagan cults were prohibited? Or after the Western Roman Empire had been extinguished in 476 with the deposing of Romulus Augustulus by Odoacer?

Once it had been the grandiose structure housing the Roman Empire and Roman Government, which has remained a model to the present day. We must be content with a reference to Herder, who called Rome 'the proud legislator for all nations' because of its outstanding accomplishments and its flawless legal system. On the other hand, Roman architecture and building technique, as well as Roman art's special achievements in painting, historical reliefs and decorative wall-painting and wall and floor mosaics, as in Pompeii, must be of particular interest to us, for this was the legacy taken up first and most intensively by the Renaissance. It lay all over the fields, in ruins, and was thus most easily accessible, whereas in the case of painting or sculpture, accidental discoveries (still rare) or deliberate excavations were required, which only began towards the end of the sixteenth century.

Roman architects were above all great handlers of mass and space-planners, and had a gift for large-scale technical assignments. As we have seen, the first Servian city wall was built in 387 B.C. following the Gallic invasions. This was the start of planned city building in Rome. The Via Appia became the first Roman highway around 300 B.C. and in the course of the next few centuries was linked up to a dense network of other roads all over Europe, which is still, in part, the basis of modern road-planning. At the same time, about 300 B.C., the first aqueduct was built in Rome, the Aqua Claudia, and was followed by countless others in Rome itself and in the provinces. These aqueducts, bringing cool drinking-water from regions of high precipitation in the mountains, often over more than a hundred kilometres (sixty miles or so) were so solidly constructed and so effective that in Rome, for instance, they quite sufficed up until the nineteenth century to supply a modern metropolis with drinking water, contained in baroque wells. The old Acqua Vergine behind the Villa Giulia still supplies many of the Roman wells to-day. That Rome continues to be called the 'City of a Thousand Fountains' and the 'Fountains of Rome' continue to be lauded by poets is all due to the ancient Romans. Nor was drainage neglected. The Cloaca Maxima, one of the most outstanding feats of engineering and sanitation in the ancient world, disposed of the sludgewaters and is still workable to-day. In 57 B.C. under Pompey the first big popular theatre was built of stone. A succeeding building, the late Roman Colosseum, was 'colossal' in every respect, and remained the largest stone building in the world devoted to public performances, until it was eclipsed in our own century by the Yale Stadium in the United States.

Even qualified historians are largely unaware that among Caesar's many and varied talents was a particular interest in town-planning. He did not live to see his ambitious projects realized, but they were partly carried out by Caesar Augustus. It was under the latter that Rome began to change from a city of brick to a city of marble. The transformation process reached its height after the fire of Nero in 64 A.D., the first 'scorched earth' policy in history to

77

77 Rome: General view. The Vatican Palace stretches north-east of St. Peter's (which we have to imagine underneath the illustration) on slightly rising ground as far as the antique manor of Bramante's Belvedere. In other words it corresponds in extent, inclusive of the Museums and so forth, to approximately what were the Belvedere's original terraced gardens. These of course were 'destroyed' by Sixtus V, who allowed a transverse wing for his library to be built there. A second parallel wing, known as the Braccio nuovo, was erected under Pius VII Chiaramonti at the beginning of the nineteenth century with the co-operation of Canova, for the purpose of housing the collection of antiquities. The roof of the Sistine Chapel can be seen at the right-hand lower edge of the illustration.

have a prior architectural plan behind it. Nero's *Domus Aurea,* Golden House, the centre of this reconstruction, was a gigantic villa-like palace area, rich in green sward, lakes and ponds.

The 'new building techniques, such as cast-metal and mortar-work (*opus caementicium*, hence our modern word 'cement'), shuttering, marble flagging and improved structural methods produced by new vaulting techniques, altered the face of the seven-hilled city. Symptomatic of the rapidly swelling population and the growing scarcity of land were the multi-storeyed houses that had grown up in the city centre, new in appearance and turning their façades and corridors to the street, with balaconies and columned halls, while their rear wall, which looked over a courtyard, was neglected. The town-palace architecture of the nobility took over features of the Italic country villa with garden parterres, while the Imperial fora, with their widely spaced axes, temples, staircases, columned halls and basilicas gave rise to representational pleasure grounds of monumental proportions. The Roman market basilica, a hall with several naves and heavy tunnel vaulting, earmarked for legal hearings and marketing, proved to be a future model for Christian architecture. Most of the monumental structures of the Empire period still survived in the fields of ruins, being practically indestructible—the Forum Romanum and the Palatine, the Capitol, Colosseum, Baths of Diocletian and Caracalla, Castel Sant' Angelo (Mausoleum of Hadrian), Arch of Constantine, Arch of Titus, and the Pantheon, to mention only the most important.

So far-flung were the boundaries of the ancient city that it was not until this century that modern Rome penetrated beyond the Aurelian brick wall

118

surrounding the city, proof of the enormous area Ancient Rome covered by the standards of antiquity. With the beheading of the Apostle Paul on the road to Ostia and the crucifixion of Peter on Mons Vulcanus in the year 64, the Christian history of Rome begins, along with the history of the Popes and Bishops of Rome. Their names have come down to us, though with no very precise details because the first Popes, Linus, Anacletus, Clement, Alexander, Sixtus, Evaristus, Telesphorus and Hyginus, in the first and second centuries A.D. were the hunted ringleaders of a rebellious sect consisting of slaves, freed prisoners, foreigners and social misfits, a body that met together in secret, in the skilfully camouflaged underground premises of their cult, cellars and catacombs. Even midway through the third century cruel persecutions of the Christians took place under Decius, Valerian and Diocletian, until the Edict of Tolerance from Milan (313) brought freedom of conscience and equality for Christians. The Church of Rome was able to expand without hindrance in the Empire's last year. It sent out missionaries freely, came to an understanding as regards the legacy of classical art, culture and philosophy in such a way that—progressing via assimilation—it did not simply cast aside what was left of paganism but took it over, a principle that was to be applied again in later church history. The first Papal Palace on the Lateran emerged from a classical imperial palace, while the Lateran Baptistery was built on the foundation walls of a classical Piscina, and the Pantheon was turned into a Christian church. Rome's most important churches were built in the fourth and fifth centuries and still mark the city scene to-day. They all followed the basilica plan adopted from the time of the Empire, though for Christian purposes it was redesigned, with a commanding central nave, flat roof and apses. The imperial 'arch-basilicas' of San Giovanni in Laterano, San Paolo fuori le Mura and St. Peter's predecessor, Old St. Peter's, plus the parish-churches of Santa Maria Maggiore, San Lorenzo fuori le Mura, Santa Constanza, Santo Stefano Rotondo, San Pietro in Vincoli, San Clemente and others, belong to this group, with their splended mosaic and marble work, which is still preserved.

The fate that had been predictable since the centre of gravity shifted East and the capital of Christianity moved with Constantine to Constantinople in the year 330, took place when the great migrations began. In 410, 455 and 546 the Visigoths under Alaric, the Vandals under Gaiseric and the Ostrogoths under Totila attacked the city, plundering and carting off whatever their horses and swiftly-assembled baggage-trains could carry. The Northern cavalry enriched themselves on the bankrupt estates of the old Roman Empire, yet were unable to remove the most valuable treasure of all: the monumental fields of ruins which were falling more and more into decay, mercifully covered with humus, and as pasture-land immune to the researches of modern archaeology; or else plundered by quarry-owners and lime-burners. The population meanwhile rapidly declined. When Romulus Augustulus was deposed in 476 there were only some 25,000 left out of 750,000 to 1,500,000 inhabitants of the Imperial City.

After three hundred years of decline, the rise of the Papacy, and hence of the city itself, began about the middle of the eighth century. The outstanding and shrewd Pope Stephen II (752–757) embarked on a major political campaign. Under the protection of Pepin, King of the Franks, whom he anointed a second time in St. Denis, he beat back the threat of the Longobard King, Aistulf. Pepin and his sons thereafter styled themselves 'Patricius Romanorum', Protector of the Romans.

Pepin wrested from Aistulf the Exarchate of Ravenna and the Pentapolis (the territory of the five seaside-towns, Rimini, Pesaro, Fano, Sinigaglia and Ancona on the East coast of Italy) and presented them to the Pope (the 'Pepin Gift', 754). These, together with Rome, formed the nucleus of the later Papal Territory. Subsequently the Pope raised claims to political sovereignty independently of Eastern Rome, basing his right to autonomy on a cunningly forged document from a French monastery, the 'Gift of Constantine' according to which Constantine the Great transferred the western half of the

Following pages:

78 Rome: Vatican Library: The vaulted hall, over 70 metres (227' 6") in length, was erected by Domenico Fontana in 1588 on the instructions of Sixtus V and is made even more splendid by the wall frescoes. The types of decoration are reminiscent of the School of Raphael 'grotesques' in the Loggias of the Vatican and the Villa Madama. Pope Nicholas V (1447–1455), a passionate collector of books and connoisseur of literature, had laid the foundations of the Vatican Library, which Sixtus IV (1471–1484) extended. To-day, with 25,000 medieval manuscripts, 7000 incunabula, 600,000 handwritten documents and 950,000 printed works, it is regarded as the most important library in the world.

Empire to the Bishop of Rome and recognised the primacy of the Eternal City
over all other churches. It is one of the ironies of history that this forgery was
later unmasked within the religious circles of the Papal Roman Court.
Lorenzo Valla (1405–1457), a highly-qualified philological secretary to Pope
Nicholas V (1447–1455), founder of the Vatican Library, was able, by means
of textual criticism, to ascribe the document to the Pepin era.

A new chapter in the history of Rome and the Papacy begins with
Charlemagne's coronation by Pope Leo III in Rome at Christmas in the year
800. It became a matter of symbolic political significance for German
Emperors to go to Rome for the coronation. One German Emperor, Otto II,
died in Rome and was buried in Old St. Peter's (983). His successor Otto III
(983–1002), a religious man and touchingly Utopian, tried to achieve his
dream of a new 'Roman Empire' in Rome and resided for a time in a palace on
the Aventine Hill.

But the holy alliance between the German conception of Empire, the
Italian Papacy and the Eternal City remained but a dream, which disappeared
in the course of conflict between the Popes and Hohenstaufen Emperors,
though not without fostering Dante's Utopian vision of a 'world monarchy'.

In the Middle Ages Rome was ruled by powerful city families who were
often little more than robber-knights or successful highwaymen with
artificially constructed family-trees. Bloody feuds raged between them. They
had settled in borrowed shells, the ruins of ancient buildings, like hermit-
crabs. There were the Counts of Tusculum, the Crescenzi, the Frangipani,
Pierleoni, Colonna, Orsini, Savelli and Anguillara. Fortified eyries were built
in theatres, baths and stadiums into which they withdrew when fighting flared
up between 'Papists' and 'Imperialists'.

But the genius of the city continued to operate unseen and the shades of the
past were not completely gone. Under Arnold of Brescia in the mid-twelfth
century and particularly under Cola di Rienzo in the middle of the fourteenth
century the citizens of Rome tried to make the idea of a Roman City-State on
the old classical model a reality. Cola di Rienzo is already a completely
Renaissance figure. During the period when the Papacy was under the
worst threat in its two thousand-year-old history, the exile to Avignon
and the manipulation of the Pontificate by the French crown (1309–1377),
this political adventurer tried to reconstruct the Roman *res publica,* by careful
interpretation and implementation of historical records and practice. He
banished the nobles, appointed himself to the tribune of the people (1347) and
proclaimed a republic. The fact that this produced nothing but a 'marvellous
comedy' (J. Burckhardt) was due to the rottenness of Italian political
conditions, and not to Cola di Rienzo or to lack of interest in the national
past. In 1354 Cola di Rienzo lost his life at the hands of the same 'Plebeians'
whom he had tried to help to a class-consciousness of the ancient Roman
type.

Meantime the population of Rome had shrivelled to a lamentable 20,000
and the buildings and town-walls of the ancient world wrapped the provincial
community round like an oversized garment. But the crisis now reached its
turning-point. After the years of the Great Schism (1378–1417) when the
'Rock of Christ' split into the two alternatives of Pope in Rome (Urban VI) or
Pope in Avignon (Clement VII), and Christendom was about to lose its way in
heresy, superstitition and witch-hunting, the root-and-branch reform
movement in the church resulted in the schism being overcome and in a
strengthening of the Papacy throughout the political world. The Popes now
felt themselves to be sovereigns and practical politicians. After the Rienzo
interlude, the energetic Cardinal Albornoz (1353–1368) won back the city for
the Curia, and gave it a constitution on the ancient mode, the 'Egidian
Constitutions', which lasted till 1816.

The Roman Popes of the Renaissance, who came from the most important
princely families in Rome and the rest of Italy, introduced one of the most
brilliant eras in the Eternal City, often compared with the flowering of
Ancient Rome under Augustus. The churches' 'Babylonian Captivity' in

79

Avignon had produced a feeling for Court life, and the nerve to acquire the necessary financial resources. The Curia was transformed into a gigantic finance house. Everything connected with spiritual office and the salvation of the faithful cost money, a lot of money, whether it was the distribution of official positions, benefices, privileges and letters of pardon, commissions (the bestowal of office) and 'reservations' (prior 'booking' of office) or indulgences, the remission of the penitence required by the church, which could now be obtained for cash instead of via crusades and pilgrimages. Naïve religious souls like the Carmelite preacher Adamo of Genoa thundered against simony (the sale of offices). In 1494 he was found murdered in his bed. Corruption thrived, especially under Pope Sixtus IV and Innocent VIII. 'Where Sixtus had obtained money by the sale of spiritual favours and offices, Innocent and his son built up a bank of secular favours, whereby pardon could be obtained for manslaughter and murder by paying high taxes. One hundred and fifty ducats went into the Papal Treasury for every penance, and anything over, to Franceschetto. Towards the end of this Pontificate Rome

122

was swarming with protected and unprotected murderers' (J. Burckhardt: *Art and Culture of the Renaissance in Italy* 1860). Figures like Pope Alexander and his odious children Lucrezia and Cesare Borgia, whom historians have attempted to erase from Italian history's roll of honour as Spanish 'foreigners' (Cesare in his Spanish fashion used to slay bulls in the courtyard of his palace, in solitary rituals) were no worse than their environment. The fact that they held prominent positions has caused them to be doggedly remembered. This was the reason why certain Humanist circles in Italy and Germany were secretly anticlerical, though, be it remarked, never anti-religious or atheistic. It was also the cause of the Utopian pressure of the period for a 'New Church' and a real reformation, which assumed concrete shape in Luther, and—paradoxically enough—facilitated the continuance of the Papacy in Rome by producing the Counter-Reformation in defence.

Political and personal immorality are not always incompatible with the highest artistic taste. Thus during the Renaissance Papacy in Rome we have the spectacle of the noblest pictures being painted, the choicest sculptures being created, whilst at times only a few hundred yards away human beings were being tortured, strangled, poisoned or stabbed, and the most sacred values of Christendom hawked around with the utmost cynicism, as if in some cattle-market.

Rome experienced an upsurge in architecture. Beginning with Sixtus IV and Innocent VIII and ending with the Baroque Popes, an attempt was made by deliberate recourse to classical architecture to restore ancient Rome with its great axes of road, squares and outstanding points of reference. As elsewhere in Italy, the study of antiquity became fashionable. Flavio Biondo's descriptive text *Roma instaurata,* written towards the end of the fifteenth century, became an obligatory text, while as early as 1443 a Roman reporter was waging a campaign against the vicious habit of using ancient marble for lime-burning, 'for the newer buildings in Rome are pitiable and it is the ruins that are beautiful!' Documentary evidence to the credit of the Curia's cultural policy are the frequent Papal ordinances in the late fifteenth and throughout the sixteenth century prohibiting the destruction of ancient monuments and works of art under threat of punishment. Papal architectural policy in the city and the study of antiquity went almost hand in hand, and the best artists of the time devoted themselves to the new task of making Rome the cultural centre of the world. These included Leonardo da Vinci, who had been in Cesare Borgia's service as a military engineer in 1503, Raphael and Michelangelo.

As far back as 1373 a small obelisk had been dug up near the Pantheon. The famous 'Boy with the Thorn' was recovered in the same way about 1450, and in 1506 the 'Laocoon', followed in 1510 by the Belevedere 'Apollo'. From 1540 onwards systematic excavation work was carried out in the Baths of Caracalla, and the 'Farnese Bull' as well as the 'Farnese Hercules' were found. Next came excavations in the Baths of Constantine (from 1550), and the discovery of the two 'Dioscuri of Monte Cavallo'. 1570 or 1606 saw the 'Medici Venus' and the famous painting of the 'Aldobrandini Wedding' complete the list of findings. Even to-day thirteen ancient obelisks still adorn Rome's most important squares. They all lay in the ground till they were excavated towards the end of the sixteenth century, and included the obelisk of St. Peter, found in 1586, and three others, those of the Lateran, Santa Maria Maggiore and Piazza del Popolo, all found in 1587.

The notorious 'Sack of Rome' by an army of mercenaries belonging to Emperor Charles V (1527) occurred just when Rome was being planned anew, and so left hardly a trace in the Renaissance picture of the city. Nevertheless parts of Raphael's noted Villa Madama fell prey to it. The completion of Rome's grandiose architectural reorganization was reserved for the Early Baroque period and thus falls outside our survey. Roman art is rooted in two historical and political institutions—the Roman Empire and the Papacy. These twin roots gave out branches, clambered up each other, supported each other and eventually came together to form the trunk out of

80 Rome: The Vatican, Sistine Chapel. General View. The smooth architecture of this simple store-room was created under Sixtus IV, who consecrated the chapel in 1483. The frescoes on the long walls and the twenty-eight paintings of popes between the windows were also carried out during his Pontificate, mainly by Tuscan and Umbrian painters. The chapel owes its fame, however, chiefly to Michelangelo's frescoes in the vaulting and his 'Last Judgement' on the altar-wall. Raphael's celebrated series of tapestries (now in the Vatican Museum) executed from 1515 to 1516 served to cover the lower third of the walls. This costly décor confers on the Sistine Chapel the effect of a shrine, containing the noblest of relics. It is reserved up to the present day for the most important ecclesiastical events in the Catholic world, the election of a Pope for example.

Following pages:
81 Rome: Michelangelo's 'Last Judgement' (Detail) 1534–1541. The Vatican. Sistine Chapel. Christ judges the world. The interceding Madonna on his right is surrounded by saints, martyrs and figures from the Old Testament. We recognise Adam on the left, and on the right the equally gigantic figure of Peter with, at Christ's feet, the greatest martyr, Bartholomew, holding in his hands his skin. Christ, with a great gesture of His right hand, is dividing those far beneath him, awakened to the Last Judgement by the sound of the Last Trump, into those saved and those who are damned. The picture is an excellent illustration of the technique of the buon fresco practised from the beginning of the fourteenth century and also by Michelangelo. Following preparatory sketches (up to original size), the draft was transferred to the ceiling or walls by the aid of finely-pierced boards, the holes in which had been powdered over with charcoal. This final draft had to be covered with fresh chalk, however, if the colours were to combine well with their background. Since any schematic 'squaring' would have rendered the work more difficult the work was done in what were known as 'daily tasks'. Only as much of the prior drawing was covered with chalk as could be painted in a day, and the outlines of the body were followed, so as to have points of reference available. These 'daily tasks' can be seen clearly in Michelangelo's 'Last Judgement'.

which, in the High Renaissance and Baroque periods, the city's present artistic shape grew.

'Let us admit, however, that it is a sad and sorry business to pluck ancient Rome out of the new city' (Goethe *Italian Journey*, 5 November 1786). But this was a task to which every artist whose ambition it was to work in Rome had to address himself. Even if he had no desire to, this was carried out unconsciously. Those familiar with the ancient art of Greece had also to reorientate themselves in Rome. Monumentality, architectonic plans that included in their dimension mountains and valleys as contained open spaces; weighty yet broad vaulting; powerful pillars with heavy architraves over them instead of columns that were 'visible at a glance'; sculptures larger than life and free-standing, not backed by a protective architectural framework; paintings in which every figure was placed for all eternity; outside staircases; victory columns and wide triumphal arches covered all over with reliefs; the elevated *gravità romana,* the weight of Roman seriousness, does not confront only the modern visitor, but had to be assimilated by artists, with an eye that was alert and took in everything. None of them escaped these impressions. They were shaped and stamped one and all by this city's radiance, and if from now on they painted, built and sculpted 'differently', i.e. in the 'Roman' way, it was not a question of external pressure but of a humble and yet proud, of an active and conscious submission. Florence was open to every artistic personality who was free to develop his own individuality. An artist born in Venice was encouraged to remain Venetian, giving himself over to the ebb and flow of the city and to its inspiration. But Rome shaped its artists and shaped them with all the weight of its existing century-old and yet still valid traditions. Florence is the city of discovery, innovation and experiment. Venice remains in the intellectual and spiritual condition in which it always existed. Innovations come out of it of themselves, and as a matter of course. But Rome reaches *consciously* back into tradition and so finds its way to the new, which even today is still involved with the past.

Rome was never a city of young styles, of joyfully experimental or exploratory ideas, but has always been a city of maturity. Only when a style has reached full maturity has Rome solemnly and sonorously taken it up, as though in final consecration. When Brunelleschi, Donatello and Masaccio created the Renaissance in Florence almost overnight, in about 1420, the Papacy was going through a period of serious crisis. One schism followed another and every legitimate pope had to contend with several anti-popes. They seldom managed even to set foot in Rome, but lived in Florence or Bologna, or eventually in exile in Avignon. Eugenius IV (1431–1447) was the first pope who managed to return to Rome, which was by then in a state of total decay. He at once started rebuilding it; but if he was to embellish his residence he and his successor Nicholas V, another art-lover, had to send for painters and sculptors in Florence and northern Italy, as well as Venetian mosaic artists such as Gentile da Fabriano, Pisanello and Donatello. Fra Angelico started working on the former Vatican chapel of the Sacrament. Nicholas V summoned to Rome the brilliant Florentine architect Leon Battista Alberti so that he could start work on rebuilding St. Peter's. He also employed Benozzo Gozzoli, Andrea del Castagno and Piero della Francesca as painters. Under Sixtus IV della Rovere (1471–1484), Verrocchio, Ghirlandaio, Botticelli, Perugino and Pinturicchio—Florentines, Sienese and Umbrians—were working in Rome.

It was not until the eve of the High Renaissance, in 1503, that Julius II managed to make Bramante, Michelangelo and Raphael, all of whom he had brought to Rome, feel so attached to the city that they failed to return to their home towns when their commissions were completed. Instead they remained in Rome and became 'Romans', since the artistic legacy that Rome could offer now fitted in with the style and ambitions of the period. Rome therefore remained the centre of the arts and the capital of the golden age of the High Renaissance. Its supremacy lasted until the Sack of Rome in 1527, when the city was plundered and devastated by Imperial Spanish mercenaries and French troops.

Rome had thus been able, as it were, to catch up on the art of the Early Renaissance, with the help of Florentine, northern Italian and Sienese artists. The almost exclusively religious art of the Gothic and Romanesque periods had passed it by, virtually without leaving a single trace, since its centres were in Cluny and Cîteaux, in the imperial 'national art' of the great cathedrals on the Rhine (Worms, Mayence, Speyer) and in the Ile de France, the cradle of Gothic architecture ranging from Saint-Denis and Chartres to Rheims and Amiens.

Italian art had without a doubt set its face against the verticality of Gothic, to replace which other forms had been found: broadly spaced-out areas and wide arcades instead of the sharply pointed type. The cathedrals of Pisa, Florence, Siena and Orvieto are there to bear witness. The mendicant orders, Franciscans and Dominicans, had built gigantic churches everywhere that impress themselves on the city scene but Rome had remained entirely unaware of all this.

Yet on the threshold of Roman art stands one of the freeest creations in all religious art, the Early Christian basilica, which seems to hold in contempt the entire classical legacy, particularly as regards vaulting. Only a few decades separated the greatest Roman example of vaulting and cross-vaulting, the Maxentius Basilica, with its massive cross-vaults and barrel-vaulting, from the old St. Peter's Basilica with its open roof-framework which leaves all the timber raftering visible. Amid all the expensive and splendid late Empire vaulting it was the late Republican or early Empire market and courtroom basilicas, in the style of the Basilica Julia or the Basilica Aemilia on the Forum Romanum, or the Basilica Ulpia on the Trajan Forum, that served as guide in building the first church in Christendom. These were lengthy structures with a high central nave and low aisles over which galleries could be placed, with a flat, coffered roof, or open rafters, vestibule and a semi-circular apse on one of the narrow sides.

The decision to refer to secular Roman basilicas in constructing early Christian community assembly halls was logical and consistent. The function of both was to concentrate a large number of people in one spot, where either the Roman orator was speaking or the Christian priest celebrated mass. The ancient Greek or Roman temple would have been quite inappropriate as an architectural model since only the priest was allowed to approach the divinity in the inner sanctum, and the audience remained outside.

None of the early Christian basilicas in Rome had towers—the Campanili allotted them to-day all belong to the twelfth or thirteenth century—since the liturgical custom of summoning the parish to worship by means of bells came into use only in the ninth century. All of Rome's early Christian basilicas, with the exception of St. Peter's, have come down to us substantially intact. The most venerable, such as San Giovanni in Laterano or Santa Croce in Gerusalemme, were of course converted to the Baroque style in the seventeenth and eighteenth centuries. Santa Maria Maggiore, where the mosaic cycle has been fully preserved, offers the visitor the clearest picture of how it must have looked originally. Alexander VII Borgia had the finest coffered ceiling in Rome completed. Begun by Calixtus III, it is said to have been gilded with the first gold brought to Europe from America.

So much was early Christendom governed by its classical legacy in shaping the basilica that other necessary Christian religious buildings also maintained their functional purpose as conceived by pagan Roman art. Among these are the tomb structures erected over the bones of particularly pious and distinguished Christians, or martyrs. The *Tolos,* the round building, windowless but with a cupola, or in any case a central structure, was retained as a tomb not only along the Via Appia but also outside Rome. Baptisteries were also invariably erected on a central ground-plan until the High Middle Ages. Since the origin of some can be traced back indisputably to the round or elliptical Roman baths, the *caldaria* or *tepidaria* (as for example San Giovanni in Laterano), it may justifiably be assumed that the tradition of centrally-structured baptisteries is due to the fact that the ancient baths were

83

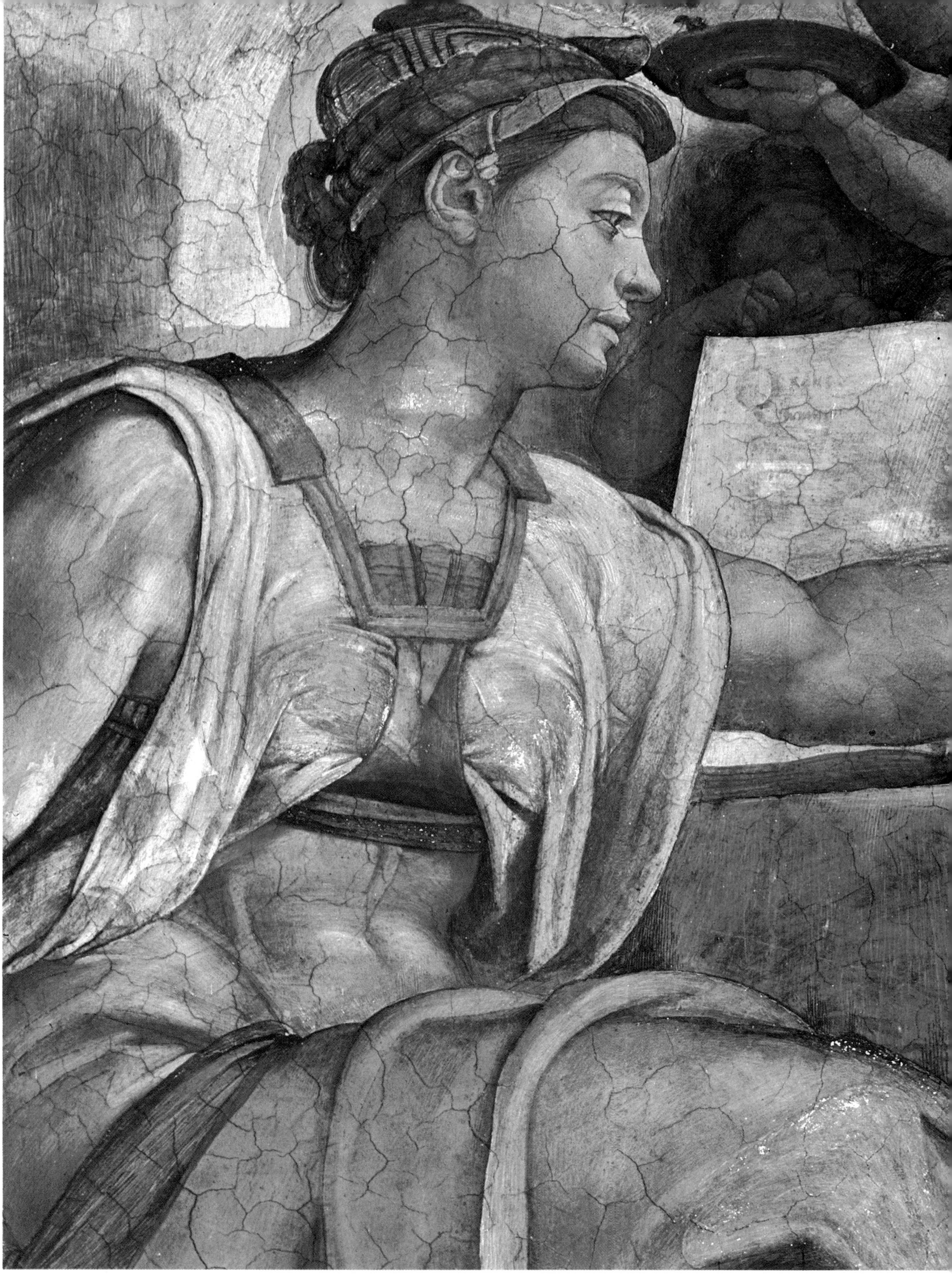

converted at the beginning of Christendom into baptismal fonts.

In the Christian West secular architecture played only a subordinate role throughout the whole of the Middle Ages. In the Rome of the period it did not appear at all. In Florence, Siena, Bologna and other Italian towns the feuding nobles built impregnable fortress-like palaces with high towers. In Venice, where there were no internal feuds, elegantly decorated Gothic palaces emerged from the water. In Rome it was quite different. There the influential noble families withdrew into the solid ruins of the ancient theatres and baths.

When the Renaissance began, however, the wealth of material which ancient Rome had left behind provided the best of object lessons and was appreciated by the architectural theorists of the time as a pattern to follow. The most important of these, Leon Battista Alberti, was, with Pope Nicholas V, the first to produce a project not confined to individual building schemes but one to be thought of as a piece of comprehensive town-planning. The project to rebuild St. Peter's was combined with new building and systematic planning of the Vatican. Streets were laid out in long-range perspectives as far as Castel Sant' Angelo, the Mausoleum of Hadrian, the farthest of the walls enclosing the Vatican State. It was this thinking in terms of great axes, and the gradation and architectural conception of successive open spaces which had been learned and understood from studying imperial baths and villa designs, that provided the impetus behind the townscape of Rome which now, and in the centuries that followed, began to emerge. 'The next step giving shape to the city occurs in the High Renaissance. Under Pope Leo X two diagonally branching streets, the Via di Ripetta and the Via del Babuino, were led off the Piazza del Popolo to form, with the old central axis of the Corso, a widespread network of streets in the shape of a fan, such as the baroque period almost invariably adopted for their founding cities, from Versailles to Rastatt and Karlsruhe.' (H. Keller, 1960).

A new rearrangement, which took in the widest areas and indeed the whole of ancient Rome followed under Sixtus V (1585–1590). The Pope was not moved in this by any artistic ideas, even though the end result was a masterly achievement in municipal architecture. He was more interested in a 'vast network of streets connecting up Rome's outstanding old churches in great vistas . . . [and] indicating the points of convergence by using the obelisks about to be erected as vertices' (D. Frey, 1924). In addition to the obelisk on St. Peter's Square put up during Sixtus V's Pontificate, the obelisks in Santa Croce, before the Lateran, on the Piazza del Popolo and in front of Santa Maria Maggiore, were re-erected under him to mark the great pilgrimage roads. His favourite church, Santa Maria Maggiore, formed the centre of this network. The shaping and architectonic designing of the squares came next. St. Peter's Square, the Piazza Navona with Bernini's Fountain of the Four Rivers, the attractive Rococo square of Sant' Ignazio, Piazza Venezia and Piazza del Popolo, which found its final form only in Valadier's classicism, all belong to the Roman scene, as does the earliest square of all, the Capitol, (Plates 72 and 73).

The Capitol, the smallest of the Seven Hills, was ancient Rome's religious and political centre. The Senatorial Palace, seat of city government, dating in its present form from the sixteenth century, stands on classical and medieval foundation walls. Michelangelo was commissioned to replan the irregular square, sloping unevenly down at the sides, once the equestrian statue of Marcus Aurelius had been brought from the Lateran to the Capitol in 1538. This bronze image of the Emperor on horseback is the one and only original that has come down to us from the ancient world. Assumed to be an equestrian statue of Constantine, the first Christian Emperor, it was therefore not destroyed. Execution of Michelangelo's magnificent designs was begun only shortly before his death. First the paving of the three-stepped oval was begun. The Emperor as Helios, the Sun-God, was to be portrayed in the centre of a radiating ellipse (Plate 73). The two lateral palaces were erected only after Michelangelo's death, but in strict accordance with his plans. Here

84 Michelangelo: 'The Expulsion from Paradise'. Detail: Head of Eve. Rome. The Vatican. Sistine Chapel. The figure of Eve seems to cower, as it were, beneath the Divine wrath. Only the features appear bold and free, full of the awareness she has acquired from eating of the Tree of Knowledge.

powerful fore-pilasters combine to form an orderly system which is colossal in its effect—the first in a secular building since the ancient world—the ground-floor resting on columns and straight architrave. The broad sloping approach (Plate 72) to the square, which is not oblong but trapezoid, is also from designs by Michelangelo, while the marble figures of the Dioscuri, from the Late Empire, provide a solemn frame for the entrance 'into the Square', *in piazza*, as the Italian language attractively puts it.

'Thus regarded, Michelangelo's Capitol represents the most powerful and profound incorporation of Italian Renaissance thinking. Antiquity is the basis and centre, but also the source of spiritual renewal. Michelangelo did

85 Sandro Botticelli: 'Scenes from the Youth of Moses', 1481–1482. Rome: The Vatican, Sistine Chapel. Botticelli's fondness for story-telling, uniting several scenes in one picture as in medieval painting, gives the fresco an Early Renaissance freshness. The wealth of charming detail almost destroys the pictorial unity.

85 not imitate classical antiquity in detail. Neither the plinth, nor the oval, nor the architecture of the palaces imitate ancient forms. On this spot we feel clearly that the ancient world is over, but that through Michelangelo's interpretation of it a concept of spiritual power has been captured which we cannot escape because it has begun to operate in ourselves.' (E. Hubala, 1968). The Capitol Square is for that matter only one of many examples of the fact that in Rome sculptures, whether classical, Renaissance or Baroque, were never erected in isolation. They had always to be seen against the background of the space, the square, in short the entire architecture.

If municipal architecture and the planning of squares covered such wide areas, it is hardly surprising that the same stylistic principle should have been adhered to in building projects that were intended at the outset to incorporate free spaces and nature herself, in villas and gardens. The artistic conception of the villa, a fine example of which, next to the Vatican's Belvedere, is the unfinished Villa Madama on Monte Mario, built by Raphael, had no need to be inspired by ancient ruins. Architects like Bramante, Raphael, Vignola, Giacomo della Porta or Pirro Ligorio got their ideas from Roman writers on architecture and from Vitruvius, from whom even the great Alberti took over entire passages, and especially from the descriptions of villas by Pliny the Younger. A villa should be built on slightly rising ground, about half way up, on a *locus amoenus,* a pleasant or favourite spot, with a fine view of nature, which would then so to speak be framed by the architecture. The view, the *prospectus,* was a legally protected piece of property in ancient Rome. Any such villa also possessed spacious gardens, shady and cool, and cryptoportici let into the revetment walls of the terraces; 'subterranean' corridors open only on one side, for a cooling sojourn on a hot day; spacious baths, in most cases also semi-subterranean, and all sorts of fountains, swimming-pools and water-displays. Recently a letter of Raphael's was found, expressing his thoughts on the final shape to be given to the Villa Madama, originally built for Cardinal Giulio de Medici, later Pope Clement VII. This letter is a word-for-word quotation from a surviving letter by Pliny the Younger in which he describes his Villa Laurentium by the sea near Rome. Though today only the shell of the villa can be seen, its shape clearly shows that at the beginning of the sixteenth century Raphael intended to build in this first-century manner, including the luxurious baths that had already been laid out in the ground-floor ashlar of the villa, which was, as it were, 'kneeling' on rising ground.

If they were to be truly perfect, gardens and squares, *villegiatura* and town needed one important feature to enliven the severity of their structure and to introduce a picturesque element—water. Many poets have sung of the swishing of Rome's fountains with their waters flowing, streaming and then lying still. Indeed in the heart of the city we are, so to speak, carried along from one square to the next by the murmuring of the water. Modern Rome's plentiful water supply is another legacy from the ancient Romans, who constructed an extensive network of aqueducts to bring water from the Sabine and Alban Hills to Rome, where it ended up in the Aqua Marcia, the Aqua Tepula, the Aqua Giulia, Aqua Paolo, Aqua Felice and many others, tumbling over fountains with decorative walls and nymphs, often embellished with statues. The Popes regarded it as a point of honour to restore the water conduits and resite the fountains in even more splendid ways, and their work in this direction won them lasting fame. After supplying the Fontana della Barcaccia in the Piazza di Spagna, the aqueduct of the Acqua Vergine, which was built by Agrippa, flows into Rome's most famous High Baroque fountain, the Trevi Fountain, a high wall decorated with sculpture over which tumble masses of water. The Acqua Vergine runs with pure spring water and the modern visitor can safely drink it.

The Piazza Navona is a completely enclosed and unified square, thanks to the architecture of the walls and the three fountains, which include Gianlorenzo Bernini's Fountain of the Four Rivers. The ground plan of the square is based on an ancient stadium dating back to the time of the Emperor

86

86   Sandro Botticelli: 'The Temptation of Christ'. Detail. 1481–1482. Rome: The Vatican, Sistine Chapel. This detail from 'The Temptation of Christ' clearly reveals what concerned the Florentine. The entire figure of the woman carrying wood dissolves in the highly-refined interplay of line and movement, beginning with the outline of the body, then travelling over the folds in the dress, to the serpent-like curling of the hair.

Domitian, and was flooded on three Sundays in summer for the 'Divertimento del Lago' (Water Festival). Access roads were closed off, and the overflow from the Fountain of the Four Rivers stopped, so that the water flowed over the edge of the fountain, and the carriages of the haughty Romans rode in a 'carousel' of water.

Roman palace-building begins almost on the threshold of the High Renaissance. The Medici, Pitti, Rucellai, Strozzi and many other palaces had long since been completed, but the Roman aristocracy was still living in the ruins converted into fortresses: the Savelli in the Theatre of Marcellus, the Orsini in the Mausoleum of Augustus, the Frangipani even in the Arch of Trajan in the Forum. In fifteenth-century Florence the owners of the great palaces were rich merchants, but in Rome they were almost exclusively cardinals, though later, in the sixteenth century, bishops and officials of the Curia and even bankers ventured to build themselves palaces. Acquiring the land often proved a difficult and tedious task, but no one counted the cost and even the earliest Roman palaces were on a scale whose splendour far eclipsed that of Florentine buildings, an unconscious tribute perhaps to the *genius loci*. Certainly in addition to the desire for comfort, a thirst for celebrity played no small part among the builders: '*Elegantiae publicae et commoditati privatae*' ('The splendour of the city and the comfort of the tenants') runs an inscription on a Milan palace dating from the end of the fifteenth century. Emphasis was laid in Rome from the start on the inner 'distribution', this too being a legacy from ancient Rome, which in its baths and villas had always cultivated the utmost comfort in arrangement and luxurious furnishings. 'No such care had been lavished on entrance-halls and inner courtyards since Imperial Rome, nor on staircases since the Cretan culture, and never before on façades. Nor was comfort neglected: medium and small rooms *(studioli,* for instance) were just as expensively furnished as the reception rooms.' (C. L. Frommel, 1973). The earliest Renaissance Roman palace is the Palazzo Venezia (Plate 67), which was begun after 1451 by the Venetian Cardinal Pietro Barbo in the grounds of his titular church, San Marco. Several architects are mentioned (Alberti, Filarete, Rossellino) but none with any degree of certainty. Externally the palace and its towers are still castle-like in their emphasis on defence. But in the inner courtyard we see for the first time the columnar system preferred by the Romans from this date onwards. It can be seen here in its pure form, with colonnades on two floors and half-columns set in front.

The Cancelleria (plate 69) is generally attributed to Bramante, but the project was begun as early as 1483 and Bramante did not come to Rome until 1499. The rhythmic way in which the façade is subdivided by means of fore pilasters and the noble proportions of the three-storeyed inner courtyard clearly make the Cancelleria the perfect Roman Renaissance palace. On the other hand (plate 70) the Palazzo Farnese, which Antonio da Sangallo the Younger started building for Paul III in 1541, though the third floor in the inner courtyard was completed by Michelangelo, already appears to anticipate baroque trends, or, to put it another way, harks back once more to the classical style of ancient Rome, though much more emphatically and deliberately. This is reflected chiefly in the very deliberate distribution of the inner space, in the way the central axis opens on to the garden above the central loggia and the expensive internal decoration. With the coming of the High Renaissance the personalities of individual artists naturally began to emerge more clearly than was possible in Florence at the beginning of the fifteenth century. As a result the Roman palaces also create a far more individual impression.

For over two hundred years, however, Rome's greatest architectural project was the rebuilding of St. Peter's, including a whole host of schemes for extending and supplementing the Vatican Palace and its surroundings. The early fourth century Christian basilica, Christendom's first church, restored and repeatedly redecorated ever more splendidly with paintings and mosaics, stood until the mid-fifteenth century, when Nicholas V, with the support and advice of Alberti, began its reconstruction, which was brought to a halt

137

87 Raphael: 'The School of Athens'. Rome:
The Vatican. Stanza della Segnatura. Carried
out between 1508 and 1511, this series of
frescoes is the culmination of Raphael's life's
work, and at the same time a complete
expression of the classical aims of the Roman
High Renaissance in style. An ingenious
pictorial programme is developed here, in a
composition that is entirely harmonious and at
the same time monumental. It introduces the
four divisions into which the medieval faculties
fell: Theology (Disputà—the Disputation of
the Sacrament, between the Fathers of the
Church); Philosophy ('The School of
Athens')—A discussion between Plato and
Aristotle concerning questions of ethics and
morality in the presence of representatives of
the most important Schools of Philosophy
in Ancient Greece, and thus a kind of
pagan Sacra Conversazione; Poetry
('Parnassus'—Apollo guiding the Muses,
accompanied by humanity's most subline
poets); and Jurisprudence ('The Bestowal of
Canon and Civil Law'). The figures in 'The
School of Athens' are recognizable in the
main: at the feet of the commanding pair,
Plato and Aristotle, are the representatives of
the exact sciences (Pythagoras, Euclid and
the astronomers). Diogenes, linking philosophy and natural science, reclines on the
stairs. The architecture in the background is
influenced by Bramante's sketches for the
rebuilding of St. Peter's.

138

8

88 Raphael: 'The School of Athens'. (Detail of Central Section). Rome: The Vatican. Stanza della Segnatura. This detail from the previous illustration shows Plato and Aristotle engaged in disputation. Both these princes of the intellect carry their attributes with them in the form of their chief works: Plato his 'Timaeus', and Aristotle the 'Ethics'. Diogenes the Cynic can be seen (right) at their feet.

Following double page:
89 Raphael: 'Parnassus'. Rome: The Vatican. Stanza della Segnatura. Apollo Musagetes, playing a violin and surrounded by his attendants, the Muses, with their musical instruments and other attributes, is seated in a hilly Olympian landscape not unlike Raphael's Umbrian homeland. Humanity's most illustrious poets, including Blind Homer and Dante (upper left), Sappho (left below), with Petrarch and Boccaccio, appear beside and at the feet of the central group.

however by the Pope's early death. It was not until Julius II, the terribile, almost fifty years later that the reconstruction project that stirred Western Christendom was again taken up. In 1506 Bramante was commissioned to work on it. He produced a pure central construction with a cupola, over the ground-plan of a Greek cross, with side-rooms, also dome-vaulted, and apses in the diagonals. His intention was to 'pile the Pantheon on the Temple of Peace (the Constantine or Maxentius Basilica).'

In 1513 Julius II died, followed the year after by Bramante. But the monumental pillars which were to carry the intersection tambour were standing, in spite of everything. Under the new direction, which was taken over by Raphael, Giuliano and Antonio da Sangallo, and Peruzzi, there was a growing tendency to deviate from Bramante's centralized conception in favour of a basilica with nave and two aisles until Michelangelo took over in 1547 and returned to Bramante's original idea, though with some significant alterations. The side halls in the diagonals, which were still basically independent churches or chapels in the Bramante version, were much more strongly integrated into the four arms of the Greek cross, thus apparently shortening them, since it was basically only a question of reinforcing the outer walls and the cupola pillars so as to allow the cupola to dominate the entire space. The cupola was Michelangelo's great concern, and the tambour was completed by the time of his death (1564). Giacomo della Porta enclosed it, and altered the outline laid down by Michelangelo, which was compressed and oppressive, in favour of 'the elegant and optimistic feeling conveyed by the onset of Early Baroque' (H. Keller 1975). (Plates 74 and 75). The central chamber, it is true, fully met the artistic ideals of the High Renaissance, but not the traditional basilica form of the episcopal and monastic churches, nor even the practical requirements of the divine service. Nor was it extensive enough, in spite of its huge size, to receive the influx of believers who wanted to visit the most sacred of churches. Paul V Borghese therefore commissioned Carlo Maderna to place to the east of it a basilica with nave and two aisles.

In 1617 the church was practically completed, but the square in front was still to be decided on. In 1586 Sixtus V had had the 25.50 metre (83' 8") high obelisk form Heliopolis—previously in the near-by Circus of Nero—erected by Domenico Fontana in the centre of the square. Maderna created one of the great fountains under commission from Paul V. The second did not arrive as a pendant until the beginning of the eighteenth century. But it needed a genius to co-ordinate and structure the whole vast area and transcendent dimensions of the square. Gianlorenzo Bernini, the outstanding architect and sculptor of Roman High Baroque, solved the problem by again harking back to the style of the late imperial period. He divided the area up into two interlocking squares (1656–1667), one great transverse oval surrounded by 17 metre (55' 9") wide colonnades consisting of four rows of Doric columns and pillars, with a straight architrave whose transverse axis is formed by the obelisks and the Maderna Fountains; and the other a trapezoid square extending and rising up to the façade of the church. The monumental open stairs leading up to the church portals repeat the trapezoid shape of the square. In this way Bernini achieved the perspective effect of making the elongation of the façade seem narrower, while the height increased, allowing it to rise more steeply without seeming to 'fall apart' (Plate 76).

Parallel with the reconstruction of St. Peter's came the extensions and alterations to the Vatican Palace (Plate 77), the equipment and furnishings of which became ever richer and more splendid. (Plates 78 and 79). Around it a number of new structures were assembled, the gem of which, next to the Belvedere and the Stanze and Loggias painted by Raphael (Plates 83–87), was a simple oblong room, the Sistine Chapel (Plate 80). Its fame and glory are the frescoes on walls and ceiling, created by the most famous painters of Umbria and Tuscany, and finally by Michelangelo in the fifteenth and sixteenth centuries. The chapel was built between 1473 and 1484 under Sixtus IV della Rovere and serves ecclesiastical purposes to-day, the most important of

SAPPHO

which is the Conclave, the election of the Pope. It was Sixtus IV also who had the wall-surfaces beneath the windows painted with a cycle of murals by Perugino, Pinturicchio, Botticelli, Ghirlandaio and Signorelli, dealing with Old and New Testament scenes rich in reference to the Pontificate of the commissioning Pope. (Plates 85 and 86). Finally in 1508 Julius II bestowed on Michelangelo the commission to paint the ceiling of the Sistine Chapel. The iconographic theme was the *ante legem* period, that is the period pre-dating the giving of the Laws on Mount Sinai. The nine crossbeams would present the stories of the Creation and the Flood in alternating large and small sections. In the others, seven prophets and five sibyls are enthroned. The four corners of the smaller central panels provide a frame for Nude Youths. 'Michelangelo painted the cycle in reverse chronological order. Instead of beginning on the altar wall with the separation of Light from Darkness, he started out from the entrance wall with the Drunkenness of Noah and painted the First Day of Creation as the last in the series of panels. The colour development inside each of the sections of the ceiling can be understood only if this is borne in mind. When the covers were removed from the first half in 1510 Michelangelo saw his picture from below for the first time. The scale of the figures seemed to him to be too small, and so in the second half he resorted to larger proportions and a smaller number of figures' (H. Keller 1975).

Clement VII de' Medici also commissioned Michelangelo (in 1533) to paint a 'Last Judgement' on the broad wall of the altar (Plate 81), which was 17 metres (55' 9") high and 13.30 metres (43' 7") broad. Here too Michelangelo was breaking entirely new ground. The twelve Apostles are present, an unusual feature, and the Madonna presses almost anxiously close to the Great Judge, interceding with the Son, who is portrayed nude and without a beard, his head and hair reminiscent of the 'Belvedere Apollo'. The quiet features 'pronounce' no resurrection or damnation. These seem to emanate from the overwhelming soul-saving gesture of the raised arm. 'Any architectonic articulation is avoided in favour of a gigantic rotatory motion: to the left we have the ascent of the Blessed, and to the right the plunging of the Damned.' (H. Keller). Under the influence of the decrees issued by the puritanical Council of Trent and the zealous Pope Paul IV thirty-four nude figures were clothed by Daniele da Volterra.

Even before that, but after the ceiling frescoes, Raphael had designed a series of tapestries, woven in Brussels, which shrouded the most important parts of the chapel.

The assimilating power of the Roman environment is exemplified once more in Raphael. The imprint of the Eternal City, whose prominent artists came almost without exception from outside, made them 'Romans'. In his Umbrian home Perugino's pupil, Raphael, was in no way an outstanding phenomenon. By Roman standards his early work must be adjudged as pale, undistinguished and at times almost boring. In Rome, however, he found his way towards a monumental form: meeting important colleagues, and above all discovering classical antiquity, helped him to become a classic. The ideals of 'classical' painting, closeness to the ancient world, absolute harmony and euphonious, symmetrical composition, and a happy convergence of balanced form and spiritual content, find their most perfect expression in Raphael. With the great frescoes in the Vatican Stanze he attains equality with Michelangelo's work in the Sistine Chapel. In the 'Stanza della Segnatura', created between 1509 and 1511 (Plates 87–90), he developed a complex series of pictures which in concentrated form presents the entire philosophical, religious and aesthetic Renaissance Cosmos. In the centre stands the *Disputà,* a *Sacra Conversazione* in new form, portraying in symbolic disputation all the great exponents of church doctrine on the supreme Christian mystery of the Holy Trinity. In the 'School of Athens' (Plates 87 and 88) Western philosophy makes its appearance in the shape of its most enlightened proponents. Out of this abstract material Raphael has woven a gripping description of actual events. The Ancient World's most important philosophical schools get to grips here with the ultimate questions

90 Raphael: 'The Deliverance of Peter'. Rome: The Vatican. Stanza d'Eliodoro. The frescoes in this room were created from 1512 to 1514 as additions to the 'Stanza della Segnatura'. Raphael here underwent an astonishing change, from the classical, calm moderation of the 'Disputà' and 'The School of Athens' to a much more expressive and active 'baroque' style, all within the space of a few years. This is particularly clear in the 'Deliverance of Peter', where the centre of interest lies in the portrayal of light manifest almost in baroque fashion. The colouring has undergone a fundamental change in order to achieve this effect.

144

affecting humanity. In the centre we recognize Plato and Aristotle, the most outstanding of the wise men. The reference made here to the Christian *Disputa* is of course deliberate. A resonant pillared hall provides the solemn background, which is reminiscent of Bramante's plans for the reconstruction of St. Peter's, which date from the same period.

91 *91 Raphael: 'The Triumph of Galatea' (Detail). Rome: Villa Farnesina. This fresco, painted by Raphael's own hand in 1514, belongs to a series of mythological and astrological frescoes carried out at the beginning of the sixteenth century for the Roman villa of the banker, art-patron and humanist Agostino Chigi by artists such as Giulio Romano, Francesco Penni, and Giovanni da Udine. After the earnest and weighty sequence of paintings in the Vatican, Raphael and his colleagues here introduce the other side of the High Renaissance, which is full of the ancient world's mythology and erotic splendour. In the Sala di Galatea (originally a ground-level loggia leading to the open garden area) a complex set of horoscopic and astrological illustrations appears on the ceiling (Baldasarre Peruzzi), together with Ovid's Metamorphoses (the lunettes) and 'The Triumph of Galatea'. Galatea glides over the sea in a scallop-shell chariot drawn by a team of dolphins, surrounded by her retinue of playful Nereids and Naiads. Her brilliant red robe, effectively contrasting with the lovely luminous figure, flutters like 'love's banner' swelling in the wind. Raphael came even closer in this tableau than in the Vatican* Stanze *to his goal and ideal, the fresco of classical antiquity, a few examples of which had just been discovered by archaeologists.*

Page following:
92 Raphael: 'Venus, Ceres and Juno'. Rome, Villa Farnesina. Garden loggia. Working under Raphael's guidance and in keeping with the free and cheerful schemes designed for the Renaissance villa, Giulio Romano and Francesco Penni painted this summerhouse with scenes from the classical myth of Cupid and Psyche, as told by Apuleius in his Golden Ass. *Raphael kept the figures on the spandrel (our illustration) for himself. Working in a classical spirit similar to that of the ancient Greeks and Romans, he came nearer to the physical ideal of classical antiquity in these vigorous and lively gods and goddesses than any other painter of the Roman High Renaissance. The ornamental motifs—festoons of fruit and foliage friezes—are by Giovanni da Udine. The curved surface above the windows (below right in our illustration) is decorated with classicizing 'grotesques'. The first authentic classical frescoes had just been discovered in Nero's Golden House at this date and this type of decoration was known as 'grotesque'* (grotteschi) *because Nero's staterooms, now covered with rubble, lay deep underground and so conveyed the impression of being subterranean grottoes.*

In the 'Parnassus' (Plate 89) Poetry is represented as the third medieval 'Faculty'. In the centre is Apollo, with his lyre transformed into a *viola da braccio*. He is surrounded by the Muses with their attributes, and accompanied by the most outstanding poets. In the left-hand upper section we recognize Blind Homer and next to him Dante's characteristic profile. Left below, with a scroll, is Sappho. An idealized Olympian hill landscape reminiscent of Raphael's Umbrian home acts as a backcloth. In another Stanza Raphael painted 'The Deliverance of Peter' from prison, by the Angel (Plate 90), in effect an extraordinarily modern representation of a 'vision of illumination', which is more effective still when we remember that the mural is sited on a wall between two windows so that natural daylight shares in the pictorial impression produced.

Raphael leads us into a purely classical world with the mythological cycle in the Villa Farnesina (Plates 91 and 92). Here he reveals the entire spectrum of the ancient world of mythology and the Hellenic love-story of Cupid and Psyche, in pictures full of grace, erotic humour and classical serenity. Contemporaries considered that these images were unsurpassable. Any 'post' or 'after' style was inconceivable. Raphael's importance in the intervening period is no longer so highly estimated, due perhaps to the adulation accorded him from the sixteenth to the eighteenth century and the ensuing nineteenth-century exaggeration. By Goethe's time he was considered to be *the* classic par excellence, and his achievement equated with Dante's *Divine Comedy*. To-day he appears to many art-lovers to be academic, dry, merely sweet and complaisant, or even cold and polished to perfection. This reversal of judgement is no doubt as unjust as his uncritical apotheosis a hundred years ago. The selection of paintings shown here for comparison may demonstrate that his genius has no reason to fear: it easily measures up to that of Michelangelo or Titian.

A second great building project of Julius II within the walls of the Vatican was the Villa Belvedere. The actual Villa, begun under Innocent VIII and destined to house the earliest and most important collection of antiquities ('Laocoön' and the 'Apollo Belvedere') following Bramante's architectural alterations to the inner courtyard, must be accorded the minimum of space in this text. The determining factor is the layout of the garden, surrounded as it is by façade walls on three levels complete with windows and pilasters, and stretching originally over three terraces from the upper Belvedere to the lower exedra. Open stairways communicate between the various terraces, the revetment walls of which, in the central axis, were here and there provided with niche grottoes and water displays. The lower garden could be flooded to arrange 'Sea-Battles' and water-ballets. In extent and conception the gardens are comparable only to the Praeneste sanctuary, which consciously influenced Bramante and Pirro Ligorio, who created the crowning exedra; or with the great imperial villas (the Hadrian, say, in Tivoli) which is why this miracle of open-space architecture is always referred to as the 'classical villa'.

'Rome is Bernini,' said Rodin, and in fact Gianlorenzo Bernini, architect and sculptor, symbolizes the last great age of Roman art, the Baroque. Together with his much more headstrong and unorthodox but no less highly-gifted opposite, Borromini, he once more enriched the seventeenth-century landscape of Rome with palaces, churches and squares representing the last and perhaps the greatest pinnacle of Roman art. Baroque signifies the 'total work of art' to which architecture, sculpture and painting, but also the decorative arts, municipal architecture and horticultural art, are subordinated. The façades of squares correspond to the concave and convex church façades, while bold vaulting constructions made it possible for painters like Andrea Pozzo or Pietro da Cortona to produce in palaces and churches gigantic ceiling paintings, brilliant in their perspective effects. Their superabundance of baroque allegories glorified the owners, or raised, with the most ecstatic religious feeling, Heavenly Father, Son, Madonna and all the saints into celestial glory. All of them, artists, Popes and saints seemed in the seventeenth century to be conscious of one duty only: to bring to completion the beauty and greatness of Rome.

Venice

Venice was a paradox
(M. Langewiesche)

A city of world rank that was never fortified.

A conglomeration of houses, palaces and churches, erected on that most insubstantial and undependable of foundations, the sea.

A state, of world rank, whose stability and political significance was based in the last analysis on nothing more than the rolling ship's timbers of its merchant fleet, but which nevertheless endured for longer than any organized state of to-day.

An organized state surrounded by enemies in its immediate vicinity, for example those who commanded the rivers flowing into the Venetian lagoon, the Po, Adige and Brenta. No maritime republic—not Pisa, Genoa or Amalfi—could have been so easily surrounded and starved into submission as Venice. That this did not happen is a tribute to Venetian statesmanship.

Venice became great not because of but in spite of its situation. It is not surprising therefore that twentieth-century Ventice still looks back on its past with pride and an awareness of tradition.

Any observant traveller who pays several visits to Venice, using the various forms of transport available to-day, comes up against this paradox even before his arrival in the lagoon city. Driving by car from Padua he reads, with

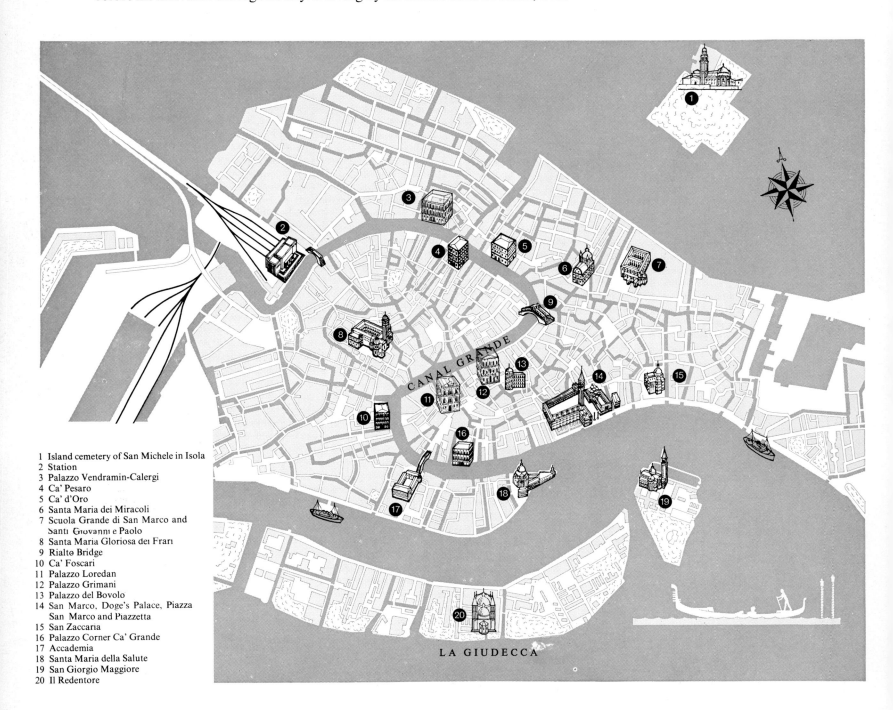

1 Island cemetery of San Michele in Isola
2 Station
3 Palazzo Vendramin-Calergi
4 Ca' Pesaro
5 Ca' d'Oro
6 Santa Maria dei Miracoli
7 Scuola Grande di San Marco and Santi Giovanni e Paolo
8 Santa Maria Gloriosa dei Frari
9 Rialto Bridge
10 Ca' Foscari
11 Palazzo Loredan
12 Palazzo Grimani
13 Palazzo del Bovolo
14 San Marco, Doge's Palace, Piazza San Marco and Piazzetta
15 San Zaccaria
16 Palazzo Corner Ca' Grande
17 Accademia
18 Santa Maria della Salute
19 San Giorgio Maggiore
20 Il Redentore

some astonishment, at the entrance to the motorway some forty kilometres (twenty-four miles) out: 'Autostrada della Serenissima'.

Above it he is greeted by the Lion of St. Mark in relief, the relevant gospel open between his paws at the words: 'Pax tibi, Marce, evangelista meus' ('Peace be unto thee, Mark, my apostle'). The same Lion sits enthroned on vertical pylons along the railway lines leading across the lagoon-embankment into the city. You can even recognize the symbol at the airport, in the middle of the industrial zone of Mestre. Arriving by sea—still the most splendid way of reaching the city—the traveller as he passes by can see the Lion on a high column above the Piazzetta (Plate 98). What is the significance of the 'Serenissima' (Serene Highness) and the Lion that still greet and welcome everyone to-day with such pride and awareness of tradition, almost two hundred years after the Venetian Republic's downfall? The Lion is the symbol of the patron-saint of an international empire, and a city-state scattered over a hundred and twenty islands in the midst of the North Adriatic lagoons. Its houses, palaces and churches were built on piles, hundreds of thousands of oak, alder and larch props. This State, apparently so vulnerable, stood longer than any other realm in our later history, be it democracy, oligarchy or government by king or emperor. Neither Greece, the 'cradle of the West', nor the Roman Empire, nor the Holy Roman Empire that encompassed and united nations, lasted as long. Venice alone can boast that in all its near one thousand years of existence no enemy conqueror ever set foot on its soil.

However select, noble and rich Venetian art appears in architecture and the fine arts, especially painting, the greatest work of art created here is the Venetian state itself. Only those who know Venice's history are able to understand and properly appreciate the art of the city.

History

The Venetians dwelt, far from the internal and external strife that was shaking the Roman Empire, on the shores and lagoons of the Northern loop of the Adriatic. Agriculture, but mainly fishing and salt-mining, gave them sustenance. The storms of the great migrations, the invasions of Visigoths, Ostrogoths, Langobards, and Huns, who destroyed Aquileia, seat of the Patriarch, in 453, drove the population further and further out into the lagoon. Only those to whom that element was native could know the treacherous nature of the shoals and the sandbanks lying under water and could make use of them for their own defence.

At the end of the seventh century, in 697, these tiny and often mutually hostile 'city-states', such as Grado, where the Patriarch of Aquileia had fled, Caorle, Eraclea, Jesolo, Torcello, Chioggia and Malamocco, united and elected a common head, the Doge. They crowned him with the sailor's cap pinched out in front, the *cornu ducale,* placed themselves under the protection of the Exarchate of Ravenna, thereby coming within the Byzantine Province in Italy.

In 809 Pepin, son of Charlemagne, took Friuli and Istria and pushed forward into the Venetian settlements in the lagoon. Chioggia and Malamocco, until then the largest settlement, were destroyed. The 10th Doge, Angelo Partecipazio, thereafter transferred the seat of government, in 811, to the largest of the islands in the most central lagoon, the 'Rivo alto', the modern Rialto. Thus Venice was founded.

Fishermen and peasants had fled to the lagoon, but with them also were well-to-do merchants from *terra firma,* who had become wealthy through the salt-trade, in Padua and Verona. Their names, Orseola, Morosini, Loredan and Pisani, the oldest aristocratic names in Europe, were to appear more than once in future on the list of Doges. These young merchant families showed the new state the only path it could take, namely trade, on their familiar element, the sea. The perils inherent in Venice's geographical and political position were also to be its opportunity.

Double page following:
93   Venice: Piazzetta with the West façade of St. Mark's and the West Wing of the Doge's Palace. The splendid façade of St. Mark's, with its coloured mosaics set in white marble filigree, links up here with the west side of the Doge's Palace almost without leaving a trace, thereby giving very clear expression to the identity of Church and State. On the right, situated in front of the Campanile, we see the Loggetta, a choice piece of architecture by Jacopo Sansovino, dating from 1537 to 1540. Behind it is the façade of the Library. The changing play of light and shadow seems to give the Piazzetta's architectural lines new and different structures at various times.

Torn between the declining but still powerful empire in the East, Byzantium, and the growing Holy Roman Empire which was able to reward its vassals and margraves, not only north of the Alps but also in northern Italy, with rich presents and domains for their loyalty and dependability, Venice developed a diplomacy which over the years became more and more subtle: *bilancia,* playing the great powers off against one another, and keeping a wary eye on new expanding forces, whether the Papal state or the competing maritime republics, Genoa, Amalfi and Pisa, the powerful city-states in Upper Italy or, later, the Hapsburgs. Venice's ambassadors were the best-informed in Europe, and reported everything back to Venice with a fidelity that was rare. Modern historians still use this inexhaustible source of information.

The merchants who brought the young state to full flower were practical, deliberate and to the point in thought and action. Yet along with their city they were bound up with the early Middle Ages. They were well aware therefore that a city, and even more a state with ambitions to rule the Mediterranean, needed a powerful and significant patron saint, and, being merchants, they knew how much quality counted. Very little was known about San Teodoro, Venice's first saint, an early Christian martyr. The fact that the first church consecrated to him was in Byzantium meant little in their eyes. But a monastery in Alexandria harboured the remains of one of the four apostles, St. Mark. The Doge, Justinian Partecipazio, dispatched a delegation to the monastery concerned in 828. The Venetians had had the best of trading relations with the Arab rulers of the territory for some considerable time. After some semblance of threat to the monastery on the part of Arabs bribed by the Venetians, the Republic's emissaries managed to acquire the saint's body for fifty *zecchini.* Concealed under a layer of pork, which to the Mohammedans was unclean, the saint reached Venice safe and sound. He is said to have performed numerous miracles during his trip over, and these were later recorded by Tintoretto in a splendid cycle which was a culminating point in Venetian painting. The saint's remains were at first lodged in the palace of the Duke, now the Doge's Palace, until the present church of St. Mark was built in his honour in the eleventh century. That meant that the priceless relic rested in the Doge's Palace church, which was what St. Mark's was, until the year 1807. The State had its patron saint, and the banner with the Lion, the saint's symbolic animal, was to wave in future from Brescia, fronting the gates of Milan, to Constantinople; from the battlements of Split and Candia in Crete; from Corfu and Famagusta in Cyprus; and from Chios and Ravenna. From now on 'Viva San Marco!' meant 'Viva Venezia!'.

Venice was still Byzantium's ally, even if only nominally, and under its protection. Trade relations were close, but the ageing city on the Hellespont had to pay for every atom of support accorded it in the expanding Republic by new concessions, wrung out of it. It was Venetian money and diplomacy that promoted relations between Byzantium and the Emperor; and Venetian ships and weapons that protected the Byzantine colonies in the Adriatic against the rapacious Saracens. When Venice, together with Byzantium, drove the Normans out of the Adriatic and Eastern Mediterranean at the end of the eleventh century, Venice's demands seemed quite modest: no territory or money, simply a trade and staple monopoly. In actual fact Byzantium was too weak to defend its Adriatic colonies, especially along the Dalmatian coast. The Dalmatian states therefore turned to Venice for help against pirates and Serbs and Croats from the hinterland. In about 1000, when the Christian West was paralysed by a vision of the imminent end of the world, the Doge, Pietro Orseolo II, began soberly and systematically to take over the Eastern Adriatic coast, a process in which Zara or Rugusa and the other towns were not exactly 'subjugated' but made the subject of alliances with one aim in mind: free trade for the lagoon city and secure bases for the Venetian fleet. The towns willingly accepted the terms imposed because Venice guaranteed their security. And as Venice in the fifteenth century united with the cities on *terra firma* so it proceeded now: *Pro summa*

94 *Venice: San Marco. Lunette on the second Northern side-entrance of the West façade. The semi-circular mosaic was created in Rococo style and carried out by Leopoldo dal Pozzo in 1728 from a sketch by Sebastiano Ricci, G. B. Tiepolo's contemporary and teacher. In a design that is still almost Titianesque it portrays the veneration accorded to the body of St. Mark by the Venetian authorities.*

fide summus amor, 'for the greatest faith the greatest love.'

Venice's successes in foreign policy were paralleled by the evolution internally of a stable political system, in which order was guaranteed by irrevocable laws. Yet there was some apprehension perhaps that in the future not every Doge would exhibit selfless devotion to the Republic. So in 1172 the Grand Council, the Maggior Consiglio, came into being. This was the political creation of a constitution which had already been put into practice, and from now on would endure for another six hundred years and even then be abrogated only under pressure from outside. The sober rationale behind the constitution was not confined within the limits of any inflexible ideology. It was as objectively conceived as the democracy of early Roman times: as élitist as the Greek oligarchy; and where affairs of state, i.e. Venice's existence, so required, almost over-cautious in the checks and balances of office.

At the top stood the Doge, elected for life by the Maggior Consiglio. Though the city had 120 of these in all, no more than half-a-dozen bearers of the recurrent aristocratic names emerged from obscurity to enter history as distinct personalities.

In their case the element of extreme good fortune or of great momentary peril was always present, as with Enrico Dandolo (1192–1205), who conquered Byzantium for Venice, or Marino Falier (1354–55), who wanted to change the constitution, and was beheaded on the steps of the Doge's Palace, his head and trunk left lying for days in the Cortile, as a warning. Francesco Foscari (1423–1457), a *condottiere*-type, and a Renaissance man of violence, decided on conquest of the *terra firma,* and had as a result to leave the Eastern Mediterranean to the Turks. Whether his decision was right or wrong, the wheel of history can never be put into reverse. In any case he was deposed because of his autocratic rule and his son sent into exile. Finally, Francesco Morosini (1688–1694), a born commander-in-chief, should be mentioned; he was able for a brief period to regain the Venetian colonies in the Levant and on the Peloponnese from the Turks. To some extent the Maggior Consiglio was the Republic's 'Parliament'. It could meet without the Doge. Originally every male 'citizen' over twenty-five years of age was a member if his family had been settled in Venice for several generations. Next to the Maggior Consiglio stood the Senate, the Upper House, so to speak, of the Venetian Parliament and its legislative bodies. The Doge and members of the Collegio met here with some two hundred elected Senators. The Collegio was the Government Cabinet and consisted of some twenty-five members elected from the Maggior Consiglio.

In the fourteenth century the notorious 'Consiglio dei Dieci', the notorious 'Council of Ten', was formed from members of the Collegio. This was an emergency measure to speed up parliamentary procedure when urgent decisions had to be taken. Practically all important matters, or those which were out of the ordinary, were discussed in secret session here. Two members of the Council of Ten were appointed State Inquisitors, with one function only, to investigate, together with a Council of the Doge's, the one crime that Venice punished unmercifully, high treason.

Independent only in appearance, therefore, it was possible for each institution to be represented in the others through committees elected from within, so that each institution controlled the other.

Any political system with a constitution based on cool and sober calculation which also excludes from government both people and citizens must try to find ways of making its abstractions not only clear to all but pleasing. Religious commitment, mystical transformation and solemn ritual were there to hand.

'Viva San Marco!' stood for 'Viva Venezia!' Not surprisingly, therefore, the Procurators of St. Mark's, the 'canons' of the state church and guardians of the patron-saint occupied a particularly high position in the state apparatus. Next to the Doge they were the highest dignitaries in the Serenissima. They alone wore purple and walked in the great processions immediately behind the Doge. And once a year the Doge, too, emerged from the anonymity of his magnificent prison to join in the glamour of public festival, surrounded by all the radiant pomp of the Serenissima. Once a year, on Ascension Day, the *Sensa,* the Doge sailed out to sea aboard the ship of state, the gilded Bucintoro, accompanied by hundreds of craft, including gondolas. No dignitary of state dared absent himself. There the Doge wed the waters again, casting his ring into the sea with the words: *Desponsamus te mare; in signo veri perpetuique domini* ('We marry thee, sea, in the sign of the one True and Eternal Lord').

In 1177 Venetian statesmanship and diplomacy triumphed for the first time over the two strongest powers of the period, Pope and Emperor. Possessed by the desire to take over northern Italy, Frederick I Barbarossa nominated three anti-popes, since the legitimate Pope, Alexander III, opposed his plans. The Emperor destroyed Milan and the Pope fled to France. Not until Alexander had placed himself at the head of the League of Lombard Towns and the Emperor had been defeated at the Battle of Legnano in 1176 did any hope exist that the two bitter enemies could be persuaded to make peace. Venice acted as mediator and arranged (or even 'forced') a meeting in Venice between Emperor and Pope, thus bringing about a reconciliation. It was Venice's first international success. For its services, from both parties of course, it demanded only customs and tax concessions.

96

In 1204 the ninety-six-year-old and almost blind Doge Enrico Dandolo led against Byzantium the army of Crusaders, which had assembled some 35–40,000 men in Venice for the Fourth Crusade. The Crusaders had come to the city in the hope that the Republic would place its fleet at their disposal to liberate the Holy Sepulchre from the Turks. After exhausting, long-drawn-out negotiations, Venice presented two conditions. Zara (Zadar) on the Adriatic coast must be won back and—here came the stunner—first of all Christian Byzantium, regarded as impregnable, must be taken. Dynastic quarrels in Byzantium provided the threadbare excuse. Basically, as was always the case when Venice had a hand in the game, it was a question of commercial profit. Byzantium held the staple monopoly for every commodity traded in the East. It was therefore able to stockpile these until they fetched the highest prices, a type of competition that had to be eliminated. And not only that. The last hour had struck for the old East Roman capital. The Crusaders did in fact burn and plunder Byzantium, but the major share of the booty passed to Venice. The ancient bronze horses, the four in hand, which ever since, apart from a brief sojourn in Napoleon's Paris, have stood above the main portal of St. Mark's (Plate 93), as well as hundreds of columns, capitals and the finest marble statuary, whether complete or in pieces—all these were brought to St. Mark's so that the southern side of the church

96 and 97 Venice: Piazza San Marco: Torre dell' Orologio (Clock Tower) erected in the years 1496–1499 by Mauro Coducci. Multicoloured marble incrustations, elegantly executed in detail, shape the structure of the three-storeyed tower, on the roof of which bronze figures, called 'Mori' (Moors), strike the hours with their hammers. The first floor contains the sundial, with the signs of the Zodiac (Plate 97) and gold and enamel inlays, while the second has a statue of the Madonna, with two panels at the sides showing the hours and minutes respectively. On the third floor is the Lion of St. Mark against a blue celestial background decorated with golden stars. The arched gateway leads through to the merceria, *market lanes stretching as far as the Rialto, which to-day remains the chief shopping-centre for Venetians and foreigners alike.*

158

became a triumphant wall of captured trophies. Innumerable reliquaries with their precious shrines enriched the Saint's Treasury. Feeling that his task had been completed, Enrico Dandolo died in Byzantium and was buried in the gallery of the Hagia Sophia.

At that time, in 1204, the Maggior Consiglio was even considering the outrageous possibility of moving to Byzantium, which would probably have decisively altered the history of Europe. The plan was rejected by two votes.

Quite apart from its plans for conquest, Venice had greatly profited from providing the Crusaders with transport, though it did incur in the process serious competition from Pisa and Genoa. By the middle of the fourteenth century, indeed, Genoa was strong enough to represent a mortal threat to Venice, unless the Serenissima managed to beat back the rival maritime republic, i.e. drive its ships out of the Adriatic at least. For a long time Genoa

had ruled the Western Mediterranean, but its vessels, under the leadership of the shrewd and courageous family of the Doria, were now penetrating into the Adriatic. They made allies of Venice's enemies, the Emperor, the King of Hungary, the Archduke of Tyrol, and even with Venice's greatest and nearest neighbour on *terra firma*, Padua, and its princely family, the Carrara. Venetian galleys, true enough, did patrol the Adriatic day and night from 1378 to 1379 to halt the advance of the Genoese fleet, but without result, despite the most strenuous effort and sacrifice. Genoa and its allies took Trieste, Grado fell, and finally, with the aid of the Carrara, Chioggia. Summoning up every ounce of their strength and material resources, the Venetians feverishly built a new fleet which in the end, if it did not succeed in winning Chioggia back, at least blockaded it for six months. In June 1380, Genoa surrendered. Venice had suffered grievous losses, but the Genoese advance had been stopped.

In 1423 Doge Tomaso Mocenigo, on his deathbed, laid before the Serenissima the following statistics: Venice had 190,000 inhabitants. Out of a trade balance of 10 million ducats, 4 million went to Venice in profits. 3000 smaller vessels sailed the seas under the Lion Banner, their crews consisting of 17,000 seamen. There were 300 large merchantmen with 8,000 sailors, and 45 galleys with 11,000, plus 16,000 ship's carpenters. Including sailmakers, ropemakers, saddlers, coopers, dockers, plus harbour and customs officials,

Previous double page:
98 Venice: The Doge's Palace. A full view of the Doge's Palace reveals how conscious of tradition people were, in the matter of architecture, for almost two centuries and how much they clung, despite much destruction, to concepts they had accepted: light and airy open ground-floors, and an apparently compact but nevertheless looser structured upper storey, with its textile-like wall pattern. The battlements obviously served no defensive purpose but were a crowning decoration only. In front stood the lagoon-city's symbols: two monumental granite columns, also imported from the East, with Byzantine capitals. One bore the statue of St. Theodore, Venice's first patron saint, and the other the original bronze figure of the Lion of St. Mark, once a chimera of Assyrian, Persian or Sassanid derivation. At the foot of the columns figural groups can still be seen, probably twelfth-century, which represent fishmongers and greengrocers, with coopers and others, indicating that the market was held on this side of the Piazzetta before the Library was erected.

almost half of the citizens and inhabitants of Venice were engaged in shipping. The Republic's arsenal was the largest dockyard of the period in the world, and could fit out twenty-five galleys in fourteen days.

Venice's houses were valued at seven million ducats, from which the city drew rents amounting to half a million. A thousand nobles, including most of the merchants, had incomes of between seventy and four thousand ducats per annum, but the size of personal income exercised no influence over individual or family ratings.

The national income that year was 1,100,000 ducats, higher therefore than that of France, England, Spain, Milan, Florence or the Curia, though by 1450 it had slipped back to 800,000. If we remember that, in addition, Venice had introduced a number of small or rather specialized industries into its territory, and gave them every encouragement, it is easy to see that the citizens' standard of living was more than satisfactory.

The glass industry at Murano enjoyed special benefits. Venice's glass factories had been moved to the island in 1291 on account of the danger of fire. Murano's population enjoyed particular advantages due to their artistic skill. They had their own *libro d'oro,* a Golden Book in which the names of their distinguished citizens were entered, just as in Venice's Great Golden Book, but the secret of the art of glass-blowing was strictly guarded. A glass-blower who left the Republic was in his absence sentenced to death. Conversely, in 1524, a glass-blower who had fled because of a murder was pardoned on his return.

Tolerance of anything which did not harm the Serene Republic was always Venice's unfailing motto. The position of the Jews up to the seventeenth century was better than in any other state. There had never been any pogroms. In 1132 over thirteen hundred Jews were living in the city. They could carry on their trade without any restriction, and even practise as doctors. Until 1374 they lived on the Giudecca (hence the name of that largest of the islands, directly opposite the city), or in Mestre. They received permission to settle in Venice itself on payment of a tax. Moneylending and usury helped them to control the trade in gold, silver and jewellery, until 1395. They were not, however, allowed to own any property, and had to wear distinctive clothing. They were also forbidden to marry Christians, or have anything to do with Christian women, even courtesans. From 1516 on they lived in the *ghetto.* This was a quarter which had originally housed foundries. In Italian the word *gettare* means, *inter alia,* to smelt metal, or cast iron.

Venice proved to be just as tolerant in times of religious fanaticism. No ecclesiastical inquisition, no witch-hunts or burning of heretics disturbed the calm, industrious life of the city. Giordano Bruno found refuge there after a restless life of wandering, until the Papal Inquisition carried him off to Rome and burned him as a heretic in 1600. Many Protestants fled to Venice after the wars of religion, from Catholic countries which forbade them to practise their religion. Books placed on the Index outside Venice were printed and published in the city, so that, as might have been expected, many of the Republic's publishers, printers, makers of woodcuts and copper-plate engravers opened up new branches.

In the late Middle Ages, when awakening self-awareness among the middle classes and manual workers led in the larger towns of the Empire and the city-republics to political aspirations, and social protest against compulsory guild 'unionization', Venice remained calm. People were comparatively prosperous. They had work, and even though the prosperous middle class, especially the merchants, remained barred from government affairs after the 'Serrata' of 1297, there was ample opportunity to acquire prominence among one's fellow-citizens as a well-to-do patron, to celebrate festivals, hold conferences, in other words establish one's position in the community.

There was in particular the institution of the *Scuole,* as they had called themselves since the thirteenth century (and before that probably either *ars* or *confraternità*). They were unique in the social and cultural history of Europe, and could be associations of manual workers for example, rather like the

100

guilds, or even ethnic groups, such as the Slavs, Greeks or Albanians living in
Venice. These *Scuole* had their own chapels and hospitals which took in
guests, and also the sick, as well as club-rooms. They 'combined the
benevolent aims of the freemasons with the devotional exercises of religious
brotherhoods'. (H. Honour, 1966). They would visit prisoners in custody and
paid for the burial services of those excuted. Members undertook religious
duties, and assisted their colleagues in time of need or sickness. Their
organizations were financed out of members' annual dues, which normally
yielded a not inconsiderable surplus, which was used to improve the club-
rooms. Every great painter in Venice, from Cima da Conegliano, the Bellinis,
father and son, to Tintoretto and Tiepolo were given important commissions
to paint chapels and club-rooms. Only Titian, prince of painters, had no time
for such pursuits. Tintoretto, for instance, known for the passion with which
he painted, as if possessed, took twenty-four years (1564–1588) to finish the
thirty gigantic frescoes on the ceiling and walls of the Scuola di San Rocco.

   At the start of the fifteenth century, soon after Doge Mocenigo had

100 Venice: The Doge's Palace: Inner Courtyard and Scala dei Giganti. Specifically Venetian-Byzantine forms were adhered to in the external structure of the Doge's Palace, even after numerous fires. The Eastern façade on the other hand, under Antonio Rizzo (1483 to 1498) and later Pietro Lombardo, took on the rich decorative forms of the Early Venetian Renaissance. In front rises the monumental Scala dei Giganti (Giants' Staircase), erected from a design by Rizzo, and dating between 1484 and 1501. It is dominated by two over-life-size figures of Neptune and Mars, created by Jacopo Sansovino in 1554, and symbolizing the fact that Venice's mastery of the seas must be upheld, by war if need be. The Doge was crowned in the podium at the top of the staircase.

101 Venice: The Doge's Palace: Golden Staircase (Scala d'Oro). This small and rather narrow stairway is the continuation of the Scala dei Giganti inside and is famous for the costly gilt stucco décor. The Doge Andrea Gritti commissioned the decoration in 1538. Sansovino and Alessandro Vittoria are named as the artists responsible for its design and execution. The stairs were solely for the use of leading citizens of the Serenissima and prominent State guests.

Double page following:
102 Venice: The Doge's Palace: Sala del Anticollegio (Collegial Entrance Hall). This was designed as a waiting-room for selected visitors being admitted to the Doge's presence. It was restored after the fire of 1574 or 1577, from designs by Palladio and Scamozzi, with richly gilt plasterwork and ceiling frescoes. The most important items are Tintoretto's and Veronese's murals, including Tintoretto's 'Minerva', who—protecting Venice and Peace—is repulsing Mars; and Veronese's 'Rape of Europa', a picture typically Venetian in that Europa does not look as though she has been raped but is cheerfully mounting the gaily-decorated bull kneeling humbly before her.

Pages 168–169
103 Venice: The Doge's Palace: Sala dello Scrutinio. (Election Chamber). The Scrutini, who belonged to the Maggior Consiglio, elected the Doge in the last resort. Decorated previously in costly fashion by Tintoretto and Pordenone, the work was again undertaken by the School of Tintoretto and Veronese after the 1577 fire. Clearly recognizable is the Venetian principle in ceiling decoration of placing the canvasses in richly carved gilt frames, which could be up to a metre (3' 3'') in depth. On the narrow side of the room stands the Arch erected in 1694, on the ancient Roman model, to honour Francesco Morosini, who was able for a brief period to win back for Venice the Peloponnese, and hence the Eastern Mediterranean.

101

presented his proud balance-sheet to the city bearing evidence of much prosperity, Venice experienced its first serious crisis. The face of the world was changing. The Mediterranean, which Venice ruled, became rather an unimportant inland sea as far as maritime commerce was concerned. On May 29, 1453, Mohammed II captured Constantinople. The very next day he entered the Hagia Sophia and while the Moslem priest was preaching the creed of Islam from the pulpit, the conqueror sent up a prayer to Allah, his face turned towards Mecca, and had Enrico Dandolo's ashes scattered to the four winds. Venice was obliged to give up the major part of the Cyclades and her colonies on Euboea. In 1492 Columbus, seeking a western passage to India, discovered the American continent. Between 1497 and 1498 Vasco da Gama became the first to round the Cape of Good Hope, thus discovering the sea-route to the East Indies. All the commercial goods from Asia which had reached the Eastern shores of the Mediterranean via the land routes, there to be loaded on to Venetian galleys, were unloaded in Spanish and Portuguese ports, cleared through customs, and marketed. Not long afterwards the Maggior Consiglio was again discussing the project of venturing a break-out from the Mediterranean into the Red Sea, anticipating the later Suez Canal. But Venice was too exhausted to undertake any such bold and epoch-making venture.

With its centuries of experience and gift of foreseeing periods of political change, Venice had understood in advance of all these events that the Republic would have to take new and opposing paths if it were to survive.

165

Open so far only seaward, especially towards the East, and interceding in land disputes only when it saw its maritime commerce threatened, the city now turned to the mainland. There farming opportunities offered themselves, in which unemployed seamen and ships' carpenters could find work. There too, now as before, lay the important trade routes to the North, which had to be grasped. Treviso, Conegliano and Castelfranco had been taken as early as 1339, to secure these same trade-routes. In 1405 Padua and Verona fell after bitter struggles with the Garrara and della Scala, as Vicenza had fallen in the previous year, while Udine and the whole of Friuli became part of the Republic in 1454. The standard of St. Mark had even flown from Ravenna's market-square, between 1430 and 1454, before the city, to its misfortune, was retaken by the Papal States. Brescia fell in 1441. Venice now found itself before the gates of Milan, which was to become its most bitter adversary. The fifteenth century thus saw Venice embark on the occupation of the mainland. Here too, however mercilessly they had once expelled, tortured and killed the ruling princes, the Venetians set up a good, peaceful and just system of government in the cities, and though columns bearing the Lion of St. Mark might be erected in the market-squares, or Venice's clock-tower and Campanile imitated in Udine or Verona, the Lion still proclaimed *Pax tibi, Marce, Evangelista meus,* and for the vassal cities the maxim held as of old: *Pro summa fide summus amor.*

The aristocracy and prosperous bourgeoisie, in the captive cities and in Venice alike, grasped the changed economic situation astonishingly quickly. The merchants became feudal barons and landed proprietors. They went to *villegiature* (summer holiday resorts), especially since poets and philosophers had been glorifying their vision of 'country-life' since the start of the Renaissance. They had their villas built by Palladio, Sanmicheli, Sansovino and other important architects of the period, but directly in front of the stately columned porticos, vineyards, orchards and tilled fields stretched away into the distance, differing entirely from the villas of Roman and Florentine patricians, where large, artistically planned Renaissance gardens comprised all the surroundings.

The quarrel with Milan lasted for decades. Both city-states were in the end exhausted, and in 1514 a mutual guarantee treaty was signed, which included the other great power on Italian soil apart from the Papal state—Florence. Meantime, however, France entered the lists, having recovered from the wounds inflicted by the Hundred Years' War with England and now unified internally. Charles VIII marched through the entire peninsula without meeting any resistance and captured Naples. Despite the 1495 alliance, the 'Holy League' between all of the Italian states, Germany and Spain for mutual help against France, Charles VIII's successor, Louis XII, again marched into northern Italy and claimed Milan. Here he touched on the interests of still-powerful Venice, whose exceedingly artful and commercially-minded diplomatic subterfuges had, moreover, also annoyed the other powers, the Pope and the Emperor. In 1508 an alliance therefore came into being between the Papal states, the French King Louis XII, Emperor Maximilian I, Aragon (i.e. Naples) and the Italian principalities of Urbino, Mantua and Ferrara. It was called the 'League of Cambrai'. The aggressive Pope Julius II excommunicated not only the Doge and the Government of Venice (in 1509) but also placed an interdict on the entire city. It was only before the gates of Padua, which had to be held at all costs as Venice's bridgehead into the *terra firma,* that the Venetians beat back the union troops in a final desperate effort. Only the fact that the League was suffering from internal dissensions had saved the Republic, at the last moment, from certain destruction. For almost 200 years Venice, in attack and defence, and usually against her own wishes, had been obliged to pledge mercenaries, money, and its best *condottieri* Carmagnola and Colleoni for wars and disputes on the mainland. Little wonder then that the Turks found it comparatively easy to take over Venice's last possessions and settlements in the Eastern Mediterranean, particularly since from 1520 onwards, in the person of Sultan

104 Tintoretto: 'Mercury and the Three Graces', 1578. Venice. The Doge's Palace: Anticollegio. A painting whose composition, in three diagonally arranged figures, giving rear, frontal and profile views, appears at first sight extremely Mannerist, yet the effect of the proportioning of the bodies and their balanced relationship to one another is completely harmonious.

Suleiman II, the Magnificent, they were led by a shrewd Regent and an outstanding general, possessed of the fanatical religious ambition to bring Europe under the Crescent. By 1529 the Turkish land-forces stood at the gates of Vienna. The Sultan had just taken from the Order of St. John the island of Rhodes, on which Venice too had had settlements. Charles V assigned Malta to the Knights of St. John as a place of refuge. Venice now possessed only one, though the most important, outpost off the Near Eastern coast, Cyprus. Caterina Cornaro, the early-widowed wife of King James II of Lusignan, had ceded the island to Venice in 1489 in return for a small residence in Asolo, which now developed into one of the most famous artistic courts of the Renaissance. In 1566 Suleiman began the encirclement and siege of Cyprus. Nicosia fell in 1570 and Famagusta was forced to surrender in 1571. The Osmanlis had guaranteed the few surviving Venetians safe passage, but they were nevertheless slaughtered and their Commandant, Marcantonio Bragadin, flayed alive.

Only now was a cry of indignation raised throughout the Christian West. Spain, the Papacy, and Genoa, which had been watching Venice's desperate battle on Cyprus not without satisfaction, concluded a treaty with Venice on 20th May, 1571 against the Turks, who were already cruising in the Adriatic. Don John of Austria, a natural son of Charles V, was in command of the fleet which in autumn 1571 met the Turkish warships before Lepanto in the Gulf of Corinth. The Christian West, but especially Venice, whose vessels attacked first, was victorious over the Crescent. Lepanto is regarded as the greatest sea-battle ever fought in the Mediterranean and has become a legend. The Allies mourned 8,000 dead, 5,000 of them Venetians, but 25,000 Turks had lost their lives out of a total of 28,000. 'Lepanto, the last and finest victory and yet a complete defeat. Everyone of note in Venice had fought and fallen there. For nothing.' (M. Langewiesche, 1940).

Nevertheless the naval victory of Lepanto delayed the Turkish advance. Not until seventy-four years had elapsed, and while Europe was bleeding to death in the Thirty Years' War, did the Turkish fleet again put to sea, to capture Venice's last bastion, Crete (1645). For three years the Turks laid siege to Candia, the capital, which had been built up by the Veronese architect Sanmicheli, a pupil of Palladio, into one of the most formidable of fortresses. The battle became one of 'attrition', almost in the twentieth-century sense, with endless bombardments and the mining of encampments and forts. The Turks lost 120,000 men. Venice, supported by Papal troops, a handful of French nobles who had once more inscribed the ideals of the crusaders on their banner, lost 30,000 dead.

At the end of August 1669 the Commandant, Francesco Morosini, surrendered and was allowed free passage with military honours. Fourteen years later he again embarked on a final expedition against Turkey, took back the Peloponnese and founded the kingdom of the 'Morea'. The banner of St. Mark even waved for a time over Athens. Only a few years later, however, the Sublime Porte had won the territory back. After nearly three hundred years of bitter struggle Venice made peace with the Turks in Passarowitz, in 1718.

The Serenissima rewarded the last of its great commanders and admirals in 1688 with the office of Doge. As a world power, 'mistress of the seas', *a bilancia* between the great powers, Venice had no further role to play in the concert of the nations. Yet its political constitution remained, and free of political responsibility, people were still full of life and wealthy enough to dance, laugh and play throughout the century of Rococo. Goldoni and Gozzi wrote hundreds of comedies which were performed in dozens of Guardi theatres. Casanova wrote his memoirs; and Guardi and Canaletto painted the city in its prime, while Giambattista Tiepolo and his sons completed in brush and palette the last precious flowering of Venetian painting.

In 1797 Venice surrendered to the troops of Napoleon without a fight. At the Peace of Campoformio he handed the city over to Austria in exchange for Flanders and Lombardy. When the revolution opened up the notorious prisons and leaden chambers, only four common criminals were discovered. On May 12, 1797 Lodovico Manin, the 120th Doge, resigned, and placed the *cornu ducale* back in the wardrobe.

The Fine Arts

"People living in a lagoon will lack any primary relationship to architecture in stone. Even when that has been mastered, feeling for the basic tectonic relations and for balance between weight and support will not be as strong as on the mainland. The real artistic strength of lagoon inhabitants will manifest itself neither in architecture nor in sculpture but above all in painting.

Wherever light can be seen changing on the water from morning till night and soft tones link up every shape and form, painting, and especially the art of *sfumato,* is bound to feel at home.' (H. Keller, 1960).

Continuity, calm, perseverance and balanced extension, all constituent parts of Venetian state policy and the basis of its government, characterize Venice's art too, which is as closely bound up with the history of the 'Serenissima' as its geographical location. In no other Italian city were the artistic traditions and movements deriving from Eastern Rome, Byzantium, so purely preserved until the High Middle Ages. San Marco (Plates 93 and 94) is a rough copy of the Justinian Church of the Apostles in Constantinople. The system of mutually supporting cupolas, surmounted by the central cupola, is the architecturally determining factor. Not only did all Venetian churches follow this system of domed churches well into the sixteenth century, if on a smaller scale—the sole exception being the city's large Mendicant churches—but the mainland churches too were based on their great model.

Mosaic and glass-blowing probably came to Venice with the extinction of the Ravenna Exarchate. Thereafter Venice was the Italian centre for mosaic art. Artists in mosaic were dispatched from here wherever mosaics had to be laid down or renewed, to old St. Peter's in Rome for instance, in the thirteenth century. The figure hovering, incorporeal and spaceless, in front of a gold mosaic backdrop remained a feature of Venetian art for the time being, whereas in the rest of Italy the first generation of great fresco painters, Cavallini and Torre in Rome, Duccio in Siena, Giotto in Florence, Assisi and Padua, Venice's neighbour, was leaving behind the mosaic work adopted from Roman or early Christian art.

Not until 11 March 1424 did the Senate officially announce the abandonment of mosaic work. Leading Florentine painters were called to Venice: Paolo Uccello, Filipino Lippi and Andrea Castagno. They painted, *inter alia,* using the *buon fresco* technique, the rooms in the Doge's Palace and a chapel in San Zaccaria. It was thus that Venice 'came to terms' with Italian painting over a century late, caught up with it in fifty years, and by the end of the fifteenth century had not only matched Florence, Siena and even Rome, but definitely surpassed them.

Byzantine painting tradition did of course die hard. In the seventeenth century the *madonneri* still survived, who painted icons in twelfth and thirteenth century Byzantine style. Domenikos Theotocopoulos, called El Greco (1541–1614), belonged to this guild during the years of his Venetian apprenticeship.

Venice's stature in the world and her commerce, spanning continents, finally revived the sense of beauty. The material and spiritual substance available was rich enough to create a brilliant centre for all the arts, and one that would last for over three hundred years.

Painting certainly does rank first among the fine arts in Venice. The workshops and studios of Venice's painting families were based just as consciously on tradition as were the business houses and banks. For generations they were definitely family professions. *Bozzetti* (drafts), workshop instructions, pattern books, sheets of sketches and preparatory drawings for the most part remained family property. With the single exception of Giorgione, no individual name appeared in the artistic workshops in Venice. The most famous families were the Vivarini, the Bellini, with their son-in-law or brother-in-law Mantegna, the Carpaccio, Palma, Robusti (Tintoretto), Caliari (Veronese), Ricci, Longhi, Tiepolo, Guardi, Canaletto and Veccelli families (Titian was a member of the latter). After Veronese's death his brothers and sons signed the pictures 'Haeredis Paolo', 'Paolo's heirs'.

When you visit the collection of paintings in the Accademia, which were collected in a fairly random fashion, you are immediately struck by an astonishing phenomenon. The gallery is on the whole chronologically arranged and the first two rooms contain large polyptychs (altarpieces

105 Paolo Veronese: 'The Triumph of Venice', 1584. Venice. The Doge's Palace: Sala del Collegio. This oval ceiling painting is located in what is possibly the most expensively furnished room in the Doge's Palace, following the 1577 fire. It portrays 'The Triumph of Venice', 'Rei Publicae Fundamentum'. Venice Triumphant is honoured by the heavenly and earthly powers, the Virtues, Divinities of the Sea, and Patrons of the Arts. The 'Master of Perspective' has here succeeded, despite the many figures, in creating overall order by a triple-zoned architectonic arrangement.

Following pages:
106 Venice: The Rialto Bridge (Ponte di Rialto). Until the first Academy Bridge was built in 1854, this was the only bridge over the Canal Grande. It was erected from 1588 to 1591, under the direction of Antonio da Ponte, following prolonged disagreement over the designs submitted by various artists, including Palladio. A single, wide-spanned arch of Istrian marble links both banks. The passageway is traditionally lined on both sides with shops (c.f. the Ponte Vecchio in Florence), leaving only a glimpse into the central arcade. The basic form is that of all Venetian bridges: a gentle ascent, with a level area in the centre supported by the level section of the bridge's semicircular arch.

105

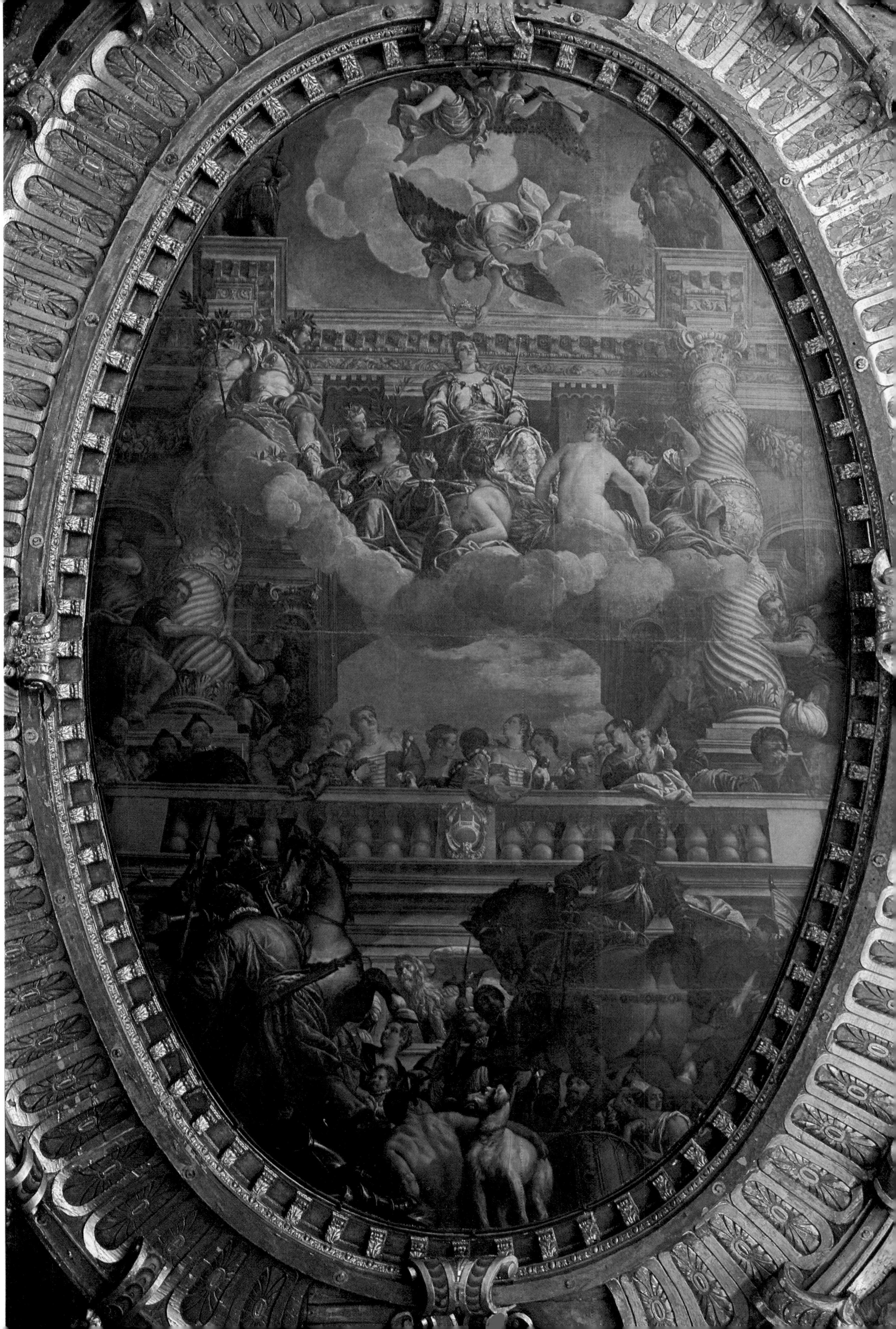

consisting of several panels with separate frames). They were painted by
Veneziano, Jacobello del Fiore, Vivarini and Crivelli, all of them working in
the Gothic manner. They all paint extremely elegant figures on a gold
background which, for all their exquisite old-fashioned refinement, are often
somewhat boring. You suddenly realize with amazement that most of these
painters lived and died in periods when such important High Renaissance
artists as Leonardo da Vinci had long since scaled their solitary peaks of
artistic greatness.

Then you go into the next room, to be confronted with what is virtually
mature High Renaissance art in altarpieces by Bellini, Cima da Conegliano
and Montegna, and Carapaccio's richly narrative cycles from the Scuole. The
use of very rich colours, blended in the most subtle way, provides a link
between the two rooms, with the *sfumato* of the tonal values, even in the series
of large altarpieces by various painters, thus creating a unity which seems
hard to explain. It also creates a lyrical mood, with the iconographic content
coming very much in second place, since the subject-matter is unique to
Venetian painting.

Of the various religious innovations we will mention first the *Sacra
Conversazione,* the 'Holy Conversation' between the Madonna and some of
the saints. It is in fact a silent encounter, since no one speaks or even gestures.
The Madonna is generally seated on a raised throne with several saints
standing beside it. One of the earliest examples of this type of altar was
created by a stranger, Antonio da Messina, who during his stay in Venice
from 1475 to 1476 painted the Pala di San Cassiano, fragments of which are to
be found to-day in the Kunsthistorisches Museum in Vienna. The real master
of this genre, however, was to be Giovanni Bellini (1430–1516), younger son
of Jacopo Bellini. The magic of his great altar paintings (Plate 115) lies
particularly in the uncompromising stillness that seems to rule in them: a
silent, solemn communing of those who understand one another without
words in their 'free' and no longer earthbound sanctity. Often angels holding
musical instruments are seated on the lower steps of the throne but do not
play. The room in which the saints have assembled round the Madonna is
sealed off to the outside world and often an aspidal flattened dome, like a
protective baldaquin, full of gold mosaic work, rises above the Blessed Virgin.
Only prolonged observation reveals the perfect compositional balance of
these paintings.

Stillness, inaction and the absence of any relation to one another on the
part of the figures represented distinguish also the paintings of Giorgione del
Castelfranco, who died young, of the plague, in 1511. In barely ten years of
work he so stimulated and quickened Venetian painting that even Titian
found it difficult to avoid his influence. Art historical research has already
ascribed nearly a hundred pictures to him, but at present his recognized and
certified *oeuvre* amounts to no more than some dozen items. Giorgione
introduced into the art of the lagoon city all the themes since regarded as
typically Venetian. He frequented humanist circles and may have been a
member of the esoteric secret societies of young Venetian nobles, probably
one reason why it is difficult to interpret the content of his pictures even today. His mythological paintings, 'poetry', idylls, landscapes and reclining
nude female figures, as well as his mysterious portraits, which say so little
about the sitter, brought a new impulse to Venetian painting and one that
fitted its temperament. Nearly all of his paintings were certainly commissioned by private buyers and in nearly all cases, except for the 'Castelfranco
Madonna', they are small in format. His 'Tempestà' in the Accademia
somehow manages to convey to us, in the smallest possible space, the
manifold presence of nature.

A thunderstorm rages in the background, and flashes of lightning
illuminate, in dazzling brightness, the towers and houses of a city. In the
foreground, however, a woman—Madonna or gipsy?—calms her child and a
youth in rather soldierly garments supports himself on a staff (or spear?).
They are relaxing by a glittering stream in the midst of the reassurance of

nature, but have no relation to each other. Everything parts them: water, meadows, a wall and the broken-off stump of a column. Atmosphere and mood, expressed chiefly in the sublime colouring, are what give the painting unity. Something similar happens with the 'Fête champêtre' (Country picnic) in the Paris Louvre. Four people, two of them men, one of whom is holding a lute, and two of them women, both nude, and all sociably disposed, are yet each isolated in a community of feeling whose absolute harmony allows of solitariness, but not loneliness.

Giorgione's 'Reclining Venus', in Dresden, is a nude but chaste feminine figure lying in an open landscape, with eyes closed, in an almost classically painted vision. This reclining nude recurs in numerous Venetian paintings, especially in Titian, and becomes a prototype which Velazquez, Goya and Manet would also feel the urge to use.

Giorgione's portraits are also veiled, to conceal their secret. 'He understands his subject as a vegetative creature and any attempt to discover character is not consistent with Giorgione's outlook. Those portrayed are not shown in action. For us they have no destiny, and no history. They manifest themselves to us only as phenomena. With such an attitude to painting it is scarcely surprising that Giorgione should have painted young people almost exclusively.' (H. Keller, 1960).

Titian, who with the portraits of Charles V, Philip II, Pope Paul III Farnese was later to become one of the most outstanding portrayers of individuals, was for a long time in his early work unable to free himself from Giorgione. 'The Knight of Malta' (Florence, Pitti Palace), the 'Young Englishman' (Munich, Ale Pinakothek) and even the 'Man with the Glove' (Paris, Louvre) remain silent and turned in upon themselves. Although Titian, 'the Prince of Painters', outshone all the other 'greats', even Leonardo and Raphael, in the eyes of his contemporaries, and was perhaps comparable to Michelangelo, who was called *il divino,* 'the divine', in his own lifetime, he remained a true son of Venice. The subdued, resonant element in his later years, visible only in the fiery glow of the gold and red in his palette; his flaky *impasto*; the deep introspection and insistent questions underlying his subject-matter, which is religious as well as mythological; the apparent stillness and quiet emanating from his most active compositions and dramatic subjects; the sudden pauses—all these features link him with Venice. Even though he was a

107 *Venice: View from the Campanile of the monastic island of San Giorgio Maggiore, giving a good impression of the lagoon-city's peculiar location. Only a narrow neck of land dominated by the dome of Santa Maria della Salute separates the waters of the Grand Canal from the broad Bacino and the large island, the Giudecca, behind which the wide lagoon opens.*

highly respected artist and much in demand—emperors and kings and princes were eager to own his work—he kept faith with his native city. Commissions from the Serene Republic, even from a tiny Venetian parish, were always just as important to him as those offered by world celebrities.

At a comparatively early age he was able to develop and benefit from the new self-awareness that emerged with the coming of the Renaissance. For instance on 20 March 1518, St. Bernard's Day, all the shops were closed because Titian's *Assunta,* 'The Assumption of the Virgin Mary' (plate 117), was due to be unveiled in one of the two great churches of the mendicant orders in Venice, Santa Maria Gloriosa dei Frari. Ridolfi, the painter's biographer, reports that the *curatore dell' opera* (the monk responsible for having the church built and furnished) objected to what he saw as the excessive number of saints present, saying that there was not enough room for them. And so it went on. In short, all sorts of criticisms were levelled at the painting. The emperor promptly offered to purchase it, whereupon the monks realized that 'art was not their métier and that reading their breviary did not impart any knowledge of art'. In 1548 Count Girolamo della Torre wrote to the Cardinal of Trent, who was staying in Augsburg during the Imperial Diet (to which Titian had also been invited to paint the portraits of Emperor Charles V and the Crown Prince (later King Philip II) as well as their defeated enemies), to the effect that 'the first man in Christendom [Charles V] wishes to communicate that everything possible should be done for Titian when he arrives in Augsburg in the way of comfort and convenience, and all avenues opened to him, so that he may pursue his work unhindered.'

Titian's working habits are also typical of Venetian painting, which was always concerned more with colour than with *disegno,* or drawing. We possess few, perhaps a dozen, reliably authenticated drawings by his hand. He laid his pictures directly on to the primed canvas and then—after the first few fleeting sketches, we are told—turned them to the wall, and did not turn them back again for weeks or even months, to gaze on them then like 'deadly enemies' and go on painting.

Tintoretto (1518–1594), Titian's great opposite, or counterpart, lived and worked at his side for a long time but never left Venice. He devoted himself solely to the ever greater embellishment of the palaces, churches and *Scuole* of the lagoon-city (Plates 104 and 123). If there ever was in Venice a stylistic trend

177

109

108

110

111

that could be called 'Mannerism', then Tintoretto was its representative. His diagonals, powerful foreshortening (either into the painting or thrusting out of it, and his unnaturally tall figures are devoid of Florentine Mannerism but inconceivable apart from the example of Michelangelo, who impressed him deeply. Above his door stood his motto: *il colorito di Tiziano, il disegno di Michelangelo*: in other words 'the colour of Titian, and Michelangelo's draughtsmanship'.

Veronese's intoxication with colour, the overwhelming development of splendour in his painting, the silken glitter and velvet glow of the garments signify the culmination of the magnificence which the state patrons wanted to see depicted. Veronese and his pupils and successors then painted the Venetian patriarchal villas on the mainland, with all the virtuosity of the *trompe l'oeil* painting whose effects still charm the beholder. Musicians sit on galleries; elegant ladies bend over balustrades; gallant gentlemen, emerging from mock doorways, greet them; while a lapdog sits on the floor in front of the framework of railings. Veronese accomplished his greatest task, however, along with Tintoretto, in painting the Doge's Palace. The residence of the Doge, the state Palace, burned down in 1577. The paintings of the Florentines who had been called to Venice at the beginning of the fifteenth century were destroyed, together with those of Pisanello from northern Italy and Titian's early work. Veronese painted one subject only, recurring in countless variations: the fame and greatness of Venice (Plate 105).

108   Venice: Palazzo Contarini del Bovolo: Scala del Bovolo, circa 1499. The Venetian palace 'open' system has been adopted here even for the round tower, with its spiral staircase, Bovolo is a Venetian dialect word for chiociola, *'snail'.*

109, 110 and 111   Venice: Sixteenth-century palaces. This series of three palaces, erected at less than fifty-year intervals, clearly demonstrates the development of Venetian architecture. Palazzo Vendramin-Calergi (Plate 109), in which Richard Wagner died on 13.2.1883, was completed in 1509. It has a completely balanced order in which each architectural element retains its own weight. In the case of the Palazzo Corner Ca' Grande (Plate 110), erected in 1537, the heightened rusticated ground-floor assumes the function of a plinth, above which rise the two upper floors. Finally, in the Palazzo Grimani (Plate 111), built around 1550, the façade is no longer divided up symmetrically by windows and columns but is broken up into rhythmically alternating broad and narrow areas, to which the alternating arched windows correspond.

Like Tiepolo, Venice's greatest eighteenth-century master, Veronese, never painted *al fresco* in the city. Frescoes did not last in the damp air of the lagoon. Veronese's ceiling frescoes in the Doge's Palace, like those of Tintoretto in the Scuola di San Rocco, are painted on canvas. Even Tiepolo's giant painting of the 'Feast of the Rosary' in the Gesuati Church, which covers the whole of the central nave, is painted on canvas. In 1508 Titian and Giorgione were commissioned to do murals for the Fondaco dei Tedeschi on the Rialto. Just one hundred years later hardly anything could be found of this single work, which was clearly executed jointly by the two painters. The damp salt air had done its work. After that Venice was careful about frescoes, however attractively its painters worked in this form on the mainland, like Veronese at the Villa Barbaro in Maser near Treviso, or Tiepolo on the stairway of the Würzburg Court Residence.

The element of continuity in Venetian culture and the natural observance of traditions handed down, to be carried on in politics as in art, can be best understood from the matchless unity of the Piazza San Marco and the Piazzetta, that open area framed by all the important state buildings, which Napoleon rightly called 'the loveliest ballroom in Europe'. The broad S-sweep of the Canal Grande, widest and most splendid of Venetian canals, here flows into the Bacino, the city's inner harbour-basin. The earliest architectonic evidence on this square—worthy of the gem which was to be mounted there—was, and how could it be otherwise, the church of St. Mark.

113

Page 179

112 Venice: Ca' d'Oro. The palace was built between 1421 and 1440 under the direction of Bartolomeo Bon. Its beauty lies not only in the extremely rich, graceful and partly-gilded decoration of column and tracery but also in the typically Venetian manner of carrying fine filigree work over a background which is indistinguishable to the eye.

113 Andrea Mantegna: 'The Martyrdom of St. Sebastian', circa 1506. Venice: Ca' d'Oro. Mantegna, son-in-law of Jacopo and brother-in-law of Giovanni Bellini, had worked mainly in Mantua, Verona and Padua before coming to Venice. Although he was a fanatical admirer of Graeco-Roman art he nevertheless paid his own tribute to Venice in the warm tones of his later manner. The saint's body is built up in a classic contrapposto, *like a Graeco-Roman statue, only the open mouth and eyes raised to heaven giving any indication of suffering.*

114 Venice: San Zaccaria: Façade. Like several other churches in Venice this too has a figure from the Old Testament as its patron saint, Zachariah, who is specially venerated in the Eastern Church. The façade of the well-known nunnery, which rich daughters of the Venetian Patriarchate taking the veil pre-ferred (and purchased their way into), belongs to the second half of the fifteenth century. Both lower floors are still devoted to the Gothicizing incrustation style, but in the upper storeys and rounded gable Mauro Coducci finds his way to the great, pure, clear forms of the Renaissance.

114

Immediately the saint's remains had been received, a church was built for him. In the year 1073 it was decided to construct a new building worthy of him, the present domed church. It was consecrated in 1094 in the presence of Emperor Henry IV, but building continued over a period of centuries without, however, altering the basic concept (Plates 93 and 94). The church was given its richest enhancement at the beginning of the thirteenth century, when the mosaics in the vestibule (or narthex) were completed, and the building decorated with items of booty from Constantinople—hundreds of columns, capitals, reliefs and mural facings of the finest marble, the most valuable pieces being brought to the south side of the church, which faces the Piazzetta and the sea. Even to-day this is the side that appears like a collection of trophies to the greater glory of the saint and the Serene Republic. No feeling

115 Giovanni Bellini: 'Sacra Conversazione'. ('Madonna and Child with
Saints'), 1505. Venice: San Zaccaria. This is
perhaps the richest of Bellini's portrayals of
the Sacra Conversazione. The Madonna,
enthroned, is holding the upright Christ-child
on her left knee. An angel at her feet on the
steps of the throne is playing a musical
instrument. On her right are St. Peter and St.
Catherine; on her left, St. Jerome and St.
Lucy. There is no communication between the
personages, not so much as a glance. Each is
quite self-contained. And yet in a higher sense
they are bound together by their inner peace,
the harmony of the composition and the
protective mosaic baldaquin, whose painted
architectonic perspective exactly corresponds
to the 'built-in' altar-frame.

116 Venice: Santa Maria dei Miracoli:
Detail of Ceiling Decoration. This little
church was built between 1481 and 1489 by
Pietro Lombardo and his school from the
finest, delicately-coloured and shaded marble.
The panelled ceiling, consisting of curves and
straight lines, is a lovely example of early
Venetian ceiling decoration.

for symmetry determines the order in which they are arranged, as in the
Classical Period or the Renaissance. They are distributed over the façade in a
trophies, the two 'Tetrarchs', a porphyry group of two Regents embracing,
seemingly arbitrary manner, their importance being indicated by the position they occupy in reference to the church interior. The most precious
which dates from the fourth century A.D.—porphyry was considered a royal
stone, so that only Emperors had statues made of it—is situated at the corner
of the south side, at the exact spot where the Treasury is located on the inside.

115

117 Titian: 'Assumption of the Blessed Virgin' ('Assunta'), 1518. Venice: Santa Maria Gloriosa dei Frari: High Altar. With this gigantic altar-painting (6.90 metres × 3.60 metres) (22′ 6″ × 11′ 7″) Titian created the prototype of the high altar-painting that remained the rule up into the High Baroque period and perhaps even for Rubens. However solidly arranged the separate groupings—the astonished and terrified Apostles around the grave, the Blessed Virgin surrounded by an angelic halo, and God the Father receiving her—the factor determining the pictorial structure is its colour composition, the guiding lines of the red tones, in their gradations.

118 and 119   Venice: Scuola Grande di San Marco. The façade of this scuola, which is now the Venice municipal hospital, was erected between 1485 and 1495. It is a masterpiece of Venetian Early Renaissance architecture, for the wealth of its coloured marble incrustation, and particularly its subtly illusionary effects in the matter of perspective. Two lions, a reference to the name of the school, seem to emerge right and left of the main portal (Plate 119). At the side, the façade joins up with the second large church of the Mendicant Orders after the Frari, Santi Giovanni e Paolo.

This corner also forms the main entrance to the Doge's Palace, the Porta della Carta, so the 'Tetrarchs' clearly represent the interlocking nature of Venice's secular and spiritual power.

The main façade on the Piazza is one of the later sections, with its five round portals leading into the narthex—the central one being higher than the others. Over them is the surrounding gallery, and above that the high, wide and rounded arches bear mosaics which are framed by white marble canopies, small spires and crockets in the Late Gothic flamboyant style. Their flowery tendrils, like petrified Burano lace, creep round the gold mosaic work. The broad West Window in the central area is almost hidden by the powerful four-in-hand bronze horses, the most precious part of the Byzantine booty, fourth or third century B.C. Greek work and the only bronze *Quadriga* to survive from the ancient world.

The next structure to be built in the Piazza and Piazzetta ensemble was what the Venetians affectionately call the *paron de casa* (the Head of the House), the Campanile (Plate 107), linking the two squares like a hinge. It rises to a height of 95 metres (313' 6'') on a square that is 12 metres × 12 metres (39' × 39'). Construction was begun in the ninth century and concluded in 1517, when it was crowned by a three metre (9' 9'') high gilded statue of the Archangel Gabriel. This figure, visible for miles, guided ships by day into the Bacino. On stormy nights a beacon-fire was lit in the bell-loft. The Campanile's particular attractiveness rests finally on two factors, apart from its extremely simple but splendidly-conceived articulation. These factors are, firstly, the colour alternations between the dull dark red brick and the crystalline, light-catching transparency of the white marble; and secondly, the harmonious balance between the horizontal and vertical elements. The soaring upwards surge of the proud, steep pilaster strips is held in check throughout by the weight of the heavy marble cornices. With a subtle feeling for the pressure of tracery the cube is gradually eased and reduced. More decorative forms, small columns in the round arched arcade of bell-storey and the balustrade arrangement, then subsume the vertical movement, which finally seems to flow with the steep pyramid roof and crowning statue of the angel into the lagoon itself. In the early hours of 14 July 1902 the Campanile collapsed. Miraculously no one was injured and the neighbouring structures suffered little or no damage. Nine months later, in April 1903, reconstruction was begun, and lasted nine years.

The Doge's Palace (Plates 93, 98, 100–103), the seat of government, was given its present form in the fourteenth and fifteenth centuries; the south side, on the Mole and sea, in the fourteenth; and the section adjoining the Piazzetta in the late fifteenth century Gothic period. The façades of the Palace even to-day reveal in the purest form Venice's peculiar attitude to architecture, which never favours what is static. To some extent the closed wall of the upper storey rests on the elegant column of the lower arcaded floor and the first floor above it, which is concealed behind a delicate curtain of colonnades, with Gothic tracery in the spandrels. Yet this high, wide area is again so gently articulated, merely by the change from the bright red and white of the stone cover, that the resulting textile-like ornamentation resembles patterned material rather than a solid wall.

Numerous fires kept plaguing the Palace, one of the severest (1483) destroying, *inter alia,* the first great painting cycles, in the interior, by the Florentine painter Pisanello. In 1577 the exterior was badly damaged and the entire treasury of paintings carried out during the High Renaissance, on commission from the state, fell victim to the flames. Tintoretto and Veronese, with their pupils, repainted the rooms (Plates 102–105) in the shortest possible time. The exterior—although Palladio hastened to put forward new plans for modernization, which were in accordance with his classical taste—was restored in its old form. On the Piazza north of San Marco rises the 'Torre del Orologio', the Clock Tower, built by Mauro Coducci and decorated with richly coloured marble incrustations (Plates 96 and 97). To-day the two *mori,* bronze human figures, still strike the hours with their hammers on the big bell.

120

120 Venice: San Michele in Isola: Façade. The church of Venice's island cemetery—lying in the lagoon some 800 metres (870 yards) from the mainland—was constructed by Mauro Coducci from 1469 onwards. In structure it is distinctly reminiscent of the façade of San Zaccaria, which is also by Coducci (c.f. Plate 114).

121

121 Andrea Verrocchio: Equestrian Monument of Condottiere Bartolomeo Colleoni, 1481–1488. Venice. Campo San Giovanni e Paolo. This most famous of Italian Renaissance equestrian statues, along with Donatello's 'Gattamelata' in Padua, was created between 1481 and 1488 by the Florentine sculptor and painter Andrea Verrocchio. A high plinth raises the bronze figure—which is executed in the most naturalistic manner, as is evident from the Condottiere's face or the decoration on the reins—away from the yellow-brown of the church walls and to some extent higher than normal, thus elevating the field-commander to 'a gladiatorial dominance'. (E. Hubala).

The entire north side of the Piazza, up to a length of 152 metres (501' 7''), was soon afterwards taken up by the Procuratie Vecchie, the Residence of the Procurators of San Marco (Plate 95). Though on the threshold of the Renaissance, this structure still retains the Byzantine-Gothicizing style of the Doge's Palace, with its graduated series of three arcades and arched windows.

Not until the Libreria Marciana, the Library, was built on the Western side of the Piazzetta, opposite the Doge's Palace, by Jacopo Sansovino (1488–1570) did the High Renaissance make its brilliant debut in these squares (Plate 93). 'Both storeys of the Library, built from 1537 from his [Sansovino's] design, are constructed on the illustrationary type of Tabularium motif, the lower floor follows the Doric, and the upper the Ionic order. The concluding . . . frieze with the putti bearing garlands, in imitation of classical fragments of reliefs, parades its Roman origin.' (J. Burckhardt, 1855).

The Library is still a piece of Venetian architecture, however, and not merely because of its rich decoration. The articulation of the second floor is un-Roman, in that the round arched opening has not been shaped and proportioned as a pillared arcade after the solid building style, but as an open colonnade, and is therefore in the Venetian tradition. And since these arches supported by paired columns are linked by short straight architrave sections to pillars behind the great columns, we arrive at the richest articulation motif in Italian art, the 'Serlio' or Palladio motif: 'The columned arcade in the centre is flanked by two colonnaded sections . . . Wherever a living reflection of plastic values was striven after, resource was had to this type of composition.' (E. Habala, 1968). Sansovino's architectural system was essentially retained in the *Procuratie Nuove,* erected from 1584 under the direction of Palladio's pupil, Vincenzo Scamozzi, on the south side of Piazza San Marco.

It was left to Napoleon to close the square by building up the west side. In 1807 a church was torn down on his orders, and the classical 'Ala Napoleonica', the Napoleon wing, was erected, based on the form of the two Procuratorates. The city's noblest work of art was thus completed simultaneously with Venice's demise as a political power.

122 Venice: Isola di San Giorgio Maggiore. The monastic island of the Benedictines owes its architectural appearance to-day largely to sixteenth century extensions and conversions, especially the reconstruction of the church, begun in 1566 by Andrea Palladio. The interior and façade of San Giorgio Maggiore became models not only in Upper Italy for many seventeenth and eighteenth century religious buildings. Though a first glance reveals the overall classical structure of the façade, yet the multistoreyed orders are highly artistically combined in mutual dependence.

122

It is not only in the area of St. Mark's Square that Venice's image has been left untouched, a rare stroke of fortune in today's world. The great churches of the Mendicant Orders too, such as Santa Maria dei Frari and Santi Giovanni e Paolo ('San Zanipolo'), with Palladio's religious buildings (Frontispiece, Plate 122), and above all the palaces along the Canal Grande, have come down to us as intact groupings. A detailed examination of the art of Venetian palace architecture from the thirteenth to the eighteenth century would exceed the limits of our survey, so rich are their forms of decoration, despite the fact that they are all based on the same morphological principles. A charming way of spending the time is to drift along the Grand Canal in a boat, seeing how the very different palace façades are in fact variations on a single theme and thus receiving a lesson in architectural style—from the Ca'd'Oro (1421–1440) past the Palazzo Contarini del Bovolo (circa 1500) to the Palazzo Vendramin-Calergi (1509) and the Palazzo Corner Ca' Grande (1537) or the Palazzo Grimani (1550) (Plates 108–112). These all have one thing in common, even as early as the thirteenth century, the wide, hospitable, inviting façade opening outward on to the Canal, a unique feature in medieval secular architecture. The central opening was often at water-level, permitting

123 Tintoretto: 'The Last Supper', 1594. Venice. San Giorgio Maggiore. Presbytery. This 'Last Supper' is the final version of a theme which Tintoretto often treated in Venetian churches. When Christ pronounced the words: 'One of you will betray me', the disciples leapt to their feet in great excitement. The deep diagonal line of the table underlines the drama of the event. The pictorial effect depends however on the flickering gleams of luminosity in which the figures of angels flash forth.

188

123

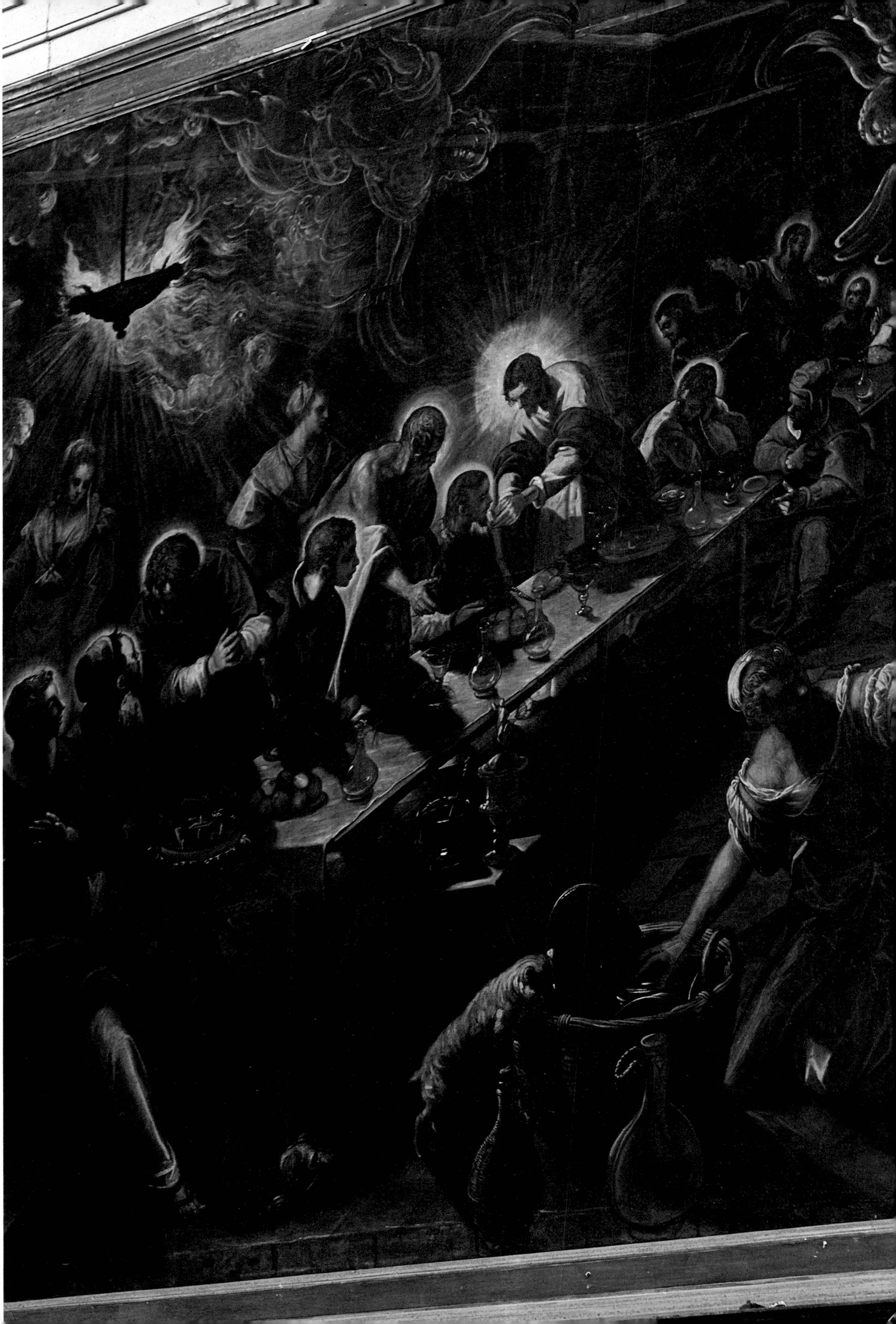

the gondola to enter the interior of the house. *Piazza,* canal and street work
their way in the freest and most open manner into the concealing four walls,
providing an insight into the essence of the medieval city

Companionship was a feature of Italian towns, an untiring need to
communicate and to exchange information and opinions in a free and easy
manner, in the *piazza,* across the yard, or from window to window. In their
open structures, the 'familiar' order of church, palace and town-hall, or of
loggia, market and monastery, around the square or ordered in a roadway,
they embody the free and inquiring spirit that has been a governing factor
since the late Middle Ages, a spirit which the modern visitor feels here, and the
Italian traveller of the Middle Ages looked to as an alternative to the walled-
in confines and political repression of the medieval world, an ideal image of
free human intercourse beneath a bright serene sky, whose indulgent climate
made it possible to go out or in, from *piazza* to salon, or street to corridor. It is
no coincidence that the architectural theory of the Italian Renaissance
defined the house as a town in miniature, and the town as a 'house' writ large,
and equated *sala* and *piazza.*

Bewitched by the perfection of organically evolved structures, the open-
minded traveller in Rome, Florence or Venice finds the basic human needs of
unrestricted communication and free social intercourse reflected in
architectural creations which even in their most monumental form do not
turn away from but towards each other, and relate not to themselves but to
something outside. The public buildings, like the private buildings of the
ruling class, express power, but seldom excessive power; self-awareness but
seldom self-aggrandizement. The free citizen's right to exist remained largely
untouched by these architectural signs of power. Nowhere did the townsman liberate himself earlier or more consistently into a freer, self-
conscious political existence than in the Italian *commune* of the fourteenth to
sixteenth centuries, or find his way towards a social identity which was soon
directed against the relics of medieval domination. It was logical, therefore,
that at the end of the Renaissance the upper classes had to bear the brunt of
city hostility. They returned to the feudal framework of the country, the
castle, the manor, the villa, from which, centuries before, they had crowded
into the towns. When the Italian aristocracy retired to the insularity of their
villegiature from about 1500 to 1550, with the 'Phantom of *piazza, commune*
and Cathedral, and the faces of lurking friends and laughing enemies before
their eyes.' (R. Borchardt), they turned their back not just on the city but on a
freedom which was no longer theirs alone.

Ancient Civilizations

EGYPT

LAND AND LIVES OF THE PHARAOHS REVEALED

Ancient Civilizations

EGYPT

LAND AND LIVES OF THE PHARAOHS REVEALED

CHIEF CONSULTANT **Professor Christine El Mahdy**

GLOBAL BOOK PUBLISHING

Managing director	Chryl Campbell
Publishing director	Sarah Anderson
Art directors	Stan Lamond
	Kylie Mulquin
Project manager	Marie-Louise Taylor
Chief consultant	Professor Christine El Mahdy
Commissioning editors	Monica Berton
	Fiona Doig
	Alan Edwards
	Catherine Etteridge
Editors	Belinda Bolliger
	Scott Forbes
	Mary Halbmeyer
	Janet Parker
	Michael Wall
Designers	Cathy Campbell
	Alex Frampton
	Laburnum Technologies
Cover design	Bob Mitchell
Design concept	Bob Mitchell
Photo library	Alan Edwards
Illustrations	Andrew Davies
	Glen Vause
Picture research	Monica Berton
	Belinda Bolliger
	Fiona Doig
	Catherine Etteridge
	Scott Forbes
	Mary Halbmeyer
	Janet Parker
	Marie-Louise Taylor
Cartographer	John Frith
Typesetting	Dee Rogers
Index	Glenda Browne
	Jon Jermey
Production	Ian Coles
Foreign rights	Belinda Vance
Publishing assistant	Christine Leonards

First published in 2005 by
Global Book Publishing
Level 8, 15 Orion Road,
Lane Cove, NSW 2066, Australia
Ph: 61 2 9425 5800   Fax: 61 2 9425 5804
Email: rightsmanager@globalpub.com.au

ISBN 10: 1 74048 056 2
ISBN 13: 978 1 74048 056 7

First published in 2005
Reprinted in 2008

Printed in China by SNP Leefung Printers Ltd

**Captions for cover, preliminary pages,
and section openers**

Front Cover: Tutankhamun being anointed by his
wife Ankhesenamun.

Back Cover: A deceased man making an offering to
Osiris, Isis, and Nephthys.

Page 1: Thoth and Anubis weighing the heart of the
deceased against the feather of trust.

Pages 2–3: Lids from Tutankhamun's canopic chest.

Page 4: A painted wooden statue of the goddess Isis.

Page 5: Glass-paste hieroglyphs covering a wooden
sarcophagus.

Page 6 (bottom): The cartonnage of Res-Paka-Shuty,
a priest of Mont.

Page 6 (center): A limestone relief showing Amenhotep II.

Page 7 (top): Pectoral jewel from the funerary jewelry of
Psusennes I.

Page 7 (center): Detail from the *Book of the Dead* of
Hirweben, Dynasty 21.

Page 7 (bottom): A painted stucco funerary mask of
a woman from the Ptolemaic Period.

Pages 8–9: The back of the throne of Tutankhamun.

Pages 10–11: From the *Book of the Dead*, the deceased
and his wife before Osiris.

Pages 22–23: Amphorae used for wine, from Abydos,
c. 3100 BCE.

Pages 70–71: The pyramids of Khafra and Khufu at Giza.

Pages 192–193: Granite statue showing Amenemhet II
as a sphinx.

Pages 268–269: The sarcophagus of Rameses III showing Ra.

Pages 390–391: A wooden sarcophagus, mask, and
mummified torso and hands.

Pages 460–461: The elaborate sarcophagus chamber in
Tutankhamun's tomb.

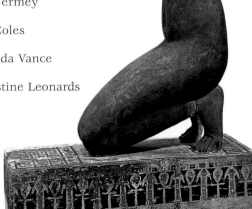

CONTRIBUTORS

Murray Adamthwaite is currently a fellow of the School of Fine Arts, Classics, and Archeology at the University of Melbourne, he also teaches at the University of the Third Age, Melbourne, in both ancient and medieval history. Murray graduated in Arts at the University of Melbourne and furthered his studies in England at the School of Oriental and African Studies, where he studied ancient history and languages. Completing a masters degree at Macquarie University, in 1990, Murray moved back to Melbourne where he completed his Ph.D. at the University of Melbourne in 1997 with a thesis on texts from the Late Hittite site of Emar on the Middle Euphrates. He has lectured several courses for the Council of Adult Education in Melbourne, and also at the University of Sydney. He has written articles for the University's Near Eastern Studies journal *ANES* (formerly *Abr-Nahrain*), and other theological journals.

Charlotte Booth has been teaching Egyptology in the U.K. for various institutions for a number of years, and is a regular speaker at numerous conferences for Egyptology societies across the U.K. She graduated from University College London with a B.A. (Honors) and an M.A. in Egyptian archeology. For her B.A. dissertation Charlotte studied the role of the Hyksos in Egyptian society, and her thesis was published in 2005. For her M.A. thesis Charlotte examined representations of foreigners in Egyptian art, and how this reflects attitudes held towards them and their role in society. She has also been published in various journals and magazines on a number of topics.

Bridget Buxton received her Ph.D. in ancient history and Mediterranean archaeology from the University of California at Berkeley in 2003, and now lectures in classics and ancient history at the University of Auckland, New Zealand. Her research interests include Roman and Hellenistic history, Classical archeology, and underwater archeology. She began writing for historical documentaries as a graduate student and now combines this with lecturing on Mediterranean archeological tours. Dr. Buxton is currently completing a book on Egypt's first Roman pharaoh, Augustus.

Dr Malcolm Choat is a research fellow in the Department of Ancient History at Macquarie University, Sydney. He also teaches on Greco-Roman Egypt and Early Christianity. His principle research is on Egypt in late antiquity (fourth to fifth centuries CE). Within this he pursues several interests, one being the use of Coptic in the earliest period (third to fourth centuries CE), another is the rise of monasticism. The basis for this work is documentary papyri, which he also edits and publishes. Additionally, he is involved in a project to collect all the papyrological evidence for Christianity in Egypt before Constantine.

Guadalupe Cincunegui has worked as an archeologist on research excavations in the United Arab Emirates and Jordan, in addition to participating in many prehistoric and historical contract excavations in Australia. She attained a Bachelor of Arts (Honors) in Near Eastern Archeology and a Master of Arts from the University of Sydney. Her major passion and interest is in the early archeology of the Middle East, especially the Neolithic and Chalcolithic of the Levant and the legal aspects of the illicit trade of antiquities throughout the world.

Fran Dorey is currently working at the Australian Museum in Sydney where she has researched and written text for major exhibitions, including one on death and the afterlife in ancient Egypt. She is also responsible for designing and implementing various programs to educate the public about a diverse range of topics, focusing particularly on archeology, paleoanthropology, and ancient cultures. She has a Bachelor of Arts (Honors) degree, majoring in archeology and ancient history, from the University of Sydney, and a Diploma in Education (Secondary) from Charles Sturt University in Bathurst. She has traveled widely through Egypt and the Middle East.

Christine El Mahdy is an Egyptologist. She started in the field as a child of seven, was reading hieroglyphs before she was nine, and now has four degrees in the subject. Today, she is Professor of Egyptian Studies and the head of the British Centre for Egyptian Studies, a distance learning provider, which she started in 2000. She has written and broadcast material on ancient Egypt for more than thirty years, as well as lecturing widely. Previous books include *Exploring the World of the Pharaohs; Mummies, Myth and Magic; Tutankhamen, Life and Death of the Boy-King;* and *The Pyramid Builder;* as well as contributing to *Mythology: Myths, Legends, and Fantasies* (2003). In all her work, she campaigns for a return to forensic archeological skills and away from mythic interpretation. Using these techniques, she is today the only Egyptologist to have declared that Tutankhamen died of natural causes, recently confirmed by the CT scans of the mummy of the boy-king.

Sherine ElSebaie is currently enroled as a senior Ph.D. candidate at the University of Toronto in Canada, majoring in ancient Egyptian religion, supported by two minors: Ancient Egyptian language and literature, and ancient Egyptian art and archeology. She obtained her masters in Egyptology from the same institution, with a thesis entitled *The Destiny of the World: A Study on the End of the Universe in the Light of Ancient Egyptian Texts*. Sherine has been a teaching assistant at the University of Toronto for the past few years in a number of courses ranging from religion to history, and archeology. Born in Cairo, Egypt, Sherine got her B.Sc. from Helwan University and worked for Ain Shams University in Cairo, teaching a course on "Ancient Egyptian art through masterpieces in the Egyptian Museum in Cairo," before moving to Canada in 1998.

Linda Evans works in the field of animal behavior and has a masters degree in Egyptology from Macquarie University, Sydney. She is currently completing her Ph.D. thesis on the depiction of animal behavior in Old Kingdom tomb scenes, which combines her zoological background with a lifelong interest in Egyptian art. She has published a number of papers on the animals of ancient Egypt and is particularly interested in the Egyptian people's relationship with the animal kingdom.

Wolfram Grajetzki is currently preparing a catalogue of the coffins in the Fitzwilliam Museum, Cambridge, U.K., and is also working on a publication of funerary material from the Second Intermediate Period found at Abydos. As part of a team working on the "Digital Egypt for Universities" project, Wolfram created over 3,000 web pages. The project aimed at providing online teaching resources for archeology in Egypt and ended in July 2003. He has studied Egyptology, Classical archeology, and prehistory, has a masters degree in Egyptology from the Freie Universität, Berlin, and also holds a Ph.D. in Egyptology from the Humboldt Universität zu Berlin. His thesis was on *The Highest Officials of the Middle Kingdom,* and was published in book form in 2000. Wolfram worked for eight years at the DASS (Database for Ancient Egyptian Coffins and Sarcophagi) in Berlin, and has been a member of numerous excavations in Egypt and Pakistan.

Nicole B. Hansen is currently finishing her Ph.D. at the University of Chicago with a dissertation entitled *Motherhood in the Mother of the World: Continuity and Change of Reproductive Concepts and Practices in Egypt from Ancient to Modern Times.* In addition, she has a B.A. from the University of California at Berkeley and an M.A. from the University of Chicago. Nicole spent many years living in Egypt where she worked as editor of the Theban Mapping Project's award-winning web site, and as field archive manager for the Giza Plateau Mapping Project. Recently, she started a new web site, Glyphdoctors.com, offering online courses in hieroglyphs and Egyptology to the general public.

Jennifer Hellum currently teaches at the University of Auckland, New Zealand, and has also taught Egyptology at Howard University, Washington D.C., at Georgia State University, Atlanta, and at the University of Toronto. She received her Ph.D. in Egyptology from the University of Toronto, Canada, in 2001 and has participated in archeological expeditions throughout Egypt, on the Red Sea coast, in the Delta, at Giza, and at Abydos for the past 12 years. Jennifer has written a forthcoming book on the building of the pyramids, and she continues to work in Egypt on excavations for other universities, as well as investigating possibilities for excavations for the University of Auckland.

Rosalind Janssen teaches Egyptology at the University of London's Birkbeck College, and also for the University of Reading and the WEA. She studied Egyptology at the University of Birmingham and University College London and now holds two master's degrees: In Lifelong Learning and in Gerontology, now teaching the latter subject at Birkbeck. Rosalind was previously Lecturer in Egyptology at the Institute of Archaeology, University College London, and before that Assistant Curator in UCL's Petrie Museum of Egyptian Archaeology. She is a specialist in textiles and the history of ancient Egyptian dress, a subject on which she has written numerous scientific articles and the popular Shire book *Egyptian Textiles* (1986). She has also acted as textile specialist on various excavations in Egypt. Rosalind is married to a Dutch Egyptologist, and together they have written *Egyptian Household Animals* (1989), *Growing up in Ancient Egypt* (1990), and *Getting Old in Ancient Egypt* (1996).

Jana Jones works for the German Archeological Institute, the American Expedition to Hierakonpolis, the French Archeological Institute, the Australian Centre for Egyptology, and the North Kharga Oasis Survey. She is completing a Ph.D. at Macquarie University, Sydney, where she attained a Masters of Arts (Egyptology). Since 1997 she has visited Egypt twice a year. As an undergraduate she studied archeology at the University of Sydney, later completing her degree at Macquarie University, majoring in modern languages. For the next ten years she designed costumes for television. Her interest in Egyptology was rekindled when she was working on a TV commercial for Cleopatra Soap, winning awards here and overseas for best costume design. She enroled in a hieroglyphs course at Macquarie University, and was smitten by the logic of the language and by the ancient Egyptians through their texts. She specializes in the analysis of archeological textiles from burials of the Predynastic and Early Dynastic periods.

Lesley Kinney has a masters degree in Egyptology from Macquarie University in Sydney and has recently submitted her Ph.D. with a thesis on *Dance, Dancers and the Performance Cohort in the Old Kingdom*. She plans to continue researching ancient Egyptian dance from the Predynastic Period to the New Kingdom. Her other special interests are Egyptian architecture, particularly the evolution of architectural engineering and idiosyncratic devices applied in Egyptian wall art. Lesley has previously contributed chapters to *Egyptian Art: Principles and Themes in Wall Scenes* (2000) and an article on *muu* dancers in the *Bulletin of the Australian Centre for Egyptology*, 2005. She presented papers on fourth-dimensional representation in Egyptian wall art at the *American Research Center in Egypt* conference in Boston, 2005 and the Conference for the *Sydney Society for Literature and Aesthetics*, in 2003.

Christiana Köhler is a senior lecturer in Egyptology at Macquarie University, Sydney, and Director of the Helwan Project in Egypt. Her main areas of expertise are Egyptian archeology, culture, history, and society in general, as well as prehistoric Egypt and the formation of the state in particular. After completion of her studies in Egyptology, Near Eastern, and Classical archeology, she graduated in 1993 from the University of Heidelberg in Germany with a Ph.D. thesis on early ceramics from Buto in the Egyptian Nile Delta. She spent the following two years on a postdoctoral scholarship at the University of Pennsylvania in the U.S.A. conducting research in Egyptology and anthropology, and has been working on numerous archeological sites in the Near East since 1987.

Anna Leffers is a Ph.D. student at Macquarie University, Sydney, undertaking a thesis on the ancient Egyptian jewelry industry, specifically examining its socio-economic changes from the Early Dynastic Period to the Middle Kingdom. She has completed a Bachelor of Arts and a masters degree in Egyptology at Macquarie University, as well as a minor thesis, which was a preliminary review of Egyptian jewelry from the Early Dynastic Period. She has participated in Macquarie University's excavations at the cemetery of Helwan in Egypt under the directorship of Christiana Köhler for the last five seasons, and has been a casual tutor in Egyptology at Macquarie University for the past three years.

Paul McKechnie has taught Greek and Roman history in the Department of Classics and Ancient History in the University of Auckland, New Zealand, since 1991. He got his first degree at St. John's College, Cambridge and started his teaching career in high schools in England, then Malawi, having achieved his doctorate at University College, Oxford. He is interested in early Christianity and in Egypt in the Ptolemaic Period. His books include *Outsiders in the Greek Cities in the Fourth Century BC* (1989) and *The First Christian Centuries* (2001).

Thomas Mudloff is currently a lecturer in Egyptology at the Field Museum of Natural History in Chicago where his specialization is Egyptian religious beliefs and the ancient hieroglyphic language. He has taught archeology and history of the ancient Near East at Northwestern University and National Louis University in the Chicago area, and lectured both in the United States and other countries. He has written articles on the history and religion of ancient Egypt and is the author of books on Egypt. Dr. Mudloff has worked for many years in Egypt, Syria, and Jordan both on excavation and with study groups in these countries. He holds degrees in Egyptology and Biblical studies.

Ezzat Refaei is currently writing his Ph.D. thesis at Macquarie University on *Funerary Beliefs and Burial Customs in Early Egypt: From the Prehistoric Period to the Beginning of the First Dynasty*. He also teaches Arabic and tutors Egyptology students. He gained a bachelor degree in Egyptology with first class honors, as well as a diploma in Egyptian Prehistory from Cairo University. In 1994 he began work at the Supreme Council of Antiquities with Dr Zahi Hawass, as an inspector of antiquities at the Giza pyramids, and then as assistant director of excavations of the pyramid complexes of Khuit and Iput, and the Teti cemetery at Saqqara. In 1997 Ezzat worked as an inspector of antiquities to the Australian expedition at the Early Dynastic cemetery at Helwan, where he worked for three seasons. Born in el Menia, Middle Egypt, Ezzat moved to Australia in 1999.

Rodna Siebels regularly gives lectures in the history and culture of ancient Egypt, as well as teaching introductory courses in hieroglyphics at the WEA, Sydney. She has tutored at Macquarie University, Sydney, where she received her M.A. as well as her Ph.D. in Egyptology with a thesis on *Agricultural Scenes in Old Kingdom Tombs*, with an emphasis on the inscriptional material found on the walls. Rodna specializes in tombs of the Old Kingdom and part of her studies at the university included fieldwork in Egypt with the Macquarie team at Akhmim.

Lori J.E. Turi has a bachelor degree in psychology from Upsala College in New Jersey, with secondary studies in theology, philosophy, and linguistics. She has taken comparative religious studies at Harvard University and has pursued a 22-year independent study in Egyptology. Her special areas of interest include Middle Egyptian hieroglyphics, Old to Middle Kingdom religious mythology and the architecture of the Fourth Dynasty. She is a freelance technical writer with over fifteen years experience who develops realistic and historically based backgrounds for game and story world design, currently working on a supplemental background publication based in the Eighteenth Dynasty royal and political structure.

Sophie Winlaw tutors for the introductory Egyptology course at Macquarie University, Sydney, where she is currently undertaking her Ph.D. in Egyptology with a thesis on the architecture of the Fifth Dynasty *mastaba* tombs at Giza. She has spent two seasons excavating in Egypt with one of the Macquarie University teams at Giza and Saqqara, two of the most prominent sites of the Old Kingdom. Before attaining her masters in Egyptology, she studied at the University of Sydney, where she graduated with honors in Classical and Near Eastern archeology. During her time at the University of Sydney, she also spent two seasons in Cyprus working on a Greco-Roman theatre site excavating and processing some of the finds. She has recently contributed to two Macquarie University publications, which record the findings of these excavations, discussing the architecture of the Giza tombs and the ceramic assemblages found at Saqqara.

Alex Woods is currently working on her Ph.D. through the Department of Ancient History at Macquarie University, Sydney. She also works part-time in the Department of Ancient History as a research assistant, helping to prepare the artwork for research publications by the Australian Centre for Egyptology. Alex has accompanied the Macquarie University team excavating the Teti Cemetery at Saqqara over a number of seasons, and presents educational talks to High School students and community groups on her experiences as a student of Egyptology and life on an archeological excavation. Alex completed her Bachelor of Arts (Honors) in Ancient history, at Macquarie, majoring in Egyptology, and her Ph.D. thesis is on ancient Egyptian art of the Old Kingdom.

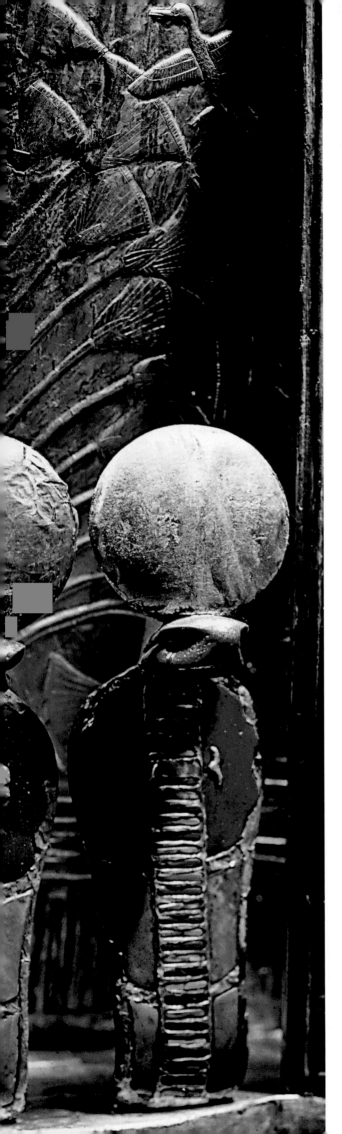

Contents

INTRODUCING ANCIENT EGYPT

Land of the Nile

Land boundaries did not exist in ancient Egyptian times. People were defined by tribal and cultural links instead—from oasis-dwellers and desert traders to city folk; from rich merchants to poor farmers; from the scorching south to the cool north.

Yet the Egyptian people were all linked together by a single feature, the river that gave them all life—the Nile.

The River

Once, in geological times, almost the whole of Egypt was covered by sea, the bodies of sea-creatures being deposited to form the limestone that now covers the area from the Mediterranean coast southward for 300 miles (480 km). This sea was flanked to the east and south by lines of volcanic hills. Their eruptions over time formed great bands of hard stones, granites, and diorites. The heat of lava flows formed beds of quartzes, from amethyst to calcite (Egyptian alabaster) and, of course, gold.

As the sea retreated, the area we today call Egypt was fed by two rivers, both bringing rich silt from the south. As time went on, the western branch silted up, forcing the stream underground where, today, it feeds and connects the line of eastern oases. Today, only the eastern branch is left, the great River Nile, which is arguably the world's longest river.

Rising from three sources in the south and leaping through chasms and gorges, the river's force is mainly spent by the time it enters the alluvial floodplain of northern Africa. Yet without the river, the civilization that we know as ancient Egypt would never have happened.

Flood!

Every year in early summer, torrential rains fell on the mountains of Ethiopia, forming rivulets, which removed rich soil. This soil, baked under an African sun, was deep red, so that the first floodwaters churned and frothed as if they were blood.

The rivulets join together to form the Blue Nile, which joins its larger lazier brother, the White Nile, at Khartoum in the Sudan. The White Nile rises beyond Lake Victoria, and for most of the year was wider and deeper than its northern tributary, but by July, the force of the Blue Nile was so great that the flood-waters dammed back the White Nile as it swung around northward.

By late July, the first floods entered Egypt from the south. The water did not arrive as a bore but rose almost imperceptibly. Fields slowly vanished until one day there was nothing left except sand and dazzling water.

Almost as soon as the floodwaters arrived, they started to decrease once more, the level dropping daily, leaving behind thick, stinking, fertile mud, too soft for ox-driven plows. Men turned out with hand plows to sow the seed behind the inexorably falling waters. As they sowed, they fell ill from heat exhaustion, river blindness, malarial fevers, and death-bearing parasites, but if they did not sow, their land would bake to concrete within hours. Although the flood season lasted for four months, the floodwaters lasted only around ten days at maximum height before beginning to fall away.

The northern sites received their waters later, but the river, now indolent, gave them silt more generously. Richest of all lands, Egypt lacked rainwater, but the Nile gave them all they needed and more. On the

Below **Temple of Luxor, overlooking the River Nile.** Some ceremonies held at the Temple of Luxor incorporated the Nile in the proceedings, acknowledging the importance of the river to the prosperity and survival of the population.

Left **Working in the fields, fresco, Dynasty 18.** The annual flooding of the Nile deposited rich silt on its floodplain, making the area very fertile, and rewarding farmers with fine crops. Most of the population worked in the fields at planting and harvest time.

world—Lake Nasser. Overnight Nubia, with many of its ancient monuments, vanished beneath the gathering waters.

For and Against

The operation of the High Dam brought dramatic results. Electricity from the dam brought the modern era to homes and industries, bringing prosperity, better health care, and longer life spans. Within a decade, the population began its inexorable explosion.

The floods were stopped, so hippos, crocodiles, and other creatures could not cross the dam and were trapped behind the wall, making Egypt a safer place. Lake Nasser became a wildlife haven where animals thrived with no natural predators. But with no soil washed down by the river, Egyptians turned to chemical fertilizers, leaching poison into their river. There was now a higher water table all year round, allowing water to seep into monuments. Within a short time, insects thrived on the still deep waters, bringing infection and misery. Without silt, the north Mediterranean coast began to erode slowly. In the south, clouds formed over the lake for the first time in history, and the average temperature dropped by 10 degrees. The ecology of the land changed forever.

The dam has brought life, prosperity, and health to Egypt. But it has also brought misery, disease, and threat, as the Egyptian people live to the north of a 300 ft (90 m) high wall of water which, if it ever burst open, would obliterate the civilization that we love within seconds.

rich, black, fertile strip, crops would ripen more quickly and fruitfully than any of its neighbors.

Damming the Flow

What the river gave, it could also deny. Sometimes the rain fell heavily; the river rose too high and houses were washed away. Sometimes the rain fell too lightly, and the river scarcely left its bed. In both cases, famine and death would follow.

There was always a dream in men's hearts to control the mighty Nile. The ancients tried to build dam walls to hold back the flow, as great walls in the south demonstrate, but to no avail.

In 1901, a small dam was opened in Aswan, forming a small lake behind it, but still allowing the inundation to occur. The electricity generated proved so useful that within a short time the dam was doubled in height. Ideas were already being formulated for the dam that would finally give control back to Egypt.

After decades of planning and design, the High Dam, or Sadd el-Ali, was finally opened in 1971. Behind it, a lake 300 ft (90 m) deep formed instantly; it was the largest artificial lake in the

Below **Aswan High Dam.** During the 18-year construction of the dam, more than 90,000 people were relocated, and 24 monuments, including the Abu Simbel temples, were dismantled and rebuilt in new locations.

The Black Land

Land boundaries today make Egypt almost as far from east to west as from north to south at its widest points. However, in ancient times, Egypt was defined as little more than the black fertile strip running along each side of the river.

Right **Limestone relief showing Bedouins dying of hunger in the desert.** Though adapted to their harsh environment, the nomadic Bedouins of the desert were at the mercy of nature and—like their riverside counterparts—they perished in times of famine and drought.

Below **Cataracts near Wadi Halfa, 1857 engraving by Louis Libay.** The dangerous rapids and cascades formed by the cataracts of the Nile, such as at Wadi Halfa, were an effective barrier to shipping.

The hills beyond this flat strip, although Egyptian on the side facing the Nile, were deemed to be "foreign." But the divisions between flat land and hills, between black land and desert, were only two of the divisions the Egyptians recognized. There were many cultural differences between north and south, and between those who lived on east and west banks. Immigrant groups, who maintained their own customs, formed many ancient settlements. Even today, the differences between the resulting individual towns are evident.

Egyptians were able to develop securely because they were protected by geography on every side. To the east and west there was open desert that was almost impossible to cross. To the south lay cataracts—rocky outcrops through which shipping could not penetrate. To the north lay marshes and the open sea, with small borders with neighbors on each side. Unlike other civilizations, the Egyptians did not need walled cities, because they felt safe from attack.

Upper Egypt

The south of the land, or the upper reaches of the Nile within Egypt, lies between Luxor and Aswan—this region was known as Upper Egypt. Less fertile than the north and hotter, its archeology is better preserved. In ancient times, its remoteness from the capital and the king meant that it was more independent and, in some periods, even broke away. Today it offers visitors many later monuments and sites to visit, including many temples from the Greco-Roman era.

Middle Egypt

This area lies south of modern Cairo and extends as far as Luxor. This is the least populated area of the country with the smallest fertile strip on each side of the river. Open to the elements, it is often the hottest place in summer and the coldest in the winter months, when there are often frosts. Archeologically many areas of Middle Egypt are still little explored and seldom visited, offering peace and tranquility to those who do venture here, as well as a taste of what ancient Egypt was really like.

Lower Egypt

North of Cairo, the river fans out and vanishes into a multitude of small canals. The land is flat and richly green. Here, the alluvial silt is thickest, the climate more temperate, and the ground the most fertile in the country. Archeologically it is still little known, as land use and damp soils make accessing ancient levels often impossible. Although kings are referred to as "king of Upper and Lower Egypt," so far as

knowledge and archeology are concerned, most of our information comes from the south.

The Oases

This curve of oases follows the line of the lost, subterranean, western branch of the Nile. Here, evidence of the very earliest settlers is generally found. The oasis-dwellers remain, as they have always been, independent of the river-folk, with their own customs and costume. In ancient Egypt, the oasis route was used for military intelligence.

Moving across the desert was never easy. Guided by Bedouins, Cambyses led his army south through the desert, bound for Siwa. Somewhere en route, the entire army vanished, never to be seen again.

Eastern Desert

Volcanic mountains flank the eastern bank of the Nile, with their granites creating one of the most hostile environments anywhere on earth. Here, little survives, scarcely even a blade of grass is found.

The mountains are penetrable only by several marked wadis or dried-up river beds. Temperatures rise to unbearable levels and there is little or no shade. In the east, quarries show very ancient working of hard stones, going back to Predynastic times. From the New Kingdom onward, the area was exploited for its gold—but this was a death sentence to those sent to work there. The Romans used Egyptian labor to extract porphyry from here— the purplish red stone prized by its emperors.

Egyptian Dependencies

From time immemorial, Egypt controlled areas of land beyond its own natural frontiers and inhabited by peoples very different from the Egyptians. These lands suffered for many centuries during Egypt's occupation and took every opportunity to rebel.

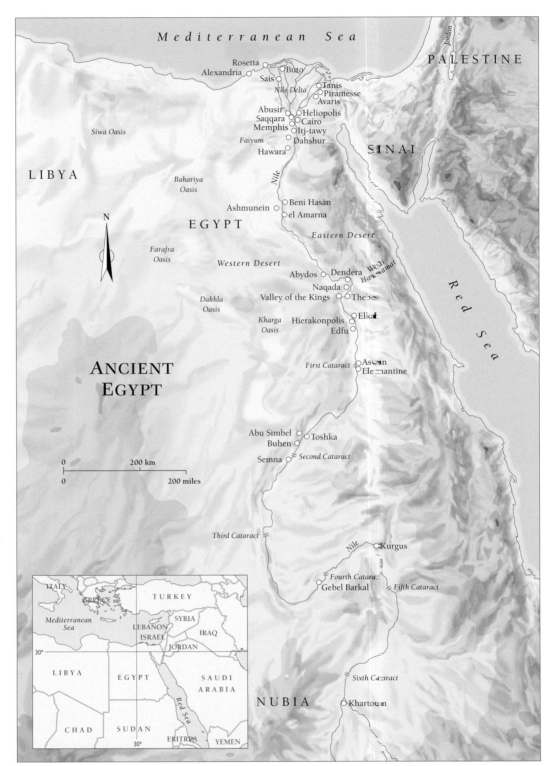

Chief of these areas was Nubia, to the south of Egypt. Nubia was itself divided into Wawat or Lower Nubia, and Kush, or Upper Nubia. For many periods of Egyptian history, Aswan was part of Wawat and not Egypt.

Another area deemed to be Egyptian was Sinai. Egyptian exploitation of the copper mines at Serabit el-Khadim degraded the landscape by cutting down and burning any locally available timber to use in furnaces.

Ancient Historians

Egyptians had little interest either in the history of their land or in their background. They believed they developed from the First Occasion, the time of Creation, when theirs was the first culture created by the gods.

Right **Fresco depicting Creation of the world, Dynasty 21**. This fresco depicts part of the story told by priests of Heliopolis, in which Geb, god of earth, separates from Nut, goddess of sky, during the Creation of the world.

Below **Granite statue of Tutankhamun, Dynasty 18**. Tutankhamun, one of the most well-known of all ancient Egyptian rulers, was given the coronation name of Nebkheperura.

Despite this, they did not have a starting point for their history but created dates from the length of time the current king had been ruling. They seemed to have had no interest in what happened before their own time.

Dates from Sites

While it may be thought that objects and monuments, which survive in great quantities, would tell us almost everything about the ancient Egyptians, this is far from true. The monuments belong to kings, not peasants, and reflect even then his public face, not his private face. Objects tell us "how," but seldom "why." Names of kings inform us when the inscription or object dated from, but give us no date. Dates list the year, season, month, and day of a king, but we have no indication when this date might be in absolute terms. When two families ruled together in different places at the same time; or when two kings ruled side by side, courtiers would always be loyal to only one, and thus only the king they served is named. Overlaps, or co-regencies, are never recorded. We do not know how long any king ruled. Today, an inscription may give us the highest date for a king; tomorrow, another inscription may be found with another date that is higher, and our history has to be rewritten.

So where do we get our names and dates from?

King-lists

Several lists of names of kings have survived—two from Abydos, one from Karnak, and one from Saqqara. It may be thought that these help—but, in fact, they are limited in use. Firstly, we know Egyptian kings by the name they were given at birth—Rameses, Tutankhamun, or Thutmose, for instance. However, Egyptians gave their kings a unique name at their coronation, such as Usermaatra Setepenra, Nebkheperura, or Aakheperkara. Egyptian kings were never given a number—this is the habit of modern history. So there was no Rameses II, for instance.

King-lists always contain only the kings' coronation names. Sometimes we find it hard to match up the names on lists with the names of the kings as we know them. In addition, every king-list was written to explain the line of descent of a particular king—in three instances out of four, from Rameses II. Hence the writer would omit names that were disapproved—so many were omitted, including all women and many families, such as the Amarna Kings. These lists never contain any reign-lengths.

Palermo Stone

The Palermo Stone is a fragmentary black diorite stone that contains year-by-year accounts of kings' reigns up to the Fifth Dynasty.

Rather like an ancient Doomsday Book, it contains items of historical and economic importance. However, the stone is broken, and the kings are shown only wearing the crown of Lower Egypt, so presumably the account comes from Lower Egypt and not Upper Egypt; so although useful for names, reign-lengths, and succession of kings, it is limited. We do not know its purpose.

Turin Canon of Kings

The Turin Canon, a papyrus written in the Ramessid period, was found in the workmen's village of Deir el-Medina. It contained a taxation list, and on its reverse was a list of names of kings from the start of Egyptian history to the end of the Old Kingdom, together with a series of dates, giving years, months, and days. At the foot, in red, is marked the number 995. However, we do not know who wrote the list or why—it may have been a very inaccurate student writing for an examination, or a priest carefully copying a list for state archives.

The papyrus is extremely fragmentary, having broken at some point after being found and before arriving into the museum in Palermo. Scholars are constantly trying to match up microscopic clues to put it back together in its right order.

While it is generally assumed that the red "995" is the number of years to the end of the Old Kingdom, this is stated nowhere. Nevertheless, the Turin Canon is still one of the best pieces of historical evidence that we have.

Manetho

When the first King Ptolemy came to rule Egypt, the Macedonian family had no idea about Egypt's long past. A priest from the delta, Manetho, was chosen to write a history for them.

Manetho was the first person to divide the kings into dynasties, in the order that we still maintain to this day.

However, his original manuscript is lost to us. All that survives are quotations in the works of other writers, and these are frequently contradictory. We do not know what sources he had available to him, nor how accurate was his copying.

We do not know what language he originally wrote in—Ptolemy I and II spoke no Egyptian, while all archives would have been in Egyptian. So did Manetho speak Greek and translate the sources into Greek before writing his account? Was it written in Egyptian and translated later? More importantly, Manetho used the coronation names of the Egyptian kings and wrote these into Greek.

Undoubtedly Manetho's original history was a fine piece of work; however, the versions that we have available to us today are far from clear.

Above **Rameses II relief, Temple of Sety I, Abydos.** Beloved and popular, the example set by Rameses II during his reign became the benchmark many successors tried to emulate.

Left **Section of the Turin Canon.** Though broken into many often discrete and tiny pieces, and written by an unknown author, the Turin Canon or Turin King-list, is one of the best clues yet to the reign-lengths of the Egyptian kings.

Propaganda and Politics

What is defined today as "history" is always colored by subjective views, by a determination to persuade the reader that our version is the only correct one. Yet even today, there can be no single accepted account of something that happens in our own time.

Given these problems of interpretation, it is all the more difficult to write of events that happened hundreds, if not thousands, of years ago. In most areas of archeology, fragmentary objects coupled with scientific correlation results in some factual basis for discussion. Slowly an "accepted" version becomes favored. However, in ancient Egypt, we are faced with far more information than most archeologists could ever dream of obtaining. Ironically, this makes the field more difficult.

History, as a scientific study, began in the Greek era, when philosophers started to question who we were, and the purpose of our existence. To find who we are, we need to find out who our ancestors were, how they lived, and what happened to them. The first man ever to investigate this was Herodotus.

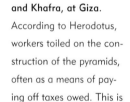

Below **Pyramids of Khufu and Khafra, at Giza.** According to Herodotus, workers toiled on the construction of the pyramids, often as a means of paying off taxes owed. This is known as a corvée system.

Herodotus

Little is known of the historical Herodotus, save that he was born in modern Turkey around the turn of the fifth century BCE.

The mainland Greek states were only in their infancy and Herodotus wanted to know who the Greeks were and how they came to live where they did. He wrote nine books of *Histories*, a word which meant "stories" rather than an academic study. Believing that the Egyptians were among the oldest races on earth, he visited Egypt almost a century before Alexander arrived and made it a Greek colony. Herodotus devoted the whole of his Book Two to an examination of the Egyptians.

It is entirely frustrating that he was one of the few eyewitnesses whose accounts we have to the remnants of living ancient Egyptian culture and yet wrote so few things that really help us. Yet

from the viewpoint of Herodotus, he was not aiming to describe Egypt, but only to explain how the Greeks may have descended from them.

We know that he did not speak Egyptian, and so he must have stayed with a Greek-speaking family in a Greek settlement, of which, we know archeologically, there were several. As a result, his "knowledge"—which came from people to whom he spoke—came from second-hand immigrant sources and not from Egyptians at all. He constantly records "what he was told." Whenever he describes a place, he adds "and I speak here as a witness"—and invariably even the physical things he describes are incorrect. He states that he saw the site from which the Nile originated, a cave between two mountains from whence the emerging water flowed both north and south. This clearly derives from an Egyptian legend of a water source, Hapi, secreted in a cave, and not from any eyewitness account. Even his descriptions of pyramids are mistaken, since he states that "their width is equal to their height"—something a mere measuring may have corrected.

It is surprising, given so many problems, that Herodotus is still relied on today in describing ancient Egypt. His description of the mummification system is still accepted even though, as a foreigner, he would not have been allowed to see it, and is still believed, thanks to him, that slaves working a corvée system built pyramids.

In the formative years of Egyptology, scholars had to use evidence that was available to them. Today, we are able to discern more readily between information that is valid and that which is hearsay, but this has come from years of experience and a great deal of evidence.

Herodotus has colored much of our thinking today. Other writers followed him—Diodorus Siculus and Strabo among others. These accounts were often supported, to an extent, by accounts in the Bible, Torah, and Koran, all of which described Egyptians as pagan polytheists who were also brutal taskmasters.

The Continuing Search

Archeology is helping us still to understand which of the sources available to us were written deliberately to color our thinking—such as religious accounts, which were written to support an argument of their own—such as the books of Herodotus; and which have been distorted and misunderstood—such as the writings of Manetho. Some sources we are still trying to understand—inscriptions and images on walls, for instance, which tell us a very biased account of life.

Despite what often seems a wonderful and rich array of information, in truth we still have little more than, as one writer stated, "rags and tatters." There is more to be found—not all of it lies under the sand in Egypt. Some of it may be buried in a museum or collection near to you. Every piece tells a story and adds to the puzzle that we are trying to piece together. Slowly, we are finding the pieces that do not belong; but until more pieces are discovered, our overall picture is little more than guesswork.

Left **Israel Stela, Dynasty 19**. Stelae inscriptions reveal much about the ancient Egyptians and their relationships with neighboring peoples. This famous stela bears the first known reference to Israel.

Below **Wall inscription, Great Hypostyle Hall, Karnak**. Preserved in stone, this inscription bears testament to the victories of Rameses II.

Dating the Pharaohs

Many Egyptologists, with many lifetimes of experience and much expertise, have written the accounts that follow in this book. They tell you, between them, a remarkable story, a story that is as up-to-date as study allows.

Right **Scribe's New Year seal**. New Year was a time of great celebration, signalling the coming of the Nile floods.

Below **Stela of Lady Taparet, Dynasty 22**. This stela depicts the sun-god at sunset and the night sky. The ancient Egyptians used celestial positioning as a guide to the seasons.

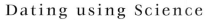

However our knowledge is growing every day. One of the constant problems we have to face every day is establishing when something actually happened. Books will always give you dates; but if you compare any two books on ancient Egypt, you will find that they often contradict each other. How can this be? As you have seen, the information on which we base our history is fragmentary. Names can be Greek or Egyptian, birth names or coronation names. But surely dates should all be the same?

Dating by Comparisons

Today we date using CE—current era; and BCE—before current era; and most peoples of the world accept that we are living in the twenty-first century.

In theory, calculating back from the present year, year 1 CE followed year 1 BCE. But nothing exists which shows us this change—it was a theory devised in the medieval period. So you will never find an object that bears an exact date—we have to calculate these dates.

One easy way to do this is by comparing information. So if a king A wrote to a king B, we know they were alive at the same time. If you dig a site in Greece and find an Egyptian ring with a king's name on it, then the Greek site has to have been built after the reign of this king. This is called comparative dating, but it does not give us exact or absolute dates.

Dating using Science

Where archeological objects do not survive well, scientific tests have been developed to find out the dates of some objects. These tests include dendrochronology, or "tree-ring dating;" thermoluminescence, or "heat-dating;" and Carbon-14 dating, or "radioactive dating."

Tree-ring dating requires substantial wood finds, together with a sequence of trees of known ages. The thickness of rings of growth is measured and can be compared with other pieces of wood to obtain an exact date when that tree grew. In Egypt, there were few large trees, no sequence of dateable trees and relatively few wooden finds, so this method is unsuitable.

Thermoluminescence tests determine when a pottery vessel

was last heated. You need a dateable sequence of pottery to do this. It is an expensive method, and is often inaccurate. We have vast quantities of pottery from ancient Egypt, none of it proving helpful in a dating context, as it lies around on the sand for centuries.

Carbon-14 is a radioactive isotope of carbon that is present in every growing organism. When the organism dies, it then decays at a known half-life. A carbon sample from any organic material can be tested, its surviving carbon-14 element counted, and this compared to a chart to check the decay rate. This result establishes a date.

Unfortunately carbon-14 does not decay at a steady progressive rate, but slows and speeds at intervals. This gives an area of doubt in dates, for instance, 1350 ± 50 years. However, this area of "vagueness" increases to obtain the greatest accuracy for a date. So 1350 ± 50 years provides you only an accuracy of 51 percent. To get an accuracy of 98 percent, the date would likely be 1350 ± 250 years. This is too vague for Egyptian use.

Sothic Cycle Dates

Luckily, we have one tried and tested method for establishing dates. The first day of the New Year was the rising of the inundation or flood.

Farmers would be awaiting the waters with eagerness, ready to start work and for fresh water and new foods. They noted, at some point in antiquity, that one of the brightest stars in the night sky, Sirius, or Sothis, reappeared after being hidden from view at exactly the time that the inundation occurred. So at the sighting of Sirius, the parties for the New Year started.

Unfortunately the state calendar, run by government officials, was divided into 365 days. They omitted the quarter-day that we account for by adding one extra day to our year every fourth year. So in the first year of the state calendar, Sirius would appear, the flood would come and the state would announce New Year's Day. Four years later, the state announced it one day before Sirius and the flood came. Another four years, and it was two days out. In fact, the two calendars only coincided once every 1460 years!

We know that the calendars coincided in 159 CE. Several Egyptian texts record the coming of the flood and the date in the state calendar when this happened. By counting backward from 159 CE, we can calculate the exact year when the event happened. By using the known reign-lengths of kings, we can start to work out which king reigned and when.

As you can see, working out dates for this book has not been easy! It has taken a great number of scholars many years and a lot of work to get this far.

We hope that you will enjoy walking through the world of ancient Egypt with us to guide you; and if sometimes the names and dates we use are not the same as those you find somewhere else, we hope you will understand.

Centuries from now, future scholars will no doubt look down upon us as mere beginners. We can only say that great buildings grow upon the strongest foundations; and in this book, we have combined to give you these foundations.

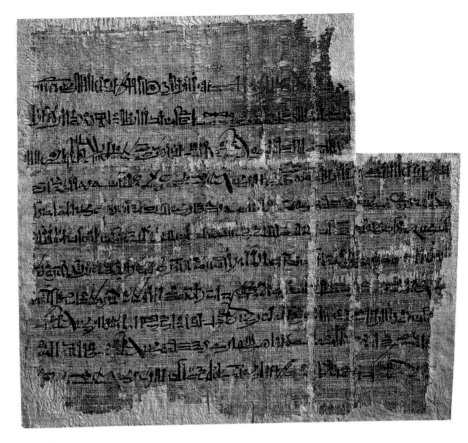

Above **Account of the Battle of Qadesh.** This papyrus details the Battle of Qadesh—a battle fought between Rameses II and his army against the Hittite forces of King Muwatalli. Such accounts assist researchers in calculating dates in Egyptian history.

Left **Bronze statue of the goddess Sothis.** The goddess Sothis (representing the Dog Star, Sirius) was associated with the coming of the Nile floods—an event that coincided with the sighting of this bright star in the night sky.

ORIGINS: PREDYNASTIC AND EARLY

DYNASTIC EGYPT

Introduction

In the past, Egyptology focused largely on the study of the Pharaonic Period, from the Old Kingdom to the end of the Ramessid Period (2686–1069 BCE). Now, however, we are delving further back, to the very roots of Egyptian civilization.

Right An early stone palette, c. 3100 BCE. This palette, with bird or other animal heads, dates from the Late Predynastic Period.

Below Ages-old Egyptian agricultural methods. With the rise of agriculture in the earliest times came a settled culture and centralized state, laying the seeds for one of the greatest civilizations.

Only in the last 50 years has research into Egypt's earliest phase of occupation become a significant area of study. The Predynastic Period (c. 5300–3000 BCE) and Early Dynastic Period (c. 3000–2686 BCE) represent a time when the foundations were laid for the development of later Egyptian culture. To grasp the roots of Egyptian civilization, we must understand how and why Egypt developed from a simple prehistoric society into a powerful nation-state.

Scholars Working Together

The construction of the Aswan Dam and the consequent salvage operation in Nubia to save ancient monuments from destruction was a turning point in the discipline of Egyptology, with experts from a variety of fields—anthropologists, prehistorians and specialist scientists—all contributing. Scholars wanted to understand the development of Egyptian civilization from its earliest roots and examine the first humans to inhabit the Nile Valley and its surrounding deserts. This meant delving into the scattered remains of the Paleolithic Period (c. 700,000–7000 years ago) and the activities of hunter-gatherer societies that were far removed from the later Egyptian civilization.

As Egyptology became more scientific, the value of excavating the sparse remains of settlement sites was recognized. Archeologists had formerly focused on excavating cemetery sites that commonly produced more spectacular finds, but there was an increasing realization that Egyptian society could not be fully understood from an analysis of mortuary evidence alone.

Michael Hoffman and his work at the settlement site of Hierakonpolis represents a significant advance in the study of the Predynastic Period. He approached his work in a holistic way, attempting to understand settlement patterns in combination with geographic and climatic conditions. In the last twenty years this study in settlement archeology has greatly improved our knowledge of prehistoric society, the development of sedentary agricultural communities, the rise of complex society, and, most significantly, the process of state formation.

An Emerging Nation

Crucial excavation work undertaken in the Delta and in Lower Egypt has also provided a more balanced interpretation of the events leading up to the formation of the Egyptian state. It now appears that Upper and Lower Egypt each developed independent communities that were in contact through trade. Moreover, the transition from small regional villages to a country controlled by a centralized state administration

was a long and drawn-out process that came about due to a multitude of inter-connecting factors.

Other areas that have been the focus of recent research are related to the rise of complex society in the Nile Valley and the archeological evidence that can shed light on this issue. For example, craft special-ization has become an area of interest as it represents a shift from domestic pro-duction to more organized industries, which are clear indicators of a growing inequality in society and a developing elite, as well as the birth of a monarchy.

Kings and Commoners

The continuing work on the remains in combina-tion with the earliest administrative and artistic records from the Early Dynastic Period has enabled a more enlight-ened analysis of the First and Second Dynasties (3000–2686 BCE) to emerge. In particular, the work by the German Archaeological Institute at the royal cemetery at Abydos has clarified the sequence of the kings of the First Dynasty, as well as the connection between these early kings and the rulers of Dynasty 0. It is now widely accepted that the Early Dynastic kings were successors of the Dynasty 0 ruling family from the city of Thinis, probably located near Abydos.

The nature of the kings belonging to the Second Dynasty is also being re-evaluated in the light of recent discoveries of at least two large rock-cut tombs at Saqqara, which appear to belong to several of these little-known rulers.

Recent Early Dynastic archeology has also attempted to understand the lives of ordinary Egyptians by studying their tombs. For example,

Left **Signs of life**. Early Egyptian settlements, often based around oases, grew by making the best use they could of the limited resources available to them.

at the cemetery of Helwan, near Cairo, an Australian archeological team is reassessing the evidence from this site, which includes the graves of the lower- to middle-class individuals from the Early Dynastic capital city of Memphis. It is hoped that the culture of early Egyptian society can be better understood, and that attempts will be made to gain further insights into the Second Dynasty.

Although there have been major advances in the understanding of the Predynastic and Early Dynastic periods, it is only through continuing efforts to excavate important archeological sites that a more complete picture of this crucial time period can be achieved.

THE FIRST SETTLERS
Early Humans

Stones, bone and ivory tools, fishing hooks, and human remains are the evidence we use to learn of Egypt's people in the Paleolithic Period. These artefacts are found in three areas: The Nile Valley, the Sahara, and the Sinai Peninsula.

Excavations of Paleolithic sites have uncovered many remnants of human occupation, allowing Egyptologists to gain a better understanding of the early inhabitants of the region and the cultural evolution that took place.

There are three clear cultural stages in the Paleolithic Period: The Lower, Middle, and Upper Paleolithic, with each one characterized by the development of different cultural artefacts, from the most basic of stone axes to evidence of more advanced domestic settlement.

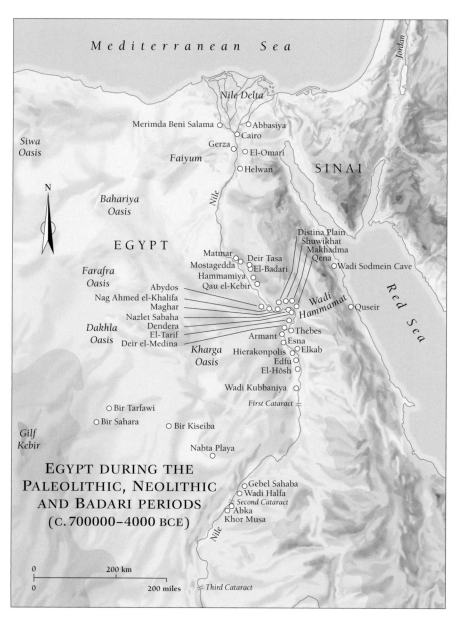

EGYPT DURING THE
PALEOLITHIC, NEOLITHIC
AND BADARI PERIODS
(C. 700000–4000 BCE)

Lower Paleolithic

The earliest stone tools found in the Nile Valley, dating back hundreds of thousands of years, are handaxes, very simple tools made from striking flakes off a stone with a pebble to produce a sharp edge. The handaxe had many functions, including cutting, chopping, digging, hacking, and hunting. These tools are also known in other parts of the world and are called "Acheulean" (after Saint Acheul in France, where the first tools of this kind were found). Acheulean artefacts were found in the Nile Valley at Abbassiya near Cairo, at Sohâg and Dendera near Qena, and in many localities in the Western Desert, Red Sea hills and Sinai.

The presence of these tools suggests that humans occupied these areas all those years ago. We know also, from studying other regions of the world, that humans in the Lower Paleolithic stage would have belonged to *Homo erectus*. However, no human bodily remains dating to this period have so far been discovered in Egypt.

Middle Paleolithic

The earliest Middle Paleolithic sites in Egypt date to around 140,000 years ago at Bir Terfawi and Bir Sahara in the Western Desert. The tools from this phase include handaxes, scrapers and flakes. Some stone tools, especially from the Western Desert, show influence of and interaction with cultures in other parts of North Africa.

The remains associated with Middle Paleolithic artefacts were probably created by Neanderthal man or early *Homo sapiens*. In 1994, at the site of Taramsa Hill near Qena in Upper Egypt, the remains of the earliest human burial in Egypt were found. This site was a mine to quarry chert for stone tools during this period. The human remains belonged to a *Homo sapiens* child and date to around 55,000 years ago.

Upper Paleolithic

The transition from the Middle to Upper Paleolithic was characterized by the production of new kinds of stone tools, blades, and bladelets,

which had already begun to appear in the Middle Paleolithic. Few Upper Paleolithic sites have been reported in the Nile Valley and Sinai. Nazlet Khater 4 (NK4), a quarrying site near Sohâg dating to around 32,000 years ago, is one of the earliest Upper Paleolithic sites in the Nile Valley. Nearby, the burial site of the second-earliest human discovered in Egypt was found.

The Western Desert has a long history of human activity. Furthermore, the recently discovered plant and animal remains at the former lake of Nabta Playa in the Western Desert, and the appearance of presumably domestic cattle perhaps as early as 11,000 years ago, indicate there were human activities during this time and that the Egyptian Sahara was indeed not lifeless.

Out of Africa?

The issue of when, where and how modern humans evolved has for decades been a subject of fierce scholarly debate. Charles Darwin was the first to point to Africa as the origin of humankind because the closest primate relatives of humans lived there.

There are two theories regarding the origin of humankind: The "Out of Africa" theory, based on the hypothesis that *Homo sapiens* developed in Africa more than 100,000 years ago and then migrated into Europe and Asia; and the

"Multiregional" theory, based on the hypothesis that *Homo erectus* migrated from Africa over a million years ago and settled in different regions of Europe and Asia and then evolved into modern humans with racial differences.

Current archeological evidence does not support the "Out of Africa" theory, because there is no evidence for the complete replacement of both Neanderthal man and *Homo erectus* by *Homo sapiens*. Some archeological findings show that they co-existed for some time.

The First Egyptians

The ethnic origin of the ancient Egyptians has also been the subject of debate for many decades. Scholars described the ancient Egyptians as either being "white", of Asiatic origin, or of African origin. There is not, unfortunately, enough evidence from the earliest pre-historic stages to find a satis-factory answer to this question.

Given Egypt's position between the two continents of Asia and Africa, and the intensive exchange between the regions from early prehistoric times, it is possible that the ethnic origins of early Egyptians lie in both continents.

Above **The Nile at dawn, near the Valley of the Kings.** The Nile has long supported human life, but erosion caused by the river itself has destroyed much of the evidence of early settlement.

Above **Prehistoric Egyptian harpoon hooks.** These tools show a great advance from the simple handaxes of the Lower Paleolithic period.

When the Desert Bloomed

The climate of a land influences everything from plant and animal life to human activity. Egypt's climate today is hyper-arid, with little rainfall during the winter months, and normally mild temperatures. But this was not always the case.

During Egypt's prehistory, the climate was very different to how it is now, enabling the first Egyptians to live and move in areas that are largely inhabitable desert today.

Climate Change

The evidence for climatic change during Egypt's prehistory comes from the areas directly adjacent to the Nile Valley—the scattered shallow basins in the Western Desert that were once sources of water, and the various oases, especially the Faiyum Oasis.

Recent studies of rocks and sediments in North Africa have revealed that the Sahara Desert has alternated between wetter and drier phases over the last 20,000 years. The current dry phase only began around 4,500 years ago; before that, for a period of some 3,500 years, what is now desert received enough rainfall to support animal and human life, at least on a seasonal basis. Only when the rainfall belt began to shift southwards did the grasslands to the west and east of the Nile Valley start to dry out, eventually giving rise to the desert we see today. In other words, between 6000 and 3500 BCE the Eastern Desert would have been a savannah-like zone, humid enough to support the kinds of animals we see in prehistoric rock art.

Recent studies of the paleoclimate suggest that, during the Pleistocene Age (c. 2,000,000–10,000 years ago), the climate in Egypt was arid, with more rainfall in the Sahara and the western oases than in the Nile Valley itself. Rainfall during the Paleolithic Period was much higher than at present, though it probably never exceeded 8–12 in (200–300 mm) annually.

A significant wet phase, which began before 7000 BCE, was interrupted by drier stages and ended between 2900 and 2350 BCE. For example, charred wood remains from the Gilf Kebir, a vast limestone and sandstone plateau in the

Above **Limestone relief of a man feeding an antelope, c. 2400 BCE.** The antelope was just one of many animals found in Egypt in the days before all was desert.

southwest of Egypt, suggest that between 8,000 and 4,000 years ago water was seasonally available and nomadic people would have found the area favorable to live and move around in.

Changes in the climate started toward the end of the Neolithic Period and during the Predynastic Period, with a rainfall of 2–4 in (50–100 mm) annually, and were accompanied by a decline in the Nile floods and an increase in aridity. A major reduction in Nile floods began around 3800 BCE (during the Naqada I Period), and continued into the Early Dynastic Period.

A number of environmental changes also had an effect on the temperature. Although not much is known regarding the temperature changes during the Paleolithic Period, the study of vertebrae of fish found at Hierakonpolis shows that there was a slight increase in the annual winter temperature during the Predynastic Period.

Animal and Plant Life

With the climatic change came a change in animal and plant life. Hunting and gathering was the main source of food in the Paleolithic Period, as shown by the extensive animal and plant remains found.

During the prehistoric period a wide range of wild animals and a rich spectrum of edible plants inhabited the Nile Valley and adjacent regions. Excavations at the prehistoric sites of Bir Terfawi (west of the Nile Valley), Deir el-Fakhuri in the Isna area, Wadi Kubbaniya, and Nabta Playa, have yielded numerous remains.

Hippos and Hartebeests

Remains have been found of a startling array of animals: White rhinoceros, an extinct Pleistocene camel, wild ass, different species of gazelle, antelopes

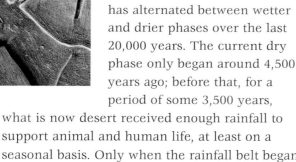

of various sizes, wild cattle about twice the size of modern cattle, hartebeest, hippopotamus, scimitar horned oryx, giraffe, African elephant, African wild cat, North African porcupine, fox, golden jackal, warthog, ostrich, turtle, striped hyena, striped ground squirrel, Barbary sheep, goat, cope or brown hare, and birds of different sizes.

For early inhabitants of the Nile Valley fish was also an essential part of the diet. The most important species was the catfish, harvested in great quantities during its annual spawn, believed to occur at the beginning of the flood. Remains of large catfish over 2 ft (60 cm) long were found, as well as Nile perch, barb fish, a kind of water snail, and molluscs.

Nutgrass and Dom Palms

Archeological evidence suggests there was a savannah-type grassland to support both animal species and humans. Plant remains include a broad spectrum of species, including wild nutgrass (a type of sedge, a soft starchy vegetable), fern, dom palm, wild wheat and barley. Also, grinding stones and sickle blades with a glossy sheen (the result of silica from cut grass stems), appear in the late Upper Paleolithic.

These favorable conditions would have facilitated human inhabitants to adapt and modify their subsistence accordingly. This also enabled them to experiment with the domestication of animals and the cultivation of plants, which led them into the Neolithic Period.

Left **Predynastic art.** This charming carving of a gazelle, c. 3100 BCE, is made of calcite, also known as "Egyptian alabaster."

Below **More than an oasis.** The Eastern Desert, in which today one can find only the occasional oasis, was once a savannah-like zone where animals roamed.

From Hunters to Farmers

The shift from hunting and gathering to food production was one of the most important cultural transitions in early Egypt. The origins of agriculture lie in the desert adjacent to the Nile Valley, from a time when there was enough rainfall for wild grain to grow.

Below **Precious water.**
An oryx takes a drink while it can. The supply of water, particularly from the Nile, dictated changes in early Egyptian farming and society.

Exactly how farming methods that allowed for the development of food production came to the Nile Valley is not known, but the archeological evidence points to two possible sources.

Origins of Farming
The first is southeast Asia, where agriculture began around 9000 BCE, and became well established by around 7000 BCE. The evidence suggests that the farming patterns in early Egypt were based on the adaptation of crops and livestock originally domesticated in southeast

Asia, and over time some indigenous African plants were added to the economy. On the other hand, recent discoveries of Neolithic communities in the Eastern Sahara point to the Western Desert as the possible origin of agriculture and animal domestication in ancient Egypt.

The archeological evidence from the Western Desert and its various oases indicates that there were moist conditions from around 7500 to 4700 BCE. This period was associated with the human occupation of almost all the Egyptian oases by hunter-gatherers and in the south by herders

of cattle. In Nabta Playa, two kinds of cultivated barley were identified in a Neolithic context dating to around 6100 BCE. On the other hand, in the Nile Valley the earliest evidence of agriculture dates to about 5000 BCE, and consists of cultivated crops and domesticated livestock found at the Faiyum Oasis and in the Delta.

Fertile Flood

While crops were mostly non-Egyptian in origin, the farming techniques were Egyptian. Two different types of farming existed, one based on the natural patterns of the Nile flood, and the other, less common due to the increasingly arid climate, relying only on natural rainfall. Neolithic villages were situated on slightly higher land, and during the inundation of the Nile they would have looked like islands surrounded by the flooded fields.

There is evidence to suggest that crops were first cultivated casually by people who were still hunter-gatherers and who had the choice of a range of subsistence strategies due to very favorable environmental conditions. Early Neolithic settlements were loosely organized with a low population density, and were often seasonal. The plowing season in ancient Egypt was short, since the land was in an ideal condition for farming for a very limited time.

Crops cultivated by the early farmers included emmer wheat, barley, peas, lentils, and flax. Grains were harvested using flint-bladed hand sickles fixed into wooden sickles, and were probably cleaned by sieving, before being stored in basket-lined storage pits, as practised in the Neolithic sites of Faiyum A, Merimda Beni Salama, and el-Omari.

Animal Husbandry

The animals used by the ancient Egyptians during the Neolithic Period were of two sorts: Domestic and wild. While wild animals such as fish, fowl, hippopotamus, oryx, gazelle, and elephant continued to contribute to the subsistence economy of the period, most of the animal resources for meat, skins, fibers, feathers, dairy products, and labor were obtained from domesticated animals such as cattle, sheep, goats, and pigs.

The choice of the species to be domesticated was mainly based on the temper of the animal; this eliminated some species like gazelle

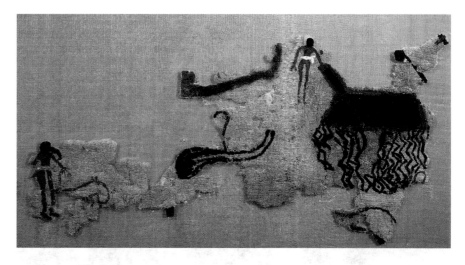

EARLY HOUSES

Early houses varied from simple round or oval huts to mud-brick rectangular houses with storage facilities. The houses were often partly subterranean, with a flexible structure of wattle and daub. Their walls were usually coated with a mixture of mud and chopped straw. A clay house model in el-Amra from the Naqada II Period represents a rectangular house with slightly concave walls. The door, shaped in a raised relief, is surmounted by a lintel resembling a wooden beam. In the upper part of the door there is a roll, probably representing a mat curtain (an architectural element that became common during the Pharaonic Period). Two double windows are located on the opposite side of the door.

Above **An early dwelling.** This delicate cloth fragment depicting two men and a simple hut dates from around 4000 BCE in the Predynastic Period. It was found in the necropolis at El Gebelein, from which it was taken to form part of one of the world's most significant collections, at the Egyptian Museum in Turin, Italy.

and deer, because they are not suitable for herding. Among the early domesticated animals in ancient Egypt were sheep, goats, cattle, water buffalo, pigs, donkeys, cats, and dogs.

Animal domestication in ancient Egypt began for several different reasons, including the need for additional resources due to population growth and environmental changes, and the need for a reliable source of meat, dairy, and labor. Animal husbandry proved to be more productive and reliable than hunting. It also had a social impact on the community, as social ties were often established with the exchange of animals.

Once the inhabitants of the Nile Valley had proceeded into a fully developed Neolithic society with permanent villages, animal husbandry, plant cultivation, and pottery production, this mode of subsistence would not change for the next several thousands of years of Egyptian civilization.

Left **Vessel from the Naqada I Period, c. 4000–3500 BCE.** Part of the magnificent Egyptian collection in the Louvre, Paris, this vessel is incised with a drawing of a antelope-like animal.

Life in the Oases

The archeological evidence indicates that the western oases—particularly Dakhla and Faiyum—through their contacts with the Nile Valley, contributed greatly to the early development of the Neolithic and Predynastic cultures in Egypt.

Right **Spearhead, c. 5500 BCE.** Inhabitants of the western oases in this period were still mainly hunters, and would have made use of weapons such as this.

More than this, these two oases fulfilled a critical role by acting as points of contact between the Nile Valley and cultures in North Africa.

Dakhla Oasis

Dakhla Oasis is located to the south of the Western Desert. It is believed that the Dakhla was occupied by hunter-gatherers during the Paleolithic Period, and that the area was probably abandoned during a hyper-arid period due to climatic changes between 50,000 and 12,000 years ago.

During the Holocene Period (10,000–2200 BCE) three local prehistoric cultures are attested: The Masara, Bashendi, and Sheikh Muftah. The Masara (c. 7200–6500 BCE) corresponds to the Epi-paleolithic Period in the Nile Valley. The inhabitants were highly mobile hunter-gatherers and their flint tools included burins, scrapers, blades, and flakes. During Bashendi A (5700–5000 BCE), the area was also inhabited by hunter-gatherers. The material remains of their culture include fine bifacial knives, hearths, a variety of arrowheads, grinding stones, ostrich eggshell beads, and animal bones identified as coming from wild species.

Bashendi B (4550–3250 BCE) indicates a transition to the Neolithic, with findings of faunal remains mostly of domesticated cattle and goat; stone tools such as knives, arrowheads, and polished axes; and beads, marine shell pendants, and bracelets. Sheikh Muftah is a Neolithic culture which began during the Bashendi Period and continued to overlap with the Old Kingdom occupation in the oasis. Their tools included piercers, scrapers, arrowheads, rectangular knives, sickles, grinding stones, and copper fragments. Pottery was also found, including shreds that resemble the black-topped ware of the Nile Valley.

Faiyum Oasis

The Faiyum Oasis is 50 miles (80 km) southwest of Cairo. In ancient times, the Faiyum was the delta of an earlier version of the Nile. The oasis developed around a vast freshwater lake—Lake Qarun (also known as Moeris)—which lay at the heart of the oasis. The lake was linked to the Nile by a channel (Bahr Yussef), and therefore was flooded annually along with the Nile. It has been suggested that, at the times when the flood receded, the bottom of the lake would have been exposed and the areas around the lake's shores would have been teeming with plant and animal life.

The excavations in the Faiyum Oasis have yielded two cultural phases at the site: An Epi-paleolithic Phase (Faiyum B), and a Neolithic Phase (Faiyum A).

Below **A farming life.** The shift from hunting to farming began around 5000 BCE at locations such as the Faiyum Oasis. By the time of this tomb illustration (c. 1200 BCE) it was the dominant way of life.

During Faiyum B (c. 8000 BCE), the site was occupied by highly mobile hunter-gatherers around the perimeter of the lake, who relied heavily on fishing from its waters—this is indicated by the large number of fish bones (mainly Nile catfish), and small, bladed stone tools discovered. They also hunted wild gazelle, hartebeest, hippopotamus, and other animals. No remains of domesticated animals were found, and the plant remains were mainly reeds and other marsh and swamp plants.

Establishing a Culture

By the time of Faiyum A (c. 5000 BCE) people continued to rely on fishing, and hunted wild animals such as hartebeest, gazelle, hare, cattle, hippopotamus, elephant, and crocodile. Yet they now also had some domesticated animals such as cattle, sheep, goats, and pigs, and domestic plants, including emmer wheat and barley.

Faiyum A sites have not yielded significant evidence for houses, except for a few possible traces of postholes, a large number of hearths and basket-lined granary pits used as storage facilities, potsherds, and stone tools. It has been suggested, however, that people lived in reed huts similar to those at Merimda Beni Salama.

Stone artefacts of the Faiyum A include flake tools, bifacial tools, polished and flaked axes, bifacial sickle blades, knives, arrowheads, grinding stones, stone discs and amazonite beads. Also found were small bone objects, such as needles, pins, and borers, as well as ostrich eggshells.

The pottery of the Faiyum A was of a coarse material with a high amount of straw and no decoration. It includes cups, bowls, cooking pots, and large dishes with four handles.

No traces of a cemetery were found, but recent excavations by a Polish expedition have yielded a Qarunian burial in the north of the oasis, close to the area inhabited by the Faiyum B people, which dates probably to around 7000 BCE. The burial is of a 40-year-old female who is lying in a contracted position on her left side, with her left hand under her head and her right hand covering her face; her head is pointing east and facing south.

The archeological evidence indicates that the people of the Faiyum A were not essentially an agricultural community, but rather a mobile culture who lived in the site on a seasonal basis in temporary dwellings, and relied heavily on the natural resources of the lake.

It has been suggested that Faiyum was abandoned around 4000 BCE, as Egypt moved into the Neolithic Period and animal domestication and agriculture became an essential way of life. These natural resources were not available on a large scale in the Faiyum. The inhabitants may have moved to the Nile Valley, where Neolithic villages were well established.

Above **The Faiyum Oasis as it looks today.** This once-populated site was abandoned c. 4000 BCE, as the Nile Valley and other areas proved to be more suitable for a growing culture.

Above **A hearty meal.** Hunting the hippopotamus helped to sustain the populations of the oases, in an era when there was much more water than today.

Villages Along the Nile

Where a population lives reflects the environmental, social, economic, and political conditions of the area. During the Neolithic Period in Egypt, the population probably defined itself according to geographical rather than political boundaries.

The archeological record indicates that the early Neolithic villages in Egypt were usually located near the riverbanks, on desert promontories, or at levees.

The Oldest Settlement

In the Faiyum Oasis, although hundreds of hearths and basket-lined granary pits have been found, no substantial evidence of dwellings has been recorded, though this may be due to the fact that the site was investigated in the 1920s when archeological techniques were not well developed. It is instead Merimda Beni Salama, in the Nile Valley, that represents the oldest fully developed Neolithic site.

The postholes and fragments of wooden posts found in the lower levels at Merimda indicate that the inhabitants lived in oval wattle-and-daub huts. In some huts a central wooden post supported the roof, and one dwelling was divided into two rooms of unequal size. The entrances of the huts faced away from the northwestern and western wind.

The uppermost layers at Merimda indicate that the settlement at that time consisted of a large village of dwellings and workspaces. The dwellings were mostly oval pits, sunk into the ground and with walls built up above the ground more than a meter high. The houses were arranged in rows on either side of a winding alley. Entry to the huts was via a step made of wood or the tibia of a hippopotamus placed against a mud wall. A pottery jar was often placed against the wall or embedded in the floor for water. The dwellings contained hearths and ring stands for fire trays.

A Growing Economy

The economy of the Neolithic villages was mainly based on agriculture, animal husbandry, hunting, and fishing. This led to the growth of the population, and the development of permanent settlement sites.

The pottery of the early Neolithic Period is relatively coarse, handmade of alluvial silts with simple shapes and little decoration. The later sites around the area of Badari, such as Mostagedda, Hemamia, and Qau, yielded more pottery types: Black-topped ware, red-polished vessels, and the rippled pottery which is a distinctive characteristic of the Badarian culture. Stone vessels were not very common during the Neolithic Period; a few bowls and jars of stone such as calcite and basalt were found. The flint tools of the Neolithic Period reflect the effect of the move to agriculture. Stone implements of the period include bifacial sickle blades, axes with polished edges, points, end and side scrapers, large knives, and flake tools.

A unique artefact from Merimda is a small human clay head; it stands as the earliest known representation of a figure with human features found in Egypt so far. Three ivory figurines were also found at Badari; such figurines may have been used in fertility rites or may represent ideas relating to fecundity and procreation.

THE HUMAN IMAGE

The representations of the human image in the art and archeology of early Egypt included sculptures, paintings, and reliefs. A clay human head from Merimda Beni Salama and three female figurines from Badari are the earliest examples of the human image. Males and females are usually standing, and rarely seated. The sexual features are emphasized; such representations may have been used in fertility rites or may have been connected to ideas about procreation. A common motif for female figurines was a stylized form with the arms raised over the head.

Left **Male ivory statuette, c. 4000–3500** BCE. Made of hippopotamus tooth ivory, this early figurine shows the emphasis on sexual features typical of the period.

Neolithic Cemeteries

Cemeteries of the Neolithic Period, especially in Lower Egypt, were relatively close to settlements (such as el-Omari and Merimda), and over time, as the settlements expanded towards the cemeteries, they sometimes overlapped. This led to the early theory of the house burial in prehistoric Egypt, but this notion has since been rejected through research.

As the population density in the Nile Valley was still very low, Neolithic cemeteries have a relatively small occupancy; about 185 graves were reported at Merimda, 50 at el-Omari, and 293 at Badari. Burials were round or oval shallow grave pits. Skeletons were usually wrapped in reed mats or animal skin and placed on their side in a contracted or semi-contracted position. At the beginning of the Neolithic Period there were no grave goods, but these were increasingly included during the Late Neolithic, including pottery vessels, stone tools, and jewelry.

Many early Neolithic graves display little evidence of social distinction, but at el-Omari, in grave A35, an adult male was buried with a long staff in front of his face. The northern side of the grave pit has the remains of posts and postholes. This could indicate that this man had enjoyed a special status within the community. Furthermore, analysis of the Badarian burials suggests that there is an association between the number of grave goods, the size of the graves, and the occupants. In other words, those with larger graves had access to more resources and better grave offerings than other members of the society. Clearly, these individuals held a different or higher status in relation to the majority of individuals within the Badarian society, which indicates social ranking.

Above **The Naqada Desert.** This desolate landscape was once home to a culture that laid the foundations of Egypt's sophisticated civilization.

Left **Egyptian idol?** It is thought this Neolithic terracotta figure is the head of an idol. It was found at Merimda Beni Salama, site of the earliest dwellings found in Egypt.

From Farmers to Traders

Understanding the nature of the relationship between Egypt and its neighbors during the prehistoric period is crucial to developing an understanding of the evolution of complex society in early Egypt.

During this time, Egypt had a vast network of contacts with the outside world, although it is not always easy to interpret these contacts because they varied through mutual influence, trade, adaptation, and conquest. This difficulty is due to chronological problems and uncertainties with the archeological context, because some objects and motifs appear in Egypt while others appear in other cultures, and there is debate among scholars on who influenced whom and which culture adapted particular materials. With the exception of Maadi, most of the archeological data comes from funerary contexts only, which does not always make the data representative of a culture.

Below **Trading place**. Buto, in the far northwest of the Delta, as it is today. In early times Buto was a trading hub with strong links to the Levant.

Early Trade Relations

During the Neolithic Period, Egypt's contact with western Asia included the exchange of lithic tools and domesticated plants and animals, sometime after 6000 BCE. The earliest findings at Merimda Beni Salama indicate possible contacts with southwest Asia, represented by the decorative motifs on Merimda's pottery, which has

parallels in Syria and Jordan. The Red Sea shells, galena (lead sulfide), and grey flint found at the site of Merimda and el-Omari indicate trade relations with the Red Sea and the Sinai Peninsula. Also, the presence of turquoise and steatite beads found at Badari demonstrates early contact with the Sinai area.

The Chalcolithic Period (c. 4000–3000 BCE) in ancient Egypt was characterized by market and trade centers, and interregional trade. The site of Maadi is regarded as a major commercial center, where some of the inhabitants were active traders and made use of the geographical proximity of their village to both Upper Egypt and the Delta via the Nile River, and to the Levant via the Wadi Digla, which led east to the Bitter Lakes and the Red Sea, and passed through to northern Sinai, thus linking Egypt with the Levant. The existence of domesticated donkeys at Maadi suggests that they were used in the land transport of commodities. Maadi, it seems, was a trade, marketing, and redistribution center, where traders would come from different places in Egypt and the Near East to exchange exotic, locally made, and imported products. The site would have acted as a trading hub of imported products to the more isolated areas in Egypt.

The archeological evidence indicates that the Maadians exchanged their local and imported products with Upper Egypt. Imported products found in Maadi include combs, palettes, maceheads, stone tools, pottery vessels, ivory, and hard stones. On the other hand, basalt vessels, certain ceramic styles, and copper were exported to Upper Egypt. For example, what could be a fine Maadian copper axe was found in a tomb at the site of Matmar in Upper Egypt.

Maadi contains five large house structures whose architecture is clearly of non-Egyptian origin and has its best parallels in the Levant—evidence that much of the economy of Maadi was based on trade, with direct contact with foreign traders. The houses were built using local Egyptian materials and consisted of an oval subterranean pit, with part of it sunk into the ground, measuring 10 x 16 ft (3 x 5 m) and up to 10 ft (3 m) in depth. There is also evidence that they were roofed with wood and matting. The walls of one house were faced with stone and mud-bricks.

Levantine Influences

Another site with influences from the Levant is Buto, which is located in the far northwest of the Delta. Here archeologists have found local pottery styles that were clearly made with Levantine manufacturing techniques, again indicating the presence of foreigners.

Other imported products from western Asia included ceramics, copper, large flint nodules and tools, lapis lazuli, shells, pigments, resins, oils, cedar wood, and asphalt. Egyptian materials also appeared in Levantine sites and consisted largely of small finished products from what may have been specialized workshops, such as gold, pottery and calcite vessels, and faience beads, amulets, small palettes, pins, flint artefacts, maceheads, and ivory vessels.

Scholars are debating if a number of small ceramic cones found at Buto could indicate contact with northern Syria and Mesopotamia, where such objects were used as architectural decoration. The evidence at Buto, however, is inconclusive, as these clay cones have not been found in association with any buildings. Further evidence of trade with Mesopotamia comes in the form of cylinder seals and artistic motifs that the Egyptians adapted to their ideologies.

Apart from the exchange of commodities between Egypt and her northern and eastern neighbors, there is also evidence to suggest that Egypt imported commodities from the south, such as elephant ivory, animal skins, and ebony. While the exchange of products during the Neolithic Period appears to be of a more haphazard character, the valley inhabitants during the Chalcolithic Period managed to establish and maintain interregional exchange networks with their neighbors, and these allowed the emerging elites access to and control of long-distance resources. This is evident in the elite tombs where such resources have been found.

Above **Pot from the Naqada II Period, c. 3500 BCE.** Pottery of this sort was one of the major items of trade in ancient Egypt.

Left **Stone palette in the form of a ram, c. 3500–3100 BCE.** Ceremonial objects such as this were regularly traded between Egypt and its many neighbors.

Craft Specialization

The Predynastic Period in Egypt was a time of great technological innovation. Nowhere is this more evident than in the advances made in the production crafts, from pottery and stone vessels to metal objects and jewelry.

Right **Carved dagger, c. 3500–3100 BCE.** The intricately carved battle and hunting scenes on the hippopotamus ivory handle of this dagger show the growing sophistication of craft at this time.

This rapid development is directly linked to the growth of agricultural production, which enabled a section of the Egyptian population to escape subsistence activities and instead focus on the production of material goods. Increasing social differentiation and the growing demand for luxury products ensured that these craftworkers became full-time specialists in their fields. The skills they acquired laid the foundation for the establishment of highly developed production industries that were vital for maintaining the rising elite and in forming the Egyptian state.

Ceramic Innovation

Ceramic production underwent a series of progressive changes throughout the Predynastic Period. During the Early Neolithic, the ceramics produced were primarily simple vessels, made from Nile silt clay. From the Chalcolithic Period,

highly polished, red-bodied vessels with black tops were typical. Pottery of this sort has been found in the graves at Badari.

During the Naqada I phase, black-topped ware continues to be produced, but with larger and more complex shaped vessels being characteristic. Pots with a red background and white painted decoration are also typical.

The most significant development in pottery production during the Predynastic Period, however, is evident in the ceramics that are typical of the Naqada II phase. For the first time a type of clay known as Marl clay was used, requiring a greater level of skill in production and firing methods. This clay was used to make the so-called "decorated" and "wavy-handled" wares. By the time of the Naqada III phase, however, ceramics had become more utilitarian in character, lacking decoration, with large wine jars and beer jars used for storage purposes being most typical.

Below **Naqada II stone vessels, c. 3500–3200 BCE.** The stone vessel industry started to flourish in the Predynastic period with the manufacture of valuable and intricate jars.

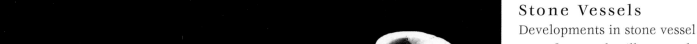

Stone Vessels

Developments in stone vessel manufacture also illustrate the rise toward craft specialization and the growth of dedicated workshops. From Naqada II, stone vessels become more common and were typically made from basalt, but other hard stones were introduced, such as porphyry, breccia, and serpentine.

Simple shapes continued in use in Naqada II, but more complex shapes, with drilled tubular handles, become standard. By Naqada III the stone vessel industry was at its height, producing vast quantities of highly polished vessels from a much larger range of materials, including calcite, siltstone, limestone, and dolomite.

DANCE

Stylised representations of "dancing" female figures were depicted on decorated pottery vessels during the Naqada II Period. These figures were shown with curving arms raised above their heads and were often shown in association with images of boats. Three-dimensional female figurines in the same style have also been found. It is still difficult to determine whether these "dancers" were meant to represent the ordinary female form or early protective goddesses. The exaggerated hips and breasts of the figurines would at least suggest that they symbolized fertility. It is possible that they represent women involved in ritual dances, which were connected to society's increasing emphasis on religious and ritual practices.

Objects of Adornment

The technical knowledge of Egyptian craft-workers is also apparent in Predynastic jewelry. With its focus on objects of adornment, the Badarian culture established the first phase of a jewelry industry that by pharaonic times would be producing highly sophisticated pieces of jewelry, both in terms of skill and artistic vision. Necklaces and bracelets of semi-precious stones, shell, ivory, and metal were all found at Badari. The manufacturing process required to produce these pieces was highly sophisticated, with stone beads requiring a time-consuming drilling process, and copper and gold beads being hammered into shape. Further evidence of the experimental nature of the Badarian craftworkers is seen in the use of glazed steatite beads, which were the precursor to faience technology.

The later Predynastic Period showed further developments in jewelry production, with metal and stone jewelry becoming more regular in shape and of superior quality, and the production of faience becoming highly developed.

Molten Metal

The Predynastic Period also sees the emergence of a sophisticated metals industry. Although rare, simple copper objects manufactured from the native metal have been found at Badari. Gold was also used in the production of jewelry from this time onwards. Occasional copper tools from Naqada I and II include axes, pins, and fishhooks. However, at the site of Maadi, situated at the edge of the Delta, a significant amount of copper ore and copper objects was excavated.

These finds would suggest a commercial connection between Maadi and the cultures of the southern Levant that were extracting and processing copper from the Sinai.

With the end of the Predynastic Period, the metals industry had clearly developed such a level of technology that copper tools could be made from molten metal and shaped in a mold. The extremely high temperatures required for this process demonstrate the knowledge craftworkers had of metal casting that would form the basis of this specialized industry from the Old Kingdom onwards.

Above **The Nag ed-Der Desert**. The raw materials of pottery were in good supply in this arid region, and there was great experimentation with both the materials and methods of pottery in the Naqada Period.

Cemeteries

Burials are one of the most important sources for archeological studies, as they provide valuable data on the funerary and religious beliefs of the early Egyptians. These humble graves are the precursors of the magnificent pyramids of later times.

Right **Curled in death.** Early graves such as this were oval in shape, and bodies were accordingly placed in a contracted position. Graves later became more rectangular, perhaps in response to the use of coffins.

This data is also useful as a basis for reconstructing social structure and cultural beliefs in the absence of information from settlement sites.

The Afterlife

Some scholars believe that burial customs were only practiced by the upper classes of Egyptian society, while those of the lower class simply disposed of their dead in the Nile River or left them exposed in the desert. This is an unsubstantiated theory, and one can say that there is no evidence to support the idea that only a small portion of the population received a proper burial.

The position of the burials and the existence of grave goods in many excavated tombs suggest that some sort of death ritual was associated with burial, which probably indicates the existence of religious or supernatural beliefs, due to the connection between death and religion in most societies. In ancient Egypt, death was regarded as part of the chaos that disturbed the order and stability of life. Therefore, the ancient Egyptian tried to overcome death by viewing it as the end of one form of existence and the beginning of another—the afterlife.

Ancient Egyptian beliefs about the afterlife were in tune with the rhythms of Egypt's natural environment and were usually represented in burial customs. The idea of resurrection and rebirth came from understanding the cycles of nature—night and day, sunrise and sunset, seeds springing from a plant that then dies, and the connection between human life and the agricultural cycle. The afterlife is best observed in relation to the ancient Egyptian god of the dead, Osiris, who was also a god of vegetation and was frequently painted green.

Mound

Pots   Skeleton

Burial Customs

The major cemeteries of the Naqada II Period are located in Hierakonpolis, Naqada, Abydos, Gerza, and Minshat Abu Omar, with the richest tombs situated at Abydos and Hierakonpolis. The cemeteries were separated from the settlement sites, and combine a large number of tombs with various grave types. The graves varied from small oval or round holes with a limited number of grave goods, to large rectangular burial chambers subdivided by mud-brick walls with storage facilities for a large number of grave goods. Each grave usually contained one single body, and in some cases two, an exception being Tomb T15 at Naqada where five bodies were discovered.

The dead were normally buried in a contracted position, with the legs drawn up and the hands in front of the face, laid on either the left or right side with the head usually to the south, facing west. However, this position was not a fixed pattern, as there are variations not only between the cemeteries but also within a cemetery. The body was usually wrapped in an animal skin, reed mat, or linen cloth.

Recent excavations at the site of Adaïma, and at Hierakonpolis, indicate the presence of early artificial mummification during this early period of ancient Egypt—a practice that was once believed to have only started during the Old Kingdom. Children were usually interred in

Below **Ceramic double-necked vase, c. 4000–3100 BCE.** This unusual vase—at least by today's standards—is decorated with plant designs.

small graves, but they were also buried in large pottery vessels. There were coffins made from basketry, air dried pottery, and wood. The use of the coffin in this period may explain why tombs were to become more rectangular in shape.

Grave goods varied according to the wealth of the grave owner. With the graves becoming larger with storage magazines, grave goods started to be placed separately from the tomb owner, with only the essential goods—jewelry, cosmetic utilities, and weapons—being placed on and around the body. Grave goods included pottery, stone vessels, flint and copper tools, clay objects, figurines, jewelry, cosmetic utensils, palettes, knives, and elaborate knife handles.

Cemeteries had a relatively large population density, particularly in the major regional centers such as Hierakonpolis, Naqada, and Abydos. The variations and diversity of the graves of the Naqada II Period indicate a growth in the social complexity of the society during this time.

Animal Burials

Recent investigation of the animal graves in the Predynastic Period indicates that animal graves fall into two distinctive categories: Animals buried within human graves, and animals buried in an independent grave within the human cemetery. Animals buried within

human graves include sheep and goats (from Maadi), and gazelles and dogs (both from Matmar). These animals were sacrificed at the time of the burial of their owner to accompany them to the afterlife, or were regarded as grave goods. This practice would depend on the species of the animal. Animals buried in independent graves are thought to reflect some sort of a sacred animal cult or divine powers in animal form. Animals with independent graves include dogs (Badari, Maadi, and Heliopolis), sheep, and goats (Wadi Digla and Heliopolis). Also recently discovered was the burial of an elephant at Hierakonpolis in the elite cemetery (HK6), dating to 3600 BCE. This is the only known elephant burial in ancient Egypt.

Above **Pre-dynastic terracotta vessels**. These simple pieces, showing the "black-topped" style of the time, are from the necropolis at Hammamiya.

MUMMIFICATION

New excavations and modern research methods are rewriting what is known of the origins of artificial mummification. The traditional view is that artificial mummification began during the Old Kingdom (c. 2600 BCE), with some isolated earlier occurrences. Recent excavations by the Hierakonpolis Expedition in the "working class" cemetery HK43 at Hierakonpolis in Upper Egypt provide startling evidence of

unusual funerary practices and the early treatment of the human body around 3600 BCE. A limited number of intact burials reveal careful bandaging of the neck and hands in layers of fine linen impregnated with resinous substances, wrapping of internal organs in linen and reinsertion into the body cavity, as well as evidence to suggest decapitation and re-articulation of the body. Microscopic

examination of textiles in the Bolton Museum from early twentieth-century excavations at Badari and Mostagedda suggests that similar wrapping procedures began as early as the late Neolithic Period.

Right **An early mummy**. Recent studies have pushed back our estimate of when mummification-like practices began.

Market Centers

The excavation of settlement sites in Egypt has become a matter of great interest, as these sites allow us to understand the development of urban centers in the late Predynastic Period, which led eventually to the formation of the Egyptian state.

Much of the work on these sites has been done in the last twenty years, as we have come to realize their value to our understanding of ancient Egyptian civilization.

Urbanization

Recent excavations have established that at this time there was a shift in settlement patterns from small, scattered villages to larger concentrations of people living in urban communities. This move would appear to be linked to the need for a centralization of resources as Egyptian society became more complex. The desire of the early rulers to control natural resources and interregional trade also played a major role in the growth of market centers.

As religion became more important, particularly in order to maintain the authority of the ruling class, these towns also acted as centers of religious worship, where local shrines were established to pay tribute to the regional gods. In addition, the formation of these cities encouraged the development of an early administrative bureaucracy and economic system, which was an essential prerequisite for the creation of a centralized Egyptian state.

Archeological evidence would suggest that the Upper Egyptian sites of Naqada, Hierakonpolis and Abydos/Thinis (Thinis is the capital of the Thinite region and is probably located just north of the cemeteries at Abydos) had all developed into major market centers by the Naqada II Period (c. 3500–3200 BCE), and that Lower Egyptian settlements, such as Buto and Minshat Abu Omar, were also important at this time.

Access to Resources

It appears that the concentration of early populations at these sites was primarily based on their access to highly valued natural resources or their strategic geographic location. In Upper Egypt, Naqada was advantageously located at the mouth of the Wadi Hammamat—a dried-out riverbed—which gave direct access to the Red Sea, as well as a range of natural resources such as gold and siltstone, ensuring the growth and increasing power of this early market center. The name Naqada (or "Nubt") in fact meant "Gold Town."

Abydos/Thinis was likewise geographically positioned to take advantage of resources available in the Eastern Desert, as well as being closer to regional centers in the north of Egypt, promoting trade relations. It was also the closest major settlement to the western oases, which meant that it would have been well placed to control goods imported from the Western Desert

EGYPT DURING THE NAQADA I AND II PERIOD (C. 4000–3200 BCE)

TOMB 100

Tomb 100 at Hierakonpolis (also known as the Painted Tomb) was discovered in the early 1900s and dates to Naqada II (c. 3500 BCE). It is the earliest known painted tomb in ancient Egypt. The tomb consists of a large rectangular room with mud-brick lined walls, with a freestanding brick wall starting about halfway from the eastern wall. Its images are painted in black, white, and red on a yellow background, and depict the tomb owner dominating powerful animals, men engaged in fighting scenes, men hunting animals, and five different types of boats. The styles of the scenes are similar to those found on the decorated pottery from Naqada II.

Right **The earliest paintings.** Despite damage to the walls in the Painted Tomb, it is easy to make out the images of boats, humans, and animals adorning them.

and Africa. Hierakonpolis, located in the south of Egypt, largely controlled trade from Nubia and trade in exotic products that originated in sub-Saharan Africa, such as elephant ivory, ebony, and rare animal skins.

Control of Trade Routes

In Lower Egypt, urban centers also appear to have developed at strategic locations. For example, the site of Minshat Abu Omar, situated in the eastern Delta would have been in a prime position to undertake trade either overland or oversea with Palestine and the Near East. The western Delta site of Buto became one of the most important urban centers in the lead-up to state formation, probably because of its control of highly valued resources being imported from Syria and Lebanon, such as cedar wood. Long-range trade with Mesopotamia would also have been important for these settlement sites, as this relationship gave access to resources such as lapis lazuli, which came from more distant locations.

An Economic Hub

At the settlement site of Hierakonpolis it is also evident that these early cities acted as centers for craft production and local trade, which played an essential role in the increasing social differentiation and economic development necessary for state formation. At

Hierakonpolis there is evidence of a range of manufacturing industries, such as ceramic and jewelry workshops. This centralization of production meant that these towns acted as economic hubs where local trade could take place between different members of the community. The high population density in these cities also guaranteed a balance between supply and demand, with transactions in essential and prestige products necessary for the growing elite, who were no longer involved in agricultural activities and wished to distinguish themselves from the rest of the population.

Below **Naqada II Period pots.** Pots of this period were simply yet elegantly decorated. The one on the left shows geometric patterns while the other features boat designs.

Emergence of the Elite

With the transformation in the Neolithic Period from hunting and gathering to a society that produced its own food and had a surplus of life staples, an opportunity arose for a group of individuals to gain a higher status in the community.

It is assumed that such a group of powerful individuals may have emerged because of wealth, bravery, knowledge, or age. This group probably took the leadership in their villages, and had access to more resources than the rest of the population.

Wealthy Graves

As early as the Neolithic Period, the beginning of social distinction can be seen in the cemeteries. The wealth in some graves at el-Omari, Badari, and Naqada is expressed by differences in grave size, grave goods, and the preparation of the body, and indicates the emergence of social ranking. It has been suggested that such high-status persons deliberately distinguished themselves from the common people, and wished to take their wealth with them into the afterlife.

During the Naqada II Period, major centers started to appear, such as Hierakonpolis, Naqada, and Abydos. The discovery of rich and large tombs in these centers indicates that there were elite members of the community buried at these major sites. At Locality 6 at Hierakonpolis, large, elaborate tombs were discovered. Some had

WAVY-HANDLED POTTERY

In the late nineteenth century, in order to establish a chronological sequence for the Predynastic Period, the great Egyptologist Flinders Petrie founded the relative dating method of Seriation, which was largely based upon the degeneration of "wavy-handled" pottery. This type of pottery originated in Palestine and was soon incorporated into the Egyptian ceramic repertoire but was transformed over time to fit in with their more specific requirements. It evolved from its original globular shape, which incorporated two wavy handles, to a smaller and thinner version with a scalloped decoration that encircled the entire vessel. Finally, the vessel body became more cylindrical in shape, with a simple rope impression completely replacing the original wavy handles. By identifying changes such as this, a useful system of dating was developed.

Below **Tomb U-j at Abydos**. The objects found at this site, particularly a royal *heka* scepter, clearly indicate that it was the tomb of a king.

postholes, indicating that they once had wooden roofs and fences, and one stone-cut tomb has associated animal burials. It has been suggested that these tombs belonged to the Dynasty 0 chiefs of Hierakonpolis, and possibly the stone-cut tomb belonged to a king known as Scorpion II. Furthermore, a number of wealthy child burials were recorded at Hierakonpolis, indicating that wealth was not only displayed in the adult tombs of the elite, but in the tombs of their children as well.

Cemetery T, located at Naqada, is of particular significance and was used mainly during Naqada II and III. It is the richest cemetery, with elaborate tombs, which indicates the presence of a local elite class. The cemetery consists of 69 tombs—the smallest of the three Predynastic cemeteries at Naqada—suggesting that it was exclusively for high-status individuals. The tombs were large and lined with bricks, similar to Tomb 100 at Hierakonpolis, but with a vaulted beamed roof.

The grave goods found at Cemetery T were exceptional and varied in type, quality, and quantity to the nearby cemeteries. For example, one tomb contained 80 separate pottery storage jars. The grave goods included decorated ware, wavy-handled ware, red ware, black-topped ware, stone vessels, jewelry, imported goods such as shell and stone beads, stone tools such as flint knives, scrapers, arrowheads, green slate grinding palettes with malachite and hematite pigment stones, copper awls and adzes, amulets, and ivory objects. Clearly, the wealth of these tombs indicates the presence of an elite class that explicitly displayed its higher status through elaborate tombs and diverse grave goods.

Tomb U-j

The most convincing example of the power of the regional kings is displayed in Tomb U-j at Abydos. The sheer size of the tomb and the wealth demonstrated by the number and quality of the grave goods would suggest that the tomb owner, known as Scorpion I, was a man of great influence and authority. In addition, the inclusion of the first written administrative records documented on small ivory labels would support the fact that at this time some kind of administrative class and system had come into being. The inclusion of a great number of imported goods, including over 700 imported wine jars, must further support the fact that this individual was extremely wealthy and had access to luxury goods imported from the Near East. The most significant piece of evidence, however, is the fact that a *heka* scepter—which was to become an enduring and potent symbol of kingship in the Dynastic Period—was placed in the tomb. Combining all these factors, it is logical to conclude that the owner of Tomb U-j was a king.

Left **Fragment of a stone palette showing a hunting scene, c. 3500** BCE. Members of the growing elite differentiated themselves by the quality of the stoneware and other goods they placed in their tombs.

Below **Diggings at Hierakonpolis**. This famous site has yielded some of the most significant treasures of the Naqada Period.

Contact or Conquest?

How and why the regional centers of Predynastic Egypt became a unified state is still a matter of contention among scholars. The problem lies in the imbalance in the archeological evidence from this transitional period.

Above **Pre-dynastic weapons**. Stone mace-heads such as these are seen in artwork of the period, such as the Narmer Palette (pictured opposite).

Below **Trade links**. A linen fragment from Gebelein, c. 3500 BCE, showing boats with rowers on the Nile.

In the past the debate has focused on mortuary data primarily from Upper Egypt, and it is only recently that excavations in the crucial Delta region and settlements in the south have facilitated the construction of a more holistic account of state formation. From this fresh evidence it appears that the unification of Egypt was a gradual process that began in Naqada II with the rise of complex society, and was the result of a multitude of dynamic forces that eventually established all of the elements required for the creation of the first-ever territorial state.

Unification Theories

Petrie's theory that the transition in Egyptian culture was due to the invasion of a dynastic race from the northeast is now seen as old-fashioned. In the 1950s Kaiser, a German scholar, attempted to reassess the nature of the transition from prehistoric to pharaonic Egypt. He believed that the Naqada culture had used military might to subdue the more peaceful agriculturalists of Lower Egypt, and forcefully imposed their culture and beliefs on them. His view of the transition was also supported by traditional inter-

pretations of the Narmer Palette, a ceremonial stone tablet depicting King Narmer, which saw this artistic work as representative of an actual historical event. This analysis saw Narmer subduing the Lower Egyptians, destroying cities, taking captives, and wearing the crowns of both Upper and Lower Egypt, symbolizing his reign over both lands.

However, it is now clear this is a simplistic view and that the unification of Egypt was a much more complex process that happened over an extended period of time, and was caused by a multitude of factors. Most scholars now believe the Narmer Palette does not commemorate an actual historical event, but simply depicts the ideology and power of kingship.

Transition to a State

One key prerequisite for state formation was the concentration of larger groups of people in urbanized market centers under the control of strong regional monarchs, which can be seen at the Upper Egyptian sites of Naqada, Hierakonpolis, and Abydos. In these economic hubs, major social and economic developments occurred mainly as a reaction to the growing power and mounting needs of the elite class.

Craft specialization and manufacturing industries were of extreme importance, as the upper class required more prestigious products to include in their graves, separating them from the rest of society. In turn this created a focus on interregional trade and access to raw materials. This desire for goods not only provided an environment for competition between regional monarchs, but also produced the conditions in which writing and an administration became essential to the organization and maintenance of the flow of commodities between different areas.

In Lower Egypt urban centers and regional monarchs appear to have existed concurrently with those in the south. They too had their own craft production industries and technological innovations to provide for the burgeoning class of administrative officials. Trade and the constant

Right **Detail from the Narmer Palette, c. 3000** BCE. King Narmer, wearing the white crown of Upper Egypt and with macehead in hand, smites a defeated enemy.

contact between these "city-states" meant that these communities were also able to exchange cultural, religious and social ideas. By early Naqada III, a string of interacting regional polities existed all along the Nile River.

The First Rulers

It is evident that the sequence of rulers from the Predynastic Period to the early First Dynasty is unbroken at Abydos, indicating that the earliest kings came from this city. Therefore, at some point the Thinite ruling family must have taken control of a larger area, eclipsing the importance of other early market centers.

It is still unclear how this took place—whether through military conflict, economic necessity, or negotiation. However, it would appear that the first step involved incorporating Hierakonpolis and Naqada into a larger, more powerful southern kingdom. From here, the Thinite rulers appear to have also gained control over the north, beginning at the apex of the Delta, which was to become Egypt's capital, Memphis. They then incorporated the Delta communities in a final expansion, culminating in the unification of Upper and Lower Egypt.

Ceramic evidence at Buto suggests the transition was gradual, with no evidence of military conflict, destruction of the town site, or bodies having died in traumatic circumstances. The final mechanisms used by the Thinite rulers to unify the country under a single monarch are still open to debate. Whether they used military force, coercive tactics, or diplomatic negotiations can only be confirmed through more intensive archeological investigations, particularly in the Delta region.

Powerful Art

A central theme in pharaonic ideology is the need to balance the forces of "chaos" and "order". Throughout Egyptian history, the king is seen to be a force keeping disorder at bay through his relationship with the gods and his strength and power.

This belief developed from the iconography of leadership that is portrayed in various scenes from the Naqada I Period (c. 4000–3500 BCE) onwards. In these artistic works the leader is commonly shown in control of the natural world, dominating his enemies, controlling wild animals, and in several cases actually destroying towns and taking living prisoners. These images clearly display all the elements required of a strong leader, which by the end of the Predynastic Period represented the king. The king had to be all-conquering on the battlefield, subjugate his enemies, and restore a balance and harmony to the world through his strength. By the time of the unification of the state of Egypt, this iconography of power and kingship was clearly established and would continue to be in use throughout pharaonic history.

Iconography of Leadership

One of the earliest examples of this ideology of leadership, as expressed in an artistic form, comes from Tomb 100 (or the so-called "Painted Tomb") at Hierakonpolis. It not only exhibits images of the natural world, but also depicts man as a dominating force over that world. Most significant is the image of a powerful figure standing between two lions, holding them apart with his bare hands. Symbolically this image represents a leader who has control over all the chaotic forces around him, and this scene is typically known as the "master of the lions" motif.

A similar representation is shown on the unprovenanced Gebel el-Arak knife handle, which dates to Naqada IId (c. 3300–3200 BCE), where a leader is positioned standing between two lions, keeping them at bay through his strength and power.

In several artistic representations from the Predynastic Period, the ruler is also depicted as a strong and powerful animal. On the Narmer Palette he is shown on the reverse side as a bull, destroying what appears to be a city. He is also shown as a bull on the Bull Palette and as a lion destroying an enemy on the Battlefield Palette. Although these images do not specifically continue to be used in the iconography of kingship into the Pharaonic Period, the themes illustrated in these artistic representations are widespread. The king is constantly shown as the dominating force in the universe, but this message is communicated in a different form.

The representation of the king "smiting the enemy," however, was to continue in use

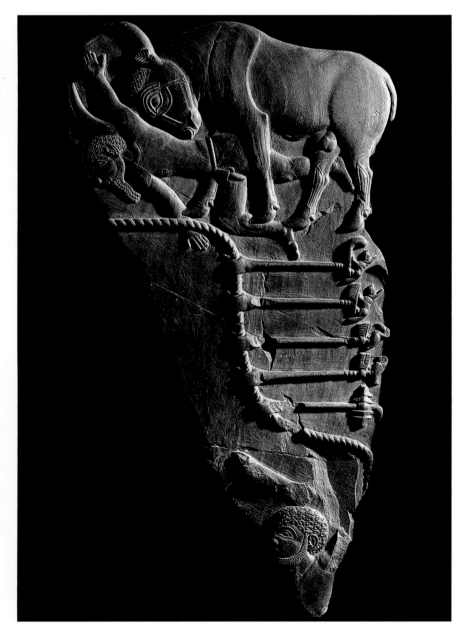

Below **Bull Palette, c. 3300–3100 BCE.** In this scene the ruler is represented as a bull, goring and crushing a hapless enemy.

throughout Egyptian history as one of the most enduring and powerful expressions of leadership. It is illustrated in its earliest form on a ceramic vessel found in Cemetery U at Abydos, dated to Naqada I, where an early chieftain is shown with his arm raised over a group of three captives, ready to bludgeon them to death. A further example of this striking motif comes from Tomb 100, where a ruler is depicted towering above three captives who have their hands tied; his arm is raised, ready to strike them down. This image clearly shows a ruler subjugating his enemies.

However, the culmination in the development of this early ideology of kingship is most remarkably seen on the Narmer Palette. In the central scene the king is shown "smiting the enemy." He stands above a kneeling individual with his arm raised, mace in hand, ready to crush this enemy with his brute strength. King Narmer is also shown wearing the dual crown of Upper and Lower Egypt on either side of the palette and his form is depicted on a much larger scale, so that he is clearly

distinguished by his size. This ceremonial palette combines a range of images in which the king is seen as all-powerful, and establishes several elements of the king's regalia and iconography, such as wearing the bull's tail and false beard, that maintain an enduring and unique representation of the king throughout Egyptian history.

Above **Abydos today.** Ancient tombs at this site have yielded striking images of royal power, on ceramic vessels and other objects.

THE EARLIEST HIEROGLYPHS

The earliest hieroglyphs were used to identify individuals by name using pictographic and phonographic signs for the name, as on the *serekh*. During the Early Dynastic Period, hieroglyphs were used to depict commemorative events, as on the Narmer Palette. They were also used on gravestones and funerary stelae, like the ones from Helwan, where pictographic signs were used in lists depicting different types of offerings, such as the leg of an ox, loaves of bread, linen, beer, and fowl. Some of these pictographic signs were developed later into hieroglyphs. Egyptian hieroglyphs were generally written from right to left, but also horizontally and from left to right, the reading depending on the direction of the signs. Early hieroglyphs appear on a wide variety of objects, such as gravestones, pottery, stone vessels, seal impressions, wooden and ivory labels, palettes, and funerary stelae. Despite advances in our knowledge of hieroglyphs in general, the meaning of some of the early hieroglyphic signs still remains uncertain.

motion	hill country, desert	cat	sail upstream	book	weep	chariot
man, son	jubilation	woman, widow	bee, honey	plant	beer pot, drunkenness	star

Left **Hieroglyphs representing the meaning of a word.** In their earliest forms, hieroglyphs were simple pictures of things or concepts, known as ideograms. Even when a group of hieroglyphs came to represent the sounds of a word (phonograms) it was sometimes followed by an ideogram that confirms the meaning of the word. These are known as determinative signs.

What Makes a King?

The king was seen as a divine being who ruled over the whole of Egypt and was the connection between the people and their gods. The country was seen to descend into chaos when the power of the king weakened.

The question of "what makes a king?" is more difficult to answer when looking at the period leading up to the unification of Egypt. It is clear that from the First Dynasty hereditary kings ruled over Egypt, but what about those rulers of Dynasty 0, or even the regional leaders of Naqada II, who were buried in unique tombs and were clearly distinguished by the society as the highest of the elite class?

Egypt's Earliest Rulers

Dating to Naqada II, Tomb 100 (or the so-called "Painted Tomb") at Hierakonpolis provides some of the earliest evidence for the ideology of kingship in Egypt. Although the tomb is not particularly large compared with other elite burials at the same site, the painted decoration is unique and the "master of the lions" and "smiting" scenes depicted reveal that the owner of this tomb was most probably one of Egypt's earliest regional monarchs.

The process of unification was gradual, and in early Naqada III or what is commonly referred to as Dynasty 0, Egypt was at least to some extent culturally unified. At this time there is increasing evidence for a group of regional rulers who had control over small city-states. These rulers can be identified largely because of the fact that their names were written within the *serekh*, which was the standard way of identifying a king in the Early Dynastic Period. (The *serekh* was a symbol that incorporated the palace facade design, which represented the royal residence, and was surmounted by the Horus falcon—a

Below **Triumphal procession of King Narmer.** This detail from the Narmer Palette (c. 3000 BCE) shows Narmer, wearing the red crown of Lower Egypt, inspecting his defeated enemies.

ABYDOS

Abydos was the burial ground for the nearby settlement site of Thinis, and is situated in Upper Egypt. In the Predynastic and Early Dynastic periods, Abydos became a major power center and the Thinite rulers provided much of the impetus needed for the transition of Egypt into a unified state. Most significantly, Abydos is the location of the royal necropolis, and the rulers of Dynasty 0 and the First Dynasty were buried here. Tombs of the last two rulers of the Second Dynasty have also been uncovered. This would suggest that the Early Dynastic kings, who ruled from the capital of Memphis, actually originated from Thinis and that, instead of being buried in the capital, they wished to be interred in close proximity to their ancestors. Abydos is also the place where a number of these early kings built their massive funerary enclosures, which probably served a ceremonial or ritual function.

Right **Royal titles.** These seals, made either from stone or bone, depict the names of early rulers such as Hathor and Pepy I, as well as animals and other features.

expression of the new royal ideology. Thus the use of writing in early Egypt falls into three different categories: Economic and administrative, royal ideology, and funerary contexts.

Three Uses of Writing

Writing was used to manage the economy, to collect revenue for the ruler's budget (taxes needed to be raised), and then to redistribute the income among the ruler's kin and to the officials and workers who worked for him. Early hieroglyphs appear on seals, impressions, and labels, and in the form of pot marks to identify goods, places, titles, and taxes. From this evidence comes the theory that writing was first developed for economic and administrative purposes. This particular use for writing underpinned a complex network of trade and administration as more resources came under royal control during the Naqada III Period.

The second use of early writing was as an expression for royal ideology, such as the *serekh*, commemorative palettes, maceheads and labels. The *serekh* is the earliest expression of royal identity: The king's name is written inside a palace facade surmounted by the figure of a falcon (Horus). *Serekhs* are found on vessels, labels, seals, and seal impressions, and in rock art. The iconography on palettes, maceheads, and labels usually represents the king engaged in a symbolic action such as "smiting the enemy" and during festivals, such as the sed-festival (a renewal of the king's rule with a ritual killing usually performed on a statue, practiced every 30 years throughout pharaonic Egypt). The representations of these events were usually accompanied by hieroglyphic signs, although in many cases their translation remains uncertain.

The third use of writing in early Egypt was in funerary contexts, such as on stelae found in private burials of the Early Dynastic Period. The stelae usually represent the tomb owner sitting in front of an offering table with a list of his or her titles, and a register of the offerings that the tomb owner desires to receive. The most famous of the early stelae are those discovered in the cemetery at Helwan, south of Cairo.

Left **Early writings.** A First Dynasty (c. 3100–2890 BCE) limestone stela, found at Abydos.

Horus: The Royal Force

The ancient Egyptians' concept of sacred kingship was unique, as well
as being fundamental to their culture. It held a significant meaning
for all levels of Egyptian society throughout pharaonic history.

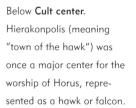

Right **Touched by the gods.** This stela of the Third Dynasty ruler Qahedjet shows him being kissed by the god Horus, affirming his divine right as king.

It is important to note that there was a slight distinction between the divine office of kingship and the king as a person. The king himself was not simply regarded by everyone as a mystical divine being; otherwise we could not explain ancient reports about conspiracies and the assassination of kings. However, being the representative of a divine office and the dominant force in ancient Egyptian society, the king was at the apex of the religious, political and social institutions of Egyptian culture, and held divine power and authority of this office as the god Horus embodied in the person of the king.

Below **Cult center.** Hierakonpolis (meaning "town of the hawk") was once a major center for the worship of Horus, represented as a hawk or falcon.

Followers of Horus

The sky god Horus, in his falcon form, is associated with Egyptian kingship during the Predynastic and Early Dynastic periods, and went on to become a popular deity throughout the Pharaonic Period. It has been suggested that the early Egyptians found in the soaring falcon their perfect metaphor for majesty. The Turin Canon, dating to the New Kingdom, refers to the Predynastic rulers as the "Followers of Horus." During the Pharaonic Period, Horus was usually depicted as a man with a head of a falcon or a hawk and played an important role in the myth of the gods Osiris and Seth. As a son of the goddess Isis, Horus was worshipped under the name Harsiese—the god who performed the opening of the mouth ritual on his dead father, assuring his succession to the throne. Horus was regarded as a national god, and so was worshipped in different regions. His

major cult center during the Early Dynastic Period was probably at Hierakonpolis (literally meaning the "town of the hawk").

The worship of Horus was practiced right throughout the Dynastic Period; he was also associated with the town of Edfu, which is at the site of the ancient city of Mesen, where he was worshipped as part of the triad with Hathor and their child Harsomtus. An impressive Ptolemaic temple exists which is associated with this cult; it attests to the longevity of the veneration of Horus.

Divine Association

The kings of early Egypt expressed their association with the divine in different ways. One of the most common ways was the association of their names and what they represented with the god Horus, in what is known as the *serekh*, or the Horus name. The king's name was written inside a palace facade sign that was surmounted by the figure of a falcon, representing the god Horus. Therefore, the Horus name combined the name of the king, the palace, and the god Horus as one entity; this probably meant that the king was seen as Horus in the royal palace.

An ivory comb of King Djet shows the outstretched wings of Horus hovering protectively over the *serekh* of the king. Scholars suggest that this representation on the comb is one of the earliest and most concise theological depictions; it combines the celestial god Horus and the king, and presents the ideology that the king fulfills his role as Horus on earth, under the protection of the celestial Horus. It is also suggested that the royal names and titles associated with Horus may have symbolized and enforced the political role of the king, such as the name of *Hor-Aha*, which means "Horus (as the king) the Fighter."

Being at the apex of a divine institution, the king was expected to fulfill the duties of the sacred office, assuring the power and authority of the office, keeping the social order, and strengthening the protection and prosperity of the country. The king was the protector of

Egypt not only against its enemies, but also against universal chaos. Conversely, a divine association also allowed the kings to legitimize their actions because they acted by "divine command."

The iconography of the Early Dynastic Period clearly enforces the idea that the king had absolute power and authority. The king is usually represented with an array of royal regalia, such as the royal crowns and scepters, a bull's tail, and special garments. The king was also the head of the military and ultimately responsible for protecting Egypt's borders, actively supported by the god Horus. He was frequently represented dominating dangerous or mythical animals, such as hippopotami or bulls, or symbolized by such animals, thus incorporating their supernatural powers.

Above **A king's power.** A ruler in the earliest Egyptian times was designated by a *serekh*, showing the falcon (representing Horus) atop the king's palace.

BATTLES FOR CONTROL
A Nation is Born

Late in Dynasty 0 (c. 3200–3000 BCE), there is evidence for the existence of a number of regional kings. It appears these rulers were in control of local polities and that monarchs almost certainly existed concurrently in the north and south of Egypt.

Although it is difficult to determine the extent of power these rulers held from the scanty evidence available, it is clear that by the First Dynasty the Thinite ruling family incorporated their local kingdoms into a single territorial state.

Competing Monarchs

The names of a number of contemporaneous early kings have been found at a collection of sites dating from early Naqada III, suggesting that there were several competing royal households. As a powerful regional center, Hierakonpolis must have been ruled by a succession of early monarchs. King Scorpion II, recognized from his macehead deposited at the site of Hierakonpolis, was in all probability a king from this site. Another likely ruler is attested in two inscriptions in the southwestern desert.

In the other major Upper Egyptian site of Abydos, large tombs belonging to Scorpion I, Iri-Hor, and Ka have been identified through inscriptional evidence. These rulers were directly linked to the kings of the First Dynasty who were buried in the adjacent cemetery.

Several other *serekhs* potentially name competing kings from Lower Egypt. The name of one Dynasty 0 ruler was found in the eastern Delta and Turah. The *serekh* has proven unreadable but it is strong evidence for the existence of a king who held power in Lower Egypt. Several *serekhs* from Tarkhan and Minshat Abu Omar have also been attributed to a likely Lower Egyptian ruler identified as "Horus Crocodile."

The use of the *serekh* design by both Upper and Lower Egyptian polities to designate their monarchs would suggest that rulers were not only competing for control of natural resources and trade routes, but were also vying for the right to rule. Contact between these "city-states" must have made it essential for the rulers to delineate themselves, and the use of the *serekh* with the Horus falcon clearly distinguished them as semi-divine. It may have also been critical for kings to prove themselves on the battlefield and expand their power base in order to maintain the trust and allegiance of their subjects.

Administrative Centralization

Economically these regional kingdoms were also becoming progressively more interconnected, as they were forced to rely on one another for certain commodities. The site of Memphis became increasingly important in order to facilitate trade relations between the market centers of Upper and Lower Egypt. Situated at the apex

EGYPT DURING THE UNIFICATION PERIOD (C. 3200–2682 BCE)

of Ka has been found on pottery vessels in Lower Egypt, and Narmer is one of the most well attested kings of this time, with his *serekh* being found as far afield as southern Palestine.

By Naqada IIIb the dominance of the southern towns of Naqada and Hierakonpolis had been eclipsed by Abydos. The next stage in the process of state formation was the incorporation of Lower Egypt into the already vast kingdom of Upper Egypt. Narmer was probably one of the key players in extending the command of Thinite rulers to Memphis and the Delta region in this final consolidation of power.

The unification of Egypt under a single king represents the culmination of a gradual process, resulting in the world's first territorial state. By the First Dynasty,

of the Nile Delta, this region experienced a period of growth from around Naqada IIIb (c. 3100 BCE). The discovery of a cylinder seal designed with an empty *serekh* at the large Memphite necropolis of Helwan also supports the idea that administrative officials were being employed from Memphis and that a centralized economy was in development.

The Final Stage

With competition and contact growing exponentially between regional market centers or early city-states, it appears that the kings from Abydos were specifically rising in influence. The name

Egypt was ruled by the Thinite royal family from the newly established capital city of Memphis. This king had power over a vast geographical area from the Mediterranean Sea in the north to the First Cataract of the Nile in the south. He had control over a large body of administrative personnel and a highly organized economy, as well as being viewed as the link between the people and the gods. The Early Dynastic Period was therefore a time of consolidation of the king's new role as "master of the universe."

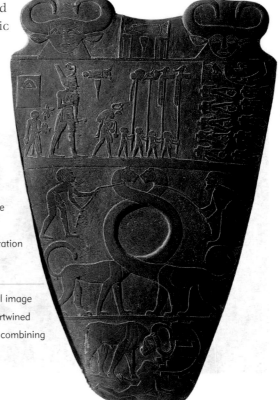

THE NARMER PALETTE

Found in the "Main Deposit" at Hierakonpolis, the Narmer Palette represents one of the earliest attempts by the Egyptian culture to demonstrate its emerging beliefs through art. The palette depicts the ideology of kingship that became such a significant part of later pharaonic society, while also incorporating an early version of Egyptian artistic conventions. On one side are images of the cow-goddess Bat, Narmer wearing the crown of Lower Egypt, and a central image displaying two mythical animals with their long intertwined necks

forming a circle. On the other side Narmer is shown wearing the crown of Upper Egypt while "smiting" his enemy. The Narmer Palette is significant because it offers an early representation of the unification of Egypt.

Right **Two become one**. The fascinating central image of the Narmer Palette—two creatures with intertwined necks—expresses the unity that came with the combining of Upper and Lower Egypt.

The Dynastic Beginning

A detailed account of political developments in the Early Dynastic Period is not possible due to the lack of archeological evidence of the time, and the questionable reliability ofl ater historical accounts and their record of the succ ession of kings.

Right **A queen among kings.** Early Egyptian rulers were, it seems, exclusively male. This stela mentions the one woman, Merneith, to almost break this line. She ruled as Queen Regent until her young son, Den, grew old enough to rule.

Below **Hieroglyphs for the rulers of Egypt.** The hieroglyphs in this king list (reading down the columns) show the Horus name of rulers from the First Dynasty.

Although the sequence of kings for the First Dynasty is now well established, the order of Second Dynasty kings is still uncertain. It is also difficult to present with any accuracy the time span of each king's reign. However, by examining the fragmentary inscriptional and archeological evidence of the Early Dynastic Period, it is possible to identify key themes, innovations, festivals, and events. Specifically, the Early Dynastic Period can be described as a time of technical innovation, of expanding trade relations with neighbors, and an increasing growth in the divine rule of the king.

Kings of the First Dynasty

The succession of kings in the First Dynasty has now been validated. Several later king-lists, such as the Turin Canon and the Palermo Stone, attest to the sequence of rulers, which is also supported by the third-century BCE Egyptian writer Manetho in his history of Egypt, written

about 2,500 years after the Early Dynastic Period. Although these accounts generally corroborate one another, it is difficult to determine their accuracy, as they were probably based on records copied and re-copied until no longer faithful to the original. However, the order of the First Dynasty kings has also been recorded in more contemporary sources in the form of two mud sealings discovered at the royal necropolis at Abydos.

The earliest dated necropolis sealing belongs to the reign of king Den, and lists the rulers of Egypt from Narmer and Aha to Djer and Djet, ending with the reign of Den. The identity of the first king of the First Dynasty and the person who should be identified with the semi-mythical Menes, who Manetho claimed united the two lands of Upper and Lower Egypt, is a matter of some debate. The two main candidates are Narmer and Aha, but it is still not completely clear which ruler should be given this honor. However,

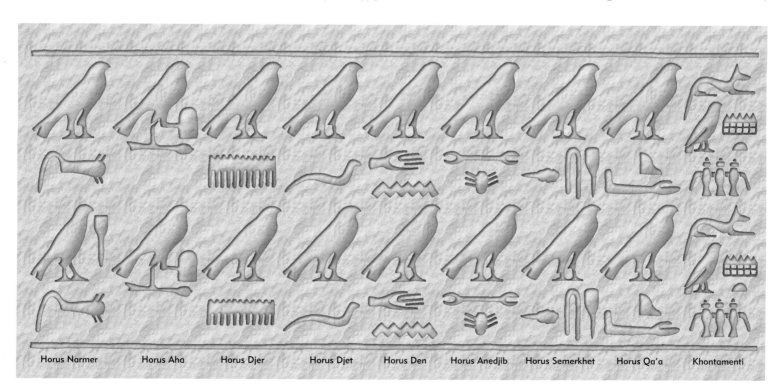

| Horus Narmer | Horus Aha | Horus Djer | Horus Djet | Horus Den | Horus Anedjib | Horus Semerkhet | Horus Qa'a | Khontamenti |

Narmer was included in the succession of kings on both necropolis seals from Abydos, and his reign is widely attested throughout Egypt.

The seal of Den also mentions Merneith, who was probably Den's mother. It is understood that her inclusion in this king-list rests firmly on the basis that Djet's reign was relatively short and that with his death he left the throne to his son Den, who was a young child at the time. Consequently, Merneith would have taken on the role of Queen Regent until Den reached maturity and could rule over the country by himself. Merneith's tomb on the Umm el-Qa'ab (the royal cemetery at Abydos), positioned among the tombs of the First Dynasty kings, would support the notion that she was the first woman to hold such a powerful position in Egypt and that her role was legitimate and recognized by subsequent rulers.

The other necropolis seal from Abydos dates to the reign of Qa'a and supports the sequence found on Den's earlier seal. However, it also includes the other kings of the First Dynasty, giving a complete list of all its eight rulers. After Den, this includes Anedjib, Semerkhet, and Qa'a.

Kings of the Second Dynasty

The sequence of kings from the Second Dynasty is still uncertain because later historical sources do not agree on a common succession, and there are few contemporary accounts which could shed light on this issue. The most important piece of evidence, providing a relatively firm order for the first three kings of the Second Dynasty, is a small statue housed in the Cairo Museum, which lists Hetepskhemwy, Nebra, and Nynetjer as a group. The sequence of rulers after that is more difficult to determine, with evidence for kings named Weneg, Sened, Nubnefer, and Sekhemib probably situated in the middle of the sequence. It is fairly certain that among the last kings of the dynasty was Peribsen, followed by Khasekhemwy.

It has been asserted that there was some kind of breakdown in power in the middle of the Second Dynasty and that several of the kings only ruled over part of Egypt. This idea is based on several key developments that occurred at this time, which include: A decrease in the importation of foreign goods, which coincides with the Second Dynasty; the shift in the royal necropolis from Saqqara back to Abydos; and the introduction of the god Seth to the royal name with the reign of Peribsen. It is very possible that a discontinuation in power did occur, but, without further support from the substantive evidence, this view must be seen as mere speculation.

Above **Later beliefs.** The Egyptians of later periods believed that instead of early kings, the god Osiris was buried at Abydos.

City of the Dead

Archeological evidence of Egypt's Early Dynastic capital, Memphis, is scarce. Yet its necropolis at Helwan can provide information on issues such as the size of the population, the material culture of the period, religious beliefs, and social standing.

Moreover, the study of the developments that occurred in ceramic styles can assist greatly in providing more accurate dating criteria for tombs or features from the Second Dynasty—a period that is not well attested in the archaeological record.

Excavations at the site of Helwan during the 1940s and 1950s, and more recently from 1997 onwards, uncovered over 10,000 graves of the lower to middle classes of Egyptian society, complementing the elite cemetery of Saqqara on the other side of the Nile River. These tombs ranged from simple pit burials with only scarce grave goods to large stone-lined *mastaba* tombs, which had ample space for the storage of a wealth of funerary goods, and were clearly reserved for the higher echelons of society.

THE FIRST LADY

Women in ancient Egypt enjoyed an equal role in both society and religion. Titles of princesses and queens appeared as early as the First Dynasty. Queen Neith-Hotep (meaning "the goddess Neith is content"), whose name was found in a tomb at Naqada and on an ivory fragment from Helwan, was probably the wife of King Narmer and the mother of King Hor-Aha of the First Dynasty. Neith-Hotep's tomb at Naqada is a large elaborate *mastaba* with a niched palace facade on all four sides. The substructure of the tomb is contained within the superstructure and is above the surface of the ground. The superstructure contains 16 rooms, the substructure contains five, and in the middle is the main burial chamber.

Tomb Architecture

Simple oval pit tombs continued in use throughout the Pharaonic Period, but the larger tombs of the First and Second dynasties underwent a gradual evolution in form, incorporating

Below **Looking good— even after death.** Wealthy Egyptians, both male and female, were frequently buried with necklaces, bracelets, and other jewelry.

innovations in funerary architecture. In the First Dynasty rectangular pit tombs were common, normally with the deceased placed in a contracted position with their head facing either to the north or south. Some kind of mud-brick superstructure was typical, used to mark out the position of the burial for the deceased's family. By the Second Dynasty, subterranean tombs that were accessible by a staircase were common. They could consist of one or more chambers, normally with small niches to house the grave goods. A large limestone slab, known as a portcullis stone, often blocked the entrance to the tomb: This was an attempt to ensure the security of the deceased and his belongings. However, this device was largely unsuccessful at Helwan, as the vast majority of tombs have been robbed in antiquity, and sometimes they have been plundered several times over, leaving only a fraction of the original evidence for modern archeologists to study.

Left **Digging in Memphis.**
Having been a major
archeological site in the
mid-twentieth century,
the Helwan necropolis
at Memphis has again,
since 1997, become an
active site for study.

Grave Goods

The number and quality of the grave goods
found in the tombs at Helwan clearly show that
material possessions had become an essential
feature in the tomb for the sustenance of the
deceased in the afterlife—no matter what their
social status. Pottery is found in abundance in
tombs of all social classes, particularly because it
was not a target for tomb robbers. In the Early
Dynastic Period, large, utilitarian storage vessels
were most common, used to supply the deceased
with wine, beer, and grain after their death.
Bread molds are also prolific and would have
produced the bread used in offerings to the dead.
In addition to these items of food, an extended
funerary repast usually accompanied the
deceased, which could include large cuts of
meat and poultry. Stone vessels attest to the
fact that the Early Dynastic Period was a
peak in their production. Their fine
quality and frequency would also
suggest that the state had
become involved in acquiring
the raw materials and manufacturing process required to
produce these vessels.

Beautiful ivory pieces have
also been uncovered in the
graves, which include small

cosmetic spoons and sticks, gaming pieces, and
inscribed inlays for boxes. Jewelry was also an
important part of funerary goods, with both
men and women having been found with ivory,
shell, or bone bangles. Beads and amulets strung
into necklaces and bracelets incorporate semi-
precious stones such as carnelian, amethyst, and
garnet or the artificial glazed imitation faience.
The remains of various copper objects also attest
to the growing importance and use of metals
during this period in Egyptian history.

Funerary Stelae

The most significant discovery from Helwan,
however, is a group of over 40 inscribed stone
blocks known as stelae, which were placed in the
tomb's superstructure. These stelae commonly
show the deceased seated in front of an
offering table, sometimes with a linen
list, and act as a precursor to the
beautiful funerary stelae which
become so characteristic of
the Old Kingdom. These stelae
from Helwan also frequently
give the name of the tomb
owner and their titles,
providing some of the earliest
evidence for writing in the
whole of Egypt.

Left **Too stale?** Bread was
buried in tombs to sustain
the dead in the afterlife.
This is in fact not a loaf
but a bread mold.

Memphis

There were three major religious and political cities in early Egypt: Hierakonpolis, Abydos, and Memphis. During the Early Dynastic Period it was Memphis that became the main cultural and administrative center.

Below **Early Dynastic ivory statue.** This exquisite figurine of a woman was found at Abu Rawash.

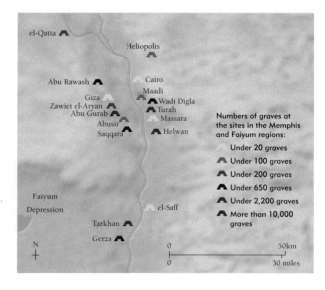

Numbers of graves at the sites in the Memphis and Faiyum regions:

Under 20 graves
Under 100 graves
Under 200 graves
Under 650 graves
Under 2,200 graves
More than 10,000 graves

Memphis was Egypt's first capital and the administrative center during the Early Dynastic Period and the Old Kingdom, and retained a significant religious and political position throughout ancient Egypt.

The Perfect Site

It seems that the choice of Memphis as the capital during the Early Dynastic Period was influenced by the strategic and geographic location of the site. Memphis lies on the northern end of Upper Egypt, and the southern end of Lower Egypt, where it was easy to administer the entire country, especially the Delta region and the internal and foreign trade routes. By contrast, the other major cities of Abydos and Hierakonpolis were considered too remote from the vast expanse of the Delta. Memphis was established near the ancient sites of Helwan, Maadi, and Tura.

Scholars suggest that the Memphite area must already have been acting as a point for transport and communication before the unification of Upper and Lower Egypt, not only between the south and the north, but also between Egypt and its trading neighbors in the ancient Near East.

In ancient Egypt, Memphis had as many as three names: *Ineb-hedj, Men-nefer,* and *Hut-ka-Ptah. Ineb-hedj* probably means "white fortress" or "the white walls," which may suggest that the city was surrounded by a wall or some other enclosure. About 2,500 years later, the great Greek historian Herodotus— whose writings have yielded much of great value to modern Egyptologists—wrote that the legendary king Menes, considered by the ancient Egyptians to be the first king of Egypt, raised a dyke which protected Memphis from the inundations of the Nile. This information could support the wall reference in "the white walls." The later name *Men-nefer* appears to come from the name of the pyramid complex of King Pepy I of the Sixth Dynasty at

Saqqara. *Men-nefer* means "established and beautiful." *Hut-ka-Ptah* is the name of the temple of god Ptah in Memphis, which the city was later named after, and it may also, it is believed, be the origin of the name *Aegyptus* or "Egypt."

The Memphite necropolis of the Early Dynastic Period consists of many large cemeteries: Saqqara, Abusir, and Abu Roash on the west bank of the Nile River, and Helwan and Tura on the east bank. The cemetery at Saqqara contains the *mastabas* of the high officials of the Early Dynastic Period, and the royal tombs of the Second Dynasty. Helwan represents the largest Early Dynastic cemetery in Egypt, with more than 10,000 graves excavated in the 1940s, and recent excavations revealing a considerable amount of information about the general population of Egypt's first capital.

The most obvious monument at the site of Memphis so far found is the temple of the god Ptah, dating to the New Kingdom, and the remains of the palace of Mernptah, the successor of Rameses II.

Where is Memphis Today?

Pinpointing the location of the early city is fraught with difficulty. The problem is that potential sites are covered by modern buildings and meters of alluvial deposits—a result of the Nile River changing its trajectory over the

the Nile River changing its trajectory over the millennia, possibly destroying the remains of the city. A recent geographical survey of the Memphite region, undertaken by the Egypt Exploration Society, has revealed valuable information regarding the topography of the site in ancient Egypt. This information suggests that, during the Early Dynastic Period, the early settlement of Memphis lay on the west bank of the Nile River close to the elite tombs of northeast Saqqara and the modern village of Abusir. By the time of the Third Dynasty the northern parts of the settlement and the cemetery were, as far as can be deduced from the evidence, abandoned as the river receded, and the settlement gradually shifted south toward the modern village of Mit Rahina.

The earliest known archeological strata of Memphis that have been excavated so far date to the First Intermediate Period at Kom el-Fakhry, which lies to the south of Mit Rahina. On the other hand, the earliest graves at Helwan predate the elite tombs at Saqqara and the beginning of the First Dynasty, which is the traditional date for the foundation of Memphis. Furthermore, the cemetery at Helwan is the largest and most socially diverse cemetery dating to the Early

Dynastic Period, not only in this region, but in the entirety of Egypt. Given that the poorest inhabitants of Memphis were buried here, not just the wealthy, it would be difficult to argue that they traveled over a long distance and across the river to bury their dead. Therefore the actual location of Early Dynastic Memphis might lie on the eastern side of the river rather than the western side.

Above **Tomb of the Apis bull.** A nineteenth-century engraving of this famous tomb in Memphis.

Below **First Dynasty vases.** These alabaster vases are shaped as milk jars supported by rope slings.

WRITING HISTORY

Ancient Egyptian writing probably started sometime around 3200 BCE, and was in use until the Roman conquest. Egyptian writing was characterised by four distinctive scripts: Hieroglyphic or "holy" signs, Hieratic, Demotic, and Coptic. Hieroglyphic signs mainly depict details and were used for sacred carving on temples and tombs. Hieratic was a cursive form where only the distinguishing details of the sign were drawn; there was also a hieratic script for personal correspondence on stone, potsherds, and papyrus with pen. Demotic, a more abbreviated cursive script developed from the hieratic, began in the seventh century BCE, and was used for personal and official documents. Coptic, developed between the third and sixth centuries CE, is the ancient Egyptian language written in the ancient Greek alphabet, with additional letters derived from the demotic. It is still in use today within the Egyptian Church.

Royal Tombs

Already in the Early Dynastic Period, the kings of Egypt were constructing monumental tombs. These tombs served the purpose not only of housing their bodies after death, but also of storing a wealth of grave goods.

These enormous structures were clearly meant to distinguish the ruler of Egypt from the rest of the population, and to emphasize both his affluence and power. The supremacy of the ruler was also demonstrated in his ability to take servants with him to the afterlife, who were buried alongside their king, perhaps as a result of human sacrifice. The construction of immense funerary enclosures, which probably served a ceremonial or ritual function, was a further striking display of their authority.

The location of the royal tombs of the First Dynasty has been a matter of some debate, with a number of scholars claiming that Saqqara was the burial ground of the earliest kings. However, it has now been clearly established, based on archeological and inscriptional evidence, that the monumental *mastaba* tombs at Saqqara belonged to members of the elite class from this period, and that the royal cemetery is located at the site of Umm el-Qa'ab in the region of Abydos.

Above **Table for the serpent game, Second Dynasty.** In this early Egyptian game, players had lion- or lioness-shaped pieces, and threw sticks to move.

First Dynasty Tombs

The royal tombs of the First Dynasty underwent significant architectural and stylistic developments. The tomb of Aha, the probable founder of the First Dynasty, was a large, rectangular tomb constructed of mud-brick and divided into three chambers with 34 subsidiary burials accompanying his grave. The tombs of kings Djer and Djet continued in this style, but their burial chambers included a series of recesses, and the number of subsidiary burials increased dramatically, with 338 interments surrounding the tomb of Djer alone. The reason for these subsidiary burials is still ambiguous, but it appears the servants of the king were meant to accompany him to the afterlife in order to continue their duties. Whether they were sacrificed at the time of the king's death is still uncertain.

The tomb of Den added several architectural features to the standard burial chamber and storage rooms of the tombs of his predecessors. For the first time a staircase led down into the burial chamber from the northeast, which allowed for the completion of the tomb before the death of the king: The security of the tomb was protected by a large blocking (portcullis) stone. The burial chamber of Den's tomb also incorporated a paved floor of granite. The tombs of kings Anedjib, Qa'a, and Semerkhet were similar, but on a smaller scale than those of their predecessors.

Second Dynasty Tombs

The early rulers of the Second Dynasty moved their burial ground to the site of Saqqara where two, maybe three, large gallery tombs have been uncovered: One attributed to either Hetepsekhemwy or Nebra, and the other to Nynetjer. They were carved into the bedrock and the rooms do not follow a regular plan but simply extend from a central entrance corridor out to either side. There is no evidence for any superstructures, although it is possible that some kind of feature was built to mark the location of the tombs, and was destroyed by future building works. From this time onwards there are no subsidiary burials accompanying the royal tombs, and it appears that this practice was discarded in the Second Dynasty.

The character of the royal tombs of the other Second Dynasty kings is uncertain as they have not been located to date, with the exception of the tombs of the last two rulers of the dynasty: Peribsen and Khasekhemwy. These kings were both buried with their First Dynasty predecessors at Abydos. The reason for a return to the

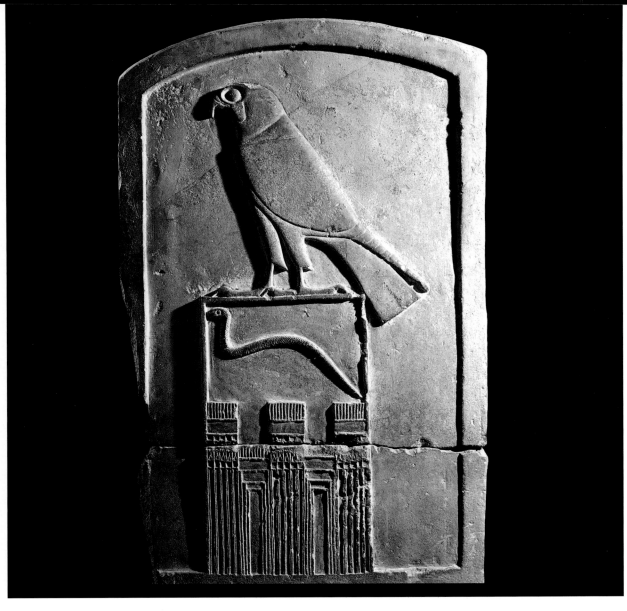

Left **Limestone funerary stela from Djet's tomb at Abydos.** This First-Dynasty stela features a hieroglyph containing a serpent and a falcon (Horus).

Abydos royal cemetery at this time remains difficult to determine. It is possible that these two rulers wanted to emphasize their lineage with the preceding dynasty and perhaps their right to rule over the country. The tomb of Peribsen largely returned to the style of architecture favored by the rulers buried at the site of Abydos. The tomb of Khasekhemwy includes a burial chamber and storage rooms, but he deviated from the earlier style of architecture by creating a more elongated structure, which was probably a result of the tomb having been built in several stages. Another interesting feature is that the burial chamber was lined with limestone blocks, acting as a precursor for later royal tombs fashioned out of monumental stone.

Funerary Enclosures

The majority of kings buried at Abydos also built huge funerary enclosures closer to the Nile Valley, which were probably the precursors to the monumental funerary temples built by the kings from the Old Kingdom onwards to celebrate the cult of the king. The exact purpose of these enclosures is unclear, though they may

have served some kind of ceremonial function or, as in later Egyptian history, may have been the focus of the funerary cult of the king. The funerary enclosure of Khasekhemwy remains an impressive testament to the power and wealth of these early kings even today, with its inner mud-brick wall rising out of the sand to an amazing height of 36 ft (11 m).

Below **Plenty for all.** These solid vessels are amphoras for wine, dating from around 3100 BCE.

Saqqara

One of the most striking developments with the expansion of the Egyptian state was the growing importance of an elite class, which had access to resources that must have been distributed directly from the king.

Right **Fine work**. An elaborately carved furniture leg, showing the type of workmanship that had formerly been only for royalty but now spread to the elite.

The members of the elite would have had very close connections with their ruler, would have served in the administration of the country, and in all probability would have been part of the royal family. The extent of their wealth and power is most remarkably seen in the size and character of their tombs and their conspicuous consumption, as attested by the wide range of grave goods.

Below **A mastaba**. Tombs such as this were popular among the administrative class, with many examples to be found at Saqqara.

The cemetery of this elite class during the Early Dynastic Period is located at Saqqara, an ancient burial field close to the old capital of Memphis, on the western side of the Nile River. Although these large structures were originally thought to be the royal tombs of the kings of the

First and Second dynasties, it is now clear that the tombs at Saqqara belong to those in the highest positions of power in the early Egyptian state. One of the original reasons for attributing these *mastaba* tombs to royalty was the sheer size of the superstructures and their characteristic niched facade, which was an architectural feature of the royal palace, affirming the significant place reserved for these individuals within Egyptian society.

Tombs of the Elite

The tombs of the elite at Saqqara consisted of subterranean chambers covered over with enormous *mastaba* superstructures. These

WHAT IS A MASTABA?

Mastaba literally means "bench" in Arabic, and a style of tomb from the Early Dynastic Period was given this name because its sloping walls resembled the benches commonly found outside Egyptian houses. Starting from the First Dynasty, pit tombs began to incorporate this type of superstructure to demarcate their position, enabling relatives of the deceased to visit and provide offerings for the tomb owner. Their shape may also reflect religious beliefs in the afterlife. At this time they were constructed out of mudbrick and were solid structures, with those of the First Dynasty incorporating the niched palace facade design, which can be seen in a range of examples from Saqqara. Second Dynasty *mastabas* were simpler in design, normally only including niches in the eastern wall. These tombs also included a substructure that commonly consisted of a burial chamber and smaller rooms to house the grave goods required for the afterlife.

superstructures were made out of mud-brick, with complex niched panelling commonly plastered and painted with geometric designs, which may be reminiscent of the woven mats used during the First Dynasty. They were normally composed of a series of separate compartments that were filled with sand, creating a solid core structure. The substructure typically included a large burial chamber with extra rooms for the storage of grave goods.

In the early First Dynasty, the subterranean chambers were only accessible at the time of the burial of the deceased, because the *mastaba* was simply built above the open pit after its construction. It was not until later in the First Dynasty, after the royal innovation in the tomb of Den at Abydos, that a staircase entrance was introduced. This meant that the superstructure could be built before the death of the tomb owner and that the burial chamber and additional rooms could be accessed after his death. This new feature of elite tomb architecture, however, meant that the tombs were more vulnerable to tomb robbers, and therefore, following royal tradition again, these graves incorporated large portcullis blocking stones to safeguard their possessions needed for the afterlife. These new innovations can be seen in the architectural structure of Mastaba no. 3505.

A unique feature of some of these *mastabas*, such as no. 3504, is the inclusion of hundreds of clay ox heads, which had real horns attached. They may have functioned as a kind of offering, or may have been representative of the animals themselves, which would have accompanied the deceased into the afterlife, providing sustenance and possibly a workforce for agricultural production. However, this element is distinct to the tombs at Saqqara and it is difficult to determine their purpose with any certainty.

Displays of Wealth

The wealth of these individuals is also demonstrated by the quality and quantity of the grave goods that they stored in their tombs. The graves not only contained a vast amount of pottery and stone vessels; in several tombs, like no. 3471 and no. 3507, substantial quantities of copper tools, gold jewelry, and other luxury products such as ivory inlays and furniture were also found. These products included imported materials like lapis lazuli, and must have been obtained by the king through trade links with other civilizations. Moreover, the high-quality manufacture of the goods suggests that they were produced by specialist craftworkers, probably in royal workshops, and distributed by the king to this select group of people.

Below **An official's treasure, c. 2950 BCE.** This gaming disk, showing the hunting of gazelles, is from the tomb of a chancellor called Hemaka. The elite copied royalty in the placement of precious goods in their graves.

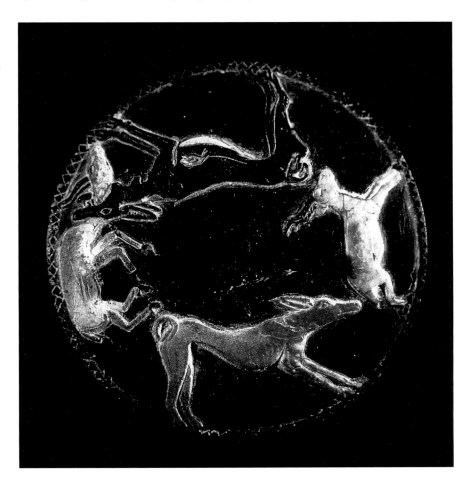

PYRAMIDS: THE OLD KINGDOM

Introduction

Spanning over five centuries (2686–2160 BCE) and four dynasties of rulers, the Old Kingdom was characterized by strong central administration and powerful divine kings. They instigated a time of relative peace and stability for Egypt.

Under these conditions, society prospered from mining and trade, and the pursuit of excellence in art, architecture, astronomy, and medicine was encouraged. The wealth of the state was channeled into creating symbols of power—palaces, monuments, and unparalleled tomb constructions—that left an indelible mark on the landscape and in history. This was the Age of the Pyramids.

Ironically, much of our knowledge about life in the Old Kingdom comes from the ancient Egyptian obsession with death and the afterlife.

The tombs, wall paintings, inscriptions, grave goods, and bodies the ancient Egyptians left behind shed valuable light on a period that is relatively "dark" in terms of its written history. Excavations at important Old Kingdom sites like Saqqara and Memphis supplement the sketchy details that exist regarding the lives and intrigues of kings, courtiers, and officials. The recently discovered workers' village and tombs at Giza also provide us with some insight into the common people and the organizational systems that harnessed the nation's workforce.

Below **Khafra's Pyramid at the necropolis at Giza, veiwed from the mortuary temple of Menkaura's Pyramid.** It is the only pyramid to have retained some of its original white limestone facing.

The wealth and power that created and sustained the Old Kingdom ultimately led to its demise. Too much fell into officials' hands and the period ended in a web of corruption, conspiracy, and political fragmentation. Inscriptions in Sixth-Dynasty tombs preserve some tantalizing hints as do the works of the priest-historian Manetho. Aided by a lingering drought and depleted treasuries, the nation entered a time of division and disorder known as the First Intermediate Period.

Left **Painted bas-relief from the *mastaba* tomb of the official Ptahhotep, at Saqqara.** It features the exquisite wall decorations of Old Kingdom tombs.

This preoccupation with death was just one part of a complex belief system. Other evidence surviving from this period shows that life at all levels of society was governed by religion. It was found in nature and the rise and fall of the Nile, and reflected in the worship of the king and state gods, the veneration of local deities, and the philosophy of *maat*, or universal order. The Egyptians called their interactions with the divine, *irt ht,* "doing things" or, *nt,* "regular procedures" and the tangible remains of these activities can still be seen today.

The King as a Ruler and a God

The ultimate responsibility for maintaining the divine order of things lay with the king. He was the chief priest and, as the son of Ra and incarnation of Horus, a god in his own right. The king was also expected to be a benevolent ruler and successful military leader. This heavy weight of obligation and expectation made it necessary to delegate duties to appointed officials, many of whom are known from their extravagant tombs or deeds recorded in inscriptions.

Females also rose to prominent and powerful positions. In the Sixth Dynasty Nebet, mother-in-law of Pepy I, became vizier of Upper Egypt (it would be 1,500 years before another woman filled this role) and Nitocris, the last ruler of this dynasty, was Egypt's first female "king."

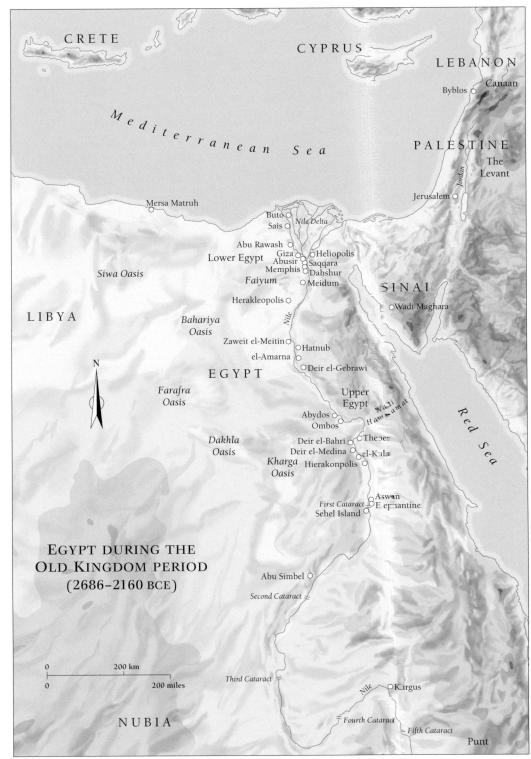

EGYPT DURING THE OLD KINGDOM PERIOD (2686–2160 BCE)

The King as God

The idea of divinity in kingship existed in Egyptian belief from before the First Dynasty. The king was not merely considered divinely inspired or mandated; he was venerated as an actual god with divine origin.

Below **Scene from a painted papyrus *Book of the Dead*.** The deceased and his wife before the underworld god Osiris.

Early references to the king identify him as *netcher* (the god) or *nefer netcher* (the good god). The divine nature of the king was a concept central to Egyptian ideology and his role was the intermediary between the gods and the people by divine right. Only he could speak with the gods and secure their goodwill. Through proper action and reverence, he would directly ensure peace, prosperity, and harmony for all of Egypt and its people.

A Good God

The foundation of the king's role originates in the legend of Osiris and Horus. Osiris was the good god, once the great and wise king of all Egypt. His jealous brother Seth, god of chaos, killed him and dismembered his body. In her sorrow, his wife Isis gathered his 14 body pieces and, with the assistance of Anubis, joined them together into the first mummy. Isis and Nepthys, in the form of kites, beat their wings to breathe life into Osiris. He rose and impregnated Isis with their son and heir, Horus. No longer permitted to rule on Earth, Osiris became the king of the Underworld, lord of eternity in the court of the dead. Horus went on to contend with Seth and eventually defeated him, taking his rightful place on his father's throne.

The Role of Divinity

The king's purpose was to fulfil the Horus role, to ensure Egypt's prosperity. He was an essential part of the divine order and it was believed that without him, Egypt would fall to chaos. One of the king's highest duties of office was to safeguard and uphold the principles of *maat*, divine truth and justice, through pious acts of devotion and just leadership. He also had secular functions, including military commander, judicial administrator, and religious leader.

Though a living incarnation of Horus, it was only after death that he would truly ascend to godhood. Complex funerary preparations were made to ensure his continued benevolence as a god in the afterlife. Duality shaped every aspect of Egyptian thought in religion and daily life, but nowhere so clearly as in the belief in the king as man and god together.

The divine authority of the god-king was identified with his coronation and ascension to the Horus throne, while before coronation the young prince was referred to as the Horus in the nest. Upon death, the king's divinity changed as he became one with Osiris in the underworld. He achieved true godhood and immortality after life, the final expression of the dual nature of the god-king. Immortality would be insured and inscribed for eternity in his burial chambers and his temples.

Inscriptions for Immortality

In early formal records, the king's name was written in a serakh panel. This was an outlined palace facade crowned with a falcon representing Horus, which expressed his representation as the living Horus on the throne. The name of Narmer, a late Predynastic king, was inscribed on a serakh panel on the necropolis seal at Den, giving the earliest evidence of these concepts. The serakh panel of Khasekhemwy, the last king of the Second Dynasty, is uniquely crowned by images of both Horus and Seth. This shows a shift in the ideal form of divinity at that time. By the end of the Third Dynasty, the king's name had moved from the serakh panel to the familiar knotted loop of the cartouche.

The perception of the king's divinity altered slightly with Fourth-Dynasty King Djedefra, who made a change in his title, becoming the first king to identify himself as "son of Ra." This marked the beginning of a departure from the concept of the king as god incarnate. The epitaph "son of Ra" would remain part of the pharaonic titulary for dynasties to come. It would also eventually lead to a more sophisticated separation of thought in the dual concept of the king as a man and the office of the king as divine.

PHARAOH OR KING?

Per-aa (pharaoh) means palace, the great or royal house, and did not designate the king himself until the New Kingdom period (c. 1550 BCE). In earlier periods, the word for king varied according to the function that was being referenced. Hem (commonly translated as majesty, but more literally "body") was used to indicate the king's physical presence, while nsw (nee-soo, king) or nsyt (ne-soot, kingship) denoted his office and administrative duties.

Right **Cartouche of Nyuserra, a Fifth-Dynasty king.**
A cartouche is a round or oval-shaped ring, a container for the heiroglyphs of the king's names. This cartouche, carved in pink granite, adorns his pyramid at Abusir.

Belief and Faith

Elements of faith permeated daily life, from the divinity of the king to the common supplication of household deities. Between the Third and Fourth Dynasties, the focus of belief shifted from its emphasis on Horus to the growing influence of Ra.

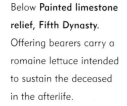

Right **Wooden bust from Saqqara, Fifth Dynasty.** This is possibly a portrait of the priest Ka-aper. The gleaming inlaid eyes are made of rock crystal.

This is evidenced by the king's name now being written in a cartouche ring instead of the traditional serakh panel, by the addition of "son of Ra" to the king's titles, and in the increasing importance of solar elements in funerary structures—most notably the Giza pyramid complex and the solar temple of the Sphinx.

Numerous regional cult deities still existed. Egypt had 42 nomes (provinces or districts) along the Nile Valley believed to be a reflection of Predynastic chiefdoms. Most housed their own cult center with local priesthoods and favored gods. Some had different versions of the creation mythology, attributed to different creator deities and complete with their own

Below **Painted limestone relief, Fifth Dynasty.** Offering bearers carry a romaine lettuce intended to sustain the deceased in the afterlife.

version of the divine family. The Egyptians found no contradiction with this. Evidence suggests that when they encountered foreign worship, they were inclined to incorporate it into their own local customs.

Religion and Magic

Religion was seamlessly interwoven with everyday life; the belief in magic and ritual practice cannot easily be separated. The word for magic, *heka*, cannot be isolated from religion as it encompassed the concepts of universal creative energy and divine power. The influence of the gods affected nearly everything. There were rituals and spells assisting with such concerns as household protection, prosperous

crops, childbirth, healing, and illness. The common person could make supplications to household gods such as Bes, Taweret, or Thoth, who offered protection and wisdom to deal with everyday problems.

Small statues, amulets, wands, and protective charms were numerous, and the images associated with deities were often incorporated into everyday items of furniture or tools. The community had a number of people capable of helping others with crafting spells and rituals, interpretations, and utilizing *heka* on their behalf, such as priests (*wab*), midwives (*rekhet*), physicians (*sunu*), or charm craftsmen (*saa* or *sau*). This would all be common practice not separated from daily activity, as there were no central places for worship outside of grand festivals or major religious gatherings. Living was infused with magic and ritual; there was no concept of religion as separate from existence. The divine was inherent in every action.

Priests and Temple Duties

The cult or god temple was the center of social and economic life in the community, though it is probable that only priests and temple workers were allowed inside. The common petitioner could come here to leave offerings or supplications, give thanks, or make petitions in the outer court or entryway, which might be adorned with lists of invocations or spells for guidance, but would be allowed no further.

Offerings supported the priesthood, workers, their families, and the poor. The temple was a sanctuary of the god, not a church. Few priests would have been involved in the daily rites and perhaps only the high priest directly tended the image of the god. All who entered the temple were required to maintain strict ritual purity, including cleanliness, purification of the body, removal of body hair, avoidance of taboo foods, and abstinence from sexual intercourse for a number of days before serving the temple. Most priestly positions were not full time; some served for only a month or two before returning to other jobs.

The priests performed daily rituals involving burning incense and pouring libations to the god. Food offerings were brought, and the statue was moved and cleaned, washed, perfumed, dressed in fresh linens, and adorned with makeup and jewelry each morning. Lesser rituals were performed at noon and evening before the temple was sealed for the night. Song hymns, and dance also played an important role; they were believed to please, nourish, and placate the gods. Music was probably part of daily reverence but was also important for public participation in festivals and processions held throughout the year. These were occasions of great celebration when many could attend the gods' rite. People would travel great distances to participate in a particular cult center's festivals.

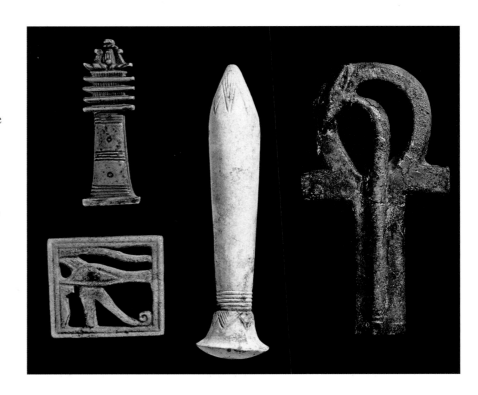

Above **A variety of ancient Egyptian amulets, held in the Turin Museum, Italy.** Clockwise, from top left, these are: An adjed pillar, a papyrus bud, an ankh, and a wedjat eye.

Significance of the Afterlife

Adherence to *maat* (leading a just, moral life) would ensure favorable judgment from the gods and admission to the afterlife, the Fields of Hotep ("fields of offerings".) This was a paradise where the deceased enjoyed a perfect version of life in the Nile Valley, with abundant food, drink, and a closer association between their eternal souls and the gods. The Egyptians had a complex idea of the "soul." Comprised of many facets, the *ka, ba,* and *akh* were of greatest importance in the afterlife. The *ka* was the spirit, or spiritual energy, believed to require tending and sustenance in the form of food offerings left for the deceased. The *ba* was the form of the physical body that allowed the deceased to move around in the afterlife. Mummification ensured the necessary preservation of a complete *ba*. The *akh*, or transformed spirit, united the *ka* and *ba*, allowing the deceased rebirth and eternal life.

Gods and Goddesses

The ancient Egyptians had an extensive pantheon of gods. They varied from small, local cults to gods of prominent political and social influence. Constant advances in linguistics enrich our understanding of their significance.

Various regions of Egypt such as Memphis and Hermopolis had different versions of creation mythology. The elements of Egypt's oldest creation myth come from the Pyramid Texts recorded in Heliopolis.

In the beginning there was Nun, the primordial waters of chaos. The god Atum (later known as Ra-Atum) created himself out of Nun. He had nowhere to stand, so under him was raised the pyramid-shaped *benben* stone as the first land. Atum contained both male and female elements, so he copulated with his hand and swallowed his seed. He conceived and spat out Shu, the god of air, and vomited (or sneezed) out Tefnut, the goddess of moisture. Shu and Tefnut mated and gave birth to Geb, the god of earth and Nut, the goddess of the sky. Geb and Nut lay together and produced four children: Osiris, Isis, Nepthys, and Seth. Atum then ordered Geb and Nut separated by Shu, who raised Nut's body above his head, creating the division of earth and sky.

The Greeks call these first nine gods the Ennead. The Egyptian word for this concept, *Pesdjet*, could mean either a group of nine gods or an unnumbered group of gods making up a pantheon or family. The first five gods represent the cosmic principles of sun, wind, water, earth, and sky. The last four pertain to the divinity of kingship and the Osiris–Horus mythology, validating the duality of the god-king.

The Egyptian Pantheon

After Atum, the gods of the Ennead begin with Geb, the husband of Nut. He guides the dead to the Afterworld and gives them refreshment. He is usually shown lying reclined under his wife

Right **Papyrus after tomb painting, Valley of the Kings, Thebes.** The sky goddess Nut, studded with stars, arches over the sky, held up by Shu. Geb is shown beneath her in a typical reclining pose.

THE MANY FACES OF RA

Predynastic beliefs attribute Atum as the sun-god and Horus as a god of sky and sun. As the Old Kingdom theocracy gained power, earlier beliefs were incorporated with the expanding popularity of Ra, and the Osiris–Horus mythology. Atum became Ra-Atum, the rays of the setting sun. Osiris became the divine heir to Atum's power on Earth and passed his divine authority to his son Horus. The king as "Horus on the throne" was a direct heir to the gods. "Ra" eventually became a precedent for identities of the sun-god, as a description of the physical presence of the sun. Deities were also elevated in status at different times by adding Ra to their names.

Horus was reflected in Ra-Herahkti associating the morning sunrise with a falcon in flight and in Heru-Behdeti as the solar disc between falcon's wings. As the ram-headed deity Auf, Ra sailed the solar bark through the Duat at night before his re-emergence in the morning. The scarab-headed god Ra-Khepri pushed the midday sun being across the sky in imitation of scarab beetles pushing balls of dung, which the Egyptians saw as a symbol of rebirth. Amun was a primitive elder god called "hidden" or "unknowable" and was reinterpreted in the New Kingdom as a manifestation of the sun-god, represented by the solar disc and titled Amun-Ra, king of the gods. The Aten, a literal name for the sun disc, was elevated by Akenaten in the Eighteenth Dynasty as the only sun-god of a monotheistic state religion, which was abolished immediately after his reign.

Right **The god Ra-Atum was associated with the setting sun.** Ra became a prominent god from the Fifth Dynasty. Other gods such as Atum incorporated Ra into their names and kings suffixed theirs with "son of Ra."

with his elbow and knee raised in the air to symbolize Egypt's hills, while Nut, goddess of the heavens, arches over both Geb and Shu as a starry, naked female whose fingers and toes touch the earth. Shu is the god of the dry wind and husband to Tefnut. His eternal duty is to support Nut arched over Geb, which prevents the universe from falling to chaos. A daughter of Ra, Tefnut is often depicted with the head of a lioness wearing the solar disc.

Osiris, the "good god," is lord of the dead and the Underworld. Originally an earth god of vegetation, he is shown mummified, with green or black skin, holding the crook and flail. His wife, Isis, is depicted with the throne hieroglyph or the solar disc between cow horns on her head. She is a powerful goddess of magic and secrets; as the mother of Horus she is mother to the king and the human link to divinity. She occupies a position in the pantheon similar to that held by the Virgin Mary in Christianity.

Seth is the god of chaos, storms, and the elemental force of opposition. He is best known for the murder of his brother Osiris. Seth appears with the head of an unidentified, possibly mythical, animal with the face of an anteater or donkey and long, squared-off ears. His wife, Nepthys, is a funerary and protective goddess, whose role seems to be to second the duties and actions of her sister Isis.

Horus, the son of Osiris and Isis, is the falcon or falcon-headed sun-god who represents the king's divinity. He has many forms and is closely associated with Ra, as his son and heir, and as the champion who avenges Osiris and defeats Seth. The sons of Horus are the guardians of canopic jars and are all depicted mummified. Imsety is the human-headed guardian of the liver, representing the south and protected by Isis. Hapi is the baboon-headed guardian of the lungs represents the north and is protected by Nepthys. Duamutef is the jackal-headed guardian of the stomach, representing the east, and is protected by the ancient goddess Neith. Qebehsenuef is the hawk-headed guardian of the intestines, representing the west, and protected by Selket, the scorpion goddess. They were retrieved from Nun by Sobek, the crocodile god, and born from a lotus flower.

Left **Hieroglyph of the god Geb from Heliopolis.** This early Old Kingdom relief, dated c. 2600 BCE, names Geb, one of the nine gods of the Egyptian Ennead, the gods of creation.

Gods for all Occasions

The animalistic form of many Egyptian gods is often a source of fascination. Anubis is the jackal-headed god of embalming. Epithets used with his name include "lord of the sacred land," and "he who is in the place of embalming." Priests performing the "opening of the mouth" ceremony during embalming often wore jackal masks. Anubis is identified as either the son of Ra and Nepthys, the son of Osiris and Isis, or the son of Osiris and Seth's wife Nepthys, but adopted by Isis, and thus a reason for hatred between Seth and Osiris. Ophios is a Predynastic jackal-headed god whose name means "opener of the ways." He bears the king's standard, the *shedshed*, on which the king ascends to the sky and guides the deceased to the right path into the Underworld. As protector and pathfinder, he is sometimes associated with Ra.

Bast is a daughter of Ra, the goddess of fire, cats, and sunlight. In her cat guise, she is a gentle household protector of pregnant women. Her son Nefertem is a solar god associated with perfumes and alchemy. The duality of Egyptian expression also associates Bast with Sachmis, the eye of Ra. She is the lioness-warrior who personifies war, violence, and destruction. The wife of Ptah, she was created by the fire of Ra's eye to punish the wicked. Mafdet is an early dynasty cheetah or leopard-headed goddess who protects against scorpions and snakes, especially in the Underworld. She is shown with braids and a snake headdress, or as a leopard climbing an execution pole and predates both Bast and Sekhmet.

Apophis is the giant snake that represents the powers of opposition and chaos, and battles against the bark of the sun-god each night as it sails through the Underworld realm of the Duat. Selket is the scorpion goddess, protector of the embalmer's tent and guardian of Apophis when he is imprisoned in the Underworld. The frog-headed goddess of childbirth is Heket and midwives are sometimes called servants of Heket. Khnemu, one of the oldest gods, is the ram-headed god of sculpting and pottery who sculpted the first humans on his potter's wheel. Nekhbet and Wadjet are the "two ladies" of the pharaonic titulary and protectors of the king. Nekhbet, the vulture goddess of Upper Egypt, is sometimes called the right eye of Ra and is depicted by vulture's wings. Wadjet, the cobra goddess of Lower Egypt, is symbolized in the *uraeus* worn on the pharaoh's headdress as an indicative mark of royal authority.

Other gods are intellectually conceptual in nature. Hu is the divine word and his name is the sound of the first sacred utterance, "hooo," while Sia represents mental perception and the touch of the divine. Maat stands for divine justice and truth and is symbolized by her ostrich feather. Heku personifies the divine force of magic. Benu is the rising sun, associated with

Left **Turquoise statuette of Thoth.** The god of learning and wisdom, Thoth was represented with the body of a man and the head of an ibis.

Right **Painted limestone decoration, Eighteenth Dynasty.** King Amenhotep II drinks milk from the cow-goddess Hathor.

GREEK	EGYPTIAN
Isis	Aset, Ast
Osiris	Usir, Wesir, Unnefer
Seth	Sutekh, Set
Nepthys	Nebt-het, Nebhet
Horus	Hor, Heru
Hathor	Het-heru
Thoth	Djehuty
Anubis	Anpu
Bast	Bastet
Apophis	Apep
Phoenix	Benu
Sachmis	Sekhet, Sakhmet
Khnemu	Khnum
Ophios	Wepwawet
Khons	Khonsu, Khensu
Thueris	Taweret

Above **The names of Egyptian gods that are most familiar** to us are actually their Greek translations. Some of them are listed above, alongside their Egyptian names and spelling variations.

Left **The jackal-headed god Anubis, Eighteenth Dynasty, Valley of the Kings, Thebes.** This painted limestone decoration is from the tomb of Horemheb, a general under Amenhotep IV and Tutankhamun.

Ra-Atum standing on the *benben* stone, and also with the *ba* of Ra. The *bennu* is a fiery bird that is reborn from its own ashes, and is believed to be the origin of the legend of the Greek phoenix.

Many gods enjoyed lasting and popular cults, such as Ptah and Thoth. Ptah, the creator deity of Memphis, is the god of architects and craftsmen. He is mummified, holding an *ankh* and a *djed* scepter. Thoth is the god of wisdom, the scribe of the gods and the inventor of writing and the hermetic arts of magic. He records the balance of *maat* in the judgment of the dead and is credited with writing the *Book of the Dead*. He is depicted either as ibis-headed and holding a scroll and pens, or as a baboon. Khons is a primitive moon-god associated with the left eye of Ra. He is possibly an early form of Thoth, depicted as a hawk-headed man wearing a lunar disc.

Hathor is a cow-goddess of love, happiness, women, fertility, and music, shown as a woman wearing a headpiece of cow horns around a solar disc. In earlier versions she is Horus' mother, but both she and that role are later associated with Isis. Bes and Thueris are popular household deities who protect children. Bes is a god of war, music, and dance, depicted as an ugly dwarf in animal skins. Taweret, a semi-humanoid hippopotamus, is guardian of women and childbirth.

The primitive and Predynastic gods are less well known. Andjety, a primitive precursor to Osiris, was depicted with crook and flail and associated with kingly power and rebirth. Bat was a sky goddess gifted with divination. Shown mostly on amulets as a cow-woman with curly horns, she is thought a possible precursor to Hathor. In the Pyramid Texts, the king is represented as "Bat with her two faces" (past and future).

Two Predynastic gods, Hapi and Min, were associated with water. Hapi was a Nile god shown as a man with the fertility aspects of a woman, usually with papyrus reeds on his head. He was responsible for causing the annual inundation, while Min was a god of fertility and rain, shown as a bearded man with Amon's headdress and a thunderbolt in one hand. The king was associated with Min when he fathered the royal heir. One of the oldest goddesses is Neith, depicted as holding a bow and arrows and wearing the red crown. The gods requested Neith's advice to settle disputes. She is Sobek's mother, and in some accounts, the mother of Ra before his emergence from Nun. Sobek is shown with the head of a crocodile; reptiles were honored and worshipped in Crocodilopolis, to placate him.

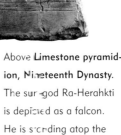

Above **Limestone pyramidion, Nineteenth Dynasty.** The sun-god Ra-Herahkti is depicted as a falcon. He is standing atop the snake-god Apophis.

the gods. By presenting this symbol thus signified his primary association with *maat* and his legitimacy as the ruler of Egypt.

Non-royals and *Maat*

The Egyptian people were also expected to value *maat* and to live their lives in agreement with its principles. Instruction manuals (known collec-

After death, the deceased declared in a "negative confession," and the degree to which they had lived a just life was evaluated by weighing their heart against either a small figure of Maat or a feather. Only the souls of individuals who had embraced *maat* were declared "true of voice" and allowed to pass into the afterlife.

having Egypt during the French army's expedition. Painted relief of the pharaoh before Sekhmet and Maat, from the portico of the great temple, Island of Philae.

The Meaning of *Maat*

Maat is a fundamental philosophical concept permeating every aspect of ancient Egyptian culture. Though no single word can encompass all its complex meanings, *maat* is often translated as truth, justice, balance, and harmony.

Below Goddess Maat, Fourth Century BCE. Painted and gilded wood with applied glass paste.

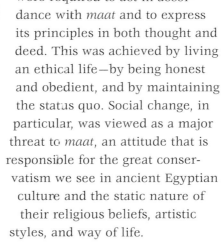

Maat was believed to be the order inherent in life made manifest in the endless cycle of nature as well as in the eternal presence of the king. *Maat* came into existence at the moment of creation and thus represented the perfect state of the universe. Nevertheless, universal harmony was vulnerable to *isfet*, the forces of chaos and disorder that threatened to constantly disturb the equilibrium of life.

To combat this challenge to cosmic order, all living things were required to act in accordance with *maat* and to express its principles in both thought and deed. This was achieved by living an ethical life—by being honest and obedient, and by maintaining the status quo. Social change, in particular, was viewed as a major threat to *maat*, an attitude that is responsible for the great conservatism we see in ancient Egyptian culture and the static nature of their religious beliefs, artistic styles, and way of life.

The Goddess Maat

The goddess Maat was the personification, the physical manifestation, of this

for the first time during the Fifth Dynasty, when the goddess appears to have become the focal point of a cult. The titles of royal officials from this period (for example, "prophet of Maat") also suggest that a priesthood was devoted to her worship. However, no temple was erected in her honor until the New Kingdom. In religious mythology, Maat was the daughter of the sun-god Ra, and sister of the air-god Shu.

The King and *Maat*

One of the most important duties of the king was to maintain *maat* on a national level, a function that he fulfilled by ruling in a just manner, serving the gods, and exerting control over nature and the enemies of Egypt. His commitment to this task can be seen in literary, ritual, and artistic form. From the Fourth Dynasty, many kings expressed their devotion to *maat* by incorporating the term into their royal titulary (for example, the epithet, *nb maat*, "possessor of *maat*") or by forming part of their name with *maat* (for example, *neb-maat-ra*, "lord of truth is Ra," the principal name of Amenhotep III).

The monarch's role as the protector of universal order could be represented graphically. Images of the king executing foreign prisoners, for example, symbolized his control over chaos, while those of hunting wild animals (particularly the unpredictable hippopotamus), emphasized

Below An anorthosite-gneiss statue of Khafra. The falcon god Horus is embracing Khafra's head with its wings outstretched. Khafra wears the nemes headcloth and false beard of a king.

Sneferu, the first king of the Fourth Dynasty, completed the first true pyramid. Called the Red Pyramid, it was created after he built and abandoned the Bent Pyramid and probably finished the Meidum pyramid. He also constructed a number of smaller step pyramids, making him the most prolific pyramid builder of the era.

Sneferu's first wife was Hetepheres I, his half-sister and mother of his sons Khnum and Khufu. His second wife also had two sons, Netjerape and Nefermaat and he had at least five more children by other wives or consorts.

A well-liked ruler, Sneferu bolstered the power of the ruling family line by giving official titles and positions to relatives. He maintained control over the nobility by keeping a tight rein on lands and estates. He conducted military excursions into Sinai, Nubia, and Libya, and began trade arrangements with Lebanon for the acquisition of cedar.

Among the most famous kings is Sneferu's successor, Khufu. Known to the Greeks as Cheops, he built *Ahket Khufu*, the Great Pyramid. Unlike his father, stories depict Khufu as a cruel tyrant. The Greek historian Herodotus recorded a tale illustrating Khufu's reputation in which the king sends his daughter to work in a brothel, raising money for his building projects.

His reign is estimated varyingly between 17 and 63 years. He maintained a military presence in the Sinai and Nubia to protect mining interests and campaigned to extend the southern border of Egypt. Khufu fathered at least a dozen children with his many wives and consorts. His first wife Meritates was the mother of Kawab and daughters Hetepheres II and Meresankh II. Khafra was his son by his second queen, Henutsen, while a Libyan consort is believed to be the mother of Djedefra, Bakara, and Khamerenebty I.

Djedefra, the Fourth Dynasty's third ruler, presents some mystery. It was once believed he murdered Kawab for the throne and was himself later murdered by Khafra, but recent discoveries have thrown this into doubt. While there is evidence of a religious schism between Djedefra and the rest of his family—explaining his move away from the burial ground of Saqqara to construct his mortuary complex at Abu Rawash—he also completed his father's burial. This makes it improbable that he was "out of favor." His name is recorded as provisioning and arranging the burial of the funerary boats at the Great Pyramid. An interesting discovery at Abu Rawash led to the theory that perhaps Djedefra, not Khafra, created the Great Sphinx at Giza. The sphinx statue found at Abu Rawash is believed to be the first of its kind. Djedefra married Hetepheres II, his half-sister and the widow of his brother Kawab. His chief wife, Khentetenka, was the mother of three sons, Setka, Baka, and Hernet, and one daughter, Neferhotep I.

The fifth king was Djedefra's younger brother Khafra, who ruled between 25 and 66 years. Khafra is best known for building the second pyramid at Giza. He is traditionally credited with the creation of the Sphinx, based on its location and his resemblance to the monument, but existing statuary shows a strong resemblance between Khafra and Djedefra. Khafra had many wives, including the daughter of his brother

18 and 26 years. He built the third and smallest of the Giza pyramids, but died before its completion. His son Shepseskaf finished it. Menkaura's five wives included his two half-sisters, and he fathered at least six children.

Shepseskaf was the last Fourth-Dynasty king. His reign, troubled by political unrest, lasted only four to seven years. The government began to fall apart, and various political and religious factions vied for independence. He chose to create a large *mastaba* at Saqqara instead of a pyramid. An unusual monument, it is constructed of large granite blocks, cased in limestone and shaped like a huge sarcophagus. Shepseskaf had one wife of record, his half-sister Bunefer. Their daughter Khamaat married Ptah-Shepses, a high priest of Memphis.

The King-lists

King-lists help Egyptologists piece together the story of the Egyptian kings. These lists are some of the oldest known written records of the royal succession. One such record is the Turin Canon, found in 1823 by Napoleon's Proconsul, explorer Bernardino Drovetti. Compiled in the time of Rameses II, it lists most of Rameses' predecessors, from rulers far back in the Predynastic Period to the Second Intermediate period. The papyrus was badly mishandled by Drovetti and is now in fragments. Manetho's history was written circa 271 BCE for Ptolemy II. His book covered Egyptian history from 3100 to 332 BCE, and he was the first to create the divisions of dynasties. The original is lost; only later quotes of it still exist. The Palermo Stone is a record of the first five dynasties and Predynastic Period rulers. The pieces are in various museums, including Cairo, London, and Palermo, Italy.

The Abydos king-list was discovered on the walls of the Temple of Sety I. It is incomplete; likely only favored or approved rulers were included. Notable exceptions to the list include the Eighteenth-Dynasty pharaohs Hatshepsut and the heretic Amenhotep IV.

Above **Part of an inscribed slab featuring a king-list.** Made of limestone with residual paint, it is from the temple of the Nineteenth Dynasty pharaoh, Rameses II, at Abydos.

Left **Red quartzite statue of Djedefra, a Fourth-Dynasty king, from Abu Rawash.** It is 10⅜ inches (26.5 cm) in height.

Life as a God-king

The king, who was both head of state and religion, shouldered a heavy burden of responsibility. He was expected to dispense justice, perform religious functions, and supervise public works, as well as lead military and trade expeditions.

Right **Painted fragment of a limestone ostracon.** Acrobats, dancers, and other skilled performers were frequently called on to entertain ancient Egyptian royalty.

The insurmountable list of activities and duties he was expected to perform made it necessary to delegate duties and appoint deputies. These include the vizier, who oversaw the affairs of state, and high priests, who performed the religious ceremonies, on the king's behalf. There were also army officers and ambassadors who helped organize Egypt's military and trade campaigns.

Mediator of Heaven and Earth

The king was meant to use his divine influence to benefit the economic and spiritual aspects of Egyptian life and to improve the lot of his subjects. The success of kingship was closely bound to the success of the annual Nile inundation; a bad Nile and the subsequent shortage of food augured a troubled reign. As a divine king, his intervention with the gods could restore or ensure the harmony of the universe (*maat*).

The king was also expected to be a warrior king and lead his army into battle. Successful kingship was often immortalized by epic depictions of the king in battle, participating in victory processions and smiting the enemies of Egypt.

Daily Life

Like the cult statues of deities, the king's body had to be fed, washed, robed, and adorned with the appropriate regalia on a daily basis. This daily toilet was performed by attendants of the private apartments of the king called *khenty-shey*, who may also have served as bodyguards. Titles associated with music have been discovered in the tombs of *khenty-shey* excavated at Giza, suggesting that the *khenty-shey* were also skilled musicians.

THE SED-FESTIVAL

After 30 years of rule, a king would celebrate a jubilee called a sed-festival, although lesser regnal periods are recorded for the sed-festivals of numerous kings. This ceremony consisted of various rituals of renewal and regeneration enacted by the king to reinforce his standing as a strong and viable ruler.

A picture of the sed-festival of Djoser has been found in a subterranean chamber beneath the Step Pyramid, in which he is shown running between two structures, perhaps signifying the borders of Egypt or the unification of the two lands of Upper and Lower Egypt. An impressive structure in the Step Pyramid complex was used as a backdrop for Djoser's sed-festival. The courtyard is surrounded by chapels, probably representing the shrines of gods from various provinces. A double pavilion at the end of the courtyard is thought to have contained two thrones representing Upper and Lower Egypt.

Right **The heb-sed court of Djoser.** It fronts the chapels in the funerary complex of this Third-Dynasty king. His pyramid, which can be seen in the background, was the first to be built of stone.

His Majesty's Pleasure

The official day appears to have begun with a meeting with the vizier to order what was required of the king's deputy in affairs of state. The king would also hold audience at the "balcony of audiences," from which he was able to confer gifts on deserving subjects and receive ambassadors, gifts, and tributes from conquered lands.

Palace design, with its broad courts, frescoed halls, gardens, and pools, suggests a life of splendor and opulence with many opportunities for leisure. Pictures of the king hunting suggest that this was a favored leisure pursuit while reinforcing the king's virility. The palace apartments also included a royal harem.

Food consumed by the wealthy in Egypt included oxen, pig, domesticated and wild poultry, and fruits including dates, figs, and pomegranates. Honey, figs, and almonds were particularly prized foods. Honey could be used to make cakes. While beer was readily available to the working classes, wine was only consumed by the wealthy.

Judging by the number of titles held by performers attached to the court and in the king's service, music and dance performances may have been a regular component of the king's daily schedule. The popularity of pygmy dancers is immortalized in the enthusiastic letter from Pepy I to Harkhuf, who was transporting a dancing pygmy back to Pepy's court. The Westcar Papyrus even relates the antics of a magician summoned to the palace to entertain King Khufu, who somehow managed to experience boredom. The Westcar Papyrus also relates that Khufu's predecessor, Sneferu, put the burden of state at bay by participating in a boating party in which he was apparently accompanied by 20 beautiful maidens.

What Price, Divinity?

All the opulence of palace life came at a price. Life as a king was plagued by the constant anxiety of plots against the king's mortal life and there are a number of conspiracies dating from the Old Kingdom. One from the reign of Pepy I is recorded in the tomb of the court official Weni. Another is suggested by the historian Manetho as occurring in the reign of Teti (for which a good deal of evidence has recently been uncovered in the Teti cemetery at Saqqara). While some features may be more myth than fact, another conspiracy almost certainly ended the reign of the unnamed brother of the female king, Nitocris, and was the reason for the subsequent demise of her reign at the end of the Old Kingdom.

Left **Limestone relief, Fifth Dynasty.** Tomb decorations frequently depict hunting scenes. From the mastaba of Akhhetep in Saqqara, this scene shows a bird hunt in progress. Hunting was a favored pastime of Egyptian kings.

Imhotep the Innovator

When Djoser—the second king of the Third Dynasty—decided to have a tomb
built for himself, he fortuitously chose Imhotep to oversee the construction work.
Imhotep was his vizier and his high priest at Heliopolis, the holy city of the sun.

It was also known as the capital of learning.
Imhotep did not merely supervise the work, he
had a vision for what a royal tomb should be.
He erected not a large *mastaba* for the king as
was the norm but a step pyramid surrounded by
a large complex in Saqqara. Moreover, all of this
large building work was entirely out of stone.

Stone for Building

The use of stone as a building material was
known to the ancient Egyptians well before
this time. They used it in their architecture in a
limited way in small buildings along with other
light materials (wood, reeds, and mud-brick).
But to change the design of the royal tomb
and to use stone on such a monumental scale
was an enormous feat.

Djoser must have been most impressed for
he had the base of a standing statue representing
him to bear his royal name along with the name
and titles of his genius architect, Imhotep,
in beautiful hieroglyphic signs. The statue is
gone, but the base was found in the entrance
colonnade inside Djoser's complex and it is
now kept in the Egyptian Museum (in Cairo).
It is a testimony for the exceptional royal favor

Below **Base of statue
bearing Djoser's name
beside the name and
titles of Imhotep, his
architect.** Both names have
since been associated.

bestowed on Imhotep, for no man was ever allowed to officially record his name on a royal monument.

Imhotep must have had a tomb somewhere in Saqqara, next to the king he served, though none has so far been discovered. Yet the memory of Imhotep as a great intellectual survived. The ancient Egyptians believed he recorded his wisdom in a literary work and was hence considered by them as patron of scribes. It was in his honor that scribes during the New Kingdom poured water from their pots before starting to write.

The image of Imhotep evolved even further; he became the son of Ptah, the god of Memphis. And during the Late Period, hundreds of bronze statuettes showing him as a seated man unrolling a papyrus sheet on his knees were made. By the end of the Late Period, he became a healer and a chapel at Saqqara was erected for him, which became a destination of pilgrimage for the ill and the crippled. He was also invoked "to give a son to everybody begging for it, a wife to everybody imploring it," as the Egyptian prayers put it.

Imhotep's Fame Throughout the Ages

During the Greco–Roman Period, the cult of Imhotep gained more fame and spread all over Egypt and Nubia. His chapel at Saqqara was called the Asklepieion by the Greeks who equated him with their god of medicine, Asklepius. Several sanctuaries were dedicated to him in many temples. At Deir el-Bahari, in the temple of Queen Hatshepsut of the Eighteenth Dynasty, a chapel was added during the Ptolemaic Period where Imhotep and Amenhotep son of Hapu, another deified man who was the vizier of Amenhotep III, were venerated; not as patron saints but as gods up until the second century CE.

It is also during the Ptolemaic Period that a text was written in the name of Djoser and his vizier Imhotep.

The text, known as the Famine Stela, is carved on a granite rock on the island of Sehel, near Aswan. It describes a terrible period of famine in Egypt caused by low levels of Nile floods for seven consecutive years during the reign of Djoser. The king calls Imhotep and asks him what to do. Imhotep answers only after consulting the papyrus rolls in the library. He reveals to the king that Khnum, the god of Elephantine, an island facing the modern city of Aswan, is the protector of the Nile sources. The king then pays a personal visit to the temple of Khnum, and this god finally sends enough water to grow food to end the famine. In gratitude, after the advice of Imhotep, the king endowed the temple of Khnum with the strip of land over 70 miles (113 km) long south of Elephantine. The temple was free to use the revenues and the taxes of this area. This story, which is set in the time of Djoser and based on a natural disaster that hit Egypt from time to time, is written in a Ptolemaic style and language. It is believed by modern scholars to be a fabrication by the priests of Khnum during the Ptolemaic Period to justify the rights of the temple of Khnum to certain lands in Nubia. And what could be more convincing than a story where the name and acts of the well-respected Imhotep was mentioned?

Above Imhotep built a stone buttressed wall with 13 dummy gates around Djoser's pyramid complex. The only true entrance is pierced into a bastion in the southeastern corner.

Left Bronze statuette depicting Imhotep with a papyrus on his lap. These were popular from the Late Period onward, when he arose as a deified man, then as a god.

The Step Pyramids

Saqqara—whose modern name appears to derive from the funerary god Sokar —is a vast desert plateau, lying some 16 miles (25 km) to the south of Cairo. It is part of the necropolis of Memphis, which was the capital city of the Old Kingdom.

The site of Saqqara has burials dating from all periods of ancient Egyptian history (from the First Dynasty up until the Late Period) but it is visited today mainly because of its Old Kingdom monuments, dominated by the all-imposing Step Pyramid of Djoser.

The Step Pyramid of Djoser

Djoser's Step Pyramid is the earliest pyramid in Egypt. However, a *mastaba* of mud-brick at Bet-Khallaf, 12 miles (20 km) north of Abydos, is also attributed to Djoser, the purpose of which is still debated. One possibility is that this *mastaba* was built as a cenotaph. Another is that it was the king's burial place—following with the traditions of the earlier dynasties—but it was later renounced in favor of a more majestic monument in the north. Another theory purports it may be the tomb of a high official during Djoser's reign. Nevertheless, scholars agree the actual burial place of Djoser is his Step Pyramid at Saqqara.

Posterity made no mistake in attributing the art of building with hewn stone to Djoser's

Below **Djoser's Step Pyramid is the focal point of a complex built entirely of stone**. It contained unique structures that would not reappear in later pyramid complexes.

PYRAMID GRAFFITI

The simplicity and elegance of the complex of Djoser were very much appreciated by its ancient Egyptian visitors—mostly scribes who came to the site during the Eighteenth and Nineteenth Dynasties over 1,000 years after its completion. They left graffiti in the Houses of the North and the South, recording their names, the dates of their visits, and how they found the complex "as though heaven were within it, Ra rising in it." All the graffiti are in black ink written in hieratic, a cursive form of the hieroglyphic script. One scribe was extremely outraged at the sight of all the graffiti that he scorned his predecessors: "My heart is sick when I see the work of their hand ... I have seen a scandal, they are no scribes such as Thoth has enlightened." He recorded his disdain in graffiti next to the others.

Right **The House of the South, much like that of the North, has four fluted columns engaged to its facade.** The structure, being a dummy for the administrative office, has little space inside it. This is where ancient visitors to the site recorded their admiration for the monuments they saw.

architect, Imhotep. Imhotep's pioneering work started with the use of small limestone blocks to build a square *mastaba* (206 feet or 63 m long and 26 feet or 8 m high). This *mastaba* was then extended to the east to incorporate a series of shafts, giving access to the burials of royal family members. The initial *mastaba* was then enlarged to become rectangular and to support three smaller *mastabas* on top. This four-stepped pyramid had a height of more than 130 feet (40 m). A later phase increased the volume of the building and the number of the superimposed *mastabas* to six. The Step Pyramid's final measurements were about 460 feet (140 m) by 385 feet (118 m) and it rose more than 195 feet (60 m) in height.

Under the Step Pyramid

A maze of galleries is reached through a tunnel opening several yards (a few meters) away from the northern face of the pyramid. Some of these galleries are lined with tiles of blue faience (one of these faience walls was removed and is now on display at the Egyptian Museum in Cairo). The galleries also contain panels showing the king running in the ritualistic race during the sed-festival. The king is designated on these panels as Horus Netjerikhet; the name Djoser is used from the Twelfth Dynasty onward.

Other galleries were filled from floor to ceiling with stone vessels: Around 40,000 of all shapes (such as bowls, dishes, jars, etc.),

and of different stones (Egyptian alabaster, diorite, schist, etc.). Most of them bear the names of the kings of the first two dynasties, some are those of Netjerikhet. The burials in a number of these galleries were plundered in antiquity. Two alabaster sarcophagi were found; one of them contained the bones of a child aged eight. Even the burial chamber of the king, lined with granite, and entered through a hole in its roof sealed with a granite plug weighing 3.5 tons, was robbed.

In 1821, the Prussian Consul-General von Manutoli found the remains of a mummy inside this chamber, but it was lost at sea when the ship carrying it to Prussia sank. A century later, parts of the same mummy, including a mummified leg, were found in the same chamber. They are believed to be parts of Djoser's body.

Left **Under Djoser's pyramid, the walls of some of the galleries are lined with blue faience tiles.** This panel in full is 6 feet (1.8 m) high and 6³⁄₅ feet (2 m) wide.

Around the Step Pyramid

The Step Pyramid was the focal point of a
complex. Elevating this superstructure to
195 feet (60 m) in height allowed Imhotep to
make it discernible from Memphis and higher
than the enclosure wall he built around the
complex. This wall was 33 feet (10 m) high and
measured 1,782 feet (545 m) by 906 feet (277 m).
It is buttressed like the walls of earlier *mastabas*.
The wall has 14 gates, 13 of which are simula-
tions and only one, at the southeastern corner,
is the true entrance. A narrow corridor, the stone
ceiling of which imitates palm logs, leads to a
long colonnade. The columns, copying in stone
the earlier reeded supports, are engaged to the
main walls of the colonnade by piers. It seems
the architect who built the Step Pyramid felt
tense about having the roof of the colonnade
supported by freestanding columns. The
colonnade ends with a small rectangular
hall; its roof lies on eight columns set in
four engaged pairs. Crossing this short
hall through a passage with a stone door
imitating a half-opened wooden one
leads to an open-air court.

To the right is the pyramid; to the
left is an enigmatic rectangular structure
with an arched roof. The subterranean
galleries under this structure, like
those under the pyramid, have faience
tiles, panels of the king, and a burial
chamber. Egyptologists call
this structure the Southern
Tomb. A chapel annex-
ed to it has a deco-
rative frieze of
cobras on the
upper part
of its walls.

The open court contains two B-shaped low
structures. They are possibly the limits between
which the king would perform the ritualistic
running. He then changed his clothes in a small
structure to the east, named today "Temple T."
Afterwards he proceeded to the sed (jubilee)
court to pay his respects to the divine statues
niched in the chapels arranged against the
eastern and western walls of the court. The king
was then crowned on a large stone platform at
the southern end of the court. This platform has
two short flights of stairs leading to the thrones
of the Two Lands placed side by side on top of it.

North of the jubilee court are two structures,
the House of the South and the House of the
North. Their facades are adorned with four
engaged fluted columns, much like the Doric
order, yet far earlier than the Greek type. The
Houses of the South and the North are believed
to be the representations of the administrative
offices from which Djoser managed Egypt's
affairs. These structures are massive stone
dummies, with not much space inside them.
This is because the complex structures were
to be used in the afterlife by the resuscitated
king, and would then, through the power
of magic, be fully functional.

To the north of the Step Pyramid are the ruins
of the funerary temple and beside it to the east
is the *serdab* (the Arabic word for a closed room).
The latter leans against the inclined casing of
the pyramid. Its northern wall has two apertures,
allowing tourists today to gaze upon a seated
life-size statue of Djoser inside the room (this
statue is a replica; the original is in the Egyptian
Museum in Cairo). The initial purpose of the
apertures though was to allow the king to watch

the circumpolar stars at the northern sky, the Imperishables as the Egyptians called them.

Reviving Imhotep's Work

All of those buildings between the pyramid of Djoser and the enclosure wall were unexcavated prior to 1920, since earlier archeologists were more interested in the pyramid than the mounds surrounding it. In 1927, archeologist Cecil Firth asked French architect Jean-Philippe Lauer to help him reconstruct the complex, which was badly destroyed but whose ruins could be put together. Lauer continued the work after Firth's death in 1931, with the help of James Quibell, then others until the late 1990s. After carefully studying the remains, their architectural technicalities, and ancient Egyptian depictions of the same buildings, Lauer was able to raise the buildings above the remaining bases of the walls.

The Buried Pyramid of Sekhemkhet

In 1951, Zakaria Goneim, Chief Inspector of Saqqara, began excavating a plateau lying southwest of Djoser's complex. The works revealed part of a large unfinished buttressed enclosure wall. On the wall, the name Imhotep in red ink was found; whether or not this designates the architect of Djoser as the designer of this complex is uncertain. Also unearthed was a step pyramid, which was left incomplete, with construction ramps still around it. Had this pyramid been completed, it would have been higher than that of Djoser, with seven steps.

In 1954, the mortuary temple to the north of the pyramid was found. Further north, the descending passage leading to the substructure was discovered. This passage was interrupted on three intervals by three intact blocking walls. On a part of the passage floor, a thick bed of clay concealed hundreds of stone vessels; also found was a collection of jewelry against its eastern wall. This included 21 bracelets and a small gold box in the shape of a bivalve shell. Some pottery jars were found, which were sealed with dry clay impressed with the Horus name Sekhemkhet, a king unknown up until those discoveries. The complex appears to be his.

The passage leads to a chamber roughly cut in the rock. In it lies a sarcophagus carved out of a single block of Egyptian alabaster. It has no upper lid, but rather a vertically sliding panel is used to close one of its ends. The fact that the

sarcophagus was sealed with plaster, and the remains of a floral wreath were on top of it, attracted wide publicity. One month after the find, and a week after the press was allowed to take pictures, the tight panel weighing 500 lb (227 kg) was lifted after two painful hours, in the presence of senior officials of the Antiquities Department. To the astonishment of all, the sarcophagus was empty. Moreover, it apparently never contained a body.

After this disappointment, work continued on the complex. The subsequent excavation seasons revealed more than 100 storage rooms around the sarcophagus chamber, more stone vessels, and an ivory plaque on which is recorded a list of linens. All the storage rooms were unfinished. The fact that Sekhemkhet reigned for six to seven years according to the ancient records may indicate his premature death, which would account for the unfinished state of his complex.

Above **The colonnade of Djoser's complex has 40 stone columns that imitate earlier reeded supports.** The columns are joined to the main walls of the colonnade by piers.

Above **The unfinished enclosing wall of Sekhemkhet's buried pyramid. His complex is near Djoser's Step Pyramid at Saqqara.**

Below **An ivory plaque found in Sekhemkhet's pyramid. It features an incised list of linens.**

Goneim's death in 1959 halted the work on the site and Lauer resumed the excavation in the 1960s. About 65 feet (20 m) from the pyramid, he discovered a *mastaba*. Its superstructure was quarried by later stone searchers. The burial chamber contained a wooden sarcophagus with the skeleton of a royal child, two years old. Fragments of gold leaf once covering the sarcophagus were scattered around it. Further work in this complex may yield more surprises.

THE UNFINISHED PYRAMID

At Zawiet el-Aryan, another pyramid lies a mile (1.5 km) north of the Layer Pyramid. Excavations by Barsanti between 1905 and 1912 revealed a trench leading to a pit. The pyramidal superstructure was never built. The burial chamber had large granite blocks covering its floor where an oval sarcophagus with a cemented lid was sunk. The sarcophagus was empty.

Until his death in 1917, Barsanti was convinced the real burial chamber was still to be discovered. Some of the limestone filling blocks of the pit had quarry marks with the name of the owner. This was believed to be Nebka, the first king of the Third Dynasty. But because of the large dimensions of the blocks, and the possibility that the name could be read Bikka—an obscure ephemeral king between Khafra and Menkaura—the Unfinished Pyramid could date to the Fourth Dynasty. In 1954, both the trench and the pit were cleared of sand to shoot scenes on pyramid building for an American film on ancient Egypt.

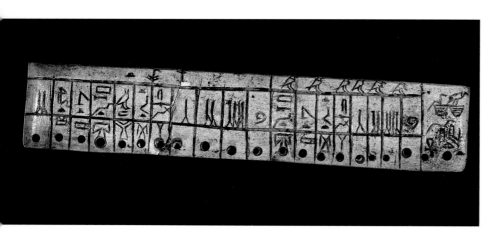

Museum of Fine Arts of Boston, archeologists George Reisner and Clarence Fisher excavated the pyramid as well as the cemeteries surrounding it. Tombs of the first three dynasties were found. One Third-Dynasty tomb contained bowls bearing the name of Khaba, which led scholars to attribute the Layer Pyramid to him. According to Reisner and Fisher's investigations, the pyramid was intended to have seven steps.

It consists of a square nucleus against which 14 independent layers of masonry have been laid. The courses of these layers were not laid horizontally, but they were sloped toward the interior. The excavators believed that the technique of adding layers of masonry to a central core was a new introduction. But the discovery of the Buried Pyramid of Sekhemkhet in 1951, and further investigation of the pyramid of Djoser, showed this technique was normally used to build step pyramids.

Some Enigmatic Provincial Step Pyramids

There are seven smaller square-based step pyramids rising in their modern ruined state to 20 feet (6 m) in height and around 65 feet (20 m) in length. One at Elephantine is built of granite; another, made of sandstone, is situated 3 miles (5 km) south of Edfu. The rest are limestone: At el-Kula (3^3/$_4$ miles or 6 km north of Hierakonopolis), at Ombos, at Sinki (5 miles or 8 km south of Abydos), at Sila in el-Faiyum, and at Zawiet el-Meitin (4^1/$_4$ miles or 7 km south of Minya).

Based on their building technique, all of these pyramids are dated to the Third Dynasty. But an expedition led by the University of California and the University of Brigham Young in the 1980s to excavate the pyramid of Sila refuted this assumption. They attributed this pyramid to the reign of Sneferu, the first king of the Fourth Dynasty, as a stela inscribed with his name was found during the excavations. No passage leading to a burial chamber was found in any of these pyramids. Hence, they cannot be burials. They can be cenotaphs, or as the German archeologists—who also investigated them in the 1980s—proposed they were erected in these provincial locations as symbols and reminders of the royal power residing in Memphis.

The Layer Pyramid at Zawiet el-Aryan

Zawiet el-Aryan, a site located 13 miles (21 km) south of Cairo—between Giza and Saqqara—was chosen by Khaba, the fourth king of the Third Dynasty, for his monument. The project was not achieved. What remains today are the lower courses of the pyramid rising for 65 feet (20 m) in height. The structure was noted by archeologists as early as 1840, but its entrance was found only in 1900 by Alexandre Barsanti, an architect with the Antiquities Department. From this entrance, a staircase leads to a sloping passage until it joins a shaft. There it makes a turn south leading to a burial chamber. Another passage to the north leads to a gallery with 32 chambers. Nothing was found in this substructure, and it looks like no burial ever took place in this pyramid.

Ten years later, heading a joint expedition between the Harvard University and the

Left **A dish of hard stone found in Sekhemkhet's pyramid.** It was among other stone vessels of different shapes.

Transition to True Pyramids

Over the next 20 years, the step pyramid design would evolve rapidly toward the smooth-sided design of the true pyramid. The first change occurred in the pyramid at Meidum—a step pyramid that had been dressed up as a true one.

Roughly 50 miles (80 km) south of Cairo, off the road to Faiyum, is the site of Meidum. It is dominated by a pyramid of peculiar shape. Standing in an impressive desert setting overlooking cultivated fields, this pyramid represents the final development of step pyramids.

WHO BUILT THE PYRAMID AT MEIDUM?

On the walls inside the mortuary temple, graffiti from the Sixth Dynasty mentioned Sneferu, founder of the Fourth Dynasty. This king was believed, as further graffiti left by visitors during the Eighteenth Dynasty show, to be the builder. But two other pyramids at Dahshur were certainly built by Sneferu. Did he build three pyramids? Or did Huni, the last king of the Third Dynasty, die before finishing his stepped pyramid at Meidum? Most Egyptologists believe Sneferu finished his predecessor's tomb while transforming it

into a true pyramid. Yet among the *mastabas* at Meidum are those of Sneferu's sons Nefermaat and Rahotep, each with his wife. No family members of Huni nor his officials are buried at Meidum. And Methen, a powerful official of his, is buried at Saqqara. Was he buried next to Huni's tomb, which still awaits discovery?

Below **The *mastabas* beside the Meidum Pyramid date to Sneferu's rule, as does Nefermaat's *mastaba* (below). This could mean Huni did not build the pyramid.**

The Meidum Pyramid

The structure first began with a seven-stepped pyramid. In a later stage this was enlarged and increased in height to convert it into an eight-stepped pyramid. Each step in the overlay was built higher than the corresponding step in the previous seven-stepped design. Finally, when the builders were almost done casing this pyramid, they received orders to fill in the steps, and case the whole structure, to achieve a true smooth pyramid. It stood 300 feet (92 m) high, 470 feet (144 m) square at the base, and had an angle of inclination of 51° 50'. Because most of the upper part of the outer smooth casing and several steps of the eight-stepped pyramid design were quarried away in antiquity, the pyramid appears today as a huge stepped tower.

It was the English archeologist, Sir Flinders Petrie, later dubbed the father of modern Egyptian archeology, who extrapolated the construction phases through which this pyramid went. He did this by observing the remains of the pyramid from the outside. Petrie's theory was verified when he returned to the site 20 years later. His assistant Gerald Wainwright bore a tunnel through the masonry from the eastern face of the pyramid during the 1910–12 seasons. Wainwright discovered 10 successive layers until he reached a point believed by him to be compact masonry, which would be the nucleus the layers leaned against, decreasing in height from the innermost layer to the outermost. Stone courses of these layers were sloping inwards, while those of the casing were laid horizontally.

In 1926, Ludwig Borchardt, a German Egyptologist and architect, reinvestigated the portions of a mud-brick path enclosed between two walls of coarse stones found by Wainwright some 980 feet (300 m) to the east of the pyramid. Borchardt had also searched in vain for other similar walls to the south of the pyramid, which were observed by Ernest Mackay, Petrie's second assistant. Borchardt believed the mud-brick way to the east and the virtually existing one to the south to be remains of the construction ramps.

In 1929–30, archeologist Alan Rowe headed the Museum of the University of Pennsylvania's expedition that re-examined the finds of Petrie and his assistants. The next important work took place in 1983–84, when the Egyptian Antiquities Organization cleared the sand and debris off most of the northern face of the pyramid revealing the intact outer casing at the bottom.

Inside the Meidum Pyramid

The entrance is in the northern face, about 100 feet (30 m) from the ground. It opens to a passage, 185 feet (57 m) long, which penetrates the superstructure at an angle of 28° and descends into the natural rock below. The passage then continues on a horizontal level for 30 feet (9 m) to a point once closed off by a wooden door. Two recesses, wider than they are deep, open out of the two sides of the horizontal corridor.

The purpose of these recesses is obscure. Archeologists believe they were most likely to be storage spaces for plug-blocks too large to be lowered down the passage after the burial and which would be used to seal access to the burial chamber. This latter chamber is reached through a vertical shaft directed upward at the end of the horizontal corridor. The shaft opens in the floor of the burial chamber at its northeastern corner. The limestone-lined chamber, mainly built in the core of the superstructure, with its floor at rock level, has a splendid roof consisting of seven overlapping layers in the form of a corbelled vault. In 1891, Petrie discovered the remains of a wooden coffin inside this room.

Left **The corbelled roof of the burial chamber in the pyramid at Meidum.** It has seven overlapping layers of stone.

Below **The intact outer casing is visible at the bottom corner of the northern and western faces of the pyramid at Meidum.** This was finally revealed when the pyramid was cleared of sand and debris in the early 1980s.

The Meidum Pyramid Complex

The structures surrounding this pyramid are very different from the fanciful sed-festival complex of Djoser. Moreover, they were what was to become the standard arrangement of future pyramid complexes. An enclosure wall delimits the area around the pyramid and contains, apart from the main pyramid, a small subsidiary stepped pyramid to the south. This early example of a subsidiary or satellite pyramid might have inherited the obscure function of the southern tomb of Djoser's complex. To the north of the pyramid, lies a large *mastaba*, a structure that will not appear within the enclosure in future pyramid complexes.

Against the middle of the eastern face of the pyramid—not the northern face, as in Djoser's complex—is the mortuary temple. It is a simple structure with an entrance in the southern corner of its front wall; it opens into a passage leading to a chamber. The latter opens to an unroofed court in the middle of which lies a limestone altar flanked by two tall limestone stelae with rounded tops. These are devoid of the expected inscriptions recording the names and titles of the king.

At a point in the enclosure wall, almost opposite the temple entrance, an opening gives access to the causeway: A long unroofed path, bound on each side with a stone wall. The causeway linked the pyramid to the valley temple. A rise in the level of the Nile bed made the excavation of this temple difficult due to the sodden condition of the area.

Below **Clearing away sand during nineteenth-century excavations at Dahshur.** This illustration by Paul Philippoteaux shows they are using the same woven baskets still used today.

Sneferu's Pyramids at Dahshur

At Dahshur, $2^{1}/_{2}$ miles (4 km) south of Saqqara and 31 miles (50 km) north of Meidum, are two pyramids belonging to Sneferu. The southern pyramid is known as the Bent or Rhomboidal Pyramid, while the northern pyramid is now more often called the Red Pyramid. Both were visited during the seventeenth and eighteenth centuries, and were properly explored by Perring, an English archeologist and engineer, in 1839. De Morgan, a French archeologist and geologist, examined them in 1894–1895. Since then, it was established that the northern pyramid belonged to Sneferu while the southern pyramid was attributed to Huni.

Finally, in 1945, the Antiquities Department created a section for pyramid studies under the direction of the architect Abdel Salam Hussein. His systematic excavation of the Bent Pyramid revealed quarry marks in Sneferu's name on its foundation blocks at the corners, establishing the pyramid's ownership. Hussein made the same discovery at the northern pyramid, which reaffirmed Sneferu as its builder. The death of Hussein after an operation in the USA in 1949 put an end to his work. In 1951, the newly appointed director for the project, Ahmed Fakhry, undertook fruitful excavations on the complexes.

The Bent Pyramid—A Project Gone Wrong

This pyramid measured 226 square yards (188 sq. m) wide and 330 feet (101 m) high. The

angle of slope is 54°, maintained to a height of 160 feet (49 m) then reduced to 43°. This change in angle is what gives the pyramid its shape and its popular names. Several theories were formulated to explain the angle change. The most tenable is that if the original angle were maintained, the weight of the masonry would have crushed the inner chambers. Indeed, these had cracks plastered in antiquity. The Bent Pyramid has strangely preserved most of its casing blocks. These were laid in its lower part in the inclined fashion of the step pyramids. The blocks above the change of angle are laid horizontally as in future pyramids.

Inside the Bent Pyramid

The entrance at the northern face is 39 feet (12 m) above the ground. Sockets on either side

of it were for a flap door, now gone. A sloping passage of 28° and 258 feet (79 m) long dives into the subterranean rock. It ends in a horizontal corridor with a corbelled roof 39 feet (12 m) high. To reach the next chamber, one has to climb a modern ladder up to a point 20 feet (6 m) above the floor of the corridor. This chamber also has a 39-foot-high (12 m) corbelled roof. On its southern wall is an opening to a vertical blind shaft. Another opening hidden near the ceiling leads to a rough passage ending at a point in the horizontal section of another passage.

This second passage is part of a corridor sloping up to the west face of the pyramid, where its entrance at 108 feet (33 m) above ground was hidden by the pyramid's outer casing until 1951. Perring was the first to get into the horizontal section of this corridor through the rough passage. He described the two portcullises he saw at each end of the horizontal section. These are blocks sliding from storage recesses in the side walls. The block, beyond which was the ascending corridor leading to the outside, was lowered and plastered on both sides, while the portcullis supposed to bar access to a chamber was still in its recess.

The chamber, built within the core of the superstructure on the ground level, has a corbelled roof 52 feet (16 m) high and its floor was built up to 13 feet (4 m) high with small stones. When these layers of stones were

Above **The Bent Pyramid showing its double slope (background).** Enough was left of its valley temple (in the foreground), to determine its plan.

Left **The Bent Pyramid has retained most of its casing blocks.** These are laid in its lower part sloping inward (detail seen on the western face). The stones above the change of angle are laid horizontally.

Right **The corbelled vault of a chamber within the Red Pyramid built by Sneferu.** It was possibly an attempt to reproduce a staircase to heaven inside the first true pyramid.

removed in 1946–47, a framework of cedarwood poles was found running along the walls and across the chamber. The purpose of this frame-work could have been to dissipate pressure off the walls. The inner structure of this pyramid is quite intriguing and its second entrance to the western face is unique.

The Bent Pyramid's Complex

The complex consists of four elements. There is the eastern mortuary temple, a structure simpler than that of Meidum, with an alabaster altar under a shelter and two large stelae, at each of its sides, carrying the name of Sneferu. Mud-brick additions were made to this temple during the Middle Kingdom and the Ptolemaic Period, when the cult of Sneferu was revived.

During that latter period, incense burners were deposited on the altar and remained undisturbed until Fakhry found them. There is a southern subsidiary true pyramid: While clearing its faces, Fakhry discovered the re-mains of a chapel to its north and the bases of two huge limestone stelae to its east. A part of one of those stelae was found. It depicts Sneferu in relief identified with his title and names. Finally, an unroofed causeway runs from the northern side of the enclosure wall in a 2,289-foot (700-m) long curve until it reaches what is believed to be the valley temple.

Below **The pyramidion at the Red Pyramid.** This is the pointed top stone. It was found when the eastern base of the Red Pyramid was cleared.

The valley temple is a rectangular building with two stelae inscribed with Sneferu's names and figures in front of it. The temple's entrance to the south opens into a long hall adorned with a frieze representing female offering-bearers, the personi-fication of royal estates in Upper and Lower Egypt. The hall flanked by two rooms on each side leads to an open court. On the northern side of the court were six shrines where statues of the king were sheltered, preceded by a portico on 10 pillars in two rows. The reliefs covering the temple walls were destroyed when it was used as a quarry. Thousands of fragments showing Sneferu at cere-monies and in the company of gods were recovered.

The First True Pyramid

One mile (1.5 km) north of the Bent Pyramid is the Red Pyramid, built of local reddish lime-stone, which explains its modern name. Its fine limestone casing is mostly lost today. The pyramid is 264 square yards (220 sq. m), 324 feet (99 m) high, with an angle of 43° (less than the common 52° of future pyramids). It is the first geometrically true pyramid, a squared-based building with four equal, smooth triangular sides meeting at the apex. Moreover, it is the second largest pyramid after Khufu's pyramid at Giza, since it exceeds the volume of that of Khafra.

Inside the Red Pyramid

The entrance at the northern side, 92 feet (28 m) above ground, opens into a descending passage (196 feet or 60 m long) that runs horizontally for 23 feet (7 m) when it reaches ground level. It leads to three chambers with corbelled roofs, the type so cherished in Sneferu's pyramids, as if the king wanted to reproduce step pyramids inside his true pyramid. The first two chambers are on the same level with 39-foot (12-m) high roofs; the third with a 49-foot (15-m) high roof is reached through an opening 25 feet (7.5 m) from the floor of the middle chamber. The latter is exceptionally placed directly under the apex. The remains of a male were found in the last chamber in 1950 and are believed by some to be those of Sneferu. Debate among Egyptologists on the burial place of Sneferu is still ongoing.

Around the Red Pyramid

The complex of this pyramid has not yet been cleared, apart from the eastern mortuary temple unearthed in 1982 by the German Institute of Archeology in Cairo led by Rainer Stadelmann. The temple, more architecturally elaborate than its predecessors, revealed larger-than-life-sized representations of Sneferu carved in relief. Another important finding while clearing the temple debris was the pyramidion, a pyramid-shaped block set last during construction at the peak of the pyramid; it was broken into several fragments. It is now pieced together and displayed near the pyramid. In the light of available evidence, it seems Sneferu built a step pyramid at Meidum but later decided to be buried under a true pyramid. The undertaken project was miscalculated, resulting in a bent pyramid. The king gave orders to transform the Meidum Pyramid into a true one while a new project was inaugurated to the north of the Bent

Pyramid. If we count the enigmatic pyramid of Sila, Sneferu has then built at least four pyramids, which makes his pyramid-building activity by far the greatest among Old Kingdom rulers.

PYRAMID NAMES

The pyramids were not mere royal tombs. They were sheathes protecting a form of life during its resting phase. Those sheathes, the pyramids, were given names. Each pyramid had an identity, closely linked to the king it protects and to the individual inspiration it exhales. The northern pyramid of Sneferu, today known as the Red Pyramid, did not bear that name when it was completed. It was called "Sneferu gleams." And the southern pyramid, now called the Bent Pyramid, was "Sneferu gleams in the south." Both pyramids were cased with the finest white Turah limestone: One can imagine how difficult it was to gaze at them when bright sunlight reflected away from their sides. The funerary cult of Sneferu was celebrated in those two pyramid complexes for at least the next 300 years, as attested by a tax-exemption decree from the reign of Pepy I during the Sixth Dynasty.

Below **The Red Pyramid built by Sneferu, Khufu's father, at Dahshur.** It is the first true pyramid and the precursor to Khufu's Great Pyramid at Giza.

PYRAMID CONSTRUCTION
The Pyramid Complex

The royal pyramid complex was a necropolis, a city of the dead comprised of numerous tombs, temples, and monuments that were intended to provide a palace to sustain the deceased during the afterlife.

The complex contained over a dozen specific buildings and structures; each was designed to fulfill a unique function in seeing to the king's eternal needs. A boundary wall enclosed the pyramid and its inner court. A second perimeter wall, usually made of mud-brick, surrounded the entire pyramid complex.

The Pyramids and Temples

The pyramid was the central structure, a monument to glorify the king and ensure his ascension to the heavens on the celestial path of the sun. Early step pyramids were designed as staircases to the heavens. The later smooth-sided design more closely resembled the sun's rays descending to earth and echoed the shape of the *benben* stone, where Atum stood at the creation of the world. The walls of the pyramid

itself were unadorned until the reign of Unas, whose burial chamber contains the first version of the Pyramid Texts.

The south and southeastern sides of the pyramid are the traditional locations of the small satellite pyramids. Their purpose is uncertain, but they may have contained statues of the king to house his *ka* (soul). Other satellite pyramids were the cult pyramid and the tombs of the queens or the king's mother.

After the main pyramid, the most important structure was the mortuary temple. These were elaborate buildings with columned halls, sanctuaries, statues, inscriptions, and storage rooms. As pyramids became less extensive toward the end of the Old Kingdom, the focus shifted to grander and more complex temples. From Sneferu's reign onwards, the mortuary temple

Right **The Great Pyramid of Khufu at Giza is the largest of all pyramids.** It is surrounded by a huge pyramid complex including living areas for cult attendants, valley and mortuary temples, boat pits, tombs, and a causeway.

was always located on the eastern side of the pyramid. The temple may have served as the last place for the king's funerary rites before interment or perhaps as a shrine to honor the king in the afterlife and preserve his name and splendor. By the Middle Kingdom, the tombs were completely subterranean and the mortuary temples became the impressive and lasting monuments of the kings.

The mortuary temple in the pyramid complex connected to the valley temple below by a long causeway. This was the primary access to the complex and the entryway for the king's arrival both in life and after death. It would also later provide a center for his ongoing worship and cult. The walls of both temples were inscribed and decorated with images of the king and the gods, often depicting the king's prowess and great accomplishments. Some scholars believe the valley temple was where the mummification rites were performed before the procession bore the king's body to the mortuary temple. However, archeological examination has revealed that the king's coffin would not have likely been able to fit through the passage from the mortuary temple to the pyramid courtyard, and so the true purpose of the temples and their design remains uncertain.

Tunnels and Chambers

With the exceptions of both Khufu and Sneferu, the king's burial chambers were located in subterranean structures under the pyramids; buried in the same style as their predecessors beneath the earlier *mastabas*. As the monuments grew more elaborate, so did the underground burial structures; they expanded to designs that included multiple tunnels, shafts, wells, chambers, and locks to deter potential tomb robbers. The most unusual design in the Old Kingdom chambers was under Djoser's pyramid, which showed a progression of changes in burial styles. It combines the shaft construction found in the Early Dynasty tombs with the Aswan granite-style of burial chamber found in later pyramids, such as Khafra's.

Boat Pits, *Mastabas* and Tombs

The boat pits are sited around the main pyramid. Boats played an important role in Egyptian religious belief back to the earliest history, being associated with the sun-god and safe travel through the Underworld and into the afterlife. The boats interred in the complex were provisioned for the king's metaphysical journey. There is debate as to whether they were actually used as funerary boats or if they were created solely to represent the solar bark the king would need to travel across the sky after his rebirth as the sun-god. Two of the boats in the pits on the south side of Khufu's pyramid have survived. One has been excavated, reassembled and placed on display in the Solar Barque Museum.

The complex also held *mastabas*, shrines, and temples for important officials, such as the king's vizier, and members of the royal family. It was considered a high honor to be buried in the royal complex. It was believed that burial in proximity to the king's tomb would impress the gods and influence their judgment upon the deceased, granting a greater chance of immortality in the afterlife.

The royal pyramid complex was a vital element in Egyptian belief; it provisioned the king for his journey to rebirth and his eternal existence. These cities continue to be a key component to understanding the purpose behind the construction of the pyramids.

Above **The causeway of Unas' pyramid, the last king of the Fifth Dynasty.** As with most pyramid complexes, it connects the valley temple to the mortuary temple.

Above **Detail of the ceiling of Unas' tomb, Saqqara.** His sarcophagus room is decorated with stars and its walls are inscribed with the first of the Pyramid Texts.

Building the Pyramids

The pyramids represent the greatest engineering marvel of the ancient world. Many theories have been proposed as to how they were built. Popular ideas depict thousands of oppressed slaves laboring under a pharaoh's whips to construct the Great Pyramid.

This Hollywood-style image owes its origins to Judeo–Christian biblical stories, which in turn may have been influenced by the writings of the Greek historian Herodotus in 450 BCE. But the pyramids were built over 2,000 years before Herodotus recorded his histories and the Egyptians of his time knew little more than myths and legends themselves.

In Herodotus' account, we are told that the Great Pyramid and its complex took approximately 30 years to build with the forced labor of gangs of 100,000 men. Ten years were spent building the road to move the stones to the construction site and another 20 on the pyramid itself. Herodotus claimed the road was half a mile (1 km) long, 60 feet (18 m) wide and had walls up to 48 feet (15 m) tall. The construction of the underground chambers was done at the same time the road was being made. In discussing those chambers, he wrote that the king's burial chamber was like an island, surrounded by a channel of water diverted from the Nile.

The pyramid itself was built like steps. Then, Herodotus stated, the remaining stones (it is thought he referred to the casing stones) were lifted with timbers. These were used to raise the stones from tier to tier. He wrote of two methods told to him: one which seems to resemble a sort

GRAFFITI AND THE WORK GANGS

As a more complete picture of how the pyramids were built emerges, the story of the workers becomes clearer. Egyptologists now believe the Giza workforce was organized into two large crews. They were divided into five units called *za* in Egyptian, translated as *phyle* by the Greeks. The *zas* of the Old Kingdom had unique unit names that included the names of the kings, such as "Friends of Khufu" and "Drunkards of Menkaura." The *zas* were further subdivided into divisions of perhaps 200 men. The divisions each had unique names to identify their work gang, such as "perfection" or "endurance." These gangs may possibly have been competitive with each other.

At various places in the village excavation, archeologists have found where the gangs left graffiti identifying their group's name and bragging of what work they had done. One such graffiti marking was found in the uppermost relieving room over the king's chamber in the Great Pyramid. Comprised of hieroglyphics reading "Friends of Khufu," it includes a cartouche with the king's name. It is the only place in the entire pyramid where Khufu's name has ever been found.

of scaffolding made of many timbers, and a second in which the timbers are reused over and over, carried up the tiers with the stones and applied as levers. Herodotus said that the pyramids were completed from the top to the ground, which indicates these stones were lifted to the upper levels first. The others were placed in turn, working down toward ground level. As the triangular casing stones were put in place, they filled in the angles of the stairs and created the smooth, polished sides.

Though no written record detailing the construction methods of the pyramids from the actual construction period has yet been found, modern archeologists have been dispelling the old images by uncovering clues to what is a very different picture. Excavations of workers' villages like the one on the Giza plateau

Below **The village workers' houses and tombs in the necropolis at Deir el-Medina, Thebes.** Pyramids required vast numbers of workers, who were housed in similar villages.

leave impressions of far fewer workers than Herodotus estimated. Evidence shows that those who lived in the villages were fed and very well treated, and even received the best medical attention available at that time.

Scholars now estimate that the work gangs numbered perhaps 200 men per group. Egyptologist Doctor Mark Lehner believes there were barracks that housed up to 2,000 workers in the non-agricultural seasons. Workers were divided into organized labor gangs that were probably employed on a rotating basis. The population of the entire village was probably between 20,000 and 30,000 people, including butchers, bakers, craftsmen, officials, and the workers' families.

In some places, the workers seemed to exhibit pride in their impressive accomplishments by leaving their gang's graffiti behind.

Choosing a Site

Of course, before the village was constructed or any building project could begin, the king would first have to determine where his house of eternity would stand. This was a vitally important consideration so the locations for building such monumental structures had to be very carefully selected. The pyramid had to be built far enough above the annual floodplain to avoid to water damage, yet close enough to the Nile to allow for river transport of building material and access for the king's visits to the construction site. Reasonable proximity to the king's capital city and a natural quarry site that was relatively close was also an important requirement. Last, the location would have to be stable and solid enough to withstand the weight of the completed monument.

Below **Limestone relief from the *mastaba* tomb of the Fifth-Dynasty official Ti.** It shows stone-workers carrying blocks of stone tools and a bucket.

Preparing the Site

Once the site was chosen, workers would remove all the rocks and debris, to create a level surface to build on. This was probably accomplished by digging shallow trenches parallel to the intended walls and possibly in a crosshatch pattern, filling them with water and marking along the level of the water. Then uneven areas could be cut down or filled in with solid rubble to match the waterline as was needed. The exception to this would be any solid rocky outcroppings near the center of the structure, which would be left in place to support the core.

Before the foundation could be established, the alignment of the walls would need to be determined. By observing where the stars rose and set around the northern celestial pole and bisecting the two points evenly, a north–south alignment could be determined. A right angle from this would also give them the east–west alignment line. Measurements using specific lengths of rope from the alignment lines would make it possible to mark off the squared base of the foundation with remarkable precision. The process of preparing the site is thought to have

taken six to eight weeks of work. However, this process was not merely groundbreaking; it was also a significant religious event and certain foundation rituals and religious observances would have been performed throughout the construction process. The first of these, called *pedj-ses* (the stretching of the cord) would have been either actually or symbolically done by the king. This ritual would have been associated with establishing the astronomical alignment of the walls.

Other rituals would have included the purifying of the ground, the ceremonial creation and placement of the first trench or guideline, the burial of any honorary foundation items, and perhaps even the placement of the initial foundation stone. Items in the foundation pit were often symbolic of particular gods or of the building tools and materials to be used. Other stages of construction may have had ceremonial requirements as well.

Building the Pyramid

Construction began with the core, which would be built around any usable rocky outcroppings left on the foundation. The subterranean and lower inner chambers would be constructed first and the walls built around them.

As the structure grew, the workers would face the challenge of raising two- to 10-ton blocks up onto the growing levels. Despite Herodotus' accounts of levers and lifting equipment, ancient Egyptians in that time period did not have pulleys or wheels. The heavy building stones were dragged to the structure by ropes attached to wooden sledges. A Middle Kingdom wall painting depicts 63 men dragging such a sledge loaded with a 25-foot (8-m) stone statue. One worker pours liquid on the ground in front of the sledge while a fore-man beats out a count to coordinate the workers.

Two theories exist about the use of ramps to raise the blocks to the necessary level. The first proposes a long, straight ramp leading from the quarry area to the level of construction on the pyramid. While this would provide the easiest and most direct route, it is estimated that by the time the ramp could have reached the top layer of the pyramid it would have a greater volume of material than the pyramid itself.

The second theory is of a series of smaller ramps that wound up the sides of the pyramid.

These would require less building material but this idea poses two problems. The stones would have to be dragged a much greater distance up these ramps and, as the ramps extended with the structure, the stones would have to be maneuvered around relatively sharp corners. Also, the ramps would obscure the sides of the pyramid as they grew, making it more difficult to take measurements and check angles.

Egyptologists, Doctors Zahi Hawass and Mark Lehner, have discovered the remains of such ramps between the Great Pyramid and the stone quarry to the southwest of the pyramid. The composition of the remains of the ramp is mostly gypsum and limestone chips, mixed with a type of clay called tafla. These materials, when mixed together, would have created a hard and solid ramp, which it is believed would have supported the heavy building stones being moved.

Above **View of the inner rooms in the _mastaba_ tomb of Kagemni, Sixth-Dynasty vizier, Saqqara.** In pyramids such chambers had to be constructed first.

Left **A nineteenth-century painting by the Italian artist Luigi Ademollo.** It is of the "second pyramid of Gizeh" being opened by archeologist, Giovanni Battista Belzoni, in 1822. It reveals the thickness of the pyramid's walls.

Below **A Fourth-Dynasty seated statue of a man, possibly a scribe.** It is made of dazzling white limestone, the stone used to encase the pyramids.

Pyramid Chambers

The upper chambers in some pyramids would have had to be constructed as the structure grew. The Grand Gallery in the Great Pyramid has a massive corbelled vault ceiling that was created by setting the opposed pairs of stone blocks slightly closer together than the pair below. This created the vaulted ceiling while still supporting the weight of the structure above it. Over the king's chamber are a series of low, flat-ceilinged relieving chambers, with the topmost room having a peaked ceiling. It is believed these were designed to lessen the load pressing down on the ceiling of the king's chamber. The graffiti in the topmost of these rooms is the only writing found in the pyramid; it is also the only internal evidence that links the structure to Khufu.

The Great Pyramid also has one unique feature—the narrow, rectangular shafts that reach at upward angles from the king's and queen's chambers to the outside of the pyramid. Examination of these structures, too narrow to be passageways, show that the tunnels were created as the pyramid was built and not drilled through the rock afterwards. Each block would have needed the correct channel carved out at the exact angle before it was set into place. Such effort indicates that these shafts were considered very important.

Building Materials

Much of the coarse building material for the main body of the pyramids came from the adjacent stone quarries and was usually a low grade of limestone. Some of the inner walls and floors for important rooms and chambers used specialty materials brought in from more distant locations, such as pink granite, white limestone, basalt, or alabaster. The casing (outer) stones of the pyramids were also created with white limestone, polished to make the structure shine in the sun. The ancient Egyptians transported these various types of stone over considerable distances, a feat nearly as impressive as the construction itself, given the available methods and technology of the time.

Limestone of various qualities and colors is found all over Egypt, but the main source of white limestone is from the Tura quarry on the east bank of the Nile near Cairo, less than 6 miles (10 km) away from Giza. Limestone from Tura would be rough-cut in the quarry then transported by oxen-dragged sledge to the Nile, loaded onto a raft and sent across the river to the Giza construction site docking area. Once across the river, another sledge would be used to drag the stones to the construction area where they could be precisely shaped and angled by finishing craftsmen before being lifted into place. The casing stones of the Great Pyramid alone required 144,000 white limestone pieces.

The other specialty stones were quarried and transported in the same way, but many came from much greater distances and some of them required skilled handling. Basalt was found to the north of the Faiyum Depression, which is nearly 62 miles (100 km) from Cairo. The lake there became connected to the Nile each year during the annual flood, making it possible for basalt stones to be more easily transported. Alabaster is a very fragile stone. Quarried from large pits or underground mines, this soft mineral requires careful handling because it "bruises" easily. It was found in the region near Amarna, now known as Luxor, over 370 miles (595 km) to the north. But pink

Aswan granite, an exceptionally hard stone, would have needed the furthest transportation. To quarry the granite, workers had to drill guide holes in the rock face to create channels to cut in, or force out, wedges of blocks much larger then they needed and cut them down later. Aswan, known as the gateway to the Nubian desert, is over 560 miles (900 km) north of Cairo, a substantial distance to transport large pieces of granite by raft. After the major construction was complete, the finishing stage was reached.

Finishing the Pyramid

The facing blocks of polished white Tura limestone were put into place. Scholars agree with Herodotus' analysis that this was done from the top down. Stones were placed and polished as the workers moved down the face, dismantling the ramps as they worked their way back to the ground with the finishing stage. The final result was a brilliant white, shining monument visible for many miles—truly an appropriate tribute for the earthly manifestation of the sun-god.

Above **A relief from the wall of Unas' causeway at Saqqara.** It shows boats being used to transport granite columns from Aswan. Pyramids were sited near the Nile to enable transport of vast quantities of stone.

TOOLS OF THE TRADE

The ancient Egyptians used simple but effective tools to accomplish amazing engineering and architectural feats. Their tools included such things as carpenter's squares to check the precision of right-angled corners; plumb lines, builder's threads, and straight edges for alignment and creating vertical lines; a measuring arm at the length of a royal cubit (20 inches or 52.3 cm); bronze and copper chisels and points, stone wedges, wooden and stone mallets and flint tools for carving, decorating, and smoothing stone faces; and wood and metal bores, ground against sand and fine pebbles, to drill holes and hollow areas of stone. Sand, gypsum, limestone, and clay were mixed to create a solid mortar.

Their measurement, cutting, and placement of two-ton or greater blocks of stone were so precise that even 3,000 years later there are stones fit together so closely that a credit card or knife blade cannot be inserted between them.

Right **A variety of Old Kingdom Egyptian tools, dated to c. 2400 BCE.** These items are made from bronze.

Alignment and Symmetry

The oldest known measurement system originates in two important Mesopotamian cultures, Sumer and Babylon, which influenced the development of geometry and higher mathematics. They were the key to the absolute precision of the pyramids.

Right **Part of the Rhind Mathematical Papyrus from Thebes, Fifteenth Dynasty.** Written in heiratic script, it deals with the volumes of rectangles and triangles, and explains how the Egyptians calculated the proportions of the pyramids. It is held in the British Museum in London.

Below **Nineteenth-century engraving of Giza.** This bird's-eye view reveals the symmetrical perfection of the design and layout of the necropolis.

Based on their systems the Egyptian mathematician-priests brought these sciences to the height of mastery in the construction of the pyramids. The early Egyptians developed highly precise geometry built on three basic units of measurement. Through much of their history, the royal cubit was a fairly stable measurement, about 20.59 inches (52.3 cm). The *shesep*, or width of the palm, measured one-seventh of a royal cubit, and the *yeba*, or digit, was one-quarter of the *shesep*.

The mathematical sophistication in the Great Pyramid's precision is evident in its near symmetrical sides, with a base less than a 0.590-inch (15-mm) deviation from a perfect square. The pyramid sits on a surface that is more precisely leveled than that of most modern buildings. The

pyramid was originally 480.9 feet (146.6 m) tall, with a base of 755.81 feet (230.37 m) per side, yielding a perimeter of 3,023.23 feet (921.48 m). When you divide the perimeter by twice the height, you get approximately 3.14 (pi), the same result as dividing 22 *sheseps* by 1 royal cubit. To calculate the slope of the sides, the Egyptians used a measurement called the *seked*, expressing the slope of an incline by the number of *sheseps* and *yebas* of rise per cubit of horizontal run. This calculation is echoed in the modern trigonometric function of finding the cotangent of the ratio between the height and half the base length of a triangle, such as the side of a pyramid.

The Rhind Mathematical Papyrus, which appears to be a teaching text written c. 1650 BCE, offers queries on these mathematical concepts. It poses problems such as how many bricks would be needed to build a ramp x cubits long and y cubits high, calculating a pyramid's height given its *seked* and base, or finding the radius and area of circles given their diameter. This emphasizes the importance of the Egyptians' knowledge of the value of pi, traditionally attributed to the Greek mathematician Archimedes, but the records of the Egyptians' grasp of these advanced mathematical concepts date to nearly 1,600 years before Archimedes' time.

The Pyramids' Alignment

The Giza pyramids line up precisely on a north–south axis, which means each face squares off

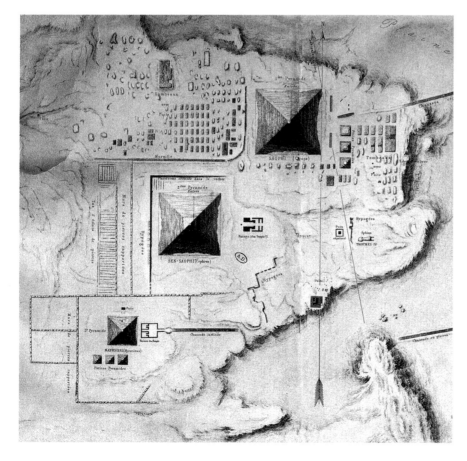

to a true direction. The Egyptians' precision in the Great Pyramid's alignment is within three-sixtieths of a degree of true north by modern calculations, a smaller deviation than is found in some modern observatories. But one aspect still puzzled researchers—how the ancient Egyptians were able to orient on true north. In the period of pyramid construction, the rotation of the stars had not yet aligned the star Polaris with the northern celestial pole, so the ancient Egyptians did not have a pole star for orienta-

tion. Moreover, the compass wasn't invented until nearly 200 BCE, in China.

Egyptologist Doctor Kate Spence provides two key pieces of information. She reconstructed the Old Kingdom location and pivot points for two stars that were in a rotational pattern near the northern celestial pole—Kochab, in Ursa Minor and Mizar, in Ursa Major. According to her findings, by watching for the vertical alignment of these two stars, the Egyptians would have been able to find true north. By calculating when this alignment of the stars took place, she established a date for the construction of the Great Pyramid with only a five-year margin of error.

Above **The pyramids at Giza, showing Menkaura's pyramid with its satellite pyramids.** The straight sides and square base of the true pyramids were built using exacting measurements and angles.

THE PYRAMID INCH

The Great Pyramid inspires endless theories equating its measurements to "hidden knowledge." One popular theory claims the pyramid's perimeter in inches equals the 365.24 days in a solar year. However, current measurements list the perimeter as 36,269.45 inches (92,124.403 cm), so how is this justified?

In the mid 1800s, the correlated works of writer John Taylor and Professor Charles Piazzi Smyth created the "pyramid inch," a measurement equaling 1.00106 British inches (2.5426924 cm), based on measurements taken in the Great Pyramid's Entrance Passage and its alignment to the star Alpha Draconis in 2170 BCE. Using earlier measurements of the base at 9,121.4193 British inches, the perimeter suddenly becomes 36,524.352 pyramid inches—a perfect match. It is also a number unfounded in the 20.59 inches (52.3 cm) of the royal cubit, and no evidence exists for early Egyptians using that unit of measurement. It does show, however, that any theory can be proven with sufficient mathematical creativity.

As Above, So Below

The pattern of the three pyramids on the Giza plateau reveals another kind of alignment. Khufu and Khafra's pyramids orient on one diagonal, but the third pyramid of Menkaura is slightly askew from that line. Astronomical observation provides the explanation. The position of the pyramids corresponds in a one-sixtieth scale mirror-image to the three stars on the belt of the constellation Orion, which is associated with Osiris. The Milky Way was thought to be the Nile in the sky, a representation of the Duat in Osiris' kingdom where the king was judged before taking his place among the stars. The Giza plateau provides an earthly image of the Afterworld, perhaps meant as a celestial roadmap for the king to find his way to eternity.

Below **A ruler with Eighteenth-Dynasty pharaoh Amenhotep III's name.** This architectural tool is made of gilded wood and has a leather case.

Art and Sculpture

Egyptian art at the dawn of the pyramid age reflects many of the qualities associated with the entire Old Kingdom period: beauty, innovation, optimism, purpose, and quiet dignity. Their exquisite art still remains entrancing today.

Right **One of 11 wooden panels from the tomb Hesyra, at north Saqqara.** The dignified portrayal of this Third-Dynasty official was an early trend in Old Kingdom tomb art.

Royal Wall Decoration

The early pyramids were undecorated, but the stone walls of temples associated with these funerary monuments were frequently adorned with bas-reliefs—embossed carvings over which a thin layer of plaster was applied and then painted. The subjects of these royal wall scenes were the rituals of kingship, particularly the sed-festival (a ceremony that celebrated the renewal of royal power), the ruler's interaction with the gods, and his role as protector of world order.

Little remains of this early decoration as many pyramid temples were dismantled in later periods and their stones reused in other build-ings. However, the quality of the artwork can be gauged from recovered fragments. The earliest examples occur in a chamber built beneath the Third Dynasty Step Pyramid of Djoser at Saqqara. These depict the imposing figure of the king participating in the sed-festival on limestone panels carved in delicate, low relief.

After the pyramid reached its true form in the Fourth Dynasty, decoration was applied to the walls of temples devoted to the mortuary cult of the king. Reliefs from a temple associated with the Bent Pyramid of Sneferu, for example, display a procession of young women, each the personification of a royal estate, bringing food offerings to sustain the spirit of the dead king. Fragments reveal these figures were surmounted by the image of Sneferu performing rituals and embraced by deities, such as the lion goddess Sekhmet. The reliefs are carved in a high, bold style, differentiating them from those of the later pyramid complex of Khufu, which have a lower

and more rounded contour. Stylistic changes such as these often enable Egyptologists to identify the mortuary complex from which displaced relief fragments originated.

Private Wall Decoration

The earliest application of bas-relief in the mud-brick tombs of private individuals consisted of intricately carved and painted limestone slabs

depicting the deceased sitting at an offering-table, which were set in niches cut into the tombs' exterior eastern wall. However, after stone-lined chapels began to be built within the tomb superstructure, the increased wall space allowed the use of relief and the repertoire of scenes to be expanded. Walls were then divided into horizontal bands within which were carved lively images of the tomb-owner receiving offerings, the slaughter of animals, and scenes of everyday life, such as agricultural pursuits, hunting, and boat-building.

Artistic Innovation

A number of artistic innovations occurred during the Third and Fourth dynasties. For example, in the tomb of Hesyra at Saqqara, representations of the deceased official were carved upon 11 wooden panels installed along the west wall of his corridor-length chapel. The dignified figure of Hesyra displays many attributes that were to become standard features of the human form in Egyptian two-dimensional art: A youthful, idealized body with head and feet in profile, but eye, shoulders, and torso presented frontally. Hesyra's chapel also preserves some of the earliest known images of daily life, including a marsh scene featuring a crocodile.

The inventive spirit of the early Fourth Dynasty is best exemplified in the tomb of Prince Nefermaat and his wife Atet at Meidum, which contains two stone-lined offering rooms. In Atet's chapel, an inscription beside the image of her husband states "he made his pictures in a drawing that cannot be erased." This refers to a new technique in which the shapes of figures and hieroglyphs were sunk into the stone walls and the resulting indentations filled with colored

paste. Unfortunately, Nefermaat's "permanent" images did not last, as many of the inlays have since fallen out. Nevertheless, the surviving reliefs introduce a variety of new scenes, including a delightful image of the tomb-owners' son playing with animals.

Both chapels were eventually enlarged by the addition of plaster-covered brick corridors that were each painted with elaborate scenes. Much of the original artwork has been destroyed, but the technical brilliance of the paintings can be determined from a few remaining fragments, particularly a frieze displaying six foraging geese. These birds, a species not seen in Egypt for 150 years, once formed part of a larger wall scene that also depicted men trapping birds in the marshes and plowing with oxen. This, and other beautifully painted pieces, reveals the height of artistic expression that was achieved during this early stage of two-dimensional art in Egypt.

Above **Painted deep relief from the Fifth-Dynasty tomb of Iru-Ka-Ptah, at Saqqara.** This style of relief became more prominent in later Old Kingdom dynasties when larger chapels provided more wall space.

Below **The Meidum geese freize from the tomb of Nefermaat and Atet.** This exceptionally well-preserved piece of Old Kingdom tomb art reveals the technical excellence achieved by early artists.

Left **The royal triad:** Menkaura is flanked by the goddess Hathor (left) and the personification of a nome (right).

Royal Sculpture

Egyptian statuary was intended to present a timeless, idealized image of the subject rather than a personal portrait. To achieve this, all statues conformed to a style, which, in the Old Kingdom, was characterized by a strictly frontal orientation, block-shaped forms, and heavy modeling. The powerful and eternal nature of kingship was well conveyed by such a style.

Royal statues were made from a range of materials, including wood, ivory, limestone, granite, and alabaster. Examples produced during the early Old Kingdom range in size from a tiny 3 inch (7.5 cm) ivory statuette of King Khufu, to larger-than-life-sized images, as indicated by a late Third-Dynasty granite head of an unknown ruler, which alone measures 21 inches (53 cm) long.

One of the earliest, and most imposing, examples of royal statuary is that of Djoser. This life-sized, limestone statue was found in situ in the sealed *serdab* room of his pyramid, indicating that its function was to receive his *ka* (spirit) after his death. The massive figure of Djoser, seated on a throne and swathed in a ritual cloak, is somber and formidable, elements that produce an overwhelming sense of majesty.

Many royal effigies have a transcendent quality that evokes strongly the king's divine status. One such example is that of Khafra, whose splendid statue depicts the king seated on a high-backed throne. Upon this perches a falcon, symbol of the god Horus, which embraces the head of the ruler with its outstretched wings. Yet surprisingly, although the object is quite beautifully rendered, it is carved from anorthosite gneiss, a rather nondescript stone. It has recently been

discovered, however, that when the statue is exposed to strong sunlight, particles in the stone cause it to radiate with a deep blue glow. It has been suggested that this celestial color and luminosity may have alluded symbolically to the king's association with Horus.

This statue is one of more than 20 similar images of Khafra that once graced an open hall in his funerary complex. However, some royal statues were kept hidden, concealed in wooden shrines situated in the deepest recesses of mortuary temples. These statues were the object of daily rituals performed by temple priests. In Sneferu's temple at Dahshur, for example, six chapels were built against its rear wall, each of which contained a statue of the king.

The most important function of royal statues, however, was to highlight the elevated position of the ruler and his role as mediator between gods and people. This is epitomized in an exquisite Fourth-Dynasty statue of King Menkaura, who stands proudly while flanked by two female figures. One is the personification of an Egyptian province, the other represents the goddess Hathor, who subtly communicates the relationship between the monarch and the gods by gently holding the ruler's hand. This triad makes a powerful statement about the nature of kingship in the Old Kingdom.

Private Sculpture

Statues of private individuals were produced in wood and ivory, but the most common material was limestone. Most were plastered, then painted in bright colors, and many were provided with inlaid eyes. Their purpose was to receive offerings for the spirit of deceased individuals, so

MUTILATED HEADS

Some of the most enigmatic funerary objects produced during the pyramid age were white limestone busts known as reserve heads. Thirty-one heads have been found (27 from Giza alone), all of which date from the early Fourth Dynasty. Each was found in either a burial chamber or tomb shaft. Most are well modeled with a smooth finish. However, many appear to have been damaged intentionally soon after they were produced, either by removing the ears or gouging the cranium from the crown to the nape. Neither the purpose of the heads nor their systematic mutilation has yet been explained.

they were installed in either the tomb's chapel or the adjoining *serdab* (statue-room) after they had undergone a ritual known as the "opening of the mouth." The name and titles of the tomb-owner were often placed on the statue base or elsewhere on the figure, yet, in keeping with the style of the Old Kingdom, the statues themselves were provided with few personal features.

The near life-sized statues of Rahotep and his wife Nofret display many of the attributes that characterize private statuary of the early Old Kingdom, including disproportionately large heads, short necks, thick ankles, and heavy limbs. The severity of their appearance is somewhat alleviated, however, by their painted skin and jewelry, and startling rock-crystal eyes.

Seated and standing figures were common during this period but a rare pose is displayed by the Third Dynasty statue of Hetep-di-ef. He kneels with his hands resting upon his knees, in an attitude of prayer. This pose and the inscribed image of a pyramidion topped by a sacred *bennu*-bird upon his right shoulder, suggest that Hetep-di-ef may have served as a funerary priest.

Group statues also occur, mainly of married couples. One of the most touching is of the dwarf, Seneb, whose wife holds him in a loving embrace. Sadly, such signs of tenderness disappear from private statuary by the early Fifth Dynasty.

Above **The exquisitely well-preserved painted limestone pair statues of Rahotep, a high official, and his wife Nofret, from their *mastaba* in Meidum.** Rahotep was probably a son of Sneferu.

Giza's Layout

Modern Giza is accessed by two main roads—one from the north leads to Khufu's pyramid and another from the east ends near the Sphinx's forecourt. The latter is the same direction from which the ancient Egyptians would have approached.

Right **There are numerous mastabas in Giza.** This columned chamber with niche statues is from the *mastaba* of Sixth-Dynasty official and overseer of pyramids, Meryra-nefer.

They crossed the Nile from the east bank, and followed the causeways westward. Dominating the plateau are the three pyramids of the kings Khufu, Khafra, and Menkaura running on a south–west diagonal through the site. Khufu's is the northern-most and the largest. Khafra built his pyramid on a precise south–west diagonal to his father's and on slightly higher ground, creating the illusion that it is bigger. The third pyramid, belonging to Menkaura, is much smaller and is not along the same diagonal line as the other two, being just over 300 feet (90 m) to the south-east. The sides of each pyramid are aligned to the cardinal points of the compass.

Subsidiary Structures

Each pyramid is surrounded by the remains of subsidiary structures which were a necessary part of the dead king's cult activities. These include the valley temple that originally stood on the Nile canal, a mortuary temple on the eastern side of the pyramid, and a causeway linking the two.

Smaller cult pyramids and offering places were also incorporated into the complex, and several boat pits have been discovered next to Khufu's and Khafra's pyramids. In addition, the massive Sphinx is near Khafra's valley temple—

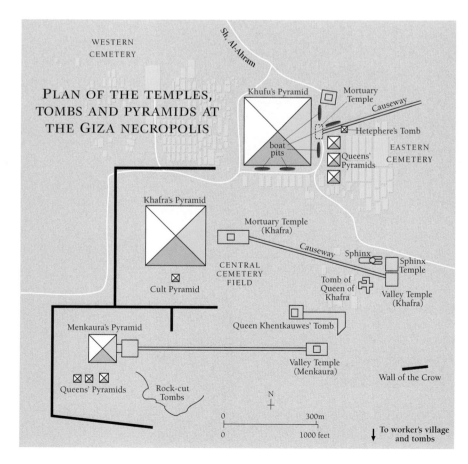

PLAN OF THE TEMPLES, TOMBS AND PYRAMIDS AT THE GIZA NECROPOLIS

WESTERN CEMETERY

Sh. Al-Ahram

Khufu's Pyramid

Mortuary Temple

Causeway

Hetephere's Tomb

boat pits

EASTERN CEMETERY

Queens' Pyramids

Khafra's Pyramid

Mortuary Temple (Khafra)

Causeway

Sphinx

Sphinx Temple

CENTRAL CEMETERY FIELD

Cult Pyramid

Tomb of Queen of Khafra

Valley Temple (Khafra)

Menkaura's Pyramid

Queen Khentkauwes' Tomb

Valley Temple (Menkaura)

Wall of the Crow

Queens' Pyramids

Rock-cut Tombs

N

0   300m

0   1000 feet

To worker's village and tombs

TOMB ROBBERY

Tomb robbery was by far the oldest profession in pharaonic times. By the Middle Kingdom, royal tombs were being systematically plundered. Spells aimed at warning off the robbers adorned pharaohs' coffins.

The Twelfth-Dynasty Pharaoh Amenemhat III threatened that god would judge anyone who disturbed his tomb, but to no avail. Coffins began to be locked, and intricate systems of portcullises and rock-blocked passages became integral to tomb structures but the robbers always knew—literally—exactly where the bodies were buried.

The Middle Kingdom scribe Ipuwer bemoaned the sacrileges: "Behold, those who were entombed are cast on high ground, and the embalmers' secrets are thrown away." Paneb, a tomb worker at Deir el-Medina, was charged with stealing from the tomb of Sety II. However there was large-scale bribery, and the high officials who prosecuted the thieves were often themselves involved in what became, during the late Ramessid period, virtually state-sponsored theft as gold and jewelry were recycled back to the treasury. Faced with such widespread desecration, priests disinterred many royal mummies and took them to new hiding places. Now some of the survivors have at last found a final resting place —in the mummy room at the Cairo Museum.

Right **A nineteenth-century engraving by Italian artist Luigi Mayer.** It shows the chamber and sarcophagus in the Great Pyramid, at Giza. Like all Giza's pyramids, it was plundered in antiquity, so Khufu's body was never found.

---

an imposing facade to this funerary complex. Also adjoining the pyramids are the remains of a series of smaller pyramids, *mastabas*, and rock-cut tombs that were for the kings' wives, family members and important officials. The largest and most impressive of these are the eastern and western cemeteries around the Great Pyramid. Among the dignitaries buried in the western cemetery is Hemiunu, Khufu's vizier and overseer, and in the eastern field is the tomb of Queen Hetepheres. South of the Sphinx are the recently discovered workers' village and burial grounds. These are separated from the royal burial sites by the great stone wall known as the Wall of the Crow. Remains of this wall can be seen to the east of Menkaura's valley temple.

Below **Two pyramids of Giza on the Giza plateau.** This royal necropolis includes three major and several minor pyramids.

The Great Pyramid

The Great Pyramid of Khufu rises above the Giza plateau, a mountain of stone that has become the icon of both modern and ancient Egypt and a silhouette recognizable worldwide. No other pyramid ever achieved its size and grandeur.

Above **Nineteenth-century engraving by Italian artist, Luigi Mayer.** This illustration reveals the discovery of a passageway between the second and third galleries of the Great Pyramid.

It would not be until the nineteenth century that modern technology would create a taller building—the Eiffel Tower. During its 4,500-year history, Giza's sands have been trodden by Alexander the Great, Julius Caesar, and Napoleon. Millions of people have scaled the stairs to its entrance and many renowned archeologists have investigated its secrets. The ancient Egyptians knew it as the "horizon of Khufu," while others have called it the "granaries of Joseph," "the mountain of the pharaoh," an astronomic observatory, and even an alien outpost.

The truth is simpler. It was built by Khufu, second king of the Fourth Dynasty and son of Sneferu, as his tomb, his "house for eternity," and the mechanism by which he would achieve immortality. He chose the new site of Giza in order to outdo his father's massive monuments at Dahshur and spent the entire period of his 23-year-reign overseeing its construction. Work finally ceased when he died about 2566 BCE.

Direct Ascent to the Afterlife

Pyramids were more than just tombs, they were designed to emphasize the divine connections of the king and assist his ascent to the gods. By introducing a new shape—the straight sides of the true pyramid—Khufu was making a significant statement regarding his strengthening affiliations with the sun-god Ra. This innovative design moved beyond the primeval mound motif of earlier pyramids and became a stylized replica of the *benben*, the sacred symbol of Ra. Emphasizing this connection between the king and god

Right **The Great Pyramid.** In its symmetry of design and precision of construction, the Great Pyramid of Khufu, known by the Greeks as Cheops, surpasses any other ancient structure ever built.

Left **Interior passageway** of the Great Pyramid of Khufu, at Giza, in a nineteenth-century engraving.

may have underpinned the decision to place the burial chamber deep within the superstructure, rather than beneath it, as had been common practice. The design probably also intended to replicate the journey of the sun's rays from a single point in the sky to Earth and provide a smooth pathway by which the king could journey to the heavens.

Extraordinary Measurements

The statistics of the structure are astounding. It sits on 13 acres (5 ha) of land and has sides just over 755 feet (230 m) long. It originally stood 481 feet (147 m) tall (it has lost 33 feet or 10 m in height due to the removal of stone.) It contains about two million limestone blocks cut from the local quarry, each weighing between two and 15 tons. This achievement in mass and height was balanced against the symmetry obtained through design and construction. The blocks were precisely positioned, the base an almost perfect square with side lengths differing by only 0.1 percent and each face perfectly oriented with a cardinal point of the compass. Around this core was a casing of white limestone, brought across the Nile from nearby Tura, which would have created a dazzling effect when lit by the sun.

Internally Intricate

The interior is one of the most intricately designed of any pyramid. To reach the burial chamber of the king, a series of corridors, chambers, blocked passageways, galleries, and shafts had to be negotiated. Some were designed to fool tomb robbers, though ultimately unsuccessful; the purpose of others remains unknown.

The original entrance is partway up the north face, a design to ensure the dead king could ascend directly to the northern stars. The initial corridor diverges after 65 feet (20 m), with one tunnel leading to an unfinished chamber carved into the bedrock, another ascending for 130 feet (40 m) into a horizontal passage. One side of this passage accesses the queen's chamber, a small unfinished room probably intended to house a *ka* statue of the king rather than a queen's burial, and the other leads to the grand gallery. This steeply ascending tunnel, 154 feet (47 m) long and 28 feet (8.5 m) high, is considered a masterpiece of engineering, with its corbelled roof and sliding-granite blocking systems to deter thieves.

A low passageway connects the top of the grand gallery to the burial chamber, located at the exact center of the pyramid. The granite sarcophagus, the only surviving tomb item, still lies in its original position oriented with the directions of the compass. There are no wall decorations or inscriptions, apart from graffiti left by the original workers—the only intriguing features are narrow shafts, similar to those found in the queen's chamber. Originally thought to be airshafts, investigations with robot cameras revealed that they were sealed. Perhaps their function was religious rather than utilitarian and they were designed to help Khufu's spirit, or *ba*, travel to the outside world.

Right **Khufu's only image.** Despite the vast size of his pyramid, the only statue known of Khufu is tiny. Made of ivory, it was discovered at Abydos.

The Great Pyramid Complex

As with his pyramid, Khufu set the standard for the future with his enormous pyramid complex. This was where he would spend eternity—his palace in the afterlife and the focal point of his worship as a god-king.

Right Stone stela, from the Fourth Dynasty. This small stela showing animal reliefs was discovered in Khufu's pyramid. It is presently held in the Turin Museum in Italy.

It was designed to last forever, a dynamic site incorporating temples, living areas for cult attendants, boat pits, and subsidiary tombs for those important enough to share his afterlife. The complex's main focal points were those monuments essential to the king's funerary rites and ongoing cult activities—the valley and mortuary temples, the causeway, and small cult pyramid. Their role in the perpetual cycle of the king's rebirth is emphasized in their east–west alignment, symbolizing the link with the sun-god's daily voyage across the sky.

Today, the complex is poorly preserved with most of the structures lying in ruins. Some remain buried beneath centuries of urban construction and pieces of others exist in walls of later buildings, placing a modern spin on the ancient definition of eternity.

Below Cairo's backyard. Cairo's urban sprawl butts up against Giza's pyramid complex. Khufu's Pyramid, the largest of the three, is in the foreground.

The Nile Connection

The portal to the complex was the valley temple, located on the edge of the Nile with ramps leading from the river harbor to its entrance. This temple was the location for the initial funeral rites and may also have housed the king's body during the embalming process. Much of the remains lie under suburban Cairo so reconstructing its full ground plan is proving difficult However, limited excavations show it to be of standard design with living areas around the temple, probably for those who served the king's cult as priests or employees of the estates.

A causeway connects the valley temple to the rest of the complex. This 2,650-foot (810-m) long ceremonial walkway was used to transport the king's body during the funeral procession, symbolically linking the tomb to the life-giving waters of the Nile. Based on comparisons with other causeways, it was probably covered, with slits in the roof for light, and the walls decorated.

Curiously Plain

At the end of the causeway lies Khufu's mortuary temple, the least elaborate of its kind at Giza. Because it was the focus for the cult worship of the dead king, it was on the eastern side of the pyramid, adjacent to the perimeter wall surrounding the tomb's base. Constructed mainly from limestone with pink granite and limestone sheathing, its outer sanctum consisted of an entrance hall that opened on to a columned courtyard with basalt paving and decorated walls. At the back of the courtyard was the entrance to the inner sanctum.

This contained a niched chapel, storage rooms, and an offering hall with a false door. The door, on the back wall directly against the side of the pyramid, allowed the dead king's *ka,* or spirit double, access to his food offerings, and also provided the focus for rituals and prayers.

Additional offerings for the king were placed in a small cult pyramid not far from the temple on the southeastern corner of the main pyramid. This housed a statue of the king's *ka* and ensured that he was well provided in the afterlife.

Mysteriously Missing Images

The complex was surrounded by burials of the king's relatives and officials. Most of these were *mastaba* tombs in the western and eastern cemeteries, however three of Khufu's female relatives were buried in the queens' pyramids to the east of his pyramid. The northernmost may be for Hetepheres, his mother, though her grave goods were discovered in a nearby shaft. The middle one was probably for Meretites, his chief wife, and the third, based on an inscription in the pyramid's mortuary chapel, was Henutsen's, his half-sister. Two boat pits, now empty, are associated with these pyramids.

Interestingly, no images of Khufu were found in any part the complex. His only surviving portrait is a 3-inch (7.5-cm) tall ivory statue discovered at Abydos. For a king remembered for the size of his tomb, this is one of the smallest pieces of Egyptian royal sculpture ever found.

IN PRAISE OF SEWERAGE

Archeologists can thank modern sanitation for helping them locate Khufu's valley temple and causeway. For many years, references to the exact location of these structures were based on guesswork, but in 1990 workers installing sewerage systems under the streets of Nazlet el-Samman, a village to the northeast of the Giza plateau, came across parts of these buildings. Enough remains survived to help archeologists determine the original path of the causeway as it led from the valley temple. Excavations also revealed sections of dark green basalt paving, a 26-foot-thick (8-m) mud-brick wall that may have been part of a living area around the valley temple and the remains of a limestone wall marking the harbor of Khufu. The Egyptian government is making plans to move some of the residents from this site so excavations can be completed.

Above **Khufu's pyramid; engraving by the Italian artist Luigi Mayer, 1804.** The top of the pyramid commands an excellent view of Giza but at this time much of the complex was still buried in sand.

The Boat Pits at Giza

Adjacent to Khufu's pyramid are five pits designed to hold the king's boats. Similar pits also exist in the tomb enclosures of other kings. Some still held the rotting remains of boats, however most were emptied in antiquity.

Right **Solar bark painting.** This Nineteenth-Dynasty relief shows similarities with Khufu's bark in its shape, canopy, and oars. It also reflects the sacred nature of these vessels, with the god Khnum passing through the underworld attended by Hathor and Horus.

Two of Khufu's pits contained boats in such an amazing state of preservation that one has been reassembled, providing us with the first definitive look at an ancient vessel and one of the few large artifacts belonging to this king. The first evidence for their existence was discovered in 1950 when architect and archeologist Kamal el-Mallakh noticed a line of mortar around a pair of what looked like rectangular pits on the south side of the Great Pyramid. Workers uncovered huge lime-stone slabs over the easternmost of the two pits, and a cartouche of Djedefra, Khufu's successor. It took el-Mallakh four years to convince his superiors that this find was significant enough to be investigated. In 1954 one of the slabs was finally raised on the eastern pit, revealing the boat still lying inside.

Khufu's Boats

Unfortunately, the boat lay in over 1,200 pieces, as it had when first placed in the pit over 4,500 years ago. Each piece was painstakingly removed for preservation and rebuilding—a giant jigsaw puzzle that took 10 years to put back together. When finally completed, the boat measured 142 feet (43.3 m) long and 19 feet (5.9 m) wide and was shaped like the papyrus reed boats of Predynastic times. However, it was made of the more expensive and durable Lebanese cedar wood and acacia. Instead of nails, the planks were stitched together by ropes of vegetable fiber running through a series of U-shaped holes. The deck held a large cabin for the king and a smaller one that was probably for the pilot.

BUILDING A 3-D JIGSAW PUZZLE

Reconstructing Khufu's boat was an extraordinary task involving intensive research, guesswork and 10 years of back-breaking work. The specifics of ancient boat design were unknown and the team spent months practicing on scale-models and watching Nile boat builders ply their craft before they even started rebuilding. Using the way the timbers had been arranged in the pit as a guide, leader Hag Ahmed Youssef Mustafa and his team started on the first of five attempts to rebuild the boat. On the fourth attempt, they discovered that many of the planks were marked with signs by the ancient builders, indicating where they fitted together. This greatly assisted with final modifications and confirmed much of the work already done. The rebuilt boat is now on display in a museum next to its original pit where it stands as a memorial to the technical expertise and artistry of its ancient builders.

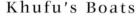

Left **Khufu's solar bark rebuilt.** The boat was originally lashed together with wooden pegs and rope made from local grass. The boat was reconstructed using the same materials.

There was no mast or sail, and the boat was propelled by 10 oars, with another two for steerage.

The second boat pit was examined in 1987. A hole was bored through the limestone to insert a small camera into the pit for taking measurements of the air contents. This confirmed that the pit contained a boat; however, the decision was made to preserve this boat as it lay, so the pit was resealed indefinitely.

The Boat's Purpose

Debate still rages over the purpose of the reconstructed boat. Had the king traveled in the boat, either when he was alive or during the funerary procession when his body was carried across the Nile to his tomb? Or was the boat built purely for use in the afterlife?

The two southern boat pits are irregular in shape and different from the other rectangular pits, which suggests they may have been built for boats that were to be dismantled and buried. This would be the expected treatment for boats connected with the funeral rites as they had special religious significance. Supporting this theory is the abraded appearance of some of the timbers, possibly made by movement of the ropes when the boat was in use. However, shavings of cedar wood and acacia found in the pit indicate the boat may have been made where it was buried. If so, the boat probably had a symbolic purpose and was built to help Khufu travel in the underworld and afterlife, or journey with the sun-god Ra across the skies.

Perhaps the answer lies somewhere in the middle. The different shapes of the boat pits and their locations around the pyramids suggest that they may have had different purposes. Some of the boats could have been for the afterlife and others, like the rebuilt one, may well once have carried Khufu's body.

Right **The Solar Boat Museum at Giza**. On the southern side of the great pyramid of Khufu, the museum holds the full-size reconstruction of this ancient boat, discovered in pieces in a pit beside the pyramid.

Mystery of Hetepheres' Tomb

On the east side of the Great Pyramid a photographer working for archeologist George Reisner set up his equipment to take pictures. The leg of the tripod scratched against some plaster, revealing an entranceway to an underground stairway.

The year was 1925, and this simple accident was soon to lead to the opening of one of the oldest intact royal tombs ever discovered in Egypt—as well as the unfolding of a mystery that may never be solved.

The team believed the stairway led to the tomb of someone important, but it would be 10 years before they would learn exactly whose. A 92-foot (28-m) vertical shaft filled with rubble separated the stairway from the chamber, protecting the entrance from grave robbers, and delayed its opening by modern archeologists. What they eventually discovered exceeded their wildest imaginations. Inside lay a room full of priceless artifacts, many inscribed with the name Queen Hetepheres, a wife of Sneferu (c. 2613–2589) the first ruler of the Fourth Dynasty, and mother of King Khufu.

Below **A fragment of a beaded cloth from Hetephere's tomb** re-created in cross stitch. The original garment is unknown but may be a sed cloak worn by Khufu or Hetepheres to celebrate a jubilee festival.

The Burial Chamber

The first glimpse into this chamber is recorded by Reisner: "Looking in from a small opening, [we] had seen a beautiful alabaster sarcophagus … Partly on [it] and partly fallen behind it lay about 20 gold-cased poles and beams of a large canopy." In fact, the objects inside it were so spectacular and of such an early date that, for a short while at least, this discovery eclipsed that of the New Kingdom tomb of Tutankhamun made by Howard Carter just a few years earlier.

The excavation of the burial chamber was difficult and conditions were often dangerous. The space was small, allowing for only two people, parts of the ceiling were unstable, and the objects themselves were fragile and often poorly preserved. But the results were worth the effort: exquisitely made furniture including a bed, two armchairs, and a carrying chair; several wooden boxes and a leather case for walking sticks; smaller items, such as copper tools, sheets of goldfoil that once embellished many of the objects, and 20 silver bracelets inlaid with turquoise, carnelian, and lapis lazuli.

The burial chamber also contained a large alabaster sarcophagus. Despite the fact that the chamber and vertical shaft appeared intact, there was no body inside. Just as puzzling was the alabaster canopic chest found in a sealed recess in the west wall. The chest was divided into four compartments, three of which still contained the preserved internal organs, wrapped in linen and lying in a solution of natron and water.

Whatever Happened to the Queen's Body?

Reisner proposed an explanation for the mystery of the queen's missing body and the lack of a superstructure to her tomb. He believed that Hetepheres must have died in the early years of Khufu's reign and was buried at Dahshur, near Sneferu's pyramid.

Her tomb was then broken into and her body stolen. Khufu removed the remaining items to Giza where he quickly constructed a new tomb for his mother. This would explain some of the anomalies of the burial chamber such as the damaged side of the sarcophagus and the objects found in the bottom of the shaft thrown there after the chamber was sealed.

However, there is no evidence she was ever buried at Dahshur and it is unlikely that her son

would have buried her with broken and violated tomb equipment, or that any tomb robber would have left the valuable jewelry behind.

Modern scholars who disagree with Reisner have made alternative suggestions. American Egyptologist Doctor Mark Lehner also believes that Hetepheres died early in her son's reign but was buried in this hastily dug shaft, rather than at Dahshur. The superstructure to the burial chamber was then built but abandoned when plans for the eastern field were altered to fit Khufu's mortuary temple. Instead, three smaller pyramids were built and her body was reburied in one of these (though there is no trace of it there today).

But why did they leave behind the canopic chest containing the organs and what was the reason for burying the queen in such haste? Egyptologist Doctor Zahi Hawass suggests instead that Hetepheres was originally buried in the northern-most of the three pyramids and later moved to the shaft burial. Her body was probably stolen when much of Khufu's complex was vandalized during the First Intermediate Period (c. 2160–2055 BCE). Priests connected to the complex could have moved the remainder of her funerary items into the shaft. Why though, did the robbers leave behind the valuable artifacts that still appear in the tomb?

Many crucial questions remain unanswered. Whatever the mystery behind this tomb and its owner, its objects have provided a glimpse into the life of Old Kingdom royalty that has yet to be surpassed.

Above **The shaft of Hetepheres' tomb, discovered by Reisner.** This tomb contained spectacular artifacts along with her sarcophagus, but no body.

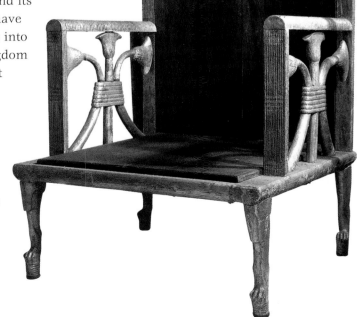

Right **Queen Hetepheres' sedan chair, discovered in her tomb at Giza.** It now resides in the Egyptian Museum (in Cairo).

Khafra's Pyramid

Khafra's pyramid sits in an elevated position at the center of the Giza plateau. The middle of the three great pyramids, it has a distinctive appearance as the only one retaining some of the original white limestone casing on its apex.

Right **Gneiss statue of Khafra from his funerary temple at Giza.** Khafra is protected by the falcon god Horus, which sits behind his head. The stone this statue is made from emanates a deep blue glow in sunlight.

Khafra, a son of Khufu, ruled from about 2558–2532 BCE, succeeding his brother Djedefra (who was buried further north at Abu Rawash). His pyramid and complex were constructed during his reign and finished on his death. Today, they rank among the best-preserved examples of these monument types and provide insight into the layout of a typical pyramid complex.

The Elevated Pyramid

Khafra built his pyramid—known as "Khafra is great"—on a rocky outcrop next to his father's, possibly taking advantage of the elevated ground to increase the height of his pyramid and offer greater stability. With a height originally about 471 feet (144 m) (though now only 448 feet or 137 meters) and sides 694 feet (215 m) long, it is only marginally smaller than the Great Pyramid but does not appear to have been constructed with the same precision and attention to detail. The limestone blocks of the core were laid with wide joints and in uneven layers and the corner bases did not align with the apex, creating a slight twist at the top of the pyramid.

The pyramid's internal layout is relatively simple. Access is via two entrances on the north side of the pyramid. The lower entrance, in use today, cuts through bedrock at the base and leads to an unfinished chamber that may have once held funerary items. The upper entrance, 39 feet (12 m) above ground, opens on a descending passageway, which levels out before connecting with a tunnel ascending from the lower chamber, and continues to the burial chamber.

The burial chamber, oriented east–west, is cut partially into the bedrock and has a gabled roof of limestone blocks. It lacks any decorative elements and the only funerary item that remains is Khafra's granite sarcophagus, although the lid lies broken by tomb robbers. The only other features of note are a shallow pit that probably contained the canopic chest and two narrow shafts that may have held support beams for a wooden structure that has since disappeared.

A Well-preserved Complex

One of the best-preserved Old Kingdom pyramid complexes, Khafra retained traditional elements

Below **The granite temple of Khafra, at Giza.** The complex surrounding Khafra's Pyramid at Giza is unique for its highly innovative architecture.

THE TEMPLE OF THE SPHINX

The Sphinx faces equinotical east, directly into the rising sun. In front of the statue are the ruins of a temple. The design resembles the construction of temples dedicated to the sun-god in the later Fifth Dynasty. The temple floor plan contains an open-sky court with 24 columns that might represent the complete hours in a day, and a dozen statues, one for each hour of daytime. To the east and west ends are recesses, or sanctuaries, probably associated with rituals for the rising and setting of the sun. It is the most precisely aligned solar temple of the time-period, however it is believed to have been unfinished and never dedicated to use by its creators. In the Eighteenth Dynasty, it was reconstructed and put into use by Amenophis II.

such as the valley and mortuary temples, causeway, boat pits, and cult pyramid, while incorporating several innovations in architectural design. Around these is a scattering of subsidiary tombs and, lying near the entrance to the complex, the monuments that have made it famous—the Sphinx and Sphinx temple.

The complex is entered through the eastern side of the valley temple, via two ramps leading from the Nile harbor. The innovative construction methods used in this temple, including the use of massive core blocks of limestone, are still evident and partly responsible for the preservation of this building. The central element of the temple is the large T-shaped hall that still contains many of its original 16 granite pillars and once held 24 statues of the king (one survives, in the Egyptian Museum in Cairo). On the roof, accessed by a ramp from the hall, is a small courtyard originally believed to have been used in the embalming process, although recent excavations in front of the temple revealed traces of a ritual purification tent that possibly served this function. Another door from the hall opens on to the 1,619–foot (495-m) long causeway that connected the valley and mortuary temples. Although now in ruins, it was probably covered and lined with granite in the same manner as the temple.

The mortuary temple sits on the eastern side of the pyramid, alongside the 33-foot-wide (10-m) paved area and inner perimeter wall that encircled the entire base of the pyramid.

This temple, the largest of its era, set the standard for future designs with the incorporation of five elements for the first time—the entrance hall, open courtyard, statue chapels, storehouses, and the offering hall at the rear of the temple. The courtyard was also impressive. Once adorned with statues and colorful reliefs, it was positioned so that the rising sun reflected off the limestone casing of the pyramid and illuminated the open area, perhaps symbolizing the daily rebirth of the king with the sun-god.

The complex also contained five boat pits, all now empty, outside the mortuary temple and, on the south side of the pyramid, the ruins of a smaller cult pyramid for worship of the king's *ka*. To the west are the remains of what are believed to have been storehouses and workshops used in the maintenance of the king's cult.

Below **Khafra's Pyramid at Giza** still retains a little of the original white limestone facing at its peak, allowing a small glimpse at the pyramids in their original glory. The temple of Menkaura can be seen in the foreground.

The Sphinx

The Great Sphinx majestically guards the Giza Plateau, its presence facing the rising sun. The monument depicts the head of an Old Kingdom king, clad in a "nemes" headdress and merged onto the elongated body of a lion.

THE DREAM STELA OF THUTMOSE IV

Between the paws of the Sphinx stands a red granite slab on which the famous Dream Stela was recorded in the Eighteenth Dynasty by Pharaoh Thutmose IV. Discovered circa 1816 by the Italian explorer and sea captain Giovanni Battista Caviglia, it tells the story of Thutmose IV as a young prince. Seeking rest while hunting lions in the desert, the prince fell asleep in the shade of the Sphinx's head and while there he received a dream. The Sphinx, identifying himself as Hor-em-akhet (Horus on the Horizon), promised the prince the throne of Egypt in return for clearing the sand and restoring the monument. Thutmose arranged major restoration of the Sphinx and did become pharaoh as promised. History reveals this as a retelling of an Egyptian folktale but it demonstrates the mystery and regard that even later Egyptians held for the statue.

Below **The dream stela sits between the Sphinx's front paws.** In ancient Egypt, dreams were believed to be a tool to divinely prophesize the future. Thutmose IV's dream was fulfilled when he was made pharoah, despite not being the the first-born son and crown prince.

The Arabs named it *Abu el-Gol* (Father of Dread). In Greek mythology, the Sphinx became a deadly female who guarded the Theban road, posing riddles, and strangling the unworthy. The word sphinx was attributed to the Greeks, probably derived from their native verb *sphingein* (meaning to strangle, throttle), explaining the creature's role in Greek mythology. The Egyptians themselves called it *shesepankh* (meaning living image), invoking the Old Kingdom belief of the statue as a living image of the god Khepri-Ra-Atum, the triple aspect of the sun-god in morning, afternoon, and evening. This echoes the Greek riddle of the Sphinx, which asks: "What walks on four legs in the morning, two legs in the afternoon, and three legs in the evening?" The answer is man.

Size and Shape

The Sphinx is the largest single-stone carving in existence, created from a solid outcropping of variegated limestone. The head is carved from hard, gray-toned limestone; the body is softer, yellowish limestone, with the base of the statue harder then the head and more brittle. The remains of its ruined temple indicate an open ceiling with a view of the statue, and western and eastern wall alcoves that might have been used during ritual observances honoring the sun.

The Sphinx measures over 240 feet (73 m) long and 60 feet (20 m) from the courtyard floor to the top of the head. The face itself is 13 feet (4.1 m) wide. Even in Egyptian history no other monument has surpassed it. The closest to date is the 50-foot (18-m) high faces of Mount Rushmore in the USA, which took over 14 years to create with explosives and drilling tools.

When Was the Sphinx Built?

Traditional Egyptology and archeology place the origin of the Sphinx in the Fourth Dynasty, circa 2500 BCE. Geological evidence claims the body is older than the head, supported by patterns of weathering and water erosion that geologists John Anthony West and Robert Schock say

indicate the body was created between 10,000 and 7,000 BCE. Archeological study has not uncovered any evidence to support the existence of a pre-Egyptian Nile culture of sufficient organization to be responsible, which casts significant doubt on the geological age in orthodox Egyptology. The statue itself cannot be directly dated by any current methodology, so the question is still unanswered.

The Sphinx's creation is most commonly attributed to Fourth-Dynasty King Khafra. This belief acquired support with the discovery of Khafra's name on the famous Dream Stela. However, the king's name does not appear in the customary cartouche (the oval ring surrounding a king's name) and is only a fragment of a name believed to be Khafra's, so it is an inconclusive relationship. This attribution

is also strengthened by statues and belongings of Khafra discovered by Egyptologist Auguste Mariette in 1853 in a temple south of the Sphinx.

More recent discoveries seem to challenge Khafra's relationship. His elder brother Djedefra, first king to call himself "son of Ra," may have created the monument. A head of Djedefra thought to be the first Sphinx statue was discovered in Djedefra's unfinished funerary complex in Abu Rawash, near Giza. Also, in 1996, a New York detective concluded through measurement and analysis that the face of the Sphinx was proportionally closer to Djedefra than to Khafra. To date, there is no evidence that conclusively proves who built the Sphinx, and analysis is further muddied by the possibility that the head has been redesigned since its creation.

Above **According to Greek mythology, the Sphinx** was an evil half-woman, half-lion demon who asked all passersby the answer to the riddle of the Sphinx, strangling anyone who did not answer correctly. When Oepidus finally gave the right answer, she threw herself to her death.

Left **French chocolate box.** Visitors have been so impressed by the statue of the Sphinx that its image has frequently been used in merchandising.

Above **Head of colossal sphinx at Giza by Luigi Mayer,** *Views in Egypt,* **1801.** During Napoleon's unsuccessful campaign to conquer Egypt, as his out-numbered, heat-exhausted soldiers headed toward Cairo they stumbled upon the awe-inspiring sight of the Sphinx and pyramids.

Right **A bad nose job.** There are many theories about how the Sphinx had its nose blown off, with dates varying from 1378 up to the 1940s.

The Changing Sphinx

The Sphinx and its temple complex underwent revisions and changes in later dynasties, especially the Eighteenth and Nineteenth. The area also became a popular entertainment and gathering center in the later Roman period, which obscured much of the original construction and purpose. In addition to erosion and reconstruction, the Sphinx has sustained other damage over the years. The uraeus, head plumes, and beard are gone, there is damage to the face and body, and the famous nose is missing.

Popular theory ascribes the damage to the nose to target practice from Napoleon's artillery-men, or to British and German soldiers in World Wars I and II. Arab conquerors that raided the necropolis might be responsible for the damage. However, the most likely culprit is the Islamic cleric Sa'im al-dahr. Accounts from 1378 note his disapproval of the heathen idol and his desire to remove it, specifically mentioning the nose, making it probable that he was responsible for its destruction.

Restorations to the Sphinx are attributed to the reigns of Thutmose IV and Rameses II by evidence of the various stelae and accounts that have been found. Further restorations were also made in Roman times, consisting of re-covering the paws and flanks where they were eroded or flaking. Marcus Aurelius is reputed to have repaved the entire floor of the Sphinx's courtyard, one of the largest efforts in the monument's ancient history.

Enter the Archeologists

Many explorations have been made of the Sphinx, each one unburying it from the sand that constantly re-covered it. In the 1840s, the explorers Caviglia and Vyse discovered a chapel between the front paws and uncovered the Dream Stela. They also found several stelae from Rameses II. Caviglia hoped to find a tunnel running under the Sphinx all the way to Khafra's pyramid but this didn't exist. Looking for hidden chambers, they blasted a hole in the Sphinx's back, but none were found. The persistent belief in hidden chambers and tunnels in and beneath the Sphinx exists to this day, unsuccessfully sought by numerous explorers.

Only three entrances into the Sphinx have ever been discovered, with one being the entry in its back opened by Caviglia and Vyse. The other two consist of an entrance near the tail about 30 feet (9 m) long, and a short, dead-end entrance on the north side discovered in 1926 by Baraize. More recently, while using seismographic equipment during examinations of erosion damage, Kent Weeks claimed there is evidence of hollows and chambers below the paws and to either side under the Sphinx. Rumors persist of the constant discovery of underground tunnels, but exploration of any of these alleged spaces has not been permitted to date.

In 1853, Auguste Mariette again cleared sand covering the statue and was the first to note the boxy attachments at the base of the Sphinx, discovered to be New Kingdom shrines. In 1925, Emile Baraize engaged in the most extensive repairs to the statue in modern times. He cleared most of the sand and built a retaining wall to contain it, echoing walls built for Thutmose IV's restorations. Baraize's work included plugging the hole created by Caviglia and Vyse. He created cement extensions of the damaged nemes to support the neck, filled in the cracks in the face, put an iron plate over a hole in the top of the head, filled in erosion fissures in the haunches and replaced repair blocks from older restorations that had fallen off. Baraize also found Greek and Roman period stelae, and evidence of work done by Ramesses II and Amenhotep II.

Doctor Selim Hassan cleared over 325,000 cubic yards (approximately a quarter-million cubic meters) of sand and debris from the site, publishing his findings in 1940. Among them is the Amenhotep stela telling of a visit to the Sphinx similar to the later, more embellished dream stela. Doctor Hassan's work was the last large-scale clearing project required and regular maintenance has prevented the statue being reburied since then.

Restoring the Sphinx

The Egyptian authorities have been organizing restoration work since 1955. In the 1980s, restoration attempts included attaching thousands of limestone blocks and injecting chemical additives into the stone. This process failed, the additions flaking away, and the previous restoration attempts on the left shoulder crumbled off.

More recent restoration and exploration has been carried out. Current plans consist of stopping the flaking of the limestone surface, reconstructing areas of masonry, and removing and correcting old restorations that were unintentionally damaging. However, dangers to the survival of the Sphinx include changing climate, seepage and water damage, pollution, modern transportation vibration, and the rise of local population, leaving its future uncertain.

Above **Sphinx excavations during the 1890s.** Work on the site continues today, with restorations led by the site director, Doctor Zahi Hawass for the Egyptian Council of Antiquities, and the Sphinx Restoration team, supervised by the Egyptian Minister of Culture, Farouk Hosni.

THE ROYAL BEARD

The Sphinx originally had the false beard that denotes kingship though various stelae have shown the Sphinx with the wedge-shaped beard of a pharaoh or the curled beard indicating divinity. The reasons for the royal beard are obscure today, but nearly all images of pharaohs are shown with one, including a woman who held the throne as king. The similarity of word roots between the concepts of hnsk (braided hair), hnsktyw (wearing braided side-lock), and hnn (phallus) could indicate the importance of the beard in representing the fertility and masculinity of the king. It could also explain why a female reigning as king (the title adopted by a ruling queen) might adopt the custom to create an impression of legitimacy. The Sphinx was similarly depicted and the remains of the Sphinx's beard are on display in the British Museum.

Menkaura's Pyramid

In Giza's southwest lies the funerary complex of Menkaura. The smallest of the main pyramids, it is still the dominant feature among the ruins of a causeway, two temples, three subsidiary pyramids, and a scattering of rock-cut tombs.

Right **Alabaster seated statue of Menkaura.** Found in the ruins of his pyramid temple at Giza, this statue measures 92.5 inches (231 cm) high, and is held in the Egyptian Museum (in Cairo).

Menkaura succeeded his father Khafra around 2532 BCE and ruled for about 18 years (although possibly as long as 26). His monuments were constructed throughout his reign, though many were incomplete when he unexpectedly died and so were hastily finished by his son and successor Shepseskaf.

The Empty Pyramid

The ancient Egyptians referred to his pyramid as "Menkaura is divine." It originally stood 217 feet (66.5 m) tall with base sides of 357 feet (109 m), but lost 10 feet (3 m) in height as stones were removed at various times throughout history. The core is made from limestone blocks and cased with white limestone in the upper section and pink granite around the base. It is the only Fourth Dynasty pyramid to use granite casing, some of which still lies near the entrance on the north face of the pyramid.

The entrance, which is about 13 feet (4 m) above ground, opens on to a 100-foot-long (31-m) descending corridor. At the bottom is a small room decorated with some unusual carved stone panels—the only purely decorative feature found inside one of the Giza pyramids. The corridor continues to the large rectangular antechamber, now lacking the objects that originally filled it. From here, the passage descends, passing a side room containing six wall niches that once held funerary items or statues, before terminating in the burial chamber.

The rectangular burial chamber differs significantly from Khufu's and Khafra's in that it is oriented north–south and cut completely into the bedrock below the pyramid. It is still lined with its original pink granite. The only tomb object remaining when explorers Perring and Vyse entered the pyramid in 1837 was the king's empty basalt sarcophagus. This was removed so it could be sent to England; however, the ship it was on met with disaster and the sarcophagus now lies on the bottom of the Mediterranean.

Right **Menkaura's pyramid is flanked by three satellite pyramids.** These may belong to his queens, but it is uncertain. His own pyramid is one-tenth the volume of Khafra's.

REINVENTING ARCHEOLOGY

A renowned archeologist, George Reisner spent more than half his life excavating in Egypt. From the early years at the sites of Naga ed-Deir, Quft, and Deir el-Ballas, he went on to lead the 1905–27 Harvard University–Boston Museum expeditions at Menkaura's pyramid complex. Reisner also excavated much of the rest of the Giza plateau including Khufu's western and eastern cemeteries, and his mortuary temple and queen's pyramids. His scientific excavation methods, including organized numbering systems and precise documentation, altered the course of archeology at Giza and led to the implementation of modern archeological practices. Born in America in 1867, he died at Giza in 1942, where he is buried.

A Lost Pyramid Complex

As with his pyramid, much of Menkaura's complex was unfinished at the time of his death. Shepseskaf hastily completed the two temples and the causeway in mud-brick rather than stone, a decision that meant few remains survive today. In contrast to Khufu's and Khafra's complex, no boat pits have yet been discovered.

Archeologists have been able to reconstruct the original appearances of the temple and they determined that both followed architectural conventions. The valley temple, at the entrance to the complex, contained an antechamber flanked by storerooms at the front, an open courtyard in the center, and an offering hall at the rear surrounded by additional storerooms. The mortuary temple, on the eastern side of the pyramid, had a rectangular courtyard leading to a portico around which were storerooms and niches, and, at the rear, the inner sanctuary and offering hall.

Valley temple excavations revealed further significant discoveries. Additions to the building were made in the Fifth and Sixth Dynasties, indicating it was still in use as a cult temple and possibly a palace. Evidence was also uncovered of workshops and lodgings that may have belonged to builders or to the priests maintaining the cult of the dead king. In the rear storerooms several exquisite statues were found featuring Menkaura in triads with Hathor and various local deities, and in dyads with an unknown queen. No trace of the start of the 1,995-foot-long (608-m) causeway was found near the temple, indicating that it did not reach the valley temple and was never finished.

Included in the complex are the subsidiary burials of Menkaura's family and officials. To the south are three small pyramids whose owners are unknown, although one may have been for his chief wife and sister, Khamerernebty II. To the northwest of the valley temple is the tomb of his daughter Queen Khentkawes. Adjacent to this tomb are the remains of a small town, surrounded by a thick enclosure wall, that could have housed either workers attached to the complex or pyramid builders.

Above **The funerary temple of Menkaura at Giza**. Menkaura's pyramid was completed by his son Shepseskaf but during the Fifth and Sixth Dynasties, his temples had additions made, suggesting his cult was still significant.

The Workers' Village

Building the pyramids and their complexes was a major feat of construction. It was also one of organization. The thousands of workers—the overseers, masons, artisans and laborers—required somewhere to live and food to eat.

They also needed workshops, offices, and places to store tools and building materials. A "city" for the pyramid builders must have existed but until recently it appeared they had vanished without a trace. In 1988, Egyptologists doctors Mark Lehner and the director of archeology at Giza, Zahi Hawass, instigated a joint excavation at the south-east edge of the plateau. Over a decade earlier some remains, including bone, ash, flint, and pottery had been found here, indicating this to be a likely location for the "workers' village." Eventually, the sand yielded its secrets. The ancient settlement currently extends approximately 2,130 feet (650 m) south of a wall known as the "Wall of the Crow" or "*Heit el-Ghurob*," though it could extend further under the modern settlement. This massive stone wall divides the mortuary complexes on the Giza plateau from the worker's village. It is 654 feet (200 m) long, 33 feet (10 m) high and 33 feet wide. A monumental gateway set into the wall is capped with three huge limestone blocks to form an architrave. The workers from the village would probably have walked through this gate daily on their way up to the necropolis to labor over the construction of the pyramids.

Bakery and Food Areas

The village is largely made up of two huge production areas, which run parallel along either side of a paved street. The foundations of one, a bakery, contain a raised hearth, storage areas for bread moulds, and a number of dough vats. Near the bakery is another large building. It is divided

Below This Fifth-Dynasty painted limestone relief depicts workers making and baking bread. Along with the pyramid builders, many other such workers lived in the village at Giza.

inside by low benches separated by narrow troughs paved with clay. The bones of vast numbers of Nile catfish and schal fish were found embedded in these troughs, suggesting they had been used to sort the fish while they were being prepared for cleaning, salting, and drying. Bones of young cattle, sheep, goats, and pigs, as well as plant grains, have also been found in this area along with a flint knife. Apparently this structure was used to prepare many types of food.

Barracks and Housing

A number of long rectangular buildings have been found grouped together near the food production areas. Internally these structures are subdivided lengthways into two long chambers, each with a number of mud-brick platforms placed at intervals down its length. The excavator of this site, Doctor Mark Lehner, believes these platforms were beds for the temporary workers employed to build the pyramids. He tested this theory by asking his workers to lie down on the platforms and discovered that they would accommodate the height of modern Egyptian workers. From this re-creation, Lehner postulated that each building housed between 40 and 50 people in a dormitory fashion. He then calculated that the barracks complex could house a workforce of approximately 1,600 to 2,000 individuals.

At the southern ends of the dormitories are rectangular enclosures divided into two chambers. Ashy deposits present in some of these chambers indicate they were used as kitchens. One suggestion is that these enclosures were self-contained domestic units, possibly occupied by the supervisors of the workers who were housed in the attached dorms.

Administration Building

A huge double-walled structure near the village area appears to have functioned as a royal administration building. Its extent is not presently known as it is still partially buried beneath a modern soccer field. It contains a court filled with large mud-brick silos, probably to store the grain being processed in the village bakeries. There is also a series of chambers dedicated to the production of copper and alabaster vessels. The discovery of loom shuttles and weights suggests weaving activities were carried out in this building. A vast number of counting tokens, which would have been used as a form of

accountancy, have been recovered. Finding these tokens along with numerous mud-seals bearing the names of Khafra and Menkaura suggests the items produced under this roof were controlled by the central government; that is, the king.

In 2002 a new security wall was being built around the entire Giza plateau. As this structure would encroach on the eastern edge of the village, Doctor Lehner set about clearing the area. To his surprise, he discovered the foundations of a wall that separates an eastern settlement from the worker's village. Unlike the village, this settlement appears disorganized and crowded. The foundations of over 45 rooms have been found containing mud-lined bins, ashy deposits, and courtyards with small granaries. Such features suggest that the occupants of this town were more self-sufficient than the villagers. Therefore, it seems likely that this township housed the skilled craftsmen and overseers who lived at Giza on a more permanent basis than the rotating workers of the village.

Above **Laying sewerage systems in suburbs east of the Giza plateau in 1990** revealed the remains of an ancient village. It was now possible to reconstruct the lives of ordinary Egyptians who built the pyramids.

Left **Mummified bread.** The remains of a vast number of standard-sized ceramic bread moulds found at Giza led archeologists to believe they discovered Egypt's oldest known large-scale bakery.

The Workers' Cemeteries

In 1990, just after the first remains of the workers' village were uncovered, a tourist riding a horse stumbled upon a previously unknown mud-brick wall. This was reported to Zahi Hawass, who determined that the "wall" was actually a tomb.

The tourist was out riding just to the west of the cemetery when he found the wall. As more and more of the graves there gradually became uncovered, it became increasingly likely that this was the cemetery for the people who built the pyramids and the officials who organized them. Two cemeteries were discovered—the upper cemetery, defined by an enclosure wall, is reserved for the tombs of artisans and craftsmen, while the lower cemetery contains over 600 tiny burials of workers.

The Tombs and Their Rightful Owners

The tombs of the upper cemetery take on various shapes. Some have a stepped dome, which covers a simple rectangular grave pit. Others are *mastabas* designed with small external courtyards. A few of the larger tombs are constructed in the shape of a small mud-brick pyramid. This is similar to the design of some of the tombs of craftsmen at the New Kingdom site of Deir el-Medina which, like the settlement at Giza, had been established for individuals responsible for constructing and decorating the nearby royal tombs.

The majority of the tombs of Giza's upper cemetery have mud-brick chapels, which contain crudely inscribed false doors. Their occupants recorded titles on these false doors, revealing the responsibilities they held at the pyramid site during their lifetimes. For example, one of the tomb owners is the overseer of the side of the pyramid, while other individuals hold titles such as director of workers or inspector of craftsmen.

The lower cemetery, though containing some larger tombs, is dominated by the small tombs or graves of the poorer workers. Most were less than a few feet square, some had rubble, mud, or leftover stones to mark their gravesites, but the majority were simple holes in the ground. Many of the bodies were lying in the fetal position with the face directed to the rising sun. Grave goods were limited and included smaller items like knives, pots, and jars for beer—even the poor wanted to take something to the afterlife. Although mostly anonymous, these remains tell us that some of these workers were women.

Above **Part of a Fifth-Dynasty painted limestone relief from the *mastaba* of Khaemreou, at Saqqara.** It shows craftsmen fashioning a statue. It is now known that workers such as these were buried in cemeteries adjacent to the pyramids.

BREWING BEER

Hieroglyphs within an upper cemetery tomb at Giza belonging to a man called Nefer-thieth identify him as overseer of the palace. However it is possible that he may also have been involved in the production of bread and beer as many of the wall scenes in his chapel depict these activities.

Beer (*henket*) was the most readily available alcoholic drink and was drunk by adults and children. Not only was it a social lubricant, it was also a suitable offering to the gods. It was supplied to employees of the state as part of their wages.

Beer was made both by brewers and in private homes, usually prepared by women. Water was poured over partially baked cakes of barley bread, which were mashed. Dates, honey, or spices could be added and the mixture was left to ferment in a vat before being sieved into a jar. The result was a thick, soup-like brew that was mildly alcoholic but also very nutritious. Getting drunk was not only commonplace, but socially acceptable. Indeed in a banqueting scene from the tomb of Paheri, a woman guest compliments her host by confirming her intention "to drink until I am thoroughly drunk," while another guest says, "Let the cup come to me. It is only right that we should drink to the health of our host!" For religious festivals, during which drunkenness was considered particularly appropriate, a stronger mixture was often brewed.

Right **Making beer with dates, painted limestone decoration from the tomb of Rekhmira, an Eighteenth-Dynasty vizier,** at Thebes. Giza workers were given beer three times a day. Egyptologists have found five different types of beer and four of wine.

Revealing Skeletal Remains

Due to the simplicity of the worker tombs, they have been virtually ignored by tomb robbers. Thus the bodies within them lie generally undisturbed. These bodies were not mummified—during the Old Kingdom this practice was in its infancy and available only to the elite—so the bones were carefully examined in the hope of extracting the life-stories of their owners.

There are significant differences between the skeletal remains of overseers, officials, and artisans to those of the laborers. The former had less rigorous daily lives and better diets, however

they still faced disease and old age. Laborers' skeletons had the most interesting stories to tell—about the damage sustained by their bodies over their lifetimes, the type of work they performed, and their treatment by the authorities.

Nearly all of their skeletons show signs of arthritis, degenerative spinal disease, and compressed vertebrae caused by heavy lifting. Analysis has also shown that most of the male workers died between the ages of 35 and 40. Females died five to 10 years younger. Though there are no written records or wall reliefs showing women carrying out the physical tasks required of the men, the condition of their skeletal remains suggest they did perform similar work. They had more damage to their bones than would be expected if they had been doing simple household jobs, including the arthritis and spinal conditions evident in the male skeletons. One woman, who died in her thirties, had bone degeneration in her neck and backbone, indicating that she had been carrying heavy loads on her head since childhood.

However, the skeletons also showed the workers had access to medical attention. There were many cases of fractures, particularly of the upper arm and leg bones, which had healed completely. There are even two instances of men who had undergone successful amputations. Such insights suggest the pyramid builders were not slaves as previously thought, but conscripted workers who were treated humanely.

Above **A view of the workers' tombs at Giza.** Those built for wealthier individuals often had mud-brick chapels, some with inscribed false doors.

The *Mastaba* Tombs of Giza

An important part of the Giza necropolis' structure and history are its numerous *mastabas*, a style of tomb. While pyramids entombed the highest ranking royals, the kings and queens, *mastabas* were used to bury their children and important people.

WHAT IS A MASTABA?

The term *mastaba* is derived from an Arabic word meaning "bench" as they resemble the benches found in front of some modern-day Egyptian houses. These low, rectilinear superstructures or above-ground masses are constructed of either mud-brick or stone.

Their first known use dates back to the Early Dynastic Period at sites such as Abydos and Saqqara. At this time, they take the form of a simple structure, which is subdivided into chambers by brick partitioning and roofed with timber panels. Later developments refined this basic design, so by the Fourth Dynasty this type of tomb generally consisted of a stone rubble core surrounded by outer casing blocks of limestone which sloped outwards from a flat roof.

Left **These ruined pillars of a *mastaba*** are part of the remains of a tomb in Khafra's pyramid complex at Giza.

A Royal Cemetery Site

Rudimentary *mastabas* began to appear on the Giza Plateau as early as the Archaic or Early Dynastic Period, covering the First and Second Dynasties. One of these tombs can be dated to the Second Dynasty from the discovery there of funerary goods with jar-sealings bearing the cartouche of Nynetjer, the third ruler of that era.

But it was not until the Fourth Dynasty that we see a huge increase in the number of *mastabas* at Giza. Khufu, the second ruler of the Fourth Dynasty who built the Great Pyramid, is also considered responsible for laying out the *mastaba* fields to the east and west of his pyramid. Though Giza was not used as the Royal Necropolis after the end of the Fourth Dynasty, a vast number of important officials of the Fifth and Sixth Dynasties continued to construct their *mastabas* here.

The Greater Giza Cemetery is made up of three major fields—the eastern, central, and western. Each of these is characterized by a large pyramid, one or more subsidiary pyramids, and a varying number of *mastabas*.

Giza's Eastern and Central Cemetery Fields

The eastern cemetery, dominated by the Great Pyramid, contains a row of three subsidiary pyramids, to the north of which is the tomb of Khufu's mother, Queen Hetepheres. It also has an area dedicated to *mastabas*, many belonging to the children of Khufu and his queens. They are identified by their royal title, "son/daughter of the ruler's body."

One of these *mastabas*, referred to as G7110-7120, is inscribed for Kawab, a son of Khufu, and one of his wives Hetepheres II, who later married the ruler Djedefra. Unfortunately Kawab's tomb, like so many others from this cemetery, has sustained a considerable amount of damage over the years. The tombs further to the east are occupied by individuals who held royal titles, as well as by non-royals of the Fourth to Sixth Dynasties.

On the southern side of Khufu's pyramid, the GIS cemetery is formed by a row of 10 *mastabas*, a couple of which are owned by Fourth-Dynasty men who held a royal title, like Khufuzedef of tomb GIIIS. However, the majority of these tombs belong to Fifth and Sixth Dynasty officials who held important administrative offices.

Immediately south-west of Khufu's pyramid is the central field. This contains Khafra's pyramid, a large tomb built for Queen Khentkawes I, the associated pyramid town, and the Sphinx. Khafra's descendants are interred in rock-cut tombs that are carved out of the cliff face to the south of Khafra's causeway.

For example, the tomb of Nebemakhet, LG 86, inscribes a text which states he is the son of Khafra and Meresankh III, the latter of whom owns tomb G7530-7540 within the

eastern cemetery. The *mastabas* constructed within this cemetery are later than those that are rock cut, dating to the Fifth and Sixth Dynasties and are owned by Khafra's more distant relatives as well as officials.

Further south again, Menkaura constructed the smallest of the three Giza pyramids. He is probably responsible for building the three small pyramids just south of his own. Little is known of the final resting place of his descendants as there is only one rock-cut tomb cut into the cliff face south of the causeway of Khafra's pyramid, which belongs to Khuenra, a son of this ruler and Khamerenebty.

Giza's Western Cemetery Field

The western cemetery is characterized by a number of Fourth-Dynasty *mastabas*. These are arranged into north–south rows divided by streets and separated from each other by east–west avenues. This rigid organization has not been observed at earlier Egyptian cemeteries. These tombs are dedicated to men and women of the Fourth Dynasty who are thought to be the distant relatives of the owners of the pyramids, particularly Khufu. For example, the owner of *mastaba* G1225, Nefertyabt, holds the title "king's daughter."

Left **Mastaba** of Idu, a Sixth-Dynasty official at Giza. This *mastaba* scene shows him seated before an offering table, his wife kneeling under his chair.

Below **Mastaba** of Meryranefer, an early Sixth-Dynasty official at Giza. These statues of the deceased are set into a niche in his tomb.

Above **Mastaba of Kagemni, Sixth Dynasty.** Vizier and inspector of priests during Teti's reign, he is buried at Saqqara. In the innermost room is a stone offering table. It sits before a false door inscribed with autobiographical heiroglyphs attesting to his good deeds and career achievements.

Some of the western cemetery tombs constructed during the Fourth Dynasty were not occupied until the subsequent dynasty. Other, impressively large, Fifth-Dynasty tombs belong to high officials or mortuary priests serving a Fourth-Dynasty ruler or a royal descendant.

Some Fifth-Dynasty *mastabas* belonged to prominent aristocratic families. For example, a group of tombs is occupied by three generations of the Seshemnefer family, all of which hold scribal titles as well as high administrative offices. However, by the end of the Old Kingdom much of the grid-like organization of the original western cemetery had been lost. Many of the streets had become blocked by the construction of small *mastabas* that encroached upon and destroyed the exterior of earlier tombs.

Tomb Decorations of Feasts

The Fourth-Dynasty western cemetery at Giza is constructed with a shaft to the burial chamber cut into the tumulus or body of the *mastaba* and a simple external chapel made out of stone or mud-brick. In the back wall of 15 of these early *mastabas*, there are slab stelae decorated with raised relief and set into emplacements.

These rectilinear stone slabs, like the one found within tomb G1201 of Wepemnefret, are generally inscribed with the name of the individual and their titles, many claim to be the "son/daughter of the king" or an "acquaintance of the king." These stelae also have an area inscribed with offering lists of items of food, drink and clothing (linens). Also included is the figure of the deceased seated on a stool before a table, which is laden with loaves of bread and surrounded by further inscriptions that detail requests for other offerings.

The ancient Egyptians took every precaution to make sure that their physical needs would be met in the afterlife. The decoration of these slab stelae reiterate this fact, as they even went to the extent of providing images of food, drink, and other necessities in the event that physical offerings could not be brought to the tomb by the living. Their belief was that these representations could symbolically nourish the body if they were deemed necessary. The fact that these stelae represent the only inscribed or decorated elements of these *mastabas* indicates that they are considered essential pieces of burial equipment.

Right **Painted limestone stela from Giza, Fourth Dynasty.** Wearing a leopard skin wrap over her dress, the princess Nefertyabet is seated on a stool before a table of offerings. Heiroglyphs of various meat dishes are intended to maintain her sustenance in the afterlife.

Right **Bas-relief statue of the official, Idu, from his** *mastaba* **at Giza, early Sixth Dynasty.** This statue of the royal scribe, showing some residual paint, stands in a recess in the wall.

False Doors and Wall Scenes

A slightly later western cemetery tomb belonging to Weneshet, a royal female, has an external chapel with a false door in its back wall. Usually a stone feature, it acts as a barrier between the realms of the living and the dead. It represents a point at which the deceased could receive offerings brought to the tomb. It is designed like an actual door with an architrave and door-jambs, though the area where one would expect the door recess to be is blocked.

The false door may be considered a development of the slab stelae as it incorporates the offering table scene found on the latter into its upper sections. The example from the chapel of Weneshet is flanked by door-jambs, which are decorated with raised relief images of the deceased, members of her family, and offering bearers.

In the eastern cemetery a group of eight twin or double *mastabas* is arranged into four north–south rows. The first is positioned closest to the subsidiary pyramids. These *mastabas* are characterized by their elongate shape and have either a chapel cut into both ends of their eastern facades or a single chapel at the southern end with both internal and external components. This type of tomb is representative of a short-lived, yet distinctive form of the *mastaba* which is only utilized for Khufu's immediate descendants and their spouses.

Their chapels are designed with at least one false door. The walls are decorated with raised relief scenes with similar content to that found on Weneshet's false door. The chapel of Kawab illustrates cattle herders presenting livestock to the tomb owner and those of Khufukhaf I and Meresankh III represent butchery scenes showing oxen being slaughtered to provide meat to sustain the deceased. Scenes depicting painters, sculptors, and metalworkers preparing objects to furnish the tomb of the deceased are also represented in these tombs. The same types of scenes are also found in the rock-cut tombs of Khafra's descendants, including Nebemakhet and Nikaura.

SONS OF RA

First Fifth-Dynasty Kings

The Fifth Dynasty was a period in which the cult of the sun-god Ra reached its zenith, with the kings of this period expressing their devotion to the god in numerous ways. Most included Ra as an element of their own name.

They built and endowed sun-temples for the god's worship. During this dynasty, the king's birth name (nomen) was regularly written in a cartouche prefixed by the title, "son of Ra," which was first introduced at the end of the Fourth Dynasty.

Userkaf Moves the Necropolis

Userkaf was the first king of the Fifth Dynasty. His background is obscure, though it is possible that he was a descendant of a secondary branch of Khufu's family. It has been suggested that Userkaf was a grandson of Djedefra by his daughter Neferhetepes. His father is unknown—perhaps the high priest of Ra, Sakhebu, as suggested by Papyrus Westcar. He married Khentkawes, a daughter of Menkaura, a union that probably ensured a smooth transition to the new dynasty. His reign was only short—the Palermo Stone records three cattle counts during his reign, a system of taxation that took place every two years, so he must have reigned for at least six years. Userkaf's birth name means "his *ka* is powerful."

Although little of the details of his reign are clear, we know he was the first king to build a sun-temple at Abusir (apparently a replica of the one at Heliopolis) which the Palermo Stone reveals was named "the stronghold of Ra." He also moved the Royal Necropolis away from Giza, and built his pyramid at north Saqqara, just east

of the Step Pyramid. Unusually he constructed his mortuary temple on the pyramid's southern side, possibly because there it would have been bathed in sunlight all day. The pyramid was called "pure are the places of Userkaf."

Sahura and the Palermo Stone

Sahura was probably the son of Userkaf, rather than his brother, as the Papyrus Westcar would have us believe. His mother was Queen Khent-kawes. His name means "he who is close to Ra." He married Neferthanebty, by whom he had four sons. None of their offspring succeeded to the throne, for reasons unknown. Sahura also continued to promote the cult of Ra by building a sun-temple, "the Field of Ra" at Abusir, where he also inaugurated the Royal Necropolis, erecting his pyramid and mortuary temple at this site.

Rather more is known of Sahura's reign, due largely to the Palermo Stone, scenes from his mortuary temple, and the rock inscriptions at Sinai. The Palermo Stone records expeditions sent to Nubia to obtain malachite, to Punt to obtain myrrh (80,000 measures), and to the Wadi Maghara in the Sinai for turquoise. Another expedition ventured into Nubia, west of Abu Simbel, to collect diorite, a hard stone usually reserved for carving royal statues. Sahura also conducted a military campaign against the Libyans, and sent a trading mission to Byblos, the port where the Egyptians obtained their supplies of cedarwood. His mortuary temple confirms these details, with scenes depicting aspects of these various missions and expeditions abroad. We also know that he presented a solar bark to Ra at his temple at Heliopolis and made generous offerings there.

The Lesser-known Neferirkara

Neferirkara was probably another son of Userkaf and Khentkawes, and therefore a brother of Sahura. His name means "beautiful is the *ka* of Ra." Very little is known of his reign. The Palermo Stone records that he built a wall enclosing the solar bark in his sun-temple,

Above **Head of Userkaf, Fifth Dynasty.** This schist statue was found in Userkaf's sun-temple at Abusir. It measures 13 inches (34 cm) high.

Right **Relief from Sahura's funerary temple at Abusir, Fifth Dynasty.** It includes deities of plant shoots, fertility, and water. Sahura died 14 years and nine months into his reign.

his own mortuary arrangements and build a sun-temple, "the delight of Ra," at Abusir, where he copied the essential elements of the original sun-temple of Heliopolis. All of this work was completed by the end of his reign.

The relief scenes from his temple attest to the celebration of the king's jubilee or sed-festival, an important ritual observed by Egyptian kings throughout the pharaonic period. It was a ritual of renewal and regeneration observed by the king for the first time after he had ruled for a period of 30 years, and henceforth at more regular intervals of three or four years. It was basically a re-enactment of the king's coronation, and reconfirmation of his rulership. The scenes of Nyuserra's jubilee festival are some of our earliest records of this important ritual.

Nyuserra, like his predecessors, sent expeditions to the turquoise mines at Wadi Maghara in the Sinai. Here a surviving scene carved into the rock depicts the king smiting his Bedouin enemy in typical fashion: Grasping the poor chieftain by the hair and poised in the act of bringing the royal mace down upon his head. Elsewhere there is a reference to an expedition to Punt during his reign to procure assorted exotic goods. The location of Punt is much debated, but it was reached by sailing along the Red Sea, and probably covers parts of modern Sudan, Eritrea, and Ethiopia.

Nyuserra's pyramid, "enduring are the places of Ra," is the last known pyramid built at Abusir.

It was during this period that the various court officials and provincial governors rose to greater power and influence than ever before, their resulting wealth reflected in the large and elaborate tombs they built to house their mortal remains. One such official was Ti, who possessed a string of important titles and married a royal princess. For most of his career he was in the service of Neferirkara and Nyuserra, dying at some point during the latter's reign. He built a magnificent tomb at Saqqara, the decoration of which stands today as a tribute to the mastery of the relief artists of the mid-Fifth Dynasty.

Menkauhor's Missing Temple

The reign of Nyuserra's successor, Menkauhor, is very poorly known, though an inscription at Wadi Maghara records that he sent a mining expedition there. He still observed his predecessor's allegiance to the cult of the sun-god, with his own name expressing this devotion: "the souls of Ra are eternal." Menkauhor built a sun-temple called "the horizon of Ra." Though its location is still unknown, for some reason he did not build it at Abusir.

Above **Painted relief, Fifth Dynasty.** Funerary procession and rites before the deceased at the tomb of priests Khnum-Hotep and Ni-Ankh-Khnum in the sun-temple of Nyuserra.

Left **Section of limestone relief with residual paint** from the *mastaba* tomb of Fifth-Dynasty official Ti, from Saqqara. It depicts people pounding flattened reeds to make papyrus scrolls for writing. Papyrus was used in Egypt from around 3000 BCE.

The Sun-temples at Abusir

The Fifth-Dynasty kings expressed their devotion to Ra by building elaborate temple complexes close to their own mortuary establishment at Abusir. They apparently modeled these structures on the temple at Heliopolis, or "sun city" in Greek.

Right **Exterior of a Fifth-Dynasty funerary chapel** at Abusir is in the tomb of the priests of Ra, Khnum-Hotep and Ni-Ankh-Khnum.

Originally the city of On, this city was the cult center for the sun-god's worship. Through the allegiance of these kings, Ra became the supreme god of the state. A creation myth formed the basis of sun worship. At creation, a mound emerged from the primeval waters of Nun with the god Atum upon it. He copulated with himself to create Shu (air) and Tefnut (moisture), who produced Geb (earth) and Nut (sky). Shu separated them by lifting Nut into her rightful position in the sky. A heron dwelt on the *benben* stone, and was adored as the sacred bird of Heliopolis, where it was regarded as the *ba*, or soul, of Ra. At some point, Atum, a creator god, coalesced with the sun-god, Ra, the two worshipped as Atum-Ra. Eventually Atum would come to be worshipped as the setting sun, and Ra the heavenly body at its zenith.

The Sun-temple's Purpose

The exact purpose of the sun-temples at Abusir is not entirely clear but their similarity to the royal mortuary complexes suggests a funerary function, perhaps as a mortuary complex for the sun. The sun was understood to undergo a kind of death during the night hours, only to emerge reborn at the beginning of each new day. Therefore, the sun-temple may have been constructed

as the night abode of Ra. Alternatively, as the king was thought to merge with the sun-god at death, the temple may have been intended to emphasize this association. The temple was clearly a place where the communion between the sun-god and the king could occur, thereby ensuring the prosperity of Egypt.

Surviving relief scenes from the temples illustrate both the life-giving powers of the sun and the part the king had to play in Egypt's welfare. In the sun-temple of Nyuserra, a chapel is dedicated to the three seasons of the Egyptian calendar, each represented as human figures over whom Ra has the prevailing influence. The temple causeway is devoted to scenes celebrating the king's sed-festival, or renewal ceremony.

While most sun-temples are in a ruinous state, those of Sahura, Userkaf, and Nyuserra preserve enough information to reconstruct some main features. They were built in three main parts: A valley temple with a causeway, providing the only access to an upper temple, which was

THE OBELISK

A feature of the Fifth-Dynasty sun-temples was an obelisk, which was the focal point of the sun-god's worship. The obelisk represented the *benben* stone, which emerged from the waters of Nun at the time of creation. It was the first object upon which the rays of the rising sun shone, and to commemorate this occasion, Egyptian obelisks were usually surmounted by a gilded pyramidion. Old Kingdom obelisks are not the tall, slender structures we see in front of New Kingdom temples, but a much wider and shorter version. The obelisk was regarded as the dwelling place of Ra, and as such the place that would capture the first rays of the rising sun.

surrounded by an enclosure wall. Userkaf's valley temple and causeway seem to have been aligned with the stars that would have arisen just before sunrise in around 2498 BCE. It has been suggested they served as a kind of astronomical clock for dawn sacrifices. The upper temple consisted of a vestibule leading into a large courtyard dominated by an obelisk placed on a truncated pyramid-shaped pedestal. The obelisk was made of white limestone and was probably around 120 feet (37 m) tall. An altar was placed in front of the obelisk. Nyuserra's altar has survived, constructed from five blocks of alabaster carved into the shape of four *hetep* hieroglyphic signs (*hetep* meaning altar, offering, peace, or satisfy) around a circle. This arrangement spells out the message, "may Ra be at peace/satisfied."

In the northeastern corner of the enclosure wall was a "sanctuary of the knife," probably a slaughterhouse where sacrificial animals were butchered. Rows of alabaster basins have been excavated, which may have been used to purify the animals and collect the blood. We know from the Palermo Stone that during the reign of Userkaf, two oxen and two geese were sacrificed daily in the sun-temple.

Officials of the period were appointed as priests to serve in the sun-temples and carry out the requisite daily rituals. It is from their tombs, where they list their many titles, that we know the names of the various sun-temples, even those that remain hidden under the sands of Abusir.

Above **Sporting competition between boatmen.** Relief from a *mastaba* in Nyuserra's sun-temple.

Below **Sun-temple of Nyuserra,** Fifth Dynasty.

Last Fifth-Dynasty Kings

Documentation for the last two kings who ruled in the Fifth Dynasty is somewhat scarce. However, what does survive suggests that the cult of the sun-god was beginning to lose its influence and officials were gaining power.

Right **The "famine relief" from the complex of Unas at Saqqara.** It depicts foreigners dying of hunger during a famine, probably near Egypt's border.

In this period, mortuary cults reflect a growing interest in the god Osiris as lord of the dead, and this god's name and titles were regularly included in prayers of offerings in private tombs.

Djedkara Abandons Abusir

Often referred to by his birth name Isesi, Djedkara's throne name, meaning "enduring is the *ka* of Ra," continues to reflect an allegiance to the sun-god. Despite this, he is not known to have built a sun-temple dedicated to Ra and he abandoned Abusir as the royal burial ground. Some Egyptologists regard this as evidence of the waning influence of the cult of Ra, whose priesthood would have become increasingly powerful with the pre-eminence of the sun-god. From this period onward, the cult of Osiris can be seen to gain momentum, with this god's name now more regularly featured on the false doors of private tombs.

The historian Manetho claims a 40-year reign for Djedkara, while the Turin Canon records only 28 years. Either way, he ruled long enough to celebrate his sed-festival, the evidence for which is provided by an inscribed vase dating to his

reign. Despite a relatively long rule, there is very little surviving documentation to attest to its details. Inscriptions at Sinai indicate two expeditions to mine for copper and stone in the region at 10-year intervals, and another in Nubia provides evidence of a mission to obtain diorite from the quarries near Abu Simbel. The autobiography of Harkhuf, from the mid-Sixth Dynasty, provides indirect evidence of an expedition into the Land of the Horizon Dwellers (probably Punt), when he comments that an official named Bawerded also brought back a pygmy from this region during the time of King Isesi.

The officials of this period continued to acquire unprecedented wealth, power, and influence, a fact betrayed by the opulence of the tombs they constructed, particularly those belonging to the viziers Rashepses, Ptahhotep, and Senedjem-ib. Despite this, the state continued to run efficiently as we can see from the evidence of the Abusir Papyri, where it is clear that a well-organized system was maintained to oversee the various mortuary establishments of the preceding Fifth-Dynasty kings.

Djedkara's pyramid, named "Isesi is beautiful," is today called el-Shawaf, "the sentinel" because of its position on a mound at Saqqara, where it overlooks a nearby village. It is in a very poor state of preservation.

Unas Drops the Ra Title

Unas, the last king of Fifth Dynasty, signaled a departure from his predecessors by omitting Ra from the royal name. This may have been his way of demonstrating that the ascendancy of the priesthood of Ra was over. At various periods in Egyptian history, the king had to contend with powerful priesthoods whose wealth and influence almost rivaled that of the king, particularly as their temples were usually exempt from taxation. Evidence suggests that at the end of Fifth Dynasty, the king was obliged to curb the growing power of the priesthood of Ra at Heliopolis,

Below **Unas's pyramid at Saqqara.** This very long causeway connects the mortuary temple to the valley temple, which lies to the southeast.

while in the New Kingdom it was that of the god Amun at Karnak that needed to be reined in.

The Pyramid Texts

Though Unas ruled Egypt for roughly 30 years, his reign is poorly documented. He is perhaps most famous for his pyramid at Saqqara, called "perfect are the places of Unas," where for the first time the walls of the burial chamber were covered with inscriptions. Carved in vertical lines, the incised hieroglyphs are filled with blue pigment, and provide the soul of the deceased king with 228 spells necessary to guide him on his journey to the next world, overcoming any hostile forces along the way. These Pyramid Texts are the oldest religious texts from Egypt, and were adapted in later times to form the Coffin Texts in the Middle Kingdom and the *Book of the Dead* in the New Kingdom. However, unlike the latter two, the Pyramid Texts were the exclusive preserve of the royal dead, enabling the king to reunite with his divine father, Ra, and pass eternity crossing the sky in his solar bark. In the Old Kingdom, this was beyond the hopes and expectations of an ordinary individual.

Causeway Decorations

The Unas causeway was decorated with a variety of scenes carved in relief, some of which are still very well preserved. There is great variety in the subject matter, with representations of laborers on the royal estates gathering figs and honey, and harvesting grain. In other scenes, we see craftsmen working in copper and gold, and ships transporting granite columns for the royal mortuary temple. Additionally there are representations of a hunt for wild animals, bearded Asiatics arriving in ships from Byblos, and rows of offering bearers. Most famous is the scene sometimes referred to as the "famine relief." This scene depicts starving people, their ribs prominent in their emaciated bodies, leading scholars to suggest that this represented a time of famine in Egypt. The people, however, look more Asiatic than Egyptian and the scene may therefore represent the circumstances of foreigners not fortunate enough to enjoy the bounty and security of life in Egypt under the benevolent rule of the king. It would be most un-Egyptian to record an adverse event or circumstance within the Two Lands.

Above **Bas-relief depicting offering bearers, from Ptahhotep's *mastaba*.** The opulence of this Sixth-Dynasty vizier's tomb attests to the increasing wealth and influence the administrative officials had achieved by this period.

First Sixth-Dynasty Kings

While the new dynasty began without any apparent social or political up-heaval, the calm was not to last. A series of plots, betrayals, and conspiracies soon emerged to unsettle the smooth running of the Two Lands.

Teti and his Four Daughters

Teti, the first king of Sixth Dynasty, married Iput, the daughter of his predecessor, and by doing so legitimized his claim to the throne. In her funerary temple, Iput described herself as the daughter, wife, and mother of a king of Egypt, a reference to Unas, Teti, and their son Pepy I, respectively. Teti's own origins are less certain, though there are several references to his mother Seshseshet, after whom he named all of his daughters. Fortunately each daughter had a second name appended to Seshseshet, otherwise we would never be able to determine which one was which. The identity of his father remains unknown.

Below **Pyramid of the first Sixth-Dynasty king, Teti, at Saqqara**. Largely a pile of rubble, it was discovered by the French archeologist Auguste Mariette in 1853.

It is usually claimed that the transfer of power from Unas to Teti went smoothly, though the Horus name Teti adopted, *Setep-tawy*—"he who pacifies the Two Lands"—would suggest otherwise. Royal names incorporating the expression *setep*, "he who pacifies," were usually only adopted in times of difficulty. Archeological evidence indicates that the last two viziers under Unas were severely punished for some reason, and consequently deprived of their tombs, thereby indicating a crisis of some kind had arisen. One of these tombs, reassigned to Teti's daughter Seshseshet–Idut, is one of the most frequently visited tombs at Saqqara today.

Despite any initial difficulties, the country remained stable and prosperous, and the power of the official classes continued to grow. Teti endeavored to control his administration by appointing members of his own family to high positions and, in particular, by securing the allegiance of senior officials through royal marriages. For example, he married his daughter Seshseshet–Waatetkhethor to the vizier, Mereruka; Seshseshet–Nebukhetnebty to the vizier, Kagemni; and another Seshseshet to Isi, who was the first holder of the newly created position of vizier of the south. By doing so he sought the goodwill and loyalty of the most powerful men in the land, both at the capital and in the provinces.

According to the historian Manetho, Teti was murdered by his bodyguard and, while there is no direct evidence, the information revealed by the autobiography of Weni gives this claim some substance. Teti was buried in his pyramid at Saqqara, the walls of the burial chamber inscribed like that of his predecessor with spells from the Pyramid Texts. Several items have been excavated from his mortuary temple, including a miniature alabaster sistrum inscribed with Teti's name and a plaster death mask, possibly a portrait would one do so again until the Twenty-sixth Dynasty. We can only conjecture as to why Pepy chose to honor his mother-in-law in this way, but clearly she had demonstrated her trustworthiness in some way. An obvious conclusion is that she, along with Weni, helped expose the harem conspiracy. The royal line continued with both wives presenting the king with children, Ankhnes-Meryra I giving birth to Merenra and a daughter, Neith, while Ankhnes-Meryra II was to bear Pepy II.

The Mystery of the Statue

In 1897 the pieces of two beaten copper statues were excavated from a pit at the Temple of Horus in Hierakonpolis. A beautiful gold falcon head, also dating to the Sixth Dynasty, was found at the same site. The larger statue was easily identified as a portrait of Pepy I because an embossed inscription gives his name and title. The smaller statue, which had been dismantled and placed inside the larger, was thought to be Pepy I's son Merenra. The plates of copper had originally been nailed over a wooden core, the timber having completely decayed over the passage of time. The statues were reassembled and are now on display in the Egyptian Museum (in Cairo). The detail of the smaller statue indicates that it originally wore the royal uraeus. This consisted of a cobra and a vulture, attached to a crown or headband. They represented the goddesses Wadjet and Nekbet, of Lower and Upper Egypt respectively. The uraeus was worn by the ruler to indicate his dominion over both halves of the Two Lands. Egyptologists saw this as evidence that a co-regency existed between the two. This would have been the first of many co-regencies in Egyptian history, created by Pepy I to settle, once and for all, the order of succession. In such an arrangement, the ruling monarch named his heir as co-ruler, the latter acting as the minor partner.

Recent studies, however, have proved the statues originally shared a single base and are both of Pepy, represented as a child and as an adult. If a co-regency did exist between the two, we will need to look elsewhere for the proof.

Foreign Affairs

We know there were several missions abroad during Pepy I's reign, including mining expeditions to the Wadi Hammamat, Hatnub, Wadi Maghara, and Sehel Island. From Weni's autobiography we learn of five military forays into the region of Palestine to put down rebellions by the tribal "sand dwellers." In the Old Kingdom, Egypt did not wish to expand borders but did seek the products of its neighbors, fiercely protecting its trading routes to maintain a steady supply of these items. Rebellions among the so-called sand dwellers would have disrupted the caravan routes, and it is doubtless for this reason that Pepy sent an army under Weni's command to restore the uninterrupted flow of produce from the Levant to Egypt.

Royal Burials

Pepy built his mortuary complex at Saqqara, naming his pyramid Men-nefer, "enduring and beautiful." Like his immediate predecessors, the walls of Pepy's burial chamber were also inscribed with spells from the Pyramid Texts. Three small pyramids were built nearby to house the remains of three of his queens.

Left **The smaller of the two copper statues,** it is probably of the young Pepy I. The other is the oldest-known large-scale metal statue. They were discovered in 1897–98.

The Vizier Mereruka

Mereruka was a high official who served as chief justice and vizier under King Teti, the first king of the Sixth Dynasty. He held an unusually large number of titles connected to the administration of ancient Egypt in this period.

Mereruka also held various honorific and religious titles, plus some relating to the personal service of the king. His tomb, one of the largest in the Old Kingdom, is constructed entirely out of limestone blocks and made up of 31 rooms. His *mastaba* is positioned in the first east–west street of the Teti cemetery, north-east of Djoser's Step Pyramid at Saqqara. The interior walls are decorated in magnificently carved raised relief, depicting detailed and elaborate scenes of daily life. The tomb is

divided into three sections; the largest belongs to Mereruka, with the other sections belonging to his wife, Seshseshet and their son, Mery-Teti.

Family Ties

Inscriptional evidence suggests that Mereruka was born into a family of high status with connections to the Fifth-Dynasty viziers. His father Meruka was buried at Giza and his mother Nedjetempet was a sister of Seshemnefer III, a vizier under the late Fifth-Dynasty king, Djedkara. Possibly owing to his family lineage, Mereruka married Seshseshet, who held the title of "eldest daughter of the king of his body" and was most probably the eldest daughter of King Teti himself. Mereruka and Seshseshet had a son, Mery-Teti, who was the grandson of King Teti and vizier under King Pepy I. Mery-Teti built his tomb in the same complex as his parents.

Mereruka held an unusually large number of titles. Among his more significant administrative titles, he was the chief justice and vizier, overseer of the six great courts, overseer of the house of silver as well as overseer of the two granaries and overseer of all the works of the king. He also held the rare title of overseer of the house of weapons and overseer of the protection of all royal palaces which, in previous reigns, was entrusted to viziers and individuals in high positions of power. He also held high priestly offices in the cults of many gods including Ra, Min, and Anubis.

THE ART OF GRIEF AND DESPAIR

One of the most beautifully carved and detailed scenes found in Mereruka's tomb is the funerary procession, which provides an excellent example of the different aspects of the ceremony performed by the ancient Egyptians in the Old Kingdom. The most evocative aspect is the depiction of a group of female mourners who are shown in an extreme state of grief, hitting their heads, pulling their hair, and raising their arms in despair. The walls of Mereruka's burial chamber are also extensively decorated, which seem to be restricted

to high officials during this period. The scenes include depictions of piled food offerings, granaries holding grain, stacks of folded linen, and two offering lists. Mereruka's elaborately decorated tomb includes an extensive repertoire of artistic depictions and is a superb example of the height of Old Kingdom art as well as the skill of the ancient Egyptian artist.

Above **Mereruka's funerary procession.** This painted relief is from his *mastaba* in Saqqara, one of the most highly decorated.

Mereruka's *Mastaba*

The large *mastaba* of Mereruka was constructed out of blocks of limestone. These blocks were most probably cut and transported from Tura, a quarry in use during the Old Kingdom. It was located on the east bank of the Nile opposite the ancient capital of Memphis. The tomb of Mereruka includes a false door, situated in the customary position in the west wall of the main offering chapel and a *serdab*, to hold the *ka* statue of the tomb owner. A life-size statue of Mereruka himself in a striding posture is set into

the north wall of the impressive pillared hall. The statue was placed inside a niche reached by steps and raised above the ground level, creating a powerful and striking first impression of the tomb owner on entering the pillared hall. The *mastaba* incorporates a vertical shaft measuring 47 feet (14.5 m) deep. It led to his very large burial chamber, which was lined with limestone blocks and decorated. The burial chamber includes a massive inscribed limestone sarcophagus.

Mereruka's *mastaba* contains 10 rooms elaborately and beautifully decorated in raised relief. His tomb's wall art depicted is typical of the Old Kingdom, showing scenes of daily life, including the tomb owner fishing and catching birds, agricultural activities, and jewelry manufacture. Yet the tomb of Mereruka also includes several unique and rare scenes, such as a desert hunt depicting a Nubian ibex being torn apart by nine hunting dogs. Another shows Mereruka painting the pictures of the seasons of the year, while in another he is being entertained by his wife, who is seated on a bed playing the harp.

Above **Limestone relief panel with residual paint from the *mastaba* of Mereruka.** It depicts an agricultural scene—people making haystacks and gathering ears of corn.

Left **Statue of Mereruka, in an alcove of his tomb.** His well-preserved *mastaba* is the largest single tomb in Egypt.

Weni and the Harem Plot

An important source of information for the Sixth Dynasty comes from the tomb of an official named Weni, whose long career spanned the reigns of Teti, Pepy I, and Merenra. He may have uncovered a harem conspiracy that led to King Teti's murder.

The details of his career survived in an autobiographical inscription, carved in 51 columns of carefully executed hieroglyphs on a wall in his tomb at Abydos. It is now housed in the Egyptian Museum (in Cairo).

Weni began his career during the reign of Teti, serving as an overseer of the storehouse, a minor position, suggesting he was a man of fairly humble origins. With the accession of Pepy I, Weni was promoted to overseer of the robing room, with the rank of companion, a favored courtier. He was also made inspector of priests of the king's pyramid.

Egyptian titles are of a somewhat esoteric nature, not all of them being fully understood, however it is clear that Weni was moving up in the world with his official positions bringing him into closer contact with the king and court. Weni himself tells us that the advancement was due to his excellence, resulting in the king's favor. Egyptian autobiographical inscriptions are certainly not noted for their modesty.

Above **Head of a stone statue of a prisoner of war found in the pyramid complex of Pepy I at Saqqara.** Pepy I was served by Weni, who became known for his tactical genius in battle.

Weni and the Harem Conspiracy Theory

Before long, the king appointed Weni to the more senior position of overseer of palace officials, while at the same time expelling four others of a similar designation. His duty was now to guard, escort, and attend the king and, as such, was part of the king's bodyguard.

We are not told why the other four men were dismissed, however the recent discovery of the tombs of four such officials at Saqqara may provide answers. All four tombs have been subject to a deliberate and systematic campaign to eradicate the memory of the tomb owner, with all names and images carefully chiseled from the walls. According to the Egyptian

historian Manetho, Teti (the first king of the Sixth Dynasty), was murdered by members of his bodyguard, men bearing an identical title to those dismissed by Pepy I. It would seem that the men were found out, punished, and denied eternal life by the desecration of their tombs. The erasure of the name from the tomb may reflect the death penalty: to have one's name spoken by the living was an avenue to eternity, and to have it erased was to condemn the spirit of the deceased to oblivion. Punishment, therefore, applied to this world and the next, with no hope of parole or redemption.

On a Fast-track to Career Advancement

Weni's career suddenly took an unexpected turn when the king asked him to act as judge in a secret case bought against Queen Weret-Yamtes. This was an extraordinary promotion, particularly as he was to be the sole judge.

Normally the vizier, who was also chief justice, would preside over such a case. Unfortunately the text does not reveal the nature of the accusation against the queen, nor why the vizier was excluded from the proceedings. However, from the archeological evidence that does exist, we do know that the name of a vizier was deliberately excised from an important inscription of Pepy I, and the tomb of a vizier of the same period was desecrated. Only the most heinous crime would warrant such treatment.

Egyptologists today believe that the autobiography of Weni alludes to a harem conspiracy—a plot to kill the king by a minor queen in order to secure the throne for her own offspring, with the assistance of the vizier. It is assumed that Weni's extraordinary advancement to senior positions, normally beyond the expectations of a lowly storeroom guard, was because he was the one who discovered the plot and revealed it to the king. We do not know the outcome of the trial, Weni using its existence merely as a prop to display the depth of his royal favor. The queen's fate is unknown.

First Commander, then Governor

Weni was next appointed commander-in-chief of an army, raised by the king from all Egyptian provinces. They were to take action against the Asiatic sand-dwellers, tribes of the Sinai and Southern Palestine, who were rebelling against Egyptian subjugation. He was appointed over far more high-ranking officials, at a time when his most important title was that of overseer of palace officials. The more senior officials, who included chamberlains, overlords of provinces and senior administrative heads, led only one contingent each. The sand-dwellers were clearly determined troublemakers, as Weni was obliged to undertake five campaigns to quell rebellions in this region.

Weni reached the pinnacle of his career during the reign of Merenra, with his appointment as governor of Upper Egypt. Now based in Upper Egypt at Abydos, Weni was responsible for the collection of all revenues due to the king from the south and was also charged with the procurement of various materials for the king's pyramid: granite from Elephantine, alabaster from Hatnub for, and basalt from Nubia. All of this, he is pleased to record, was achieved with the utmost speed and efficiency.

Above **A Bedouin in the Sinai Desert**. Weni went into the Sinai to battle a group of people known as the sand-dwellers at least five times.

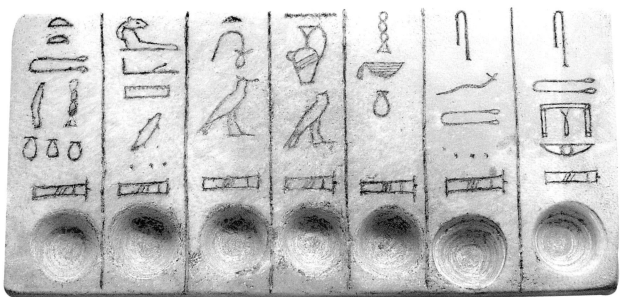

Left **Weni served under Teti until the king was subsequently murdered.** This offering tablet comes from a tomb in the cemetery of King Teti, Saqqara.

Last Sixth-Dynasty Kings

Pepy I was succeeded first by Merenra, his son by Ankhnes-Meryra I and then by Pepy II, his son by Ankhnes-Meryra II. Merenra reigned for only five years or so before his early death brought his brother to the throne.

Right **Cartouches of King Pepy II.** These are fragments of Pyramid Texts from the walls of his pyramid in Saqqara, near Djoser's Step Pyramid.

Because both women married Pepy during the year of the king's twenty-first cattle count (that is, the forty-second year of his 50-year reign), both boys must have been very young when they came to the throne, and probably required a regent to rule on their behalf.

Mysterious Merenra

Not many details of Merenra's reign are known. It is possible that he was his father's co-regent in the last years of Teti's reign. The discovery of a small gold tassel, inscribed with both names, may provide the evidence for this political arrangement. Worn hanging from the king's kilt, similar items from later periods are usually indicative of a co-regency.

We know Merenra appointed Weni as governor of Upper Egypt at Abydos. As governor, Weni was responsible for procuring various stones for the king's pyramid complex. The trip to Nubia to obtain granite also involved cutting five navigable channels in the Nile near the First Cataract, to facilitate the transport of the stone back to the capital. The burial chamber of his pyramid, called "Merenra shines with splendour," was inscribed with passages of the Pyramid Texts. The mummy of a young male wearing the side-lock of youth was found in the sarcophagus, though it is not certain that these are the remains of Merenra. It is possible that this is a later, intrusive burial.

Long-reigning Pepy II

As a young child of no more than six years when he came to the throne, Pepy II ruled Egypt

PYGMIES AND DWARVES

The highlight of Pepy II's reign was the arrival of a pygmy, or *deneg*, brought back from Central Africa by Harkhuf. A scene from a Fifth-Dynasty tomb at Giza shows a pygmy performing a dance with a group of women, perhaps the "dance of the God" referred to in a letter by the youthful king.

More common in Old Kingdom tomb scenes is the dwarf, or *iwhw*, who is represented with the typical pathological signs of achondroplasia: Thickset body, shortened limbs and large head. While they can often be found in charge of an official's personal effects, or perhaps leading his pet monkey and/or dog, the most common setting for the dwarf in these scenes is in jewelry

workshops. Here they are set to work manufacturing the broad *wesekh* collars that adorned Egyptian nobility. It seems their manual dexterity was much prized in the production of jewelry.

Several tombs belonging to dwarves have been excavated at Giza and Saqqara. It should be remembered that not all Egyptians had sufficient means to build and decorate a tomb, and these individuals built theirs in the Royal Necropolis. They were clearly well-respected members of society. The most famous dwarf is Seneb, the master of the king's wardrobe, whose beautiful tomb at Giza yielded a masterpiece of Egyptian art. The statue, now housed in the Egyptian Museum (in Cairo), shows Seneb seated with his wife and two small children, the latter occupying the space in front of his short, folded legs.

Left **Painted limestone statue of the dwarf Seneb with his children and wife Sentyotes** from his *mastaba*, which is in a place of honor near Khufu's pyramid at Giza.

Right **These heiroglyphics describe an expedition to find the summit of a pyramid.** It was probably created in the Sixth Dynasty during reign of Merenra. From South Saqqara, it is now held in Egyptian Museum (in Cairo).

through his mother, who acted as regent during her son's minority. An inscription at the Wadi Maghara, dating to the second cattle count of his reign, attests to her regency status, giving prominence to her name and titles and representing the queen wearing the crown and uraeus. In the Brooklyn Museum, an alabaster statue of Ankhnes-Meryra II, with a youthful Pepy I seated on her lap, is sometimes referred to as a regency statue because of the emphasis it gives to the queen. During the first years of Pepy's reign, any missions abroad, such as that recorded by Harkhuf, were probably commissioned by Ankhnes-Meryra II. Her brother Djau, who succeeded their mother, Nebet, as vizier during Pepy II's reign, is thought to have been the young king's tutor. Pepy II is known to have had four wives: his half-sister Neith, Iput II, Wedjebten, and Ankhesenpepy.

Manetho claims that Pepy II ruled Egypt for 94 years and died in his hundredth year. A reference to his thirty-third cattle count is the highest surviving date for Pepy II, crediting him with a reign of at least 66 years. During his long reign, the wealth and power of the provincial governors grew at an alarming rate, as their allegiance to the king diminished. Their positions were no longer dependent on royal appointment, but had become hereditary. In addition, Egypt's control over her trade routes was becoming less secure, and several officials were killed during tribal skirmishes. For example, the ship-builder, Anankhet and several of his men were killed by tribesmen when they were constructing ships for the king at the Wadi Hammamat. Harkhuf's successor, Pepynacht, also known as Heqaib, was obliged to lead a recovery mission to bring back their bodies.

Harkhuf's Travels

Our understanding of Egypt's relations with her southern neighbors is brought into sharp focus with an inscription relating to the activities of an official who led several expeditions into Nubia during the reigns of Merenra and Pepy II.

The autobiographical inscription of Harkhuf, the Governor of Upper Egypt, was carved in 52 lines on the facade of his rock-cut tomb at Aswan. The text is a typical autobiography, first listing the many titles he held in the service of the king. Among his numerous titles, Harkhuf was a count, overseer of Upper Egypt, treasurer of the king in Upper Egypt, sole companion, lector priest, and overseer of interpreters, the most important of these cited first.

Expeditions into Nubia

According to his autobiography, Harkhuf led three expeditions south during the reign of Merenra. The first was to the land of Yam, in Nubia, which roughly corresponds today with Sudan's modern Kerma. Accompanied by his father Iri, Harkhuf's mission was to "open the road to this foreign land," suggesting this was an exploratory expedition to discover new trade routes. The expedition took seven months and he returned with all kinds of unspecified products from the region. The objective of his subsequent missions was to keep the trade routes open, and possibly extend them, as well as obtain goods from these new regions. Harkhuf was always accompanied by a military unit, conscripted for just this purpose.

The second expedition lasted eight months, and traveled along the "Ivory Road" through the lands belonging to a confederacy of three Nubian tribes. The strength and number of Harkhuf's troops encouraged cooperation from the Nubian chiefs, and he was able to exact gifts from them for the Egyptian king. He explored these regions, which he claimed had not been visited by Egyptian officials before, and again returned with a large quantity of produce.

On his last trip for Merenra, Harkhuf traveled along the "Oasis Road." It passed through several western oases (perhaps Farafra, Dakhla, and Kharga) on the trip to Nubia, rather than follow the Nile Valley. When he reached Yam, he discovered that its chief had departed on his own punitive mission—to smite the *Tjemeh* (Libyans).

Harkhuf set off in pursuit and managed to defuse the situation, though he does not explain how this was achieved. He continued his trading mission, leaving Yam with 300 donkeys laden with incense, ebony, various oils, leopard skins, elephant tusks, throwing sticks, and "all kinds of good things." The chiefs of the confederated tribes of Nubia provided him with an escort to guide his party through the mountainous regions of Nubia and gave him cattle and goats as well. The king was so delighted with the results of this mission that he dispatched ships laden with date wine, cake, bread, and beer to meet the returning party.

Below **A stela of Pepy II from his mortuary temple at south Saqqara**. Harkhuf served under this king as well as under Merenra.

The Pygmy From the Land of the Horizon Dwellers

In the second year of his reign, Pepy II again sent Harkhuf to the land of Yam. Having arrived in Nubia, he set about the usual business of collecting the produce of the land, and in so doing managed to obtain a pygmy "of the god's dances" from the Land of the Horizon Dwellers. (The term "horizon dwellers" was a vague designation for the peoples of remote regions to the east and southeast of Egypt.) This had previously been done by another official in the reign of Djedkara, the pygmies being much sought after to perform a special dance to honor a god (unspecified, but probably Ra). Harkhuf sent a dispatch back to the capital informing the king of his recent acquisitions, including that of a pygmy.

The proudest moment of Harkhuf's career came with the delivery of a personal letter from the king himself, expressing his pleasure at the successful outcome of this trading mission. The king particularly expressed delight in the procurement of the pygmy, for as he writes, "my majesty desires to see this pygmy more than the gifts of the mine-land [Sinai] and Punt."

Pepy II was still a child, probably no more than eight years old, and it is evident that he could barely contain his boyish enthusiasm at the prospect of seeing this pygmy. He promised Harkhuf all manner of rewards for the pygmy's safe delivery, and offered considered advice as to how this could be best achieved:

When he goes down with you into the boat, appoint excellent men who shall be around him on both sides of the boat. Beware lest he falls into the water, when he lies down in the night. Appoint excellent men who shall sleep around him in his cabin. Inspect ten times in the night...

Though the letter does not tell anything of the expedition's return to the capital, it is doubtless that Harkhuf delivered this prize safely, for he would never have included this letter in his tomb autobiography, had he failed. The weathered hieroglyphs containing the boy king's letter can still be read today on the facade of Harkhuf's tomb.

Above **Hypogeum of the Elephantine princes, on the left bank of the Nile at Aswan.** Many officials of the last dynasties of the Old Kingdom are buried at Aswan, including Harkhuf.

Left **Harkhuf's tomb at Aswan reveals his life story in its inscriptions.** Besides asking passersby to bless him with prayers offering him endless food and beer, he promises to seize anyone who dares enter it "like a wild fowl."

Egypt's Administrators

In the Fifth and Sixth Dynasties Egypt was administered by a well-organized central bureaucracy. The king was theoretically in control but a hierarchical system of officials saw to the day-to-day running of the state on his behalf.

Below **Painted limestone statue of Ranefer, an early Fifth-Dynasty high priest of Ptah and Sokar.** It was found in the funerary chapel of his tomb in Saqqara.

The capital at this time was at Ineb Hedj, "the white wall," a reference to the whitewashed walls surrounding the city. It is often called Memphis in modern references, a Greek name derived from a corruption of Mennefer, name of the nearby pyramid of Pepy I at Saqqara.

The Vizier

The vizier, or *tjaty*, was still the most senior official in the land and by the end of the Fifth Dynasty he had accumulated an impressive array of titles. These reflected the range of responsibilities that were part of his office: the overseer of all the works of the king; the overseer of the scribes of the royal documents; chief justice; overseer of the two granaries; and overseer of the two treasuries. The last two reflect the dual nature of the Egyptian state, which comprised Upper and Lower Egypt. So the vizier authorized any activities relating to the courts, the treasury, the granaries, tax collection, and the organization of labor. Interestingly, he never seems to have been given control of any military, trading, or mining expeditions.

In The Fourth Dynasty, the vizier was always one of the king's sons, but by the Fifth, this was no longer the case. Nevertheless, the king endeavored to maintain a close relationship between the vizierate and the throne in some way, either by passing it to other family members, or by marrying the prospective vizier to a royal daughter.

Toward the end of the Fifth Dynasty, another vizierate was created and henceforth there was a vizier for *Ta Shemau* (Upper Egypt) and one for *Ta-Mehu* (Lower Egypt). This was probably a response to the increasingly complicated bureaucracy, requiring someone based in the south to administer the region efficiently. It would also give the king a representative in a region far from his capital. The vizier for Lower Egypt was based at Memphis, and always seems to have had the greater prestige of the two. His counterpart was sometimes based at Abydos, but the southern capital seems to have varied with each new vizier.

Provincial Administration

Egypt was divided into nomes, or provinces, each administered by its own district governor, or nomarch. His title was great overlord of the province. There were 20 nomes in Lower Egypt and 22 in Upper Egypt. The great overlord was responsible to the vizier, and ultimately the king, for the efficient running of his province, and the collection of any local taxes due to the Royal Treasury. One of his most important responsibilities was the maintenance of the irrigation channels in his province, for without them the seasonal crops would fail. The great overlords resided in their provinces, and were eventually buried there as well. Originally the nomarchs were promoted to this rank by the king, but by the Sixth Dynasty these positions had largely become hereditary, with each governor passing his overlordship to his eldest son. Over time the provincial rulers became increasingly more independent and showed progressively less allegiance to the throne.

Other Officials

Beneath the vizier and the great overlords were the many officials working in the various government departments. All Egyptian officials in the Fifth and Sixth Dynasties were the bearers of numerous titles, rather like "the lord high everything else," in the operetta, *The Mikado*. The titles can generally be divided into three classes: Honorific, religious, and bureaucratic. The honorific titles attested to the official's relationship to the king, the most common titles being: Acquaintance of the king, confidant of the king, sole companion, and hereditary prince. Every official also bore several religious titles, such as *sem* priest or *waab* priest of the king, though he probably acted as a priest in a part-time capacity, called on for temple duty at certain specified times. The most numerous titles are those pertaining to the service an official performed in the administration. A brief summary of a few of these titles demonstrates the range and variety of work undertaken: Overseer of linen; overseer of fishermen; overseer of commissions; director of scribes; privy to the secrets of the king; overseer of all vegetation.

Clearly a prerequisite for a career in administration was the ability to read and write, as nearly every official lists scribe as part of his portfolio of duties. Sometimes the title is more specific, listing the particular department for which he acted as scribe—scribe of the king's documents or scribe of the storehouses. Officials often commissioned statues of themselves as scribes, seated with their legs crossed and a sheet of papyrus stretched across their lap. These were placed in their tombs.

Left **Inside the *mastaba* of Idu, an early Sixth-Dynasty inspector of priests and overseer of scribes**. Located at Giza, it shows a false door with a statue of the deceased.

Below **Painted limestone relief from the *mastaba* of Fifth-Dynasty official, Ti, in Saqqara**. It shows cattle being driven across a river.

Kings' Faithful Retainers

Any ancient Egyptian who had sufficient means to do so, built and decorated a tomb to house his mortal remains. The tomb was called "The house of the *ka*," and was the place where the spirit of the deceased, or *ka*, lived on for eternity.

Right The wall at the entrance to the *mastaba* of the official Rahotep and his wife Nofret, Fourth Dynasty, at Meidum. He was possibly a son of King Sneferu.

This was not an undertaking to be taken lightly or left to one's advanced years. Life in ancient Egypt was often of a precarious nature and few lived to what we would describe as a good old age. Consequently, when a young Egyptian began his official career, he usually started work on his tomb, taking time and care to ensure it would be ready for him when the time came. Despite this, the evidence reveals that many tombs had to be completed in haste due to the sudden demise of the intended occupant. Conversely, those who did have sufficient time to complete the tomb usually left one small part incomplete as a reminder to the gods that they were not yet ready to take occupation.

Mastabas and Rock-cut Tombs

In the Fifth and Sixth Dynasties, the officials continued to build *mastaba* tombs in the Royal Necropolis, usually close to the pyramid of the king they had served. The tombs of this period are

generally much larger than those of earlier dynasties, reflecting the increased status of the official classes and their growing wealth. However, they almost certainly required royal permission to build in the Royal Necropolis, and tomb inscriptions reveal that the king regularly rewarded good service by endowing the tomb with some of its more costly features. For example, we know the king provided the official Weni with the sarcophagus, false door, and offering table for his tomb.

In the provinces, the great overlord and his officials built rock-cut tombs in the cliffs overlooking the Nile Valley. The basics of these tombs were identical to those of *mastaba* tombs: One or several rooms to serve as chapels for offerings, and a shaft cut into the floor leading to the burial chamber. As in *mastaba* tombs, the false door and its altar were the focal points of the chapel and it was here that food offerings were left for the deceased. The walls of the chapel were decorated with scenes of daily life.

Magical Wall Scenes

The attainment of eternal life depended on a number of things, according to Egyptian belief, in particular the perpetual supply of food for the *ka* and the preservation of the deceased's name. While it was preferable that fresh supplies of food were delivered to the tomb daily, it was possible to obtain this sustenance magically

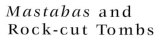

CASE OF THE NAME-CHANGING STATUE

In 1860, a beautiful 44-inch (112-cm) statue of sycamore wood was excavated from the sand near Userkaf's pyramid at Saqqara. The statue was the standing figure of a plump individual standing with his left foot forward and holding a staff. The workers were considerably taken aback by this discovery, remarking on its resemblance to a local village headman, the Sheikh el-Beled. The name has stuck, and the statue is usually referred to as the Sheikh el-Beled. In fact, it is the *ka* statue of a Fifth-Dynasty official by the name of Ka-aper. Given the importance placed on an individual's name by the ancient Egyptians, he would probably not thank them for this new designation.

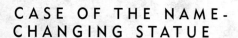

Left The life-like carved wooden statue of official Ka-aper. The eyes are made of rock crystal and rimmed with copper.

Right **Painted limestone false door of Iteti**, with a statue of the deceased set into the opening, from his *mastaba* in Giza. His many titles included inspector of priests of the pyramid of Khafra and inspector of the great house.

from the wall scenes, which regularly depict the supply of food. Alternatively, prayers could bring about a similar result. Tombs usually had a prayer of offerings inscribed on the entrance, and/or on the false door. These included a fairly standard formula requesting "bread and beer, ox and fowl, alabaster and linen, and everything good and pure for the *ka* of ..." The hope was that anyone who passed by the tomb would recite the prayer, naming the recipient, and in so doing bring these items to life. As an indication of the deceased's worthiness for this honor, he listed all the titles he had accrued in the service of the state and sometimes included an extensive autobiography of his career.

Preserving One's Name Forever

If all else failed, life eternal could be achieved if one's name was spoken by the living, and to this end an individual's name was inscribed in his tomb at every opportunity. The inclusion of the autobiography also served as a reminder of his good service and worthiness to be remembered. The ultimate punishment was to have one's name obliterated from living memory. There are many examples of officials condemned to eternal oblivion by the erasure of their names from their tombs as the ultimate punishment for crimes against the state.

Lost Bodies

To live forever, the body of the deceased was supposed to be preserved to provide a resting place for the *ka*. If for some reason the body was lost, the Egyptians placed lifelike statues of the deceased in the tomb to serve as an alternative. Portraits of the deceased on the walls also served this purpose. The Egyptians were certainly masters of the contingency plan.

LIFE IN THE OLD KINGDOM

Agriculture

Some important Old Kingdom tomb scenes relate to the annual cycle of the principal crops, barley and emmer wheat. By the Fifth and Sixth Dynasties, the scenes had expanded to include most of the processes involved in this cycle.

Right **Wooden linen chest from an Old Kingdom tomb at El Gebelein.** Flax was used to weave linen for clothing, with the wealthiest Egyptians wearing the finest cloth. Royal linen was so fine it was semi-transparent.

These scenes were set out in a series of sequential episodes over several registers in the tomb chapel. While they were probably included to provide a perpetual supply of food via the agency of magic for the deceased, they serve as a window into the past, revealing the agricultural practices of the Egyptians in this period.

The Agricultural Year

The Egyptians divided their year into three seasons of four months' duration. The first season was *akhet* or inundation, lasting from July to October. In this season, the waters of the Nile covered the land. When these waters eventually receded, a thick layer of fertile black silt was deposited over the land, hence the name the Egyptians gave to their country: *Kemet* or the Black Land. With the land under water, it was impossible for the Egyptian peasant to

continue any farm work, and it is believed that many were conscripted to work on state building projects for the duration of *akhet*.

Following inundation came the season of *peret* or emergence, which lasted from November to February. During this season, work on the land resumed, with the land boundaries restored, any flood debris cleared and the soil prepared to receive the new season's crop. The scenes of the agricultural cycle bear witness to some of these activities.

Though not common, some tombs show a group of peasants breaking up the heavy soil with hoes before the plowing teams began their work. All agricultural scenes include one or several plowing teams working over the field, creating planting furrows. The dynamics of the team are always the same: Two cows pulling a plow, steered by a plowman, with a second

RENDERING ACCOUNTS

Many of the official classes had considerable land holdings, their estates being worked by the peasants who occupied the land or lived in the towns it encompassed. At the end of *shemu*, an accounting of the total harvest was required by the landowner. A proportion of the yield, the lion's share, was retained by the owner, a proportion was allotted to those who worked the land, and a proportion was required as a taxation payment to the state. The local leaders of the towns on the estate were responsible for ensuring an accurate account of the total yield was delivered and that there were no discrepancies. A common motif in tomb decoration is the rendering of accounts, where these village headmen are brought before the overseer of the house and his

scribes, to bear witness to the accurate assessment of the various dues required.

This was an occasion when punishment was meted out to those who failed in their responsibilities. For those guilty of serious transgressions in the performance of their duties, the punishment was severe. In the Sixth-Dynasty tomb of Mereruka, one of the headmen has been stripped naked, tied to a post, and given a severe beating by several officials. Viewed in this light, modern systems of taxation do not seem quite so harsh.

Right **A scribe accounts for the harvest in a fresco from the tomb of Menna.** It is in the Valley of the Nobles, Qurna, at Thebes. He was a scribe under Thutmose IV, an Eighteenth-Dynasty pharaoh.

peasant always in attendance, keeping the beasts in line. The plowing team is usually followed by a sower, who cast seed into the newly created furrows. The seed was then trampled into the soil by a flock of sheep, guided over the field by several shepherds wielding whips, to keep them under control. Scenes dating to the second half of the Sixth Dynasty often exhibit highly naturalistic details that bring the action to life. For example, there is often a fairly unruly flock of sheep depicted with several individual animals heading the wrong way.

The last season of the year was *shemu* or harvest, lasting from March to June. The main focus of the agricultural scenes is on the activities that took place in this season, when the crops were harvested, transported, and processed before finally being stored in granaries.

Harvesting Crops

The first activity of *shemu* was harvesting the crops planted the previous season. Tomb decoration does not make any reference to work undertaken in the field during the maturation of the crop, instead moving immediately from scenes of sowing to those of the harvest. The principal crops harvested in these scenes, and in reality, were barley, emmer wheat, and flax.

Flax was a vital crop for it provided linseed oil and, more importantly, the fibers from which they could manufacture linen. It was the first crop of the year to be harvested, and is always represented as such in tomb decoration. The scenes show the crop being harvested while it still bore blue flowers, indicating that the fibers were destined for the production of fine linen. If courser material was required, for sacking or for

rope, the crop was left to dry out a little before
harvesting. The stems were always pulled from
the ground, never cut, for cutting would stain
the fibers and render them unsuitable for the
manufacture of fine, white linen.

The cereal crops of emmer wheat and barley
were harvested next. Barley was probably the
more important of the two, as it was used as
cereal for making bread, while its germinated
form produced malt for brewing beer. Emmer
wheat was used for flat bread and pastry. Often
the accompanying inscriptions tell us which
of the two crops was harvested below, many
tombs indicating fields of both. The crops were
harvested using a wooden sickle, with short
flint blades glued into the cutting edge.

The size of the harvest scenes varied according to the space available. In large tombs such
as that of the official Ti, the harvest scenes are
spread out over several registers with numerous
field hands at work, while in some of the smaller
provincial tombs only two or three harvesters are
represented in this process. The Egyptian artist
often included naturalistic elements to give the
scenes more life: Field hands stopping to drink
from a flask, quail wandering through the crop,
and sometimes a flautist playing a tune in
accompaniment to the work.

After the crops were harvested, the sheaves
were bundled up and placed in large stacks to
await transport to undergo further processing.
The next stages follow the harvest scenes in a
series of registers continuing down the wall.

Transporting the Harvest

The harvested sheaves were piled up on tall
stacks at the edge of the field until they could be
transported to the threshing floors for further
processing. The threshing floors were probably
located, as they often are today, on the outskirts
of the local village. The sheaves were placed in
baskets, or rope sacks, which were then loaded
onto donkeys. A scene in Ti's tomb demonstrates
this activity, with four field hands struggling to
maneuver a heavy sack onto a waiting donkey.
Once loaded up, the donkeys were escorted from
the field, with several people in attendance,
usually wielding sticks to punish any signs
of recalcitrant animals. In the tomb of Ity at
Gebelein, the artist included a donkey bearing
the blood-smeared wounds inflicted by the
handler's stick. Tomb scenes are often very
realistic in the rendering of work undertaken in
the field. The harvest transport scenes indicate
that young boys, or adolescents, were often co-
opted into assisting with work on the estates.

Threshing, Sieving, and Winnowing

After arriving at the threshing floor, the sheaves were unloaded and again stacked until required for threshing. At that time the harvested grain was spread out on a circular area of ground, prepared with a surface of trodden clay. Herds of donkeys or cattle were driven over this floor to break up the sheaves, and in so doing separated the straw and husks from the seed. Tombs usually show one floor operated by donkeys and another by cattle. We do not know if this represented two different stages in the threshing process, or if it signified either animal could carry out the process. At all times, field hands were required to supervise the animals, ensuring that they kept moving in a circular formation around the threshing floor.

After threshing, the grain required further processing to remove any remaining chaff or other extraneous matter. This was achieved by winnowing and sieving, tasks undertaken by women, according to Old Kingdom tomb scenes. Captions above the women refer to them as "the five crew," though the meaning of this term is no longer clear. It has been suggested that the women worked in groups of five, but the numbers of women depicted in surviving scenes do not give any support to this notion, with anywhere between

two and seven women engaged in this work. They dressed in short skirts and usually wore scarves, probably because part of their work involved tossing the grain into the air to allow the breeze to carry off the lighter chaff. This was done using a pair of wooden winnowing scoops. One woman was always in charge of a sieve, into which the grain fell from the winnowing scoops, sifting out the remaining impurities. A third woman used a long brush to sweep away any chaff that was left on top of the processed grain.

Above **Limestone relief from the Fifth-Dynasty** *mastaba* of Akhhetep at Saqqara. It shows donkeys being worked in the fields, carrying heavy loads.

Storing the Harvest

Once the five crew's work was completed, the processed grain was carefully gathered in baskets from the piles assembled at their feet, and taken to the granaries for storage. All of this was carried out under the watchful eye of an overseer, and the amounts gathered and stored carefully recorded by a scribe, seated nearby. Archeological evidence supports the accuracy of the rows of granaries depicted on tomb walls. The granaries were represented as adjoining, tall structures of mud-brick, standing on a raised platform. The grain was deposited in an opening in the domed roof, reached by a flight of stairs, and it was extracted via a trapdoor near its base.

Below **Painted limestone relief from Ti's** *mastaba*. Farm workers make a haystack on land that has been made fertile by the annual Nile inundation.

WEAVING LINEN

In mid-November, after the Nile floodwaters receded, farmers scattered flax seeds in their fields then sent sheep in to trample them in. Three months later harvesting began. The youngest plants made the finest linen cloth; the oldest were used to manufacture rope. Flax fibers were spliced, spun, and woven. One illustration suggests women moistened the fibers by putting the threads into their mouths during the spinning process. The hand-spindle, a stick weighted at one end to maintain momentum, was the most common method used. Once the flax fibers had been spun into a yarn, the warp threads were placed onto a loom. While flax was the most widely woven material, the Egyptians also made clothing from wool—dyed and spun at both Lahun and Amarna—and goat's hair.

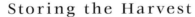

Death and Funerary Ritual

For the ancient Egyptians, to lose one's identity and be forgotten was to lapse back into the primeval waters of chaos and oblivion. So abhorrent was the concept that they became obsessed with the preservation of their identity and memory.

Right **A Fifth-Dynasty limestone sarcophagus.** It is from a tomb at el-Gebelein and is now housed in the Egyptian Museum in Turin, Italy.

This was achieved by carving their image, or even just their name, into durable materials such as stone or, if they were wealthy enough, building stone funerary monuments and even preserving the body for eternity.

Burial Practices of God-kings

Initially, only royalty could aspire to eternal life in the hereafter, but a process referred to as the "democratization of the afterlife," in which high officials and the nobility gradually adopted similar aspirations, was well under way before the end of the Old Kingdom.

Fundamental differences remained between the burials of royals and the elite; only the king could aspire to being buried in a pyramid, a device aimed at facilitating the resurrection of the king and his ascendance into an afterlife with the gods. Solar barks, boats required to navigate the netherworld in the company of the gods, were also only the prerogative of the king and could not be used by anyone else.

The Pyramid Texts, magical spells and instructions for the king's progress through the netherworld, are only found decorating the walls of the pyramids of royals. It was not until after the Old Kingdom that these texts were inscribed inside the coffins of elite non-royals. Elite Old Kingdom tombs are instead covered with scenes of life and the kind of afterlife pursuits to which the tomb owners might aspire, such as hunting in the marshes.

After death, immediate steps were taken to preserve the body. Mummification in the Old Kingdom was not very successful and little remains to hint at the process used then. The Egyptians left no records detailing the mummification process, but by examining one surviving Old Kingdom mummy, the body was apparently wrapped in linen and smeared with a plaster or resin coating, molded to resemble the deceased. The body inevitably decomposed leaving only the plaster shell, few of which have survived intact. Ironically, some bodies of the very poor buried directly into desert sand, have been well preserved due to the perfect desiccation of sun and sand. Many examples of this form of mummification have survived. By the New Kingdom, the technique was much refined and the process was clearly recorded first-hand by Herodotus.

RITUAL SACRIFICE AND BUTCHER QUEENS

The Acacia House, an Old Kingdom performance institution, was associated with two diverse activities, both occurring at the funeral—the ritual sacrifice of cattle and the performance of dances which appear to have held significance as metaphors for fertility or rebirth.

Curiously, the title *sehedjet seshemtyw shendjet* (director of butchers of the Acacia House) was held by no less than six queens (Hetepheres I and II, Meresankh II, III, and IV, and Khentkawes but only one man (Peher-Nefer). Given that the butchery of cattle required considerable strength and precision, it is unlikely that these queens actively participated in the slaughter; rather they appear to have had a directorial role presiding over funerary sacrifices.

Left **Detail of the head of a statue of Peher-Nefer.** He was director of butchers of the Acacia House during the Fourth Dynasty. This statue is from the necropolis at Saqqara. It is now housed in the Louvre Museum in Paris.

The Funeral Procession

Our understanding of royal funerals comes largely from tomb scenes of high officials. It is unclear if the funerary procession, as depicted on Old Kingdom tomb walls, took place after death, or if it was celebrated during their life as a status show and to reinforce their afterlife expectations. Some depictions of funerary processions unambiguously show the tomb owner participating in the event in a form that can only be the living person, suggesting that the scenes are of funerary ritual rather than a funeral *per se*.

An inscription in the *mastaba* of Mereruka reads, "setting out from the house of the estate to the beautiful West." The funerary procession began at the house of the deceased and set forth toward the Nile. Many servants would carry the funerary furniture, offerings of clothing and food to sustain the deceased in the afterlife, and unguents for the funerary rituals.

At the head of the official party was the wife, sometimes titled *Djeryt* (translating as Kite, the

Above **The falcon god Horus performs the opening of the mouth ceremony on the deceased Rameses II**. A Nineteenth-Dynasty pharaoh, this relief is from a small temple he built at Abydos.

bird of prey the goddess Isis used to search for her dead husband). In the Old Kingdom, the association of the deceased with Osiris was officially reserved for kings. However, the titles *Djeryt Wrt* and *Djeryt* appear next to two female mourners in their stations at either end of the coffin on the funerary barge depicted in the tomb of the vizier Ptahhotep.

The title *Djeryt Wrt,* meaning Greater Kite, alludes to the form Isis assumed in order to search for her dead husband Osiris, while *Djeryt* translates as Lesser Kite, and is associated with Nephthys, the grieving sister of Isis and Osiris. The association of these two female mourners, in the funeral of a non-royal, with the goddesses Nephthys and Isis from the Osirian legend, suggests that by the end of the Old Kingdom this funerary aspiration had crept into the funerals of officials.

Behind the Kite, pallbearers carried the coffin but it is unclear whether the deceased was inside the coffin or whether the body joined the cortege at the purification tent on the other side of the

Nile. The other people in the official party included the lector priest, who read scriptures from the sacred scrolls during rituals enacted at stations along the way, the *sem* priest who organized the crossing of the Nile, and the *wet* priest who was associated with the embalming process.

At the riverbank, the *sem* priest set about the arduous task of organizing transportation of the entire cortege to the west bank. This included all the mourners, servants, funerary furniture, the *ka* statue, the coffin, the food offerings and unguents, as well as the live animals to be used for transporting the catafalque (the coffin and its sled) across the desert and to be slaughtered for the funerary feast.

Once disembarked on the other side of the Nile, the party set off across the desert to the necropolis. In most depictions, the coffin is placed on a sled and dragged by cattle. Pouring liquid in front of the sled eased the friction of the sled against the sand, the same principle employed to aid the transport of stone blocks during pyramid and temple construction.

Dancing and Feasting

Dance was a prominent feature of the funerary procession. In many scenes, dancers are shown solemnly stepping in unison in front of the coffin. The dance is performed with the arms held high above the head in an arc. Much more lively dances, performed in pairs, accompanied the funerary processions as depicted in the provincial tombs of the nobles, Djau and Ibi, both interred in the rock-cut tomb near Deir el-Gebrawi.

In other tombs, such as the tomb of Debeheni, an official at Giza, and in Mereruka's *mastaba* at Saqqara, dances take place at the door of the tomb, usually performed by maidens of the Acacia House. Humorous records of the hungry asides of impatient guests at the funerary feast survive from the tombs at Saqqara.

Ritual and Offerings

The opening of the mouth ritual, intended to vivify the *ka* statue of an individual by opening the mouth, nostrils, and eyes, was enacted at the tomb door. The statue was intended to house the *ka* of an individual in case the body disintegrated.

The procession of grave goods up the stairs to be placed into the tomb was often enacted while music and dance was performed near the tomb, as seen in Debeheni's tomb The interment of the deceased was an vast undertaking involving placement of a heavy stone lid on the sarcophagus. Once the body was interred, the doors were closed and plaster seals were put in place. An offering of food from the funerary feast was left for the sustenance of the deceased, and the mourners and officiants made their way east across the Nile, to return to the land of the living.

Left **Funerary statue of Mitri, a high-ranking official in the late Fifth to early Sixth Dynasties.** Made of stuccoed and painted wood, it is from his *mastaba* at Saqqara.

Below **The entrance wall of Teti's funerary chamber is covered in heiroglyphics.** These are the Pyramid Texts, which contain spells intended to assist the deceased in the afterlife.

THE *MUU* DANCE

The story of Sinhue shows that dances occurred at funerals: "The dance of the *muu* is performed at the door of your tomb." These enigmatic personages were male funerary dancers. They are depicted wearing short kilts. On their heads are crowns made from aquatic plants, either woven reeds, as in the example from the tomb of the vizier Nebkawhor, or papyrus buds as seen in the Old Kingdom tombs of Seshseshet-Idut (a daughter of Teti) and the vizier Ptahhotep II. The *muu* are associated with the dead souls of the ancient kings of Buto, a Lower Egyptian pilgrimage site, and this may account for the resemblance of their most characteristic headdress to the crown of Lower Egypt.

There is strong evidence to suggest that the *muu* were originally ferrymen, employed to transport pilgrims to holy sites situated in the Delta and accessible only by water. Later, a stylized version of this ritual was enacted within the necropolis precincts as a substitute for the original pilgrimages. It is this enactment which is depicted in the only three Old Kingdom examples, outlined above.

In later periods, the *muu* expanded their repertoire, performing a dance in pairs, usually near the door of the tomb, and another ritual dance in which they met the cortege at the edge of the necropolis, the threshold separating the world of the living from the world of the dead. Another station of the *muu*, dating from the Middle Kingdom, shows the *muu* standing inside an architectural structure overlooking a garden with iconography associated with the holy sites of Sais, Buto, and Heliopolis. These figures have been interpreted as guardians of the necropolis.

Daily Life

The wall scenes in Old Kingdom tombs are an invaluable source of information about daily life during this period. They reveal many fascinating details about how these people lived that would otherwise have remain hidden.

While the themes represented in these tombs may have been selected for their symbolic value, perhaps creating a perfect hereafter where an individual expected to pass eternity, the models used were those the Egyptians were familiar with. They recreated life as they knew it along the Nile valley, albeit a life without the usual trials and tribulations.

Below **Workers butchering a cow.** This painted limestone relief is from the *mastaba* of the Fifth-Dynasty Princess Sesh-seshat-Idut, at Saqqara.

Fishing

Fish were a cheap and abundant source of food and many tombs have representations of the Nile teeming with many of the varieties in the diet of ordinary Egyptians. In such scenes, the various techniques used to catch fish are on display with some individuals using a simple hook and line, while others gather in fish using hand nets. Basket traps set on the river bottom can also be seen. The most common and the most detailed fishing scenes are those involving the use of a dragnet. Spread out over two registers, the scene has two groups of haulers facing each other, as they heave on a rope connected to the large net beneath them. One edge of the net is weighted with metal or stone sinkers to help drag the net through the water, gathering huge numbers of fish in the process. The artists went to some lengths to render realistic scenes of activity on the Nile, including the plants and animals that could be found in the watery depths. In the tomb

of Ankhmahor, for example, a hippopotamus is about to unwittingly deliver her baby into the waiting jaws of a crocodile. In another tomb, mating turtles and crocodiles are represented among the fish below the owner's papyrus skiff.

At the conclusion of the fishing excursion, we often see baskets of fish being carried away to be gutted and filleted. Sometimes this is followed by a scene where the fish is cooked in a pan over an open fire. There are also scenes where baskets of fish are offered for sale at a local market.

Fowling

The reeds and marshes along the Nile were the habitat of a great variety of bird-life, and poultry was clearly an important part of the Egyptian diet. Clap-nets were regularly used to trap large numbers of birds, the nets spread out over a pond to wait until a sufficient number had gathered on it. A signalman hiding nearby would alert his men when it was time to haul on the strong rope attached to the net, trapping the birds as it closed over them. Many of the birds were kept in cages until such time as they were slaughtered for the table. Almost every tomb also included the tomb-owner standing on a skiff in the marshes, using his throwing stick to bring down birds rising from a papyrus thicket. This appears to have been a favored leisure pursuit of the upper classes.

Building Boats

Because of the importance of the Nile, it is not surprising that many tomb scenes are devoted to other activities taking place along its banks, apart from fishing and fowling. We often see men gathering papyrus stems, tying them in bundles, and carrying them across their backs to the boat-makers. Three or four men usually worked together to manufacture papyrus skiffs, tying the bundles together tightly with flax ropes. These skiffs were the basic means of travel on the Nile for the ordinary Egyptian, providing the means to transport small items, or undertake a little fishing

in the middle of the river. Sometimes peasants rowed these boats alongside their cattle during river crossings, ensuring the animals stayed together. Again, the Egyptian artist used this occasion to demonstrate the perils of the deep, with crocodiles lurking in the water ready to seize the opportunity of an easy meal. Other scenes depict these boats ferrying objects down the river, and sometimes the ferrymen indulging in a little good-natured sport with their fellow river travelers, using their steering poles to knock their rivals into the water.

Butchery

Butchery was another theme represented in most tombs, with one or several beasts, usually cattle, slaughtered. These scenes are included in a mortuary context, with the cuts of meat destined for the offering table of the deceased to provide eternal sustenance. Despite this context, we see the techniques normally employed by butchers in the pursuit of their work. The animal was first lassoed and manhandled to the ground so that its legs could be hog-tied and then tethered to a floor ring. The butchery knife was honed on a sharpening stone attached to the butcher's belt, and the animal's throat cut. The beast was then dismembered by a team of butchers working together.

While there are also representations of a range of other activities in Old Kingdom tombs, this examination covers some of the more common themes of tomb decoration and allows a glimpse into how the ordinary Egyptian passed his day.

Above **Boatmen engage in a sporting competition.** This bas-relief is from the *mastaba* of the Sixth-Dynasty official Ptahhotep, at Saqqara.

Below **Fishing with weighted hooks, a Sixth-Dynasty bas-relief from the *mastaba* of Kagemni at Saqqara.** He was vizier and inspector of priests during the reign of Teti.

Entertainment

Scenes of the wealthy being entertained by music, dance, children's games, and board games were a popular decoration in Old Kingdom tombs. Music and dance were enjoyed as part of the religious calendar and at the sed-festival of the king.

Right **A raised relief depicting dancers and soldiers in the entourage of the nobleman Ti.** The carvings in his *mastaba* at Saqqara are among the Sixth Dynasty's finest.

A number of vocational institutions existed, such as the Acacia House, which was associated with funerary rituals, and the *khener*, an ensemble of musical performers attached to temples, the court or commissioned by the funerary estate of individuals. From the titles of performers, we know many other performers were also attached to the court of the king and even the pyramid cult of the dead king.

Music and Dance

The most popular Old Kingdom orchestral instruments were the harp and flute, and most orchestras included at least one singer. There were flutes with different pitch ranges and a double flute constructed with parallel pipes. While drums are not attested until the Middle Kingdom, other percussion instruments such as clappers, castanets and the sistrum were in use during the Old Kingdom. However, they do not appear to have been incorporated into orchestras. Instead, they are shown in dance scenes, usually held by the dancers. The sistrum is also attested in ritual contexts.

Orchestral and dance scenes are usually depicted on separate registers indicating that they were not performed together. Rather, dance

scenes appear, almost without exception, accompanied by a group of rhythmists who clap the beat. Most Old Kingdom dances were performed in unison, rather like modern-day chorus lines. Popular unison dances included one characterized by a pose in which the arms are raised in an arc above the head resembling cow's horns and another in which the arms are raised up as if in salutation. Both of these dances were performed as secular entertainment and at funerals.

A strenuous unison dance, in which the leg is kicked high to the front while the torso is thrown precariously backwards appears to have been associated with the cult of Hathor. In most representations of this dance, a disc attached to the end of a long tress of hair swings in counter-motion to the dancers' movements. Another dynamic dance performed in unison, but with the dancers running in different directions, may have had its origins as a hunting or war dance as it is sometimes performed with boomerangs. The dancers' bodies are twisted back, with the limbs arranged in a manner resembling a swastika.

Pair dances were also popular, sometimes depicted as couples performing in unison and sometimes performing different steps in series. Most pair dances represented at Giza and Saqqara are rather sedate in nature, whereas the pair dances which appear in the tombs of provincial nobles are much more energetic. Even in partnered dances, men and women are never shown dancing together. The pair dance steps represented in sequence in the Seshseshet

Below **A section of a Fifth-Dynasty painted relief from Saqqara.** Held in the Egyptian Museum (in Cairo), it shows a flautist and a singer.

Right **A female dancer performs, in a relief decoration from a Fifth-Dynasty tomb in Saqqara.** The various dance scenes from Old Kingdom tombs reveal much about entertainment during that time. Egyptologists have been able to recreate some ancient dances.

chapel in the *mastaba* of Mereruka, may be the world's earliest choreographic notation. Many other dance steps are represented, including the pirouette and a high-stepping march.

The mirror dance, performed by young girls, is associated with the cult of Hathor because the participants perform a chant referring to Hathor in the tomb of Mereruka, and hold mirrors and hand-shaped clappers, both significant objects in the cult. The objective appears to be to catch the reflection of the clappers in the mirror.

Fun and Games

The boys' game of prisoner, which is captioned with the term *khebi* (dance) in one example, may have been a coming-of-age enactment. There are two scenes or motifs associated with this boys' game. The first is a group of naked youths running, usually escorting a bound prisoner; the second shows a scuffle inside a hut or enclosure in which one youth is subdued by four others.

The board game of *senet*, which appears to be the forerunner of chess, was played by moving pawn shaped pieces on a grid of 30 squares. Each player probably had seven pieces and the number of progressions in a move was determined by throwing sticks or knucklebones. Unfortunately, the rules of *senet* have not been preserved.

GAMES CHILDREN PLAY

Children played games similar to those still played in Egypt and elsewhere today. A game resembling a tug-of-war was executed by two opposing teams, not with a rope, but by the front two opposing partners holding hands and leaning back. A whirling or pivoting game, in which a central figure holds two other players, one in each hand, appears in several tombs. Another game shows a boy balancing on the shoulders of a team of others as they move toward a goal. In another, two children are shown clinging to the back of another who crawls. A contest between two boys involved throwing sticks at a target, and there are many representations of wrestling.

Women

Women in Egypt appear to have enjoyed greater freedoms and respect than many of their counterparts in other ancient societies. The only known documents, from the New Kingdom, indicate that women were equal to men in the eyes of the law.

Below **Khufu's daughter, Princess Nefertyabet at her funerary feast.** The stela includes food and cosmetics for the afterlife.

Among many other benefits, women could own and dispose of property as they saw fit. Though no equivalent documentation exists from the Old Kingdom, there is nothing to suggest that the situation was very much different during that time.

A woman's primary responsibility was in the home, as revealed by the most common female title: *Nebet per,* or lady of the house. The Instructions of Ptahhotep advise a man how to handle a woman in her domain, if trouble is to be avoided:

> *Do not control your wife in her house, when you know that she is efficient. Do not say to her: Where is it? Fetch it! When she has placed it in the correct place. Let your eye watch in silence. Then you know her skill. It is a joy when your hand is with her. Many do not know this! If a man desists from trouble at home then he will not meet its beginning.*

Clearly it was believed a woman was best left alone to run the house without male interference.

Women in Art

Egyptians placed great emphasis on family life, and marriage and children were encouraged as the ideal. Tomb decoration regularly depicts a husband and wife in loving embrace, with their children in attendance. Old Kingdom statues of a man and his wife are also very common, the wife often draping an arm around her husband's shoulders or waist. While the wife is sometimes represented in tomb scenes as a very diminutive figure at her husband's feet, this is not always the case. Many images of a husband and wife have the pair depicted in similar proportions, suggesting a close partnership between the two. The women are always represented with paler skin tones to men: Usually a creamy yellow, while the men are a dark brown or red. This was an artistic convention perhaps used to suggest women were more accustomed to the shade of the house. Interestingly women portrayed working in the field

COSMETICS

No self-respecting Egyptian lady would be buried without her mirror. In the afterlife, as in life, appearances were all-important. Even in Predynastic times, women used their fingers to mix a paste made from malachite on their stone palettes. It was mined in the Sinai and Eastern Desert and used as a bright green eye paint. Later the fashionable color was black, and the paste—derived from a galena-based form of kohl—was applied with a "kohl pencil." The eye paint may have had a religious significance, but it was also a disinfectant.

Ocher was used as a form of rouge, while oils were applied and henna used to color hair. The rich employed their own hairdressers and, as a further enhancement of the body beautiful, women apparently had tattoos which have been found reproduced on figurines. A mummy was discovered with a tattoo of the god Bes on her thigh.

are also depicted with pale skins, working alongside their tanned male counterparts. In tomb art, the woman is always represented at her youthful best—slim and taut.

Feminine Occupations

Apart from her work in the house, women could have additional occupations. Women from the upper social ranks commonly held priesthoods, usually in the service of a female deity, such as Hathor or Neith. Like her husband, she probably did not serve in the temple on a full-time basis, but provided service at prescribed intervals. Priestess duties probably included performances of ritual dances and/or songs for the goddess. In tomb scenes female dancers and orchestras comprised entirely of women perform, both probably included as part of a temple ritual. A woman close to the court sometimes held the honorific titles, royal acquaintance or royal ornament, but her preference always depended on that of her husband.

Women also worked at weaving, turning flax into fine linen on horizontal looms. There are several surviving tomb scenes portraying the rewards given to female weavers for this work in the form of broad gold collars. It is difficult to understand the full range of female activity, as women did not possess nearly as many titles as men. While there were female overseers (such as overseer of weavers) they always related to supervising women workers, never men.

Female Burials

Women could, and did, build their own tombs if they had the means to do so. More usually however, provision was made for a woman's burial in the tomb of her husband. Just as they shared a home in life, they would continue to do so in death. Usually a shaft leading to a burial chamber was cut in the tomb for the wife, and a false door inscribed with her name was placed overhead in the chapel. Sometimes she shared her husband's false door, with her name and image cut into one of the jambs. By so doing, she would receive all the blessings that would come to her husband.

Above **A painted limestone pair statue of the Fifth-Dynasty official Raherka and his wife Meresankh**. Such statues reveal a close bond between husband and wife.

Right **A servant woman kneading dough.** This Fifth-Dynasty limestone statue indicates baking was a female occupation.

End of the Old Kingdom

The exact cause for the decline and collapse of the Old Kingdom is unknown, but it is believed Pepy II's very long reign was a factor. In the second half of his reign it seems the king was no longer capable of exerting his control and influence over Egypt.

The ever-expanding power and independence of the provincial governors had undermined royal authority, with these overlords acting more like rulers than faithful servants of the crown. It is possible that the years of granting tax exemptions to temple estates had depleted the treasury as well. In granting vast estates to temples and to individuals, the king had hastened the process of land ownership shifting away from the central administration.

Tomb autobiographies of the late Old Kingdom indicate that all was not well along Egypt's borders either. Pepynakht Heqaib's mission to Palestine to bring back the body of an Egyptian official slain by the sand dwellers, as well as a subsequent mission to Nubia to crush a rebellion among native tribes, indicate that Egypt's trade routes were also being compromised.

Pepy II's Successors

The years following Pepy II's death are unfortunately very poorly documented, consequently very little is known of the period. He was succeeded by Merenra II, who was probably the son of Pepy II and Neith. The Turin Canon records a reign of only 13 months for Merenra. The Greek historian Herodotus, writing in the second half of the fifth century BCE, when these events were already ancient history, claims that Merenra had been murdered.

Below **The courtyard and tomb of Pepynakht Heqaib, on the Nile at Elephantine.** Missions by this Sixth-Dynasty governor proved there was trouble along Egypt's trade routes.

Merenra was succeeded by his sister and wife, Nitocris, who was the last ruler of the Sixth Dynasty. There is no surviving archeological evidence to support her reign, though the Turin Canon mentions her name. All our information regarding this queen comes from late sources. Manetho, a priest during the reigns of two Ptolemaic kings, wrote that Nitocris was: "Braver than all the men of her time, the most beautiful of all women," and he records a reign of 12 years for the queen. Herodotus claims that Nitocris avenged the murder of her brother by slaying all those responsible. She invited all the Egyptians she knew to have been involved, to attend the inaugural ceremony of a large underground chamber she had built. While the ceremony was taking place, she flooded the chamber by opening a concealed conduit pipe, drowning the assassins. The veracity of Herodotus' version of events has not been confirmed by any archeological evidence.

Dynasties Seven and Eight

With the death of Nitocris, Manetho describes a period of "70 kings in 70 days," which although an exaggeration, describes the chaos that followed the fall of the Sixth Dynasty. In reality there were probably only 17 kings, possibly descendants of the ruling house of Pepy II, who ruled from Memphis for a period of about 20 years. The king-list in the Temple of Seti I at Abydos provides the names of the 17 kings, about whom virtually nothing else is known. Only one has left any tangible proof of his reign: Kakara Ibi, who built a small pyramid to house his mortal remains along the causeway of Pepy II's pyramid complex. Kakara's pyramid was the last to include verses from the Pyramid Texts, but the pyramid itself is a very poor relation to those of his forebears, covering only 37 square yards (31 sq. m) and built entirely of mud-brick.

Change and Chaos

Periods with rapid changes in administration over the space of only a few years are never conducive to the maintenance of good government, and so it proved in Egypt. The kings of the Seventh and Eighth Dynasties could only exert any influence in the region immediately surrounding the capital. Elsewhere the regional governors held sway over their own provinces, and cast covetous eyes toward the territories of their neighbors. Ankhtifi, the provincial governor of the third nome of Upper Egypt, records that he found his province: "Abandoned by him who belonged to it, in the grip of a rebel, under the control of a wretch." The Lamentations of Ipuwer paints a more graphic picture: "I show you the land in turmoil. What should not be has come to pass. Men will seize weapons of war. The land will exist in uproar...The land is diminished, its rulers are many."

As if this were not trouble enough, evidence suggests that Egypt also suffered years of drought during this period, and subsequently severe food shortages. The state of the Nile is described by Ipuwer: "Dry is the river of Egypt, one crosses the water on foot." With a weakened central authority, there were no longer sufficient grain supplies kept in reserve to survive this disaster. Tomb biographies refer to the "painful years of distress" that had to be endured as a result of a particularly bad drought along with civic unrest.

Eventually the land was divided into two separate parts, with a ruling family established at Herakleopolis and another family rising to rule in Thebes. The Two Lands were now divided, a period referred to by Egyptologists as the First Intermediate Period.

Above **Relief of fishing and hunting birds in the marshes.** A scene from the tomb of Sabni, at Aswan, a Sixth-Dynasty governor. By this time, such officials were wielding their increasing power.

Left **Marble bust of the Greek historian, Herodotus, c. 485–25 BCE.** Of the little known about the end of the Old Kingdom, some comes from his fifth-century records.

CHANGE AND CONTINUITY: FIRST INT
SECOND INTERMEDIATE PERIOD

Introduction

After the collapse of the Old Kingdom, Egypt was ruled in the First Intermediate Period by several local nomarchs, more or less independent of the king residing in the north. Few monuments of these kings are known, demonstrating a stark decline in royal power.

Above **Senusret I, Twelfth Dynasty.** One of the many achievements of Senusret I was the establishment of a building program that saw temples and monuments erected across the country.

Right **Faience figurine of naked lady with tattoos.** Faience objects were made from quartz particles. This striking figurine is a fine example of the Egyptian craftsmanship of the Middle Kingdom era.

Only one small pyramid of the period has so far been identified. Several of the southern nomarchs seem to have fought against each other, but only a few of these took over parts of the royal titulary. At the same time, the provinces were flourishing to an extent not known before, showing a general spread of wealth around the country.

A United Egypt

The unification of Egypt finally came from the south, where kings ruling from Thebes managed to overcome the north after decades of warfare, creating a new period of unity now known as the Middle Kingdom.

In the eyes of the ancient Egyptians, the Middle Kingdom is the classical period of their history. These days, we might sooner think of the Old Kingdom with its monumental pyramids, or the New Kingdom with its vast empire, but the ancients clearly had a different view. Some kings of the fourth century adopted names of Middle Kingdom rulers, evidently because they were seen as especially powerful figures of the past. Temple inscriptions of the Greek and Roman period refer to the foundation of the buildings under Middle Kingdom kings. The language of the period was considered as classical, and was used in temple and tomb inscriptions up to the Roman period, although the later stages of the Egyptian language were being used in daily life. The art of the period was also regarded as classical. Late Twelfth Dynasty royal sculpture is, in its realism, almost

without parallel in Egyptian history. Even for small object types, the period reached the highest standard. The jewelry of the Middle Kingdom is certainly the finest ever produced in Egypt.

Despite all this, relatively little survives from this period. The temples and many tombs of the Middle Kingdom were built in the finest limestone. These temples were mostly destroyed very early on in rebuilding projects. The limestone used was quarried away for other temple buildings or, in the Roman Period, to be burnt for lime. With this destruction, long texts of the kings and biographies of officials once placed on the walls of the buildings were destroyed, leaving gaps in our knowledge about the period. Just a handful of surviving examples demonstrate that the temples and tombs were, indeed, once decorated with long descriptions of kings and officials.

The eight kings of the Twelfth Dynasty ruled for almost two hundred years, making the period one of the most politically stable in Egyptian history. The dynasty saw some of the most important rulers of Egypt come to power— such as Amenemhet I, the founder of the dynasty, and Senusret I, who was the first king to systematically build temples across the country (his obelisk at Heliopolis is the earliest one still standing). Other rulers of the Twelfth Dynasty included Senusret III, whose military campaigns were famed as far away as classical Greece, and Amenemhet III, who built the famous "labyrinth" visited and described by many Greek and Roman writers, but now totally destroyed. The Twelfth Dynasty ended with the rule of Queen Sobeknofru, the first Egyptian woman on the throne for whom we have contemporary monuments.

Regional Development and Diversity

The political fragmentation of the country in the First Intermediate Period had resulted in different local styles. Each region developed its own traditions, and these were still vibrant in the Middle Kingdom, surviving the reunification of the country. The coffins, tomb decorations, sculpture, and even pottery types became quite distinctive from one region to the next. The fragmentation of craft production was strengthened by the fact that in the Middle Kingdom there were still many nomarchs effectively ruling small local territories under the overall control of the king. Provincial cemeteries in the Middle Kingdom were richer than ever before or since. Even people of modest status might be buried in decorated coffins, and were sometimes equipped with expensive objects such as gold jewelry. In the Twelfth Dynasty, the capital moved from Thebes in the south to Itj-tawy in the north. Only at the end of the Twelfth Dynasty is a trend toward centralization visible. The great tombs of the nomarchs in the provinces disappear, whereas more building work can be seen around the royal residence and in the south at Thebes, which became the second city of the country in the Thirteenth Dynasty.

The End of the Middle Kingdom

The Middle Kingdom ended in a long chain of short ruling kings—the Thirteenth Dynasty. Little is known about these kings or the links between them. However, despite this apparently unstable political situation, the country functioned under the efficient administration installed in the Eleventh and Twelfth Dynasties, without significant changes. The end came only when, at a point perhaps late in the Thirteenth Dynasty, people from Palestine took over the eastern delta fringes and founded Hyksos rule over the north of Egypt. The southern part of Egypt remained under the rule of Egyptian kings, residing at Thebes; these kings finally managed to expel the Hyksos, and went on to found the New Kingdom.

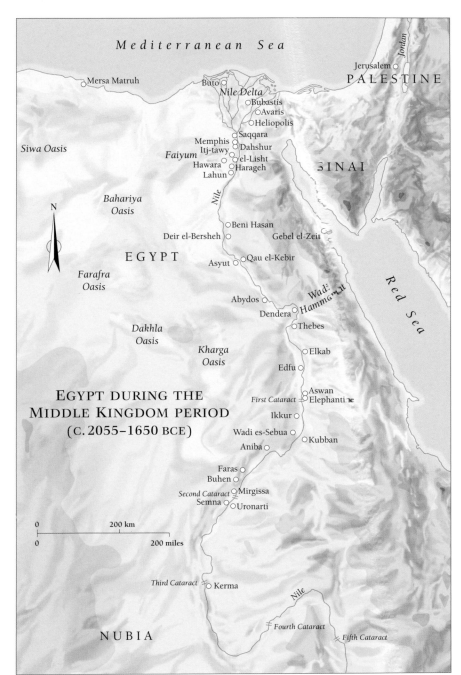

EGYPT DURING THE MIDDLE KINGDOM PERIOD (C. 2055–1650 BCE)

Left **Jewelry and utensils of the Twelfth Dynasty.** During the Middle Kingdom, the skill of artisans reached new heights of excellence, as seen in these examples discovered at Tod, which utilize gold, silver, and lapis lazuli.

THE FIRST INTERMEDIATE PERIOD
Collapse of Ultimate Power

The decline of the Old Kingdom is epitomized by the way its pyramids and tombs progressively dwindled in size and quality. Such projects were a drain on Egypt's wealth, which was already diminishing due to climatic changes across the Near East.

Right **Ivory head rest inscribed with name of Pepy II.** While there are numerous exquisite artifacts that date back to the time of Pepy II, it is his lengthy reign that left an indelible mark on Egyptian history, as it is believed to have played a role in the fall of the Old Kingdom.

More arid conditions had meant a greater reliance on the Nile as a source of irrigating the land, and this, in turn, caused further problems as the Nile floods became less frequent than in earlier times. This reduced frequency, often coupled with low floodwater levels, resulted in water shortages, famine, and death. Much of this most probably occurred during the long reign of the Sixth Dynasty's King Pepy II.

By the Ninth Dynasty, Ankhtifi states "All of Upper Egypt was dying of hunger and people were eating their children," which although this was probably an exaggeration, it gives an indication of the problems faced by Egypt at this time.

Fragmentation

Pepy II ruled for 94 years, the longest reign in Egyptian history, and this is thought to have contributed to the demise of the Old Kingdom. Pepy bestowed gifts and wealth upon his favored officials, diminishing the royal coffers while the wealth and power of the nobility increased. Due to this, in the latter years of his reign, the centralized state at Memphis started to deteriorate, as the power of the local nomarchs increased. They

started building elaborately decorated tombs in the nome capitals, and barely acknowledged the sovereign in Memphis.

The demands of commitments made by the Old Kingdom to foreign powers to establish and maintain foreign relations also contributed to the deterioration of the royal treasury.

End of an Era

When Pepy II died, the slowly deteriorating centralized government broke down completely and Egypt was divided, with nomarchs ruling over different areas simultaneously. Manetho states that the Seventh Dynasty was made up of 70 kings who reigned for 70 days, which although not accurate, does give an indication of the instability of the period.

The Eighth Dynasty, believed to have been descendants of Pepy II, ruled from the Memphite region, and comprised of approximately 17 kings over 20 years. However, they left very little evidence of their reign other than a small pyramid belonging to King Qakara Iby. Asiatics were said

A DECLINE IN GOOD TASTE: ART OF THE FIRST INTERMEDIATE PERIOD

The First Intermediate Period was a time of new artistic developments and innovations, often with characteristics identifiable with certain regions.

In the Gebelein region, animal hides were painted in patterns and unrealistic colors (pink asses and gazelles). New colors were also introduced, including orange, lemon yellow, and gray-blue, and in the tomb of Setka at Aswan, each register was painted with a different background color.

In the Theban region, the human figures were depicted as very tall and slender, with large oval eyes that filled the upper part of the face, wide noses, large ears, and protruding lips. Even the bread on the offering tables was presented as long and thin. At the end of the First Intermediate Period, when the Eleventh Dynasty reunited Egypt, these innovations were abandoned in favor of Old Kingdom proportions and style.

to be ruling the delta north of Memphis at this time, and the Ninth Dynasty ruled over Middle Egypt from the city of Herakleopolis Magna.

As with the Eighth Dynasty, there were frequent changes of ruler in the Ninth Dynasty, although they appeared to be ambitious and after 30 years, the Herakleopolitan Tenth Dynasty had gained control of Middle and Lower Egypt and the Theban Eleventh Dynasty ruled Upper Egypt up to the boundaries of Herakleopolis Magna.

The most important monument of the Ninth Dynasty is the tomb of Ankhtifi, the nomarch of the Second and Third Nomes of Upper Egypt, located at el-Moalla, 19 miles (30 km) south of Thebes. Ankhtifi records in his autobiography that he held both religious and administrative titles, and the two key events in his life were an expedition against the Theban nome, and the pacifying and reorganization of his own nome at Edfu. These were probably small-scale events, in which Ankhtifi was not especially successful, and there is no evidence of a successor to his position.

New Beginnings

After an extended stalemate, the Theban King Mentuhotep II succeeded in overthrowing the Herakleopolitan kings, with the aid of the newly reinstated resources of Nubia. Although Mentuhotep II brought an end to the civil wars, he focused his attention primarily on the southern region and there were complaints of neglect from the borders of the delta. The remainder of the dynasty concentrated on improving the status of Egypt. The start of the Twelfth Dynasty saw a truly unified state, over 100 years after the collapse of the Old Kingdom.

Left **Pyramid of Pepy II, located between Dahshur and Saqqara.** Pepy II was the last king of the Old Kingdom. His death after a reign of 94 years, signalled the beginning of a period of great unrest and upheaval for Egypt.

Life in the Province

The First Intermediate Period was a time marked by political disorder and profound cultural changes. The events and changes experienced during this turbulent time left a legacy that extended into the Middle and New Kingdoms.

Below **Grove of date palms** *(Phoenix dactylifera).* Dates were a significant crop for the ancient Egyptians. Not only did the palms yield fruit, the timber was used for building purposes, and leaves were utilized in basket-making.

Typically, information about political and cultural turmoil comes to us from "official" sources such as the inscriptions of kings, provincial governors, and scribes. How then, in the face of political and social turmoil, did normal Egyptians exist and adjust?

Unfortunately, archeological research into settlement sites of this period is problematic; nonetheless, burials of this time, despite demonstrating a significant deviation from burials of the past, indicate that day-to-day life remained relatively unchanged for most Egyptians.

Wealth for Everyone!

During the First Intermediate Period a considerable number of Egyptians were either independent farmers or herders who cultivated their own land holdings, or the lower-classed *meret* who worked plots of land owned by wealthy land owners. It is also apparent that some Egyptians increased their land holdings by serving as priests in mortuary cults, while others probably employed themselves as part-time craftsmen.

As a result of the agrarian nature of Egyptian society at this time, many Egyptians would have lived with the yearly fear of low Nile floods and potential famine. Such subjects appear as regular concerns in texts from this period, and while there has been much speculation over the years as to the exact nature of the environment in Egypt during this period, drought and famine were topics that could be used by the local authorities to legitimize their power and establish social dependence.

Local Rule, Local Fighting

Whatever the regularity of day-to-day life, the First Intermediate Period was one of political conflict, and hostilities often broke out between the different nomes and their nomarchs. Evidence attesting to these hostilities at this time is demonstrated on stelae from the region of Koptos. Here, many stelae portray the deceased with bows and arrows, rather than carrying their tools or staff of office. Moreover, the large number of these stelae completed by fathers, friends, and brothers points to the fact that death may have come before the children of the deceased were old enough to arrange the proper funeral services.

One of the greatest changes for the local populations in Egypt during the time of the First Intermediate Period was the presence of local rulers. During the Old Kingdom, provincial rulers were directly in control of their region, under instruction from the king who governed from the

turn, created a widening gap of social and cultural inequality between the majority of Egypt and its rulers, and it was during the First Intermediate Period that this gap was narrowed.

Change in the Province

Changes in the centralized system of ruling appear as early as the Fifth Dynasty, when provincial governors were posted within their regions on a hereditary basis, resulting in powerful provincial families. The economic structure of the country also changed as a result of a decentralized system. Previously, economic resources were concentrated in the royal city and redistributed to the provinces—in the First Intermediate Period provincial governors had direct access to their local wealth.

Decentralizing the government of Egypt provided a social and cultural renaissance for provincial regions previously outside the sphere of the capital city. The provincial lifestyle must have changed notably as iconographic patterns, textual models, and religious and ritualistic knowledge flowed from the capital to the outskirts of Egyptian society. Provinces began to retain their own specialist professionals and artisans, and their own local produce, rather than allowing these to be exploited by the royal court. The production of local arts and crafts, as well as locally controlled government, led to economically and culturally more complex rural centers.

capital city. Provincial governors were loyal to the capital for many reasons, including their dependence on the king for income and other resources. The centralized governing style of the Old Kingdom meant that little of the monumental architecture or cultural achievements seen in the capital were found in regional centers. This, in

Left **Agricultural methods.** Agriculture remains a mainstay of the Egyptian economy, and while modern-day Egypt has embraced many technological advances in agricultural techniques, there are also methods still in use that remain relatively unchanged from the time of the ancient Egyptians.

BURIALS AND TOMBS: DEMOCRACY IN DEATH

The bulk of archeological information on all periods of Egyptian history comes to us through their cemeteries. In the First Intermediate Period there is a notable change in both the size and number of cemeteries and tombs. The increase in numbers could be for a variety of reasons, but the two most common theories are that either the stable conditions during the Old Kingdom led to a population explosion, or that there was a major population growth during the First Intermediate Period as a result of more efficient use of local resources.

The changes in the sizes of tombs has been called the "democratization of the afterlife"— an opportunity for the general population to utilize burial elements traditionally reserved for the very wealthy or royalty. A good example of this "democratization" is the marked increase

in specially made tomb artefacts, whereas during the Old Kingdom the graves of the lower classes contained artefacts used during the life of the tomb owner. While the use of non-functional tomb objects is not new in Egypt, it is the first time that they appear in the tombs of the non-elite. The appearance of these objects indicates that both the demand and the finances of the general population were enough to warrant and support a class of craftsmen specializing in "non-functional" items. These non-functional artefacts vary from boats, workshop scenes, and mummy masks, to wooden representations of people known as shabti figurines.

Below **Stela of Iri, First Intermediate Period.** The importance of the afterlife in Egyptian culture is celebrated on this limestone stela, which portrays a young couple presenting offerings to a deceased couple.

Crises and Opportunities

While the First Intermediate Period appears to have been a time of unrest for Egypt's rulers, it presented a unique opportunity for nomarchs, or provincial governors, to establish their own regions of dominance.

Opposite page **Model granary, First Intermediate Period.** Striving for self-sufficiency in the nome, nomarchs sought to control local resources. Grain crops—such as barley and emmer—were harvested and stored in granaries.

Below **Training the militia.** This fresco from Beni Hasan, Upper Egypt, shows soldiers undergoing the rigors of military training.

That the nomarchs were extremely influential and powerful figures can be seen in the autobiographical and biographical inscriptions in tombs from this period, where feats of heroic humanitarian deeds and military prowess are emphasized. While these inscriptions may be biased, it is certain that some of the recorded events took place, although perhaps not in circumstances as glorious as those described.

The Role of the Nomarch

Nomarchs were appointed for leadership as early as the Fifth Dynasty. Like other branches of administration in ancient Egypt, the position of nomarch was hereditary—a process that led to the development of powerful local families.

Nomarchs established residency in their ruling district, where they controlled the administration of the resources of the area, were responsible for the nome militia, and assisted the population on behalf of the king.

The placement of the nomarch away from the capital and in a rural center was a break away from the traditional form of centralized rule, and while it is likely that the move was intended to enhance the efficiency of provincial administration, it indicated a change in the socio-economic patterns fundamental to the existing system. In effect, this change also gave the nomarch access to the resources available within his territory, which in turn could be transformed into power over the local population.

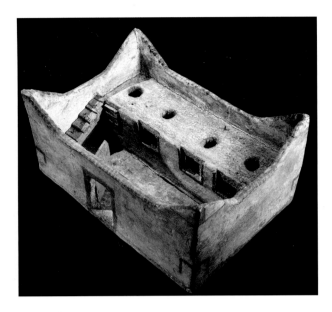

Not only were the nomarchs responsible for administration and the militia, they were also entrusted with the well-being of the population. There are some accounts from nomarchs (Ankhtifi in particular) of caring for their population by feeding and clothing them while the rest of Egypt was starving. This has led to speculation as to the environmental conditions in Egypt at this time, and whether falling Nile floods resulted in mass famine as described in the accounts of Ankhtifi. Regardless of whether natural events were the cause of a famine, at a time of conflict such as this it would have been extremely difficult for farmers to tend to their crops—many of the men would have been conscripted to fight in the nome militia; furthermore, raiding armies often burnt the crops of their enemies.

Militias—the New Heroes

Throughout the Old Kingdom, the central administration had relied on nomarchs to organize the population within their nome for military service and/or expeditions. During the First Intermediate Period, the military experience of the nomarchs and the loyalty of their troops emerged as a decisive factor in struggles for ascendancy. From tomb inscriptions and graffiti, we are aware that nomarchs were loyal to either the rulers of the north or the south and that they were active in campaigning for victory against the opposing force. One of the most well-known accounts about the role of the nomarch in the battle for supremacy is that of Ankhtifi, a nomarch loyal to the Herakleopolitan rulers, who recorded his autobiography on the walls of his tomb, recounting a military campaign against the Thebans.

ANKHTIFI

Ankhtifi was a nomarch during the earlier part of the Herakleopolitan rule of Egypt. We know about him as a result of his rock tomb situated near el-Moalla and the autobiographical text that is inscribed in its pillars. While biased, this text does provide us with an ideal guide to the biggest issues of the First Intermediate Period, as well as an idea of the political atmosphere of Upper Egypt at this time.

In his autobiography Ankhtifi tells us that he was active in restoring peace and order to the nome of Edfu, and that in sympathy with the Herakleopolitan rulers he led a military campaign against the Theban rulers. He also claims that during a time of great famine and disorder he was responsible for feeding the hungry and clothing the naked.

From texts of this period, economic crises appear as one of the great issues, and it was not uncommon for nomarchs to take advantage of a bad situation in order to legitimize their power.

Crises had evidently become socially significant as a context in which personal power and independence could be legitimized, and this observation probably helps us to understand why the issues of famine and sustenance were so pivotal in Ankhtifi's autobiography.

One of the most interesting aspects of the war narrative in Ankhtifi's autobiography is the absence of any mention of the king, and it would appear that at this time the king was not mentioned, even in passing, as an authority to control the distribution of power. The absence of the king in such a text demonstrates the shift away from the traditions of the Old Kingdom, where the king had been the sole source of legitimate authority. Under Old Kingdom leadership, all actions of the nomarchs relied on the king's command. At the conclusion of the Old Kingdom, when the power of kingship faded, a more open situation emerged in which local rulers could act in accordance with their own aims. The nomarchs began to rely on their own power bases, and their sole concern was to defend their position from other nomarchs. The rivalry between nomarchs means that often successes are over-emphasized in order to legitimize a familial power base. Ankhtifi's autobiography must therefore be considered very carefully within the context of its time and in light of other material evidence.

Below **Tomb of Ankhtifi at el-Moalla.** The inscriptions on Ankhtifi's tomb have provided an informative, though biased, insight into events of the time.

The Herakleopolitans

In times of battle it is the winner who writes the history. For the Herakleopolitans, their loss to the Theban dynasty means that little is known about the kings who made up the Herakleopolitan dynasty and ruled for a period of probably around 185 years.

According to Manetho, the Herakleopolitan dynasty was established by King Khety, a fact that is confirmed with inscriptions referring to the kingdom in the north as the "house of Khety." What is not known is where Khety came from, or how he came to take power at the end of the Old Kingdom.

Position, Position, Position...

The Herakleopolitan rulers derive their name from their seat of power, Herakleopolis Magna, a city in the north of Egypt that was situated in an important strategic position, acting as the gateway from north to south. The Herakleopolitan province, protected from northern invaders by its geographical position, had derived great benefit from the increase in trade as a result of the colonization of Nubia. All the Herakleopolitan rulers appear to have ruled from Herakleopolis Magna, although the final ruler of the dynasty is buried in the ancient royal necropolis of Saqqara, indicating that they probably thought of themselves as within the tradition of Memphite rulers. The fact that several of the early rulers took on the name of Pepy II, last king of the Old Kingdom, supports this idea, and it has been suggested that the first kings of the Herakleopolitan dynasty were sons or grandsons of Pepy II.

Lack of monumental architecture for the Herakleopolitan dynasty has been interpreted as indicating a failure by the kings in establishing a powerful centralized system in the style of the Old Kingdom state. However, the lack of evidence may simply represent a gap in the knowledge of this area of Egyptian archeology. A greater part of the information available regarding the Herakleopolitans comes from monuments constructed by private individuals. The epigraphic evidence exists mostly as biographical inscriptions centering on the war between the Thebans and the Herakleopolitans from the tombs of the "overseers of priests" at Asyut. The evidence from Asyut is important, as it later emerged as a significant military stronghold in Upper Egypt during the later part of the Herakleopolitan reign.

Powerful Connections

The Asyut texts mention the king in some detail, and a strong connection appears between these "overseers of priests" and the king, with some claiming close personal ties and aristocratic connections. This would seem to indicate that the Herakleopolitan kings relied on nomarchs who could be trusted to remain loyal to the king on the basis of close personal connections. Regardless of their loyalty to the king, the nomarchs regarded their nomes as their primary concern, and it was here that their true loyalty lay.

Below **Fresco of agricultural workers carrying grain, from the tomb of Iti at Gebelein, First Intermediate Period.** Famine was an ever-present threat as the floodwaters of the Nile became increasingly unreliable. In successful seasons, the toil and hardship of sowing and harvesting were rewarded with a bountiful harvest.

Cultural Development

Archeologically, there is difficulty in establishing whether the Herakleopolitan dynasty is to be considered a new cultural entity, mainly due to the lack of key groups of material that can be firmly dated in dynastic terms. What the archeological evidence does present is evidence for the simultaneous development of material culture in the north and south of Egypt. The Herakleopolitan populations were buried with similar objects to the populations of the south—objects such as wooden models of servants and workshops and cartonnage masks.

Judging from the archeological evidence, the Herakleopolitan communities appear to have undergone similar patterns of social and cultural development to the rest of the country. The major difference in material culture lies in the shapes of pottery vessels, with vessels manufactured in the north during the First Intermediate Period adhering more closely to the Old Kingdom tradition than those manufactured in the south.

Left **An array of weapons among the funerary items of Chancellor Nakhty, 11th Dynasty.** Conflict was rife during the First Intermediate Period, as rivalry between nomes frequently escalated into military action in a bid for control of all Egypt.

INSTRUCTION TO KING MERYKARA

The reputation of the First Intermediate Period as one of political, cultural, and intellectual obscurity and decline is false, with written evidence in particular indicating that quite the opposite occurred. Resulting from the turmoil of the period, the Egyptian population was forced to deal with the collapse of some of the most fundamental principles of their society and to reconsider their position within the universe. The decline of royal power, and the hostilities that waged for control and rule of Egypt further served to weaken the image of divine power and Egyptian royalty. The State was no longer present to protect the population, leaving them unprotected and exposed to violence, famine, and social upheaval. The resulting anguish is distinguishable in the literary works of the First Intermediate Period, which demonstrate an almost unparalleled level of pessimism in all genres of work.

One of the most well-known Herakleopolitan texts is *The Instruction of Merykara*. This text is dated to the Herakleopolitan period, as its author is thought to have been the predecessor of the Herakleopolitan king Merykara—probably Khety III. The text is known from three remaining incomplete copies made in the Eighteenth Dynasty, and the fact that this text was copied on multiple occasions indicates the esteem in which it was held. In the instruction, Khety III passes on to his son the secrets of success in life and work. Apart from reproducing the stereotypes of literature of this time, Merykara's instruction is characterized by a total honesty on the part of the king, who does not hesitate to acknowledge his own errors, and encourages his son to look after his nobles and officials in order to avoid any further confrontations. The text is quite valuable in the context of Herakleopolitan studies, as there is so little other information relating directly to the kings of this dynasty.

Right **Writing materials.** Besides papyrus, the ancient Egyptians used a range of materials for writing and record-keeping, from bone to pottery fragments (ostraca).

The Rise of Thebes

During the First Intermediate Period, one of Egypt's most famous cities, Thebes, began to play a pivotal role in the country's history. The God Montu was the most important deity of the region.

Right **Terracotta offering bowl, inscribed with a letter from a mother to her deceased son, Thebes, First Intermediate Period.** The importance of Thebes gained momentum during the First Intermediate Period. Though remains of the time are limited, those that have been discovered give us a glimpse of life in Thebes.

While the Thebans of the First Intermediate Period did not control as much of the country as the Herakleopolitans, they left behind many more remains. Our knowledge of Thebes during this period, however, still remains rather scanty.

A nomarch named Intef ruled the Theban nome and oversaw its priests. He also called himself "king's confidante at the narrow gateway to the south" and "great overlord of Upper Egypt," and probably controlled an area as far north as Dendera. Intef was considered to be the ancestor of the Eleventh Dynasty, and later Senusret I dedicated a statue in his honor at Karnak

Temple. Intef was followed by Mentuhotep I—who was post-humously designated a king on a statue dedicated to him hundreds of year later—and Mentuhotep's son Sehertawy Intef I, the founder of the Eleventh Dynasty. Sehertawy Intef I rebelled against Herakleopolitan control, and declared himself king. He was recognized as such in the First through Sixth Nomes.

Intef II fought against the Herakleopolitan rulers Khety II and Merykara. He was succeeded by Nakhtnebtepnefer Intef III, probably his son, about whom very little is known due to the scantiness of remains, although he seems to have maintained control of the regions conquered by

WAHANKH INTEF II

Wahankh Intef II, the brother of his predecessor Intef I, ruled for fifty years. He called himself King of Upper and Lower Egypt and Son of Ra, titles implying that he had a divine mandate to rule all of Egypt. During his reign, he carried out military campaigns and extended Theban control southward to Elephantine and northward to the southern boundary of Asyut, recapturing Abydos and releasing prisoners from its prisons.

Intef II re-established the royal tradition of patronage of the temples through his building projects. Remains of his monuments have been found at Karnak (the earliest remains found there),

and he erected chapels of Satet and Khnum c Elephantine, in the First Nome.

Intef II must have been a dog lover, for he left a stela in front of his saff tomb depicting himself and five of his hunting dogs.

Right **Statue of ram-headed god Khnum.** At Elephantine, Wahankh Intef II erected a chapel to honor Khnum, a god associated with creation and the Nile floods.

his predecessors. He was succeeded by a man who was probably his eldest son, Nebhepetra Mentuhotep II, who would finally reunite Egypt.

Officials of the Time

The Theban rulers were able to gain control of a larger area of Egypt through the work of a number of faithful officials. A general named Djary led the fight against the Herakleopolitans and their king, Khety, taking the city of Thinis, until then a bastion of the Herakleopolitan nome, and extending Theban control to the Tenth Nome. The battle at Abydos may have taken place in the local cemetery, resulting in the destruction of several tombs. However, Djary was subsequently given the task of revitalizing the ten nomes then under the rule of Wahankh Intef II, who provided ships for carrying out this mission. Hetepy was a skilled administrator of the three southernmost nomes under Intef II. The treasurer Tjetjy was taken into the confidence of Intef II and continued to serve under his son.

Saff Tombs

At the northern end of the Theban necropolis at al-Tarif, across from Karnak, which later was to grow into the biggest temple complex, a new type of tomb was developed in the First Intermediate Period. Known as saff tombs (from the Arabic word meaning "row"), they consisted of a long, wide, sloping courtyard cut into gravel and marl at the lower edge of the desert, at the rear of which was a facade consisting of a row of pillars (hence their name). Beyond this facade, carved into the cliffs, were offering chambers and burial crypts. An inspection carried out 1,000 years later in the Twentieth Dynasty indicates that there were remains that suggested that the tombs may have been topped with pyramidal structures, but no remains of them are found today.

Many private individuals built such tombs, but the largest of all was possibly constructed for King Intef I, and is known as the Saff Dawaba. The courtyard was surrounded by burials of his followers. His successors also built saff tombs.

Left **Ruins of Thebes by Karl Richard Lepsius (1810–1884).** The ruins of the once-powerful city of Thebes are captured in this evocative 1842 image.

The Battle for Supremacy

The battle for supremacy began when a dynasty of rulers from Herakleopolis Magna took control of Egypt toward the end of the Old Kingdom. They faced immense opposition, but none greater or more dangerous than that from a dynasty of rulers from Thebes.

Right **Wooden votive figurine, 11th Dynasty.** Bitter enemies in the struggle for power, the Herakleopolitans and the Thebans battled sporadically for almost a century. As an added measure to their arsenal, figurines such as the one pictured here, which represents an enemy, were used in magic rituals.

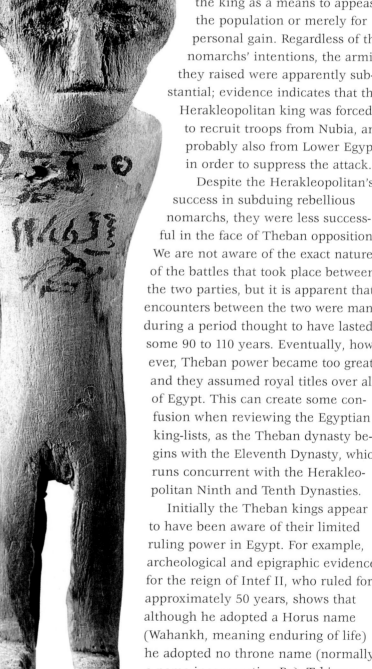

Evidence indicates that the Herakleopolitans incorporated the name of Pepy II, the last Old Kingdom king, into their own, in an attempt to legitimize their power or perhaps because they were truly Pepy II's descendants.

The Adversaries of the Herakleopolitan Dynasties

The history of this period is not clear, however there are some epigraphic sources that provide us with a picture of what the First Intermediate Period may have been like as the power and influence of the Theban nomarchs increased into supremacy over the Herakleopolitans, and eventually Egypt. One of the earliest records of hostilities between the two competing dynasties comes from the tomb of the nomarch Ankhtifi at el-Moalla. In his autobiography, Ankhtifi writes that he is loyal to Neferkara (who was perhaps the third ruler of the Herakleopolitan Ninth Dynasty), and that he campaigned with his own militia on behalf of the king against the rebellious nomarchs of Thebes and Koptos in the south of Egypt.

Probably a short time after the campaign recorded by Ankhtifi, a band of nomarchs from Middle Egypt also rose up against the Herakleopolitans. Graffiti found at the Hatnub quarries bears testament to the longstanding dissatisfaction with the Herakleopolitan ruler at this time. Unfortunately, although these texts are quite vocal in their dissatisfaction with the king, they do not name him. It is debatable as to whether the nomarchs of Middle Egypt rose up against the king as a means to appease the population or merely for personal gain. Regardless of the nomarchs' intentions, the armies they raised were apparently substantial; evidence indicates that the Herakleopolitan king was forced to recruit troops from Nubia, and probably also from Lower Egypt, in order to suppress the attack.

Despite the Herakleopolitan's success in subduing rebellious nomarchs, they were less successful in the face of Theban opposition. We are not aware of the exact nature of the battles that took place between the two parties, but it is apparent that encounters between the two were many during a period thought to have lasted some 90 to 110 years. Eventually, however, Theban power became too great and they assumed royal titles over all of Egypt. This can create some confusion when reviewing the Egyptian king-lists, as the Theban dynasty begins with the Eleventh Dynasty, which runs concurrent with the Herakleopolitan Ninth and Tenth Dynasties.

Initially the Theban kings appear to have been aware of their limited ruling power in Egypt. For example, archeological and epigraphic evidence for the reign of Intef II, who ruled for approximately 50 years, shows that although he adopted a Horus name (Wahankh, meaning enduring of life) he adopted no throne name (normally a name incorporating Ra). Taking a throne name would have indicated a strong belief in divine kingship and hereditary power. Unfortunately few

representations of Intef II have survived, making it impossible for us to know whether he adopted symbols of kingship on his statuary.

The most valuable piece of evidence from the reign of Intef II is his biographical stela, which recounts his openly hostile policy toward the Herakleopolitan kings in Abydos. Intef II's biography also details what can only be described as an extremely expansionist policy regarding Upper Egypt. The combination of these two activities led to what appears to have been as many as several decades of war in a relatively small region between Abydos and Asyut. There is a record of at least one counter-attack by the Herakleopolitans on a fragmentary inscription from the tomb of an "overseer of priests," Ity-yeb, in Asyut. However, an inscription from the tomb of the son of Ity-yeb demonstrates that any success achieved by the Herakleopolitans against the Thebans was short lived.

The Demise of Herakleopolitan Rule

Unfortunately no records remain detailing how the Herakleopolitans were finally defeated by the Thebans. However, there are a number of instances where we are able to fill in some of the blanks. For example, given the strategic importance of the town of Asyut for both of the warring parties, and the fact that the name of the ruling nomarch and his family disappears after Theban unification, it seems likely that Asyut was taken with some force.

After the collapse of Asyut, Herakleopolitan rule appears to not have lasted for much longer and, from this time on, Theban power dominates and the process of unification of Upper and Lower Egypt commences.

Above **Limestone stela of Wahankh Intef II (2112–2063 BCE), 11th Dynasty.** Details of the victories of Wahankh Intef II are depicted on this stela outside his tomb at el-Tarif.

Left **Head of wooden statue of Chancellor Nakhty, 10th Dynasty.** This impressive statue of Chancellor Nakhty was discovered in his tomb at Asyut. The town was the setting for many years of war between the Thebans and the Herakleopolitans, and finally fell to the victorious Theban forces.

The Two Lands Reunited

The son and successor of Intef III, Mentuhotep II, was one of the most important kings of ancient Egypt and the founder of a new era. He unified the country after many years of fighting and the politically unstable First Intermediate Period.

Mentuhotep II is therefore the first king of the Middle Kingdom, the classical period of Egyptian history. Despite his importance, there are amazingly few facts preserved about his reign and its most important political event. It is even not yet known with accuracy at what point during his reign that the reunification occurred. Nor is it certain that this was one single event, such as the conquest of the northern capital, or whether it comprised a more complex sequence of episodes. All references to it are indirect and in recent years some researchers have even proposed that the final unification was a peaceful, rather than a military, event.

What's in a Name?

One of the most important indications for Mentuhotep II as unifier of Egypt is the naming of the king. During the course of his reign the king changed his royal names at least twice. This caused some confusion among earlier researchers, they assigned each set of names to a separate king. Nowadays, it is generally agreed that these names refer to one person, and that they reflect different stages in his status as ruler over parts of, and then the whole country.

In the last part of his reign, the Horus name of Mentuhotep II was as the "unifier of the two lands." The Horus name was the oldest part of the royal titulary, and certainly its most formal element. It identified the king as Horus on earth, and it seems significant that the king changed this name.

It should also be noted that only in the closing years of his reign did Mentuhotep II bear the full royal titulary, consisting of five names, while at the beginning he had only two names. This full titulary might express his status as ruler over the whole of Egypt.

Below **Stela of Irtysen, a sculptor during the reign of Mentuhotep II.** The rebuilding process of a united Egypt during the reign of Mentuhotep II saw artisans drawn away from their home base to building projects where their skills were in demand.

MEKETRA'S TOMB

By the early Middle Kingdom, painted wooden models depicting daily life replaced earlier paintings and reliefs found in noblemen's tombs.

Discovered in 1920 by American archeologist Herbert Winlock on the west wank of Thebes, Meketra's tomb contained an undisturbed chamber with the finest and most extensive set of painted and gessoed wooden models (twenty-four in total) ever found, giving a glimpse of life on Meketra's estate.

Two of the models depict a house fronted by a pillared porch and rain gutters alongside a lush garden of trees surrounding a pond.

Other models show servants dressed in real linen garments, brewing beer and baking bread, spinning and weaving, carpentry, cattle breeding, and butchery.

Meketra's work as "treasurer of the king of Lower Egypt" took him up and down the Nile, and models depicted his traveling boat, his pleasure yacht, his skiff for hunting birds and fishing, fishing canoes, and a kitchen tender for meal preparation, all made with riggings of real twine. There were also models of servants bringing the goods that Meketra needed in the afterlife to his tomb.

In addition to this limited evidence there are also some signs of military actions under the king, which might relate to wars against the north. On a stela of a private man, called Intef, datable to the early years of the reign of Mentuhotep II, is mentioned a "year of a rebellion in Thinis"— clearly a reference to a civil war. Another official, named Henenu, said in his biographical inscription found on a stela in his tomb that "he suppressed the South, North, East and the West."

On the decoration of a small chapel set up by the king at Dendera, the place where the goddess Hathor was worshipped, the king is shown in a unique scene smiting two plant stems, which seem to symbolize Upper and Lower Egypt. Beneath this main scene, two gods are depicted, at least one with a falcon head, performing the "unification of Upper

and Lower Egypt." The scene belongs to the standard program of royal temples of all periods. The "unification of Upper and Lower Egypt" was one of the symbolic tasks carried out by the king when he started his reign. On an annals stone of the Old Kingdom this event describes the beginning of a new reign. However, in the case of Mentuhotep II we would like to see this symbolism as referring to his main achievement, the reunification of Egypt.

Other evidence of the reunification comes from the arts. With the founding of a new unified Egypt the king started a huge building program, and for this he certainly needed more artists

than were available in Upper Egypt and there is indeed enough evidence that craftsmen and artists from Memphis appeared now in the south in Thebes. This only seems possible because the king ruled over the north.

King Mentuhotep II is certainly one of the most important Egyptian kings. However, his reign exemplifies how little we know about certain political events. The formation of a new Egyptian state at the end of the Third Millennium BCE is still a big open question and we will only know more about it when, in the future, more sources—such as biographical inscriptions—come to light.

Above **Detail of palace facade, on limestone sarcophagus found at Deir el-Bahri, 11th Dynasty.** To date, few remains of the First Intermediate Period have been found. Inscriptions on remains such as this limestone sarcophagus hold vital clues to events, people, and places of the time.

THE MIDDLE KINGDOM
Nebhepetra Mentuhotep II

Ancient Egyptians of later periods regarded King Nebhepetra Mentuhotep II as one of their most important kings. Scenes in later temples and tombs depict Mentuhotep II in the company of the great Egyptian rulers, King Menes and King Ahmose.

The three kings, Menes, Mentuhotep II and Ahmose were each the founder of one classical period. Menes was regarded as the first Egyptian king of all. Ahmose was the founder of the New Kingdom and the king who defeated the Hyksos. Nebhepetra Mentuhotep II is evidently regarded as the creator of the Middle Kingdom. Despite his importance to the Egyptians and his long reign of fifty-one years, surprisingly few facts are known about King Mentuhotep II. The exact date of his reunification of Egypt is uncertain. Mentuhotep II was the son of Wahankh Intef III and of the "king's mother" Iah. His main wife was Tem, who also had the title "king's mother" Tem, bore him his successor, Sankhkara Mentuhotep III.

Reinstating the Vizier
With Egypt reunited, the king faced the task of stabilizing and reorganizing the whole country. This is most clearly visible in the administration and the building program of Mentuhotep II. Prior to his reign, the organization of the royal court of the Eleventh Dynasty seems to have been based

Right **King Mentuhotep II (2055–2004 BCE)**. This king conducted several military campaigns against foreign countries. In this limestone relief the king is shown wearing the white crown of Upper Egypt and holding a mace. He is subjugating a foreign enemy, probably a Libyan.

on the model of a provincial court or perhaps just that of a private household. Mentuhotep II introduced new administrative positions that were more appropriate for running a country the size of Egypt. The most important of these positions was the office of vizier. Head of the state administration during the Old Kingdom, the vizier again became second only to the king in importance.

Building a New Future

Mentuhotep II also launched a monumental building program on a far larger scale than is known for any previous ruler in the dynasty. Each king of the Old Kingdom had concentrated construction activities, almost exclusively, on his pyramid complex. If the surviving monuments offer a reliable guide, this policy changed dramatically in the Middle Kingdom. Blocks with the name of the king carved in finest relief have been found at all major temples in Upper Egypt, demonstrating that the king renovated or even rebuilt a series of provincial temples. For this task the king needed teams of trained artists and craftsmen, more than would have been available in Thebes, his capital at this time. Some workers are known to have arrived from the North, where they had worked before for the Herakleopolitan kings, and there must have been many more.

Military Might

As the first king in perhaps a hundred years to rule all Egypt, Mentuhotep II conducted several military campaigns against foreign countries, doubtless to demonstrate his new power. In the tomb of Intef, the king's general, the siege of an Asiatic fortress is depicted, indicating that the king campaigned in Asia, most likely in South Palestine. Rock inscriptions in Lower Nubia imply that military action took place in the South. This area was especially important for its raw materials, notably gold.

He Who United Two Countries

In his long reign, Mentuhotep II changed his royal titulary several times. His royal names clearly reveal the political program of an Egyptian king. At the beginning of his reign he was called Horus: Seankhibtawy Mentuhotep, but at some later date he became the first king of the Eleventh Dynasty to acquire a throne name: Nebhepetra. He changed his Horus name after or during the unification of the country into Horus: Sematawy—"who united the two countries."

MENTUHOTEP'S QUEENS

We know the queens of King Nebhepetra Mentuhotep II primarily from their burials in the funerary complex of the king at Deir el-Bahri. Some of their tombs, found intact, were equipped with very beautiful sarcophagi, coffins and jewelry. The principal queen was a woman called Tem, who bore the title "king's mother" to denote her elevated status as mother of his successor. Tem is of non-royal origin, unlike Neferu, the sister of the king, who had a beautiful rock-cut tomb next to the funerary temple of Mentuhotep II. There is no evidence that Neferu and Mentuhotep II had children. This marriage might have been purely formal, perhaps reinforcing the divine status of the king. Inside the king's funerary complex a further six women were buried. Five of the women had the title "king's wife". Unlike other queens, these women were also styled "priestess of Hathor," giving the impression that they formed a kind of divine harem around the ruler. Above their burials there were chapels with scenes depicting the women together with their king and bearing the title "king's wife". Three— Ashait, Kawit, and Kemsit—also had sarcophagi decorated on the outside in relief, but this time the women were shown without the king and without the title "king's wife."

Right **Ashait, a royal lady of the court of Mentuhotep II**. Limestone relief from Ashait's sarcophagus at Deir el-Bahri.

A Monument for a Great King

As the reunifier of Egypt, Nebhepetra Mentuhotep II constructed for his own eternal cult a funerary complex on a suitably magnificent scale. His monument would stand the test of time and inspire the architects of Hatshepsut some 600 years later.

His Eleventh Dynasty predecessors had been buried in large colonnaded tombs that were carved out of the gently sloping rock-face in Thebes West. This type of tomb is known as a "*saff* tomb." Though impressive structures, these *saff* tombs were evidently not regarded as distinctive enough for a great king of Egypt.

Below **Temple of Mentuhotep II (2055–2004 BCE)**. This impressive funerary complex was constructed near Thebes at Deir el-Bahri.

Mentuhotep II Funerary Complex
Nebhepetra Mentuhotep II chose a new burial ground not far away, but closer to the high-rising Theban mountains. The mountains provided an appropriate setting for Mentuhotep II's funerary complex, at a place now called Deir-el Bahri.

His unique building was erected in several phases. At its core was a platform adorned at the front with square columns. On top of this platform was a second smaller one, this time adorned all around with columns, and reached by an impressive ramp. This second platform was crowned by a structure of unknown shape. Most likely it was a pyramid shape, as Ramesside

documents end the name of the complex with a pyramid-sign. However, some Egyptologists have argued that there was a third platform. Six chapels of royal women, who were buried in shaft tombs beneath, were found at the back of the second platform, between the columns.

Behind the core building, directly in front of the mountain rock-face, a broad courtyard, also adorned with columns, led to a great hall with eighty columns. This is Egypt's oldest such columned hall. At its end stood a statue of the king in a rock-cut niche.

The Earliest Human-shaped Coffin

The burial chamber of the king was reached via a 492 ft (150 m) long tunnel which started in the middle of the courtyard, where there was also an offering table or a related structure. The burial chamber at the end of the tunnel lay about 148 ft (45 m) beneath the level of the courtyard. The chamber was almost entirely filled by an alabaster shrine. The chamber had already been looted in antiquity, but it still contained the remains of a wooden coffin and of canopic jars. The coffins are the oldest examples from Egypt that feature a human-shaped lid. Curiously, another chamber lay beneath the temple, reached via another long corridor starting under the great courtyard in front of the temple. This second chamber contained a wooden coffin, inscribed with the name of the king. Beside it was a statue of the king, depicting him as black-skinned, wrapped in linen. This is evidently a ritual burial, but its precise function and meaning remain obscure. One proposal is that this place was originally intended for the king's burial, but was used as ritual statue burial when the king decided to be buried elsewhere.

The Symbolism of Reunification

The great open courtyard in front of the temple building was adorned with trees and with statues depicting the king. The entire complex was surrounded by two walls and could be entered via a broad open causeway coming from the east, where there must have been a valley temple, now totally lost. The main building was richly decorated with reliefs. Only fragments are preserved. They show parts of battle scenes, depictions of the king among the gods, and processions of courtiers identified by title and name. The funerary complex of Mentuhotep II combined Upper and Lower Egyptian elements, and was evidently charged with the symbolism of reunification. The crowning structure in the middle (the pyramid) seems to follow Lower Egyptian traditions, while the long rows of columns at the front are borrowed from the *saff* tombs of Mentuhotep II's predecessors, a typical Upper Egyptian tomb type.

Tombs of the Courtiers

Around this funerary complex, mostly carved into the cliff-face, were the tombs of the king's courtiers. The tomb of the king's general, Intef, was decorated with paintings and reliefs. The tomb of Khety, decorated throughout with fine reliefs, included depictions of the king in the tomb of a private individual—for the first time in Egyptian history. Khety is known from many sources and seems to have had an exceptionally important position under Mentuhotep II. In some reliefs in a desert valley (Shatt er-Rigal) he is shown together with the royal family, and he was also involved in the sed-festival—the royal jubilee—celebrated after thirty years of the king's reign.

One of the successors of Mentuhotep II started a similar mortuary temple on an impressive scale a little farther south from Deir el-Bahri. However, this site was abandoned at an early stage of construction, leaving the complex of Mentuhotep II as a unique finished complex in the history of Egyptian architecture.

Right **Mentuhotep II.**
The king wears the double
crown of Upper and Lower
Egypt and a white jubilee
robe in this painted
sandstone statue.

The Foundation of Itj-tawy

Amenemhet I left Thebes, and chose another site for his capital and final resting-place. He founded Itj-tawy at the border between Upper and Lower Egypt, the point that Egyptians regarded as the geographical center of their country.

Right **Limestone relief depicting Senusret I in the protective embrace of the god Ptah (c. 1918–1875 BCE)**. Senusret I succeeded Amenemhet I as king.

Sehetepibra Amenemhet I is the first king of the Twelfth Dynasty. He held already the powerful position of vizier during the reign of Nebtawyra Mentuhotep IV, last ruler of the Eleventh Dynasty. As the vizier he was mentioned in a number of rock inscriptions at the Wadi Hammamat. He had guided an expedition of 10,000 men to the area to quarry stone for the king's sarcophagus. How a vizier finally managed to become Sehetepibra Amenemhet I, king of Egypt, is not yet known, but it seems possible that his expedition of 10,000 men is directly linked to his rise to power. Little is known about the first years of his reign, but Amenemhet I may be the king who started a huge funerary complex at Thebes similar in style and size to the complex of Nebhepetra Mentuhotep II. This site was left unfinished at an early stage.

Establishing a New Capital

The reason the king chose Itj-tawy for his capital and final resting-place is unknown. One explanation is that Thebes lies too deep in the south of Egypt to act efficiently as capital of the country, as it is so far from all other major centers. Memphis is much more suitably positioned, close to the economically important fertile Delta plain, and to the main trading routes to Asia. In the Middle Kingdom, connections with northern neighbors became increasingly important, so it comes as no surprise that Amenemhet I moved north. There is evidence that initially he tried to establish his capital at Memphis, but, for reasons unknown, in about the twentieth year of his reign, he built a totally new city named "Amenemhet, Seizer of the Two Lands." Amenemhet-itj-tawy is generally abbreviated to the name Itj-tawy.

Below **Abandoned stone coffin lid (from the Middle Kingdom)**. The site of the ancient capital, Itj-tawy, has never been located.

As well as being situated near the border of Upper and Lower Egypt, the new capital was approximately 13 miles (20 km) south of Memphis, a sufficient distance for it to function as an independent urban center. Its location demonstrated that Amenemhet I was the real ruler of both halves of Egypt. This must have been important to him, as several works of literature and contemporary inscriptions of officials indicate that the king had to fight against enemies within his own country during civil disturbances. With the foundation of a new city, the king might have sought to disarm or to deflect many of his enemies. In the low desert close to Itj-tawy the king built his pyramid and his officials erected their tombs.

Old Kingdom Influence

With the foundation of this new capital, the culture of Egypt changed and the court came under intense Memphite influence. In Memphis, the traditions of the Old Kingdom were still very strong, even at the end of the First Intermediate Period. Craftsmen and artists worked in age-old traditions, using the models that had been passed down the centuries. For his funerary complex in particular, Amenemhet I adopted Old Kingdom forms. This is most obviously visible in the pyramid, which self-evidently resumed Old Kingdom practice, rather than continuing the more recent Theban architectural developments.

The Glory of Itj-tawy

Itj-tawy very quickly became the most important cultural and political center and would remain so throughout the period of the Middle Kingdom. Under Amenemhet I's successor, Senusret I, the city generated its own style and influenced the rest of Egypt. This influence is even evident in more mundane object types such as pottery vessels. New coffin styles were first modeled in Itj-tawy then copied in other parts of Egypt.

A very interesting indicator for the art production in the city during the Thirteenth Dynasty comes from Hierakonpolis, a town far in the south. The stela of a local priest of Horus, named Horemkhauf, records that the priest made a journey to Itj-tawy to collect, in front of the king, a new image of the god Horus for the temple at Hierakonpolis. Even in the Thirteenth Dynasty the king of Egypt resided in the city of Itj-tawy and the royal workshop there still produced items for the whole country.

The Lost City

Almost nothing is known about the capital city of Itj-tawy and its architecture, palaces, and temples. Even its exact geographical position was for a long time under discussion.

The site of el-Lisht is likely to be the closest location to the lost city, as the cemeteries there teem with tombs from all periods of the Middle Kingdom and all social levels, rich and poor. This wide range of tombs only makes sense if there was a major population center in the area. The name of Itj-tawy is often written in hieroglyphic script with the sign of a fortress, indicating that at least one quarter of the city was fortified, perhaps the palace and the administrative offices. After the Thirteenth Dynasty, Itj-tawy lost its importance forever. More than one thousand years later it is mentioned on the stela of Piy. Under the Romans "Itj-tawy" still could mean "capital" in hieroglyphic inscriptions, but by then the capital was Rome and the old glory of Itj-tawy was long gone.

Above **Painted limestone statue of Senusret I.** Under this king, Itj-tawy developed its own style and influenced all Egypt.

Senusret in the Faiyum

King-lists suggest that Amenemhet I and his son Senusret I had a co-regency, reigning together for about ten years before Senusret I ruled for a further 33 years. They were the first Egyptian kings to reclaim and cultivate the Faiyum.

Right **Senusret I, son of Amenemhet I.** Co-regent then ruler during the Twelfth Dynasty, Senusret is depicted in this limestone statue from el-Lisht.

Amenemhet I had to confront many problems inside Egypt. In comparison, the reign of Senusret I seems to have been quite stable. However, two inscriptions refer to a big famine in the 25th year, and other sources imply disturbances, perhaps in connection with that starvation. Senusret I is best known for his amazing temple-building program, covering every region of Egypt. Under his son and successor, Amenemhet II, who also had a long and stable reign, Egypt flourished. Senusret II, most likely the son of Amenemhet II, reigned for less than a decade. Senusret II sited his pyramid at Lahun, at the entrance to the Faiyum, a highly significant choice of burial-place.

Below **Senusret II funerary complex (Twelfth Dynasty).** Senusret II built his pyramid at Lahun, at the entrance to the Faiyum. His burial-place was signficant; the Faiyum area was favored by the Twelfth Dynasty kings.

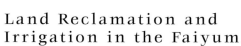

Land Reclamation and Irrigation in the Faiyum

The Faiyum is a large fertile basin just west of the Nile valley. This "river oasis" is fed from a side branch of the Nile, known today as the Bahr Yussef, that drains west into Lake Moeris, the Faiyum lake, that was once freshwater but is now saltwater.

The level of the lake varied over time, immediately impacting on the history of the area. In earlier times the lake was large, and the basin full of marshland, making it unfit for agriculture. In the Old Kingdom there is little evidence for settlements of any size in the Faiyum. Over time, Egypt needed more agricultural land to support its growing population. In the early part of the Old Kingdom such land seems to have been available in the Nile Valley itself, and marshland in the Nile Delta was being reclaimed for farming. However, by the end of the Old Kingdom the most accessible Delta marshes had probably been turned into farmland, so the Middle Kingdom kings had to look for new suitable land. It is possible that nature came to their aid with a massive drop in the level of the Faiyum lake. Unfortunately, agriculture in the Faiyum is not mentioned in Egyptian inscriptions, as these focus on pious donations to various deities, without describing the more practical side of ruling the country. Most of the evidence for the cultivation of the Faiyum is therefore indirect, deduced from the royal building activity there and accounts from much later sources.

Middle Kingdom Monuments

The crocodile god, Sobek, is one of the leading deities of Egypt, and his center of worship was Shedit, capital of the Faiyum. In the late Middle Kingdom he became one of the main gods of kingship, doubtless as a result of the rising importance of his province. However, the first steps of a cultivation program to reclaim the Faiyum basin might have been taken already

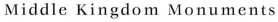

Right **Pillar from the temple of Senusret I.** This pillar or obelisk was erected at the king's temple in Heliopolis. It is known as the Northern Pillar and it became a cult center for the god Atum.

under Amenemhet I. His capital, Itj-tawy, is nearby, and the choice of location might have been influenced by this proximity. Other direct royal activity in this region took place under Senusret I.

Senusret I erected a monolithic round-topped pillar near Shedit. The pillar still stands today and its top is decorated with reliefs. The main royal monuments in the Faiyum bear the names of king Senusret II and king Amenemhet III, both buried at its edge.

An Artificial Lake?

Near the pyramid of Senusret II at Lahun, a great dyke cuts across the entrance to the Faiyum. This allows control of the inflowing waters of the Bahr Yussef, an important step towards efficient cultivation. However, although the dyke starts close to the pyramid of Senusret II, its date is uncertain: New geo-archeological investigation is needed to reveal this. About 1500 years later, Herodotus, the Greek writer, reported from his visit to Egypt that the Faiyum lake was artificial. He writes after describing the labyrinth:

"And even more wonderful is the lake Moeris...This lake has a circuit of three thousand six hundred furlongs or sixty schoeni...It has been dug out and created by the hand of men, as can been seen from the lake itself as there are two pyramids in its middle on top of it with a colossal stone figure seated on a throne."

The lower parts of these figures, known as the Biahmu colossi, still stand today. The figures depicted Amenemhet III, the king most prominent in this area. He was buried at the very edge of the Faiyum, in Hawara. Several temples in the region were built in his reign. The Biahmu colossi are enigmatic monuments, as there is no trace of a temple behind them.

After the Middle Kingdom, the Faiyum attracted little royal interest, except during Ptolemaic times, when numerous small towns flourished around the "oasis", with active cults for Sobek, and for the king who built the greatest monuments here, Amenemhet III.

Karnak and Amun

The Sun cult had dominated devotion in the Old Kingdom, yet by the New Kingdom the following of the deity Amun was clearly pre-eminent. The origins of this cult of Amun coincided with the rise of Karnak in the Middle Kingdom.

During the First Intermediate Period, the Old Kingdom base at Memphis disintegrated. A dynasty emerged that managed to displace the northern nomarchs, now little more than warlords. At the same time a new southern dynasty arose, based at Thebes (modern Karnak), capital of the fourth nome of Upper Egypt. Conflict between North and South erupted. Many casualties resulted, but at last the South was triumphant.

The Patron Deity of Thebes

With this Theban victory over the northern Herakleopolitan kingdom, a formerly obscure provincial town now shot into prominence. The king credited with the conquest of the North was Mentuhotep II. Through a series of engagements he managed to subdue the Herakleopolitans and reunite Egypt.

This political ascendancy eventually meant that the patron deity of Thebes, Amun, likewise became prominent, although this development did not happen immediately. For the interim period, Montu, a local war god, enjoyed royal patronage and the kings of this time bore the birth name Mentuhotep. Under the Twelfth Dynasty kings, however, Amun was combined with the Old Kingdom sun deity, Ra, as Amun-Ra. The Theban cult would dominate all Egypt in the following centuries. The New Kingdom kings built on the legacy and would elevate Amun in his own right.

Constructing a Southern Capital

The extent of Middle Kingdom Thebes has only been revealed by relatively recent exploration. The New Kingdom pharoahs levelled much of the great city that the Middle Kingdom had bequeathed and erected their elaborate temples over it. The Middle Kingdom remnants that have been unearthed demonstrate the bureaucratic control of urban planning typical of the period.

Other examples of this urban planning can be seen in Kahun and at Abu Ghalib in the Delta and at Buhen, far to the south in Nubia.

From small beginnings the Twelfth Dynasty kings expanded the Theban complex according to a rigid state-planned layout. The complex was surrounded by solid walls running east–west and north–south and the settlement continued into the Second Intermediate Period.

QUEENS' JEWELRY

When Flinders Petrie returned to the site of el-Lahun in 1914 he found, among shaft graves in the area of Senusret II's pyramid, the grave that belonged to the princess Sit-Hathor-Iunet, daughter of Senusret II. Although the grave had been looted in antiquity, the robbers had missed a niche hiding three ebony caskets. These caskets contained a rich hoard of personal jewelry and cosmetics.

Among the prize pieces were a royal *uraeus* (sacred serpent); a magnificent gold diadem featuring a cobra and rosettes; a silver mirror supported by the head of Hathor; and pectorals displaying in a cartouche the prenomen of Senusret II.

Earlier, in 1895, Jacques de Morgan had investigated tombs at Dahshur, belonging to Mereret and Sit-Hathor, of the family of Senusret III. At this site the items he found included two floral circlets of gold, and a pectoral bearing the prenomen of Senusret III.

The magnificent jewelry items found at these Middle Kingdom sites are among the most exquisite surviving examples of Egyptian design.

Below **The Pectoral of Mereret, sister of Amenemhet III.** This gold pectoral, inlaid with carnelian and glass, depicting the king was found at Dahshur.

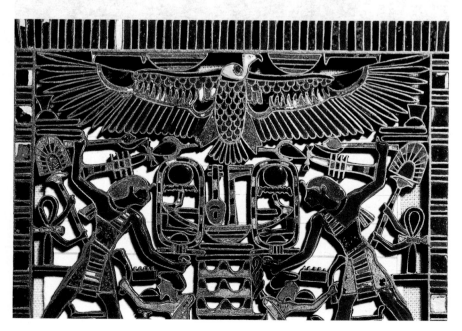

Middle Kingdom Workmanship

Some of the exquisite workmanship of the Middle Kingdom has been recovered, for example, the kiosk-shrine of Senusret I that was reassembled from blocks discovered near the base of the Third Pylon at Karnak.

On the other hand, domestic pottery from the same period is rather coarse, displaying the simple incised patterns that are characteristic of other Middle Kingdom pottery findings.

The Legacy of Mentuhotep I

By far the most spectacular construction from the Middle Kingdom is Mentuhotep I's mortuary temple at Deir el-Bahri, on the western bank of Thebes, opposite Karnak. Innovative for the time, this amazing temple was built on different levels.

A terrace stands on a forecourt and at the rear of both levels are colonnades with reliefs showing the king's military prowess. The inner part of the temple is a hypostyle hall leading to the tomb itself. Beneath the temple platform is a tunnel leading to a cenotaph, under which had been interred a painted statue of Mentuhotep.

The coloring and stance of Mentuhotep's statue identify him with Osiris, while the eastward orientation of the temple itself would probably identify it with the sun deity.

Adjacent to this temple is the mortuary temple of the later and more famous Hatshepsut of the Eighteenth Dynasty, who in many ways has eclipsed the reputation of the earlier monarch.

During the New Kingdom the mortuary temple became part of the Amun complex of temples in the Karnak–Luxor region, and it is classified as an Amun temple in which the king had taken residence. While more strictly it is a New Kingdom development, the Amun temple is nevertheless built on themes inherited from architectural achievements of the Middle Kingdom.

Above **Senusret I Kiosk.** The king's kiosk has been reconstructed at Karnak and is known as the White Chapel or altar of repose.

Left **Uraeus belonging to Senusret II.** This gold and enamel ureaus (the sacred serpent protective element worn on a king's crown) is from the pyramid of Senusret II at el-Lahun.

Middle Kingdom Pyramids

The Twelfth Dynasty kings revived the architectural tradition of pyramid burials. They modeled their pyramid complexes on those of the Old Kingdom, sometimes closely, but also incorporated some innovative building techniques.

Above **Decoration on statue of Senusret I.** The relief on limestone statue shows the symbolic union of Upper and Lower Egypt, from the king's mortuary temple at el-Lisht.

Kings of the Old Kingdom and First Intermediate Period had been buried in the north, far from Thebes. The first two Middle Kingdom pyramids, for Amenemhet I and his son, Senusret I, were also erected in the north, at el-Lisht, near the new capital, Itj-tawy.

Pyramids at el-Lisht

Both pyramids were constructed of loose limestone blocks and just covered with a more stable casing also in limestone. The pyramid of Senusret I had an inner skeleton of stone walls giving the building greater stability, while the spaces in between were filled with loose blocks and even with sand. This pyramid complex is the best-preserved example from the Middle Kingdom. It is a remarkably faithful copy of a late Old Kingdom complex, showing how precisely the architects of the king followed older prototypes. As in the Old Kingdom, there was a valley temple, and a causeway connecting the valley with the pyramid temple, the latter built directly in front of the pyramid. Around the pyramid were two walls, one enclosing the pyramid and pyramid temple, the outer wall enclosing several smaller pyramids for royal women. The inner wall was decorated with the Horus name, the first of the five royal names of an Egyptian king. This name identified him as a particular manifestation of the god Horus on Earth. The pyramid temple was richly adorned with reliefs and statues.

In the Old Kingdom the whole pyramid complex had one name. In the Middle Kingdom each part of the complex had its own name. In the case of Senusret I the pyramid was called "Senusret watches the two lands". The whole complex or one of the pyramid temples had the name "United with [cult] places is Kheperkara" (the throne-name of Senusret I). The pyramid town was called "May Senusret appear."

King Amenemhet II, son of Senusret I, chose Dahshur, instead of el-Lisht, for his burial place. Dahshur had been an important royal cemetery in the early Old Kingdom. Amenemhet II's pyramid has not yet been fully excavated.

New Building Techniques

Senusret II moved to another site for his pyramid, much farther south, at Lahun on the edge of the Faiyum. His is the first Middle Kingdom pyramid constructed mainly in mud bricks. There was again an inner skeleton of stone walls but the spaces in between were filled with mud bricks, not stone.

There are other innovations in this building. Since the Old Kingdom, the entrance of the pyramid had always been in the north, with the burial chamber in the middle of the building. At Lahun the entrance was in the south, outside the building and next to the tomb-shafts for the burials of several royal women, as if it were just another shaft tomb. The burial chamber was no longer in the exact middle-point of the pyramid; it was set to the south but slightly off-center. Around the burial chamber there were several corridors, making the burial chamber a sort of island in the middle. One suggestion is that this layout echoed the burial place of the underworld god Osiris, who became one of the main gods of Egypt during the Middle Kingdom. Trees were planted around the foot of the pyramid, another feature that evokes the tomb of Osiris. There was a small pyramid for the king's wife and a funerary

temple. Far to the east was a valley temple, next to a planned town named "Kahun". Unfortunately, all these monuments were found very much destroyed.

Senusret III built a pyramid, also with brick core, at Dahshur. Perhaps its most remarkable feature is the great temple next to the pyramid, where the cult of the dead king was performed. The pyramid of Senusret III contained a second pyramid temple on a much bigger scale. Though almost entirely destroyed, thousands of relief fragments show how richly the temple was

adorned. It seems that here the cult of the king is being formulated in a new way, in a temple explicitly for the cult of the king as god. Near the king's pyramid were smaller pyramids for royal women.

Prototypes

Amenemhet III erected two pyramids. One was located at Dahshur, the other at Hawara, where the king was most likely buried. The blocking system of the building is especially elaborate, with huge stones ingeniously manoeuvred into the corridors after the burial. The burial places of the rulers Amenemhet IV and Sobeknofru are not known. The internal layout of Amenemhet III's Hawara pyramid became the prototype for Thirteenth Dynasty pyramids. These were much smaller, and most are unfinished, but the blocking systems were more complex than at any time in Egyptian history.

Left **Pyramid of Amenemhet III.** This pyramid had an elaborate internal layout that became the prototype for later pyramids. A huge temple, later known as the "labyrinth" stood in front of the pyramid.

Below **Pyramid of Amenemhet I (Twelfth Dynasty).** Erected at el-Lisht, this pyramid was constructed of loose limestone blocks covered in limestone casing.

Gold: Nubia and Egypt

In the eyes of the ancient Egyptians, the Middle Kingdom ruler Senusret III was clearly one of their most important kings. Nowadays we would consider Khufu or Rameses II as the great kings, but for the Egyptians it was Senusret III.

Herodotus and Manetho reported that Senusret III conquered great parts of Asia, perhaps confusing his campaigns with those of the New Kingdom rulers, but certainly demonstrating the magnitude of the king's reputation. In fact, surprisingly little is known about Senusret III and his activity in Asia, as only a few Egyptian texts mention them. We are better informed on his military campaigns in Nubia.

Control of Nubia

Nubia, or more precisely, Lower Nubia, is the land directly south of Egypt along the Nile. It is not very fertile, and was never densely populated. However, the country is rich in raw materials, so it always attracted Egyptian expeditions and campaigns. During the Old Kingdom, an Egyptian trading post was based at Buhen, but the surrounding countryside was probably not under Egyptian control. Only in the Middle Kingdom was this area occupied, and the territory down to the Second Cataract conquered then placed under permanent control. Most Middle Kingdom rulers took part in Nubian campaigns but there is little evidence that Mentuhotep II or Amenemhet I intended to conquer the country. Only in year 18 of Senusret I was there a big military campaign in Nubia that seems to have led to permanent control. Strong fortresses were built at several points for security purposes and these were manned by Egyptian garrisons.

The Gold Land

The most important raw material from Nubia was gold, but copper mines and important stone quarries were also valued. The gold mines lay largely in the Eastern desert, from the level of Koptos in Egypt to past the Second Cataract. The exhaustion of gold mines in the Egyptian deserts made those in Nubia more important. Egyptians of the Middle Kingdom did not mint coins, but gold was treated as a kind of currency. Near Eastern texts refer to Egypt as the Gold Land. This wealth is largely based on the Nubian mines.

MIDDLE KINGDOM FORTIFICATIONS

Perhaps the most impressive architectural remains of the Middle Kingdom are the fortresses built by Senusret I and Senusret III in Lower Nubia. Although there must have been fortresses at the border between the Nile Delta and Palestine, only those in Nubia are well preserved. These Nubian sites did provide excellent examples of military architecture, but sadly they are now beneath the waters of the Lake Nasser. Investigations revealed that the forts were all constructed in mud bricks with massive walls over 16 ft (5 m) thick. At Buhen, an inner fortress is within the vaster area marked by the outer walls; the original height of the inner walls has been calculated as approximately 26 to 29 ft (8 to 9 m) high.

Each of the fortresses seems to have had a specific function. At the southern end of the Second Cataract, the fortresses of Semna-West and Kumma marked the southern border of Egyptian-controlled Lower Nubia. The Buhen fortress may have acted as the administrative center of Lower Nubia, judging by the numerous seal impressions and tiny papyrus fragments found there. Some fortresses had granaries to supply the troops stationed there. Nubian settlements found near other fortresses indicate that the fortresses were built in part to keep a local population under control.

Left **Limestone stela of the Nubians, Middle Kingdom.** During this period Egypt controled much of Nubia. More than a thousand years later it was Nubia which controled Egypt.

Above **Map of the king's gold mines.** The most important raw material from Nubia was gold.

The Southern Limits of the Empire

Conquest of the region was consolidated in the reign of Senusret III, who led several military campaigns into Nubia and built additional and still mightier fortresses.

The reason for these new campaigns after Senusret I is not entirely clear, but there may have been rebellions, or perhaps Senusret I had not conquered the country, but only inserted fortified trading posts at certain points without controlling the country in between.

Another factor might have been the rising power of Kerma, south of the Third Cataract. In the Second Intermediate Period, Kerma came to control Lower Nubia and even invaded Egypt. Some rock inscriptions indicate that the campaigns of Senusret III penetrated further south, but the border was kept at the Second Cataract. Here the king erected stelae confirming in words the southern limit of his empire.

Senusret III in Nubia

Senusret III went on to build a channel at the First Cataract to maintain better communications with Nubia and provide easier transport for freight. During his reign Lower Nubia came under Egyptian administration. Based on this activity, King Senusret III was worshipped as a god shortly after his death, especially in Nubia.

Left **Gold engraved pendant, Middle Kingdom.** Egypt's reputation as the land of gold was based on riches from the Nubian mines.

Amenemhet III

Amenemhet III was the last important ruler of the Twelfth Dynasty. After an especially long co-regency with his father, Senusret III, which perhaps lasted twenty years, Amenemhet III ruled Egypt for about forty-five years.

Below **Amenemhet III (1831–1786 BCE).** Head and torso of a limestone statue of the king, from Hawara.

In many ways Amenemhet III brought to completion the work of his predecessors of the Twelfth Dynasty, notably in their focus on the Faiyum. In his reign, control of Nubia appears solid, as there are few references to military activity. The king seems to have concentrated all his energies on grandiose building projects, in particular, his burial complex.

The Hawara Pyramid of Amenemhet III

At the very beginning of Amenemhet III's reign, work started on a pyramid for the king at Dahshur. However, the building was constructed on soft ground, and serious cracks developed in the stone blocks lining the corridors. As a result, the pyramid was deemed unsuitable for the burial of the king, although it was used as a burial place for several royal women. For his own burial, the king chose an entirely different site with a second pyramid complex. The new pyramid was erected at Hawara, not far from the pyramid of Senusret II, and even closer to the Faiyum fields. Several rock inscriptions at the Wadi Hammamat record the quarrying of blocks of hard stone during this reign. The building name of the Hawara pyramid, Ankh-Amenemhet—"May Amenemhet live," is mentioned in one of these Wadi Hammamat inscriptions, as well as on papyri found at Lahun, the town from which the building work seems to have been organized.

The Hawara pyramid has a length of 200 cubits (about 344 ft or 105 m), and was perhaps 190 ft (58 m) high, as were most pyramids of the Twelfth Dynasty. Its core was of mud brick, and the structure shows several important innovations. The burial chamber was reached via several corridors, secured through a complicated system of blocking stones. The burial chamber was carved out of several huge blocks of quartzite (silicified sandstone), one for the whole lower part and three for the roof. The monolithic block for the floor and walls of the chamber must be about 110 tons (112 tonnes) in weight, making

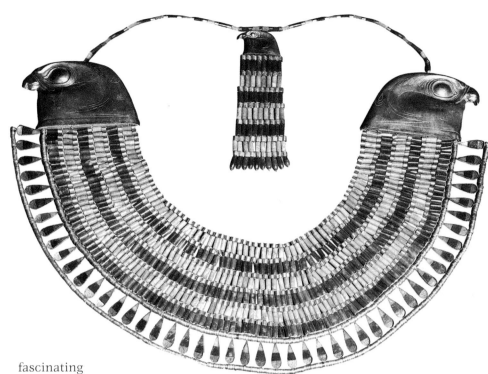

The King's Daughter

The burial had been disturbed in antiquity, but remaining in the chamber was the sarcophagus of the king. Alongside it was a second sarcophagus for the king's daughter, Neferuptah.

The excavator of the pyramid believed that the king's daughter was buried with him. However, decades later another excavator found the smaller pyramid of Neferuptah, about two kilometres southwest of the king's pyramid. Neferuptah's intact burial chamber still contained her jewelry and other important objects, revealing that she was not buried next to her father, as might have been originally intended, but in her own tomb. Perhaps Neferuptah died later than her father and it wasn't possible to re-open Amenemhet III's pyramid after his burial, so a new tomb was started for his daughter.

Unraveling the Labyrinth

A huge temple, known later as the "labyrinth" stood in front of the pyramid of Amenemhet III at Hawara. Several classical authors described this temple as one of the most beautiful and fascinating buildings in Egypt. Not much of the labyrinth is preserved, because in Roman times it was quarried away. It seems that the temple consisted of a web of columned halls and courtyards, richly decorated with reliefs and hundreds of statues, many of them unique in type and appearance. This building and its sculpture may have inspired Amenhotep III, much as the latter's Colossi of Memnon seem inspired by the colossi of Amenemhet III at Biahmu.

Above **Collar of Neferuptah, daughter of Amenemhet III**. Gold collar featuring hawk's heads, inlaid with colored glass and semi-precious stones.

"CINEMATOGRAPHY" IN TOMB PAINTINGS

In several early Twelfth Dynasty tombs, notably those at Beni Hasan, complex compositions of athletic activity are painted on the chapel walls, with pairs of wrestlers arranged in series across several registers. The wrestlers are depicted in an array of different detailed positions of man-to-man combat, wearing only loincloths. In each pair one man is a light skin color, the other darker, doubtless to distinguish them graphically from each other, rather than as an indication of ethnicity. Art historians have noted the cinematographic effect of these multiple scenes, reading the varying positions as one following the other. However, on closer inspection, the sequences do not create that effect. No one pair is depicted in a position resulting from the previous one or leading to the next. Instead, the artist seems to have wanted to show all the possible moves in wrestling. Furthermore, the siege of a fortress is generally depicted alongside these scenes. The intention may have been to show the recruits on a training field, then fighting in a war and perhaps putting their training into practice.

Left **Sphinx of Amenemhet III**. Gray granite sculpture of Amenemhet's face with a lion's mane, from Tanis.

Royal Statuary

During the Middle Kingdom, statues became much more publicly visible as well as grander in scale. The appearance of the royal statues also changed, displaying a new emphasis on individual features.

Old Kingdom statues produced for the cult of the dead were placed in a "serdab," a small chamber in the tomb chapel mainly reserved for statues of the tomb owner and his family. Tomb statues were probably a substitute for the deceased if the body was destroyed. Most of them show a generalized image without individual features. This is also true of royal sculpture, with the majority of Old Kingdom examples coming from pyramid temples, and only a few from local temples or chapels. During the First Intermediate Period and Middle Kingdom, smaller statues, often made of wood, were placed directly next to the body of the deceased in the underground burial chamber, instead of in the serdab.

In another departure from tradition, Middle Kingdom statues, even of non-royal individuals, were often placed in temples, so the person depicted would be close to a certain god and could share in the offerings. During the Middle Kingdom, temples seem to have become far more monumental, and befittingly were often equipped with royal statues much larger in scale than those of the Old Kingdom. Middle Kingdom statues were prominently positioned,

Right **Statue of Senusret I.** This colossal black granite statue, found in the king's mortuary temple at el-Lisht, displays the "expressionless beauty" typical of the early Middle Kingdom.

rather than hidden away in tombs or pyramid temples, where they were accessible only to a small number of people.

Expressionless Beauty

The new function of statues had a direct influence on their appearance. Sculpture of the early Middle Kingdom often shows shared rather than individual features. Especially in the early Twelfth Dynasty sculptures, strong Old Kingdom influences are visible. In the pyramid temple of Senusret I at el-Lisht, a set of partly unfinished statues show the king enthroned. In terms of craftsmanship, the figures are quite perfect, but the faces seem almost expressionless.

There are few certain examples of statues depicting either of the king's successors, Amenemhet II and Senusret II. One colossal sphinx of Amenemhet II has a face with individualized features, though still ageless or "idealized."

A Pessimistic Appearance

Under Senusret III royal sculpture changed drastically. The face was no longer youthful and ageless. Instead it had heavy eyelids and lined cheeks. Surviving works vary considerably in detail, and the effect is described differently by different art historians. A colossal example found in Karnak shows the face of a strong, energetic ruler with indications of lines under deep-set eyes and around the level mouth. Other images of the same ruler also show lines in the face, but with the ends of the mouth downturned, a rather pessimistic expression to modern eyes. Over a hundred statues have been attributed to this king, although only a few retain a part inscribed with his name. However, the face of Senusret III is so distinct that there are generally no problems in attributing any uninscribed statues to this ruler. The expression on the faces of these figures is often described as sad or pessimistic, but we should be cautious about taking an overly subjective view. These works come from another culture with very different concepts of kingship.

One recurrent Egyptological interpretation has noted a correlation between sculpture and certain works of literature, dating mainly to the late Middle Kingdom. The literature of this period also expresses a rather pessimistic world view. However, the precise dates of composition are inferred rather than explicitly recorded, and it might not be possible to relate trends in different art forms to each other.

Age and Experience

The features of Senusret III are mirrored in non-royal sculpture of the late Twelfth Dynasty. A central focus of all these images may be age rather than pessimism. In the Old Kingdom, statues tend to convey an ageless appearance whereas in the late Middle Kingdom, the depicted person seems either young or old. This is interesting, as few members of Egyptian society actually reached old age. Instead of the blank, open eyes of earlier tradition, late Middle Kingdom sculptors carved deep-set eyes that gave the effect of the figure genuinely looking at an object of view. In contrast to the lined face of the king, the rest of the figure is still idealized, conveying the athletic body of a youth. The Senusret III style continued to generate masterpieces in both royal and private sculpture into the Thirteenth Dynasty.

For Senusret's son, Amenemhet III, there are generally two types of royal sculpture. One shows a young king, the other type an older, ostensibly more experienced king. Whether these types of representation are to be connected with the actual age of the king remains unknown.

The statues of Amenemhet III are less remarkable for the features of the faces, an attenuated version of the style of his father, Senusret III, than for the innovative positions and costumes in which the king is shown. Life-size sculptures show him with leopard-skin, necklace and thick-braided hair, or as a sphinx with a long lion-mane instead of the royal headdress. Many of these forms of statuary are unique to the reign of Amenemhet III and perhaps come from his vast pyramid temple at Hawara.

Above **Granite statue of Amenemhet III.**
This statue depicts the experienced face of King Amenemhet III.

Left **Fragment of black granite head, Senusret III.**
This fragment, from Medamud, features the "pessimistic" appearance common to statues of Senusret III.

Bureaucracy

As in other periods of Egyptian history, bureaucracy played a prominent role in both administration and daily life during the Middle Kingdom. The use of administrative titles in society reflects a highly developed bureaucracy.

Right **Painted wood model of scribe Intef (c. 1975–1640 BCE).** Egyptian scribes recorded almost every kind of transaction on papyrus.

In most historical periods, Egyptians were identified in inscriptions by their administrative titles. Evidently, these titles formed part of their identity in much the same way that personal names did.

The bureaucracy worked on different levels. Besides the king, the royal court consisted of officials in higher and lower positions. Certain institutions had branches around the country. At a regional level, the nomarchs had their own local courts. Private estates also had to have their own administrative systems.

The Palace Administration

At the palace, "ministers" were identified by their ranking titles and the most important of these was "royal sealer". These ministers were responsible for the different branches of the palace administration. The three main sectors were the commodity stores, the military and workforce, and the scribal offices. Outside the palace, but perhaps attached to it, the "great enclosure" was an institution that seems to have organized labor in the late Middle Kingdom. It appears that the State forced people to work for it when needed. One surviving papyrus lists people running away from the great enclosure, an indication of how arduous work could be at this institution.

Nomarchs and Stewards

At the more local level, the provinces in Middle Egypt, and perhaps also in Lower Egypt, were under the charge of the nomarchs. The nomarch had a staff of lower officials, each with different tasks. However, in the middle of the Twelfth Dynasty these nomarchs were replaced by governors or mayors, who were only responsible for one town and the surrounding region and fields.

During the late Middle Kingdom administration of the provinces was more centrally controlled from the capital. Estates belonging to officials, or to towns or institutions, had their own administrator(s), most often holding a title translated as "steward" (literally: "Overseer of the house"). Not surprisingly then, steward is the most common title of the Middle Kingdom.

The Ancient Records

Although papyrus must have been very expensive in ancient Egypt, there is abundant evidence that officials recorded almost every administrative transaction on papyrus. These organic documents have little chance of survival, but many fragmentary examples were found at the town site of Lahun, on the desert edge.

Several documents ended up in tombs, perhaps by accident, perhaps as a sign of status. A set of four papyrus rolls found in a tomb at

Naga el-Der contains the accounts of building work in the region under Senusret I. One exceptional surviving document records the accounts of the Theban palace in the Thirteenth Dynasty.

In the late Middle Kingdom seal impressions and the sealing of goods became increasingly important. Hitherto they appear only sporadically. At every archeological site of the late Middle Kingdom, literally thousands of seal impressions have been found. Most scarab seals with a name and title also belong to this particular period of time. It might indicate a fundamental change in administration, or perhaps just the wish for more control.

The Question of Slavery

Egyptologists have constantly wondered whether Egyptian society was relatively free or offered little personal freedom for the individual. There is evidence that Egyptians who did not belong to the class of bureaucrats could still gain wealth. From the Middle Kingdom there are many well-equipped tombs of people without any titles who seem to have gained their wealth outside the State administration, perhaps from working as farm-owners, craftsmen, or traders.

Above **Limestone stela of Sobekhotep (c. 1938–1755 BCE).** This Abydean stela depicts a middle-ranking official of the Middle Kingdom and his wife.

DID SLAVERY EXIST?

There is no Egyptian word translatable exclusively as "slave," but the question of whether the ancient Egyptians had slaves or not is still open to discussion. Egyptologists once assumed that such amazing buildings as the pyramids could only have been built with slave labor. However, others argue that free people inspired by religious ideas built the pyramids.

Reportedly, the Egyptian kings conquered foreign territories and captured thousands of people. Taking the example of the Roman Empire into account, it might be concluded that these captives became slaves. It is also possible that they were transferred to uninhabited regions in Egypt to be settled as farmers. The texts do not tell us what happened.

Several Egyptian texts mention the legal transfer of rights to people. Officials were sometimes awarded with the gift of a high number of men and this might represent a form of slavery. Doubtless, a great part of the population lived in a status similar to the serfs of the Middle Ages. These people were attached to certain estates, which belonged to officials or to the king, and they had to deliver most of their production output to the estate owners. However, it seems likely that the people still had some measure of personal freedom. They might have been able to work on their own fields and sell their own products. Egyptian workers were not just a gray colorless mass of humanity, as is sometimes assumed.

Left **Slave beaten by master (c. 1400–1390 BCE).** A scene depicting the practice of slavery was found in this New Kingdom tomb fresco.

The Nomarchs

During the Middle Kingdom, the nomarchs had considerable economic power. The inscriptions and artefacts found in the elaborately decorated nomarchs' tombs at Beni Hasan demonstrate the importance of these provincial governors.

At the beginning of the First Intermediate Period, Egypt was split into different political units. Local nomarchs ruled more or less independently from the king in Memphis. However, few nomarchs assumed the title of king—perhaps only the Theban rulers. Early on, the Theban kings had eliminated nomarchs in their territory, and replaced them with local governors who were responsible only for their own town and perhaps the country-side around it. These Theban appointed governors no longer ruled a whole province.

In the territory under the Herakleopolitan kings the development was different. The Herakleopolitans did not eliminate the power of local nomarchs. They used them instead as allies in the struggle against the Theban kings. This is most clearly visible in the tombs at Asyut, where long biographical inscriptions record events around the wars against the Thebans. Despite the Theban conquest of the North and Mentuhotep II's reunification of Egypt, the power of these nomarchs was not destroyed, and they kept their influential and powerful positions.

There is evidence that the kings of the Eleventh Dynasty and early Twelfth Dynasty installed new nomarchs at certain important places. The sequence of nomarchs at Beni Hasan starts in the Eleventh Dynasty after the unification. At Meir, Rifeh and Qaw el-Qebir the nomarchs appear only at the beginning of the Twelfth Dynasty, indicating that in these places Amenemhet I or

Senusret I installed important families, presumably those who were especially loyal to the new dynasty. There are several references to civil war in the early Middle Kingdom, and it is possible that the kings placed loyal people at strategic points to stabilize their power in the more insecure regions.

The Magnificent Tombs of the Nomarchs

The nomarchs are known mainly from their magnificent tomb chapels in Middle Egypt. The best preserved, though not the most important, were found at Beni Hasan. These tombs are decorated with paintings showing the tomb owner, his family and servants, and the lower officials working for him. They have the usual workshop and agricultural scenes, familiar from elite tombs of the Old and New Kingdoms, and some more unusual depictions. Several Beni Hasan tombs have depictions of soldiers in training and the siege of a fortress or town. Paintings in one tomb at Deir el-Bersheh depict the transport of a colossal figure, while those in a tomb at Meir (the latest decorated tomb) depict only women. The women are performing various tasks or functioning as offering bearers. The latter scenes might be connected with the cult of the goddess Hathor, who was the main deity of Qusae, the town near Meir.

By far the largest and most magnificent tombs, sadly much destroyed, are to be found at Qaw el-Qebir, where the no-marchs of the Tenth Upper Egyptian province were buried. The Qaw tombs were richly adorned with statues, reliefs and paintings of a very high quality, demonstrating the economic power of the nomarchs. The lower officials, often depicted in the tomb, were

Right **Wooden state of Hapidjefa, governor of the province of Asyut (c. 1918–1875 BCE).** Hapidjefa was a nomarch during the reign of Senusret I.

buried in front of the nomarchal tombs. Most surviving Middle Kingdom coffins come from these subsidiary tombs.

Relationship with Royalty

Each local court was in many ways a smaller version of the royal court. There was no vizier, but the nomarch had a treasurer, responsible for the valuables of the estate, and a steward, who was the administrator of the estate fields.

The nomarchal tombs at Beni Hasan are well known for their long biographical inscriptions, which record how the owner built local temples and cared for his people.

Some of the nomarchs of the Middle Kingdom even counted the years of their "reigns" as the king did. However, although the nomarchs were very powerful and acted almost independently, they often refer in their inscriptions to the king and they always emphasised their loyalty.

Changing Burial Customs

The biggest and most beautiful tombs were all built under Senusret II and Senusret III, the only exception being the largest tomb at Qaw el-Qebir, datable under Amenemhet III. Surprisingly then, by the next generation there are no nomarchal tombs. The last dated nomarchal tomb at Beni Hasan is decorated with one inscription only. In the last tomb at Meir the nomarch's coffin was inscribed with his name and titles but the tomb is undecorated. It has been argued that Senusret III eliminated the nomarchs as they were too powerful, but researchers are now more cautious about the apparent decline of the nomarchs. Few of the larger tombs can be dated securely and changes to decorations might be connected to changing burial customs. It is important to remember that titles of nomarchs ("governor" and "overseer of priests") still occur after the reign of Senusret III.

Above **Interior of tomb at Beni Hasan.** The best preserved nomarchal tombs are at Beni Hasan (Engraving by Hector Horeau, 1841, *Panorama of Egypt and Nubia.*)

Above left **Sarcophagus of Governor Ibu.** Nomarchal tombs near Qaw el-Qebir have yielded finds such as this Middle Kingdom sarcophagus of Governor Ibu.

Osiris: A New God is Born

Osiris was first mentioned in the Pyramid Texts, the earliest collection of religious texts associated with the royal funerary ritual. The most complete record of the death and resurrection of Osiris comes to us from Plutarch.

The Pyramid Texts, inscribed on the walls of the burial chamber of King Unas, and appearing in pyramids until the end of the Old Kingdom, contain allusions to the myth of Osiris. In the second century CE, the Greek historian, Plutarch, gave his account of the myth. According to Plutarch's version, Osiris was a living king who was murdered by his jealous brother, Seth.

Below Fresco depicting the Pilgrimage to Abydos (c. 1390–1352 BCE). The earliest cult center of Osiris was at Abydos.

The Myth of Osiris

Osiris was guest of honor at a feast during which Seth pledged a magnificent chest to the person who could fit into it. When Osiris was inside the chest, Seth had the lid sealed with molten lead and thrown into the Nile, drowning his brother. The chest drifted to Byblos, from where it was retrieved by Osiris's wife, Isis. The chest was then was stolen by Seth. Seth cut the body of Osiris into 14 pieces (this number varies in different accounts) and scattered the pieces throughout Egypt. Isis searched for the pieces and buried them where they were found. As a Nile carp had swallowed the phallus, a false one had to be made. However, in the Egyptian accounts, Isis and her sister Nephthys reassembled the dismembered corpse. It was mummified by Anubis, becoming the first mummy. Isis turned herself into a bird, and conceived her son, Horus, by hovering over the mummified body. Horus eventually avenged his father's death, seizing the throne from Seth. Osiris became king of the underworld, and Horus the living king. This became the basic tenet of the royal funerary cult of Osiris.

Osiris as a Metaphor for Rebirth

Osiris is almost always depicted as a mummy wrapped in a white cloak or shroud, with the royal insignia of flail and crook in his protruding hands. He wears the white crown of Upper Egypt, sometimes with added side feathers, or the *atef* crown (a tall, conical crown featuring side plumes and ram's horns at its base) and a false beard. These symbols of kingship reflect the original function of Osiris as a god of the royal dead. His hands and face are often painted green, symbolizing his association with the fertility of the land, a metaphor for rebirth.

Identification with Osiris

The aim of the "resurrection" spells in the Pyramid Texts was to identify the dead king with Osiris, so that the king too could be reborn by sympathetic magic:

"Lo, the King is in front of the gods, equipped as a god, his bones fastened together like Osiris."

However, from the late First Intermediate Period, identification with Osiris was no longer the prerogative of royalty. As a result of the "democratization of the afterlife," all non-elite individuals could be resurrected as Osiris.

The texts, which had been inscribed on the walls of the pyramid tomb chambers, were now fused into a series of spells and utterances known as the Coffin Texts. These appeared on the coffins of non-elite, private individuals. The deceased non-royal was now referred to as "Osiris of X", and many of the iconographic features associated with Osiris appeared in private funerary art.

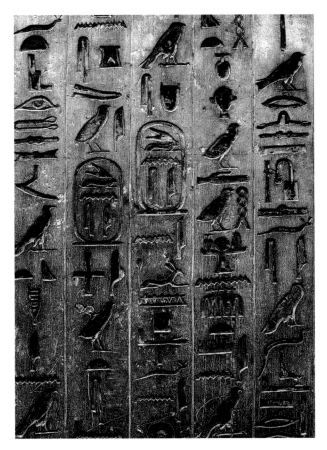

Left **Pyramid Text from the sarcophagus room of King Unas** (c. 2450–2325 BCE). The Pyramid Texts included magical formulas, rituals and prayers that were aimed at identifying the dead king with Osiris.

The Cult Centers

Dating from at least the late Old Kingdom, the earliest cult center of Osiris was located at Abydos, in Upper Egypt. Osiris was also connected with Busiris in the Delta and with Heliopolis, the center of the *Great Ennead* (the nine creator gods). At Abydos, Osiris appears to have absorbed the identity of the earlier jackal god of the necropolis, Khenti-Amentiu, taking on his title of "Foremost of the Westerners" (ie., the dead). Abydos was believed to be the place where the head of Osiris was found, and the site became an important center of pilgrimage during the Middle Kingdom.

HELPERS IN THE AFTERLIFE: SHABTI FIGURES

Mummiform funerary figurines known as *shabti* were an integral part of Middle Kingdom tomb furnishings. They were in the image of the deceased owner as a mummy, and intended to substitute for his physical body in magically carrying out unpleasant agricultural tasks in the afterlife, such as the maintenance of the irrigation systems. Figurines from the First Intermediate Period were crude and made of clay and wax, but the Middle Kingdom figurines of painted wood, stone, and faience were mostly fine works of art. The faience was a non-clay product of crushed quartz or quartz sand, with a soda-lime silica glaze. Some *shabti* were provided with a miniature coffin. Numbers ranged from one *shabti* per burial to as many as 365. Some *shabti* were inscribed with a magical incantation for "causing *shabti* to do the work of their owner in the realm of the dead."

Left **Middle Kingdom *shabti* in painted wood.** These funerary figurines were designed to accompany the deceased.

The Coffin Texts

The Coffin Texts is a body of over one thousand funerary spells. The spells were often inscribed on and inside the coffins of private individuals in the Eleventh and Twelfth Dynasties and appeared on tomb walls, mummy masks, and papyri.

Many of the Coffin Text spells were variants of the Pyramid Texts. Those texts were first carved on the walls of the burial chambers of King Unas, and appeared in the pyramids of the kings and queens of the late Old Kingdom (c. 2500–2200 BCE). The purpose of the texts was to ensure that the dead pharaoh was transformed into a god in the afterlife.

COFFINS

The most important innovation in funerary practice in the First Intermediate Period and Middle Kingdom is the use of funerary texts on coffins of non-royal individuals, as part of the "democratization" of the funerary cult. The rectangular, wooden coffin's exterior was inscribed with bands of protective text. A pair of magical *wedjat* eyes, the lunar eye of Horus, were painted on one side, level with the face of the mummy, which lay on its left side on a headrest, "looking" out to the world of the living.

The coffin interior was elaborately decorated with a frieze depicting provisions for the afterlife, such as garments, jewelry, furniture, tools, and weapons, as well as ritual objects and royal insignia that would enable the deceased to be resurrected as Osiris. The objects were grouped meaningfully so headrests were at the head end and sandals at the foot. Below the frieze were extracts from the Coffin Texts.

Another innovation was the anthropoid, or mummy-shaped coffin, which reproduced the appearance of the mummified body wrapped in a shroud with the head exposed, reflecting the iconography of Osiris. The anthropoid was placed inside the rectangular coffin.

Below **Middle Kingdom sarcophagus.** Coffin friezes depicted provisions for the afterlife and objects that would enable the deceased to be resurrected as Osiris.

Guides to the Netherworld

The texts were grouped in the pyramid according to one of three categories: Protective, ritual, or personal. Magical, "protective" incantations were intended to ward off dangerous, harmful creatures, such as snakes and scorpions. "Ritual texts", were to be spoken while the funerary rituals were carried out (these included "offering" and "resurrection" spells in which the deceased was addressed as Osiris). "Personal" spells, which the dead king himself used, were intended to help the king to leave the pyramid and pass safely to the next world.

During the Old Kingdom, these funerary texts were reserved exclusively for the king, although some aspects of the Pyramid Texts, such as the "offering" ritual, appeared in private burials. Elite private individuals sought inclusion in the royal funerary cult by being buried as closely as possible to the pharaoh. This can be seen in the *mastaba* tombs in the vicinity of the pyramid complexes at Giza and Saqqara. *Mastaba* tombs are a tomb with a rectangular, bench-like superstructure connected to a subterranean burial chamber by a shaft. The proximity of their tombs to the king's burial-place gave individuals access to an afterlife, but one in which they continued their earthly status, and did not become divine.

Democracy and the Afterlife

After the Old Kingdom collapsed, a process described as "democratization of the afterlife" took place. Imitation of royal funerary prerogatives by officials and their families, especially in the identification of the deceased with Osiris, now guaranteed that ordinary people could attain divine status in the afterlife. In the Pyramid Texts only the deceased king could be called "Osiris". In the Coffin Texts and later texts, all dead individuals had the title of Osiris and they could re-enact the myth of resurrection, as long as they proved their worthiness.

The coffin was, in effect, a microcosm of the pyramid chambers, in which the mummified person was surrounded by the magical texts. The "resurrection" ritual of the Pyramid Texts continued to be used. Its underlying theme was the transition of the deceased from this world to the next. The "offering" ritual, which consisted of short spells accompanying the presentation of food and other offerings, was replaced by a list of the offerings. A frieze illustrating these objects was painted around the top of the four inner sides of the coffin. However, most of the Coffin Texts belong to the category of "personal" spells, such as instructions for crossing water, or climbing a ladder. These instructions are metaphors for transition to the next world.

The Book of Two Ways

A new feature of burials in the early Twelfth Dynasty was a series of spells that were written on the floor of the coffin.

These spells were often illustrated with a map and drawings, to safely guide the deceased's spirit on its way to the afterlife. This "guide to the hereafter," known as the Book of Two Ways, described the demons and obstacles that would be encountered, and provided the special knowledge necessary for successfully negotiating them.

The knowledge included the correct answers to questions that would be asked by the ferryman before he took the deceased across the "Winding Waterway." This was a river that borders the "Field of Reeds," one of the final destinations.

Above **Pyramid texts in pyramid of King Unas (c. 2450–2325 BCE).** The Pyramid Texts were first carved on the walls of the king's burial chambers.

Left **Wooden sarcophagus (New Kingdom).** The mummy-shaped coffin is known as an anthropoid.

Funerary Customs

The basic tenet of ancient Egyptian funerary beliefs was that death was an interruption, not an end. Everything was based on the belief that eternal life continued after death: "You have not gone away dead, you have gone away alive."

Life after death was dependent on the preservation of the body by mummification, and the enactment of funerary rituals that would guarantee a safe passage to the afterlife. Provision of funerary equipment in the tomb was another essential.

Democratization of Funerary Customs

Changes in funerary customs in the Middle Kingdom reflected changing funerary beliefs. The so-called "democratization of the afterlife" made access to divine status in the afterlife available to lower-ranking individuals. The Old Kingdom Pyramid Texts, basically reser-ved for royalty, ensured that only the king would become a god in the afterlife. Whereas the king would automatically have access to the hereafter, the Middle Kingdom Coffin Texts of non-royal Egyptians introduced the theme of moral judgment, which the dead had to pass before becoming immortal. The Texts were inscribed on and inside the wooden coffins of private individuals. Although both solar and Osirian concepts existed simultaneously in the Pyramid Texts, the Osirian religion had the greater appeal for common people. The deceased "became" Osiris, who was the prototype mummy.

Right **Wooden figure of a woman (c. 1975–1940 BCE).** Placed in burial sites, these figurines were proabably intended to be symbols of rebirth in the afterlife.

Housing the Dead

During the First Intermediate Period, modest rock-cut tombs predominated in the provincial centers, usually with only a small stela outside. During the Twelfth Dynasty, large rock-cut tombs with a decorated chapel and courtyard reflected the changing political scene.

Wall paintings included the ritual boat journey of the mummy of the deceased to Abydos, the cult center of Osiris. Many private individuals made the pilgrimage to Abydos to erect their memorial chapels and stelae in the proximity of the god.

Mummification

Mummification techniques were not highly developed at this time. More effort was expended on the external wrapping than on the internal preservation of the body.

There was a huge increase in the amount of linen used, especially with the addition of whole, folded, sheets wrapped around the body and also placed in the coffin. Red linen was included for the first time. Molten resin was applied to the body and some of the inner wrappings, but many of the bodies were badly preserved underneath.

Amulets and funerary jewelry magically protected and empowered the deceased. These were wrapped inside the bandages. The jewelry may have belonged to the deceased in life, but some objects, such as the protective broad collar, could be specifically made for funerary purposes. The Middle Kingdom was the high point in ancient Egyptian jewelry production, in terms of both technical refinement and design. Gilded and painted cartonnage mummy masks (made of layers of linen or papyrus stiffened with plaster) appeared in the First Intermediate period, and they continued to be used throughout the Middle Kingdom.

Afterlife Essentials

Painted wooden models of scenes of agriculture and food production magically ensured eternal supplies for the owner in the afterlife. With the decline of these model scenes in the mid-Twelfth Dynasty, and a reduction in the use of Coffin Texts on the interior of coffins, a new range of ritual objects appeared in burials. The objects included magic wands and rods, sticks and staves, many of which had previously been illustrated on the frieze inside the coffin. Objects were considered to have the same magical power as texts, and they could be independently activated by supernatural means. Curved "wands" carved from hippopotamus tusks were decorated with processions of wild animals, monsters, and deities holding knives to ward off harmful powers. Magical rods had a similar function, and both wands and rods offered magical protection in life as well as death. Sticks and staves as symbols of office, together with bows and arrows, were commonly included in the tomb.

Small funerary figurines, sometimes encased in miniature coffins, represented the deceased in his mummified form. The figurines were intended to serve as a substitute for the actual body, if it should be destroyed. These figurines subsequently developed into *shabti* figures, servants for the afterlife. Naked female figurines with pronounced sexual organs were frequently included in the tomb. They have been variously identified as fertility figures, dolls, or concubines. They were often found in cult places and domestic contexts, where they were probably meant to promote fertility. In a burial context the function of the figurines was probably as symbols of rebirth. Blue faience hippopotami, decorated with motifs of vegetation, were probably associated with fertility through the regenerative effects of the Nile inundation. Faience model offerings of food and pottery were also included.

The graves of poorer individuals were often simple shafts, without a chapel or offering table. To receive offerings, clay platters were placed at the mouth of the shaft. Food such as bread, vegetables, and a trussed ox were modeled into the surface. A spout ensured that offerings of water could escape. More elaborate models in tombs of poorer individuals were of pottery houses, erroneously termed "soul houses" by early excavators. The model houses included offerings and a libation basin or pool in the courtyard.

Above **Wooden model of a cook from Asyut (c. 2000 BCE)**. Models of food production ensured food supplies in the afterlife.

Below **Terracotta model houses (c. 1975–1640 BCE)**. Model houses left in tombs reflect the architecture of the time.

A Model for the Afterlife

During the First Intermediate Period and the early Middle Kingdom, fine painted wooden tomb models were used to represent the afterlife. The models replaced the predominantly limestone figures of servants that were found in Old Kingdom tombs.

Wooden models appeared in large numbers in non-royal tombs. These were intended as magical substitutes for servants, or to represent the continuance of food production in the afterlife.

Right **Painted wood procession of offering bearers (c.1950 BCE)**. The figures represent the delivery of produce to the tomb owner from his mortuary estates.

Food Production in the Afterlife

The models were placed on the lid of the coffin or on the floor around it. Probably the largest collection of Middle Kingdom tomb models comes from the burial chamber of Djehuty-Nakht, a nomarch (governor) in provincial Deir el-Bersheh in Middle Egypt. This fascinating and extensive collection consists of more than 45 scenes and 55 boats.

The most intact collection of models is from the Eleventh Dynasty tomb of Meketre, a high official buried south of Deir el-Bahri, on the west bank opposite Luxor. It comprises 24 models representing the official's entire estate and fleet of ships, giving a view in miniature of the workings of a community.

Two ochre-colored residences, with colonnaded porches, a copper-lined watertight pool, and elaborate gardens reflect the domestic architecture of the Theban area. Each model scene is housed in the building in which the activity took place. The butcher's shop depicts the slaughter of cattle and has miniature cuts of meat hanging in the upper levels. The granary is a complete building, with silos inscribed with the names of different varieties of corn. The brewery and bakery show every step of the production process, from the initial grinding of the flour to the finished product, with loaves and sealed beer jars stacked in baskets. Female spinners and weavers in the weaving workshop record each stage of the process of linen production.

Meketre and his sons are shown overseeing the counting of the cattle, and as passengers on two of the wooden boat models. All the figures were carved from coniferous wood and painted as if dressed, but pieces of linen had been added to nearly all of them to represent clothing.

Servants to the Tomb Owner

In addition to a procession of men and women carrying offerings, two superb half life-size figures of female offering bearers have been found. One figure carried individually carved

wine jars in a basket on her head, the other meat and bread. Each held a live duck by the wings in the right hand. The figures personified the mortuary estates, which were parcels of land endowed by the tomb owner to provide produce and an income to sustain his mortuary cult after death. They echo the Old Kingdom wall paintings, where processions of figures brought produce to the tomb owner from his estates.

Model Soldiers

Military scenes were a frequent theme in Eygptian wall paintings. During the periods of unrest, the governors of the nomes (provincial districts) recruited and trained both foreign mercenaries and local troops to protect Egypt.

Spectacular model soldiers from the tomb of Mesehti at Asyut in Middle Egypt reflect this practice. Forty dark-painted Nubian archers, holding bows and arrows and wearing traditional decorated red kilts, were arranged on a board, marching in rows. Egyptian pike-men in white kilts, holding lances and shields covered in animal hide, were grouped on another board.

The models were realistically executed. No two figures are exactly alike.

The Nile in Miniature

Boats comprised the largest group of each model assemblage. The collection of Meket-Re included boats for extended travel on the Nile, which were followed by fully equipped kitchen tenders. There were also fishing canoes, with crew hauling in fishing nets, and papyrus sporting boats for fishing and fowling in the marshes by the tomb owner in the afterlife.

Boats with a funerary and religious function continued to be part of the tomb assemblage after the models fell out of favor. Boat models represented the re-enactment of the voyage to Abydos for the burial of Osiris, with whom the deceased was symbolically associated. In addition to the Osirian cycle, the solar bark in which the sun-god Ra traveled through the underworld at night and across the sky by day, was also represented in some tombs.

By the Twelfth Dynasty, model scenes of daily life appear to have been less popular, and were replaced by the quite different *shabti* figures.

Left **Making bread and beer, stuccoed and painted wood models (c. 1975–1640 BCE).** Models representing the production of food in the afterlife also reveal details of daily life in Egypt, such as the processes of brewing and baking.

Left **Egyptian army models from Mesehti's tomb at Asyut (c.1938–1755 BCE)** Reflecting military themes in tomb wall-paintings, forty realistic Egyptian model soldiers were placed on a board with forty Nubian model archers.

Middle Kingdom Kahun

An array of artifacts and valuable papyri were found in the Middle Kingdom pyramid town of Kahun. The Kahun site has yielded evidence that enables scholars to reconstruct life in a typical Egyptian urban community during the period.

The times of Egyptian prosperity were those periods when the entire country was united under a central administration.

The Middle Kingdom emerged from the victory of the Theban kings over their northern rivals. When Amenemhet I seized power from the somewhat shadowy Mentuhotep IV, the Eleventh Dynasty concluded. The usurper established a new dynasty and, in a short time, a new capital in the Faiyum region at Itj-tawy ("Seizer of the Two Lands"), most likely near the modern settlement of el-Lisht at the northern entrance to the Faiyum. Over the course of the Twelfth Dynasty the whole region was to have a face-lift.

The center of this very fertile basin is Lake Birket Qarun, known as Lake Moeris to the classical authors. The Faiyum was opened up for agriculture in a way not seen during the Old Kingdom. The connecting channel (the modern Bahr Yusef) became the lifeline of the water supply as the Twelfth Dynasty pharaohs widened and deepened it for irrigation purposes.

New towns emerged in the Faiyum region, especially when the royal necropolis, and the associated mortuary cults, were relocated to el-Lisht, near the new capital.

Below right **Tomb model of house with portico.** Model houses reinforce the evidence provided by the Kahun excavations.

A New Town in the Faiyum

One such pyramid town was the well-planned settlement of Kahun, lying near the modern el-Lahun. The town's ancient name was *Hetep-Senusret* ("Senusret is satisfied"). It was initially established to house the construction workers for the pyramid of Senusret II, along with their families. Flinders Petrie investigated Kahun in the 1890s, and again in 1913, and he found a whole array of artifacts and valuable papyri. In some of the papyri are hymns eulogizing the king in what is clearly part of the funerary cult maintained in this priestly community.

Kahun Excavations and the Meketre Tomb Models

Assisting our knowledge and understanding of the actual remains of Kahun are several tomb models that demonstrate daily life in Middle Kingdom Egypt. These models were obtained from the near contemporary Eleventh Dynasty tomb of Meketre, Chancellor to Mentuhotep I.

Two model houses among this collection correspond closely to the wall remains of units along the northern side of Kahun's main east-west street. This helps us to reconstruct with some confidence the actual appearance of a typical

SEMNA IN NUBIA

When Senusret III subdued Nubia he secured control of his now extensive empire by building a series of forts.

Since surveillance is essential to security, the Egyptians sent patrols for which they used local Nubians. An intriguing set of documents known as the "Semna Despatches", which turned up in a tomb in Thebes, has shed interesting light on the conduct of these patrols.

Dating to the reign of Amenemhet III, these Semna Despatches reveal a close scrutiny of all people movements, including

that of travelers, traders, and boat traffic. The aim was to regulate closely the conduct of the Nubian community under Egypt's immediate control and wider contacts with regions further south.

The royal officials at Thebes wanted to be fully informed of all developments in minute detail.

This was in line with the policy of Senusret I, as proclaimed in his stele, that no Nubian may cross his appointed boundary in either direction, except those in legitimate trade or diplomacy.

Middle Kingdom house, at least one from the middle to higher levels of society.

The outer walls of a house in Kahun would have presented a rather stark facade. However, the interior usually revealed a complex of rooms and courtyards, the showpiece being a court, colonnaded on its southern side, and adorned with a tree-lined garden, in some cases the trees lined a central pool. In the Kahun examples a reception room, again supported on columns, and another adjacent court are visible.

In these larger houses are granaries of such capacity that together they must have supplied not only the respective households but also other residents of the town of Kahun. The Meketre tomb models again help our understanding. A granary in one model is similar to remains at Kahun. The granary model depicts labourers filling sacks while scribes record the amounts, presumably for rations administration, and taxation, in what was a highly bureaucratic society. Calculations from the dimensions of the granaries, and from known ration sizes, indicate that the population exceeded five thousand citizens.

The houses of Kahun frequently contained various artifacts such as pottery (often blue-glazed), tools and farm implements, remains of linen cloth, furniture, musical instruments and games, including a game piece that is similar to a draught-board. Even a rat trap has survived the centuries in Kahun. The combined evidence of the Kahun excavations and the Meketre models reveals a picture of life in an Egyptian town.

The Kahun Papyri

The other main yield of the Kahun finds was the cache of papyri. Some of the papyri are yet to be studied fully, but it is possible to discern the structure of society, legal procedures, organization of labor, and knowledge of medicine and mathematics in Ancient Egypt. The town had a mayor, by now the norm for Egypt, and offices for the peripatetic royal vizier and other government officials. One papyrus, a household list from a priest of the mortuary cult of Senusret II, describes a veritable entourage of brewers, cooks, and general laborers of the community.

Legal papyri such as wills show the procedures of inheritance. In one will a priest transferred both his office and property to his son who would continue in office. In other records, an architect leaves his property and slaves to his brother, an architect and priest. The brother then turns it over to his wife.

From a modern standpoint, the medical knowledge revealed in these texts is a mixture of both scientific insight and superstitious magic. In a gynecological text, diagnostic techniques for pregnancy demonstrate insight, but some prescriptions for feminine ailments are quite dangerous.

The texts show that Kahun is both administered and structured according to the Egyptian bureaucratic ideal.

Above **The Pyramid of Senusret II at Lahun.** Kahun lies at the foot of this pyramid.

Below **Pleated linen robe, Middle Kingdom.** Linen, musical instruments, and papyri survived at Kahun.

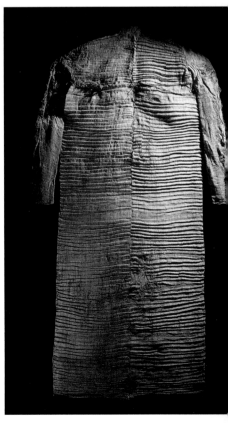

Foreigners in Egypt

Despite Eygpt's relatively isolated geographical setting, there is extensive evidence of foreign contact. Throughout Egyptian history there was interaction with foreign neighbors and with the immigrants who came to live in Egypt.

Below **Vases from Asiatic tributary states (1878 engraving by Achille Prisse d'Avennes).** Asiatic products have been found in Middle Kingdom sites.

To the west and east of Egypt lies the desert. The south borders on Lower Nubia, which was never densely populated. However, the impression of geographical isolation is certainly false, for Egypt had contact with both the Nubians and the Asiatic people. Not only were they neighbors, both Nubians and Asiatics became part of the Egyptian population.

The Nubians

The Old Kingdom hieroglyphic inscriptions refer to people called *Nehesyu* 'Nubians', most often simply portrayed in modest military or domestic positions. Stronger links between Egypt and its southern neighbor are to be expected, as there is no natural border between the two countries.

Nubians appear again in the First Intermediate Period and Middle Kingdom sources. Nubians in Egypt are still shown in the same roles, as soldiers and servants. On the sarcophagus of queen Ashait, two Nubian servant-women are depicted, demonstrating that some Nubians were employed at the royal court.

Nubian archers were renowned for their abilities. A remarkable wooden model troop of forty Nubian soldiers was found in the tomb of the nomarch Mesehti of Asyut. The Nubian soldiers can easily be identified by their dark skin and by their foreign dress, which is evidently of painted leather.

There is little evidence that Nubians reached the grander positions, but one exception might be an official with the relatively high title 'great scribe of the treasurer' and the name 'Nubian' (*Nehesy*), known from several scarab seals. In the Second Intermediate Period there is a king with the same name. In neither case, though, is it known whether these men were really Nubians, or whether they received their names because they had especially dark skin at birth. The reason for this invisibility of Nubian people, especially in higher positions, might be that the Nubians rapidly became integrated into Egyptian society and so were no longer presented as a separate ethnic group.

The Asiatic Peoples

People from Asia, even from South Palestine, are not often mentioned in earlier Egyptian sources. Literary works set in the First Intermediate

Period refer to Asians entering the Delta, and Amenemhet I building the "Walls of the Rulers" at the eastern border of the Delta to stop this immigration. An inscription of Amenemhet II from Memphis records a campaign against two Asiatic cities, ending with the deportation of over 1500 *aamu* "[Semitic-speaking] Asiatics" to Egypt.

Many Semitic names appear in documents of the Middle Kingdom and there are some people with Egyptian names who are referred to as "Asiatic" (*Aam*), as if they dropped their foreign names, but chose to keep their identity.

Most of these Asiatic people were servants in lower and middle positions. They appear as cooks, weavers and workers in palace storerooms or on the estates of Egyptian officials. However, many other immigrants might have received an Egyptian name; so those not identified as Asiatic would then not be visibly foreign to us.

Nubian Burials

Initially, it seems that most Nubians quickly became Egyptianized. However, this pattern did change in the Thirteenth Dynasty. Small cemeteries with Nubian burials appear throughout the land, especially in Upper Egypt.

The tombs are round surface burials, with the dead placed in a contracted position. Archeologists named these burials Pan Graves, because the first tombs found were rather shallow holes. Typical hand-made Nubian pottery vessels were placed beside the body in the graves.

These graves must have belonged to small bands of Nubians employed by Egyptians or entering the country as nomads. Burial-goods, such as archery wrist-guards, indicate that these Nubians certainly served as soldiers. The buried may include the desert Nubians that were referred to as *Medjay* in Egyptian sources.

Asiatic Settlements

The archeological evidence for immigration from Asia is utterly different. The eastern edge of the Delta is rich in settlements and the burials of people from South

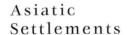

Above **Asian and Egyptian war chariots and weapons (A. Racinet, *Historical Costumes Vol 2*, 1888).** Despite military conflict over the centuries, foreigners also worked within Egypt as soldiers.

Palestine, dating to the end of the Middle Kingdom and Second Intermediate Period.

Clearly, at the end of the Middle Kingdom a substantial wave of migration came from Asia to Egypt. Asiatic peoples settled in Egypt at the fringe of the eastern Delta, but with these settlers there is little evidence for any assimilation, at least in the first generations.

Thirteenth Dynasty Palestinian Mansion

A great palatial mansion found at the main site of the region at Tell el-Dab'a is in the Egyptian style but has yielded many finds of Palestinian culture. In the tombs behind this palace the remains of a statue show an Asian official. The statue was certainly produced in an Egyptian workshop but the hairstyle and the costume are foreign. Evidently these Asiatic immigrants employed Egyptian craftsmen and artists for their own products.

The palace dates to the early Thirteenth Dynasty, and shows that by this time Asiatic immigrants could become wealthy in Egypt. Culturally, these people were the basis for the later Hyksos domination of the country that occurred during the Second Intermediate Period.

Left **Asiatic family arriving in Twelfth Dynasty Egypt (1878 engraving by Achille Prisse d'Avennes).** Asiatic immigrants settled in the Delta region of Egypt during the late Middle Kingdom.

Egypt and Crete

Around 2000 BCE the Minoan culture on the Greek island of Crete developed into a civilization with all the signs of a high culture. From early on there is evidence for at least indirect contact between Egypt and Crete.

Crete is the first European civilization. The Minoan of Crete had all the features of a developed society, such as writing, full-figured art, palatial centers and towns.

Little is known about how contact between Crete and Egypt worked, if Egyptians ever reached Crete or Cretans reached Egypt before the early New Kingdom. Egyptian objects found on Crete include a number of fine stone vessels, dating to the Old Kingdom, possibly indicating that contact was made during that period.

THE TOD TREASURE

El-Tod (or Tod) is the modern name of the ancient Egyptian town Djerty, not far from Thebes. Here there stood a temple for the war god, Montu. Excavations uncovered four bronze boxes in the temple foundations, two with the name of King Amenemhet II. The boxes contained an unexpected find: 153 silver bowls and numerous smaller objects, mainly Near Eastern cylinder seals of lapis lazuli, but also a silver Minoan seal with a spider-motif. The silver bowls are all of non-Egyptian appearance. Because of their high value there are almost no comparable

finds. Such objects, if not lost or removed to a tomb, were usually soon melted down to reuse the metal. It is therefore not easy to determine where these bowls were made, but, on stylistic grounds, the Aegean seems plausible. These findings, together with imported Minoan pottery from other sites, provide important evidence for international trade around 1900 BCE.

Below **The Sanctuary of Tod (c. 1900 BCE)**. Excavations at this temple site revealed Minoan objects inside boxes marked with the name of King Amenemhet II.

Direct Trade Links

In the third millennium BCE Cretans produced stone vessels. Some were similar to Egyptian examples, so Egyptian prototypes might have influenced the production of this object type. Despite this evidence for contact between the two cultures, the nature of this contact is uncertain. Possibly, Egyptian vessels were brought to Crete via other centers or by other seafaring people of the eastern Mediterranean.

At the end of the First Intermediate Period scarab-shaped amulets developed in Egypt. Intriguingly, both imports and local imitations appear at about the same time on Crete. In western Asia only imports are found until a few centuries later. This difference in the reception of Egyptian items is perhaps the strongest indication of direct trade between Crete and Egypt.

At about the same time, c. 2000–1900 BCE, the spiral motif first appears as an independent compositional element in Egyptian art. This motif had long been popular in the Greek islands, and it now became common in Middle Kingdom Egypt. Since the scarab motif had somehow traveled from Egypt to Crete, perhaps the spiral motif moved in the other direction, imported into Egypt from Crete. It could, though, have developed in Egypt independently.

Minoan Pottery in Egypt

The late Middle Kingdom provides more tangible evidence for contact on the Egyptian side. Minoan pottery vessels or sherds (pottery fragments) were found at several major sites, notably Lahun, Abydos, and el-Lisht. At Lahun, the number of fragments encouraged the excavator of the site to imagine that Cretans worked here on constructing the pyramid of the king Senusret II. However, only palace-ware was found, and only a few vessels, so this is unlikely, particularly as there are no other indications for Cretans at Lahun. Minoan pottery found in Egypt belongs to a type known as Kamares ware, painted to evoke the effect of metal vessels. The imitations show how much Egyptians appreciated these artworks.

Their open form makes the vessels unsuitable for transporting material, so presumably they were imported for their own sake rather than for any contents. Minoan vessels of the same type and date have been found in smaller numbers in Cyprus and Syria–Palestine, suggesting a trading circuit around the eastern Mediterranean.

Egyptian Artifacts in Knossos

There is debate over the nature of the trade between Egypt and Crete, how substantial it was, and what materials were involved. Some researchers think only certain luxury objects were exchanged between the Egyptian court and Minoan palaces. Many traded goods do not survive well in the archeological record, notably oil, food, textiles, and metal. Fortunately, a rare example of Minoan silver has been preserved at el-Tod. As so little pottery survived, the Minoan pottery found in Egypt might form just a small percentage of the objects exchanged. The occasional Egyptian objects on Crete might also belong to this trade. The most famous example is the Middle Kingdom statuette of a man called Weser, found in later levels at Knossos in Crete. The date the statue left Egypt is unknown.

Several New Kingdom depictions and references to "*Keftiu*" are identified as references to Minoans, but Middle Kingdom sources provide only one ambiguous written reference to Crete, in the "Laments of Ipuwer," dating to the very end of the period. One passage from this ancient "Lament" reports that Crete lacked embalming material because Egypt no longer acquired cedar from Byblos in Lebanon, further evidence that a trading circuit was established.

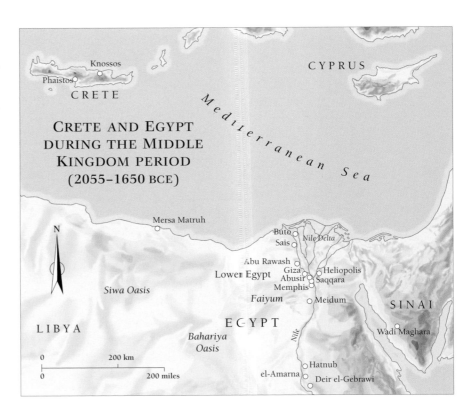

CRETE AND EGYPT DURING THE MIDDLE KINGDOM PERIOD (2055–1650 BCE)

Above **Map showing Egypt and the island of Crete.** There is some evidence of direct trade between these countries during the Middle Kingdom.

Left **Minoan palace on Crete.** Objects were exchanged between the Egyptian coast and Minoan palaces.

Middle Kingdom Decline

The spectacular pyramids and mortuary temples of the Old Kingdom still stir the imagination, while the glories of empire and the era of Rameses "the Great" evoke admiration. By comparison, what was the legacy of the Middle Kingdom?

The Middle Kingdom was the "classical" period of Egypt, producing great literature that was assiduously copied by later scribes. It was the era of the powerful and productive kings of the Twelfth Dynasty, the reclamation of the Faiyum for agriculture, and the foundations of Egypt's later empire. However, the Middle Kingdom was also characterized by decline.

Fading Glory

When the glory days of the Twelfth Dynasty concluded there were no spectacular monuments or stirring exploits to leave to posterity. Amenemhet III, the last king of note before the

Twelfth Dynasty faded out, reinforced the economy of Egypt. He left two significant pyramids, one at Dahshur, the other at Hawara, but the Hawara pyramid was the last of any importance.

After a shadowy namesake and a queen, Sobeknofru, concluded the Dynasty, an obscure period of decline, confusion, and disarray known as the Thirteenth Dynasty ensued.

The Turin Canon, a piece of papyrus inscribed with a list of the names of Egyptian rulers, mentions at least fifty kings, and most likely more, ruling within a period of around 150 years. Various theories are proposed to explain the weakness of the Thirteenth Dynasty, as opposed

Below **The Turin Canon,** (fragment from the Egyptian Museum, Turin). Lists that show the lengths of the kings' reigns provide clues to the succession of Thirteenth Dynasty rulers.

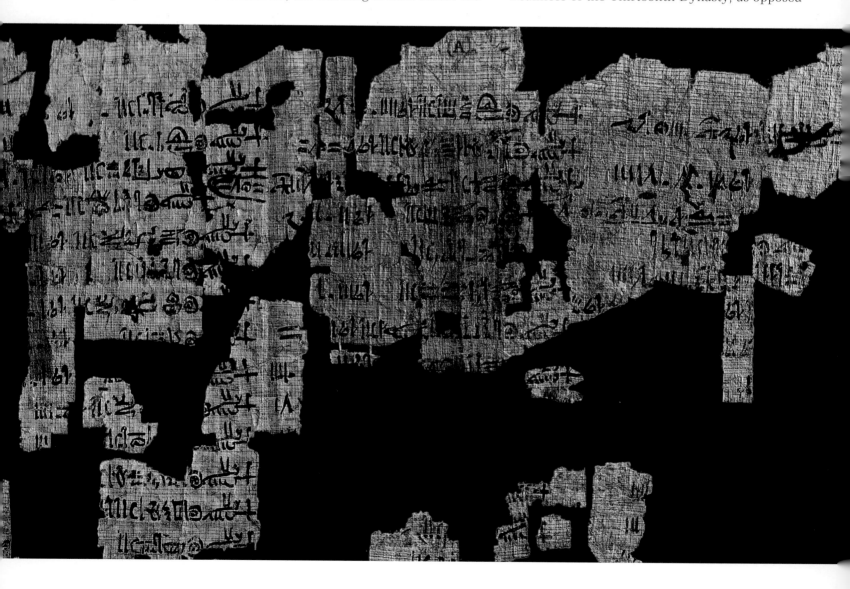

to the previous period of greatness, but facts about the dynasty are obscured by the fragmentary nature of the evidence.

A Weakened Kingdom

One theory envisages that a series of figurehead rulers, manipulated by the more stable line of viziers, were appointed and then dismissed at will. However, closer inspection of the source material for the Thirteenth Dynasty reveals a different picture. While there was an initial period of instability, when a succession of kings ruled for three years or less, a second phase saw a stronger group of kings with longer reigns. A third phase witnessed the break-up of the dynasty with a contemporaneous Fourteenth Dynasty ruling from the city of Xois in the Delta.

Especially in the early part of the Dynasty, non-royal monuments rarely refer to the king, nor does the king appear in the standard prayers in funerary inscriptions, indicating that the power of the king and palace has declined in popular estimation.

Finally, around 1720 BCE the so-called Hyksos or "Desert Princes" invaded the northern part of the country, sacked the city of Memphis, and ruled from Avaris in the Delta.

Known Kings of the Thirteenth Dynasty

Some kings of the Thirteenth Dynasty are known fairly well, while others are known only from scattered fragments. Aside from its fragmentary character at crucial points, the Turin List is less than comprehensive. At least ten kings from Upper Egypt are mentioned in other records. However, this may support the view that the Seventeenth Dynasty was simply the Thirteenth relocated from Itj-tawy to Thebes, when the Egyptian state contracted to rule Upper Egypt alone, possibly in the time of Merneferra Ay, c. 1720 BCE.

According to the lists on the Turin Canon, Hor is one of the earlier kings

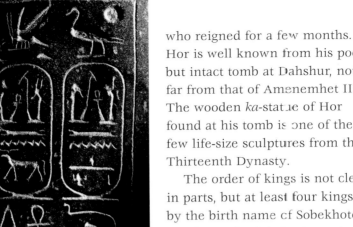

who reigned for a few months. Hor is well known from his poor but intact tomb at Dahshur, not far from that of Amenemhet III. The wooden ka-statue of Hor found at his tomb is one of the few life-size sculptures from the Thirteenth Dynasty.

The order of kings is not clear in parts, but at least four kings by the birth name of Sobekhotep stand out, the Sobek element indicating adoption of the crocodile deity of the Faiyum, which became a mark of the dynasty. In a later phase, the royal power seems to have reasserted itself with the successive rule of three brothers, Neferhotep I, Sobekhotep IV, and Sithathor, although the latter was probably only a prince. A relief from Byblos in Lebanon depicts Neferhotep with the local prince, Yantin, kneeling before him as his vassal. Meanwhile, four life-size statues of Sobekhotep have been recovered, and he is known to have secured the Nubian borders with a show of force.

The Rise of Avaris

The interesting feature of this period, now becoming clear from the excavations of Manfred Bietak in the Delta, is the prodigious growth of Semitic settlements around the area of Tell el-Dab'a, the ancient Hyksos capital of Avaris. Although the history of occupation stretches back to the First Intermediate Period, expansion increased dramatically in the late Middle Kingdom and into the Second Intermediate period. Typical houses in the region display a plan similar to counterparts in Palestine, and the burial customs of the area are also typically Semitic for the period.

The other outstanding features of the dwellings are the wall frescoes and pottery styles that show strong connections with the Minoan civilization of Crete. Again, the explanations of these phenomena vary, but they do help to build up a picture of an obscure and hitherto little understood phase of Egyptian history.

Left **Cartouche of Hyksos king on a sphinx from Tanis (c. 1630–1520 BCE)** The Hyksos influence in Egypt increased during the late Middle Kingdom, especially in the Delta.

Below **Statue of Awibra Hor with Ka headdress (c. 1300 BCE).** Hor is one of the known Thirteenth Dynasty kings. This life-sized wooden statue is from his tomb at Dahshur.

THE SECOND INTERMEDIATE PERIOD

The Rise of the Hyksos

At the collapse of the Middle Kingdom, Egypt was in a state of political and economic upheaval, leaving the throne open to invasion from any foreign group with the power to take it. The Hyksos took advantage of this opportunity.

Right **Ahmose continued the campaign of the previous two Egyptian kings against the Hyksos.** He was ultimately successful in their final expulsion from Egypt.

They overthrew the petty kings who were claiming sovereignty in different areas of the Delta region. At the beginning of their reign the country was divided into three, with the Hyksos Fifteenth Dynasty ruling in the eastern Delta, the Fourteenth and Sixteenth Dynasties ruling in the western Delta and the Seventeenth Dynasty ruling from the Theban region. Manetho records that the Hyksos rise to power was easy—without a battle—and the archeological record supports this.

Provincial Rulers

Contrary to popular belief the Hyksos did not invade Egypt in the Second Intermediate Period, but were already settled in the eastern Delta, primarily at the site of Avaris (modern Tell el Dab'a). There

had been an Asiatic population at this site for more than a century prior to the Hyksos period. As the Hyksos community was well established in the Delta region they would have had local support when the first Hyksos king rose to power. The first four Hyksos rulers of the Fifteenth Dynasty (thought to be Shamuqenu, 'Aper-'Anati, Sekerher/Salitis and Khyan) used the *hka haswt* title (which means "rulers of foreign lands"), although Khyan abandoned it when he gained control over Upper and Lower Egypt later in the dynasty. It could therefore be suggested that the Hyksos rulers did not have the ambition originally to call themselves by typical Egyptian royal titles and seemed content with ruling the Delta with only provincial power. The lack of evidence of the first three kings of the Hyksos Fifteenth Dynasty coincides with this small-scale local ambition.

Rising Ambitions

When Khyan ascended to the throne he started a military campaign southwards with the intent of conquering all of Egypt and earning the title

Right **"Kamose the Brave" led an expedition to Avaris.** Despite his minimal military success, he boasted to Apepi: "Behold, I am drinking of the wine of your vineyards...I am hacking up your place of residence, cutting down your trees."

THE OTHER HYKSOS CITIES

Petrie identified Tell el Yahudiya, in the Delta, as a Hyksos settlement. The square mud-brick settlement is enclosed in a 60 ft (18 m) sand bank with a 200 ft (60 m) slope leading to the eastern entrance. This sand bank was surrounded by a 40 ft (12 m) high wall, which was removed in the nineteenth century for building material. There were five graves within this enclosure, each containing Hyksos scarabs. One was a gold-mounted scarab inscribed with King Khyan's name, which would give the earliest possible date of 1621–1581 BCE for this grave and the settlement.

King of Upper and Lower Egypt. He
waited for 20 years at Memphis
gaining strength and support before
campaigning further southwards to
conquer Abydos. The ambition of
Khyan and the following king
Apepi increased. During the reign
of Apepi, the strongest of the
Hyksos kings, the southern boundary of Hyksos control was at
Hermopolis and the northern
boundary was at Pi-Hathor between
Tanis and Bubastis. However,
evidence of isolated Hyksos points
of control at Nefrusi (in Middle
Egypt) and Gebelein (south of
Luxor), which would have secured
a safe trading passage from Avaris
to Nubia, indicates the extent of
their power. This could also suggest
that the Theban Seventeenth
Dynasty were vassal rulers of the
Hyksos kings with the Hyksos
Fifteenth Dynasty being in control
of most of Egypt.

The Egyptian literary evidence
describes the Hyksos destruction
caused on their campaigns southwards. However, these sources were
written after the expulsion of the
Hyksos with the purpose of reinforcing ideologies of Egyptian
kingship, and there is very little
archeological evidence to support
this mass destruction.

Warrior Kings

Despite this relatively peaceful
take-over the Hyksos are well
known for being a warrior nation,
and in the majority of burials at
Avaris there are a number of
Syro–Palestinian weapons included
as grave goods. Although Avaris

was a fortified city, it does not seem to have
been engaged in battle and the reinforced
enclosure wall was not built until the very end of
the period at the start of the campaigns of the
Seventeenth Dynasty against them. This does
suggest that the campaigns of the Hyksos to
conquer all of Egypt were met with minimum
retaliation, until the very end of the period when
the Seventeenth Dynasty had gathered enough

manpower to initiate a campaign to expel them.
The warrior skills of the Hyksos were proven
when it took three generations of the Theban
Seventeenth Dynasty to gain control of Egypt
from these kings. Both Seqenenra Taa and
Kamose probably died in battle with the Hyksos,
leaving the completion of the campaign to
Ahmose, who expelled them from Egypt and was
the first king of the Eighteenth Dynasty.

Above **The Hyksos intro-
duced the composite bow
into Egypt.** They also
adopted the use of the
chariot at the same time
as the Egyptians near the
end of the Intermediate
Period.

Who Were the Hyksos?

The Egyptians referred to the Canaanite inhabitants of Avaris as *Aamu*, a term that generally meant Asiatic and could be applied to any inhabitants of the Syro-Palestinian region. The rulers of these Asiatics were known as *hka haswt*.

The term "Hyksos" is Greek and derived from the title *hka haswt*, meaning "ruler of foreign lands." One of the most debated issues regarding the Hyksos rulers is their country of origin, although it is widely agreed that they were "Asiatic."

Below **The earliest image of the Hyksos comes from the Twelfth Dynasty tomb of Khnumhotep II at Beni Hasan**. It depicts a trading party bringing eye-paint to Egypt. The leader, Absha, is at the front of the group and is identified as *hka haswt*.

Clues in Names and Material Culture

The material culture from the Hyksos strata at Avaris is closely correlated to the last stage of the Middle Bronze Age II in the Syro–Palestinian region. There is also evidence to suggest there were Mesopotamian influences within the Hyksos material culture. Many of the burials at Avaris contain composite bows, scimitars, cylinder seals and toggle pins, all of which have Mesopotamian origins. Even the vaulted tombs themselves are influenced by Mesopotamian culture. However the objects used are of traditional rather than contemporary Mesopotamian design and were in use up to 750 years prior to their arrival in Egypt. This could suggest that these objects did not reach the Hyksos directly from Mesopotamia, but arrived indirectly through trade relations.

On the "Amada stela" of Amenhotep II the Hyksos are listed alongside the *retenu*, a general term used by the Egyptians for the Palestinians, suggesting the Egyptians regarded the Hyksos as a different ethnic group from the Palestinians. However, it is generally believed that the Hyksos

were Canaanite in origin, and this is reflected in the material culture from their capital city, which is primarily Canaanite in origin and design. The most obvious Canaanite practices carried out at Avaris were servant burials across the tomb entrances and the donkey burials.

Through the study of names, Mesopotamian influence is further suggested. A record of the Theban Seventeenth Dynasty wars against the Hyksos mentions the capture of a female slave called Ishtar-ummi. Her name belongs to a northern Mesopotamian culture and not the Canaanite culture, where the name would have been Astarte-ummi. Unfortunately the study of names does not provide accurate evidence of the origins of the individual.

Primary Hyksos Kings

There are six probable rulers of the Hyksos period, settled in the Delta region, who reigned for a total of 108 years. Their names all have a western Semitic origin.

Shamuqenu (1649–? BCE) and 'Aper-'Anati were the two earliest kings of the Fifteenth Dynasty, and are identified from a single scarab seal bearing their names. Their reign length and regions of power are unknown.

Sekerher/Salitis (? –1621 BCE) is attested by a stone door-jamb from Avaris, which bears both Egyptian royal titles and the *hka haswt* title, and is the only monument that includes both. This door-jamb indicates that Sekerher/Salitis had built a monumental building (temple or palace) at the capital.

Khyan (1621–1581 BCE) is one of the better-known kings of this period and it is thought he

may have ruled for approximately 40 years. He started his reign under the title *hka haswt* and then adopted the traditional Egyptian titles. His eldest son was Yanassi, who was probably his intended heir although he never in fact came to the throne.

Apepi (1581–1541 BCE) came to the throne amidst a violent usurpation of the rightful heir Yanassi, and was the most ambitious of the Hyksos kings. He also ruled for approximately 40 years and gained control over most of Egypt during this period in power.

Apepi had a son and a daughter and it has been suggested that he was married to a Seventeenth Dynasty Theban princess Tany, which would have been a traditional way to seal peaceful alliances between ruling houses.

Khamudi (1541–1540 BCE) was probably the last king of the Fifteenth Dynasty and the Hyksos period and ruled for only a year before Ahmose expelled the Hyksos from Egypt. Only three scarab seals, two in Jericho and one that is unprovenanced, attest this king.

There are a number of other kings mentioned on scarabs indicating there was an internal struggle for power with different kings ruling different areas, or there was distribution of scarabs to those who were not kings. Scarabs may have been issued to crown princes or may record earlier names of the six primary kings.

Above **Trade brought the Hyksos to Egypt.** This reconstructed engraving from Beni Hasan shows an Asiatic group of men wearing elaborately patterned clothes, with short pointed beards and shoulder-length hair.

Above **Limestone relief cartouche of Apepi.** His long reign was both the zenith and the nadir of Hyksos rule.

Memphis

One of the real problems regarding the Hyksos in Egypt has been the application of the sequential dynastic structure to the archeology of the country, with the assumption that it was a cultural unity during this period.

Above and below **The appearance of new styles of pottery ware is indicative of political and cultural change.** This can be seen with the rise of the Hyksos and transition to the Middle Kingdom.

The nature of the Hyksos culture is just now presenting itself in its true light due to the recent work at such places as Avaris and Tell el Yahudiya. Additionally, the removal of many monuments from Memphis and the Memphite region in general, and their dispersal to Avaris and other locations in the north, must be assigned to the Hyksos. Ancient records lead us to believe that the destruction in the north was quick and that Memphis was taken by the Hyksos soon after their appearance and pillaged. Indeed, later tradition was to credit the Hyksos king Apepi with having founded Memphis. This may, however, refer to nothing more than some construction work on a palace in this city.

New Ceramic Style

The archeological evidence, while still sparse, would seem to lend credence to this scenario. A new style of ceramic ware appears suddenly at Memphis and becomes well established in a very short period. It is represented by a transitional phase and corresponds to the historical period under consideration. From the extant evidence we possess, there appears to be a steady development within the style of the Middle Kingdom ware until this period is reached. At this point substantial changes can be seen. The nature of these changes takes the form of a difference in the "fabric," or type of material used for manufacture and the decoration found on the pottery itself. Additionally, some general shape changes can be seen in the deposits.

The introduction of this new ceramic style fits well with the period of the Hyksos incursions. This is a period that must have lasted for at least 40 years if we include the first 20 years of Ahmose's reign and add the supposed periods of his two predecessors who were also engaged militarily with the Hyksos. It would seem at this point that there is archeological evidence to support the idea that the Hyksos did inhabit the city of Memphis for a time at least. The pottery workshops

that supplied Memphis suddenly changed their style. An earlier change like this can be seen at the time of the Middle Kingdom. The site of Lisht exhibits a new style of ceramic ware when it became the capital during the Middle Kingdom. All of this gives support to the account given in Manetho's history and cited by Josephis where he describes the ease with which the Hyksos gained control of Egypt. His account tells us that the Hyksos had appointed one of their number as king. His name is indicated as Salitis and he was said to have had his seat at Memphis from where he collected tribute from both Upper and Lower Egypt.

Over a period of some 20 years then this Sekerher/Salitis—historical sources indicate that these names refer to the same king—probably based at Memphis, ruled a kingdom consisting of the Nile Delta and the Nile Valley as far south as Gebelein (south of Thebes). The reference here to the extent of the area under Memphite and so Hyksos control, would give some credence to the story of the "Quarrel of Apepi and Seqenenra".

One archeological thread yet to be tied together is the appearance of a small number of pieces of Kerma cooking pottery at Memphis and Kerma beakers found at Saqqara in a burial. The necropolis of Saqqara has long been regarded as the cemetery of the capital at Memphis. This pottery hails from far to the south and may be an indication of Nubian mercenaries serving in the Theban army at the end of this period. These mercenaries were likely part of the army that drove out the Hyksos at the beginning of the Eighteenth Dynasty.

ARCHEOLOGY OF A CITY

It is surprising that a city of the importance of Memphis throughout all of Egyptian history has so far given us very little by way of archeological information concerning this period. In fact little real evidence of the Hyksos Middle Bronze Age culture exists beyond the eastern Delta area.

The lack of large Hyksos-related public architecture at the site does not mean, however, that the Hyksos had no real power in the region. The last 20 years have seen sites such as Memphis give up information that previously had either been missed or ignored due to the difficulties encountered excavating in areas where the water table is high. The ceramic evidence found at Memphis has helped tie together the many loose ends in the historical record. Many of this important city's secrets are still to be found in its stratified layers of occupation. The evidence being unearthed here indicates that the culture of the city did evolve but did not fundamentally change until into the beginning of the Eighteenth Dynasty.

Below **Engraving by the German KR Lepsius, c. 1845, showing an area of the ruins at Memphis.** Excavations at the site have shown how sophisticated techniques for the study of pottery reveal Egyptian history in the context of cultural change.

Avaris

The wall of his early Eighteenth Dynasty tomb at Elkab tells us how Ahmose son of Ibana followed his king into battle when the Egyptians besieged Avaris. The king noted his bravery against the Hyksos and presented him with the "gold of valor."

Below **Large stele of Kamose.** The hieroglyphic inscription celebrates his victory over Apepi, though it was the following Egyptian king, Ahmose, who finally defeated the Hyksos.

Such military biographies are rare in Egyptian tombs and Ahmose's provides us with one of the only written records of this campaign. It gives insight into this period of Egyptian history and the life of a man who rose through the ranks when animosity ran high in the country.

Biography of a City
After enduring years of the humiliation of Hyksos control of a large portion of the land, the Theban king Ahmose I, finally succeeded in overthrowing the city of Avaris, their capital. The site is located in the eastern Delta and is known in Arabic as Tell el Dab'a. The presence of the Hyksos in Egypt and indeed, the entire period itself is best represented at the site of Avaris. Around 1785 BCE the Twelfth Dynasty lost control of the country and occasioned the rise of the Thirteenth Dynasty at Thebes while a Fourteenth Dynasty arose at the Delta town of Khasuu. The Hyksos, themselves located in the Delta, then gave rise to the Fifteenth and subsequent Sixteenth Dynasties at Avaris. Manetho then recognizes a Seventeenth Dynasty again in Thebes and gives us the dynastic history, at least of the Hyksos period, as 1650–1540 BCE.

In geographic terms, the site of Avaris itself lies in the northeastern Nile Delta at the Pelusaic branch of the Nile. This would have been a particularly strategic location for contact with the eastern Mediterranean where both sea and land routes join.

Expansion
The site consists of three mounds with the central one showing evidence of a large town of Twelfth Dynasty date. This town expanded in size during the Thirteenth and Fifteenth Dynasties. It is on this site that archeological evidence shows a palace and several associated structures and at least three occupational levels that can be attributed to the kings of the Fifteenth Dynasty, that is, the Hyksos. It must be noted however, that no specific king can be identified with this residential complex, and in fact may represent an aggrandized example of an elite house of the Middle Kingdom.

While based in Memphis, it is probable that Sekerher/Salitis came from a family of local rulers of Avaris belonging to the Fourteenth Dynasty. As such the actual power base remained at Avaris. At this time, a rapid expansion of the city can be seen to several times its original size. This was undoubtedly due to an influx of population

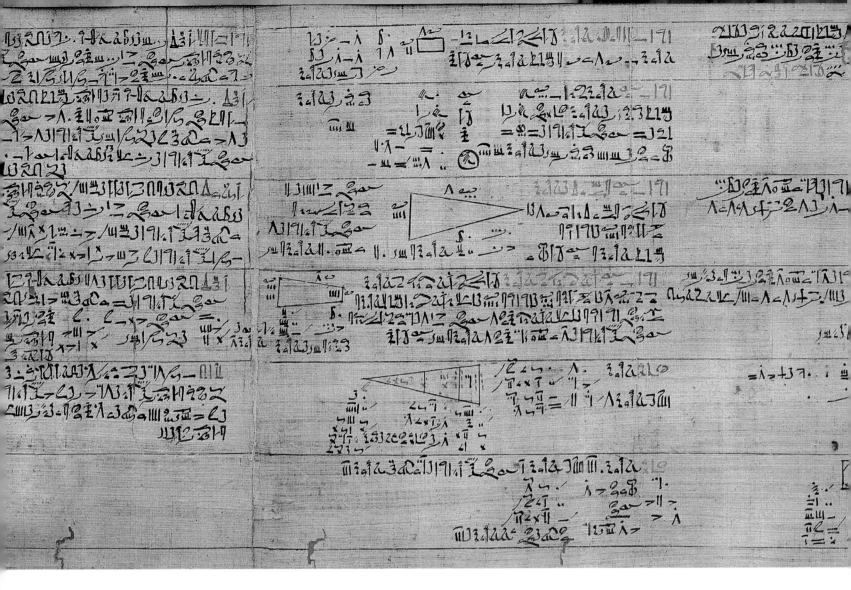

Above **Rhind Mathematical Papyrus of calculations.** This papyrus is part of the wealth of written sources from the period, along with the Turin Papyrus, one of the most extensive "king-lists," and Manetho's fragmented history Aegyptica.

from the area of southern Canaan. The Turin Papyrus tells that the Hyksos ruled for around 100 years and that the second last ruler reigned for something in excess of 40 years. This king has been identified as Apepi whose lengthy reign can be verified by the Rhind Mathematical Papyrus where a regnal date of year 33 is indicated. Additionally he must be placed towards the end of the period since he was contemporaneous with kings Seqenenra Taa and Kamose, the last two kings of the Seventeenth Dynasty. Finally, Apepi is attested from the palace area at Avaris, his name on a house altar of two of his subjects.

Palatial Architecture

The late Hyksos period at Avaris shows us a large structure that has been called a "citadel" at the western edge of the site. This places it at the eastern bank of the Pelusaic branch of the Nile, and shows a wall constructed of mud brick just slightly over 20 ft (6 m) wide. This wall was later expanded to 28 ft (8.5 m) in width and shows rectangular bastions slightly larger than $16\frac{1}{2}$ ft (5 m) wide at a distance of about 66 ft (20 m) between each. Behind these walls, gardens were found in two levels and an upper level showed pits for bushes that probably formed the foundation of a vineyard laid out in a pergola system. Assuming that such a fortification was not just to protect a garden, we may conclude that all this belonged to palatial architecture of the period.

There are other indications at Avaris for a Hyksos "stronghold" evidenced in the debris above the garden level. Pieces of columns, the roof of a kiosk and fragments of royal statues are among the materials that have been found. While some of this may date from the time of Ahmose, objects with royal inscriptions from the Hyksos period were also found within this area. Lastly, an altar showing the names of Apepi and Tany were found in a modern canal, which travels through this area.

Left **A bronze mirror belonging to Ahhotep, mother of Ahmose.** Ahhotep was a queen whose reign spanned the transition from the Second Intermediate Period to the New Kingdom.

Thebes

There is evidence to suggest that the Hyksos presence in Egypt was not as damaging as later sources indicated. At the close of the Seventeenth Dynasty, Kamose defined the Theban realm as extending from Cusae to Elephantine in the south.

Above **The village of Cheikh el-Qurnah, an ancient Theban town**. The region was once important for its strategic location in controling river and desert routes.

It has been suggested that this Theban realm was independent of Hyksos rule at this time. Here in the Seventeenth Dynasty the record indicated that the cultural identity, both conceptual and material, was that of the Middle Kingdom and not the Egyptianized Canaanite world of the Hyksos.

Fortified Towns

There is evidence to indicate that Theban towns in the Hyksos period may have been, at least in some cases, strongly fortified. This was surely the case concerning the towns in the area of the Hyksos–Theban border at Cusae and on the Theban–Nubian frontier at Elephantine. The model of the Middle Kingdom fortified town with its high walls, low defenses and a moat, would likely have been followed. Relying on this type of plan we can then reconstruct the appearance of Thebes in the Hyksos period, or at least get an impression of it. The city on the eastern side of the Nile was of moderate size—120–250 acres (50–100 ha) has been suggested—and may have enclosed a central area of temples and palaces. The main temple of the city would have been that of the god Amun-Ra and was of Middle Kingdom origin. Even at this time we could expect this temple to be large. Of the temples, with many stelae from the Thirteenth and Seventeenth Dynasties that tell of various military conflicts, Kamose's three describing his attacks on Avaris, excite the most interest.

It is a fact, however, that we know very little of the town environments of the period. That the towns themselves could have been quite large is borne out by archeological evidence from the period of the Middle Kingdom. There is no reason to suspect that the size of the towns, especially one such as Thebes, would have declined in size over the following years. Urban life continued to be important and large towns on the scale of Avaris at some 250 acres (100 ha), and Thebes, as suggested, would not have been

exceptional. By contrast, many towns of Middle Kingdom date were laid out in a sort of "grid" plan. This does not seem to be the case in the late Seventeenth- and Eighteenth-Dynasty towns, where a more random form exists along with a grid. Such an arrangement seems to have been the case in Thebes.

Modest Pyramids

On the west bank of the Nile beyond the cultivation area, began the vast necropolis of ancient

Right **An engraving of the ruins of Thebes, a large-scale town of the period, seen from the west**. This 1842 engraving is by the German KR Lepsius.

Thebes. The area was reserved for royalty and the elite officials of the city. The kings of the Seventeenth Dynasty built on a more modest scale at Thebes than their predecessors of the Middle Kingdom. Their pyramid tombs were built at modern day Dra Abu el-Naga and were made of mud brick. These rose at an angle of about 60 degrees and were some 33 ft (10 m) in height for the largest. A rock-cut platform served as a base for these structures and held a chapel with a stele. Close by were the tombs of local officials and their relatives.

It can be asserted, however, that the Theban kings of this period showed a military aggressiveness and a strong preference for a centralized authority that hearkened back to the Middle Kingdom. Thebes at this time produced a series of politically astute kings who laid the foundation for the reunification of the land of Egypt.

A BATTLE OF WILLS: THE QUARREL OF APEPI AND SEQENENRA TAA II

At the end of the reign of Apepi, an open conflict with Thebes began. Taa I was succeeded by Seqenenra Taa II, called "the Brave," who married Queen Ahhotep I. She would become the mother of Ahmose, founder of the Eighteenth Dynasty. The found mummy of Seqenenra Taa II, now in the Cairo Museum, reveals marks of a violent death and provides indication of the hostilities between the Hyksos and the Theban kings.

There are two surviving records of the conflict: One of these, *Papyrus Sallier I*, is the tale of the "Quarrel of Apepi and Seqenenra." While considered to be a folk tale, it has its value and its humor. In one section we are told that king Apepi cannot sleep because of the noise being made by the Hippos in a pool in the eastern part of Thebes. His request to Seqenenra is that he makes these beasts cease their noise. It is of course, impossible for Apepi in Avaris to hear these animals all the way down in Thebes, but the reference is a metaphor for the trouble that the Theban kings are causing. While we have lost the end of this tale, the outcome of the conflict is a matter of historical fact.

Kush

Kush is usually defined as the area of Upper Nubia and more directly, the specific region around Kerma and the Third cataract of the Nile. There is evidence to suggest that during the Hyksos period, Kush and its kings had come to a high level of power.

Above **Painted limestone wall decoration.** Egypt's subject peoples, Nubians and Asiatics, raise their hands in submission.

The kingdom of Kush was the principal obstacle to complete Egyptian control of Nubia. Contained on one of a pair of stelae set up in Karnak by Kamose, the last king of the Seventeenth Dynasty, he lets us know that he is quite dissatisfied with the state of affairs whereby he must share control of the country with an Asiatic on the one hand and a Nubian on the other. The stela makes it clear that such a division of the land will not continue.

It is evident in Kamose's words that he believed Nubia should be considered a part of Egypt. An intercepted letter from Apepi to the king of Kush invites him to invade the Theban kingdom from the south at the time that Kamose is warring against the Hyksos holdings. The letter states that Apepi will hold Kamose in check while Kush attacks from the south, and none will oppose them. From this we can see that Kush had developed as a kingdom of considerable strength and importance.

City of Riches

Upper Nubian excavation at the site of Kerma has revealed evidence that this was the capital of this kingdom. Kerma stands at the beginning of the Dongola Reach, an area that is an exception for the Nubian Nile, in that it is a rich agricultural area with a broad flood plain. This allowed for the growth and maintenance of a large population and the accumulation of wealth. The town was situated near to the river and contained brick houses in more that one occupational phase. To the south, there are also traces of what may have been substantial fortifications surrounding the town with a moat and walls of stone and brick construction. The main feature of the town is a structure that is referred to as the Western Defuffa. This appears to be a sort of L-shaped castle made of solid mud brick.

A staircase rose up from a courtyard opposite which was a building wing made of baked mud brick. This is the oldest known example of such brick in the Nile Valley.

The necropolis at Kerma is sited northeast of the plain and the royal cemetery here is contemporary with the Hyksos in Egypt. It extends in a strip into the desert more than 3300 ft (1000 m) long and about 2500 ft (750 m) wide. Behind this cemetery on the desert plateau tumulus graves from the Classic Kerma phase are located at the end of a long sequence of burials. Three of these are large and show internal structures of mud

brick and feature subsidiary graves. The burials were on a bed surrounded by numerous grave goods, human bodies, mostly female, and rams. In some instances, there were up to 12 bodies. The graves show a high point in Kerma culture.

The evidence here indicates that life at this time for the nobility was rich indeed. It was largely patterned upon the Egyptian court, which set the standard at this time. There was abundant wealth as indicated by the remains in the graves. Plunderers took most of the gold of course, but what has remained speaks of a society rich in material wealth. The source of this wealth must have been a monopoly on the Nubian gold trade by the kings of Kush during the period. This would have allowed them to attract the finest craftsmen and soldiers. Also, in matters of trade, Kush must have grown to great importance due to the caravan route through the western oases that allowed Kush to trade directly with the Hyksos and by-passed Thebes entirely.

The relative modesty of the burials at Thebes from the Seventeenth Dynasty may be an indication of lack of trade.

Material from the Classic Kerma Phase and Kush has been seen far to the south and also in Lower Nubia where it forms a cultural component coeval with the Hyksos and the Seventeenth Dynasty. This comes to an end with the beginnings of hostilities between the Hyksos and Kush with the Thebans. The Kamose stela indicates a military campaign against Kush by year 3 of Kamose. It has not yet been determined when Kerma fell, however the graves are the last burials of the Kerma kings.

Above **Hieroglyphs cut from applied gold leaf.** This mummy cartonnage is an indication of the wealth of Kush society.

Left **An engraving from the period between 1842 and 1849, by KR Lepsius.** It details the ruins at Philae in Nubia, with its superb examples of Roman temples.

Interregional Trade

Egypt is relatively rich in raw materials. However, there were always contacts between Egypt and her neighbors, and even regions much farther away provided other materials not available within the country.

Already in the Naqada Period, lapis lazuli was imported from Afghanistan and obsidian from Ethiopia, doubtless via other countries. For the Naqada Period,

CYPRUS AND EGYPT

There is little evidence for trade between Egypt and Cyprus before the end of the Middle Kingdom, when Cyprus was not yet a prominent Mediterranean civilization. At the time of the Egyptian Second Intermediate Period, many changes are visible on the island, including the development of towns and, later, writing. At Tell el Dab'a many burials have been found with juglets placed directly next to the head, and it can be assumed they once contained a precious liquid such as scented oil, as they have a markedly narrow neck. The juglets were most likely produced in Egypt or the Southern Levant. At the end of the Second Intermediate Period they were suddenly replaced by similarly small, handmade and painted juglets manufactured on Cyprus. Hundreds of these have been excavated on the site, the highest number outside of Cyprus, showing that suddenly, and rather unexpectedly, large-scale trading with the island began. These vessels disappeared at the beginning of the New Kingdom, to be replaced by new Cypriot and Levantine vessel types for the same or perhaps different contents.

Below **A painted limestone temple relief from Deir el-Bahri that depicts an Egyptian trading mission arriving in Punt.** This region of East Africa was the source of many exotic products.

Palestinian pottery has been found in many places in Egypt, and many Egyptian objects are known from Palestine. Most of the imported vessels were storage jars, so traded not for their form but for their contents, probably liquids such as wine or oil, both in high demand in Egypt.

Trading Highs and Lows

In the Old Kingdom, international trade appears more concentrated in certain places, and was perhaps directed by the state as represented by the royal palace. Byblos in modern Lebanon was an important port for the trade in cedar wood, as Egypt did not have timber of high quality. There are also attested several expeditions to Punt, a country reached by the Red Sea and so perhaps in the region of South Arabia or Ethiopia. These trading routes involved sea travel—Byblos is an important port, and in connection with Punt, inscriptions and depictions record ships.

During the First Intermediate Period, large-scale international trade seems to have ceased, as the king's court lost so much of its power, though small-scale cross-border trade might have continued. The break is confirmed by a detail of funerary evidence: Most First Intermediate Period coffins were made of low quality Egyptian sycamore, whereas many Old and Middle Kingdom coffins were cedar imported from Byblos.

Middle Kingdom Influence

In the Middle Kingdom, international trade became very important again. Several expeditions directed by high court officials were dispatched to Punt, and it has even been possible to identify a Middle Kingdom harbor at Wadi Gawasis on the Red Sea coast. In the late Middle Kingdom, the rulers of Byblos even bore an Egyptian administrative title and used Egyptian hieroglyphs, demonstrating the extent of Egyptian influence on this town. Nubia was important for its raw materials such as metals, stone, ivory, but also for certain woods and other luxuries. Not many objects of Asian origin have been found in early Middle Kingdom contexts.

However, this does not mean there was no trade; the imports might have been raw materials invisible in the archeological record.

In contrast many Middle Kingdom objects were found in Asia. These include several statues, which might have been brought here in the Second Intermediate Period. The people depicted almost certainly never went to Asia. For example, one statue found at Ugarit shows the vizier Senwosret-ankh with his wife and daughter. It has sometimes been claimed that this high official was on a mission in this town. However, the figure bears an inscription showing that it was originally set up in Memphis. It is likely that he never left Egypt, and the statue might have been traded long after his death.

In the late Middle Kingdom and Second Intermediate Period, Levantine storage vessels on Egyptian sites indicate intensive trade, at the same time as increased immigration from Palestine, followed by Hyksos rule in the eastern Delta. South Palestine was at this time heavily influenced by Egypt. Large numbers of Egyptian scarabs have been found there, and around 1700 BCE local scarab production based on Egyptian prototypes started in Palestine. From the Hyksos period, objects with the name of Khyan reached Hattusha (capital of the Hettite Empire), Knossos (Crete) and Mesopotamia. These might be diplomatic gifts to foreign courts, rather than trade objects.

Above **A papyrus copy of a tomb fresco**. It shows women playing the harp and lute, instruments imported from Western Asia during Hyksos rule.

Left **A small amphora typical of those imported from Cyprus to Egypt.** Amphoras were mostly used for wine and oil.

WARRIORS: THE NEW KINGDOM

Introduction

The Hyksos occupation was a watershed. Beforehand, Egypt seemed secure, and protected from invasion by geography. Afterward, the pharaohs realized that to protect their realm they had to fight. They had to become warriors.

When the Middle Kingdom kings opened their northern borders to trade, conquest, and immigration, it probably never occurred to them that the same open borders could spell their downfall at the hands of foreign invaders. But so it turned out. The Asiatic Hyksos took control of the eastern Delta, then gradually extended their influence right across the realm.

It was from Thebes that an independence movement eventually emerged. It started slowly, then led to the eviction of the Hyksos from their stronghold in Avaria. Not content with their freedom alone, the Thebans pursued the Hyksos northward, laying waste to cities, villages, and fields. As they cut a swathe across the north, they presented themselves as conquerors, and eventually the world's first empire was created, extending from Sudan in the south to the Black Sea in the north. The battle for Theban liberation from the Hyksos had given rise to a new warrior ethos that would endure for most of the New Kingdom.

Holding the Line

For the next five centuries, most Egyptian rulers fought ceaselessly to keep their borders clear from attack. A long line of kings led their armies into battle, seemingly unafraid of injury or death, and determined above all to secure Egypt's peace.

The New Kingdom kings saw themselves as victors even before they left home, for victory was always given to them in advance by the god Amun. Sword or mace in hand, these rulers led the battle and faced down, often single-handed, the threats of their rivals. By smiting their enemies, they imposed *maat*, or equilibrium, on the land and vanquished the forces of Isfet or Chaos. During their battles, Amun guided and guarded them, ensuring they emerged victorious.

But did they? How much of this was propaganda? How

EGYPT DURING THE NEW KINGDOM PERIOD (1550–1069 BCE)

many accounts tell of kings leading battles, when in fact they were not even present? Certainly no king save one—Seqenenra Taa—died in battle, and we only know that for sure because we have his mummy. Whether the kings were there or not, temple walls and inscriptions record their triumphs, while history as we know it is silent. Are these images the dream or the reality?

Sunset of the Pharaohs

The New Kingdom kings were the Supermen of their age, bestriding their world like giants for more than five centuries. As they lived by the sword, so, finally, they fell by the sword, and at the end of the New Kingdom Egypt was occupied by outsiders yet again. Thereafter, a long period began during which Egypt was continuously controlled by foreigners. It was to last until the revolution of 1952, a span of almost 3,000 years.

The kings of the New Kingdom saw their era as the sunrise of Egypt's might; we, in retrospect, can see it as the golden sunset of the pharaohs.

Above **Temple of Nefertari, Abu Simbel, c. 1279–1213 BCE**. The creation of immense temples cut into cliff faces was one of the major architectural innovations of the New Kingdom.

Left **Rameses II overpowing his enemies, painted limestone block, Nineteenth Dynasty**. Rameses is shown grasping the hair of three symbolic enemies: Nubian, Libyan, and Syrian. All three peoples contributed to the downfall of the Ramessid kings.

FIGHTING FOR FREEDOM

Rebel Leaders

An uneasy truce between the Thebans and the Hyksos seems to have endured until toward the end of the Seventeenth Dynasty, when two kings, Seqenenra Taa and Kamose, pursued a campaign to expel the occupying force.

Above **Chariot of a prince, engraving after Eighteenth Dynasty tomb decoration, 1878.** Improved transportation and weapons—often acquired from the Hyksos—helped the Thebans gain their independence.

A little south of Beni Hasan in Middle Egypt, at a site called by its Greek name Speos Artemidos, there is a small rock-cut temple dedicated to Pakhet, the lioness, built by the Eighteenth Dynasty ruler, Hatshepsut. The inscription over its door declares that she found the temple ruined by Hyksos kings. This, along with other archeological finds, indicates that the Fifteenth and Sixteenth Dynasties of Hyksos kings ruled over a territory that spread at least as far as Middle Egypt.

At the same time, farther south in Luxor, dynasties of Theban kings were ruling, although

they were cut off from the north's prosperous markets. Few inscriptions tell us of life in Luxor during these years, although two of the kings were called Sobekemsaf, a name that implies loyalty to Sobek, a deity worshipped by the rulers of the Thirteenth Dynasty. This suggests that the Seventeenth Dynasty kings were descended directly from those of the Thirteenth Dynasty.

Sobekemsaf I appears to have had two sons, Intef VI and Intef VII. Their tombs, and those of their successors, Intef VIII and Sobekemsaf II, have not been located, but it seems they were comparatively rich. Five centuries after their deaths, tomb robbers admitted at their trial in the Twentieth Dynasty to breaking into the tomb of Sobekemsaf II and his queen. The robbers found them wearing gold masks and lying in coffins of gold. They dragged the coffins outside and melted down all the gold. The tomb remains unfound to this day.

This wealth indicates that the majority of Seventeenth Dynasty kings lived in relative affluence, despite being under Hyksos rule. Furthermore, there is little evidence of any armed resistance against the northern foreign kings—until the reigns of the last two kings of the dynasty, Seqenenra Taa and Kamose.

The Struggle of Seqenenra Taa

Though his name means "Seqenenra the Great," we still do not know much about this king. However, archeological remains indicate that

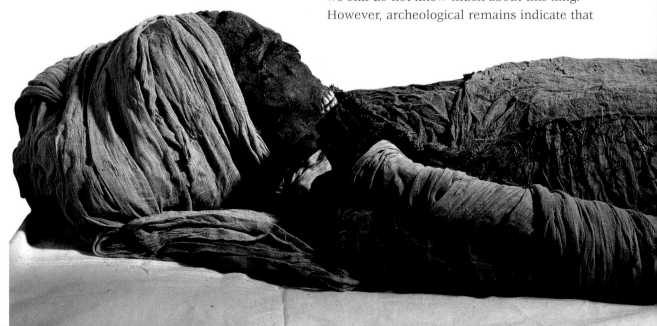

Right **Mummified remains of King Seqenenra Taa, c. 1560 BCE.** Examination of these remains, found in 1881 at Deir el-Bahri, revealed that the king had died a violent death battling the Hyksos forces.

he began an armed struggle against Hyksos rule. A papyrus, written around 1210 BCE, describes a letter written 350 or so years earlier by the Hyksos ruler Apepi to Seqenenra Taa. In the letter, Apepi complains that the hippopotamuses in Luxor are roaring so loudly that they are keeping him awake, and he asks Seqenenra to quieten them—or else! What Apepi was, in fact, saying is that the Thebans were causing trouble in the north. War between the forces broke out soon afterward, so this letter could well be the first ever recorded declaration of war.

Seqenenra Taa appears to have constructed himself a fortress behind enormous mud-brick walls at Deir el-Ballas. Large numbers of Nubian pots and weapons were found there, suggesting that a sizable Nubian force had been called upon to help the struggling Thebans.

We cannot tell exactly when or how the battles occurred. However, the mummy of Seqenenra Taa, found in the royal cache at Deir el-Bahri, shows appalling battle injuries. Wounds to his head, caused by a bronze Hyksos axe of a type found at Tell el-Dab'a (formerly the Hyksos capital of Avaria), show he was injured on the left-hand side of his head and would have lost the use of his right arm and leg. Despite this, the bones began to heal and Seqenenra Taa, though unable to walk, survived long enough to lead the army into battle a second time. This time he was killed, struck with arrows in his face and finished off by a dagger thrust into his neck as he knelt, facing his enemy.

Kamose the Brave

The campaigns of Seqenenra Taa's successor Kamose, who may or may not have been his son, are recorded in greater detail. Two stelae at the temple in Karnak recount the story of his struggle against the northerners.

The first stela describes how Kamose encounters the Hyksos armies at Deir el-Ballas and defeats them. While marching north, his men intercept a message being sent around the oasis route in the western desert. The plea has come from the defeated Hyksos king to the prince of Nubia, asking him for mercenaries to help his fight. Kamose dispatches a group of soldiers out to the nearest oasis, Bahriya, to ensure that no Nubian reinforcements can arrive by this route.

The second stela finds Kamose on his way to Avaria, sending insults to Apepi, such as "shut your mouth." Kamose led his ships northward along a waterway, probably an artificial canal or moat, and arrived at the foot of the walls of Avaria, where he set up a blockade. Here, he tells the Hyksos ruler he has "drunk the wine of your vineyards...cut down your trees...forced your women into ships' holds."

Yet, the stela makes it clear, for some unaccountable reason he then turned around and sailed back to Luxor. Once there, he led his ships and soldiers in a victory parade—despite never striking a single blow against a Hyksos enemy!

Kamose was king for less than three years. Though he declared he would "save Egypt and expel the Asiatics," he left a country still under occupation. But by the time of his death, Theban control extended to the Hyksos capital and all of Egypt was behind him. No doubt this inspired the subsequent triumph of his son Ahmose.

Above **Carved head on sarcophagus of Kamose, c. 1550 BCE**. The tomb of Kamose was found at Dra Abu el-Naga, near Luxor, in 1857. The coffin was intact, but when it was opened the body immediately crumbled into dust.

Theban Liberation

Kamose had prepared the way for the liberation of Egypt from Hyksos rule. But 11 years would pass before his successor Ahmose was able to launch an all-out attack on the Hyksos stronghold of Avaria and reunite his divided land.

Right **Limestone statue of Ahmose, Eighteenth Dynasty.** Following his conquest of Avaria, Ahmose destroyed the Hyksos' palaces and fortifications, replacing them with his own.

It appears that the Hyksos king Apepi and the Theban king Kamose died around the same time, as both disappear from the archeological record. This coincidence suggests that a disease may have been widespread, wiping out many in the country, something that happened from time to time.

Ahmose, the next ruler of Luxor, seems to have been little more than a child at the time. He was protected by his mother, Queen Ahhotep, wife of Kamose, who appears to have held the country together during the king's infancy and early youth. She may even have led troops herself.

There was thus an uneasy peace for some years as the Theban king grew up. During this time, however, the Hyksos king seems to have made no move to regain territory lost to Kamose and, luckily for Ahmose, no more challenges were issued. Was he too a child, with Fate playing an ironic role?

The Fall of Avaria

Accounts suggest that the Theban acquisition of Avaria may have taken some time to accomplish. Records show that Theban soldiers led by Ahmose sailed in troop ships up to the city walls of Avaria and instigated a siege. No account, however, says how long it lasted or how it was eventually broken.

While it continued, small divisions of Theban troops attacked nearby

towns and villages either loyal to or controlled by the Hyksos. Town after town fell, making the area ever safer for the Thebans. The next battle, one record states, "was then fought in Egypt." This implies that by that time the Thebans controlled all of Egypt except for Avaria itself.

With the Hyksos isolated, and undoubtedly Ahmose cutting off all supplies entering the city, Avaria finally and suddenly fell. No account describes exactly how it happened. It does not appear that the Thebans either broke into Avaria or felled its walls. It seems most likely that the Hyksos simply gave up, then broke out and fled, with the Egyptian army in hot pursuit.

Ahmose subsequently marched his army to the north and besieged the city of Sharuhen in southern Palestine. He was determined to see this city fall, which may indicate it had given refuge to some of the Hyksos. The siege lasted six years. During this time, regiments of Egyptians pushed even farther forward, defeating pockets of Hyksos resistance wherever they were found. Once Sharuhen had been razed to the ground, Ahmose returned south, visited Luxor

HORSES AND CHARIOTS

The lack of evidence of horses in Egypt before the Hyksos occupation suggests the occupiers introduced the animals—as well as associated technologies such as the chariot.

The Hyksos are thought to have come from modern-day Eastern Turkey or Kurdistan, and tests on the bones of ancient Egyptian horses have matched them to horses bred in that region today. The Egyptian horses stood around 14 hands tall; though light-boned, like modern Arab stock they were very powerful.

The chariots brought to Egypt by the Hyksos had wheels with four spokes each. These tended to break easily, so the Egyptians then adopted eight-spoked wheels, but that made the hubs weak. Eventually, they settled on six spokes for each wheel.

The Egyptian cavalry yoked two stallions in the shafts of their chariots. This proved to be a major liability for Thutmose III when, during one battle, besieged Hittites let out a mare in season, causing the Egyptian cavalry horses to rear and bolt!

Above **Userhet, an official under Amenhotep II, riding his chariot, limestone decoration from his tomb, c. 1427–1400** BCE. The four-spoked wheel is the traditional Hyksos design.

Below **Theban dagger with inscribed blade, Eighteenth Dynasty.** Usually made of bronze, the Thebans' blades were sharper than the Hyksos' copper weapons, giving them a significant advantage in battle.

briefly to mark his victory, and then marched against Nubia. Here, in two fierce campaigns, he ensured that any remaining Hyksos sympathizers were wiped out and that Nubia was brought back under Egyptian control.

Campaign Diaries

Much of our information for these events has come from the tomb biographies of two remarkable soldiers who fought on the Theban side. Both came from from Elkab, halfway between Luxor and Aswan, and both, somewhat confusingly, were also called Ahmose.

Ahmose Pennekhbet served in the Egyptian army under six kings, but he was only a youth when he fought in the war of liberation under Ahmose. His account of this time says merely that he served Ahmose against the city of Djahy in Palestine, where he took a prisoner and killed a man. Presumably this was one of the cities attacked during the siege of Sharuhen.

The second Ahmose was the son of a woman called Ibana and a soldier called Baba, and he is known today as Ahmose, son of Ibana. His father's mother appears to have been of foreign birth; given the situation, one wonders if she may even have been of Hyksos extraction.

Following in his father's footsteps, Ahmose, son of Ibana, entered the army of King Ahmose. He later became an admiral, but began his service in a ship called *Northern*, in which he sailed to Avaria. He distinguished himself in the battle on three occasions. But even after his country's struggle and such personal heroism, his account reduces the fall of the Hyksos city to a few words, noting laconically: "Avaria was taken. It was plundered and I took captives—three women and one man. Total: four."

The New Army

Following the wars of liberation, Ahmose and his successors continued to expand the Egyptian empire. This resulted in the development of a strong warrior ethos and the establishment of a permanent, professional army.

Below **Egyptian weapons and armor, engraving after tomb decoration in the Valley of the Kings, 1809.** The formation of a standing army led to significant developments in the refinement of weapons and military strategies.

With the expansion of the empire, Egypt was forced, for the first time in its 1500-year history, to examine its existence in the context of the Eastern Mediterranean. For centuries she had lived an isolated existence, her conscripted army serving under close relatives of a king whose authority came from birth and not from experience or ability. So-called "campaigns" seem to have been little more than attempts to protect trade routes.

During the schisms of the Middle Kingdom, however, independent militia forces had sprung up throughout Middle Egypt. Tomb paintings show them being trained, exercised to increase fitness, and issued with weapons for their task. This experience proved to be so useful that from the start of the Eighteenth Dynasty it provided a template for a standing Egyptian army.

A great deal was expected of the new career soldier, much of whose adult life, as biographies show, would be spent fighting outside Egypt. The extension of the Egyptian empire exacerbated this, with soldiers increasingly being expected to live *and* die abroad. This did not please the soldiers of Egypt, who, as *The Tale of Sinuhe* records, desired to die in their own land. Papyri show that deserters were punished severely, and their families were kept under close control until the absconder was found and returned.

Ruling by Assimilation

Conquest was one thing, but how would Egypt cope with an increasing empire, ever-extending borders and supply lines covering many hundreds of miles? Although the Egyptians established a few permanent garrisons in conquered territories, by and large they ruled their new acquisitions in a more subtle and intelligent way.

Understanding that occupied countries would breed hostility and rebellion, as had happened in Egypt under the Hyksos, the Egyptians made a point of capturing the sons of rulers from the cities they conquered. These men were taken to Egypt and placed in the *kap*, the royal school. Here they would be educated in Egyptian and learn Egyptian customs until, as they grew older, they began to forget their homeland and became Egyptians themselves. At this point, they would be returned home, where they would still be accepted as a rightful heir, but at the same time remain loyal to Egypt.

This policy allowed Egypt to control its territories with only a token military presence. Furthermore, when larger military forces were required abroad, they consisted, increasingly, of

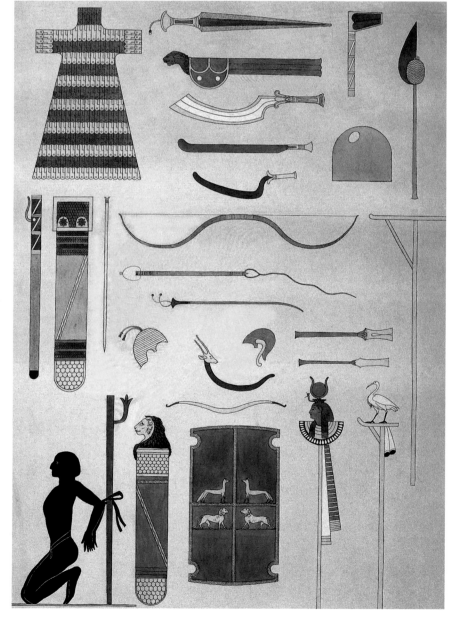

Left **Ethiopian princess arriving in Thebes during the Eighteenth Dynasty, engraving after fresco, from** *Histoire de l'art égyptien* **by Achille Prisse d'Avennes, 1878.** Expansion of the empire obliged the rulers of the New Kingdom to carefully nurture relations with neighboring realms—or attempt to subjugate them.

whole divisions of foreign mercenaries recruited from the conquered territories. In this way, more and more Egyptian soldiers were able to return to and remain at home in Egypt.

Protecting the Home Front

In the early days of expansion, while successive kings led their armies into the north, there was an urgent need to ensure that regular supplies were sent out from Egypt to the soldiers, that new recruits were conscripted and trained to replace the dead, that metals continued to be mined and smelted to replace broken weapons, and that horses should be bred and trained. In short, someone had to rule Egypt during the king's absence. This became especially challenging at certain times, most notably when Nubia, observing Egypt in crisis, used the opportunity to rebel and create problems in trade to the south, the source of stone, gold, and cattle.

Repeatedly in this period, the task of maintaining order at home fell to royal women, in particular three remarkable characters. Tetisheri was the wife of Seqenenra I and mother of Seqenenra Taa. Her grandson, Ahmose, insisted on building her a chapel with a garden and a pyramid at Abydos, the usual place for cenotaphs and monuments for kings rather than royal wives. When Ahmose was recognized as the first king of the Eighteenth Dynasty and founder of the New Kingdom, Tetisheri was venerated as the ancestor of all the subsequent kings.

Queen Ahmose-Nefertari, the wife of Ahmose I and mother of Amenhotep I, also played a very active role. However, it was Queen Ahhotep, wife of Seqenenra Taa and mother of Ahmose (and possibly Kamose), who played a major role in strengthening the dynasty.

Right **Queen Ahmose-Nefertari, wooden statuette from Deir el-Medina, Eighteenth Dynasty.** As well as Great Royal Wife and Divine Adoratrice, Ahmose-Nefertari identified herself as God's Wife and assumed the role of high priestess. She outlived her husband and her son.

The Tomb of Queen Ahhotep

Nineteenth-century discoveries confirmed Queen Ahhotep's influential role during the reigns of her husband Seqenenra Taa and son Ahmose. They also showed that she was one of the few queens to lead her troops into battle.

Below **Inlaid gold pectoral from the tomb of Queen Ahhotep, Dra Abu el-Naga, c. 1525 BCE.** The exquisitely crafted image is of Ahhotep's son Ahmose being purified with sacred water by the gods Amun (right) and Ra (left).

In 1859, the Director-General of Egypt's Antiquities Organization was the Frenchman Auguste Mariette. When he was 20, his family had inherited the estate of a relative, Nestor L'Hôte, which included L'Hôte's pioneering studies of ancient Egypt. Mariette became fascinated, and taught himself hieroglyphs and Coptic. In 1848, he presented himself at the Louvre Museum and asked if he could become an Egyptologist there. He was accepted and given a position on the staff.

In 1850, he was sent to Cairo for the first time to collect papyri the Louvre had purchased. However, having finally arrived in the place of

his passion, he refused to return home when summoned and was fired. Chance, however, led him to establish the provenance of a number of sphinxes that had recently appeared in Cairo. Shown where they had been found at Saqqara, he quickly dug up more and followed a line of them through the sand to discover the Serapeum. The Louvre immediately reinstated him, allowing him to remain in Cairo on its behalf.

In 1857, alarmed by the trafficking in antiquities and the battles fought by archeologists over their rights to dig at ancient sites, Mariette proposed to the Egyptian governor that a museum should be established in which Egypt could dis-

play its own treasures, and that an antiquities organization should be founded to control digging at sites through licenses or concessions.

Mariette was an indefatigable digger, always managing a large number of digs simultaneously in different areas along the length of the Nile. He "controled" them by sailing between them as frequently as time and tide allowed.

In 1859, he was sent a report that a fine intact tomb of a queen, complete with golden treasures, had been found at Dra Abu el-Naga, on the west bank at Luxor. As he raced south, he received word that the treasures had been stolen by a local chief, who was carrying them north to present to the governor of the province. When an indignant Mariette saw a craft heading toward them, he realized it was carrying the robbers and "his" treasure, so he threw a line to the ship, and dragged it alongside. A fierce fight ensued, during which the robber was thrown over the side. Mariette then reclaimed the jewelry.

Her Royal Titles

The body of Queen Ahhotep was found intact in a heavily gilded wooden coffin. The larger outer coffin bearing her titles "king's daughter, king's sister, Great Royal Wife and king's mother" was found later, in 1881, in the royal mummy cache at Deir el-Bahri. The titles on it show she was the daughter of Seqenenra I and Tetisheri and thus the full sister of Seqenenra Taa, to whom she was also married. As she was also the mother of Ahmose, the marriage with her brother had clearly been a full one.

It was rare in Egypt for a full sister to marry her royal brother the king, and rarer still for a child to be born of the union. It has been suggested that the ruling dynasty considered it safer during these turbulent times not to allow any third party into the family through marriage. However, the perpetuation of incestuous unions may have eventually created significant problems for their offspring.

Fighting Queen

The tomb of Queen Ahhotep was modest in size, but the coffin contained several notable treasures, including beautifully crafted jewelry. There were also two model ships made of gold and silver. However, the most startling discoveries were an inlaid bronze battle-ax and a necklace bearing three solid gold flies.

The battle-ax was inlaid with a Cretan-style griffin and called Ahhotep "Mistress of the Islands." This title suggests that she may have controled trade in the Eastern Mediterranean.

Traditionally, gold flies were awards for displays of valor on the battlefield. Such awards were rare, and virtually unheard of for a woman. They reinforce the idea that Ahhotep had played an active role in the army, as indicated by an inscription on a stela at Karnak: "She is the one who looked after Egypt's troops and guarded them. She brought back the deserters. She pacified Upper Egypt and drove out the rebels."

Indeed, it appears that Queen Ahhotep not only ruled Egypt single-handed while Ahmose was a child, but that she also conscripted, trained, and equipped her troops, *and* seems to have led them into battle herself—a remarkable achievement in such troubled times.

Above **Necklace adorned with gold flies, from the tomb of Queen Ahhotep, Dra Abu el-Naga, c. 1525** BCE. Awarded for displays of courage in battle, the flies are each about the size of an outstretched human hand.

EGYPT AND THE AEGEAN

During the early Eighteenth Dynasty, trade around the Eastern Mediterranean was controled by the Egyptians, as inscriptions and shipwrecks testify. Egypt's strongest trading links were with Crete and the Aegean islands. Excavations at Tell el-Dab'a, ancient Avaria, stronghold of the Hyksos, have revealed many frescoes identical to those at Knossos, including bulls' heads, leaping bulls, and Greek key designs. Similar designs have also been found in paintings at the palaces of Deir el-Ballas and Malkata. The Minoan griffin on the battle-ax of Queen Ahhotep has been interpreted by some as indicating that she was a Minoan princess, although this seems unlikely.

Right **Dancing bull, fresco, Knossos, Crete, c. 1700–1400** BCE. The presence of frescoes like this one in Eighteenth Dynasty buildings has led scholars to suggest that an alliance between Egypt and Crete existed at this time.

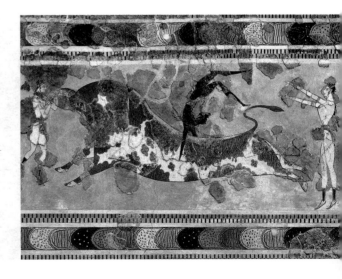

Amenhotep I

Assisted by his mother, Ahmose-Nefertari, Amenhotep I swiftly consolidated his father's military successes. He also continued Ahmose's building program and may have founded the tomb complex now known as the Valley of the Kings.

Above Rolled papyrus and writing palette, Eighteenth Dynasty. These items were found at Deir el-Bahri, where Amenhotep built funerary monuments.

Below Seated colossi of Amenhotep I and Thutmose II, Karnak. Amenhotep I constructed a number of gateways and shrines at Karnak, most of which have been rebuilt.

Ahmose, considered the first king of the Eighteenth Dynasty and founder of the New Kingdom, ruled Egypt for around 25 years. Yet he was a young man when he died. His family's right to the throne of Egypt was open to question, since they had gained it as a result of conquest over the Hyksos and not through inheritance. One scholar has suggested that some of the "rebels" against whom Queen Ahhotep fought were rival families also claiming rights to the succession.

In Ahmose's eighteenth year, a stela records a gift of large quantities of silver and gold into the temple of Karnak, presumably impoverished

during the Hyksos wars. For the first time, the name of his Great Royal Wife is given as Queen Ahmose-Nefertari, "king's daughter, king's sister, Great Royal Wife, and Divine Adoratrice." Although she had not died, this was the first time that Queen Ahhotep, his mother, had been replaced in inscriptions, though her name continues to appear for many years. It shows that, yet again, a sister had married her full brother.

Four years later, Ahmose-Nefertari is finally listed, with her other titles, as "king's mother" showing she had borne children for her brother. It has been suggested that she bore three children at least—two sons, Ahmose-ankh and Amenhotep, and a daughter Merytamun. Ahmose-ankh, however, disappeared, presumably dying young, leaving Amenhotep as heir to the throne.

Amenhotep was crowned king under the title Djeserkara around 1525 BCE. Throughout his reign he was always associated with his mother, Queen Ahmose-Nefertari. One inscription shows a wife with him, though not a Great Royal Wife, and the coffin of Princess Merytamun, found in the Deir el-Bahri cache of 1881, lists her as "Great Royal Wife." It seems likely that, like her parents, grandparents and great-grandparents, Merytamun married her brother. However, at his death Amenhotep was still depicted with his mother; so presumably his sister-wife also died young.

It is hard to escape the conclusion that at least three generations of incestuous marriages had taken their toll genetically on the royal line. A succession of children dying prematurely, a king with whom no other wives or children were associated, and who died childless at the very start of an auspicious new period, when his own claim to the throne was itself questionable—this was the worst possible scenario for the dynasty.

Last of the Family Line

The dynastic divisions we use today are based on the works of Manetho, an Egyptian priest who lived around 330 BCE, during the reigns of Ptolemy I and II, and who wrote a history of Egypt for the new ruling family. His original

son and grandson of his predecessors; Amenhotep I was his son. But the line died out with him and passed sideways into the hands of the relatively unknown Thutmose I. Why does the dynasty not start with him?

Fit for Their Kings

According to an inscription, it was an architect called Ineni, working for Thutmose I, who was instructed to find a place "that no man can see, where no man can hear" for the burials of the kings of the new Theban family. Yet the men who built the tombs in what we now call the Valley of the Kings were housed in a village known as Deir el-Medina, and the founders of this village were recorded regularly and often as Amenhotep I and Queen Ahmose-Nefertari.

This is baffling, as Amenhotep I, the last king of his family line, was buried with his ancestors at Dra Abu el-Naga. Why would he have founded a village for workmen for the royal valley if he had no intention of being buried there? On the other hand, why would his successor Thutmose I have sent his architect to choose a burial site if the village of Deir el-Medina had already been established for that purpose?

Located in a waterless area on the west bank of the Nile, at the foot of the cliffs that contain the royal tombs, Deir el-Medina was a small settlement comprising some 60 or so houses. Yet it was to become home to some of Egypt's greatest artisans, who would cut and paint tombs for centuries to come.

Left **Princess Merytamun, carved cedar coffin, Deir el-Bahri, Eighteenth Dynasty.** Merytamun's coffin refers to her as Amenhotep's "Great Royal Wife," though few other contemporary monuments attest to this role.

document is lost to us, and we do not know what sources he drew upon to write his work. The extant copies contain contradictory information.

New dynasties are usually deemed to start with new families inheriting the throne. However, it seems that on several occasions, Manetho got it wrong. The start of the Eighteenth Dynasty is a case in point. Ahmose was

PAPYRI AND OSTRACA

Far from being the forerunner of modern paper, papyrus—a word that means "that which belongs to the king"—was rare and extremely valuable. It was made from narrow strips cut from the stem of the papyrus reed laid at right angles and compressed. In a similar way to the vellums and parchments of the Middle Ages, it was often reused by Egyptians centuries later.

Ostraca (singular: ostracon) are fragments of broken pottery or pieces of stone that were written on by scribes. Some are mere slivers; others can be more than 20 inches (50 cm) long. Sometimes they bear texts written in hieratic, the cursive form of the language; others are covered with sketches.

Right **Ostracon, Nineteenth Dynasty.** The image of a window inscribed on this stone is accompanied by text that reads "Nakhtamon, you will make four like this, exactly like this, and very, very quickly, by tomorrow!"

The Valley of the Kings

The tomb complex in the Valley of the Kings near Luxor would become the burial place of the royal family for the next 500 years. Patterns of construction emerged as the tomb builders refined and perfected their methods.

There is reason to believe that by the end of the Middle Kingdom all pyramid burials of the kings of the previous thousand years had been destroyed or robbed. The kings of the Eighteenth Dynasty ruled from their palace in Memphis where the officers of the court supervised workshops and the state archives were stored for many centuries, but the family came from Luxor. So it seems reasonable that they should have chosen to be buried nearby.

The Valley of the Kings is really two branches of the one valley, situated directly behind the limestone cliffs of the west bank of the Nile. Access to the valleys is difficult because of the terrain—you must either climb the cliffs and walk across a plateau then descend on steep pathways, or you must follow the lower-lying land, as the road does today, and go northward some distance before heading south.

The main valley is presided over by a pointed hill that resembles a pyramid. Given the traditional significance of the pyramid in funerary rites, this may be another reason why the site was selected. The ancients called the peak Meretseger—"she who loves peace and quiet."

The area was easily protected and guarded. The tombs were never covered over with sand, as many believe, but merely stopped up with mudbrick doors sealed with the king's seal. Sentryposts stood on the crests of the hills. The Medjay, the local regiment used for policing the area, could see anyone entering the valleys by day or night, so there was no need to hide the tombs.

Innovations in Tomb Design

The tombs' designs were different from any tombs made previously in Egypt. Not only were they separated from the places where daily offerings of food and drink were made, but the bodies were not buried at the foot of deep shafts. Instead a deep burial chamber was created where the coffins, sarcophagi, and shrines could stand.

The limestone of the valley cliffs is soft and crumbling. The valleys are wadis, or dried riverbeds. When flash floods occur, as they do every

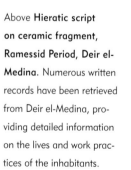

Above **Hieratic script on ceramic fragment, Ramessid Period, Deir el-Medina.** Numerous written records have been retrieved from Deir el-Medina, providing detailed information on the lives and work practices of the inhabitants.

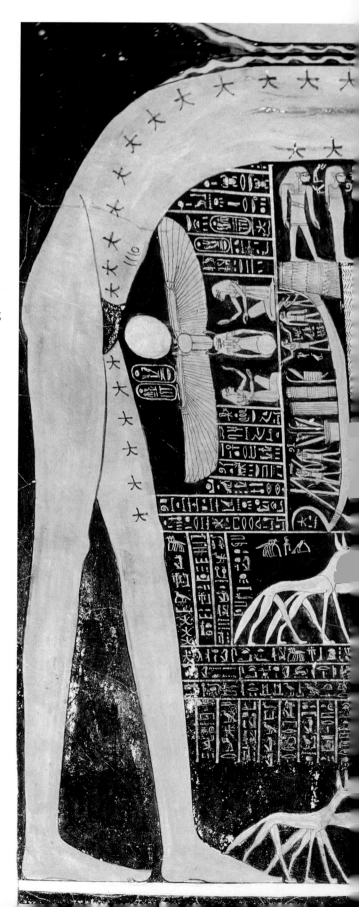

few centuries, the wadis turn into torrential rivers in a matter of minutes. The water easily penetrates the limestone, forming deep cavities. The builders at first utilized these to form the early tombs. Later, tombs were cut into the rock where the cliff met the valley floor; one, KV 62, the tomb of Tutankhamun, was cut into the valley floor itself. Those who managed the work in the Valley of the Kings must have kept records of previous tombs, including their depths and angles of incline, as the workers rarely cut into an existing tomb when building a new one.

Above **Corridor leading to sarcophagus room in the tomb of Merenptah, Valley of the Kings, c. 1213–1203 BCE.** The design of this tomb reflects the late style of long, straight chambers.

Royal tombs generally consisted of four chambers connected by long corridors. The corridors in the earliest tombs curved gently toward the burial chamber. Later tombs had right angles in their corridors; later still, the lower sections were slightly offset. The latest tombs were cut in straight lines into the rock. The reasons for the changes of design are not clear, but it may be that it was to avoid cutting into earlier tombs. Or they may have been dictated by the quality of the stone, or by contemporary ideas on access to the afterlife. If the latter were the case, it is hard to explain why the corridors changed as they did, and why the corridors follow different compass directions according to which side of the valley they were on.

Guidebooks for the Afterlife

The tombs of the Valley of the Kings were decorated throughout with brilliantly colored paintings. Unlike tombs for non-royals, which usually showed scenes from their lives, the decorations in royal tombs focused on the afterlife. Notably, they included sacred texts that would guide the deceased during the journey to their fellow gods.

No two tombs contain the same texts in the same order. Where extracts from certain texts are used, however, they are the same, implying a main body of texts from which sections were chosen. Sections of the *Book of the Dead* are used rarely, and only in very late tombs, suggesting that these texts were primarily for non-royals.

The most common text was the *Amduat*, "the book of what is in the Duat [or underworld]," which shows the passage of the sun over Earth during the day, and through the realm of the gods by night. Other common texts included *The Litany of Ra*, which links the deceased king with the sun-god, and the *Book of the Gates*, its title referring to the gate in the night, or span of hours, during which the deceased must pass through to the underworld. The ceilings were decorated with impressions of the night sky, with Nut, the personification of the sky, stretching down the center of the burial chamber.

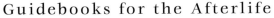

Left **The Goddess Nut arched over scenes of sun-worship, ceiling in the tomb of Rameses VI, Valley of the Kings, 1143–1136 BCE.** Goddess of the sky, Nut was said to swallow the sky at night and give birth to it again each morning.

Life in Deir el-Medina

It is our good fortune that the people of Deir el-Medina were literate, for they left behind tens of thousands of ostraca and papyri that describe their day-to-day lives in detail, providing us with a window onto a fascinating world.

Above **The god Bes, ivory carving, Eighteenth Dynasty.** Depicted as a deformed dwarf, Bes was considered the protector of women in childbirth. His image was found in many houses in Deir el-Medina.

Many of the writings found at Deir el-Medina were retrieved from scraps in the town rubbish tip. They include letters, stories and poems, personal histories, descriptions of the village, records of births, marriages, and deaths, and accounts of daily activities, including the working methods of the tomb builders.

More than 100 people lived at Deir el-Medina, mainly tomb workers and their families, but also other craftsmen such as carpenters, metalworkers, potters, and even a physician. Answering to the vizier, they received a better-than-average wage and were reasonably well educated.

The houses in the village all opened out onto a central "street," only wide enough for two men to pass each other. It is thought that even this was roofed over, turning the village into one large building. There was only one exit from the village, and this was presided over by janitors, who saw every person entering or leaving.

The workers were organized into two gangs—the gang of the east side and the gang of the west side, believed to refer to the opposing walls in the tombs. Each group was supervised by a foreman.

The men worked on the tombs eight days of the ten-day week. They left the village on the first day, sleeping overnight in huts near their work and only returned at the end of the week. They were issued with tools and pigments as they left the village. The tools were weighed against a stone, and the stone marked with the man's name. If he wanted it to be sharpened during the week, it would have to be returned to the village, checked against the stone, sharpened,

Right **Ruins of houses and tombs at Deir el-Medina.** The closely packed buildings in the foreground are the workers accommodation. On the hill in the background are the workers' own tombs.

weighed against a new stone, and reissued to ensure that none of the metal was stolen.

Registers recorded absences from work. Explanations of absenteeism included "to worship his god," "to mend the foreman's door," and "to feed the foreman's animals." One interesting excuse was "to brew his beer!" Other excuses recorded include an absence for "his day," perhaps a birthday or some other anniversary, and, simply, "sick."

On the ninth day, markets took place, at which goods made during the workers' spare time, or animals that were excess to individual needs, could be exchanged. Afterward, a local tribunal might be held, during which the whole community would listen attentively to civil cases and minor criminal cases.

Managing the Household

Although the women stayed at home, they were regarded as extremely skilled people. In the days before shops existed, a wife had to provide for every need of her family. The wife who lacked skills in any area risked the family's survival.

Wives' duties included the safe storage of the grain their husbands earned; grinding the grain for flour; baking bread; providing oil for a wide variety of uses; looking after the animals; providing water; spinning, weaving, and making clothes; and of course, giving birth to, and raising and educating, children.

Girls were trained from early childhood to become good housekeepers in their turn. The woman was entirely responsible for the daily running of the house, and was in fact dominant

to her husband in this regard. A wisdom text of the Old Kingdom urged men, "Do not say to your wife 'where is it?' when she has put it in the right place. Let his eye observe her in silence."

Women were expected to stay indoors because they were cherished. To show that they were respected and loved, they were depicted in paintings and sculptures as being fairer skinned than their husbands—this proved that they had no need to venture out into the heat of the day.

An Infancy Fraught with Peril

Infant mortality was high, and weaning a child was a risky undertaking—many died at this stage. If a child survived weaning, training for adult life began almost at once, with boys accompanying their father and girls their mother.

There was little time for play, which is borne out by the fact that few toys have been found. Those that have survived from fortunate children include balls, dolls (some with clothes to change into), and wooden toys (including some that could be pulled along the floor). There is no evidence of girls attending school, and few boys could be spared the time to be formally educated, as their income was seen as vital to family.

HEALING AND MEDICINE

According to Homer, the Egyptians were the wisest of healers. Legend recorded that Thoth wrote 7 texts among the 42 he bequeathed to mankind to aid them in medical understanding. If someone fell ill, they might try home cures first, but if this did not work, advice was sought from a specialist who consulted scrolls to match the symptoms with his text.

The physician did his best to help, but sometimes the diagnosis was that the problem was incurable. Prescriptions comprised a mixture of substances, to be taken or applied. In most cases, an amulet was shown and words were spoken—rituals aimed at evicting the evil spirit that was thought to have brought the sickness.

Above **Fragment of papyrus bearing medicinal recipe, Eighteenth Dynasty.** An extract from a medical treatise, the text includes a confident recommendation: "another perfect remedy— one measure of galena, one measure of honey, fat…"

Left **Village barber at work, painted limestone decoration from the tomb of Userhet, c.1427– 1400 BCE.** A scene that could have taken place at Deir el-Medina, the image shows a barber working on one man while others wait, some dozing in the shade.

Building a Tomb

Only the most skilled craftspeople were employed in the Valley of the Kings, though poorer work in some areas suggests that apprentices were trained on the job. The work was tightly structured, with little room for individual flair.

Right **Cartouche of King Horemheb, painted limestone decoration from his tomb, KV 57, Valley of the Kings.** Horemheb's tomb was discovered in 1908 by the British Egyptologist Edward Russell Ayrton.

Below **Tomb entrance, Valley of the Kings.** The friable nature of the terrain in the Valley of the Kings must have played havoc with the construction of the tombs.

The selection of a site for a new tomb in the Valley of the Kings—also known as the "Place of Truth"—was probably made by the foreman or overseer. However, the complexities of designing a tomb in a concealed three-dimensional space, along with the pressing need to ensure that the new tomb did not impinge on an existing one, were such that advice would probably also have come from the vizier himself, holder of the records of earlier tombs.

The first gangs on the site were responsible for cutting the walls of corridors and chambers. The two gangs worked on opposite sides of the tombs. How they measured exact right angles at floor and ceiling, and made sure that the correct angles were observed as the corridors descended into the bedrock, while at the same time ensuring that the work of each gang met exactly in the center of the corridor, is baffling, given their relative lack of technology.

Once the walls had been roughly cut, they were flattened to prepare them for the next stage. During the Eighteenth Dynasty, the walls were carefully smoothed, skimmed with a thin layer of gesso (plaster mixed with gum or resin), and then rubbed down for painting. From the reign of Rameses II onward, when workers were more rushed, the walls were left roughly faced. A 1-inch (2.5-cm) layer of mud-brick was then applied and allowed to dry. The gesso was applied to this surface. This caused immense problems, as water, due to both the rising

water-table and moisture from the evaporating sweat of thousands of workers and visitors, gathered between the stone wall and the layer of mud-brick, causing the bond between them to break down. The first indication of this might be the sudden collapse of entire sections of painted wall.

Tools of the Trade

It is generally suggested that the walls of the tombs were cut using dolerite pounders. These small balls of extremely hard igneous rock are found commonly in the desert areas in the south of Egypt. They are also found regularly around work sites, including the floors of the Valley of the Kings. However, small chips of white limestone have been found that were clearly cut from the walls of tombs and these are generally sharp-edged. This suggests that metal tools such as chisels must have been used for the initial cutting, with dolerite pounders being used afterward to smooth the walls.

What did the workers use as a light source when working underground? Today, boards covered with aluminum foil are used to reflect sunlight into the tombs and many scholars believe that this was the method used by the workers here and elsewhere. But reflective surfaces in ancient Egypt were few; mirrors were generally small and made of copper, and reflected only small areas of dim light.

However, many pottery lamps have been found in the valley. These vary from small containers for a little oil and a single wick, to multiple wick lamps, and tapering "rushlights" which fitted into wall sconces. Linen wicks were issued to the men twice a day, according to registers, while the oil for the lamps had a little salt added to reduce the smoke. The wicks appear to have burned for no longer than four hours—an unlikely origin for the eight-hour day!

Interior Decoration

To prepare for the decoration of a tomb, craftsmen were provided with "trial pieces," small ostraca marked with a grid and indications of the pictures or inscriptions that were needed. They then drew a larger grid onto the wall. In many cases, less skilled draftsmen would carefully copy the drawings from the trial piece onto the wall using red paint, while a master followed, correcting the lines in black. The background color was then added: often off-white or yellow, but rarely light blue. Details and borders were added using other colors—first lighter ones, then darker ones. No attempt was made to add highlights or any kind of shading.

Work progressed panel by panel, but not necessarily moving from one panel to the next in sequence. The unfinished tomb of the last Eighteenth Dynasty king, Horemheb, includes some areas where completed decorations stand side by side with some that had barely been started. Judging by the same tomb, however, it appears that work started at the outside and progressed into the tomb, ending in the burial chamber.

As the work went on, patches of smoke from the lamps formed on the ceilings. When all other work was completed, these patches were painted over, thus ensuring that no trace of smoke remained. In some tombs where the ceilings were not completed, smoke rings can still be seen, indicating the spots where lamps once burned.

Working on the royal tombs must have been a noisy, extremely dusty, smelly, and sweaty business. Most workers would have suffered from coughs caused by dust and soot in the lungs, and eye problems due to the dust and poor lighting. Although the end results are magnificent, it is often forgotten in viewing them just how many workers suffered to make the tombs in the first place.

Above **Wall painting, tomb of Sennedjem, Deir el-Medina, c. 1200 BCE.** Sennedjem worked at Deir el-Medina and his tomb, one of the finest private tombs in Egypt, lies in the town necropolis.

Left **Tool made of wood, leather, and bronze, from the tomb of the architect Ka and his wife, Deir el-Medina, Eighteenth Dynasty.** Sharp-edged metal tools like this one were probably used to chip away at the tomb walls.

EMPIRE BUILDERS
Thutmose I

Amnehotep I died after a reign of about 22 years. He may have had children, but none of them appear to have survived him. His only remaining successor was a soldier, Thutmose, whose claim to the throne was through marriage.

Right **The Lions' Gate, ruins of Hattusas, Bogazkoy, Turkey.** Between 1650 BCE and 1180 BCE, Hattusas was the capital of the powerful Hittite Empire, which covered most of Anatolia and extended south to Syria.

Thutmose I Aakheperkara had married his principal wife Ahmose some time before he came to the throne. It is not clear exactly when this occurred. Nor is it known precisely how Ahmose was descended from the royal family. She may have been a daughter of Amenhotep I by a lesser wife, or the daughter of his brother Ahmose-ankh. Thutmose's marriage to probably the last surviving member of the old ruling family assured his succession to the throne.

A stela in Wadi Halfa shows Thutmose with Ahmose-Nefertari, Amenhotep I's mother, who was clearly still alive and playing a major part in domestic affairs, and with his own mother, named as Senisoneb, but gives no other details.

Thutmose was elderly (at least in Egyptian terms) by the time he was crowned. He was a

Right **The Lions' Gate, ruins of Hattusas, Bogazkoy, Turkey.** Between 1650 BCE and 1180 BCE, Hattusas was the capital of the powerful Hittite Empire, which covered most of Anatolia and extended south to Syria.

career soldier, most probably a formidable leader during the reign of Amenhotep I. Soon after his coronation, a stela records a gift of gold and silver which he made to the temple of Abydos. In return, he was recognized as being descended directly from Osiris. This gave him greater credibility as ruler, which, having no blood ties to the previous king, he badly needed.

The Conquest of Kush

Thutmose I turned out to be the right king in the right place at the right time. The military campaigns of Amenhotep I had freed Egypt's borders from the Hyksos threat and had quieted Nubia, but more work was needed.

In his second year, Thutmose I led a military expedition into the south of Nubia. At the third cataract, now in Sudan, he wiped out whole tribes with ruthlessness and determination. He recorded after one battle: "The bits cut off [the rebels] were too big and too many for the birds to carry off as food." He seems to have stayed in Nubia over

THE CULT OF AMUN

Amun, who has several different identities within the groups of Egyptian deities, first came to prominence in Thebes in the Twelfth Dynasty. Represented variously as a curly-horned ram, a goose, or a man wearing the twin-plumed crown, he was served secretly by the king within the dark sanctuary of the temple of Karnak.

It had long been thought that the cult merely concerned feeding and dressing a statue of Amun. But it has recently been shown that ithyphallic images usually identified with the fertility god Min are in fact the Karnak image of Amun. It seems that the

king reenacted Amun's creation of the world in some kind of daily fertility rite.

Above **Amun as a ram, cradling Amenhotep III between its legs, polished granite, Karnak, Eighteenth Dynasty.** The combination of the head of a ram and body of a sphinx was known as a criosphinx.

Right **Thutmose I, relief carving on sarcophagus, Valley of the Kings, c. 1504–1492** BCE. Two sarcophagi from the Valley of the Kings bear the name of Thutmose I, but it is uncertain whether he was first buried there or at Deir el-Bahri, or at another location.

winter, for in the third year of his rule, he finally returned to Karnak celebrating a great victory, "with that wretched Nubian [probably the Prince of Kush] hanging upside down from the prow of His Majesty's ship." Nubia would not threaten Egypt again for many years, for the Egyptians were now able to appoint the leader of that country—known as the "King's Son of Kush"—and for the next few generations, Nubia's leaders were Egyptian rather than Nubian.

Syrian Reconnaissance

For the remainder of his reign Thutmose I campaigned regularly, every summer, in the north of Egypt. The exact identity and location of his enemies is still open to discussion, but three realms would attract the attention of Egypt's armed forces over the next century—Mitanni, Nahrin, and the land of the Hittites.

In the early Eighteenth Dynasty, Mitanni lay to the west of the Euphrates in modern Syria, with its capital at Washshuganni (a place yet to be identified). Nahrin lay across the river in modern Iraq and Kurdistan. Thutmose I was the first Egyptian king to attack Mitanni and Nahrin, although no inscription claims he defeated them. It seems rather that, like Kamose, he showed the way for later kings to follow. By the middle of the dynasty, these two realms seem either to have united or at least come to be regarded by Egyptians as one country.

The Hittite capital, Hattusas, was located in central Anatolia, and Hittite territory covered most of modern-day southern Turkey. It also extended south, impinging on a major Egyptian trade route that ran from Badakhshan, north of

Afghanistan—a major source of lapis lazuli—along what is today the Silk Road to terminate on the coast at the Egyptian city of Byblos, modern Ras Shamra. During the reign of Thutmose I, however, the Hittites were divided and no real threat to Egypt or its trade.

The Death of Thutmose I

The details of Thutmose's death are as mysterious as his origins. Even estimates of the length of his reign vary from six to eleven years. Recorded as the first king to cut a tomb in the Valley of the Kings, he has in fact two tombs and two sarcophagi. His mummy was found in the Deir el-Bahri cache, so we will never know where he was finally laid to rest.

Below **Prisoners working on the temple of Amun, Karnak, engraving after decoration in the tomb of Rekhmire, 1878.** Thutmose I's major modifications to Karnak included a new entrance, formed by the Fourth and Fifth pylons.

New Kingdom Women

In ancient Egypt, women enjoyed legal equality and some even ruled the realm, though their status depended entirely on their husband or father. The early New Kingdom saw many changes to the roles and duties of royal women.

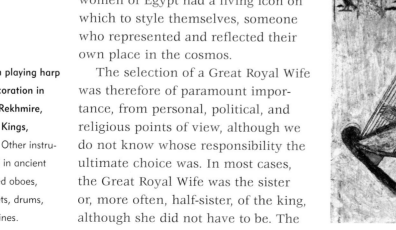

Above **Bone dish in the shape of a duck feeding a fish to its ducklings, New Kingdom.** This kind of container was used to hold eye paint, ointment, or scented body oil.

It was during the reign of Queen Ahhotep that the most significant changes in monarchical rules regarding women seem to have occurred. Most significantly, Ahhotep was the first woman to take the title "Great Royal Wife." Thereafter, the Great Royal Wife was appointed at the time of the king's succession. She was crowned alongside her husband and became owner of separate estates that had their own managers and advisers.

Another development that arose at the beginning of the New Kingdom was that when a king was crowned he became the sole intermediary between gods and men, bridging the chasm that lay between the human and the spirit worlds. Publicly he was identified with Amun, Ptah, or Osiris, all gods whose consorts bore them divine children. (Privately, however, a king was still recognized as being just a man, and often had to vie with other men to demonstrate his superior skill and power.)

Consequently, the great royal wife became a divine consort: she was Mut to the king as Amun, Sekhmet to his Ptah, or Isis to his Osiris. In the office of state, she was a link to the goddess, the female side of the divine, regarded as wise and powerful in her own right. During festivals, she *became* the goddess, to be consulted over difficult issues. So from the early New Kingdom onward, for the first time, the women of Egypt had a living icon on which to style themselves, someone who represented and reflected their own place in the cosmos.

The selection of a Great Royal Wife was therefore of paramount importance, from personal, political, and religious points of view, although we do not know whose responsibility the ultimate choice was. In most cases, the Great Royal Wife was the sister or, more often, half-sister, of the king, although she did not have to be. The Great Royal Wife's role was primarily public, social, and religious, in a "marriage" that was often no more than a public face and did not necessarily involve physical union. For the duties of childbearing often fell to other women.

Life in the Harem

During the early years of Egyptology (when Egypt was part of the Ottoman Empire), the term "harem" was applied both to the lesser wives and to the building in which they lived. It was redolent with images of sexuality, of seductive women held against their will and guarded by eunuchs— as reflected by the numerous sensuous images of harems in European art of the period.

In ancient Egypt, nothing was farther from the truth. The New Kingdom kings established women's quarters of great luxury and beauty. In contrast, the kings' own private quarters were tiny; the only beds found in them are single. For his leisure, the king would enter the world where the women chose to live. The women were guarded by the king's officers, who most certainly were not eunuchs, and in the harem they led pampered yet fruitful lives. Unlike the Great Royal Wife, however, they were anonymous and played no part in state affairs.

Right **Women playing harp and lute, decoration in the tomb of Rekhmire, Valley of the Kings, c. 1400 BCE.** Other instruments played in ancient Egypt included oboes, flutes, clarinets, drums, and tambourines.

Harems such as those at Gurob, el-Ballas, and el-Amarna show us that the lesser wives spun and wove fine textiles; played musical instruments and danced; adorned themselves with oils and perfumes; practiced makeup and hairstyling; and indulged in the latest and finest fashions. It is true that kings had their choice of women. We know that at one point Amenhotep III added 317 women from Nahrin to his harem; the following year he forwarded a letter to Nahrin saying, "Now I have sent you silver and gold, great quantities, so send me women, many of them, and with soft voices."

The aim of each woman was to bear a son who might inherit the throne. Undoubtedly, each used all her wiles to encourage this outcome, although it seems possible that, with male guards around, the king may have accepted paternity for some sons not of his own blood. The chief lady of the harem, his favorite, was given a title we translate today as "Senior Royal Wife."

Children were born in the harem, and the royal school, the *kap*, was located here. The harem women exerted great influence over their royal sons, so it is hardly surprising that most royal women were buried by their sons rather than their husbands.

The Chantresses of Amun

It is still not clear what happened to royal women when an old king died and a new one came to the throne. They were certainly not killed to accompany him, as happened in other cultures, nor is there any evidence that they were isolated somewhere, in something akin to a medieval nunnery.

Some of the younger women and more recently acquired wives may have been accepted by the new king into his own harem. Others may have been assigned a different role. The title "Chantress of Amun" was given to certain ladies of high birth, a title with its own rank, income, and status. Yet examination of the mummies of some of these women suggests they had neither danced nor played an instrument in their lives; nor were their marriages to courtiers of the highest rank after the king's death commensurate with their having been mere dancers. (The temple cult did not include dancers in any case.) It seems likely that naming a woman Chantress of Amun was a way of providing a "royal pension" and thereby allowing her to marry well.

Above **Woman giving birth, with midwife, papyrus, Nineteenth Dynasty.** Bearing a son to the king was the ultimate goal of most women in the harem. Yet, given the limitations of contemporary medicine, childbirth was a perilous undertaking.

Left **God Amun and goddess Mut, carved stone statue, Nineteenth Dynasty.** In the same way as the king was the embodiment on Earth of Amun, so the Great Royal Wife assumed the role of his consort, Mut.

Hatshepsut

Thutmose I was succeeded by a son, Thutmose, borne by a member of his harem. But a daughter by his Great Royal Wife Ahmose, named Hatshepsut, appears to have had a stronger claim to—and a greater desire for—power.

Above **Hatshepsut with Amun**, painted relief, **Red Chapel, Karnak**, c. 1473–1458 BCE. Throughout her life, perhaps to reinforce her claim to the throne, Hatshepsut emphasized her status as daughter of the god Amun.

Thutmose I had at least five children. Two sons, Wadjmose and Amenmose, did not survive childhood. Their mother is unknown, but is unlikely to have been the Great Royal Wife Ahmose, who, however, gave Thutmose two daughters, Hatshepsut and Nefrubity (the latter's fate is unknown). By a lady in his harem called Mutnefret, he had a son, also named Thutmose.

The question of succession thus became something of a problem. Although there was a son to inherit the throne, the younger Thutmose was of minor royal birth when compared to Hatshepsut, Thutmose's daughter by his Great Royal Wife. Egypt had had many regnant queens, but they had all been chosen because there was no male alternative. Yet the semi-divine status of Hatshepsut, daughter of a king and a Great Royal Wife, clearly outranked the status of Thutmose, a mere son of the harem.

The Child of Amun

It has often been said that the kings of Egypt regarded themselves as gods and sons of gods. This is an exaggeration. Only two rulers were ever depicted as being of divine birth—Amenhotep III and Hatshepsut.

An unusual relief at Deir el-Bahri, Hatshepsut's magnificent temple, shows that on the night of

Hatshepsut's conception, the body of Thutmose I was taken over by the *ka* of the god Amun. It was the *ka* that moved the body and occupied its interior, even providing the sperm or egg. The inscription says that Hatshepsut's mother, Great Royal Wife Ahmose, recognized the god by the fragrance emanating from the body of Thutmose. As a result of this miracle, Hatshepsut was regarded as a real, physical child of the god; at her delivery, the pregnant Ahmose was guided into the birthing chamber by other gods and goddesses who supervised and eased the birth.

It is hard to know, with historical hindsight, whether Hatshepsut actually believed this as a truth or used it as a political maneuver. Her father, after all, had been identified as a son of the god himself through his temple donation. It appears that either she truly believed she was the child of Amun, and thus head and shoulders above the rank of her harem-born half-brother, or that at the very least she helped spread the story, knowing it would impress the greatly superstitious Egyptians and help her seize the throne for herself. Without doubt, the example of Queen Ahhotep would have encouraged Hatshepsut to dream of attaining power.

Egypt's royal records show only the formal face of monarchy, never the private side. Did Hatshepsut despise her young half-brother? Regardless, tradition demanded that she take the accustomed position. At his coronation, she was crowned his Great Royal Wife.

Divine Adoratrice

Near the end of the reign of Thutmose I, Queen Ahmose-Nefertari, widow of the great Ahmose and mother of Amenhotep I, died a very old lady. Her mummy, found in the Deir el-Bahri cache, shows that she had scoliosis, which had left her hunchbacked; she was slightly balding, and had protruding teeth—far from the slender beauty portrayed on monuments. She had taken the title of "Divine Adoratrice," probably after the death of her husband.

This title was somewhat mysterious until it came into its own in the late Ramessid Period. At this early date it required the holder to participate in the secret cult of Amun (in a yet unknown capacity), and gave her authority, revenue, and rank in her own right, independent of her male relatives. The headdress associated with the office, a vulture-headdress made of interlinked leaves of pure gold, linked the wearer to the goddess Mut. Undoubtedly, the Divine Adoratrice thus played Mut to the god Amun during the Opet festival.

Hatshepsut inherited the title from the old queen. She was to bear it with great pride, and even during the reign of her brother-husband Thutmose II she used the title of Divine Adoratrice in preference to Great Royal Wife. Was this because she disliked the latter title? Or because the former gave her power in her own right? It seems that from the start there may have been some resentment building up in her relationship with the king.

The Unhappy Couple

It is difficult to be sure of the age of Thutmose II when he took the throne, but it is certain that he ruled for about 12 years. He left very few monuments behind him. His father, who ruled for between six and eleven years, left far more. Since the number of monuments is a good guide to reign-length, it is sensible to err on the high side and assign Thutmose I a minimum of 10 years.

Thutmose II was the child of a minor harem wife, and cannot have been more than nine when he became king, maybe even younger. Thutmose I validated his claim to the throne by his marriage to the last relative of Amenhotep I, so Hatshepsut could have been born before he became king, in which case her claim to divine birth may have been necessary to maintain her regality. Given this, she could have been 12 or older at the time of the marriage. The antipathy between the two could be partly the result of an older girl being forced to marry an almost-infant half-brother.

Above **Hatshepsut kneeling in front of Amun, carving on obelisk of Hatshepsut, Karnak, c.1473–1458 BCE.** Hatshepsut repaired and built many temples at Karnak, endearing herself to the priests of Amun.

Left **Sphinx of Hatshepsut, Deir el-Bahri, c.1473–1458 BCE.** Her subsequent creation of her own mortuary temple allowed Hatshepsut to attach her image to a major symbol of royal power, the sphinx.

Right **Ceremony of purification of mummies, decoration from the tomb of Merymaat, Eighteenth Dynasty.** The process of mummification was elaborate and expensive, and thus only available to royals and others with considerable wealth.

Thutmose II

Over
ambi
to th

Deir el-Bahri

Hatshepsut's most enduring legacy is her magnificent temple at Deir el-Bahri. Begun soon after her coronation and built over many years, it was her *Djeser Djeseru*—"Holy of Holies"—and her record and celebration of her reign.

Above **Goddess Hathor, carved column, Deir el-Bahri, c. 1473–1458 BCE.** Hatshepsut's small temple to Hathor was filled with columns adorned with the goddess's face, as well as images of Hatshepsut being suckled, or given life, by Hathor.

From the start of her reign, Hatshepsut behaved as a powerful king rather than an insecure queen. Images and inscriptions depicted her more often as male than female. At her birth, she claimed, she was given "eight *kas*, seven of them male."

Egypt had never been more prosperous or peaceful. The empire, created by her father, was calm; Nubia was servile and regularly sending "tribute;" Egypt's navy controlled trade in the known world of the eastern Mediterranean. Gold and electrum (a natural alloy of gold and silver highly prized in Egypt) flooded into the state coffers. Hatshepsut was ably assisted by many capable courtiers— Hapuseneb, priest in Karnak; Djehuty, her treasurer; and Senenmut, her steward. In short, the sun shone on Hatshepsut and she looked forward to a long and glorious reign.

As soon as she was crowned, she began work on embellishing Karnak and repairing sites that had been damaged during the occupation. Her tomb was begun in the Valley of the Kings, ultimately the deepest ever cut there. More significantly, she soon ordered work started on an immense new temple at Deir el-Bahri.

Precedents for Deir el-Bahri

The natural amphitheater of honey-gold cliffs on the west bank of the Nile at Luxor was already home to another building. This unusual monument, comprising a square base with a colonnade and probably a *mastaba* on top, was the work of Mentuhotep of the Eleventh Dynasty, one of the few kings who had also organized a successful expedition to Punt. Hatshepsut's architects designed a similar edifice, to the north of Mentuhotep's. Created in three terraces, each

approached by a gently sloping ramp, it remains one of the most original and graceful of all ancient Egypt's monuments.

Each terrace was fronted by square columns, and the columns of the top terrace were also adorned with statues of the queen as Osiris. The lower terrace walls, like the others carved in raised relief, show Hatshepsut's obelisks being transported to Karnak temple. On the middle terrace, to the north the expedition to Punt is depicted and described in detail, while to the south the walls show Hatshepsut's divine conception and birth. The top terrace depicts the Opet Festival, and the beautiful Festival of the Valley, during which the statue of Amun, set in a shrine, visited the sites of the west bank.

OBELISKS

The earliest obelisks were made of many stones cemented together and were called *benben* stones. Later obelisks, made of single pieces of granite, were fragile and delicate. Usually erected in pairs at the fronts of temples, they were carved with hieroglyphic inscriptions from base to tip and had gold peaks. Some were apparently gilded. The Romans were the first to export Egypt's obelisks to their own cities—there are 13 in Rome; only five complete ones remain standing in Egypt. The Egyptians called obelisks *tjekhenu*, "shining stones." The word "obelisk" comes from the ancient Greek *obelus*, meaning a "spit" or "pillar."

Below **Hatshepsut and her obelisks at Karnak, granite carving from the temple of Deir el-Bahri, c. 1473–1458 BCE.** It is thought that these pink granite obelisks, which still stand at Karnak, were originally coated with gold.

Amun, which was named *La Chapelle rouge*, "the Red Chapel," by French Egyptologists. Little studied until a few years ago, the stones offer a different perspective on the relationship between Hatshepsut and Thutmose III.

Carvings on the stones show both rulers being crowned in Karnak, and receiving a succession of crowns from the hands of assorted deities. Other stones show the two kings side by side, participating in festivals as equals. Both their names appear in cartouches, both wear the crown of kingship. The overall impression is of a contented partnership. Here there is no damage to Hatshepsut's name or image—and the chapel stood in Karnak for many decades after Thutmose III died.

So what of the damage to the stones from Deir el-Bahri? It seems that Thutmose III decided to build a new temple in the bay of cliffs, between and on top of the earlier temples of Mentuhotep and Hatshepsut. It is thought that when his orders to dismantle the Holy of Holies were given to the workers, some of them damaged the images, not on the orders of Thutmose, but out of frustration.

Left **Stone blocks carved with hieroglyphs and reliefs, Red Chapel, Karnak, c. 1473–1458** BCE

Hatshepsut began work on this shrine shortly before her death, and Thutmose III seems to have continued the project, though he never finished it.

was Hatshepsut-Merytra (no relation to King Hatshepsut), who is known to be the daughter of a Chantress of Amun, perhaps one of Thutmose II's harem-wives.

Thutmose's Revenge?

At the end of the nineteenth century CE, the temple Hatshepsut built at Deir el-Bahri did not exist. All that was left were piles of rubble and foundations to show where the building once stood. Much of the stone had been divided between two quarry holes situated a mile apart on the west bank. The temple, as it exists today, is the result of decades of patient analysis and reconstruction by Egyptologists.

Some of the stones found in the quarries were taken by museums contributing to the restoration and so lost to the temple. When these stones were closely examined, it was found that on many of them the image of the queen and her name had been cut out. In some cases, the damage seemed both deliberate and vicious.

Many assumed that the obvious reason for this was that once Hatshepsut died Thutmose III set about obliterating any trace of his stepmother's name, as punishment for the humiliation she had heaped upon him. This notion is still popularly held, but it is probably not the truth.

The Red Chapel

In the open-air museum north of Karnak, for many years a series of dark quartzite blocks lay neatly on stone trestles following their removal from a pylon gateway in which they had been used as rubble. At an earlier time, they had formed a kiosk or waystation of the shrine of

FESTIVAL HALL

Behind the sanctuary of Amun in Karnak temple, an open courtyard leads to the so-called Festival Hall of Thutmose III. Uniquely, this was constructed in the form of a stone tent, its columns shaped like tent poles. Inside, the colors of the painted walls are bright and fresh. An inscription lists 54 days of the year when festivals were held in the temple.

Behind the hall are the "Botanical Rooms," where exquisitely detailed reliefs show rare plants, seeds, fruits, animals, and birds collected by the king. It is thought likely that these items were actually stored here, making this the world's oldest zoo and herbarium.

Above **Colonnade of the Botanical Rooms, temple of Karnak, c. 1479–1425** BCE.

Thutmose III's Festival Hall may have been designed to resemble the tent the king used during military campaigns.

Ancient Egypt's Napoleon

Thutmose III's military campaigns bolstered and expanded the empire, notably in the northeast, and brought Egypt an influx of wealth. His energy, tenacity, and triumphs have led to him being compared to Napoleon Bonaparte.

Above **Thutmose III, painted limestone relief from Deir el-Bahri, c. 1479–1425** BCE. The king is shown wearing the crown of Amun, adorned with long plumes, ram's horns, and a sun-disk.

Right **Thutmose III smiting foreign prisoners, temple of Karnak, c. 1479–1425** BCE. Thutmose brought a multitude of prisoners back to Egypt. The more influential among them were Egyptianized and returned home as loyal vassals.

It is possible that the mummy found in the Deir el-Bahri cache and identified as Thutmose III is not that of the famous king at all. The royal mummies in the Egyptian Museum were X-rayed in 1968. At that time, DNA analysis was not technologically feasible, and blood and tissue tests were not allowed by the museum authorities, so evidence of age could only be inferred from the condition of teeth and bones. Comparing the X-rays of a mummy with X-rays of those purported to be its father and/or sons was the only possible way to check lineage. The X-rays showed that the head of Thutmose III is completely different than those of his father Thutmose II and his son Amenhotep II. In fact, the face is so different that one pathologist suggested the mummy was more likely Nubian than Egyptian. How could this be?

When the tombs in the Valleys of the Kings were robbed, the mummies were usually thrown aside. When they were later collected, they were identified only by wooden tags, and moved twice more before arriving in their final resting place in the Egyptian Museum. A body could have been misidentified at any one of these stages. That said, until blood typing or DNA can establish identities with confidence, we have to go along with the current identifications.

The body in dispute is that of a short man, only 5 ft 3 in (160 cm) tall. If it is Thutmose III, it could be said that like Napoleon and many other conquerors he was "vertically challenged."

The Battle of Megiddo

Thutmose III undertook his first campaign, to the north of Egypt, in his first year of sole rule, and campaigned almost every winter after that. His aim initially was to subdue the enemies that Thutmose I had left alone—Mitanni and Nahrin. The modest accounts of his campaigns are carved onto a wall in Karnak, 223 lines of hieroglyphic texts detailing his routes and battles.

The first campaign was triggered by a rebellion based in the Mitanni cities of Qadesh, built on an island in the river Orontes in Syria, and Megiddo. Local chiefs had gathered together and were inciting revolt. Thutmose III would have none of it, and marched against them.

The armies were to meet on the plain outside the heavily fortified city of Megiddo. Megiddo lay on an open road that led north and south across the plain. To the east lay hills that no army had ever crossed. Thutmose III sought advice from his officers as to which way he should approach the rebel army. They recommended the road, attacking the enemy either from north or south. Thutmose ignored them, and daringly chose to take his army through the Aruna Pass in the hills to the east, a gap only wide enough to take two men side by side, and fraught with the risk of ambush. Two days later, like Lawrence at Aqaba,

Left **Glass-footed drinking cup owned by Thutmose III and bearing his cartouche, c. 1479–1425 BCE.** Patterned glass vessels may have been introduced to Egypt from Syria as a result of Thutmose's campaigns, and soon became prized status symbols.

Right **Thutmose III, basalt statue, c. 1479–1425 BCE.** Images of Thutmose III vary from traditional figures in that the upper body is shown as more broad-shouldered and muscular than usual.

he emerged unexpectedly behind enemy lines. Startled, the rebels fled into the city, abandoning chariots, horses, and weapons for Thutmose's men to collect. After a siege from which there was no escape, the chiefs came out and begged the king for mercy. He collected tribute from them and left them as loyal vassals of Egypt.

Across the Euphrates and Back

During his eighth campaign, Thutmose III defeated his longstanding enemy in Qadesh, then marched onward up the Orontes to the Euphrates. It is not clear how he and his men crossed the Euphrates. It could not have been on foot, as the river was too deep and fast, and it is unlikely that they could have found suitable boats in the area. The most likely scenario is that Thutmose brought boats with him from the plains of Syria. His determination knew no limits.

Once on the east side of the river, he had a stela erected marking the event. On his return, he attacked Qadesh again, leading a chariot group. The Prince of Qadesh opened the city gates and let out a mare in season, thereby creating mayhem among the stallions in the chariots. A soldier managed to get to the mare and "slit her belly open," thus saving the king's life.

Near the enemy territory lay the unidentified land of Niy. It seems to have been the equivalent of a safari park dedicated to elephants, and open to kings and powerful chiefs for hunting. Where the elephants originated remains a mystery.

A soldier in Thutmose's army, Amenemheb, described in his tomb how, after the adrenalin rush of crossing the Euphrates, the king had to release his energy in Niy. "He hunted 120 elephants for the sake of their tusks. I cornered the largest of them which then turned and attacked His Majesty. I cut off his 'hand' while he was still alive in the presence of His Majesty, while standing in the river between two rocks."

Although such wholesale slaughter seems unforgivable today, the killing of one elephant, let alone 120, using the weapons available at the time, must have been no mean feat.

The Tomb of Rekhmire

It is rare for us to see beyond the official face of the Egyptian monarchy. But the decorations in Theban Tomb 100, the tomb of Vizier Rekhmire, reveal the workings of the kingdom's court, government, and economy.

Right **Vase sealed with cork, on a linen base, Deir el-Medina.** Given the paucity of grain earned by ordinary workers, basic vessels like this one must have played a vital role in protecting food supplies.

Below **Metalworkers smelting gold, painted limestone decoration from the tomb of Rekhmire, Qurna, c. 1400 BCE.** This is one of a series of paintings showing craftsmen working on the temple of Amun in Karnak.

The T-shaped tomb of Rekhmire, vizier to Thutmose III, is perhaps the finest on the west bank at Luxor. It is decorated with brightly painted images and inscriptions, many of which depict and describe the vizier's daily duties, relationships between king and subjects, and the farming of royal estates.

Rekhmire was born to high office. His uncle, User (who is buried in Theban Tomb 61), was vizier before him in the early years of the reign of Thutmose III. But Rekhmire did not inherit the office; clearly he earned it. He recounts how he became vizier, and an image shows him receiving his authority from Thutmose III. Beneath it, Rekhmire says of his king, "There was nothing that he did not know in heaven, on Earth, or in the afterlife." Of his own position, he calls himself "second only to the King." He tells us also that Thutmose III was a king who was concerned about his country: "His Majesty knew of everything that happened...he was Thoth, there was nothing that he did not complete."

Rekhmire died in office under Amenhotep II, no doubt wealthy, but probably also worn out by the demands of his job.

The Duties of a Vizier

When the king selected Rekhmire for office, he warned him candidly, "Take the office of vizier. Supervise everything that is done in it. See, as for the [post of] vizier, it is not sweet, it is bitter as gall."

With such an introduction, one wonders why Rekhmire should have accepted. He is warned he must be fair to everyone, an impartial judge, and cautious over his every word: "The man who judges in public, the wind and the rain carry word of what he has done." He must be calm, and must never judge friends differently than strangers: "Treat the man you know the same as the one you do not know." He is instructed that "a man who only does what he has been ordered is innocent," a surprisingly modern concept. His duty is simply to carry out justice, because "the vizier is its fair custodian since the time of God."

The inscription lists his duties, and through them we get a glimpse into the actions of government in the halls of the king. The vizier is to have a daily meeting with the king, after which he and the treasurer meet to discuss the results of the previous day's happenings and to review the actions of subordinates.

During the day, the vizier supervises all state and royal offices. He is to control the treasuries for both. He is head of the entire justice system, from hearing criminal cases to organizing the King's daily security. He is in charge of conscription for the army, and for provision of all supplies and equipment for both army and navy. During a war, he is to receive and dispatch daily messengers to the king to ensure good government when the king is absent. He is in charge

of all taxation, and thus of all agriculture. He is overseer of all state and royal workshops, and responsible for accounting for all imported and exported goods. In short, if Egypt were to be regarded as one great estate, with the land leased to tenants, the vizier would be the overall head of administration for all aspects of its organization.

Given the complexities of the Egyptian state, one must wonder whether the newly appointed vizier ever enjoyed a good night's sleep again!

Wages and Salaries

In theory, every worker received his pay monthly in the form of grain and other staples. It is usually suggested that the harvest would have been collected into centralized granaries, to be handed out as salaries. But consider the logistics. If all grain were gathered into the granaries in Memphis, all workers would have to go there to be paid—for southerners, this could take a week for each leg of the journey. Even if the grain were stored locally, payday would still be a nightmare.

One scholar has calculated that in one year of the reign of Rameses III 61,413 men were employed in Karnak alone. Receiving pay in grain—imagine the queues!—would mean that any broken sack, any grain eaten by mice, or any grain tainted by mould was lost money.

Basic pay for a worker was just enough to keep a man alive for a month. An "overseer of 10" received more than double this, and would have been quite comfortable. As workers rose through the ranks, they would receive more grain—whether they needed it or not.

A high official like Rekhmire, earning perhaps a hundred times more than an ordinary worker, would have a real problem. He would need lines of ox-carts to carry his grain; means of securing it; and then, 30 days later, like it or not, would have to return for more. With no banks to store the surplus, how did such people cope? There is, after all, only a certain amount one can eat!

Market price-lists have been found, however, showing goods priced in *deben*, a *deben* being a ring of copper weighing just under 4 oz (115 g). A sack of grain equaled one *deben*. It is thus likely that higher paid workers received part of their pay in grain, and the rest in *deben*. This would make the *deben* the world's first metal currency.

Left **Syrians and Assyrians bringing tribute, painted limestone decoration from the tomb of Rekhmire, Qurna, c. 1400 BCE.** Numerous scenes in the tomb show the delivery and inspection of tributes, the result of Thutmose III's ongoing conquests.

Below **Loading grain onto boat, fresco from the tomb of Wensu, mid-Eighteenth Dynasty.** Wensu was a grain accountant. Taxes paid in the form of grain were often shipped along the Nile to royal storehouses.

Amenhotep II

Appointed co-regent shortly before his father's death, Amenhotep II proved himself a tireless and ruthless military campaigner, but also a shrewd administrator whose firm rule allowed the empire to continue to flourish.

Below **Amenhotep II kneeling before the gods, pink granite statue, Eighteenth Dynasty.** Amenhotep is shown presenting the gods with two round wine jars.

According to a stela from Giza, Thutmose III's son Amenhotep II was born and raised in Memphis, where he spent much of his youth in his father's stables. "He adored horses and delighted in them, he was hard-working, understood their characters, and knew how to train them." His father was so impressed that he announced: "Let him be given large and fine horses from the stable of His Majesty in Memphis and tell him, 'Look after them, break them in, trot them, and care for them when they are headstrong.'"

Towards the end of his reign, Thutmose III appears to have had concerns over the succession. Two years before he died, he had his son crowned and they reigned as co-regents. Why would Thutmose have done this? He had enriched and stabilized the country more than any king for the previous two

centuries. Moreover, he was bequeathing to Egypt something none of his predecessors had been able to offer—a son and heir who was an adult. It seems probable he simply wanted to ensure that no one could usurp the throne. The Sphinx Stela records that Amenhotep II acceded to the throne "in his eighteenth year."

Displays of Prowess

From his youth, Amenhotep excelled in all physical activities. As king, he gloried in his superiority, boasting of his prowess on many occasions. His subjects were in awe: "No one knew how to manage a chariot as he did...No one could draw his bow and he could never be beaten in a running race. His arms were so strong they could not weary when rowing...he drew 300 bows to test the work of their makers."

On several occasions he displayed his talents before an appreciative public. "He entered the northern grounds and found four targets of Asiatic copper had been set up, the copper of one palm thickness [about 4 inches, or 10 cm] with 20 cubits between each of them [about 30 ft, or 10 m]. His Majesty appeared in his chariot like great Mont. He grabbed his bow and snatched four arrows. Then he set off northward, shooting like Mont in all his might, and his arrows emerged from the back of the target. This was something which had never been done in the past, except in the case of the king." As if this were not enough, other stelae say that he shot his arrows so hard that each came out of the back of the copper target and fell to the ground.

A Cruel Streak

Although Thutmose III conquered countless cities, he was always ready to make an example of a few prisoners and pardon the rest. In contrast, Amenhotep II was determined to be fierce and merciless. By his third year, the virile young king had returned from what was probably his first campaign in the north, bringing with him seven captive princes. After displaying them in a victory parade in Memphis, he sailed south to

LIFE OF A SOLDIER

At the start of the New Kingdom, expansion in the north and problems in Nubia resulted in the creation of a professional army in Egypt. We know that conscripts were called to the Memphis barracks for training, but not the length of their training or how long they served. In peacetime, conscripted soldiers were called upon to move stones for building projects, an unpleasant task.

On their marches abroad to campaign, each man carried a backpack containing 20 loaves of bread for daily rations. The soldiers were issued with weapons and sandals only when they reached the border fortresses. Conscripts were usually infantrymen, whereas charioteers seem to have been drawn from the highest levels of the nobility.

Men were able to rise quickly through the ranks of soldiers if they showed ability. Horemheb and Rameses, who both came from non-royal backgrounds, both rose through the army to become commander in chief and then king.

Right **Sennefer and his wife Merety, painted limestone decoration from the tomb of Sennefer, Qurna, Eighteenth Dynasty.** Successful soldiers frequently gained the patronage and favor of the king. A general under Amenhotep II, Sennefer was eventually appointed mayor of Thebes.

Luxor, and there executed six of them, "and hung them upside down on the pylons of Karnak, their hand [cut off] next to them." The seventh terrified wretch was allowed to live while he sailed south with the king to the Nubian capital of Napata, a journey of about seven or eight days. But on arrival Amenhotep had the prince slaughtered and his body hung on the walls of Napata.

In his campaign of year 7, once again he marched north, and most towns wisely came out to acknowledge him as king. In Palestine, one town refused to capitulate. After taking many captives, Amenhotep "made them into living prisoners. Then two ditches were dug around

them all and set on fire. And His Majesty stood over them, alone, battle-ax in his hand." In Ugarit, he slew an army of rebels to a man. On the plain of Sharon, finding an envoy bearing a message to Nahrin, he had him tied to the back of his chariot and dragged to his death.

Not surprisingly, Amenhotep II carried away more booty than all the previous kings put together. Among the plunder, he brought back numerous women. Some may have been treated as prisoners of war, others undoubtedly entered his harem. From his 30-year reign, we know the names of several sons, but no daughters. The only person to carry the title of Divine Adoratrice was his mother, and he declared no Great Royal Wife. It is hard to escape the idea that he was determined that no woman could ever do again what Hatshepsut had done to his father.

Left **Cartouche of Amenhotep II, Red Chapel, Karnak, Eighteenth Dynasty.** Amenhotep II made additions to almost all of his father's building projects and to many begun by Hatshepsut.

Thutmose IV

The success of Amenhotep II's military campaigns brought vast wealth to Egypt and by the end of his 30-year reign the empire was secure. His son Thutmose IV needed to do little but supervise trade and accept a steady flow of tribute.

Right **Thutmose IV with his mother Tiaa**, black granite statue from Karnak, c. 1400–1390 BCE. It is unclear how Thutmose acceded to the throne. Amenhotep II had numerous children and Tiaa was never acknowledged as a royal wife.

Accounts of Amenhotep II's conquests, in the form of monuments and inscriptions, suggest that he campaigned abroad only during the first 10 years of his reign. We don't know if he terrified his neighbors into leaving him alone or whether he was injured and unable to campaign after that. However, the records do reveal the prosperity of his reign.

In inscriptions in the temple of Karnak, Amenhotep II claims "the walls around it are of fine stone, the doors of finest cedar from the terraces [of Lebanon]." He says the halls were filled with food and fine things for Amun, "beyond measuring." One shrine for Amun was "made of gold, its floor of silver. It was filled with silver more beautiful than the stars of heaven; the treasury filled with tribute from all lands and its granaries bursting with plump, fresh grain filling them to the top of their walls."

In 1898, Victor Loret rediscovered the tomb of Amenhotep II (KV 35) in the Valley of the Kings. The entrance to the new tomb was littered with objects, indicating that it had been robbed in antiquity, so there was little expectation of substantial finds within the tomb. Imagine Loret's surprise then when, leaning over the sarcophagus, he saw the linen-shrouded body of Amenhotep II, the first king ever found in his own tomb. Fifteen other royal bodies were found in the side chamber. Many of them were the bodies of Amenhotep II's close family.

Below **Long-necked vase** with *wadjet* eye decoration, tomb of Kha, c. 1400 BCE. Kha was architect of some of Amenhotep II's most important buildings.

Thutmose and the Dream Stela

The oldest son of Amenhotep II, by harem-wife Tiaa, was Thutmose. Just before he became king, Prince Thutmose went hunting with friends at Giza. The day was hot, and the young prince rested in the shadow of the Great Sphinx, by then over 1,000 years old. Thutmose slept; and in his sleep, the god Ra-Horakhty came and said to him, "You are my son, I am your father; I have waited long years for you to arrive." Ra-Horakhty bemoaned the state of his statue. Later, Thutmose cleaned the sand from around the paws of the sphinx and placed

between them a stela recording his remarkable encounter. Many have said that Ra-Horakhty promised Thutmose the throne if he cleared the sand, but the inscription does not state this. Simply, the young king had experienced a profoundly disturbing encounter with his god. It was to change history forever.

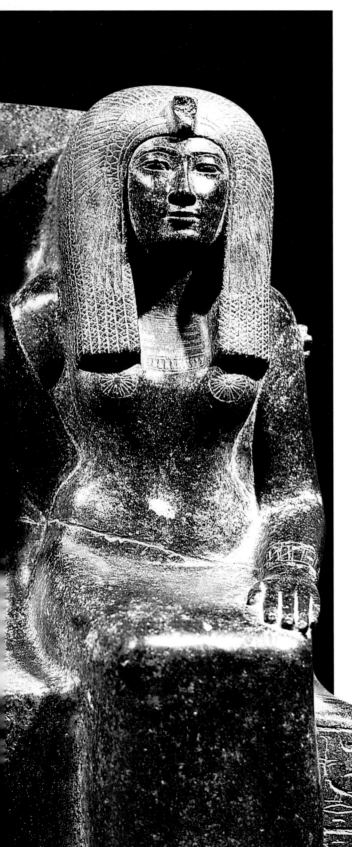

There is no evidence that Thutmose IV ever led a military campaign during his short eight-year reign. Texts in Nubia suggest that an expedition quelled disturbances in the gold-mining region. Another inscription records his marriage, to a daughter of Artatama, King of Nahrin.

Some of the finest tombs in Luxor date from the reign of Thutmose IV. Their decorations show lines of foreigners bringing tribute—Cretans carrying vases, Africans bringing exotic animals, Nubians presenting gold, and, of course, vassal states in Syria and Palestine bending the knee before the king. Amenhotep's success was such that all Thutmose IV had to do was accept the gifts and adulation. By now, all gold and all trade were in Egypt's hands.

Above **Dream stela and Great Sphinx, Giza.** For much of the time between its construction around 2500 BCE and the intervention of Thutmose IV, and again until the early twentieth century, the Great Sphinx was mostly buried by drifting sands.

The Rise of the Aten

From the time of his accession onward, the majority of Thutmose's inscriptions dedicate his monuments to Ra, or Ra-Horakhty, while references to Amun, so venerated during the reigns of his ancestors, are scarce. An increase in syncretism (the process whereby two or more deities were fused into the object of a single cult) linked gods such as Amun-Ra and Sobek-Ra. However, worship of the sun-god Ra became less significant.

According to Egyptian beliefs, the sun had many faces and identities. At dawn, before it appeared over the horizon but with its light indicating it was about to rise, it was Khepri, the cosmic dung-beetle pushing the ball of the sun into the land of the living. As it sat on the horizon, it was Ra-Horemakhet, or Harmachis—Ra who is Horus of the (east) horizon. At the fierce heat of noon, it was the Aten. As the sun set, it became Ra-Horakhty, or Ra who is Horus of the second horizon. And as it sank, it fell into Atum, the waters of the Creation.

From the start of his reign, Thutmose venerated the sun in many faces. He went into battle "with the Aten before him." This was the first time the Aten had changed from the mere sun at noon into a demi-god in his own right. From this period onward, the Aten was to play a more significant role in state affairs.

The Theban Tombs

Most of the finest painted tombs on the west bank at Luxor date to the reigns of Amenhotep II and Thutmose IV, probably because prosperity drew more talented craftspeople, as well as better training, tools, and pigments.

Above **Boat on the Nile, decoration from the tomb of Sennefer, Valley of the Nobles, Luxor, c. 1400 BCE.** As mayor of Thebes, Sennefer was responsible for the collection of taxes at several ports on the Nile.

On the west bank there are probably around 1,000 tombs of the highest officials in the land. These tombs are cut into rock, some at ground level, some approached by descending steps; most originally had tomb gardens in front of them. They are more correctly called tomb chapels, since the burial chamber, or chambers, invariably lie at the foot of deep underground shafts. Although the chapels are brilliantly painted, the burial chambers are usually small and unpainted. The chapels are small and either have one chamber, or are T-shaped, with the tomb shaft farthest away from the entrance. The location of the tomb shaft, sealed with rubble and plastered over, was marked with a stela, a false door (through which the ka might emerge), and a stone offering table. Recent years' excavations have shown that most tombs had extra shafts for other family members cut into the courtyard or garden outside.

Preparing the Tomb

During his lifetime, the tomb owner would lay aside estates purely for growing food for his mortuary cult. He would appoint a manager for these, whose duties were to bring food to the tomb two or three times a day, keeping the food for his family when the offering was over. After two or three generations, the land reverted to the family to be redistributed to later cults.

The stone sarcophagus, the stela, and the offering table all had to be provided by the king, as only he had rights to the stone quarries. The tomb site itself would have to be formally

MASTERING MUMMIFICATION

The Egyptian notion of an afterlife incorporated the belief that the body was resurrected during the final ceremony before burial, then made its way at sunset to the western horizon, where it entered the spirit world. The body therefore had to be preserved.

Modern research suggests that experiments with mummification took place over centuries and that the process was perfected during the New Kingdom. It was discovered in that era that removing the blood was the key to halting decay. So the body was desanguinated, then placed in natron (a naturally occurring salt) to absorb any remaining blood. The deceased was removed from the salt while still malleable and wrapped in bandages—it is clear from New Kingdom mummies that the fingers and toes were still soft enough at this stage to be bandaged individually. Prior to being placed in a coffin, the body was coated with resin to complete the preservation.

The mummy of Sety I is perhaps the best preserved of the era. Other fine examples include those of Yuya and Thuya, who both retain their flesh colors and look as if they had just fallen asleep.

Below **Embalming of a mummy, from the Book of the Dead, Papyrus of Konshu, Nineteenth Dynasty.** The process was supervised by a priest wearing the jackal mask of the god Anubis.

donated to the official, and, other than royals, only officials could have tombs. Ordinary people were excluded from cutting their own tombs.

The tombs were guarded by the Medjay, originally a Nubian regiment. Even so, because people regularly entered the tombs, goods were not placed within the chapels. Paintings and inscriptions provided what was needed for the dead, while the funerary prayer provided for food and drink when the mortuary cult ceased. With the name of the dead continually repeated, immortality came through the lips of posterity.

Decorations in Nobles' Tombs

In tomb decorations, each scene is painted in registers, each wall is independent of the others, and the whole is framed by elaborate border designs. The colors are bold and primary, with no shading or highlights. In every tomb, you need time to stand and stare, for you will always find amusing details that make the tomb unique.

The tomb of Menna, Theban Tomb (Th.T.) 69, is decorated with scenes of harvesting. As adults work, two little girls fight, tearing each other's hair. In the tomb of Nakht (Th.T.52), while Nakht and his wife Tawi sit at their offering table, a cat

under their chair is eating a stolen fish. Sobek-hotep was Mayor of Luxor and his tomb (Th.T.63) includes many images of him accepting tribute on the king's behalf. Hekhernekhekh was Thutmose IV's tutor, and a delightful scene in his burial chamber (Th.T.64) shows the little prince seated on his knee. Tjanuny was commander in chief of Thutmose's army and a scene cut from his tomb (Th.T.74), now in the British Museum, shows a group of overweight soldiers, like sumo-wrestlers, wearing strange nets over their kilts.

One of the finest, most richly decorated tombs in the area is that of Sennefer (Th.T.96), a general and Mayor of Thebes under Amenhotep II. When tomb cutters worked on his ceiling, they found a stratum of exceptionally hard rock. Rather than spending a long time removing it, they simply smoothed it over and painted mats on it.

Recent excavations at Saqqara have revealed vast cemeteries from the New Kingdom period, all displaying similarly impressive decorations. It appears that the sheer zest for life spread through Egypt during the reigns of these warrior-kings. Confidence had never been at a higher ebb. Fate was to decree that it would never reach such a high level again.

Above **Tomb of Sennefer Valley of the Nobles, Luxor, c. 1400 BCE.** The pergola of black grapes on the ceiling, along with numerous scenes of Sennefer imbibing, attests to his love of wine.

Yuya and Thuya

The discovery of the tomb of Yuya and Thuya, in the Valley of the Kings in 1905, stunned the world. Though it was soon overshadowed by the tomb of Tutankhamun, it remains one of the richest and most intact sites yet found.

Above **Detail from gold sarcophagus of Thuya, tomb of Yuya and Thuya, c. 1400** BCE. Appropriately for a tomb so lavishly adorned with the precious metal, this image shows the goddess Isis kneeling on the hieroglyph for gold.

According to his titles, Yuya rose to power as Master of the King's Horse, and Priest of Min at Koptos. His wife, Thuya, carried the title of Chantress of Amun, hence she was probably a minor wife from a harem of a previous king. A statue, now in the Metropolitan Museum in New York, lists the same titles for a man of an earlier generation, called Yey, leaving little doubt that the family held important posts in Koptos for several generations. However, none rose to such high levels as Yuya and his wife, for among their children were a future Great Royal Wife and a King of Egypt.

The burials of Yuya and Thuya were found intact. Arthur Weigall, then Inspector of Antiquities, described the discovery vividly: "Imagine the stuffy room, the stiff, silent appearance of the furniture, the feeling that the ghostly inhabitants of the chairs have just been disturbed." The burials lay together in one small room in the tomb. Thuya was at the back, and Yuya had been placed, rather more hastily, next to the entrance, suggesting that he died later than his wife and

that the tomb had been reopened for his burial. At some time, robbers had torn open Thuya's coffin searching for treasure. Several items were stacked in the entrance corridor, suggesting that the thieves had placed them there to be moved at a later date but failed to come back for them.

Among the finest objects were chairs, the first of their kind ever found, and a low chariot, which seems to have been designed for personal transport rather than war. The best of the chairs has scenes on its back showing offerings being made to two Great Royal Wives, Tiye and Sitamun.

The mummies are among the best examples ever to come out of Egypt. Yuya's face, reddened as in life, is crested with a shock of white hair turned slightly yellow by the embalming resins and bandages. Thuya, looking as if she is only sleeping, has a magnificent head of hair reaching down her back, deep auburn-red in color.

Yuya and Thuya earned their place in history, and in the Valley of the Kings, through their children. Their eldest, a daughter called Tiye, became Great Royal Wife to Amenhotep III. Their

youngest, a son, Anen, became a priest in the temple of Karnak. The middle son, Ay, became a loyal follower to one of Egypt's most controversial kings and eventually took the throne himself.

The Palace of Deir el-Ballas

Yuya and Thuya's connections with the royal family seem to have been established or at least greatly strengthened during the time when the king resided at the palace of Deir el-Ballas near Koptos. This little-known site was built during the reign of Seqenenra Taa as a frontier fortress to mark Theban borders with the Hyksos. It seems to have been abandoned after the first three years of Amenhotep III's reign, probably because the 200-year-old mud-brick structure was by then inadequate for the king's needs.

The palace stood on the west bank of the Nile. Opposite, on the east bank, lay the town known today as Qift, or Koptos in Greek. Koptos was the home of the ithyphallic god, Min, and it was in this temple that Yuya served as high priest. Undoubtedly, the royal family would have come to the temple to make offerings. This would have brought the young Amenhotep III, merely a child at the time, into contact with the family of Yuya and Thuya. There is a possibility that the mother of Amenhotep, a minor wife named Mutemwiya, might have been related to one of them. In any case, when she died, the care of the young prince seems to have passed to Yuya and Thuya.

Above **Funerary mask of Thuya**, gilded cartonnage inlaid with gemstones and glass, c. 1400 BCE. The elaborate coffins and funerary items in the chamber were in stark contrast with the tomb, whose walls were bare and undecorated.

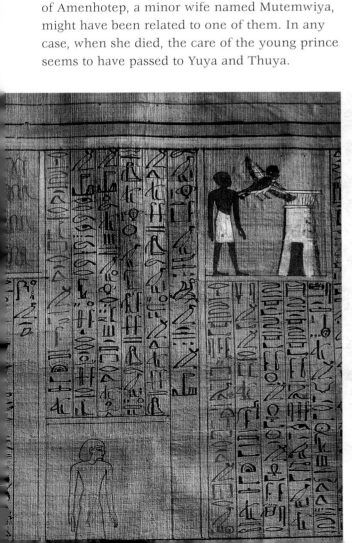

THE BOOK OF THE DEAD

The *Book of the Dead* is the name widely used for a collection of Egyptian sacred texts that have been found in numerous tombs. The English title is misleading; the Egyptians referred to these works as "Words for Coming Forth by Day." The texts included the liturgy that was required to be read during burial, and scripts that would help the deceased reach the afterlife safely.

When an individual died, the bereaved could order texts for the tomb of the deceased, choosing whichever chapters and illustrations they wanted or could afford to have transferred to papyri. As a result, no two surviving papyri are identical, although the same chapters and illustrations occur in many of them.

Left **Texts and illustrations from the *Book of the Dead*, papyrus from the tomb of the architect Kha (Th.T.8)**, c. 1400 BCE. Included in this selection of texts and scenes are a depiction of the Opening of the Mouth ceremony (far left) and an image showing a spirit leaving a body in the form of a bird (left).

The Young Amenhotep III

During the short eight-year reign of Thutmose IV, his mother Tiaa was hugely influential and held the title of Great Royal Wife. Yet it was a minor harem-wife, Mutemwiya, who gave birth to the son who would succeed Thutmose.

Tiaa held both the title of Great Royal Wife and that of God's Wife of Amun. Given that she had not been Great Royal Wife to her husband Amenhotep II, it can only be that her son elevated her to this status. Long after the death of Hatshepsut, the distrust of powerful women engendered by her reign seems to have continued. We know nothing of Mutemwiya as she was one of the lesser wives of Thutmose IV. Had she not borne a son for the king, she would have died as obscurely as she lived.

In a back chamber of the temple of Luxor, the conception of Amenhotep is shown. As with Hatshepsut before him, it was claimed that on the night of his conception the spirit of Amun entered the body of his father Thutmose IV so that Mutemwiya gave birth, in time, to Amun's son. Why should this have been recorded?

Of the Egyptian rulers, only Hatshepsut and Amenhotep made such a claim. In the case of Hatshepsut, she needed to justify her usurpation of the throne. Amenhotep had no such need, since we know of no other contender for the throne, so what was his reasoning?

A recent suggestion is that Amenhotep believed himself to be a god, unlike other kings who only assumed semidivine status through coronation. However, there is little evidence for this. The more likely suggestion is that Amenhotep recorded what he thought was the truth—his father, Thutmose IV, believed he had had the spirit of god enter into him as a direct result of his encounter with Ra-Horakhty.

Coronation of Amenhotep III

Amenhotep III Nebmaatra appears, from his titles, to have been crowned in Karnak. At his coronation, he also presented to the people his new Great Royal Wife Tiye, daughter of Yuya and Thuya—in essence, a commoner. Since it was almost unheard of for a king to take a Great

Left **The young Amenhotep on the knee of his nurse Hekarnehhe, engraving after painting in the tomb of Hekarnehhe, 1878.** Amenhotep was still a child when he ascended the throne.

Royal Wife who was not a sister, it has long been decided
that this must have been
a great love match. How-
ever, those who claim this
miss one important point.

Mutemwiya, the mother
of Amenhotep III, was a minor
harem wife of Thutmose IV,
who could only have had a harem
after he became king. Given that
Thutmose ruled only eight years, and
assuming that Mutemwiya had become
pregnant at the start of his reign, her
son could have been no more than
seven years old when he reached
the throne, and perhaps even
younger. Since it is unthinkable
that a seven-year-old boy "fell in
love" with his prospective bride, Tiye, it may
have been the influence of her father, Yuya,
that brought them together.

The First Tabloids

During the first 11 years of his 39-year reign,
Amenhotep III issued, or had issued on his
behalf, five series of stone scarabs, each about
4 in (10 cm) long, inscribed on their backs with
news about Egypt's new king. These scarabs
were circulated in their hundreds, perhaps
thousands, around the empire. The first series,
undated, lists the king's titles and announced the
selection of a wife: "Great Royal Wife Tiye, may
she live. The name of her father is Yuya, the
name of her mother is Thuya. She is wife of a
great king." The second series, dated year 2,
noted that Tiye was now his wife.

It is interesting that the scarabs included the
names of the parents of the Great Royal Wife. We
seldom know the name of one parent of a king's
spouse, let alone two, and their names were certainly never proclaimed in this manner. There
seems no doubt that Yuya and Thuya were
instrumental in marrying their daughter to
the new boy-king for their own advantage.

The second series of stone scarabs, dating to
when Amenhotep was no more than eight years
old, recorded that he had been told of the arrival
in Egypt of a herd of wild cattle. Having ordered
them to be placed inside an enclosure, he was
then permitted to sit, in safety, and shoot arrows
at them, eventually killing 170 beasts. It was the
ancient equivalent of a fairground shooting game.

The third series of stone scarabs,
in a similar vein, recorded that
Amenhotep killed 102 wild lions
in the first 10 years of his reign.
Presumably he was trying to
promote an image similar to
that of his grandfather.

In his tenth year, the fourth
series of scarabs announced
that, again like his grandfather,
Amenhotep III had married a
sister of the King of Nahrin,
Giludkhipa by name—and that she
had brought with her 317 women!
By this time the king was in his mid-
teens and undoubtedly reveled
in the presence of females within
his harem. The following year,
year 11, it seems as if he needed
to placate his Great Royal Wife. He built for her
a lake, almost one-quarter of a mile long, in her
hometown. Fifteen days later, she sailed on it.

Queen Tiye was one of the most remarkable
women of the age. Texts that date from later in
the reign record that it was she who carried out
correspondence with foreign kings on her husband's behalf. She would also play a significant
role in other events that followed.

Left **Head of Amenhotep
III, black diorite bust,
c. 1390–1352 BCE.** There
is no record of anyone
ruling as regent for the
young Amenhotep III,
though it is likely he was
assisted by his mother or
the family of his wife Tiye.

Below **Birth chamber of
Amenhotep III, temple of
Luxor, c. 1390–1352 BCE.**
To emphasize his divine
origins, Amenhotep deco-
rated this chamber with
reliefs showing the god
Amun occupying his
father's body on the
night of his conception.

Malkata

It was fortunate for Amenhotep III that he inherited a stable and prosperous country, given his age when he ascended the throne. This prosperity enabled him to embark on great building projects, such as the palace-city of Malkata.

Above **Detail of fragment of patterned glass, New Kingdom.** Many of the artifacts found at Malkata were intricately designed, to the extent that they might easily be mistaken for modern works.

As a youth, Amenhotep III seems to have been cosseted, and there must have been many in the court to look after him and indulge his whims. Moreover, his resources were unlimited. As one king wrote to him: "Gold is more plentiful in your country than sand."

After the first 10 years of campaigning and demonstrating his physical prowess, it seems that Amenhotep settled down to domestic affairs and indulged his passion for fine living and, especially, building. No other king ever built on the scale that he did, for he added to almost every site already constructed, and the monuments he raised were both massive and grand. Soldiers of the time probably spent almost their entire careers moving stone!

Amenhotep was the first king to have colossal statues cut of himself and his wife. She was always depicted at the same size, with her arm around the king, supporting him carefully. Queen Tiye was undoubtedly a little older than her husband, but their marriage was a success. In time, she bore Amenhotep six or more children.

To celebrate their relationship, Amenhotep built one of the most beautiful temples in Egypt, the temple of Luxor. He also built a *maru* or viewing place on the west bank, directly across the river from Luxor, from where the royal couple and their children could watch events in the new temple. Within months, the decision was taken to enlarge the viewing place, and the palace-city of Malkata was born.

During the reign of Amenhotep III, his chief architect was one of Egypt's great geniuses, Amenhotep, son of Hapu. Minds such as his came along infrequently in the history of Egypt.

Right **Vases and bowl, glass paste, New Kingdom.** Amenhotep's reign saw a flourishing of applied arts such as glassware and ceramics. These pieces are typical of the era's predominant patterns and color ranges.

Perhaps only Imhotep and Khaemwaset were at the same level. These men could work miracles, and the kings that they served were blessed.

Royal Quarters and Estates

The remains of Malkata and the adjacent harbor of Birket Habu today lie about a mile south of the southernmost mortuary temple on the west bank of the Nile, Medinet Habu. The sites are little visited, and excavations in the 1880s and the 1970s have barely begun to reveal their secrets.

Originally, the buildings lay on both sides of a main road that ran parallel to the Nile. Those to the east of this road have been badly eroded due to the expansion of the fertile strip. Central to the area are the remains of a great palace for the king, with a broad hall alongside. Broad halls and square edifices filled with columns are generally associated with coronations or jubilees, and in this case, both ceremonies were undoubtedly held there.

Queen Tiye had her own palace and estates, served by officials she appointed. This was separate from the harem where the minor wives lived. It would have been in one of these two buildings that her children were born and raised.

Her eldest son was named Thutmose after his grandfather, her second son was called Amenhotep after his father, and their younger sister took the name Sitamun. Unusually, Princess Sitamun appears regularly in statues at her parents' side. Later in the reign, she too would take the title of Great Royal Wife and, in time, would have her own palace here, with estates.

Among other buildings already identified is a temple to the north of the palace, and several houses where the servitors or priests lived. But most of the area still lies buried, the outlines of the low mud-brick walls just visible as undulations in the sand. Who knows what discoveries are still to be made here?

Palace Decorations

The period during which Malkata operated as a palace was the most lavish Egypt had ever known. Not surprisingly then, hundreds of fine artifacts were found at the site. The pottery was especially elegant, much of it decorated with dark red and black geometric designs. Beautiful glassware was also found, typically deep blue in color and bearing pale blue, yellow, or white lines drawn with a tool as the glass cooled, resulting in vessels of remarkable refinement.

The walls of the palace were plastered and brilliantly painted. The lower sections still bear scenes of papyrus thickets, with bulls rushing through and raising clouds of bright-plumaged birds. The ceilings, which have long since collapsed onto the floors, were finely painted with patterns and colors that were almost identical to decorations in palaces on Crete.

Many of the statues and paintings record the fashions of the era. Women's dresses developed from basic sheaths with a simple over-robe to diaphanous gowns with complex over-robes tied under one arm. The women also wore court wigs of astonishing width, length, and weight.

Foreign ideas poured in and the Egyptians seemed content to adopt them. Wealthy beyond imagination and surrounded by a peaceful and servile world, the court of Amenhotep III and Tiye must have seemed like a glittering dream.

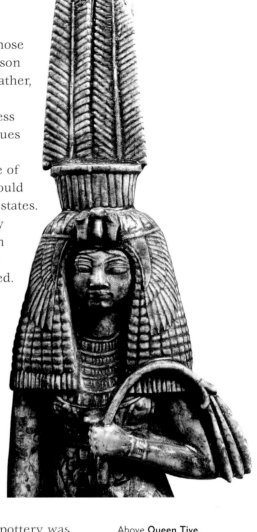

Above **Queen Tiye, wife of Amenhotep III,** steatite with green enamel, c. 1390–1352. Tiye is depicted wearing the fashions of the day: an elaborate gown and long, heavy wig.

The Temple of Luxor

One of Amenhotep's greatest works is the delightful temple of Luxor. Called the *Ipet-resyt* or Southern Harem, it was dedicated to the marriage of Amun and Mut, celebrated by the Opet Festival.

Above right Head of Amenhotep III, black diorite bust, c. 1390–1352 BCE. Amenhotep's temples and his promotion of religious festivals reinforced his position as a divinely appointed ruler.

Below Temple of Luxor. At left, steps lead up to the Abu el-Haggag Mosque, which occupies part of the courtyard of Rameses II. To the right is the entrance to the temple, to the far left the colonnade leading to the "solar" court.

There is no clear evidence of any earlier structure on the site of the temple of Luxor, although the temple itself was extended and altered several times during later periods. Indeed, it remains one of the few ancient Egyptian sites with a continuing religious role.

During the early Christian period, the sanctuary was walled off, an apse was cut behind an altar, and Coptic icons were painted on the wall —outlines of the Coptic icons remain to this day. Later, a mosque was built and dedicated to a local mayor, Sheikh Abu el-Haggag. At that time, the temple was filled with sand, so the mosque today stands halfway up the eastern wall and partially covers the front courtyard of Rameses II.

During the nineteenth century, houses were constructed for local people on top of the sand-filled colonnades. Lady Lucie Duff-Gordon, an invalid suffering from tuberculosis and living in Egypt to try to restore her health, occupied one of these houses. One winter, finding it too cold, Lady Duff-Gordon traveled down to Sudan. On her return, she found that the floor of her house had fallen into the colonnade beneath, taking her piano with it!

Later, the temple was cleared of sand and houses. But the constant rumble of traffic and the pounding of feet on the courtyards now threaten the stability of the columns. Salts, filtering upward from the ground because of the high water-table, are also causing the surfaces of the stones to "bubble" and then fall away, taking the exquisite carved reliefs with them. As one Egyptologist has stated, without action the temple will still be there in another century, but its walls will be devoid of inscriptions and images.

The Layout of the Temple

The temple is oriented approximately north–south. Visitors enter through pylon gateways that were once flanked with a pair of obelisks and colossal statues. One of the obelisks now stands in the Place de la Concorde in Paris. To the north of the pylons is an avenue of sphinxes, which originally lined the avenue from the temple of Karnak, about 1.2 miles (2 km) away to the north. The center of this avenue now lies under the main shopping street of the city of Luxor.

Rameses II built the forecourt, which incorporates a small chapel of Thutmose III and Hatshepsut; it was here that the original Opet Festival was presumably staged. Today, the chapel is attached to the back of the western pylon. The walls of the tall colonnade to the south were built by Tutankhamun, and are his only monument. The colonnade leads to the "solar" court, one of the most graceful ever built. Surrounded by papyrus-bud columns, it is truly delightful.

The columned hall beyond is relatively small, with only 32 columns, 16 on each side. The sanctuary was built by Amenhotep III, but covered with granite and carved by Alexander the Great. Side chambers include the birth chamber where Amenhotep III's divine conception was carved, today in parlous state. At the back was the *per ankh* or "House of Life," where there was once a school and copyists' workshop.

and Mut, and the birth of their son Khons. Images carved on the temple walls show Amun in his ithyphallic form, often named as Kamutef, or "bull of his Mother." The festival was one of the most popular celebrations in all Egypt and was still held during the Greek period, judging from the additions made to it by Alexander the Great.

The Opet Festivals held during the reign of Amenhotep III were undoubtedly different from others, since he considered himself the son of god. They would have celebrated his birth, enabling him to be spiritually reborn each year.

It has been suggested that the design of the temple's open courtyard represents Amenhotep's leanings toward sun-worship, following his father's revelation. However, the inscriptions on the columns do not confirm this.

Above **Pylon gateway viewed from forecourt of Rameses II, temple of Luxor, c.1360 BCE.** The standing columns between the pillars in the forecourt were carved in the image of Amenhotep III, but bear the name of Rameses II.

A Wedding Feast

The temple complex was originally dedicated to the Opet Festival, which celebrated the marriage of Amun

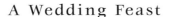

THE OPET FESTIVAL

The renowned Opet Festival took place in the second month of the Inundation season, as the waters that flooded the temples in Luxor receded, leaving the floor, columns, and sanctuary high above, like the mound upon which the world was created. Music and dance accompanied the celebrations and abundant food and drink was supplied for all who attended.

The statues of Amun and Mut were removed from their own temples, secreted

within a mobile shrine, and carried to Luxor temple to spend a "honeymoon." Nine months after returning "home," the statue of Mut would be carried to a "birth-house", to give birth, ritually, to a son, Khons.

Left **Mut, stone carving, Luxor, c. 1279-1213 BCE.** Mut had long been known as a goddess and divine mother, but her identification as the husband of Amun and mother of Khons dates from the Eighteenth Dynasty.

Egypt's Heyday

The reign of Amenhotep III was the high point of the New Kingdom and a golden age in the history of ancient Egypt. Art and architecture attained new levels of sophistication, and royal festivals were seldom more extravagant.

Above **Winemakers treading grapes, decoration from the tomb of Nakht, c. 1390** BCE. Vineyards all over Egypt provided wines for consumption at the king's lavish jubilee festivals.

Under Amenhotep III, wealth in the form of trade goods continued to pour into the country and Egypt experienced rapid economic and social development. There was a great flowering of the arts, most notably of visual arts and architecture.

The art of statuary, for example, was at its most consummate during this period. Among the most impressive examples of this art was a cachette of fine statues, mainly of Amenhotep III, found in the temple of Luxor, where it had been buried, probably during the reign of Rameses II when the temple was extended. A colossal seated statue depicted the King with Tiye, Mutemwiya, and Sitamun at his side. Now in the Egyptian Museum in Cairo, it shows the immense scale the sculptors were working on. At the time, it was the largest statue ever carved in Egypt.

Amenhotep's Jubilees

It has often been stated that jubilees, or sed-festivals, were held during the thirtieth year of the king's reign. But, in fact, most kings celebrated a sed-festival, although very few reigned for as long as 30 years. The notion seems to have been based solely on the reigns of Amenhotep III and Rameses II, which were both unusually long.

Many sed-festivals were probably held after the illness of a monarch, since one aim of the festival was to reinvigorate the king. This implies that, at least during his first 30 years, Amenhotep III enjoyed good health.

A discovery of hundreds of labels from wine and food jars at Malkata indicates that the first jubilee was held in the year 30–31. Records show that it lasted some ten months! Wine labels were particularly abundant, and it seems that enormous amounts of wine were gathered for the festival. Records of the festivities include the names of most leading officials.

Three years later, in year 33–34, Amenhotep III celebrated a second festival. Jar labels show this to have been a much quieter affair, with more food labels than wine labels. The dates only span around two weeks, and the names of officials are conspicuous by their absence.

Only five labels, all for meat, record the date of the third festival, which was celebrated in year 37 and appears to have been more like a one-day

Right **Amenhotep III in his chariot, mortuary temple of Merenptah, c. 1213–1203** BCE. This work may acknowledge both the glories of Amenhotep's reign and Merenptah's debt to his predecessor. The latter used stone from Amenhotep's mortuary temple to build his own.

party involving just a few friends. However, an illustration in the tomb of Kheruef (Th.T.192) of third jubilee celebrations shows a youthful king participating in activities associated with Abydos and the festival of resurrection in Abydos. So it may be that the third festival celebrations were not based in Malkata but elsewhere.

Twin Temples

For his first jubilee festival, Amenhotep III ordered the construction of two great temples in Nubia, one for him and the other for his wife, Queen Tiye. The twin sites lie close to each other, a few miles north of the third cataract and the Kushite capital of Kerma. The site is extremely remote. Below the second cataract, the Nile takes a wide westward turn before veering back eastward again between the fourth and fifth cataracts. The easiest way to get from the second cataract into Upper Nubia is to cut across the desert between these points, across the Belly of Rocks. This is the route taken by most Egyptian kings on their campaigns, and by caravan-traders to this day, since it cuts around 100 miles (160 km) off the journey along the Nile. Soleb and Sedeinga lie at the westernmost bend of the Nile, an area unvisited by travelers even then, although it was right in the center of the gold mines being exploited by Egypt. Both temples are still where they were built, fortunately, as the waters of Lake Nasser do not extend so far south.

Both the Soleb and Sedeinga temples are built from local sandstone. Soleb, dedicated to Amenhotep III as Lord of Nubia, invoked the legend of the Eye of Horus, which appeared in Nubia in the form of a lioness. Two magnificent granite lioness statues (now in the British Museum) were dedicated to the king. The temple of Sedeinga was dedicated to Queen Tiye, and incorporated Hathor-headed columns and images of the queen participating in the jubilee. A rare relief shows her in the form of a sphinx, the object of her family's beliefs.

The building of these two full-scale temples in remotest Nubia exemplifies the superb craftsmanship that thrived during the reign of Amenhotep III.

The Succession

An inscription in Saqqara names "the king's son, priest of Ptah, Thutmose." Given the name, it seems likely that this young man was the eldest son of Amenhotep and Tiye. He could not have been born much before the tenth year of Amenhotep III's reign, and he vanished before year 27. So Thutmose died in his mid-teens and, as yet, his tomb has not been located, though presumably it is at Saqqara.

The second son, Amenhotep, was next in line to inherit the throne. His parents seem to have regarded him as ill-suited to the task, and began taking steps to prepare him for office.

Above **Subjugated Syrians paying tribute to the King of Egypt, c. 1425 BCE.** A steady flow of tribute from vassal states bolstered the Egyptian economy, funded great buildings and art, and allowed the king to live extravagantly.

Turning toward Aten

Even in his later years, Amenhotep III continued to build on a grand scale.
During this period, references to the Aten proliferate in the king's works
and life. Even a daughter, born to Tiye, was given the name Baketaten.

Above **Gold mask of Amenhotep III, c. 1390–1352** BCE. Similar items would have been placed in the king's tomb, but all were stolen before archeologists discovered it.

Thutmose IV's divine encounter was with Ra-Horakhty, the rising sun, but for Amenhotep III it was the Aten, fully developed as the sun at midday, who emerged as the most influential deity in the life of the king.

The constant references to Aten are not the only noticeable change in artifacts from these late years. Images from the latter part of Amenhotep's reign clearly show the king as overweight. Depictions of Egypt's royal family and nobles are normally idealistic, so it is slightly discomforting to see a king depicted with such frankness.

Other unusual representations of Amenhotep III can, however, be attributed to a later change in artistic style. A headless statue, now in New York; a small stela in the British Museum showing Amenhotep seated with Queen Tiye under the rays of the Aten; a broken head of a statue in Egypt showing the king as heavy-lipped and slant-eyed—all of these images bear clear signs of bodily distortion. But rather than an actual physical change, this is a stylistic modification associated with the art of the early reign of Amenhotep's son and heir, Amenhotep IV, also known as Akhenaten.

Right **Amenhotep III wearing nemes headcloth, painted limestone statue, c. 1390–1352** BCE. Amenhotep's long reign and great wealth yielded numerous portraits of the king, allowing us to trace physical changes from youth to old age.

Appeals to Sekhmet

Just south of Karnak lay the temple of Mut in Asher. Probably on behalf of his wife Tiye, Amenhotep III made considerable additions to the temple, among them a sanatorium or place of healing. Strangely, orders were given for the temple to be surrounded by a ring of statues of the goddess Sekhmet. Sekhmet was identified as the consort of Ptah of Memphis, and was regarded as the bringer of deadly illnesses such as plague, smallpox, typhoid, and cholera. She was greatly feared and could only be assuaged by offerings.

The creation of the Sekhmet statues, each one wearing the sun-disk of Aten, suggests that some form of illness was rampant during the closing years of the reign of Amenhotep III. It also displays his strong leanings away from Amun and toward Ra and Aten.

Temple and Tomb

The construction of the tomb and mortuary temple of Amenhotep III began early in his reign. Both were designed to the finest standards. The mortuary temple was the largest ever built in Egypt and it dominated the west bank. A stela marking its back wall says "its walls are covered with gold, its floors with silver, and its doors paneled with electrum." At the entrance were two colossal statues of the king. These now stand alone as the temple behind them was demolished by later kings.

Left **Colossi of Memnon, quartzite statues, west bank, Luxor, c. 1360** BCE. These two massive statues of Amenhotep III originally stood at the entrance to his mortuary temple. Each was carved from a single block of stone and stands about 70 feet (21 m) high.

The statues are now known as the Colossi of Memnon, a name acquired when they were mistakenly identified during the Classical era as images of the Greek king Memnon. They were badly cracked during an earthquake in 27 BCE. Subsequently, dew would gather in the cracks at night; at dawn, as the heat of the sun evaporated the dew, air was sucked into the cracks, making the statues "sing." For generations, Roman leaders, including emperors, came to witness this bizarre phenomenon, many of them leaving their names carved on the statues. Around 200 CE, however, Emperor Septimus Severus ordered the cracks to be repaired, thus severing the vocal cords of these strange statues forever.

The tomb of Amenhotep, open since antiquity, lies in the western Valley of the Kings. It was excavated in 1915 by Howard Carter and again from 1989 onward by a team from Waseda University, Japan. Separate rooms were found made ready for the burials of Amenhotep's two Great Royal Wives, Tiye and Satamun.

Yet neither wife was buried here. Furthermore, the mummy of Amenhotep (or one identified as such by a tag—an identification that is still a topic of lively debate) came to rest elsewhere, specifically in a side chamber of the tomb of Amenhotep's grandfather, Amenhotep II, where it was found in 1898.

Studies show that this individual was obese and suffered severe dental erosion, caused by years of eating bread full of coarse sand grains, and dental caries, the result of eating soft, sweet foods. Both problems left him with abscesses that erupted through his jawbones. This would have been extremely painful and in turn have affected his ability to function properly. Additionally, he would have suffered stomach upsets due to the poisons exuded by his teeth and gums.

The mummy of Queen Tiye was also found in the tomb of Amenhotep II, and was positively identified through comparison with a lock of her hair found in the tomb of Tutankhamun.

Approaching the End

Toward the end of his reign, Amenhotep III began negotiations with the King of Mitanni, whose sister he had married early in his reign for the hand of his daughter Taduhepa. But partly because he sent the king wooden statues covered with gold instead of the solid gold ones he had promised, he met with little success, and it was some time before the negotiations could be completed. In the meantime, letters were dispatched from Egypt to modern-day Iraq and pleas were made for "the healing statue of Ishtar" to be sent to aid the sickly king. Both princess and statue arrived too late to save Amenhotep.

Below **The goddess Sekhmet, polished granite statue, c. 1390–1352** BCE. Sekhmet—the name translates as "power" or "force" —was thought to be the bringer of disease.

Kingdom of Gold

During the New Kingdom, the royal coffers overflowed with gold. Not only did it pour in as tribute, but also it had long been mined at various sites in Egypt. An army of skilled craftspeople was available to fashion it into a range of goods.

Gold first appeared in Egypt as nuggets that were washed down the Nile and thrown up on meanders of the river. Two cities in predynastic Egypt, Hierakonpolis and Naqada, became rich through collecting and trading in these deposits. The names of both cities contained the hieroglyph for gold. The gold actually formed within rich lodes of quartz in Nubia, between the second and fourth cataracts. It is unclear at what date Egyptian kings decided to go and seek out the gold, instead of waiting for the river to deliver it. The Palermo Stone, now in Sicily, records that in the fifth year of his reign, Sneferu (2613–2589 BCE), father of Khufu, builder of the Great Pyramid, captured and brought back to Egypt 7500 Nubian men from the area, probably to prevent constant attacks on his gold workers.

Before the building of the High Dam near Aswan, investigations were carried out to record archeological sites that would be lost under the new lake. Several were gold mines.

Digging in the Desert

Entrances to gold mines were small and the shafts dropped steeply down into the ground to great depths. Workers, probably Nubians, would crawl down, bent double, pressing their backs to the roof of the shaft to steady their descent. When a gold-bearing seam was identified, fires would be lit at the rockface, turning the entrance shafts into chimneys up which workers would have to clamber to escape. Once the fires had heated the rock, cold water dashed against the face would cause it to crumble. Workers could then bring rocks to the surface in baskets.

On the surface, larger nuggets were extracted whole. Then, saddle-querns of stone were used with rollers of volcanic stone to crush the rocks. The dust was run through water troughs, allowing the heavier gold particles to sink and be collected.

Burners on the site produced sufficient charcoal supplies to fuel furnaces—and deforest large tracts of land. The gold dust would be melted down in the furnaces then cast into rings called *debens*. The *deben* rings would be weighed individually, and could be threaded onto carriers so that none could be removed or altered. This ensured that all the mined gold would be brought back to the king. Gold dust could not be measured accurately, and even tiny amounts from a large number of bags could be pilfered to form substantial quantities. Soldiers then accompanied the convoys carrying the gold *debens* along the trade routes through Nubia and southern Egypt to the royal treasury.

Left **Gold pectoral of Rameses II, c. 1279–1213 BCE.** Supplies of gold and levels of artistry were maintained under the early Ramessid kings.

on several occasions only as the "wet-nurse" of Nefertiti, rather than "mother of the Great Royal Wife", a much more important title. (The term "wet-nurse" was, however, often used for both men and women who looked after royal children, so a more appropriate translation would be something like "carer".) This suggests that Ay was the father of both Mutnedjmet and Nefertiti, but that the mother of Nefertiti was not Teye but an earlier wife.

This in turn means that the family of Yuya and Thuya once again was linked closely to the royal family. Yuya and Thuya's daughter, Tiye, Great Royal Wife, was mother to Amenhotep IV; their son, Ay, was father to Nefertiti. In other words, the two youngsters were first cousins.

Cradle of a New Religion

Deep in the heart of Nubia, north of the third cataract, a small workers' town was excavated briefly between 1936 and 1938, in two short seasons. The area today is called Sudla and lies below a hill called Gebel Sese, but for unknown reasons the archeologists who excavated the town called it Sesebi.

Only about one-third of the town, inside mud-brick walls, has been excavated, revealing three large buildings, termed "temples" at the time. There were also two foundation deposits—small pits covered with stones containing seals and items bearing names and dates pertaining to the period when the town was founded. The names are those of Amenhotep IV; the dates from the first three years of his reign.

A little north of the site of Sesebi lie the twin temples of Soleb and Sedeinga, which played a large part in the jubilee festivals of Amenhotep III in his year 30. The dates and carvings suggest that Amenhotep IV, crowned in year 27 of his father, was sent down into Nubia to assist with preparations for the jubilee. This idea is supported by a carved block found at the city later constructed by Amenhotep IV, Tell el-Amarna. It shows the king participating in jubilee celebrations in his year 3.

Carvings in a crypt below one of the temple buildings at Sesebi show a series of traditional Egyptian deities, with offerings being made by the new king. Among them, a falcon-headed god with a sun-disk on his head is named as the Aten. It seems that Akhenaten was formu-

lating his religious ideas in this remote Nubian wasteland, where the Aten was seen as just one of a series of traditional Egyptian gods.

Shortly after the celebrations for his father's jubilee ended, Amenhotep IV left Nubia, never to return. He sailed northward in search of a site where he could build an entirely new city, devoted to the cult of the Aten. This was to become Tell el-Amarna.

Below **Amenhotep IV and Nefertiti, statue, Eighteenth Dynasty.** Nefertiti is most prominent in art of the early period of the king's reign.

Aten, the Sun-God

For centuries, the term "Aten" had been in use in Egypt to describe one of the five aspects of the sun as it traversed the sky from dawn to dusk. During the middle of the Eighteenth Dynasty, it came to represent an all-powerful god.

Right **Temple of Amun, Karnak.** This was where Amenhotep IV built his first temples to the Aten. Little trace of these structures remains, but they probably lay to the east of the temple of Amun, facing the rising sun.

Iconographically, Aten came to be depicted as a sun-disk, often with a uraeus in front of it. Rays emerge from the disk, each terminating in a hand holding an *ankh*, the hieroglyph for life. In works produced during the reign of Akhenaten, the rays are shown touching the heads and faces of the royal family, and occasionally blessing their palace.

These images were first observed in tombs discovered around the edge of the plain of Tell el-Amarna from the late nineteenth century onward. Artifacts, such as stelae from the town, showed the same image.

The later destruction of the city by Horemheb and the apparent absence of images of other deities encouraged early Egyptologists to label Akhenaten a monotheist and heretic, a proto-Messiah, centuries before his time, who was persecuted and almost destroyed by the pagans around him. A century after these ideas were first spawned, reflection and further archeological investigation prompted review.

A "heretic" is a person whose religious ideas oppose the political norm; but Akhenaten *was* the political norm and in any case the word "heretic" does not exist in ancient Egyptian. More thorough searches of the site revealed

figures of other deities in every single house in the town. Excavations throughout Egypt from the same period have yielded not one image of the Aten outside Tell el-Amarna. Moreover, many references to the Aten as god continue to be made in texts many centuries later.

This all suggests that the notion of a monotheistic revolution is inaccurate, but also that the Aten's worship was limited to one place. In other words, the Aten was considered a local god, and Tell el-Amarna, a new city, was established to provide a home for him.

Hymns to the Aten were found in several places, the longest version in the Amarna tomb of Ay. Reputedly written by the king himself, it describes the Aten as the Father of all Mankind, creator of all plants, animals, and peoples of the world, a true imageless god shared by all nations.

Temples of the Sun-God

Central to the worship of sun-gods throughout Egyptian history were open-air courts dominated by a *benben* stone, or prototype obelisk. The earliest of these, dedicated to Ra, was erected at Heliopolis, now lying under the foundations of the university of Ain-Shams (ironically, in Arabic, university of "the Sun"!). Later, in the Fifth Dynasty, other sun-temples were built at Abu Ghurab, north of Abusir, following the same

Below **Servants bringing food to the temple of the Aten,** *talatat* blocks, Tell el-Amarna, c. 1347 BCE. These blocks—whose name, Arabic for "three," derives from their width, three hand-breadths—were used widely in the new city.

design. Not surprisingly, two such temples were discovered at Tell el-Amarna. The great temple to the Aten, whose courtyards were filled with more than 300 offering tables, each with a brazier, was made to let the public make offerings to the rising sun. The royal Aten temple was a smaller version next to the palace, for the exclusive use of the royal family.

The root of Atenism was not the worship of the sun itself, but the theory that you can no more look upon the face of god than you can look at the sun at noon. Just as the sun gives life to earth, so god, invisible behind the sun, also creates and nourishes the world.

The solar temples permitted no high priest and no secrecy. Instead, Akhenaten made the Aten the king in his city, often writing his own name without a cartouche, reducing himself to a "common man." He described himself as the son of Aten and led the worship. But he offered religious democracy, whereby everyone within the city could participate equally.

Karnak and the Aten

It is commonly believed that Akhenaten was forced out of Luxor because the powerful priests of Amun in Karnak despised his new religion. In fact, nothing could be farther from the truth. Kings of Egypt chose where they worshipped and brought vast riches to those places. It was in Karnak's—and Amun's—advantage to have Akhenaten stay.

Excavation in the 1970s behind the eastern gate of the outer wall of Karnak showed that there had once been a line of columns, some 1300 feet (400 m) in length, leading to two open courtyards in the desert. Stones found packed inside several pylon-gates at Karnak as rubble infill proved to be tens of thousands of engraved blocks of limestone from these two open courts. Using early computer equipment, the stones were "reassembled."

The discoveries came as a shock. During the reign of Akhenaten, Karnak temple had been turned into the entrance to an Aten temple that stood behind it. The Aten temple remained in place during the reigns of subsequent kings, finally being demolished by Horemheb who needed the stones for his own building projects.

Thus the Atenists were not forced out of Karnak. On the contrary, part of the temple was rededicated to Aten. Local people, then had the choice of following the old cult of Amun or participating in the democratic worship of the Aten.

One thing, though, did change. With the rise of the Aten, the Opet Festival ceased. It was the ancient equivalent of canceling Christmas.

Above **Akhenaten before the sun-god Aten, royal tomb, Tell el-Amarna, c. 1352–1336 BCE.** Typically, Akhenaten is shown presenting offerings, in this case lotus flowers, and in turn being blessed by the sun's rays.

Tell el-Amarna

Like his adoption of the name Akhenaten, which took place in the same year,
the founding of Tell el-Amarna reflected Amenhotep IV's devotion to the new
religion of the Aten and his desire to cut all ties with traditional beliefs.

Above **Palace at Tell el-Amarna, from the** *History of Art in Antiquity* **by Perrot and Chipiez, 1882.** This artist's impression depicts the royal family's isolated retreat, as well as the pools and gardens that surrounded it.

Amenhotep's search for an untouched place that could be dedicated to the Aten ended in Middle Egypt, on a broad plain on the east bank of the Nile, where the cliff edges curved down to the river, both to the north and the south. No other town existed on this expanse of flat land. Furthermore, the site spoke to him, not just because of its isolation, but because in the center of the cliffs at the back of the plain, a wadi, or dried river valley, cut further east into the desert; at dawn the sun would rise directly above the wadi, cupped by the cliffs on both sides. This image was the hieroglyph for "akhet," the horizon. The new king felt he had come home.

Planning a New Capital

Fourteen boundary stelae, eleven on the east bank and three on the west bank, surround the city of Tell el-Amarna, yet maps of the site only ever show the east bank. Remarkably, the west bank, where the city cemeteries are located, has neither been mapped nor excavated.

Despite its modern name, the site is not a *tell*, a Middle Eastern term for a mound created by successive cities built on the same site. Instead, the name derives from the joining of the names of two villages: El-Till on the east bank and el-Amrah on the west bank. As at Sesebi, the archeologists made up a name that has stuck. The ancient name for the site was Akhetaten, meaning "horizon or rising place of the Aten."

Sir Flinders Petrie described the eastern plain as "roughly the same size of Brighton" and estimated that the population was probably around 50,000. In excavations, less than 20 percent of the site has been examined. In the center lay the main city, focused on the great temple.

A highway ran north to south through the town bearing wheel-tracks from chariots used by the royal family. South of the great temple, the palace buildings straddled the street. To the east lay the private apartments; to the west the public buildings and reception halls.

Housing Rich and Poor

Large houses, specially designed for the king's most important officials, occupied pride of place on the site. Lesser houses were squashed between them, while the houses of the poor, added last, often used the external walls of larger houses to support their small homes.

Many houses had their own drainage systems. Cisterns held water for the houses to use; toilets were created by placing jars underneath wooden benches; and shower-rooms had low benches where servants could stand and pour water on their employer's head. Excess water drained through a hole in the wall and out to a sewage ditch along the northern edge of the town. Along the sewage ditch were found the remains of shanty housing for the very poorest inhabitants.

Right **The ruins of the royal palace at Tell el-Amarna.** Beyond the remains of the palace, a line of cliffs forms the eastern boundary of the plain and the "horizon of the Aten," above which the sun rises each day.

THE FOUNDING OF AKHETATEN

Above **Granite stela of the scribe Nebwani, from Tell el-Amarna, c. 1352–1336** BCE. As well as the king's pronouncements, stelae at Tell el-Amarna also record day-to-day life in the city.

In the middle of his fifth year as king, Amenhotep IV took a group of loyal followers and camped on the empty plain. At sunset, according to inscriptions, he mounted a golden chariot and rode the periphery of the cliffs. Wherever he stopped, he decreed that a boundary stela would be carved from the rock face. Around 23 ft (7 m) tall, each stela listed the king and queen's titles. After his throne names, Amenhotep added his newly adopted name of Akhenaten, and that of his wife Nefertiti, who was to become known as Neferneferuaten,

beloved of Waenre. On each boundary stela, he listed the buildings to be built within his new city. As he did so he swore, "I shall not pass beyond it ever." Akhenaten moved into the city a year later, when most of the buildings were complete. There is no indication that he ever left it again.

Palaces of the Rising Sun

To the north and south of the town were two independent palaces. The northern palace, found littered with the names of Neferneferuaten Nefertiti, seems to have been a place to which the Great Royal Wife and her daughters could retreat. The Maruaten, to the south of the site, was the king's harem. The palaces could only be approached from the river, as the road did not extend that far, affording the women seclusion. Both palaces were surrounded with pools and lush gardens filled with shrubs and trees offering scent and shade.

The tombs were built in two clusters, north and south of the entrance to the wadi. A mile up the wadi, the king cut a tomb for himself, his wife, and his daughters. Looking east from the temple at sunrise, it would appear that the Aten was rising from the royal tomb itself. The layout of the town followed imaginary lines radiating from the royal tomb, like the rays of the Aten. The tomb, and so the king, was thus the source of the Aten and of life for the entire city.

Right **Bust of Akhenaten from Tell el-Amarna, c. 1352–1336** BCE. Artworks from the early part of his reign depict Akhenaten with a long face and neck, prominent chin, and full lips. These features would be increasingly exaggerated in subsequent Amarna art, almost appearing like caricature.

Amarna Art

Occupied for little more than 30 years, Tell el-Amarna was at once a unique social experiment and a microcosm of mid-Eighteenth Dynasty life. Its distinctive artworks are a window onto the lives of its court and citizens.

Above right **Stela of the scribe Ani, Tell el-Amarna, c. 1352–1336** BCE. The stela shows the royal scribe riding his chariot through the city streets.

Below **Akhenaten and Nefertiti beneath solar disk, c. 1352–1336** BCE. This work is typical of mid-period Amarna art in its distorted figures and in its intimacy, with the king and queen shown playing with their children.

Akhenaten and his court dwelled in Tell el-Amarna for just 13 years, and the city was demolished by Horemheb some 30 years or so after it was built. Its inhabitants were then forced to move away, but we have no idea where they went. This is part of the city's enduring fascination; another is its unusual and revealing art.

Archeologists and copyists who visited the tombs of Tell el-Amarna found them intriguing from the start. Abundant carvings on walls depict images of daily life in and around the city. Buildings are shown in detail, revealing exactly how they were used. The king and Great Royal Wife are represented everywhere, often in unprecedentedly frank and intimate scenes; in one scene, for instance, they are shown kissing while driving a chariot.

Updating the Canon

Egyptian art is often castigated for being stylized and repetitive with no spark of originality. However, draughtsmen were expected to copy what they were given and not to work freely. All images were drawn on ostraca or papyri onto a grid now known as the Canon of Proportion, which was set around the time of Unification.

In the case of human figures, the squares of the grid matched the size of the clenched fist of the subject. Eighteen squares covered the span from the bottom of the feet to the hairline. The central vertical line ran between the legs, and defined the edge of the hairline and the face. All features had specific positions within the grid that could not change.

Seated figures conformed to the same structure as standing ones, with no allowance made for stretched and retracted muscles. Although skilled artists might change facial expressions to form specific portraits, the style was limited.

Around year 4 of Akhenaten, the royal artists Hor and Suti were directed on new methods of art. A stela now in London makes it clear that the impetus came personally from the king. The grid was extended vertically to cover 21 squares instead of 18. At first, draughtsmen found it almost impossible to cope, unsure which sections of the body should be extended to incorporate the extra squares. At the same time, as artists' trial pieces now held in Cairo and the Louvre show, attempts were constantly being made to achieve acceptable portraits of the royal family. The results for the first few years included grossly distorted figures, with skinny limbs, elongated necks, and swollen bodies.

The fashion of the period was to wear pleated kilts—simple rectangles of linen, pleated horizontally and tied round the waist. They rode high up the back, sagged at the back of the hem and in order to stay put had to be tightly knotted at the front, with a front lappet or sash to preserve modesty. The result of this was twofold. The pleating made the kilt swell at the sides; and the tight knotting made the belly bulge over the waist, no matter how slender the wearer. The new style exaggerated these features, making hips huge and the abdomen appear distended.

For several years, it becomes impossible to distinguish male from female, let alone one person from another. We have to study the images and observe details of individual style. For instance, one person always has a pointed wig, another always has sandals; the king always wears a gown that falls to mid-calf length whereas Nefertiti's robe always sweeps the floor.

As the artists become accustomed to the changes in the grid, so the images become more conventional. By the end of Akhenaten's reign, normality is fully restored. Shabti figures of Akhenaten, found broken in the royal tomb, are indistinguishable from any other portrait style of the Eighteenth Dynasty.

Style or Symptom?

The bizarre forms of early and mid-period Amarna art have led to suggestions that the royal family suffered from various diseases. One theory offered was that they had Froelich's syndrome or acromegaly. Caused by a defect in the pituitary gland, this disease affects the output of growth hormones, resulting in parts of the body growing more quickly than others. It also reduces the sufferer's sex drive, and can cause impotence. Given that Akhenaten was married to one of the most beautiful women in history and she had six daughters, this seems unlikely.

A more recent suggestion has the royals all suffering from Marfan's syndrome, which again causes growth spurts, but is especially noticeable in the fingers, which become elongated and turn

up at the ends. Many of the figures in Amarna art display distortions of this type.

But this or any other disease is an unlikely explanation—unless every single inhabitant of the city was formerly well, then all developed the illness simultaneously, and all later recovered at the same time! What we observe is an art style and nothing more.

Types of Relief

It was the Egyptian custom to use sunken relief on the outside of buildings and raised relief on inside walls. In the former, images and inscriptions are simply cut into the stone, sometimes embellished with detail; in the latter, the background is cut away, leaving the images standing proud and then they are finely worked. The reasons for the distinction are to do with

Above **Tomb of Meryre, high priest of the Aten, Tell el-Amarna.** The use of sunken relief on interiors is characteristic of Tell el-Amarna. Meryre was never buried here and his fate is unrecorded.

Left **Harpist and singers, bas relief from tomb of Meryre, Tell el-Amarna.** Meryre, the high priest of Aten, was appointed "Chief Seer of the Disk of the Sun" by Akhenaten.

stone was three hand-spans wide. The Egyptian stoneworkers of the period were used to working on a colossal scale. In Amarna, the emphasis was also on speed. The king ordered an entire city to be built in his year 5, and one year later about 50,000 people were ready to move in. Moving large blocks required gangs to shift them. *Talatat* blocks could be lifted by a single man and moved swiftly into place.

Once walls were built, decoration was then added. Relief carvings were made before the walls were painted. The registers were not confined to one row of *talatat* blocks, but were spread over the wall to suit the designer. Scenes would continue from one block to another—making the later puzzle of restoration so much easier. When the carving was completed, the wall was painted, normally using white for the background and primary colors for the scenes. The original finished effect would have been garish to our eyes.

Royal Statuary

The tradition of carving royal statues on a colossal scale was continued at Amarna. Several royal statues have survived in various sizes and condition. The faces are universally disturbing, protuberant eyes following you with uncanny reality when you walk below them. But the statues occur in two distinctly different styles. In one, the figure wears a *nemes* striped headdress, a horizontally pleated kilt with a kilt sash, the ceremonial strap-on beard, and has the arms crossed. In the other, the figure is naked without genitalia. Both figures bear the cartouches of the Aten instead of a personal name.

The lack of genitalia on the latter type of statue has aroused much debate. Was the king being shown as sexless because he is the Aten? Could it be a comment on failed sexuality? And

lighting. Outside, sunrays will always cast shadows in sunken relief, allowing them to be seen. Inside, lamplight, diffused and soft, allows raised relief to cast stronger shadows.

In tombs of the Amarna period, however, scenes are invariably in sunken relief, probably because it was quicker to execute. Buildings in the city were built of blocks referred to as *talatat*, the Arabic word for "three", because each block of how would the king accept such a thing in any case? One scholar in the 1980s, after studying numerous images of the royal family, noted that the back of the neck of the king in early images is strongly bowed, or convex, while the back of the neck of Nefertiti is shown concave, curving gracefully to the base of the head. Using these criteria, he then established that the "naked" statues have a concave neck, and are thus Nefertiti, whereas the kilted ones have the convex neck of Akhenaten. This was later confirmed when it was realized that tomb carvings of the columned hall in the palace actually showed pairs of statues between the columns, one male and the other female.

Death and Drama in Year 12

One entire wall of the tomb of Meryre II at Amarna depicts the king and queen seated on a dais and receiving tribute from representatives of all the countries within the Egyptian empire. The festival of year 12 was significant for any Egyptian king; however, accepting a 12-year co-regency, it is likely that this festival also marked the death of Amenhotep III and the succession of Akhenaten to sole rule.

One chamber of the royal tomb at Amarna shows, in the same year, either one or two tragic deaths, depending on interpretation. In both, a girl or woman lies dead on a bier. The queen grasps the arm of her husband while both are grief-stricken. Behind them, courtiers support each other, so great is their sorrow. Certainly one of the scenes, if not both, depicts the death of the royal couple's second daughter, Meketaten. However, in one of the scenes, a courtier holds a baby in her arms. One scholar suggested that Meketaten married her father and died giving birth to their child.

However, since Meketaten cannot have been born much before year 3 of Akhenaten, by year 12 she would have been only nine years old, and, allowing time for a pregnancy, would have had to conceive at eight. This seems impossible. Another more likely explanation is that the dead girl is the little known minor wife of Akhenaten called Kiya and that the baby is the infant Tutankhamun. However, since the scenes are devoid of inscription, speculation is fruitless.

What we can take from this is that in one year Akhenaten lost both his father and his second daughter, and probably a wife, too. What was happening? Events at the end of the reign of Amenhotep III suggest that some disease may have been rampant. Whatever the case, the loss of so many members of the family must have caused immense pain to the king and queen.

Above **Meketaten, one of the daughters of Akhenaten, limestone bust, c. 1352–1336** BCE. The side lock of hair indicates that Meketaten was still a child when this likeness was created.

THE FOREIGN OFFICE ARCHIVE

In 1887 a woman digging in Tell el-Amarna for ancient mud-brick to fertilize her fields found a series of baked clay tablets with strange markings that she sold to an archeologist. Later digs revealed a total of 382 such tablets, all inscribed in cuneiform writing in the language of Akkadian. Translated, they were found to be letters from the Amarna foreign office, covering the period from the reign of Amenhotep III to Tutankhamun. They tell a tragic story of cities appealing, in vain, for Egyptian military help against the Hittites invading regions in the north. Read in sequence, the letters allow us to follow the collapse of the entire northern empire.

Left **Inscribed clay tablet, one of the so-called Amarna Letters, c. 1352–1336** BCE. This tablet is a letter from a Palestinian vassal prince to Akhenaten. Much of the king's diplomatic activity was focused on maintaining the loyalty of vassal states.

Tutankhamun

Now the most widely known Egyptian king, Tutankhamun was in his day
a relatively insignificant ruler whose origins remain obscure and whose
brief reign was almost entirely uneventful and little documented.

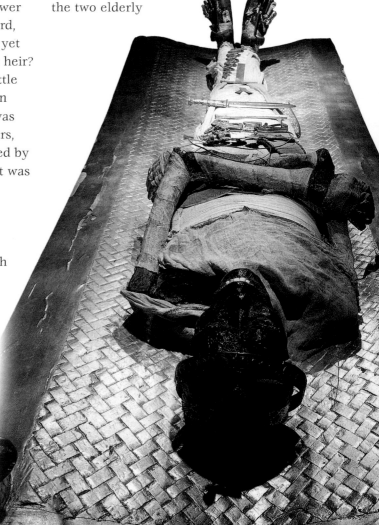

The last years of the reign of Akhenaten are shrouded in mystery. Given that he reigned as co-regent with his father for the first 12 years and with his wife Nefertiti for the last five, his reign is less substantial than most books suggest. One thing is clear. During his reign, the Hittites in Anatolia patched up their differences, united behind a single king and started to attack Egyptian holdings in the north. Letters in the foreign office archive show city after city begging for Egypt's military aid in return for their years of "tribute." Akhenaten did nothing. By the end of his reign, most of the northern empire was lost.

The death of Akhenaten in his year 17 was followed by his burial in his tomb at Amarna, as fragments found there demonstrate. He was buried mummified, in the likeness of Osiris. At his death, his wife and daughter still held power in Luxor. But soon they vanish from the record, too. Were they murdered? Did someone fear yet another female king, this time with a female heir?

Like Amenhotep III, the new king was little more than six years old when crowned. Born Tutankhaten, he inherited a kingdom that was torn apart by the events of the previous years, divided in religious beliefs, and impoverished by the loss of substantial parts of its revenue. It was not an enviable situation for a little boy.

Who Were His Parents?

It was always hoped that the discovery of Tutankhamun's tomb in 1922 would establish his identity and origins. It did not. Suspicions that he was a younger brother of "Smenkhkara" cannot be correct since it is now clear Smenkhkara did not exist.

A *talatat* block, found in el-Ashmunein across the river from Amarna and now in Brooklyn Museum, bears the only known reference to Tutankhaten as a child. He is named as "the king's son, his beloved of his own body." The epithet is a standard one,

used by Akhenaten for each of his daughters. So it seems Akhenaten was his father. But who was his mother? In recent times, it has been almost universally accepted that it was Kiya. However, we still have no evidence. It could just as easily have been Nefertiti herself. Without more evidence, we can do no more than speculate.

The boy was crowned Tutankhaten Nebkheperura in Karnak temple. However, inscriptions show clearly that he spent the next two years living in his home town of Amarna, virtually as a puppet king, while authority was taken by his last surviving relative, Ay (his grandmother Tiye's brother), who became regent in Luxor. At the same time, a previously unknown commander-in-chief of the army, Horemheb, acted as regent in Memphis. While the two elderly

Above **Tutankhamun emerging from a lotus flower, painted wood, c. 1336–1327 BCE.** For ancient Egyptians, the blue lotus flower symbolized the primeval ocean from which all life, including the king and his ancestor the sun-god, came forth.

Right **Mummy of Tutankhamun, c. 1336–1327 BCE.** This reconstruction shows how, before burial, the mummy was laid on a bed of gold. Examination of the corpse revealed that the king was 5 ft 7 in (170 cm) tall.

men divided power between them, Tutankhaten took his last surviving sister, Ankhesenpaaten, as Great Royal Wife.

In his third year, the king returned to Luxor. We know that he revived the Opet Festival, for inscriptions and images in his colonnade depict this. However, he did not restore the old religion. His golden chair, found in his tomb, bears the names of both Aten and Amun, suggesting that he adopted an even-handed approach—inside Karnak, the temple of the Aten still flourished, although the sanctuary of Amun had been restored. At the same time, he changed his birth name to Tutankhamun, though his throne name, by which the people knew him, remained the same. His wife changed her name to Ankhesenamun.

In his short reign of nine years, he achieved nothing of note. There is no evidence of any military campaign, although a stela of the year before he died states that one of his courtiers, Maya, carried out a taxation tour of Egypt, presumably to collect conscripts and supplies for a proposed campaign that did not eventuate.

Death of Tutankhamun

The mummy found in Tutankhamun's tomb in 1922 was that of a young man. The first examination in 1925 revealed no cause of death, although Howard Carter speculated that for a youth to have died, foul play was probably involved. An X-ray made in 1968 found a thinning of the bone behind the left ear, raising speculation that he may have been murdered by a blow to the head. But in 2005, a CT scan confirmed that he died of natural causes, not of foul play. It has been observed that he had a broken thigh bone and speculation suggests an infection may have brought about his death. However, since resin has been found in the break, unless he was defleshed before resin was poured over him, the fracture must have occurred after death. The cause of death is still uncertain.

The most insignificant ruler of ancient Egypt was buried in a small tomb with a jumble of objects, many of them already broken or old when he died. In comparison with other great pharaohs, his burial was minor and poor, and his

funeral was attended by only eight people, as the embalming cache in KV 54 revealed in 1907. Within a short time, people forgot he ever existed. His name, found infrequently anyway, was carved over by a later king. His tomb was forgotten.

His lack of significance was his good fortune. While other, greater, tombs were robbed, while Greeks and Romans came and went, as rulers rose and fell, Tutankhamun slept undisturbed. Only in 1922 was his repose finally interrupted, after which this minor king became perhaps the most famous ruler the world has ever known.

Above **Tutankhamun being anointed by his wife Ankhesenamun, carving on throne from his tomb, c. 1336–1327** BCE. Tutankhamun came to the throne while still a child, and married his half-sister, who was originally known as Ankhesenpaaten.

Tutankhamun Rediscovered

The discovery, in February 1907, of a pit containing remnants of Tutankhamun sparked widespread interest. But his tomb may have remained hidden if it hadn't been for the persistence of English archeologist Howard Carter.

Above **The entrance to the tomb of Tutankhamun in the Valley of the Kings.** Tutankhamun's is the smallest royal tomb in the valley, but the only one that remained unplundered before its discovery by Howard Carter in 1922.

In February 1907, Theodore Davis, concession holder in the Valley of the Kings, discovered a small pit, KV 54, containing several sealed pottery jars standing in a confusion of rags. The pots, dating from the end of the reign of King Nebkheperura, held the remains of a funerary feast for eight people, including eight floral collars. The rags were bags of natron—the dry salt used in mummification—and resin-stained cloths. In 1913, Davis named his find the "Tomb of Touatankhamanou," but few believed that this was a tomb, even of such a minor king.

The discovery of an incomplete tomb 55 a few days later changed things again. This small tomb—sealed with the title of Tutankhamun—contained material from several burials. However, a coffin and mummy were unidentifiable and the subsequent poor scientific examination of the tomb by Davis added to the confusion.

Locating the Tomb

George Herbert, Fifth Earl of Carnarvon, took the concession from Davis in 1913, just before the outbreak of World War I. Davis announced that the valleys were now empty, but Howard Carter, working for Carnarvon, thought otherwise. He believed that the tomb of Tutankhamun was still to be found. Using objects already excavated, he triangulated them on a map and focused on a small area in the middle of the Valley of the Kings, under a spoil-heap from the nearby tomb of Rameses VI. During the war years, Carter remained alone in the valley.

The first dig in the area revealed a group of workers' overnight huts dating from the Ramessid Period. Carter apparently then moved away from this site, but not before building a stone retaining wall around the area of the huts. This wall, 20 ft (6 m) tall in parts, followed exactly two sides of the entrance to a tomb that, in theory, Carter did not know existed. This, of course, was too much of a coincidence. It is certain that Carter would have looked below the workmen's huts, knowing that anything below them could not have been disturbed since the Ramessid Period. But if he knew there was a tomb there, why did he wait several years before returning to the spot?

It is well known that Carnarvon's daughter, the beautiful Lady Evelyn Herbert, had grown

CARTER AND CARNARVON

Howard Carter was a sickly child whose father taught him portrait painting. Lord Amherst sponsored him to accompany Sir Flinders Petrie to Egypt as a copyist. He first went to Egypt when he was 17, and learned archeology from the guidance of Petrie.

George Herbert, Fifth Earl of Carnarvon, went to Egypt to convalesce after a road accident that had nearly cost him his life. He loved the country and longed to dig there.

Carter and Carnarvon met in Luxor, when Carnarvon obtained a concession to dig on the west bank and Carter was asked to show him the ropes. Both men were antisocial and often abrupt, although they formed an uneasy alliance. They dug together for almost seven years before Carnarvon obtained the concession for the Valley of the Kings.

Although Carter was allowed to continue his work after Carnarvon's death, he was embittered by the new laws that prevented him taking artifacts out of Egypt. After finishing his task, he left the country for good.

Left **Lord Carnarvon and Howard Carter opening the tomb of Tutankhamun, 1922.** This contemporary recreation is by the Italian artist Achille Beltrame.

fond of the rough archeologist, much against her wealthy parent's wishes. As early as 1913, Carnarvon was considering removing his financial support from Carter to sever the links for Evelyn's benefit. Carter could be certain that one day an ultimatum would come, and he needed to counter this by dangling a tomb before the eyes of the Earl.

The moment came in the summer of 1922. After years of fruitless digging, with many tombs discovered but containing no contents of merit, Carter was told that Carnarvon was withdrawing his support. In response, Carter offered to pay the bills for one further expedition (he was penniless at the time), on condition that Carnarvon would refund him if and when Carter found a worthy tomb. Carnarvon reluctantly agreed.

A few days later, Carter returned to the spot within the wall he had built years before and set his men to dig. The first step was found in just a few hours. Two weeks later, the Earl, Carter, and Lady Evelyn removed the outer door to the tomb and faced a sloping corridor packed with rubble. After clearing this, a second door stopped their progress. Carter chipped a hole in a corner and held up a candle. It flickered with the emission of air from within, preventing him from focusing for a moment. "Can you see anything?" asked Carnarvon. "Yes," Carter replied, "Wonderful things!" The legend, and the turmoil, now began.

Political Problems

Packed with treasures, the tomb immediately drew the eyes of the world. Carter, a private and surly man, suffered under the attention. Egyptians, already straining under the leash of English occupation, seethed as an Englishman emptied the finest royal tomb ever found in their country.

At the start of 1923, Carnarvon and Carter argued bitterly and Carnarvon decided to leave. In Aswan, a mosquito bite on his cheek, cut while shaving, became infected, and pneumonia and septicemia quickly took hold. Seriously ill, he was taken to Cairo, where Carter joined him. On April 21, however, Carnarvon died.

As far as Egypt was concerned, with the death of Carnarvon the concession for the valley lapsed. Other Egyptologists were invited to examine the tomb but refused—there was little attraction as the work would be all-consuming yet the tomb forever associated with Carter.

Late in 1923, the widowed Lady Carnarvon was permitted to endorse the concession, thereby allowing Carter and his team to complete the emptying of the tomb. But at the same time the law was changed so that nothing from the tomb could leave Egypt. Despite this, Carter continued this work, finally completing the escavation in 1935.

Left **Howard Carter, at left, standing at the door of Tutankhamun's tomb, 1922.** Carter is accompanied here by Arthur C. Mace, who was carrying out excavations nearby on behalf of New York's Metropolitan Museum.

Below **Antechamber to the tomb of Tutankhamun.** This reconstruction shows the scene that met Carter as he entered the tomb. The king's riches and personal belongings packed the chambers.

The Tomb of Tutankhamun

Though small, the tomb of Tutankhamun contained greater riches than any archeologist had hoped to find. Enthusiasm was tempered by the realization of what must have been lost from the tombs of more distinguished rulers.

Despite the thousands of objects found inside it, the tomb of Tutankhamun was the smallest royal tomb in the valley and the only one found with an entrance in the valley floor. It has constantly been claimed that the tomb was prepared for someone else, perhaps Tutankhamun's last living relative and successor, Ay, and had to be relinquished to Tutankhamun as no other tomb was ready at the time of his unexpected death. But there is no evidence for this. The name of Ay is not found anywhere within the tomb. More importantly, the tomb of a nobleman was always one chamber, or T-shaped. Even the rich tomb of Yuya and Thuya conformed to this arrangement. The tomb of Tutankhamun contains four chambers, in accordance with every royal tomb.

Most royal tombs, however, have long passages between the chambers, thus making them seem bigger than they are. In Tutankhamun's tomb, KV 62, there are no such passages. The reason for this is unclear. Possibly there was no time to make the tomb any bigger, or perhaps other tombs, as yet undiscovered, limited the space available for the workmen to dig further. The neighboring tomb, KV 55, also sealed in Tutankhamun's name, would have had the same layout if completed, so it could be that the designers of the period favored a new, smaller design.

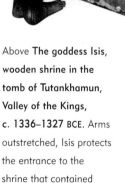

Above **The goddess Isis, wooden shrine in the tomb of Tutankhamun, Valley of the Kings, c. 1336–1327 BCE.** Arms outstretched, Isis protects the entrance to the shrine that contained Tutankhamun's coffin.

Layout of the Tomb
Sixteen steps led down from the outer door, which had been broken into at the top left corner at some time in its history. Behind it, a long sloping corridor led to a second door. Behind this, the transverse chamber, or antechamber, was crammed with large items including dismantled chariots and beds. Boxes packed underneath one of the beds hid a low entrance to a small side chamber, or annex. This contained objects that had been used by the king in his lifetime.

To the right of the antechamber, two life-sized, black-painted guardian statues flanked a large area of wall covered with a different color of plaster from the rest of the wall. Behind this lay the burial chamber itself, filled almost to the limits of its size by four gilded wooden shrines. In the right side-wall of the burial chamber, a door, never sealed off, led to another room, the Treasury. It contained the most valuable pieces found within the tomb.

The Hall of Chariots
According to an ancient sketched plan of the tomb of Rameses IV, the first chamber in a tomb, usually at the end of one or more lengthy corridors, was normally called the "Hall of Chariots." Tutankhamun's tomb provided the first opportunity to discover why this was so.

To the left of the doorway were four of the six dismantled chariots found in the tomb. Next to them, but on the rear wall, three huge gilded beds had boxes and chairs stacked on and underneath them. The middle bed, patterned like a leopard, but with the head of a cow, had wooden boxes holding joints of meat and poultry underneath it. On the floor in front of the beds were two stools and five assorted boxes. Between the guardian statues was a pile of reeds, pots, and baskets, which covered a hole in the bottom of the wall leading to the burial chamber.

The House of Gold
The annex was the most cluttered room in the tomb, with objects piled to a height of 6.5 ft (2 m). It contained more than 2000 individual items. These included beds and Tutankhamun's walking sticks, bows, arrows, clothes, model ships, and other personal belongings.

The burial chamber contained a "nest" of four shrines, with smaller objects crammed between them and inside the narrow corridor between the outer shrine and the back wall. Inside these shrines lay Tutankhamun's quartzite sarcophagus and, within this, another nest of three anthropoid coffins. Above the outer shrine was laid a blue linen cloth studded with gold rosettes to look like stars.

This was the only chamber in the tomb whose walls were painted. The back wall shows, to the right, a unique picture of Ay, Tutankhamun's successor, carrying out the "Opening of the Mouth"

ceremony. The walls of the chamber must have been painted as the room was being filled, as the outer shrine had drips of paint on it.

The Treasury

A huge shrine with carrying poles, on which lounged a recumbent figure of Anubis blocked the entrance to this room. An elaborate gilded shrine, later found to contain the king's viscera inside a canopic chest, dominated the chamber. A further two dismantled chariots lay in sections against one wall, beside chests containing jewelry and bearing model boats. This proved to be the richest room in the tomb.

Tutankhamun's Treasures

The riches found in Tutankhamun's tomb encompass a remarkable diversity of objects, ranging from the official—thrones, crowns, and commemorative artworks—to the domestic and personal, such as jewelry and clothes.

Above **Tutankhamun riding into battle, painted wooden chest from his tomb, Valley of the Kings, c. 1336–1327 BCE.** The image shows the king, wearing his distinctive blue crown and protected by vultures, charging his Syrian enemies in battle.

Right **Earring belonging to Tutankhamun, from his tomb, Valley of the Kings.** Made of gold, lapis lazuli, carnelian, and turquoise, the earring features a central motif of the king beneath a vulture and flanked by cobras.

The artifacts found in KV 62 staggered imaginations around the world, and gave rise to numerous new theories. But, on the whole, they raised more questions than they answered. Because this is the only royal tomb yet found virtually intact, we have no way of knowing how typical it is.

Many of the objects were broken and worn, or borrowed from elsewhere. Since the king was the ruler of the richest country in the world at the time, was this deliberate? Was this king buried so secretly that more precious objects could not be used; or was it the Egyptian practice to keep the new and better objects for the living?

Many of the wine-jars were old at the time of the burial. Given that the walls of these vessels are porous and the wine within will evaporate through them in less than three years, most of the jars placed in the tomb would have been empty. Was this because they would have been easier to transport, or because they were merely symbolic? Did the Egyptians

think it better to preserve good wine for those who could appreciate it? Without another tomb for comparison, we can only wonder.

Furnishing the Tomb

Although some scholars have suggested that the three huge beds in the antechamber were used for mummification, this is unlikely. Mummification is a messy business and these beds show no staining. They have sledge bases and since they match the number of coffins, this suggests they were used to drag the coffins into the tomb. Six smaller beds found in the antechamber and the annex were all for practical use. One of them was a folding bed that would have been used when traveling or on a military campaign.

Seven chairs, twelve stools, and eleven footrests were also found. Two of the chairs, the so-called "ecclesiastical throne" and "golden chair," the most elaborate of all the pieces, both bore the names "Tutankhaten" and "Tutankhamun." The golden chair, often called a throne, is unlike the others in design, having a flat seat and a back illustrated with an inlaid scene, and being heavily gilded. It is larger than most of the chairs, many of which would only hold a young child. The scene on the back of the golden chair shows the young king and his wife. Above their heads is the Aten.

If this were the throne and, as many claim, Tutankhamun reintroduced the religion of Amun and abandoned that of the Aten, how could he have spent almost 10 years sitting on a throne that proclaimed the outlawed god? The chair reinforces the idea that Tutankhamun adopted an even-handed approach to religion after returning to Luxor.

Jewels of the Crown

Although hundreds of necklaces, pendants, bracelets, earrings, and finger-rings of immeasurable value were found in the tomb, artistically many of them are crude in comparison with earlier jewels, such as those of the

the child he was at the time. Another piece, perhaps inherited, was an elaborate corselet intended for military use.

Personal Effects

Several items provide insights into the king's character and interests. Numerous bows, many made specifically for firing from chariots, and many throwsticks, combined with an illustration on a fan, reveal that Tutankhamun was an avid hunter. Of 14 writing palettes, two bore the names of Meritaten and Nefertiti—although most were unused! A simple reed stick, with a cap and ferrule of gold, was inscribed "cut by His Majesty's own hand when he was a child." Most little boys bringing home a stick would be told to throw it away, but when that boy was king of the most powerful land on earth, it was retained and preserved in solid gold!

Many of Tutankhmun's clothes show him to have been of slender build, and are dyed with brilliant colors and designs. Most touching of all were 27 gloves, made to fit the boy, each woven in one single piece—the first ever found in Egypt.

One particularly affecting object is an alabaster goblet that appears undecorated until held up to the light. Then, almost miraculously, a touching image of the king and queen appears on it. The goblet was made of two eggshell-thin layers of stone, cut to fit each other, with the image painted on the inner surface. To see it is to peer into a rare and private world.

Middle Kingdom. Three bracelets bore the names of Akhenaten and Nefertiti Neferneferuaten. Several pectorals had Tutankhamun's name altered from earlier ones. Many of the earrings were worn, despite their great size and weight—the mummy of Tutankhamun had holes 1 inch (2.5 cm) in diameter in his earlobes.

Among the most moving pieces are several pieces of regalia made for the coronation of Tutankhamun. They include a small gold and glass crook and flail, and a small gold staff bearing the king's image and measuring only 4 ft (1.2 m) tall—designed, in other words, for

Kings Ay and Horemheb

Tutankhamun died suddenly, without an heir. Two claimants to the throne then came forward: Ay, a court adviser, and Horemheb, commander in chief of the army. Their successive reigns marked the end of the Eighteenth Dynasty.

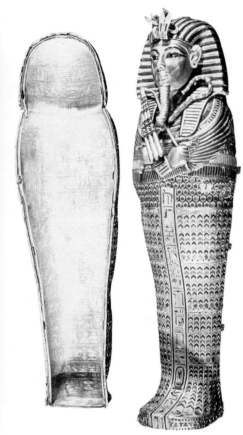

Above **Miniature coffin found in the tomb of Tutankhamun, Valley of the Kings.** This small gold case was used to hold the king's viscera, removed during embalming.

Right **Ay receiving gold from Akhenaten and Nefertiti, wall relief, Tell el-Amarna, c. 1336–1327** BCE. Images like this one must have reinforced Ay's claim to the throne after Tutankhamun's death.

Tutankhamun's sudden death is still mysterious; we only know that he almost certainly did not die from a brain tumor or a blow to the head as was once believed. The embalming cache (KV 54) shows he was mummified in the Valley of the Kings. His sarcophagus, too small for his coffins, bore the name of Nefertiti Neferneferuaten and was dragged from the neighboring tomb of KV 55, where the coffin was placed on a low bed on the floor. His viscera were placed in gold coffinettes that had belonged originally to Nefertiti Ankhkheperura. These were placed inside a container whose lid bore the erased names of Kiya.

The Secret Coronation

What was happening? Was this truly a royal Egyptian burial? One clue is to be found in the painting on the burial chamber wall. In Egypt, a new king could not be crowned until the deceased king had been buried. But on the wall, Ay is shown wearing the crown of kingship, with his names in cartouches. This is not just an "Opening of the Mouth" scene, but political propaganda, demonstrating that Ay was crowned *before* Tutankhamun was buried.

Although two mummies of baby girls were found in Tutankhamun's tomb there is no indication that they were his children. He died before he could father a living heir. His widow, the last surviving daughter of Akhenaten and Nefertiti, Ankhesenamun, then vanishes from the scene. There are no clues to say she was alive to attend her husband's funeral.

There were now only two valid claimants to the crown. One of them, Ay, was brother of Great

Royal Wife Tiye and father of Nefertiti, and had also acted as regent during the early years of Tutankhamun. The other, Horemheb, was commander in chief of the army. He had married Nefertiti's sister, Mutnedjmet, probably to validate an earlier claim to the throne. His titles outranked those of Ay, he also acted as Tutankhamun's regent, and he had the army behind him—a persuasive claim!

Yet Horemheb seems to have been absent at the time, perhaps on a military campaign. Ay managed to keep the news of the king's death from Horemheb long enough to have himself crowned. By the time Tutankhamun was safely buried and Horemheb could stake his own claim, Ay's position was inviolable.

Horemheb Triumphs at Last

Ay, however, was old and had no children, and when he died, four years later, in 1323 BCE, Horemheb asserted his claim. Ay was buried in a tomb in the western Valley of the Kings. The walls were painted by the same hands that decorated Tutankhamun's tomb, and the sarcophagus was the one originally intended for Tutankhamun. The tomb was robbed in antiquity and the mummy has not yet been found.

We have no clues about Horemheb's early life or meteoric rise to power as commander of the

armies. In 1975, his tomb in Saqqara, Memphis, was rediscovered, having been located for the first time in 1842 by Lepsius then lost again. In the tomb, a subsidiary chamber was found, containing enough fragmentary inscriptions to show it was the last resting place of Mutnedjmet. The pathologist who investigated the bones noted that the pelvic girdle was scratched, indicating that she had borne several children. One of the grooves was so deep that it suggested she might have died in childbirth.

Horemheb had married Mutnedjmet around the time of the death of Akhenaten, hinting that he was staking a claim to the throne before the accession of Tutankhamun. The hasty coronation of Ay implies that he tried a second time and failed. When he finally took the throne, he was ready to release his pent-up anger.

The Razing of Amarna

It has often been argued that Horemheb's hatred of the royal family was fired by their failure to take military action to prevent the erosion of the northern empire. Had this been the case, then his first act as king would surely have been to march north. But he did not; instead, he used the army to pull down every monument built during the Amarna period and fully restore Amun.

The city of Amarna itself, long since abandoned by all but a handful of inhabitants, was evacuated. Horemheb then removed every single stone, often transporting the building materials long distances away to make sure they were hidden from sight. He also dismantled the Aten temple of Karnak, and removed every example of Tutankhamun's name, replacing it with his own. He claimed, on the restoration stela, to be bringing peace to the land, although his Edict 150 suggests he aroused great public opposition.

By the end of his reign, it was as if an entire period of history had been erased. Ironically, the one tomb that escaped him was that of Tutankhamun. Those present at the burial, even when working for Horemheb, never betrayed the young king, allowing him to sleep undisturbed.

HOREMHEB'S EDICT 150

Unlike its neighbors, Egypt had no written legal codex. Inscriptions suggest that laws and penalties may have varied from place to place. Criminal and civil trials were held before tribunals comprised of local inhabitants. More significant trials were held either before the vizier or the king.

Following his coronation, Horemheb erected a stela in Karnak, the Edict 150 or Great Edict, which stipulated appropriate punishments for a range of illegal acts, most notably different types of civil disobedience. This implies that Egyptians rebelled against his accession to the throne.

RISE OF THE RAMESSIDS

Rameses I

Egyptians now sat in the eye of a storm without realizing it. The winds of change were behind and in front of them. This period of false calm saw the birth of a new dynasty, the Nineteenth.

Above right **Horemheb making an offering to the god Amun, granite statue, c. 1323–1295** BCE. Horemheb's Coronation Text relates how he was anointed as king by Amun.

According to one inscription, Horemheb ruled for 54 years. For many reasons, this is out of the question. Fifty-four years is the length of the longest reign of the New Kingdom, that of Tuthmose III, and it is likely that Horemheb claimed that reign-length to bring him the favor that Thutmose had enjoyed.

For an army general who was supposedly angered by the previous royal policy of nonintervention, and who knew enemies were beating on the door of the empire, it is odd that Horemheb led not one single campaign against them. Probably he was too old. Amenhotep III had appointed him general some 40 years earlier,

Right **Rameses I flanked by the gods Horus (left) and Anubis (right), decoration from the tomb of Rameses I, c. 1294** BCE. The decorations in the tomb of Rameses I have the same style as those in the tomb of Horemheb.

so he could not have been younger than 60. It seems likely that he reigned only a short period before he died. This could be further confirmed by the fact that his tomb, KV 57, was incomplete. His mummy has not been found, and no unidentified mummy from other caches fits his age. Horemheb left no heir and the throne passed to a colleague in the army, also a professional soldier, called Paramessu.

The Brief Reign of Rameses I

Paramessu was born in the Hyksos city of Avaria in the eastern Delta. He gained promotion only because of his military abilities, since records suggest his family were simply peasant farmers. He served as vizier under his friend Horemheb, then took the throne as Rameses I Menpehtyra.

His reign was brief, certainly less than two years and probably only a few months. We know almost nothing of him. He left behind no monuments except his tomb, and is known essentially as a link between eras. Manetho regarded him as the first king of the Nineteenth Dynasty.

When he died, presumably of old age like his two predecessors, Rameses I was buried in a tomb in the Valley of the Kings which, although not cut to its expected length, was at least complete as far as decoration was concerned. The hand that designed the tomb of Horemheb also designed this one, for apart from the cartouches, the scenes and coloring are almost identical.

It seems strange that Horemheb, who claimed such a long reign, should have been allocated an incomplete tomb, whereas Rameses I, who reigned just a few months, should have a finished tomb. One possibility is that the tomb we assume belongs to Rameses I was intended for

Horemheb, but that Rameses I had him moved to the incomplete tomb. In any case, it suggests that work was carried out on the two tombs simultaneously, which in turn reinforces the idea that Horemheb chose Rameses as his heir in his late years. It is unusual for anyone to have had a tomb cut before he even became king. Had Rameses died uncrowned, perhaps the tomb would have been assigned to his son, Sety.

Above **Cobra guarding the path to the underworld,** decoration from the tomb of Rameses I, c. 1294 BCE. This and a number of other decorations in the tomb of Rameses I illustrate scenes from the *Book of Gates*.

The Sideshow Mummy

From 1860 to 1999, a macabre display of "freaks," including a five-legged pig, thrilled audiences around North America. Latterly, it became a permanent display sited on the Canadian waterfront opposite Niagara Falls. Among its exhibits was a mummy, bought for £7 in Egypt in 1860 by a doctor, who then donated it to the show. Devoid of wrappings, and called, for unknown reasons, "Ossi-pumph-nofru," it excited little attention.

In 1980, a visiting Egyptologist noting its condition and crossed arms, became convinced that it was genuine. In 1999, it was bought by a museum in Atlanta. Subsequent tests revealed that it was about 3,000 years old. Moreover, comparisons of X-rays of this relic with those taken in 1967 of the royal mummies in Cairo showed an uncanny resemblance between the sideshow mummy and the mummies of Sety I and Rameses II. By then there was little doubt—this was the lost mummy of Rameses I.

In 2003, Rameses I crossed the Atlantic once more to join his son and grandson in the Egyptian Museum in Cairo. The most traveled pharaoh in history, Rameses I had finally come home.

Sety I

During the short reign of his father Rameses I, Sety served as commander in chief of the army and vizier. Although he was already elderly by the time he took the throne, he succeeded in restoring order and prestige to the kingdom.

Right Sety I with the goddess Hathor, decoration from the tomb of Sety I, c. 1294–1279 BCE. Prior to becoming king, Sety had held a number of priestly titles as well as those of vizier and army commander.

Below Sety I wearing nemes headdress and ureaus, tomb of Sety I, c. 1294–1279 BCE. As well as restoring religious and political order, Sety I revamped Egypt's infrastructure, reopening mines and digging new wells.

Rameses I's brief reign had heralded what Manetho would later classify as the Nineteenth Dynasty. Sety I was the first king of the new era to have an extended reign; thus great responsibility fell upon his shoulders to repair the damage done by his predecessors.

A Land Divided

King Amenhotep III had created a divided realm, with two capitals and two kings ruling concurrently. During the reign of his son Amenhotep IV, or Akhenaten, yet greater schisms had occurred. Confining himself to his new capital of Tell el-Amarna, Akhenaten had cut himself off from the rest of Egypt. Although the government offices in Memphis continued to function, as burials being discovered in Saqqara show, they had no leadership. Officials who operated independently were themselves a threat to the realm, undermining belief in an all-powerful king at the head of the social pyramid.

In addition, Akhenaten had deferred to the Aten as the kingdom's religious figurehead. The traditional system, which depended on the king reenacting the Creation daily in the sanctuary of Karnak, had been abandoned. According to ancient traditions, these ceremonies maintained *maat*, the equilibrium between the worlds of physical and spiritual existence. Thus *maat* itself had been threatened, and Isfet, primordial chaos, could return at any time.

The structure of government, traditional religious beliefs, and faith in the monarchy

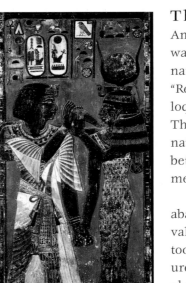

had all been shaken to the core. It was up to Sety to mend these divisions and restore full authority to the office of king.

The Renaissance Man

Among the titles he took when he was crowned, Sety I acquired the name *Wehem-mesut*, meaning "Repeating-of-Births" or, more colloquially, "Renaissance Man." This name reflected his determination to change things for the better—which, in his opinion, meant back to the old ways!

The Amarna art style was abandoned and traditional artistic values reintroduced, though this took time and many human figures carved in Sety's reign retain elements of the Amarna style. The old temples were refurbished, old towns were reinhabited, and old gods were honored with renewed and more intense worship.

Superstition grew, as everyone from the king down paid more attention to the gods, and the use of charms to restore faith in the old ways proliferated. Horemheb's tomb, when found, was filled with propitiating images of every god imaginable, as though he were desperate to reduce the damage that might have been caused. Private tombs from this time onward lost the sense of humor present in those of the previous dynasty, becoming somber and intense.

One of the few changes made by Akhenaten that was accepted and continued was the use of Late Egyptian in writing. Akhenaten had abandoned the outdated language of the past and brought writing up to date, introducing new words and contemporary idioms.

In all other fields, Akhenaten was now ignored as if he had never existed. If necessity meant that his reign had to be mentioned in some context or other, he was referred to as simply "the Great Enemy."

Reclaiming Lost Ground

Sety I ushered in a time that promised peace and prosperity. At home all seemed calm, but abroad it was a different matter. As a career soldier, his first responsibility was to restore Egypt's military prestige. He therefore began a war against the Hittites aimed at reclaiming parts of the northern empire lost under Akhenaten.

Although Sety seems to have led several different campaigns, the only one that has been firmly dated occurred during the first year of his reign. Within months of being crowned, he led three regiments north. Following the coast roads, his first aim was to secure a series of fortified towns, making them into safe ports for Egyptian merchant shipping. This implies that trade had been hampered by the loss of Egyptian territory during the reign of Akhenaten, impoverishing the treasuries. Later, Sety challenged the Hittites for the first time. Apparently, he initially met with success, capturing the key city of Qadesh. However, the Hittites soon won it back again. It was evident already that the Hittites were determined to hold their ground and continue to expand their territory at Egypt's expense.

Sety I also had to quell the rebellious Nubians, always the first to exploit any chinks in Egyptian armor. Of even greater concern was a Libyan incursion in the western Delta. Like the Nubians, the Libyans were quick to exploit what they perceived as Egyptian weakness, and seeing the western borders unmanned they flooded across. Although Sety claimed his campaign was a success, substantial Libyan settlements remained in the Delta. These settlers would be a thorn in the side of Egypt for a long time to come.

THE ARMY ABROAD

The soldier in the professional army of the Nineteenth Dynasty was well trained and equipped. The army consisted of four regiments, each of 5,000 men, plus cavalry divisions. The kings who campaigned in the north had to lead these men safely through hostile territory and find safe camp sites, guided by intelligence gathered in advance.

A little equipment might arrive by sea, but for the most part all food and other supplies either had to be brought by land in rear of the army, or foraged locally. The fighting men thus had to be accompanied by a second army of cooks, medics, animal carers, metalworkers for weapon repairs, chariot makers, clothing and sandal suppliers, and, of course, the ubiquitous accountants. When the battle was done, they had to march hundreds of miles back home again, often wounded, semistarved, and exhausted.

Above **Sety in his chariot,** **relief carving, Karnak,** **c. 1294–1279 BCE.** A whole series of carvings on the north wall of the temple of Karnak is devoted to Sety I's military campaigns.

Sety the Builder

Throughout his 15-year tenure as king, Sety I conducted an ambitious building program that altered numerous towns and cities and all major religious centers. It resulted in some of the finest buildings Egypt had ever seen.

Right **Relief decoration, mortuary temple of Sety I, Qurna, c. 1294–1279 BCE.** The painted decoration shows a sacred barque carrying a shrine and bearing the ram's-head insignia of the god Amun at prow and stern.

Sety continued Horemheb's work, eradicating any remaining inscriptions and images of the Amarna kings, and reinstating the obliterated images and names of the traditional god Amun.

He reopened long-closed quarries to obtain valuable building materials. He also increased the numbers of men working in mines in Sinai to improve copper supplies, and in Nubia and the Eastern Desert to raise yields of gold. During the Eighteenth Dynasty, supplies from the Nubian goldfields dwindled to a trickle, and although the new sites in the Eastern Desert were more productive, they were also more labor intensive. In his year 9, Sety ordered a well to be dug for his workers in the Eastern Desert. Keen to be seen as beneficent, he ordered a town and temple to be built in the same area. The routes to and from the sites were also improved and protected.

Sety commenced building works at every major temple in the land, including Memphis, Karnak, Elephantine, and Abydos. He also built a great temple in his home town of Avaria (now called Tell el-Dab'a) dedicated to Seth, his local god. The scale of his program of renewal was so vast that many of his buildings, unfinished at his death, had to be completed by his son Rameses II, who often claimed them as his own. Indeed, many of the buildings popularly attributed to Rameses were in fact initiated by Sety I.

Below **Mortuary temple of Sety I, Qurna, c. 1294–1279 BCE.** Behind the temple colonnade lie a hypostyle hall and chapels. The courtyard in front contained a royal palace where the king would reside when visiting.

The Temple of Qurna

On the west bank of Luxor, at the northernmost edge of the plain, stands the exquisite temple of Qurna. This was Sety's mortuary temple. Today it lies off the beaten tourist track, but is well worth visiting. It was originally many times larger than it appears today: The great pylons, open courtyard, and avenue of sphinxes have all been destroyed by local building.

All that is left now is the area of the hypostyle hall and the rear of the temple. The hall's facade is graceful and unusual, and was modeled on Abydos. Excavations have shown that to the south of the open courtyard there was a small palace where Sety stayed while in Luxor.

Inside, unlike Abydos, the small hypostyle hall leads to a single sanctuary. The walls, decorated with delicate raised reliefs, show Sety with his son, Rameses, crowned co-regent. To the rear of the sanctuary, small side chapels were dedicated to Amun, Mut, and Khons. To the north of the sanctuary is a small chapel to Ra in his many forms, including, notably, the Aten. Balancing it to the south is another chapel dedicated to Sety's father, Rameses I, who had not had time to build a mortuary temple of his own. The raised reliefs throughout the temple are beautifully carved and were once colored in great detail.

The Tomb of Sety I

The Italian engineer and explorer Giovanni Belzoni discovered and entered Sety's tomb in 1817, using a battering ram, according to his *Narrative*. Although the tomb had been robbed in antiquity, many items were found inside, including two wonderful series of *shabtis,* one set wooden, the other of faience, which are among the finest figures ever made.

Belzoni later exhibited his finds in London. He offered them to the government, which was unable to find the money, so everything was then offered to the public. The *shabtis* were scattered among buyers, and many of them are still unaccounted for today.

Sety's tomb was then the largest yet found in the Valley of the Kings, and its decoration remains the finest of any royal tomb. Unlike many other tombs, the walls were carved in raised relief before being completed with carefully applied details. It so impressed Belzoni's young English wife Sarah that she successfully begged him to be allowed to move in and lodge there rather than at the hotel at which she was staying. Unfortunately, in order to make access easier,

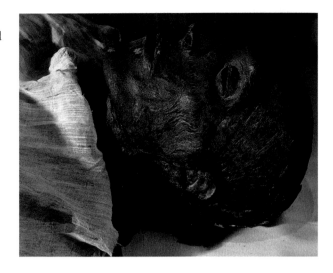

Left **Mummy of Sety I, c. 1279 BCE**. Discovered in the Deir el-Bahri cache in 1881, Sety's mummy is one of the best-preserved royal mummies ever found.

they had the pit in the entrance passage filled in. But this was designed not to trap robbers, as they thought, but as a soakaway. An unexpected storm blew up a few days later, followed by flash floods. This allowed floodwater into the tomb for the first time in its history. The water penetrated the decorations, causing huge amounts of damage, which still make the paintings unstable, though restoration has been carried out since.

The mummy of Sety I, arguably the finest royal mummy ever made, was found in 1881. Sety appears restful, sleeping in quiet repose. To be able to gaze upon the face of so great and ancient a king is a privilege beyond measure.

Below **Mortuary temple of Sety I, Qurna, engraving, 1842–49**. Following the arrival of Christianity in Egypt, the temple became a church. Many of its buildings were dismantled to provide materials for other projects.

Rameses II

Over the centuries, Rameses II has gained the most exalted reputation of any of the Ramessids, coming to be known as Rameses the Great. Yet his reputation derives, at least in part, from clever appropriation of the works of others.

Below Rameses II as a child, limestone stela, Nineteenth Dynasty. It is likely that Rameses was born before his father Sety became king.

A relief, carved in diorite, depicts Sety I presenting his son Rameses for coronation toward the end of his reign. Rameses later claimed that this co-regency lasted for seven years, although he may have exaggerated. We estimate that he could be no younger than 14 years old when he assumed sole rule, as at his coronation he acknowledged his Great Royal Wife Nefertari and acquired a harem, led by future Senior Wife Isetnefret. Women evidently pleased him greatly, and he continued to enjoy their company throughout his 67-year sole rule. Assuming the records are correct, we can estimate that he died well into his eighties.

Although like any fit and healthy boy he at first longed to campaign with his father, the novelty quickly wore off. He had his image added onto scenes of his father's campaigns, but he probably was not there; and his campaigning as sole king ended soon after his fifth year.

Crowned as Rameses II Usermaatra Setepenra, he is known popularly as Rameses the Great. Although we now question his greatness, it was never doubted by subsequent Egyptian kings, who longed to have a tenure like his. To bring them luck, they took his name and wished for a reign as long as his in their inscriptions—but to no avail!

The Ancient Versailles

Rameses' family hailed from the northeastern Delta, in or near the former Hyksos capital of Avaria. The local god here was Seth, Sutekh, or Sety, after whom his father had been named. Although it is often believed that Seth was an evil deity, this is a misconception. In the Delta, Seth was a respectable figure, venerated by locals, who guarded the lives of sailors against storms.

We cannot know if it was Sety who first chose to expand the family home into a palace, but we do know that Rameses II had it completed. The site has now been identified as Tell el-Dab'a, but in Rameses' time it was called Piramesse or *Per-Rameses* ("the house of Rameses"). The main temple was called the Per Atum. Interestingly, these two places are noted in the Book of

modern village of Qantir, and was tentatively identified as Piramesse by a number of statues of Rameses II. The original Hyksos capital at Tell el-Dab'a seems to have been swallowed up by the growth of Piramesse, which eventually spread to Qantir.

The great city enclosed houses for many high officials, a variety of temples, estates for Rameses' sons, and workshops, many of which were producing bronze weapons and armor for the Egyptian army. At the center stood the royal palace and surrounding estate. The building was made of mud-brick and probably lined with stone that was later robbed. Many statues and obelisks from Piramesse were subsequently moved to the later capital of Tanis. From Tanis, many were eventually taken as antiquities to the city of Alexandria, where they decorated the royal palace.

Piramesse lay on Egypt's northern borders, a short distance from its frontier forts, in an area that had been regarded as unsafe in the past. It also occupied what had been lush grazing land favored for livestock, an area identified in the Book of Genesis as Goshen. Consequently, foreigners settled here in large numbers, as reflected in the cultural mix of finds.

Exodus, under the names Rameses and Pithom, as having been built by enslaved Hebrews.

The development of this palace-city, modeled on Amenhotep III's palace-city of Malkata, would occupy the first 30 years of Rameses' reign. As the city was completed, foreign ambassadors came simply to gasp in wonderment, admiring its "most beautiful of balconies, its halls paved with lapis lazuli, its walls overlaid with gold."

Officials moved in to be close to this most powerful king, although government remained, as always, in Memphis. In a pattern repeated much later at the French Palace of Versailles, the court circled around the king like planets around a sun. The French kings, however, either forgot or ignored the lesson of Piramesse—that the isolated court of a strong king could later become a prison for much weaker monarchs.

Excavating Rameses' City

The site of Tell el-Dab'a was first examined in 1966. It lies a short distance away from the

Outdoing Amenhotep III

Unlike his father Sety, whose aim was to restore equilibrium or *maat*, Rameses II was always a man in a hurry. He inaugurated some building works but completed many more. In addition, he usurped statues and monuments throughout the land, claiming ownership of everything standing during his reign. To obelisks, which he could not easily change, he added columns of new inscriptions on each side of the

Left **Second court of the Ramesseum, near Luxor, c. 1279–1213 BCE.** The outer columns bear huge statues of Rameses II. With his arms crossed and holding his scepters, he is depicted as ready for rebirth in the afterlife.

Below **Column in hypo-style hall, Ramesseum, near Luxor, c. 1279–1213 BCE.** Images were drawn on pillars and walls by scribes, then colored by painters using pigments made from ground rocks and minerals.

WORK PRACTICES

Most jobs were carried out by men, although women helped in the fields at busy times. There are few clues to show how craftsmen were chosen from the agricultural communities, but it seems that they were trained on the job. Some may have followed the trade of their father. In all occupations, there was a foreman or Overseer of Ten. Above him were local, regional, and national managers, who in turn reported to the vizier. The largest employers were the temples. Workers were paid every 30 days (one month). Basic rations were one and a half sacks of emmer (about 30 gallons) and half a sack of barley (10 gallons).

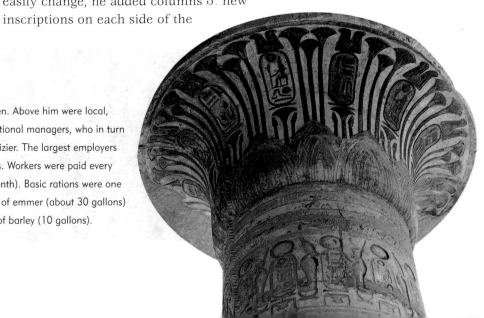

originals, making his work bolder than the earlier inscriptions. He doubled the size of the workforce in Deir el-Medina, the workers' settlement on the west bank of Luxor.

When Rameses II came to the throne, Luxor was still dominated by the building works of Amenhotep III. Rameses was determined that this would not continue. He was especially keen on usurping Amenhotep's statues, and adding front sections to Amenhotep's buildings to give the impression that they were his own.

Much of his work, though, when examined closely, was slapdash. Stones for building were not properly finished, and gaps were filled with old cement. Images were poorly designed and crudely cut. Rough tomb walls were covered with thick layers of mud to save smoothing them off, which made it easy for later tomb robbers to cut out decorations and sell them illegally. Rameses' inscriptions are huge and deep—indeed, it is said that if an inscription is deep enough for you to put your hand in it, it was made by Rameses!

Works of the Mighty

Like every other king of the New Kingdom, Rameses built his mortuary temple and palace on the west bank near Luxor. It came to be known as the Ramesseum. To build it, he appropriated materials from other temples, including many stones from the finest temple of all in the area, the temple of Amenhotep III. Unhappily for this most astute yet voracious of kings, his perpetuation of this practice meant that his own works would be plundered in turn.

The front pylon gateways are badly damaged, having been built on poor foundations on wet ground, so today you enter through the northern wall directly into the second courtyard. The northern half of the temple is missing, exposing the remains of hundreds of mud-brick buildings that once clustered round the temple. Excavations have shown that there was once an entire town here, with houses (many with upper stories), workshops, and even school buildings. The king's palace lies south of the temple.

Below **List of kings, British Museum, c. 1250** BCE. Originally housed in the temple of Rameses II at Abydos, this carved limestone slab lists Rameses' predecessors as king—or at least those he wished to be associated with!

The second courtyard, containing colonnades and Osiriform statues of the king, is dominated at the southern corner by the wreck of a massive statue. This was once the largest seated statue ever made in Egypt, carved from a 1,000-ton block of stone brought here from Aswan. Though legend has it that it fell in an earthquake, examination of the upper torso reveals many wedge holes, left when the stone was deliberately split. As the legs are also missing, there seems little doubt that at some point in its history the statue was dragged down and broken up for other projects. The feet alone, still placed in their original position and now in deep grass, are so huge that it is just possible to sit on the big toe!

Another head was removed from this courtyard by Italian Egyptologist Giovanni Belzoni, using only six ropes, four rollers, and plenty of will power! To get it out, he had to cut corners off some of the column bases, cuts still visible today. The head is now in the British Museum, where the poet Shelley saw it and immortalized the king further in his famous poem "Ozymandias:" "Look down on my works, ye Mighty, and despair."

Left **Temple of Amun,
Wadi es-Sebua, Nubia,
engraving, 1841.** This
temple was built on behalf
of Rameses II by the
viceroy of Nubia, Setau.

Rameses in Nubia

Rameses also built, or claimed as his own, many temples in Nubia. The temple of Wadi es-Sebua, a scaled-down version of a full Egyptian temple, is approached by an avenue of sphinxes, and its pylons and halls are still intact. At Aniba and Amada, Rameses added halls to the fronts of earlier temples to imply they were his own.

This period saw the introduction of the labor-saving practice of cutting temples into rock faces instead of constructing them from stone. Examples include Beit el-Wali, now moved to a new site just south of the High Dam; Gerf Hussein; and El-Derr. All three incorporated statues of Rameses II in the sanctuary alongside other gods.

Claiming Kingship

It is often supposed that every temple had a list of kings within it. In fact, only four such lists exist—and all were either written or usurped by Rameses II. One, now in the British Museum, came from the temple of Rameses II. Another, held in the Louvre, came from the temple at Karnak and lists 62 kings. The third, the Saqqara tablet, was found in a private tomb and contains 57 kings. The fourth and most complete list is still in the temple of Sety I at Abydos. On it, Sety appears alongside his son Rameses, who is holding a scroll, making offerings before a list of 76 kings from the Unification down to the Nineteenth Dynasty. The names are all coronation names, not the birth names by which we know the kings.

Although none of these lists indicates reign-lengths, they do aid our understanding of the order of rulers. But we must bear in mind that they were made as propaganda, to display a lineage with which the king wished to be associated. Many major kings are omitted, and many insignificant ones are included. All four lists omit all female kings and all the Amarna kings. The entire bottom line of the Abydos list is the name of Rameses II repeated.

Left *Djed* **pillar amulet
inscribed with the names
and titles of Rameses II,
Nineteenth Dynasty.** The
djed symbol appears as
pillars in buildings but also
in other forms including
amulets. The symbol is
associated with the god
Osiris and ideas of stability.

The Temple of Abydos

Begun by Sety I and completed by Rameses II, the magnificent temple of
Abydos contained seven sanctuaries, each dedicated to a different deity.
Prominent among these was Osiris, whose birthplace this was thought to be.

Below **Portico, temple of
Abydos, c. 1294–1213
BCE.** The temple consisted
of two courtyards with
porticos, behind which
lay two hypostyle halls
and seven chapels.

nscriptions found in and around the temple of
Abydos indicate that the area was used throughout Egypt's history. The first kings of the unified Egypt chose to be buried here rather than in
their home town of Hierakonpolis, or near their
new capital of Memphis. But although kings
revered Abydos and it is likely that earlier

temples were built on the site, no reference has
been found to a substantial building before the
temple constructed by Sety I. However, the
location of the present temple, right next to the
burial place of Egypt's first kings, and events that
occurred during its construction, suggest it was
built over earlier sacred sites now lost.

Sety's architects had the king
"mark the boundaries," a ceremony,
illustrated in the late temple of Edfu,
that involved him leaving a foundation deposit, "stretching the cord"
around the boundary wall, and dedicating the space within to the new
temple. Egyptian temples are usually
rectangular, but Abydos is different.
Two episodes suggest that this may
have been due to the presence of
earlier buildings under the sand. In
the first, Sety's workmen found an
ancient temple under the proposed
rear of the new temple. It seems that
they then changed the form of the
new building to an L-shape to incorporate the existing structure.

At about the same time, some
of Sety's workmen discovered an
ancient chamber-tomb nearby.
Although we now know it was the
tomb of King Den from the First
Dynasty, they considered it to be the
burial place of Osiris. The fragmentary remains were cleared, a new
sarcophagus added, and the site then
opened to perhaps the world's first
tourists. Over subsequent years, visitors brought so many offerings to
the site that a layer of pots accumulated, many feet thick. Consequently,
villagers gave the site the Arabic
name *Umm el-Qaab*, "mother of pots."

A Place of Pilgrimage

Abydos was dedicated to the resurrection of Osiris, through which all

THE CULT OF OSIRIS

One of the oldest gods of Egypt, Osiris is first mentioned in the pyramid texts associated with the constellation of Orion. In Roman times, Plutarch retells the Egyptian legend of how Osiris was murdered by his brother Seth and resurrected magically by his sister-wife Isis. Seth then tore apart his body. Isis collected the pieces and formed from them the first mummy that was buried in Abydos. As a result, Abydos was venerated as the burial place of Osiris and the place through which resurrection of the dead might happen. In later times, Osiris was believed to have been reincarnated as the Apis bull.

Left **Sandstone stela from Abydos, c. 1279–1213 BCE.** The lower half of the stela shows Ounennefer, high priest of Osiris during the reign of Rameses II, with his wife and parents. Above are the Abydos gods, from left to right, Isis, Osiris, Horus, and Hathor.

Egyptians hoped to be resurrected. They made pilgrimages to the temple and hoped that their *ka*, or life force, would come here after death.

Unlike every other temple in Egypt, this one was not dedicated to one local god—nor was it, as some call it, Sety's mortuary temple. Instead, it was designed with seven sanctuaries—for the Abydene triad of Osiris, Isis, and Horus, and for Amun of Luxor, Ptah of Memphis, Re-Horakhte—linked to the Aten and still venerated—and finally the sanctified Sety I, through whose efforts the temple had been built. In other words, there was something here for every pilgrim!

The pylons have now gone, leaving only the open court and the building beyond. Originally the facade had seven entrances, one to each chapel, but Rameses II had all but the central one blocked. Six sanctuaries were of standard design. Once the door closed, the supplicant stood in a barrel-vaulted room. However, the seventh, the central sanctuary of Osiris himself, had a second hidden door at the back of the chamber. Once inside the sanctuary, the king could pass unseen into the Osiris complex, the most secret of areas, where ceremonies to trigger resurrection would take place.

To the left of the sanctuaries were a hall containing the king-list, smaller chapels, and stores.

The Osireion

Behind the temple of Sety and below the surface of the ground lies a small, rectangular building of great antiquity, known as the Osireion. The square columns and massive stones of its walls, all of finely worked granite, are clearly of Old Kingdom origin and closely resemble the valley temple of Khafra at Giza. Sety had his own inscriptions carved onto these walls. In the center, a lower channeled area surrounds a raised dais. The sarcophagus of Osiris once stood on the dais, surrounded by water for most of the year, only drying out in the summer months. The coming of the annual inundation, refilling the base of the chamber, would represent the coming of fertility, regrowth, and resurrection.

Temple of Rameses II

It was left to Rameses II to complete his father's temple. As he did elsewhere, he carried out the work with inappropriate haste. Sety's construction is justifiably renowned for the grace of its carvings and brilliant colors of its decorations; by comparison, Rameses' work is crude. However, a short distance north of Sety's temple is Rameses' own. It is smaller than that of his father, and its roof remains open (unlike the restored roof of Sety's), allowing sunlight to illuminate brightly colored reliefs that still astonish visitors.

Below **Rameses II, carved relief from temple of Rameses II, Abydos, c. 1279–1213 BCE.** Only the lower walls of this temple still stand, but they bear brightly colored reliefs that must have been stunning in their day.

Egypt and the Hittites

Soon after the start of his reign, Rameses II declared war on Egypt's long-standing northern rivals, the Hittites. He proclaimed the ensuing battle a great triumph, but in truth it marked the beginning of a terminal decline.

Above **Asiatic prisoners submitting to Rameses II,** temple of Abu Simbel, c. 1279–1213 BCE. By illustrating his successes on monuments throughout the realm, Rameses promoted an image of himself as a great conqueror.

Right **Hittite god with short sword, gold statuette, fourteenth century BCE.** Many Hittite gods were guardian figures and small objects like this may have been carried for protection.

Settlers arrived in modern southern Turkey, the region of Anatolia, around 6,000 years ago. Egyptians knew them as the Kheta; we refer to them as the Hittites. To the south, in modern Syria, lived the people of Mitanni and Nahrin. Although these two peoples were once distinct from each other, by the start of the New Kingdom, the names Mitanni and Nahrin were interchangeable.

Tuthmose I did not challenge Mitanni or Nahrin but respected them as worthy rivals. In contrast, Tuthmose III confronted and subjugated them. But after he withdrew, and subsequent Egyptian kings failed to maintain a strong presence in the area, the Hittites moved in and expanded their own empire. In some instances, they did not even have to resort to military action. Akhenaten's refusal to send the Egyptian army to aid towns threatened by Hittites meant that many cities chose to ally themselves with the more powerful force. Other towns, as the Amarna foreign archive shows, were attacked and fell.

By the time Sety I came to the throne, it had been at least 130 years since a dominant Egyptian power had campaigned in the area. Little wonder that the Hittites had taken advantage. During this elapsed time, new loyalties had become entrenched. The new generation in the north did not see Egypt as overlords trying to retain power, but as invaders trying to extend their territory. For the Egyptian army, this meant that instead of marching and camping in loyal areas, they found themselves in a hostile environment.

The Army under Rameses II

Rameses must have realised that, as had been the case with his labor force, he was behind the times and needed to strengthen his army. The two regiments that had existed during the mid-Eighteenth Dynasty had already been increased to three during the reign of Sety I; yet another regiment was added under Rameses II.

Each regiment of 5,000 men comprised professional soldiers as well as some conscripts. Earlier commanders had understood the importance of training, intelligence, and communications, and titles of officers in each regiment reflected these needs. The main Egyptian garrison was in Memphis; but from here it was still several days' march through to the border, where weapons, shoes, and other supplies were issued to the soldiers. Beyond the northern frontier, they were in enemy land.

Reliefs of Sety's campaigns show Rameses was also present, but in most cases Rameses added his figure later. There is, however, clear indication of his keenness in military affairs—even if this was not reflected by his ability! During the reign of Sety I, the region of Amurru, centered on the city of Qadesh in northern Syria, rebelled. Sety led a campaign against Qadesh and met with initial success, but as soon as he left the Prince of Amurru regained control. In his fourth year, Rameses II led another campaign to retake the city. He, too, was successful, but, again, as soon as he pulled out, the Hittite King Muwatalli moved back in and annexed the area once again.

The Battle of Qadesh

At the start of his fifth reign-year, Rameses declared war on the Hittites and led his forces against Qadesh. Probably to maintain his line through hostile territory, he spread his divisions out. He led the division of Amun; the division of Re followed some distance behind; those of Ptah and Seth brought up the rear.

As Rameses approached Qadesh, a large fortified city standing on a mound on the river Orontes, his intelligence gatherers captured two Hittite soldiers. Under duress, they revealed that the Hittite army was some 30 miles (48 km) to the north at Tunip. Rameses crossed the river and pitched his tent in a shield-wall enclosure, with the division of Amun establishing the main encampment area around him.

His forces brought in two new Hittite captives, who admitted, this time, that the Hittites were in fact already encamped on the other side of Qadesh, out of view. As the division of Re approached the river, the Hittite army, in full force, at around 20,000 infantrymen, marched in formation around the side of the city, cutting off the division of Re midstream. Some men fell back, some, safely across, fled in panic through the half-ready camp of Amun, creating mayhem. Many perished in the river, both Egyptians and Hittites.

Rameses dispatched a rider at once to call on the other divisions to catch up. But they were too far behind. According to Rameses, with everyone in total panic, he called upon Amun, and with mighty arm raised, climbed into his chariot and single-handedly drove the Hittites back!

On Rameses' return, the account was carved in most of his temples, with Rameses prominent as the hero of the hour. Unfortunately, the Hittite account claims victory for them!

In truth, the battle was but a minor skirmish with no outright victor. As Rameses withdrew back into Egypt, the Hittites followed, regaining city after city. By the time Rameses was back home proclaiming a glorious victory, the Hittites were broaching the border. The empire was lost.

Below **Rameses II fighting at the battle of Qadesh, engraving after carving in Ramesseum, 1878.** Several temples, including Karnak, Abu Simbel, and the Ramesseum, bear depictions of Rameses' heroic role in this battle.

Rameses' Queens

During his long rule, Rameses II had seven Great Royal Wives and innumerable harem-wives, and sired well over 100 children. Yet such was the duration of his reign and life that he outlived most of them.

Above right **Merytamun, daughter of Rameses II, Nineteenth Dynasty.** Merytamun's necklace is made up of rows of the *nefer* hieroglyph, a symbol based on the shape of a heart, which represented goodness and beauty.

It seems that military life did not suit Rameses as much as he had hoped it would. After the battle of Qadesh he never went to war again. Several minor campaigns were mounted, but there is no evidence that the king led them. After Qadesh, for the next 62 years, he seems to have spent his life in comfort, in the delightful company of his many wives and children.

During his co-regency with his father, Rameses fathered at least seven living children by his two principal wives, plus at least 15 by minor wives in his harem. Thus he had more than 21 children by the time he was 21 years of age. During his first five years as sole king, the numbers of his children far outstripped his age.

In his temples, ranks of his sons are shown. These sons, all of whom had grown to adulthood, exceed 110 in number. This was before the end of his reign, and the total does not include the sons who died in childhood, nor any of his daughters.

Right **Queen Nefertari, decoration from the tomb of Nefertari, c. 1254 BCE.** Nefertari is shown seated in a shrine playing the game of senet. Next to her is the *ba* bird, the embodiment of the soul or personality, which takes flight after death.

Rameses' wish to be "father of millions" was probably fulfilled, as the blood of his children is no doubt in the veins of most modern Egyptians!

Great Royal Wife Nefertari

Nefertari, his first Great Royal Wife, apparently married to him at the start of his co-regency when he was about 14 years old, is of unknown origin. She was not from his own family, as she is not named as "king's daughter" or "king's sister." It is interesting that, in this as with his buildings, he was following the example of Amenhotep III. But perhaps learning from his predecessor's mistakes, he did not make public the parents of Nefertari, thus denying them the infamy accorded to Yuya and Thuya, and with it, any threat to his throne.

He seems to have loved his wife dearly. She is portrayed, in image and inscription, as exceptionally beautiful, although her mummy has not

survived. She is praised as "she at whose bidding the very north wind blows." A letter survives which she is said to have written to Queen Padukhipa of the Hittites following the peace treaty. It is stilted, and if it came from her, neither marks great intelligence nor interest in foreign affairs: "Now my land is at peace with your land; and your land is at peace with my land; and we are both at peace together forever."

She was mother to several children, including the first crown prince. If Nefertari was about the same age as Rameses, then she died in his year 25, around the age of 40, an average age for Egyptians.

She was buried in a magnificent tomb in what is today called the Valley of the Queens. In truth, almost all of the tombs here were for queens and children of kings of the Nineteenth Dynasty and later; an entire valley of queens for rulers of the Eighteenth Dynasty

therefore remains to be discovered. Images of Nefertari in the royal tomb show her slim and beautiful, dressed in diaphanous linen.

Isetnefret and Sons

Isetnefret took the title Senior Royal Wife during Nefertari's lifetime, indicating that she was a minor wife but probably first to bear her husband a son. As with Nefertari, her parentage is never mentioned. After Nefertari's death, Isetnefret was raised to the status of Great Royal Wife, a position she held for several years. Many of her children went on to greater renown, including Khaemwaset and Merenptah, Rameses' successor, albeit his thirteenth son. As yet, we have no tomb ascribed to Isetnefret, no mummy, and no funerary objects, implying that they all await discovery.

The Hittite Wives

After the deaths of Nefertari and Isetnefret, the rank of Rameses' Great Royal Wife was held, in turn, by Bintanat, daughter of Isetnefret; Merytamun, daughter of Nefertari; Nebettawy, daughter of an unnamed mother; and Henutmire, perhaps Rameses' elderly sister.

Bearing children was not, of course, their function, and as his wives and children began to die before him, Rameses realised he needed yet more heirs. At this juncture, the Hittite king brought him his daughter to marry: "Behold, the Great King of Kheta comes, bringing with him his eldest daughter, bringing with him quantities of gifts." Rameses, by now in his mid-fifties and extremely old in Egyptian terms, was pleased to accept her. She was renamed Maathorneferura.

Several years later, a stela from Coptos records a second visit of the Hittite king, "with his other daughter," also to be betrothed to Rameses. This princess is not named, nor do we know the date of the marriage. However, during the last 30 years of Rameses' reign he certainly had a Hittite Great Royal Wife.

Above **Rameses II and his daughter Bintanat, statue at temple of Karnak, Nineteenth Dynasty.** Daughter of Rameses by Isetnefret, Bintanat was a favored daughter, eventually being appointed a Great Royal Wife.

Karnak

Although the kings of the Eighteenth Dynasty enriched Karnak's treasury, the temple remained relatively small. It was the modifications made under Sety I and Rameses II that created the imposing complex we know today.

Above **Ruins of the temple of Amun, Karnak.** Built and enlarged over more than 1,300 years, Karnak consists of three major temple complexes covering more than 100 acres (247 ha) of land.

The kings of the early Eighteenth Dynasty greatly increased the wealth of the temple of Karnak. Every time they went campaigning, they would first ask Amun for victory. When their wish was granted—as it always was!—the king would hand over plunder and gifts to the temple.

Amenhotep III built the third pylon as the front of his temple. Later, he also added an open front courtyard to its east, bearing his name and image on some of the internal walls. We don't know if he began work on the second pylon in front of this courtyard. We do know that Horemheb completed the second pylon, probably to hide the *talatat* blocks from the Aten temple, which he had dismantled. However, the courtyard between the second and third pylons remained open.

Sety I appears to have started to decorate the faces of the second pylon, and the columns in the open court between it and the third pylon. When he died, much of the work was incomplete. Rameses II finished it, adding his own name. In front of the second pylon, now the front of the temple, Rameses built two colossal standing statues (of which only a trace of the feet of one remains) and an Osiriform statue showing him with his daughter Bintanat. This is still standing, though it was usurped by a later king.

The Hypostyle Hall

After the open courtyard of Amenhotep III was roofed and filled with columns by Sety I, extending the temple significantly westward, the mighty hypostyle hall—the word "hypostyle" means simply "many columns"—was only ever seen by the king and one or two of its highest officials. No member of the public was ever allowed to enter. Standing today in this hall, it seems illogical to have built on such a scale, and with such beauty, when so few eyes would ever see it.

The hypostyle hall contains 122 columns, of which the central 12 are significantly higher and broader than the others. This height difference

ORACLES

The first record of an oracle dates from the reign of Rameses II. At one point, the post of high priest was filled by a statue of Amun. To decide appointments, the statue would be placed within a shrine and carried before the candidates by priests. Amun would then "nod his assent" when passing the preferred choice.

After this, petitioners could have two alternative possibilities written on ostraca and placed in the path of the shrine as it was carried around 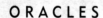 the temple. The statue would direct the shrine to the correct choice.

At the temple of Kom Ombo near Aswan, a space in the back wall of the temple allowed petitioners to ask their questions directly; a priest hidden inside the wall responded.

Right **Rameses II making an offering to Amun, carving from Karnak, c. 1279–1213 BCE.** Rameses' deference to oracles diminished his authority in the eyes of the priests.

allowed for clerestory lighting, the only light needed in this place. With the roof missing today, it is hard to imagine just how dark and majestic the hall must have appeared when complete. During the Victorian period, when much of the temple was filled with sand, it was deemed possible to hold a dinner party for at least 20 guests seated around the top of just one of the central columns!

Rameses II completed the columns, as well as usurping many earlier inscriptions added by his father, all the while proclaiming that he was "a good and dutiful son." An examination of the inscriptions on the columns reveals as many as three different layers of hieroglyphs carved one on top of the other. Around the walls, Rameses' work can be distinguished from that of his more careful forebears by its careless completion. On the outer walls, his military campaigns are shown, in particular the battle of Qadesh.

The First Peace Treaty

In Rameses II's reign-year 16, his old adversary, the Hittite King Muwatalli died. Muwatalli's brother Hattusili usurped the throne from Urhi-Teshub, the rightful son and heir. Urhi-Teshub fled south for his life and begged for sanctuary in Rameses' court. Hattusili threatened Egypt with a great war, and demanded the return of the prince. However, the Hittites were now faced with the rising power of Assyria to their east. Needing their forces to protect their borders against the Assyrians, they had little choice but to pursue peace with Egypt.

In Rameses' reign-year 21, the first ever peace treaty was drawn up. King Hattusili and Rameses exchanged warm words of regard for each other,

as did their queens. The full text of the peace treaty was carved on the south exterior wall of the hypostyle hall in Karnak. A second copy, in Hittite, was preserved in the Hittite capital of Hattusas, or Bogazkoy. Part of the agreement was that the Hittites would supply a new wife for Rameses. And indeed an inscription in Memphis states that in Rameses' year 34 the Hittite king did visit Egypt, bringing a daughter to marry the King of Egypt. In the end, the great enemies became firm allies.

Above **Temple of Amun, Karnak, viewed from the sacred lake.** Archeologists have recreated the lake that originally flanked the temple. A venue for rituals, it also symbolized the primeval waters from which all life emerged.

Left **The hypostyle hall in the temple of Amun, Karnak, engraving, 1809.** This artist's impression gives a sense of the grandeur of the hypostyle hall upon completion, when it was the largest room yet built in Egypt.

Abu Simbel

The construction of the temple of Abu Simbel was a remarkable feat of engineering, matched centuries later, in the 1960s, by the resiting of the temple prior to the creation of Lake Nasser.

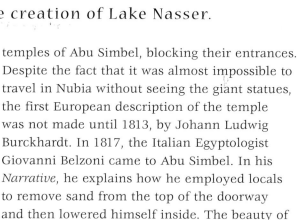

In almost every aspect of his life, Rameses II pitted himself against his glorious predecessor Amenhotep III. As Amenhotep had done, Rameses celebrated a jubilee festival in his thirtieth year, and thereafter every three years—a total of 14 at least. Like Amenhotep, he instigated a cult of himself as a god.

Every building erected by Amenhotep was either copied, extended, or usurped by Rameses. Nowhere was this more apparent than in Nubia. Here, Amenhotep III had built temples dedicated to the cults of himself (Soleb) and his wife (Sedeinga). Not to be outdone, Rameses chose to build matching "his and hers" temples on the Nile at Abu Simbel, much farther north than Amenhotep's temples, yet, like those, situated at the southernmost point of Egyptian control at the time of construction.

Discovering the Temple

For many centuries after their construction, sand tumbled down the slopes around the two great temples of Abu Simbel, blocking their entrances. Despite the fact that it was almost impossible to travel in Nubia without seeing the giant statues, the first European description of the temple was not made until 1813, by Johann Ludwig Burckhardt. In 1817, the Italian Egyptologist Giovanni Belzoni came to Abu Simbel. In his *Narrative*, he explains how he employed locals to remove sand from the top of the doorway and then lowered himself inside. The beauty of what he saw overwhelmed him. Graffiti left at the temple indicate that two other explorers, Mangles and Irby, were with him at the time.

Restoration Work

In 1873, a Victorian lady anchored on the river at the front of the temple. Amelia Edwards, a

Above **Temple of Rameses, Abu Simbel, engraving by Hector Horeau, 1841.** The engraving shows the temple as it was in the nineteenth century, partially buried by sand.

Above right **Falcon-headed sphinx, Temple of Rameses, Abu Simbel, c. 1279–1213 BCE.** The god Horus is most often depicted as a man with the head of a falcon, but occasionally he is also shown, as he is here, as a falcon-headed lion.

THE LOSS OF NUBIA

During the early years of the Eighteenth Dynasty, Egyptian kings had subdued Nubia almost as far south as the fourth cataract. The Nubians contributed vast amounts of gold and tribute to Egypt, as decorations in the tomb of Rekhmire demonstrate. But whenever weak Egyptian kings came to the throne, Nubian tribes took the opportunity to rebel. During the Amarna period, control slipped in the far south. Rameses II's temples in Abu Simbel marked the southernmost point of Egyptian control in his reign, a loss of over 200 miles (320 km) of Nubian territory. And despite the grandeur of the temples, and the power they seem to embody, the southern empire would soon crumble.

novelist, had come to Egypt to escape from the rain in Greece, where she had originally been intending to stay. Her companion for her sail was Marianne Brocklehurst. The two ladies hired a *dahabiya* each and took a leisurely holiday up the Nile, with Marianne's brother shooting anything that was foolish enough to move. The ladies themselves explored and bought trinkets to take home, including a mummy from the Valley of the Kings. This was propped up in a broom-cupboard on board, until they decided that guests coming to a dinner party one night might be offended by the smell, and therefore "had to drown the Dear Departed" by throwing it over the side.

Once at Abu Simbel Amelia decided to take a well-earned rest while the Brocklehursts sailed on to Wadi Halfeh. It started to dawn on Amelia, as she looked daily on the great carved faces of the temple, that the stone of the facade had a diagonal stripe on it, caused by the exposure of one section and the accumulation of sand on the other. Having little else to do, she ordered ladders from the nearby village, had her cook brew up some strong coffee in metal buckets,

and watched as her crew painted the lighter side of the temple to match the darker side!

While she was there, she also took "squeezes," or casts, of stelae, inscriptions, and even some of the statues, using papier-mâché or plaster of Paris. That she might have damaged the statues in doing so was not even a consideration!

The Temple of Rameses

Rameses' rock-cut temple was the finest ever built in Nubia, far larger than earlier ones. At its facade were four colossal seated statues of the king, with small figures of his mother and wife clutching the sides of his calves. At 69 ft (21 m) tall, the Rameses statues were largest ever cut by Egyptians.

The bases of the statues that form the entrance bear carvings of shackled foreigners, Semites to the north and Nubians to the south. There is little doubt that Rameses was trying to put the fear of himself into the heart of every Nubian!

Inside, eight statues of the king as Osiris flank a columned court, bold, painted eyes staring sightlessly across at each other. The side walls depict Rameses as king in his chariot, riding across the chaotic forms of his enemies, and, almost inevitably, scenes of the great "triumph" at Qadesh.

A series of six small side chambers, two to the south and four to the north, leads off this columned hall. These curious rooms are generally described as "store chambers," a word often

Above **Facade of the temple of Rameses, Abu Simbel, c. 1279–1213 BCE.** At the feet of the colossal statues of Rameses are smaller statues of his mother and children, and his wife Nefertari.

Left **The two temples of Abu Simbel, engraving after Giovanni Belzoni, 1822.** The first modern person to see inside the temple of Rameses at Abu Simbel, Belzoni removed many items from the tomb, some of which ended up in overseas collections such as the British Museum.

Above **Statue of Rameses II, Temple of Rameses II, Abu Simbel, c. 1279– 1213 BCE.** Eight massive statues of the king as Osiris dominate the first hall. Wall decorations depict the king's military exploits, including the battle of Qadesh.

Right **Hall of the temple of Rameses II, Abu Simbel, engraving, 1842–49.** Inside the temple three adjoining halls, lined by colossal figures of the king, extend for 185 feet (56 m) into the hillside.

used for any room whose purpose is obscure. The sides of each chamber are flanked by benches—too narrow, however, to store things underneath—while around the room, rectangular niches are cut into the walls. On close examination, it becomes apparent that each niche would neatly frame a person seated on the adjacent bench. This raises the question of the precise function of the temple.

Abu Simbel stands in an isolated spot with no buildings in close proximity. On the walls of the front are mounted official royal declarations in the form of small stelae. There was nowhere for a priesthood to live and nowhere for food to be prepared for offerings, unless it was brought in by river. The side rooms, along with the scale of the facade and the tied captives at the entrance, lead to the possibility that the temple served as some kind of "embassy" or government building, a kind of Egypt-in-Nubia, where meetings with local Nubian chiefs could be held on Egyptian territory.

Rameses in Many Guises

The sanctuary at the rear contains four statues, sitting side by side on a bench—Ptah of Memphis, Amun of Karnak, Rameses himself, and, finally, Ra-Horakhty, associated with the Aten cult. The temple was designed so that in February and August each year the rays of the rising sun would strike straight into the heart of the temple, through the processional way, illuminating the figures at the rear. The first statue to receive this blessing was, of

course, that of Rameses, whereas the unfortunate Ptah sat in his corner in constant darkness!

The smaller side temple, although dedicated to Nefertari, has four standing statues of Rameses at its front, flanking and protecting the two statues of the queen. Inside, it is a similar story. Although Nefertari is present in every scene, frequently Rameses is shown with her, smiting an enemy in her presence and displaying his manliness. The images of the queen are strangely tall and slender, like fashion plates. Measurements of the figures show that artists here adopted a 21-square grid to depict the queen, instead of the usual 18-square grid.

The columned hall inside incorporates Hathor-headed columns, the capital of each taking the form of a sistrum handle. On one wall, a relief shows Rameses making offerings to himself and Nefertari as god and goddess. This relief is unique in that it is the only such scene in which a wife of nonroyal origin is elevated to semi-divine status like the king.

Moving a Mountain

In the mid-twentieth century, the Egyptian government decided to build the Aswan High Dam to create a reservoir, Lake Nasser, in part of the Nile Valley. The project had been considered for centuries and planned for two decades. Construction would take more than 10 years.

An old British dam, opened in 1901, had shown how effective such a barrier could be. However, while the old dam shut off only one section of the Nile, creating a small reservoir, the new dam would inundate a huge area of surrounding land. The British dam had already partly submerged a fine temple dedicated to Isis on the island of Philae when the waters rose 60 ft (18 m). The High Dam would create a lake with a depth of 300 ft (90 m), drowning many more sites forever.

As building work commenced, the government consulted with Egyptologists and foreign governments to work out how to save these unique relics. Numerous proposals were considered. One idea was to enclose the temple complex where it stood inside a massive barrage. However, this was soon discounted.

Left **Aerial view of the temples of Abu Simbel at their new location.** Between 1963 and 1968, the temples were cut into more than 16,000 blocks, then transported and reassembled at this site.

that the sun continued to penetrate the building twice a year, as it had done for centuries. Then there was the more fundamental question of just how you move thousands of tons of rock fashioned out of a cliff face?

The decision was finally taken to saw the temple into massive blocks, lift the blocks using cranes and trucks, and then reassemble them at new sites. No appropriate cliff could be found to hold the reassembled temples, so two giant domes of sand were built over them. On the facade of each, some lines of cutting were not colored, but left lighter than the stone, to indicate for future generations how the temples were cut and moved.

The reconstructed temple is as much a miracle of contemporary technology as the original building was for the ancient Egyptians. Perhaps the greatest miracle of all is that the rays of the rising sun still reach into the temple on the very days they used to, when the king is still illuminated. The soul of Rameses must be gratified indeed.

Aside from the danger of leaks, no 300-ft (90-m) barrier could withstand the immense pressure exerted by that amount of water.

It became clear that the buildings would have to be moved from their original site. But this was way beyond any engineering feat carried out to date. Eventually, however, the United Nations Educational, Scientific, and Cultural Organization (UNESCO) proposed moving the great temples of Abu Simbel with the assistance of American and British engineers.

Not only did the temples have to be shifted 200 ft (60 m) above and 600 ft (180 m) west of their original position, there was also the vexed question of getting the orientation correct, so

Below **Temple of Nefertari, Abu Simbel, c. 1279–1213 BCE.** On the facade of the smaller temple, two pairs of statues of Rameses II flank two statues of his wife Nefertari. The statues stand 35 feet (10.5 m) tall.

The Sons of Rameses II

Many of Rameses' sons attained high positions in his court and a few even gained enduring fame. Many, however, passed away before the king did. The final resting place of the princes has only recently been relocated.

Rameses sired so many children that a future for his line seemed golden. However, he outlived many of them, and when he died after 67 years as king, his successor, Merenptah, his thirteenth son, was already a very elderly man. When Merenptah died, after less than 10 years as king, fierce rivalries broke out between his potential successors. Where one heir might be considered perilous, and two comfortable yet negotiable, the hundreds of children and grandchildren left by Rameses II made the issue of succession extremely complex.

Below The Serapeum, engraving after Mariette, nineteenth century CE. Mariette found the Serapeum by following a line of sphinxes to its door. Inside, the bulls' sarcophagi occupied niches off narrow corridors.

Khaemwaset and the Apis Bulls

Several of Rameses' children left their marks on the world, but none gained as exalted a reputation as Khaemwaset, his second son by Isetnefret. He was born toward the start of his father's reign, and was clearly distinguished from others by his intelligence and confidence. As a young man, he became Priest of Ptah at Memphis. From here, he was placed in charge of his father's project to build a new burial area for the sacred Apis bulls. The catacombs at Saqqara had been started in the Eighteenth Dynasty.

THE SERAPEUM

The Serapeum, the burial place of sacred Apis bulls, was found by the French Egyptologist Auguste Mariette at Saqqara in 1851. Apis bulls were chosen for particular signs and colorings, and were considered the reincarnation of Osiris. They lived in a "palace," officiated at festivals, had their own jewelry, and, when they died, were mummified just as a king might have been. The catacombs of the Serapeum contained many empty bull sarcophagi—each weighing in excess of 80 tons—but only one intact burial. The burials dated from the Eighteenth Dynasty to the Greco-Roman period. It is thought that earlier burials still await discovery.

Left **Worshipper praying to the Apis bull, limestone stela, Twentieth Dynasty.** Worship of the Apis bull was continued in ancient Greece and in the Roman Empire.

Khaemwaset supervised their extension. While this was underway, he spent his free time visiting the monuments of Saqqara. It is hard to comprehend that the Step Pyramid, for instance, was more than 1,500 years old when Khaemwaset visited the site. He examined most of the monuments still standing, and at each of them, carved on their face a "museum label" listing whose building it was and its state of repair. Today, many of these labels left by Khaemwaset are the only means we have of identifying the buildings' original owners.

Khaemwaset represented his father in at least the first five jubilee festivals, and his name is found in many major temples, showing he toured Egypt to do this. In his father's year 52, he became the oldest surviving son of his father, and for some years, gained the title of Crown Prince. But he died in his father's year 55, before he could inherit the throne.

Frenchman Auguste Mariette's excavation of the Serapeum revealed only one intact bull burial, preserved because the roof had collapsed on it. After clearing the debris, to his astonishment Mariette found an intact human burial in a small chamber behind the bull burial. Although the identity of the deceased is still open to question, it is possible that it is the Ramessid Egyptologist-Prince, Khaemwaset.

For centuries after his death, the sayings of Khaemwaset were handed down through the generations and he became revered as one of the greatest thinkers Egypt has ever seen.

The Tomb of the Royal Princes

In 1985, the Theban Mapping Project made an unexpected discovery. It was involved in the three-dimensional mapping of the Valley of the Kings, and was attempting to retrieve some tombs whose exact sites were not known.

Behind a pile of debris left by the English explorer Howard Carter when excavating the nearby tomb of Tutankhamun, the team found the door to the long-lost tomb known as KV 5. This had been originally visited in 1835 by James Burton, the explorer of the Nile source. He remarked on it as an unimportant, small, rubble-filled chamber. It provoked the same response in Carter, who also looked into it briefly before choosing it as the site for his spoil.

The modern explorers, led by Kent Weeks, clambered across dangerously unstable rubble into a confined space. To one side, a crawl-through seemed inviting. Once through this, they found themselves in an astonishing pillared hall. Sixteen pillars supported the ceiling of the largest chamber found in the valley. At the end of the chamber, more doorways could be seen.

The excavation of the tomb continues to this day. With the rubble cleared, the team found a network of chambers. In one of them, close to the door, human remains were found. These were of a robbed burial of three young men. A nearby inscription on the wall mentioned "sons of Usermaatra Setepenra." A papyrus now in Turin recorded robbers who admitted stripping stone from "the tomb of the royal children of Usermaatra Setepenra, the great god." This seemed to confirm that the tomb was KV 5.

By the beginning of 2005, 110 chambers and passages had been located and cleared, and tens of thousands of artifacts recovered. Passages "like an octopus with its body surrounded by tentacles," as Weeks described it, led farther and farther into the ground. Although there remains the promise of more exciting discoveries to come, much of the tomb has suffered over centuries from flooding, which has brought debris in with it. The sifting of the objects and mapping of the tomb will take many years.

Below **Figurine of Khaemwaset, c. 1279–1213 BCE.** Figurines like this one were known as *ushabti* and were made to accompany the deceased into the afterlife.

Exodus

The sacred texts of the world's three major religions recount the story of the expulsion of the Hebrews from Egypt. Yet no trace of this event appears in Egypt's archeological record. Did the Egyptians deliberately suppress the story?

Above **Story of the Exodus**, Spanish illuminated manuscript, fourteenth century CE. The images show, left to right at top, the pharaoh's order of expulsion and the plague of the first born, and, at bottom, the pursuit of the Egyptians and the parting of the Red Sea.

Prior to the decipherment of hieroglyphs, one of the main sources of information about ancient Egypt was the Bible. The Books of Genesis and Exodus recount stories of two patriarchs. The first, Joseph Zaphenath Paneah, was sold into Egypt by his jealous brothers, then attained fame and fortune by interpreting the pharaoh's dream, and eventually brought his entire family to stay. Four hundred years later, another Hebrew, Moses, was called by God to lead the enslaved Hebrews out of Egypt. When the pharaoh refused to let the slaves go, God brought plagues on the land of Egypt. The pharaoh finally let them go, then changed his mind and pursued them. God helped Moses part the waters of the Red Sea, allowing the Hebrews to escape to freedom while the Egyptian army perished to a man.

Did the Exodus Happen?

The stories are fundamental to the world's three largest faiths today. The information they gave early archeologists was unequivocal. The Egyptians were untrustworthy pagans, who became bitter task-masters. Herodotus reinforced this view, claiming that slaves built the pyramids.

Yet no reference has ever been found in Egypt to Joseph Zaphenath Paneah or to Moses. Even the plagues are unrecorded. Can it be that the Egyptians omitted to mention such critical events? Is it, as some claim, that the events were so humiliating that they preferred to ignore them?

This is very unlikely. After all, if Rameses could turn a minor skirmish into a major victory in his monuments, would it not be possible for Egyptian kings to portray the Exodus story in a way that reflected glory onto them?

The established facts are few. During the Eighteenth Dynasty the north was peopled by groups such as the Mitanni and Nahrin. By the late Nineteenth Dynasty, Israel existed—a stela dated to year 5 of Merenptah's reign notes, "Israel is devastated, its seed is no more." Although some point out, reasonably, that the word for Israel is followed by the hieroglyphs for "people" and not for "city," it remains a fact that the state of Israel could not exist before the tribes had settled and agreed on common grounds for government.

It seems unlikely that an event so potentially embarrassing and humiliating as the expulsion of slaves would have been recorded unless it actually happened. Given that many immigrants settled in Egypt and that Israel existed in the Nineteenth Dynasty, it seems reasonable that some kind of exodus took place. But when?

Dating the Exodus

No Biblical account ever names any pharaoh before 1 Kings and the name usually cited is

Pharaoh Shishak. However, the term "pharaoh," from the Egyptian *per-aa* meaning "great house," was not used before the reign of Akhenaten. Moreover, the accounts in Genesis and Exodus mention the land of "Ashur." This is Assyria, which did not come into existence much before the Ramessid Period. On the other hand, both of these clues tell us only when the account was written down, not when the events happened. Most ancient cultures preserved their stories through verbal accounts, and the stories they recounted could have occurred centuries earlier.

The first chapter of Exodus mentions "the store cities of Pithom and Rameses." These can be identified as the temple of Atum (Per Atum) and Piramesse, the city and temple built for Rameses II. This, with the mention of Israel in the reign of his son Merenptah, has suggested that Rameses oppressed the Hebrews, and that they escaped during the reign of Merenptah.

There is a problem, though. Inscriptions show that all building work stopped in Piramesse by Rameses' year 30, when he celebrated his first jubilee. This means that the workers would have been unemployed for 37 years prior to Rameses' death; and that they then demanded freedom from Merenptah, survived the plagues, raced across Sinai into the north, then formed Israel, only to be "devastated" in his year 5. While convenient, this is impossible timing.

Although we know that Israel existed in Merenptah's year 5, the inscription does not say *how long* it had already existed. In fact, the exodus could have happened considerably before his reign. One likely possibility is that the exodus reflected folk-memories of the city of el-Amarna. Here people worshipped a god "without image." When the kings left the city and it was finally destroyed, what happened to the inhabitants? Archeology guesses that they returned to their home towns. However, there were an estimated 50,000 people in the city at its high point, and they had lived their new lives for almost a full generation. If these people did indeed leave Egypt, then Egypt would have been relieved of a problem; and the king who followed them may not have been trying to recall them, but to ensure that they left.

Without more evidence, we cannot know the truth. Although it seems likely that such an event did take place, the sands of time may have hidden it from our view forever.

Above **Akhenaten, limestone bust, c. 1352–1336 BCE.** Could it be that the story of the exodus refers to the diaspora that followed the death of Akhenaten and the razing of Tell el-Amarna?

Left **Crossing the Red Sea, fresco by Bartolo di Fredi, Duomo of San Gimignano, Italy, 1367.** The fresco shows the Hebrews passing safely through the Red Sea while the Egyptian army is engulfed by its waters.

THE RAMESSID SUNSET

Merenptah

By the end of Rameses II's reign, the empire was all but lost. The golden glow that Sety I had seen as a new dawn turned out to be the burning embers of pharaonic Egypt. Rameses' son Merenptah could do little to reverse the decline.

Below **Merenptah, engraving, 1878.** Merenptah was the thirteenth son of Rameses II and the fourth son by Queen Isetnefret.

During the late years of Rameses' life, the threat from the west had intensified. Despite his self-professed mythic status and enduring appeal to the people of Egypt, from a military point of view he had been a failure. Fortresses had been built during his reign and permanently manned on the Libyan front, but to little avail. Libyans had flooded into the Delta as early as the middle of Rameses' reign. Having lived there for more than 30 years, they now considered it their home. Other settlers were eager to join them.

Chaos and Disorder

The rise of Assyria to the east of the River Euphrates meant that the Hittite realm to its west soon came under attack. The Hittites could do little to repel the Assyrian forces, and constant raids on Hittite settlements meant that crops could neither be sown nor harvests reaped. With no food from their own fields, and no powerful force such as Egypt to help defend them, the Hittites began to starve. Fear and violence drove many people out of their homes and westward to look for safer areas to live in. Wherever they ran, they pressurized local populations; in turn, they drove others from their homes.

Such disorder was not confined to the Middle East. In Crete, the Minoan civilization had crumbled and its islands had subsequently starved. In central Greece, the Mycenaean settlements had also been attacked. Throughout the eastern Mediterranean, crops had failed.

In Egypt, fortunately, the Nile continued to rise, maintaining Egyptian food supplies when others had nothing. An inscription in Karnak records that grain shipments were even sent by Merenptah to his old enemy, the Hittites. Yet Egypt would soon come under pressure.

Refugees from the collapsing civilizations began to flee by sea. Homeless and starving, these "Sea Peoples," as they became known, landed in their thousands on the coast of Libya.

Mereye, King of Libya, formed an alliance with the Sea Peoples and marched against Egypt. His army faced no resistance and, recruiting settled Libyans as it went, it marched within sight of Heliopolis and Memphis itself.

A Hollow Victory

Merenptah was at least 50 when he was crowned king. In reality, he was too old to lead the army, yet the world beyond Egypt's borders was in foment. He sent a number of military expeditions abroad in his initial years, notably to Nubia and Palestine. In his fifth year, he led his army to confront the Libyans. He claimed a mighty victory. "There was none that escaped among them. His Majesty's infantrymen spent six hours fighting them and they were cut down by the sword." Among the accounts of victory were descriptions of phalluses cut from enemies and made into piles for the god Amun.

The words, though, ring hollow, coming as they do on top of so many Egyptian claims of supremacy under Rameses. The modest lists of plunder say it all: "Libyan children, 6; horses, 12; goats, 64." The truth was that Egypt was tottering in an uncertain world.

In the same year, Merenptah's armies marched against northern realms. Although the Hittite threat had dwindled, many northern cities had been free of Egyptian control for years. Merenptah claimed victory over a wide area, from Gaza to Ashkelon and beyond. But there is no evidence that his victories achieved anything.

Death and Burial

Merenptah died after less than 10 years as king. The design of his tomb in the Valley of the Kings was innovative, notably for its long corridors. Off the entrance corridor, a small chamber was dedicated to the cult of his father. In the center of the burial chamber stood a low alabaster podium, upon which was placed the sarcophagus. Unlike the tomb of Tutankhamun, for example, where the sarcophagus contained a nest of coffins, here a nest of sarcophagi of immense weight and size protected the innermost anthropoid coffin.

The tomb was robbed soon after it was buried. Of the two outer sarcophagi, only the lids and smashed fragments of the troughs survived. The innermost sarcophagus was removed and taken to Tanis, where it was reused for the burial of King Psusennes I of the Twenty-first Dynasty. In 1920, outside the tomb, Howard Carter and Lord Carnarvon discovered a group of 13 alabaster jars used in Merenptah's burial. These bore the name of Rameses II, but had been over-carved and damaged in the process.

The mummy of Merenptah was found in the tomb of Amenhotep II, discovered in 1898. The king closely resembled his father. However, the body was in poor condition, the skin bearing patches of salt. Clearly the mummification had been perfunctory. It was a sad and sorry sight.

Left **Entrance to the tomb of Merenptah, Valley of the Kings, c. 1203** BCE. Discovered by Howard Carter in 1903, the tomb of Merenptah lies near that of his father, Rameses II.

Below **Tomb of Merenptah, Valley of the Kings, c. 1203** BCE. From the entrance, a series of long corridors leads down in a straight line through this pillared hall to the burial chamber.

The Fight for Succession

When Merenptah died, the last direct link with Rameses II was broken,
for Rameses' other children were all either dead or too old to stake a claim.
It was left to his numerous grandchildren to dispute the succession.

Right Chalice belonging to Queen Tausret, c. 1200–1186 BCE. Tausret became the third queen to rule Egypt during the New Kingdom, after Ahhotep and Hatshepsut.

In disputes for succession to a throne, one might expect that the strongest claimant would succeed. But history, repeatedly, shows the opposite to be true: The weaker the claimant, the more power those around him can exert. Following the death of Merenptah, a series of incompetent, mentally and physically weak men were maneuvered onto the throne, to the detriment of the country.

Sety II and Amenmessu

By his Great Royal Wife Isinofret II, Merenptah left a son, Sety II, who was crowned king. Despite this, a rival claimant, Amenmessu, came forward. It is likely that he was Rameses' grandson by a minor, female line and that he claimed authority, and ruled, in a different area of Egypt, probably the south. However, around his year 3, Amenmessu seems to have died. He was given a royal burial in the Valley of the Kings, but his tomb was badly smashed, probably by Sety II, who subsequently sought to erase all trace of Amenmessu's reign.

Below Temple of Sety II, Karnak, c. 1200–1194 BCE. Built of quartzite and sandstone, the chapel contains three chambers devoted, respectively, to Mut, Amun, and Khonsu, and is adorned with reliefs showing Sety II making offerings to the gods.

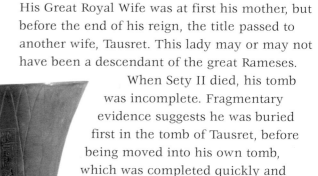

Sety II ruled afterward for only five years. His Great Royal Wife was at first his mother, but before the end of his reign, the title passed to another wife, Tausret. This lady may or may not have been a descendant of the great Rameses.

When Sety II died, his tomb was incomplete. Fragmentary evidence suggests he was buried first in the tomb of Tausret, before being moved into his own tomb, which was completed quickly and with paintings of a poor standard. His mummy was discovered in the tomb of Amenhotep II, placed in an unrelated coffin and identified only by a wooden tag.

The Syrian Connection

Arguments rage over the identity of the next king, Saptah. His mummy, also discovered in the tomb of Amenhotep II, reveals he was a weak boy who had poliomyelitis as a child, resulting in a deformed foot and twisted, shortened leg. It is known from an inscription in his tomb that his mother, Sutailja, came from Syria. His father may have been Sety II or even Amenmessu.

From the start, Queen Tausret acted as regent for the king, who besides being ill was also little more than a child. The Syrian connection is an intriguing one, for Tausret's steward and probable lover, Bay, was also Syrian. A later inscription claims he was an "upstart" or self-made man. During the reign of Sety II, he had merely been a scribe in the court. He ascribed his phenomenal rise to power, however, to remaining loyal to Queen Tausret throughout her reign, supposedly on behalf of Saptah.

Bay was buried in royal style in the Valley of the Kings, in a tomb identical in layout to that of Tausret. Although a relief near the door shows him making an offering to Saptah, throughout the rest of the tomb Bay is shown facing the gods alone in place of the king. An inscription in the tomb says it was Bay who "raised the king to the throne of his father," claiming openly that Saptah

IMMIGRATION TO EGYPT

Egypt's borders with Libya in the west and Nubia in the south were always vulnerable. During the reigns of weak kings, immigrants flooded in and were sometimes never evicted. Moreover, campaigns in the north during the Twelfth Dynasty brought back prisoners of war in such numbers that two papyri list households comprising 60 percent foreigners. And during the New Kingdom, the empire encouraged many settlers into the country, who of course brought their languages and fashions with them.

From the Twentieth Dynasty onward, immigration resulted in large non-Egyptian communities in the Delta. Excavations have shown Jewish and early Greek settlements all along the banks of the Nile.

Above **Foreign prisoners, faience tiles, c. 1180** BCE. The prisoners shown are, from left to right, Libyan, Nubian, Syrian, and Nubian.

only ruled because he permitted it. When Saptah died, Tausret and Bay ruled together for a further two years before their deaths.

Sethnakht's Short-lived Coup

On the island of Elephantine, a stela records a story of rebellion and violence. Sethnakht, usually regarded as the first king of the Twentieth Dynasty, claims that he had thrown a group of rebels out of Egypt and confiscated their goods, on the basis that their gold and silver was being used to buy mercenary troops from the north.

Their leader was Bay. There seems little doubt that Sethnakht had staged a coup. As the stela is dated from his year 2, it is believed that it took him two years to gain full control. Who he was is uncertain, but it seems likely that he was another grandson of Rameses II.

His success was short-lived, however. Soon after his coronation, he died. During his reign, he usurped the tomb of Tausret for his own use. But although his coffin was found in Tausret's tomb, a body that may perhaps be his was found in the tomb of Amenhotep II.

Rameses III

The first king for many years to inherit the throne without challenge, Rameses III fought hard to maintain stability. Yet his attempts to root out corruption in his administration eventually weakened the office of king.

Above **Hieroglyphic inscription, temple of Rameses III, Medinet Habu, c. 1172 BCE.** The inscriptions form part of an account of the military victories of Rameses III.

Above, right **Rameses III, granite statue, temple of Karnak, Twentieth Dynasty.** Ramesses III inadvertently handed greater wealth and power to religious leaders, in particular to the priests of Amun in Karnak.

Rameses III was the son and worthy successor of Sethnakht. He may have been descended from the Rameses II, but the connection cannot be traced. The previous kings had all lived in Piramesse but had still chosen to be buried in the Valley of the Kings in Luxor, probably because of the tradition established there over the centuries. More recently, however, although Memphis had not been abandoned completely, ambitious courtiers had clustered around Piramesse to extend their control over the kings, and, increasingly, opted for burial in Saqqara. Luxor had almost been abandoned. Breaking with this trend, Rameses III chose to live in Luxor, building a palace, tomb, and temple there. There is no indication that he ever lived in Piramesse.

Strike and Rebellion

Sethnakht had stopped much internal fighting in the country when he had Bay deported and his supporters quashed. Upper Egypt had a chance of peace once again. Rameses III seems to have come to terms with the large numbers of immigrants that had settled in the Delta and concentrated on development of the state instead of foreign campaigns. He started his building works soon after his coronation, the most impressive being his palace and mortuary temple, among the biggest ever built on the west bank.

The structure of government had begun to break down, however, as a result of the vicissitudes of the previous dynasty. In Luxor, several officials had become corrupt, exploiting the absence of the king. Rameses undertook to put right the injustices. The Great Harris Papyrus in the British Museum, an accounts papyrus from his reign, lists the huge numbers of families who were dependent on Karnak during his reign. To secure the lives of people impoverished by corruption, he donated vast tracts of royal land to the major temples. This land had always belonged to the king and, although it was leased to the temples, in return the state received grain and other produce as tax. Handing over the freehold meant giving up this income, with the result that the state granaries, which provided "pay" for palace workers as well as emergency back-up supplies, ran dry.

In year 29 of Rameses' reign, the workers of Deir el-Medina went on strike because they had received no pay for several months. They petitioned the king about their case, and protested nightly outside the houses of their overseers. They must have received private support from families, because it was to take seven months for the grain to flow into the granaries again in sufficient quantities to pay the staff. The loss of royal land and income would never be repaired.

Furthermore, Karnak became rich at the king's expense, and the priests who controlled that wealth were able to control the king, too.

Attack of the Sea Peoples

Ever since the reign of Merenptah, Egypt's northern coast had been threatened by a steady incursion of refugees. Outside Egypt, refugees had also gathered in many coastal towns and on the islands of Crete and Cyprus. These refugees were known generally as the "Sea Peoples."

During Rameses III's eighth year, the Sea Peoples formed an alliance and gathered a united force intent on entering Egypt. Some planned to attack on land, others by sea. Rameses appears to have been forewarned, however, as his troops were ready. The king first marched north and attacked the land force. It was arriving with women, children, and possessions in carts, ready to settle, but Rameses' army killed many of them and turned the rest back. He then sent some of his army out in boats to intercept the naval force.

The subsequent encounter, the first-ever recorded naval battle, saw the Egyptians grappling their craft alongside the enemy vessels, climbing aboard, and engaging the invaders in hand-to-hand combat. In other words, they planned the attack as they would have planned a land battle— as if the water were a mere inconvenience!

Rameses' victory, like that of his ancestor Rameses II, was recorded boldly on his monuments. But although he had turned back the tide, it was only a momentary respite, for the force against Egypt could not now be stopped.

THE EGYPTIAN NAVY

The Egyptians on the whole were poor and reluctant sailors outside the Nile Valley. Ships were designed only for riverine travel and when they did put to sea remained close to the coast rather than entering open water. Ships for troop transport and for merchant trading, from at least the Old Kingdom if not earlier, left Egypt and sailed port to port anticlockwise around the Eastern Mediterranean. A wreck discovered at Ulu Burun, of a ship transporting Egyptian and traded goods, contained bronze figures of Seth that were carried as charms

against storms at sea. Most crews comprised conscript soldiers forced to work on ships, an experience undergone and described by Ahmose, son of Ibana.

Above **Egyptian ships of the Twentieth Dynasty, painting by Rafael Monleon y Torres (1847–1900).** Egyptian vessels were relatively small, with a single mast and room for only about 50 soldiers. In battle, the Egyptians deployed ranks of archers to provide cover while they attempted to board their opponents' ships.

Left **Rameses III receiving tributes, engraving after bas relief at Medinet Habu, 1809.** While resisting invasion and dealing with corruption, Rameses III managed to organize various trade missions, including one to Punt.

Medinet Habu

Throughout the first half of his long reign, Rameses III focused much of his attention on the construction of what would be the last great mortuary temple ever built in Luxor and the most enduring legacy of his rule, Medinet Habu.

Right **Temple of Medinet Habu, engraving from Panorama of Ancient Egypt and Nubia, by Hector Horeau, 1841.** The engraving shows the state of the temple in the mid-nineteenth century, before restoration.

Below **Migdol Gate, temple of Medinet Habu, c. 1172 BCE.** On either side of the temple's eastern gateway are reliefs showing Rameses III defeating the enemies of Egypt. A matching western gateway was destroyed during the reign of Rameses XI.

Medinet Habu was built at the southernmost end of the plain of the west bank. Originally, canals led from the Nile to a quay in front of the main gate. The temple was ringed with an unusually strong outer wall of stone instead of mud-brick, giving it formidable defenses. The main gate was a three-story, battlemented tower, today called the Migdol Gate.

Inside the gateway, a broad open courtyard reveals the large pylon gates of the main temple within. These are the best to survive from the New Kingdom on the west bank. Inside the gates, two open courts led into two hypostyle halls and finally to the sanctuary.

From the first open court, a door in the south wall led outside. To the right, two limestone pillars once framed a door leading to Rameses' palace. Here, in a tiny room occupied almost entirely by a dais approached by three ranks of steps, was the king's throne. To the right side of the dais, a small side door led into an ensuite bathroom, complete with "showers" and toilet.

The temple precinct of Medinet Habu, the last great structure ever erected by a native king, became a city as well as a temple, for around its walls flourished workshops and houses that sheltered people on the west bank from attack. In the first century CE, when it was known as Djeme, the settlement expanded rapidly after villages in the area had been plundered and destroyed, and houses were even built inside the temple. Later, part of the temple became a monastery, whose abbots ruled where once the old king had sat.

The Plot Against Rameses III

Rameses III ruled for 31 years, a long and stable interlude, as Egypt's final native pharaoh. But the unrest outside the palace walls filtered inward at the end of his reign. In the harem, a Nubian wife called Tiye hatched a plot to murder him, in order to allow her son Pentawere to succeed to the throne. In the upper rooms of the Migdol Gate, the king is shown in his harem, sitting naked, with a favorite wife tending him. Perhaps this was Tiye herself; undoubtedly the upper gatehouse was the place where he sported with some of them.

Tiye persuaded one of the harem guards to carry a message south to her brother to rouse the Nubian army against her husband. More wives persuaded other guards to bring wax and other materials into the palace so that they could make

wax figures of the king and stick pins into them, and carry out other spells and charms to bring about the king's end. The plot caused mayhem in the court, and it was soon discovered.

The people involved were quickly brought to trial. The guards who had obtained supplies and taken messages from the women were found guilty and told to "go and let the punishment fall upon yourselves," suggesting that they were forced to commit suicide. Members of the internal harem staff who looked after the ladies, were also found guilty and taken away "so that their punishment falls upon them." In other words, they were executed. The final group brought before the court was the ladies themselves. The papyrus is silent as to their ultimate fate. However, it is known that the case had to be abandoned and new judges appointed after the defendants seduced the first ones!

The mummy of Rameses III was found in the 1881 Deir el-Bahri cache. It reminds many people of the mummy played by the actor Boris Karloff in the film *The Mummy*, and indeed the actor modeled his costume on this relic. Although there is no sign of violence against Rameses, it seems probable that his wives poisoned him.

Yet Rameses may have had the last word. When the Deir el-Bahri cache was found, the bodies of the kings were laid on the sand to await transportation to the museum in Cairo. As the rising sun touched the mummy, the resins softened, causing his bandages to twist and contract. To everyone's horror, Rameses' arm slowly started to rise of its own accord!

HAREM CONSPIRACIES

It is a sad yet illuminating fact that for 3000 years of ancient Egyptian history, kings were only murdered by their wives! The great ambition of each of these women was to achieve the highest rank for a woman, "Mother of the King." A king might have harems filled with hundreds of wives, but he could have only one mother! So when a king died, each wife vied for her son to inherit the throne. Harem conspiracies seem to have changed the line of inheritance at the death of Khufu (Fourth Dynasty), when Djedefra vanished and Khafra took the throne; and in the reign of Pepy (Sixth Dynasty) when the courtier Weni was asked to hear a trial of a conspiring queen. Amenemhat of the Twelfth Dynasty was murdered as a result of a harem conspiracy aimed at bringing his son and co-regent to the throne.

Above **Portico of second court, Medinet Habu, c. 1172** BCE. As well as recounting Rameses' military victories, the abundant relief work at Medinet Habu depicts the accumulation of treasures for the temple, religious festivals, and, as here, the gods.

Religion and Superstition

Egypt was always a remarkably conservative realm, where few conventions ever changed. The exception was religion, which developed significantly—in choice of deities and forms of worship—from one generation to the next.

The study of religion is one of the most complex areas of Egyptology. Herodotus described Egyptians as "religious to excess, beyond any other nation." Early Christians publicly deplored the use of idols and castigated Egyptians as the worst kind of pagans. Together, these impressions have left an image of a primitive people bent on the worship of pagan statues, whose gods took the form of animals or humans with animal heads. This is a gross misrepresentation.

Archeology, however, is a poor guide to ancient religious beliefs. Any statue found is a "god," while anything that cannot be understood is said to have had "mystic, symbolic, cultic, or ritual importance." Yet objects and monuments can never fully inform us about ancient beliefs—these ideas came only from within the people who held them. Even today, the religious beliefs of two people are not identical, so how is it possible to understand what people believed thousands of years ago?

State Religion

State religion was based on cosmologies, or Creation myths. There are several forms of these in Egypt, which have developed over centuries. Common to all, however, is the idea that before the Creation, in the days of Isfet, or primordial Chaos, there was a formless, watery void in which a primitive, massive force created the first mound of land. Light then divided from dark, noise from silence, air from water.

Later priests embellished this story in different ways. According to those of Memphis, the god Ptah thought with his mind and spoke with his tongue, and then his words became physical

reality. According to Heliopolis, a lotus grew on the first earth, and opened to give birth to the sun. From the flames rose the first bird, the phoenix, which cackled and broke the silence. According to Luxor, Amun appeared from the lotus and spread his seed over the land, thus creating all animals, plants, and humankind.

At his coronation, the king was given the powers to act as a bridge between the physical world of man and the spiritual world of the gods. He had to maintain *maat*, or equilibrium, between the two worlds. Every day in the sanctuary, he reenacted Creation to ensure that Isfet could never return. Egyptians believed the fate of the cosmos was in his hands.

Beliefs and Worship

It is unlikely that the ordinary Egyptian understood anything about state religion, for no commoner was ever allowed to enter a temple. But there was no sense of resentment. In Egyptian eyes, the farmer was just as important as the king, and if either failed chaos would result.

Festivals were among the few occasions when the inner world of the temple coincided with the outer world of the streets. On these occasions, the temple statue would be removed from the sanctuary and placed inside a shrine atop a model ship or barque. This would then be carried openly through the streets to its destination, while the temple provided the people with unlimited quantities of free wine, beer, and cooked food. Little wonder that these festivals were so popular!

Most people worshipped "domestic" gods, amulets, and figurines designed to bring comfort. Among these were Bes, a dwarf-god who presided over the home and childbirth; Tausret, the pregnant hippo, who brought children to those who could not conceive; and Hekat, a frog, who guarded against

miscarriage. Above all, everyone venerated the king, a living god, whose daily role ensured blessings on the land they worked.

Magic and Superstition

Herodotus' comment that the Egyptians were "religious to excess" undoubtedly refers not to public ceremonies, but to their total belief in the power of magic in their lives. From the Old Kingdom onward we have references to spells and charms, wax figurines and curses, which were used deliberately or accidentally to interfere with a person's fate.

Such beliefs are still prevalent in Egypt. There was, and is, an overriding fear of the Evil Eye, against which the ancient Egyptians' most powerful amulet, the *wadjat*, or healed eye, offered protection. The Evil Eye could be invoked accidentally. Allowing a healthy son to be admired in public was a certain way for the Evil Eye to bring about his death. The accidental crossing of two people's paths in childhood could be enough to bring about infertility. Mud balls containing nail clippings and hair found in ancient and modern Egypt were used to place curses on an enemy. Slips of papyrus, rolled inside an amulet, could protect against these.

The world of the ancient Egyptian was a dangerous one, where fate, demons, and curses could interfere daily with your health, prosperity, and happiness. It was this attitude to life, rather than any dependence on temples, that made them "religious to excess."

Above **The heavens, as depicted in the tomb of Sety I, Valley of the Kings, c. 1294–1279 BCE.** This image reflects the diversity of gods thought to inhabit the world beyond.

Below **Bronze statue inspired by the cult of Apis, 715–332 BCE.** Apis the bull is flanked by the goddess Isis, to the right, and a worshipper offering a lotus flower. The cult of Apis eventually spread throughout the Roman Empire.

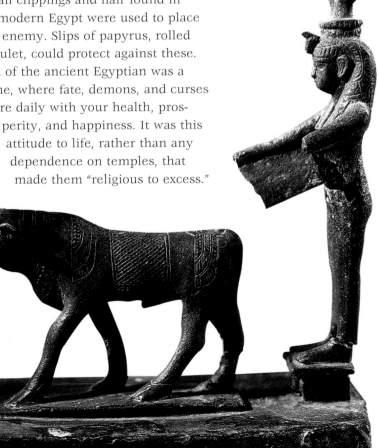

A Steady Decline

The next three Ramessid kings reigned only for a short time and presided over further erosion of the empire, continuing economic problems, and a shift in the balance of power in favor of the high priests of the temple of Amun.

Right **Tomb of Rameses VI, engraving from *Panorama of Egypt and Nubia*, by Hector Horeau, 1841.** This tomb had been known and visited since antiquity, as indicated by Greek, Coptic, and Latin inscriptions, but was not cleared of debris until 1888.

Many of Rameses III's children died young. His oldest son, Amunhorkopeshef, was given a royal burial in the Valley of the Queens. Scenes on the walls show the king with his son. The boy appears around 12 years old yet, when the tomb was first opened, the sarcophagus was there with its lid intact and inside was a tiny coffin holding the skeletal remains of a stillborn infant. Why build such an elaborate tomb for a child who never even breathed after birth? Most likely it is a reflection of Rameses III's desperation to produce a living heir.

Down the Ramessid Line

Below **Rameses III and his son Amunhorkhopeshef, decoration from tomb of Amunhorkhopeshef, c. 1184–1153 BCE.** The king, wearing the red crown of Lower Egypt, leads his son to meet the gods of the afterlife.

The remaining kings of the Twentieth Dynasty were all called Rameses, and all took throne names containing elements of the name of Rameses II in the hope of attaining protection and a long reign. However, they were as unsuccessful as their immediate predecessors.

Rameses IV, the fifth son of Rameses III, ruled for about six years. He opened up many quarries and mines that had been closed for centuries. However, four times as many guards as workers were employed, suggesting that these sites were at risk of attack. Rameses IV lived for most of his reign in Piramesse, by now almost a prison for its weak kings. In Luxor meanwhile, the priests of Karnak, following their earlier acquisition of lands, had attained great power. The head of the temple, Ramesesnakht, had established a line of succession for himself, and he now employed more men than the king.

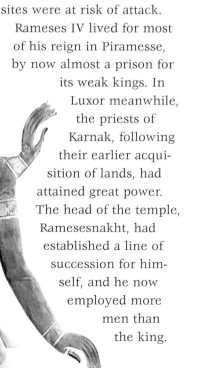

Rameses IV died a young man, as his mummy, found in the tomb of Amenhotep II, reveals. His tomb was never completed, although a sketch plan of its layout, on a fragmentary papyrus, is now in the Egyptian Museum in Turin.

His son, Rameses V, ruled for only a very short period. During this time, workers in the Valley of the Kings refused to work and a corruption scandal came to light at the temple at Elephantine. Rameses V's mummy was found in the tomb of Amenhotep II. The presence of lesions on his body suggests he died from smallpox.

The identity of Rameses VI is open to doubt. It is probable that he was a brother of Rameses IV, and thus uncle of the dead Rameses V. However, Rameses V was not buried until at least two years after Rameses VI was crowned. Little is known of his eight-year reign. His tomb is one of the finest in the Valley of the Kings, though his mummy,

too, was found in the tomb of Amenhotep II. It bore witness to later events in the valley. Inside its linen wrappings were human remains that had been hacked apart, including a woman's hand and a stray arm. The king's pelvis had been placed around his neck. How the mighty had fallen!

Amenhotep the Usurper

At the death of Rameses IV, a descendant of Ramesesnakht, Amenhotep, was high priest in Karnak. On the outer wall of the temple of Khons at Karnak, a relief shows Amenhotep alongside, and the same size as, the god Amun. Above him, his name and title, First High Priest of Amun, are written in cartouches.

According to another inscription, it was at about this time that the Nubian prince Panehsy was summoned to Egypt to fight a "war against the usurper." The death of Rameses IV, and the infirmity of Rameses V, who was already ill and dying, meant that there was no one to raise an Egyptian force to suppress Amenhotep. So the call went out and the Nubians marched 700 miles (1,100 km) across desert sands to Luxor to remove the usurper priest and his close supporters.

REVENGE OF THE NUBIANS

In the burial chamber of Rameses VI, a smashed section of his sarcophagus stands upended in the middle of the floor. Until the 1980s, it was believed that modern robbers, wanting to see if the stone contained hidden treasure, accomplished this. But a scholar pointed out that resins poured into the sarcophagus had clearly still been liquid when the sarcophagus was smashed and upended, since resin had spilled onto the cracked surface and run in vertical rivulets down the stone. Resins were poured over the body of the deceased king and hardened within a few days, so this proved beyond doubt that robbers had entered the tomb within hours of the burial of Rameses VI, smashed apart the sarcophagus, and mauled the mummy in order to retrieve any gold and precious amulets buried with it.

In an ironic twist, it turned out that the perpetrators of this robbery were the very Nubian forces that had been summoned to protect Egypt. At the end of the reign of Rameses VI, the Nubians crossed to the west bank and went on the rampage. They smashed their way into tombs, stealing gold from the bodies and leaving the tombs open and in total disarray. Perhaps the greatest irony was that for centuries the Egyptians had controlled Nubia and taken their gold. In the end, Fate allowed the gold to return to Nubia, and the Egyptians lost almost all they had ever acquired.

Left **Broken sarcophagus, tomb of Rameses IV, Valley of the Kings c 1147 BCE.** The sarcophagus was smashed by the Nubian robbers, but the mummy was found in the tomb of Amenhotep II, where it may have been placed for safekeeping.

The Last Pharaohs

Following the Nubian intervention in Luxor, the Ramessids lost control of Upper Egypt. Even in their home territory of the Nile Delta, they faced a challenge from the Libyans, who founded a new dynasty led by Smendes.

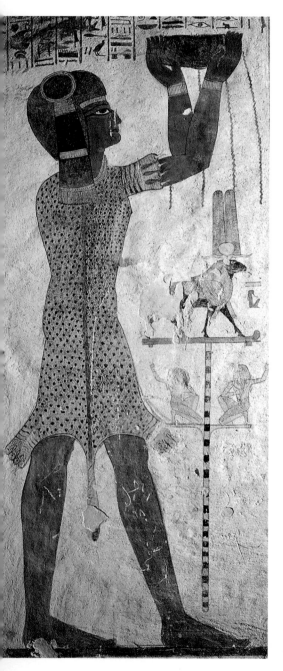

Above **Priest making a sacrifice at the tomb of Rameses IX, c. 1108 BCE.** While the priesthood generally deferred to the Ramessids, the high priests of Amun began to see themselves as their equals.

Rameses VII may have ruled for around six years, though little is known of him. He was probably a son of Rameses VI and very young. When he died, he left no heir to succeed him, and although a tomb was cut for him, it was left incomplete. He may never have been buried there, and his mummy has not been found.

Rameses VIII, according to his own inscription, may have been yet another son of Rameses III. If so, then he was elderly and presumably placed on the throne because there was no one else. His reign lasted only a few months. No tomb was ever cut for him.

We cannot know for certain exactly who Rameses IX was. He was crowned and ruled in Piramesse for around 18 years. Given the weak health of his predecessors and the lack of an heir at the death of Rameses VII, it is quite likely that he was no relation to the old family whatsoever, but took the name simply to continue the tradition.

Libyans in the Delta now started rising against the ineffectual kings and claimed the throne for themselves through a new dynasty, starting with Smendes. Although Rameses IX began some building work, it was concentrated on Heliopolis and the Delta, implying that his rule extended no further than this. The priests now had full control of Luxor.

Karnak's Renaissance

After the Nubian raid on the Valley of the Kings, it seems that the Ramessid kings abandoned Luxor to its own fate. The tombs in the valley lay open for more than a decade. With the royal tombs empty and the mummies violated, the workers from Deir el-Medina abandoned their village and settled in the safety of Medinet Habu. Assuming that that no one cared about the tombs any longer, they began to remove items that might be of use to them.

Panehsy, the Prince of Nubia summoned to suppress Amenhotep, occupied Luxor for some time before returning south. He left his son, Piankh, to rule in Karnak in his place. Piankh ignored the continuing rule of the Ramessids in the north, and instituted a new era called *wehem-mesut*, or "renaissance." His son, Herihor, became `high priest of Karnak, and the family now effectively ruled Upper Egypt.

Herihor personally undertook the cleanup operations in the valley. Keen to assert himself, he was determined to stamp out all actions that might undermine his authority. Bringing the men of Deir el-Medina into court was one way of demonstrating this in public.

Left **Earring of a royal woman of the court of Rameses XI,**
c. 1099–1069 BCE. Made of gold, the earring incorporates one row
of cobras on a winged disk and another row bearing sun-disks.

Right **Decoration from the tomb of Rameses IX, c. 1108** BCE.
The king is shown twice, to the left wearing the red crown of Lower
Egypt and to the right wearing the white crown of Upper Egypt.

The workers did admit to breaking into
one intact tomb, from which they removed the
bodies of the king and his wife, took their gold
coffins and masks, and melted down the gold,
which they then divided between themselves. It
is not clear from the trial papyri what happened
to the men, although it seems that the gold was
handed over to the judges who then divided it
up among themselves!

Buried Treasure

Although Rameses IX was succeeded by Rameses
X, probably his son, there was now an understanding that the Ramessid kings had no authority outside the area around Piramesse

The Ramessid Period was at an end. But one
final mystery remains. Carter found graffiti, left
by workmen in a hidden valley around the back
of the hills on the west bank of Luxor, which
stated that the men were working on the tombs
of Herihor and his son Pinudjem. No items from
either of these burials have ever come to light
in any collection in the world. The burials, it

seems, are still intact and awaiting discovery.
Given that these men tidied up the royal tombs
and stripped the royal mummies for their own
advantage, we can only imagine what treasures
they decided to keep for their own burials.
Should this lost tomb ever be found, it could
eclipse Tutankhamun's forever.

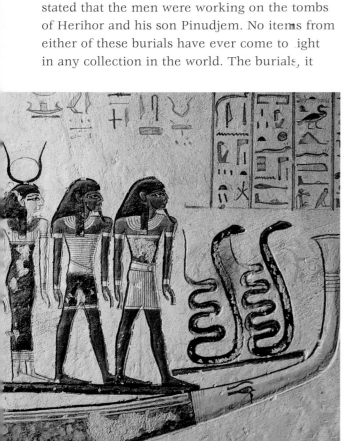

MOVING THE MUMMIES

The last tomb in the Valley of the Kings was cut for Rameses
XI, but was neither finished nor occupied. Excavation of the
tomb told a bizarre story. After they finished pilfering the
royal tombs, Herihor and Pinudjem gathered the royal
mummies together "for their safety." We know from hieratic
inscriptions on many of the mummies that the two men
rewrapped some of them and marked their identities, either
on the outer wrappings or on dockets attached to their necks.
It was unclear, though, why some mummies were left open
whereas others were rewrapped.

In their haste, the Nubians had not pillaged many of the
mummies. So Herihor and his son now stripped them, removing all gold and amulets, to enrich their own coffers, before
rewrapping them and moving them, as one single cache, to
another tomb. Inscriptions suggest the bodies lay for some
years in the tomb of Sety I, before eventually being carried
to their final resting place at Deir el-Bahri.

Left **Sacred barque, deco-**
ration from the tomb of
Rameses IX, c. 1108 BCE.
The vessel is carrying the
dead sun—depicted as
the god Osiris, complete
with ram's head—and his
entourage on their journey
through the underworld.

OCCUPATION: THIRD INTERMEDIATE

PERIOD TO ROMAN PERIOD

Introduction

The period of occupation covered by this chapter runs from 1069 BCE until the conquest by the Arabs in 641 CE. It was a time of great upheaval for the Egyptian populace, during which native rule was repeatedly overthrown by foreigners.

Below **Singing to Amun.** This bronze and gold sistrum—a rattle-like percussion instrument—belonged to Henuttawy, a singer for the god Amun in Dynasty 21. It depicts the goddess Hathor.

For millennia, Egypt had been the wealthiest and the most powerful state in the ancient Near East, the nation from which all culture and knowledge was said to originate. Little wonder, then, that it was taken over by so many foreign invaders—first the Libyans, then the Kushites from the Sudan, followed by the Persians, the Greeks, and, finally, the Romans.

A Resilient Culture

Yet Egypt did not go quietly under foreign rule. Each group of the alien sovereigns was separated by a relatively minor renaissance of native rule, at least minor enough that the Egyptians were not able to maintain their hold on their country for longer than a few years.

Despite these challenges, the people adapted with little difficulty to the new regimes, with their strange customs and requirements. The culture retained its vigor and the people their high-spirited attitude to life, and the ancient, distinguished past of the country was never forgotten. In fact, it was that past that drew conquerors to Egypt's shores; its art and culture were admired and copied by most of the foreign rulers. The Libyans, for example, assimilated so well into Egyptian society that in the royal art of this period they are indistinguishable from Egyptians.

The Divided Country

The Third Intermediate Period consists of Dynasties 21 through 24. Generally all three of the so-called "Intermediate Periods" were periods of decentralized power, with a sometimes dizzying succession of kings, many of whom were on the throne for a year or less. The first two of these periods were times during which Egypt sought to return to rule under one pharaoh. Both the Middle Kingdom, following the First Intermediate Period, and the New Kingdom, following the Second Intermediate Period, were times of great political and economic power in which the empire grew to its furthest extent and the greatest literature was produced.

The Third Intermediate Period is different; during this time, the fact of a divided rule was accepted and even exploited. Lower Egypt was governed by one ruler, Libyans in Dynasties 22 to 24, who often took the title of pharaoh and lived in one of the Delta cities. Upper Egypt was under the control of a second ruler who lived in

Thebes and generally did not take the title of pharaoh, perhaps paying nominal homage to the other ruler. Often the Upper Egyptian ruler was a member of the pharaoh's family, but this did not prevent many of these rulers from administering Upper Egypt as de facto pharaohs. Having a family member in control of Upper Egypt did not prevent a separation of powers, but did ensure no internecine strife, leaving the pharaohs to concentrate on their own areas of influence.

The pharaohs of the Late Period Dynasty 26 continued to rule a fragmented country from Sais in the western Delta. It was not until the First Persian Conquest (Dynasty 27) that the country was once again united, albeit under foreign rule. The ephemeral kings of the Twenty-Seventh, Twenty-Eighth, and Twenty-Ninth Dynasties had a tenuous hold on the throne, yet monuments in their name were erected throughout Egypt, indicating that their rule was widely accepted.

Ruling Through Amun

The religious climate of the Third Intermediate and Late Periods differed substantially from that of previous dynasties. Early in this era, the government became one that allied itself with the priests of Amun through the royal adoption of the office of high priest of Amun. In so doing, the southern general, Herihor, who initiated this action, started a trend for the rest of this era: Government as theocracy. This meant that the king was only the titular head of the country, ruling through the voice of Amun, enacting decrees that were handed down through oracles of the god.

Particularly prevalent through the Libyan dynasties, this theocratic style of government gave the kings the locally powerful backing they needed as interlopers in the royal office.

The Libyans reigned over a divided country, with an appointed high priest of Amun in the south as the chief administrator and the king in the north as receptor of the oracles and decrees. The theocracy continued to function, but the king was the font from which the decrees now flowed, rather than Amun, giving the king more power over Egypt as a whole. The dynasties that followed adopted a form of government more akin to the earlier governments of Egypt, with the king as supreme head of a united country, ruling every aspect of the government, including the priesthood of Amun.

Left **Hippo-shaped gaming table, c. 945–715** BCE. "58 holes" was a popular game in Egyptian times, using tables similar to this, but this one is unique.

Below **Meeting Amun.** This fresco from a Dynasty 26 (664–525 BCE) sarcophagus shows the deceased—on the right—being presented to the god Amun by ibis-headed Thoth.

Dynasty 21

Near the end of Rameses XI's reign, Egypt was governed by three powers: Smendes, an influential administrator of unknown origin, in the north (Lower Egypt); Herihor, a high priest of Amun, in the south (Upper Egypt); and, in between, Rameses XI himself.

Below **Sarcophagus of Psusennes I.** The impressive coffin of this Dynasty 21 king.

When Rameses XI died c. 1069 BCE, and with him the New Kingdom, Smendes proclaimed himself king, and created a set of titles linking him to the Ramessid kings. Even though he had no blood relationship to these former kings, Smendes and his rule were accepted by the priesthood of Amun in the south. On Herihor's death, Piankh assumed the role of high priest of Amun as well as general of the armies, and he passed these offices—minus the army of Nubia, which had seceded—to his son, Pinudjem, who took over in about 1070 BCE.

The Beginning of Foreign Rule

Following the death of Smendes in 1043 BCE and that of his successor, Amenemnisu, in 1039 BCE, the north was ruled by Psusennes I, the son of Pinudjem I from Thebes. In turn, the south was governed by his brother, Menkheperra. With both seats filled with members of the same family, the country had relative cohesion for a short while, until a new family ascended the throne in the north in the name of Osorkon the Elder, a Libyan, who was the son of the Chief of the Meshwesh, Sheshonq. The reign of Osorkon the Elder was a short six years, and he was followed on the throne by Psusennes II, an Egyptian, but it foreshadowed the Libyan dynasties soon to come.

Psusennes II was the last ruler of Dynasty 21, descended from the Theban commanders, and once a high priest himself. From the reign of Smendes onwards, the Theban priests of Amun supported the northern ruler, while still maintaining their status as commanders. The most telling evidence for this is the use of the northern kings' names in dating events and monuments in the south during this period. This was undoubtedly the result of Thebans being on the northern throne, and hence, familiar with both the people and the issues in the south.

Egypt, and being such was an indication of their strength and their right to rule. This did not seem to be the case with the Libyans. After the rule of Sheshonq I, the adherence to a New Kingdom ideal of kingship was not as apparent, and eventually Egypt was divided into as many as ten separate polities. These kings all took the titles of royalty, known as the fivefold titulary, one of which was the *r esu-bit* title, or King of Upper and Lower Egypt. Such a situation would have been anathema to the New Kingdom rulers, and would not have been endured. Some scholars have noted that this may betray a singular lack of understanding on the part of the Libyans of the real meaning of Egyptian kingship.

The arts of the period may also reveal this lack of comprehension in the portrayal of the king and his subjects. Egyptian kings had always had a specific symbolism in the reliefs and paintings, including certain activities previously reserved for the king. In the literature also, the role of the Egyptian king was quite precise, with certain genres of literature, such as donation stelae, reserved exclusively for the king. Yet, in this period, non-royal persons were depicted presenting offerings to the gods in kneeling and other positions that were once solely a royal privilege, and donation stelae dedicated by non-royal subjects begin to appear.

This may be seen as an offshoot of the practice of allowing for several different rulers in Egypt at one time. Certainly several of the non-royal owners of donation stelae and kneeling offering statues had also set themselves up as rulers. However, this could also be seen as a very real misunderstanding by the Libyans of the parameters of Egyptian kingship, a lack of knowledge of the liberties that must not be allowed by what were essentially commoners.

Libyans in Society

Libyans had long been one of the traditional "enemies" of Egypt, portrayed in an ethnic costume that included tattoos, long striped robes, and feathers worn as headdresses. They were a force to be reckoned with during the New Kingdom and must have caused considerable difficulty during Dynasty 21, although evidence during that period is scanty on all fronts. In all probability, they had been slowly integrating themselves into Egyptian society along the fringes of the western Delta throughout Dynasty 21. Their likely place of origin is Cyrenaica, a site along the eastern Mediterranean coast of Libya, and they appear to have been an aliterate, nomadic society. The Libyans were renowned for their military strength, and it seems to have been on this basis that they were accepted into Egyptian society with apparently relatively little disturbance to the population. Throughout their period on the throne, they are invisible both in the material archeological record and in the relief work, depicting themselves iconographically as Egyptians and leaving behind no identifiable evidence of a purely Libyan culture.

While the art and archeological remains show no difference between the Libyan culture and the Egyptian, there is evidence that they

Below **Royal scarab**. Found at Tanis, this breastplate displays the interesting workmanship of the time, including delicate turquoise inlay.

MACHIMOI

The *machimoi* (a Greek term meaning "warriors") were a warrior class in Egyptian society, originally composed primarily of Libyans. Later their ranks were filled with native Egyptians. As a class of society they were both a help and a hindrance to the throne. They were specifically a class of warrior, rather than simply an army, and as a result were powerful in their own right, with the very real potential to work against the king. The likely ballast to this latent possibility lay in the use of mercenaries by the rulers, an armed force made up of several different ethnic groups, including Greeks and Carians from Persia.

During later dynasties, in particular Dynasty 26, the mercenaries were the preferred royal military group, a situation that appeared to have been not to the liking of the *machimoi*, as they revolted during the reign of Apries in the Twenty-Sixth Dynasty and removed the king from the throne. The *machimoi* class remained a military force into the Ptolemaic period, acting as soldiers and policemen for the Greek pharaohs.

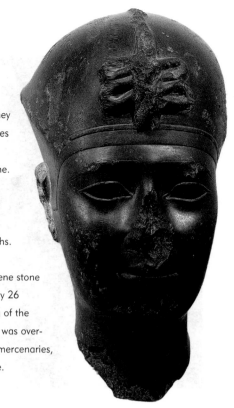

Right **Trouble in mind.** This serene stone portrait of King Apries of Dynasty 26 (664–332 BCE) suggests nothing of the troubles faced by this ruler, who was overthrown in a revolt by *machimoi* mercenaries, formerly protectors of the throne.

maintained certain parts of their ethnic identity. Most foreigners in Egypt, after a few years, took Egyptian names, thereby losing their ethnicity in the records; the Libyans consistently preserved their Libyan names. They also recorded much lengthier genealogies than was the custom for purely Egyptian rulers. Their attitude toward the kingship also differentiated them from the Egyptian kings; their tolerance for a divided country may point to a nomadic social structure.

By the time of Osorkon the Elder of Dynasty 21, they had become members of the highest rank of Egyptian society, and Libyan mercenaries had become the major part of the Egyptian army. Indeed, it has been suggested that, as early as the end of the New Kingdom, the entire Egyptian army was composed of Libyan mercenaries. It might not be such a surprise, then, that they became a key factor in the rule of Egypt relatively shortly thereafter. They managed to maintain that rule for the following four centuries, a further indication of their strength and administrative organization.

Fragmentation

Dynasties 23 and 24, while nominally Libyan, were ruled by a number of different men from a number of different centers. Most of them appear to have been Libyan, by their continuing use of the names Osorkon and Sheshonq, among other clues. The fragmentation of the Delta and other parts of the country persisted, with a number of the rulers calling themselves king,

the first of whom was Pedubastis I at Thebes. His rule coincided with that of Sheshonq III of Dynasty 22. From 818 BCE until 715 BCE, eight rulers were in power in various centers in Egypt, each reigning over relatively independent city-states, some of which were described as mini-kingdoms. This state of affairs continued until the end of Dynasty 23, with the reign of Tefnakht (c. 727–720 BCE), in the Delta. He was able, despite having only a very short reign, to consolidate his territory in the Delta as far south as Memphis. Upon his death, his son, Bakenrenef (c. 720–715 BCE), took over and ruled for an even shorter time. Bakenrenef is, nevertheless, the sole king of Dynasty 24.

Egypt had never responded well as a country, first, to the subjugation of the people by a foreign power, and, second, to a state of governmental decentralization. When the Libyan power structure began to break down, it paved the way for a new set of rulers to take the throne, which is what occurred. For the next 90 years, Egypt was to be ruled by the Nubians, a people who had long been under Egypt's yoke.

Below **Getting the eye.** This Dynasty 21 papyrus portrays an Egyptian named Hirweben kneeling to receive the eye of Horus.

The Kushite Kings

Nubia had been a vassal or province of Egypt almost since the beginning of its history, yet it now came to rule Egypt. The evidence of events in Nubia throughout Egypt's history, however, mainly relied on Egyptian presence and reportage of the area.

Below **Assyrian attacker.** The Kushites, while essentially controlling Egypt, had trouble with incursions by Assyrian kings such as Ashurbanipal.

Particularly during the period before the Twenty-Fifth Dynasty, evidence for Nubia as a whole, or "Kush" as the area was then known, is sparse, so that the means by which the eventual conquerors of Egypt rose to power is conjecture at its best.

Nubian Rulers

The first Kushite king of Egypt was Piy (c. 747–716 BCE). During the first half of his reign, Piy was content with ruling most of Egypt from Thebes, but in approximately 720 BCE, with the growing power of Tefnakht in the Delta becoming a threat, he advanced toward the Delta, to Memphis. Following the taking of Memphis by force, Piy returned to Kush and remained there until his death.

While it was relatively easy to maintain control of Egypt as far north as Thebes, it proved more difficult to keep a close eye on Lower Egypt, and Tefnakht, far from being restrained, was again gathering northern territory. This prompted the next Kushite ruler, Shabaqo (c. 716–702 BCE), to march north again and retake Lower Egypt. It was during the reign of Shabaqo that the Assyrians from Mesopotamia became a problem, in particular Sargon II. They continued to cause Egypt difficulties throughout the Kushite period, advancing and attacking Egypt within its own borders. Taharqo (c. 690–664 BCE), who was the grandson of

Piy and one of the most successful of the Nubian rulers, in terms of the amount of architecture built or restored, was himself subjugated under the Assyrian command of Esarhaddon.

The Nubian rulers were exceptionally taken with Egyptian culture, likely a product of having been their vassals for so many centuries. They worshiped Amun and paid particular attention to his temples while in Egypt. They adopted Egyptian names, many of them, and Egyptian methods of depiction in the reliefs. While they are frequently shown with specifically Nubian features, it is often difficult to differentiate between the Egyptian and the Nubian monarchs. This is found not only in Egypt but also in Nubia, which they continued to rule simultaneously with ruling Egypt. Piy's tomb, for example, in el-Kurru, the traditional burial place for the Kushite kings, is entirely Egyptian in character and decoration, except for the team of chariot horses buried close by.

Battles With the Assyrians

Toward the end of the Third Intermediate Period the Assyrians were increasingly intent on taking over Egypt. The Kushites had difficulty in controlling the Delta and preventing rebellion, a fact that the Assyrians used to their advantage. Despite a treaty signed by Shabaqo and Sargon II that lasted for approximately fifteen years, the Assyrians were taking more and more of what were once Egyptian holdings in Syria–Palestine. Taharqo launched an unsuccessful military expedition against the Assyrians in 671 BCE, which resulted in the Assyrian taking of Memphis and the retreat of Taharqo to Nubia. Esarhaddon's conquering of Memphis would not have been possible without the compliance of the rebellious leaders in Lower Egypt. When Esarhaddon died en route to put down rebellion fomented by the Nubians in Lower Egypt, his son Ashurbanipal sent a force to deal with the rebels. With this accomplished, the force returned to Assyria. The compliance of Lower Egypt upon which the Assyrians depended, however, was not one upon which they could rely, and, almost as soon as he returned to Assyria, the Lower Egyptians began courting the favor of Taharqo. Ashurbanipal's retribution was swift and terrible, slaying all but one of the members of the Saite family rulers, leaving the last, Necho I, as a vassal ruler from Sais, and his son, Psamtek, on the throne of the city-state, Athribis, located in the Delta region.

Meanwhile, Taharqo's successor, Tanutamani, undertook another expedition to the north, with the aim of reconquering territory previously taken by Piy. While he was successful in this aim, the northern rulers sending letters of surrender, it was a Pyrrhic victory, for the armies of the Assyrians under Ashurbanipal returned and traveled as far south as Thebes. They took the city, looted it, and burned it to the ground, something that had never happened before in Egyptian history, and this signaled the end of Kushite rule. The transfer of power from the Nubians to the Saites was engineered by the Assyrians. Nekau (Necho) I had died, and his son, Psamtek I, became ruler of Sais with the blessing of the Assyrians. With the retreat of Tanutamani to Napata after the sacking of Thebes, the Nubian dynasty was at an end. Unfortunately, the information we have thereafter on the final king is sparse, even in his own city of Napata.

Left **Art in miniature.** This small hinged case, of bronze inlaid with silver and gold, dates to the Twenty-Fifth Dynasty (747–656 BCE).

Below **Ptah and Anubis.** The two gods are featured on this cartonnage (the "second skin" stuck directly onto a mummy) of Res-Paka-Shuty, a priest from around Dynasty 25.

The Saite Period

The Saite dynasty is the last one that ruled a relatively united Egypt. Despite rumblings in the Delta from stubbornly autonomous principalities in the west, the rest of Egypt was ruled by one ruler at a time.

Right **Looking back.** As with much art of the Saite era, this fresco of the god Seker recalls the artworks of Pre-dynastic times.

Below **Gods of the underworld.** This Dynasty 26 fresco is from the sarchophagus of one Tachepenkhonsu.

The first ruler was Psamtek I (c. 664–610 BCE). Psamtek I's long reign of 54 years, and those of his successors in the dynasty, constituted a short-lived renaissance for Egypt, but one that brought Egyptian culture and government to a level of greatness reminiscent of the New Kingdom. Egypt's status in Syria–Palestine was briefly renewed and the art produced was of the finest quality.

An Uneasy Peace

Psamtek I was placed on the throne by Assyria, and, with its blessing, was left to rule in peace provided he did not attempt to encroach upon Assyrian land. In spite of this powerful backing, certain cities in the Delta refused to accept Psamtek I as sole ruler of Egypt, and it was necessary for him to convince them, militarily, to come to terms with his leadership. Once this was achieved, around his eighth regnal year, Egypt became more open to foreign trading markets and influences. The Saite kings were reliant on the use of foreign mercenaries in the armies, often used as foils to the power of the native Egyptian warriors, the *machimoi*. Around the same time, or shortly thereafter, a

DIVINE ADORATRICE

The Divine Adoratrice, also known as the God's Wife of Amun, was a celibate position in the great temple of Amun at Thebes held by close female relatives of the reigning king. The title has been found as early as the pre-Amarna Eighteenth Dynasty. During the Kushite period and the following Saite period, this position was used to great political advantage by the pharaohs, as a means of ensuring the loyalty of the ancient city of Thebes. It was also a position of great influence for the woman who held it, who was, in effect, the wife of the most powerful deity in the Egyptian pantheon.

Left **A powerful woman.** This statue of Karomama, Divine Adoratrice of Amun at Thebes, is of bronze inlaid with pink gold, silver, and glass.

burgeoning trade with Greece began, perhaps a natural consequence of opening the borders to foreign soldiers. The Greek and other foreign immigrants in Egypt were settled in towns in the Delta and permitted to conduct business from there, with special dispensations from the pharaohs, in particular Ahmose II (Amasis) (c. 570–526 BCE), the second-to-last king of Dynasty 26.

As well as fostering trade with certain parts of the Mediterranean, the pharaohs attempted to reclaim foreign territory in the Levant that was, in antiquity, under their rule. While initially successful in terms of capture, it proved beyond the abilities of the Egyptians to maintain the territory, largely due to the massive power and might of the Assyrian rulers, who were in the process of empire building.

A series of royal succession problems in Assyria spelled the end of the Assyrian empire, but the Persian kings of the Achaemenid family were already in the process of building an even larger and more powerful empire than that of the Mesopotamians, and it was this empire and its rulers that ultimately brought about the end of this late age of the rebirth of Egyptian values and power.

Archaization and Art

One of the hallmarks of the Saite period for Egyptologists is the extremely fine quality of the art that hearkens back to the greatest periods of Egyptian culture, the Old and Middle Kingdoms. Not only does it appear that the best artists were fostered in the court, but, more importantly, there seems to have been an explicit desire to imitate the artistic scenes and iconography in Egypt's brilliant past. This is found in the copying of certain funerary reliefs, which must have been well known to both the artists and the people requesting them. Generally, these reliefs were so faithfully reproduced that, on first glance, they cannot be distinguished from the original scenes.

This phenomenon is well known in Egyptian art and literature, and has been given the term "archaization." Throughout Egyptian history, artistic or literary reference to the past through the use of archaic forms of the language and through the duplication of certain standard artistic representations was used to pay honor to the luminous and magnificent history of Egypt's renowned culture. Archaization reached its apogee during Dynasty 26. It is notable that the scenes chosen for reproduction were not ones featuring royalty and great deeds, but homely scenes involving, for example, a woman sitting under a tree picking fruit, a baby in a sling across her chest. It seems it was the notion of a great legacy of "being Egyptian" that was the principal behind archaization, not a reflection of Egypt's great ancient kings.

Following the Saite period, while certain artistic styles were adopted by foreign rulers in Egypt, never again was the art and literature so precisely imitated.

Below **The finest of work.** This intricately decorated sarcophagus belonged to Lady Oudjarenes, who lived during Dynasty 26.

The First Persian Conquest

With the defeat of Psamtek III by the Persian Cambyses II at Pelusium in 525 BCE, the final Egyptian renaissance was at an end. The Egyptians were no longer a match for the Persians, who were stronger militarily and strategically.

This defeat of Psamtek III, who was one of the Saite kings, rulers of an era in which earlier Egyptian culture was revered, signaled the beginning of a new period of foreign rule.

The Achaemenid Empire

There is some question in the contemporary literature concerning the Persian rule, whether it was a tremendously difficult burden for the Egyptians to bear, or whether the Persians made serious attempts to adapt their rule to the Egyptian culture and religion. According to contemporary Egyptian sources, the Persians showed respect for the Egyptian religion and native way of governing. According to classical sources, however, the Persians were the epitome of the harsh overlord, with no thought or feeling for the Egyptian sensibility.

Cambyses II was responsible for an infamous incident that occurred during an attempt to gain control of the oases. While marching to Siwa oasis, he lost an entire army to the desert sands, never to be seen again. Whether apocryphal or factual, this story left the impression, likely false, of incompetence on the part of Cambyses that remains to this day.

Whatever the case, when Cambyses II died in 522 BCE a rebellion took place that was put down within three years by Cambyses II's successor, Darius. At this time, he regained complete control of the country. Darius seems to have continued his predecessor's policy of maintaining and rebuilding temples, thereby paying homage to the native deities and propagandizing at the same time. Much of Egyptian government did

Left **Military might.** This fifth-century BCE frieze, from the palace of the Persian king Artaxerxes II, shows two resolute archers, reminding all who saw it of the Persians' power.

not change; the workings of the bureaucracy remained the same, and this gradually led to an Egyptianizing on the part of some of the Persian administrators put into place by the kings.

What did change was the upper levels of government. The Persians installed their own men in the most important and influential positions. Supreme among these was a satrap or governor, making Egypt a Persian satrapy or province and thus part of the empire. As such, the Egyptian government officials were expected to act in accordance with the desires and needs of the Persian Empire. Yet, the history and former power of the Egyptian administration lent it a certain sense of pride and entitlement. Xerxes, Darius' successor, was not as fastidious as previous kings in paying attention to Egyptian customs and religion, but later kings made great efforts in that direction. If this was intended to win over the Egyptian people, it failed.

Despite the apparently generally benevolent rule of the Persians, there were a number of reasons for the Egyptian rebellions that arose later in Dynasty 27. The Persian king ruled from Iran, and, although a satrap was installed in the king's place, the king was still an absentee landlord. The Egyptians were renowned throughout the Mediterranean as xenophobes, and this would have made alliances between Egypt and Persia uneasy at best. Persia's presence in Egypt did nothing to prevent local rebellions from being fomented, and in fact the absence of the king, coupled with Egypt's aversion to foreigners generally and foreign rulers specifically, likely propelled the idea of rebellion from thought to action.

Rebellion

The primary rebellions, those that contributed in the most productive way toward the eventual expulsion of the Persians, were led by Amyrtaios, from Sais, and Inaros the son of Psamtek III. Amyrtaios was descended or claimed to be descended from the Saite kings of

Dynasty 26. Both had the support of Greek troops, which strengthened their numbers and aided in the overthrow of the Persians. Inaros was first in the sequence, and declared himself king, having gathered support throughout the Delta. Amyrtaios was one of the gathered allies, and together they retook Egypt as far south as Memphis. At this point, the Persians retaliated. The Greek troops that had accompanied Inaros' and Amyrtaios' forces abandoned the fight and fled. Inaros was taken and eventually executed. The Persian leader allowed Inaros' sons to rule from the Delta, and wisely avoided visiting repercussions upon them that might have incited rebellion once again. This kept the peace in Egypt for a short while, 30 years or so, but with the death of Artaxerxes, Darius II ascended to the Persian throne in 424 BCE. His reign was similar to that of the first Darius; however, Egypt was ripe for revolt again. With the death of Darius II in 404 BCE, the grandson of Amyrtaios, also named Amyrtaios, declared himself king, after approximately six years of covert actions. There was no response to this from the Persians, likely due to their own succession difficulties.

Above **King Darius I (521–486 BCE).** This relief shows Darius on his throne at Persepolis in Persia (Iran). The Achaemenid kings preferred to rule from Iran rather than basing themselves in Egypt.

Left **Persian jewelry.** This Dynasty 27 earthenware amulet bears the name of Darius I.

The Last Independence

Dynasty 28 consisted of one king, Amyrtaios, whose reign was short: 404–399 BCE. Yet he managed to take the country out of the hands of the Persians and put it back into the hands of an Egyptian native. This was accomplished as far south as Memphis.

Right **Well protected.** The figure of Dynasty 30 king Nectanebo II receives protection from a god-like falcon. In this time of turmoil, he would have needed of it.

As the Delta had always been the most vulnerable to attack from outside—and during the latter part of Egyptian history this was particularly true—it was very important to ensure that this part of the country was held as securely as possible, an almost impossible task.

Ephemeral Kingship

Evidence for Dynasty 29 is scanty, as with so much of this period, but what is available shows that each of the three primary kings who made up the dynasty—Nepherites I, Hakor, and Nepherites II—had short reigns, and that those reigns were turbulent, ending in their assassination or deposition from the throne. The entire dynasty lasted only 20 years. Nepherites I (c. 399–393 BCE) was likely a military man from Mendes in the eastern Delta,

Below **Sphinx of King Nepherites.** The king was to have very little time to contemplate such artworks, ruling for only a few years.

and is thought to have been of Libyan descent. How he took over from Amyrtaios is unknown, whether it was through a coup or on Amyrtaios' death. A contemporary papyrus states that Nepherites I went to war against Amyrtaios and had him executed in Memphis. Thereafter, he established Mendes as his new capital, and may have had his coronation at Memphis or Sais, likely with a political agenda. What little archeological evidence is left of his tenure on the throne indicates that he was intent on renewing Egypt, along the lines of Dynasty 26, and thus, his royal Horus title was the same as Psamtek I. His reign lasted only six years, according to the king-lists, although the last regnal year on a monument attributed to him is the fourth.

After Nepherites I, the rulers of two separate groups reigned for less than a year each, one for only a few months. Following these ephemeral kings was Hakor, who had a reign of 14 years. During this period, Hakor seemed bent on legitimizing his right to the throne, although succeeding kings represented him as a usurper of the throne with no true royal ties. His son, Nepherites II, ruled for only a short few months before being deposed by Nectanebo I, the first king of Dynasty 30.

Staving off the Persians

The military during this entire period was peculiarly powerful, given the short-lived reigns of its rulers. This is particularly true of the reign of Hakor; he managed to hold off the Persian armies with a military force that was considerably better organized and maintained than it had been in the near past. The Egyptian army was now operating under the rule of a single man, which aided greatly in keeping it loyal, and

Right **Immortal warrior**. One of the "immortals," the elite corps of the Persian army. The Persians remained a constant threat during this period, and eventually regained the control they had had earlier.

the navy was exceptional, the best in the world at the time. Added to these factors, the army contained Greek mercenaries, who fought in the Delta to great effect. The Greeks also had strong feelings against the Persians, which helped with loyalty to the Egyptian king.

The Persian army was intent on recapturing Egypt; together with Cyprus, these two countries were the last in the Near East to become part of the Persian Empire, hence for the Persians it was especially important to regain an Egyptian foothold. This made a strong military force an urgent necessity for the Egyptians, and for three years Hakor was in a good position to withstand advances by the Persian armies. The death of Hakor was an unfortunate turn of events for Egypt; as with so many of the pharaohs during this period, he left Egypt in an unstable position regarding his succession. When his son succeeded to the throne, he was rapidly overthrown by the ruler of the rival Delta city of Sebennytos. This internal strife had the effect of destabilizing the armed forces and left Egypt in a precarious state, vulnerable to outside attack.

THE LAST EGYPTIAN-MADE TEMPLES

The rulers of Dynasties 28 and 29 were quite spectacularly short-lived and unstable, especially when compared with the heyday of Egyptian history. Yet, despite this disability, the rulers of these dynasties were able to put into place building programs that added considerably to the monumental structures at Karnak on the east bank of Thebes and Medinet Habu on the west bank, as well as at Elephantine, among other southern sites. In the north, work was done at Mendes, the capital of Dynasty 29, Memphis, and Saqqara. The building programs seemed primarily to have consisted of adding portions to already existing structures; however, this was a time-honored Egyptian method of leaving one's mark, and had the added element of honoring those pharaohs who had gone before, by recognizing their great architectural achievements.

Nectanebo I and II

Upon gaining control of the Egyptian throne, Nectanebo I had himself crowned at Mendes, as his predecessor, Nepherites I, had done, and thus began the final native Egyptian dynasty. The struggle for the throne and the successful succession are unclear, there being no records for this particular issue; however, it seems likely that Nectanebo I was a member of the royal family of Dynasty 29, using the Delta as a base, without neglecting Upper Egypt under his rule.

The primary concern during the reigns of Nectanebo I and his successors was the ongoing Persian threat from the east. In order to counter this, the pharaoh built a series of fortifications along one of the eastern branches of the Nile in the Delta, the Pelusiac. When the Persians attacked, with the Greeks (their allies at the time), they were forearmed with knowledge of the Egyptians' preparations along the Pelusiac,

and began their renewed assault on Egypt along the Mendesian branch, which led into the Mediterranean nearer the center of the Delta. This attack was ultimately unsuccessful due to mistrust between the two allies—Persia and Greece—and a timely Nile inundation that rendered the landscape impassable; the Egyptians were able to counter the attack and drove the invaders out.

In 365 BCE, Nectanebo I put forth his son, Teos, as the successor to the throne. Teos, the general of the royal armies, was involved in repelling the Persians; upon gaining the rule of Egypt from his father, he helped pay for the necessary military campaigns by taxing the Egyptians heavily, an action that was likely instrumental in his ultimate downfall. While on campaign in the Levant with his grandson, the future Nectanebo II, his own son, Tjahepimu, declared Nectanebo II king, replacing Teos.

Nectanebo II assumed the rule of Egypt at a time when the ancient Near East was in turmoil, largely due to problems with succession in Persia. This period of instability in the Persian royal house provided the satrapies throughout the Near East with the space to rebel against the Achaemenids' unwelcome rule, and Egypt helped by providing troops for a rebellion by the city of Sidon. Once the Persian succession to the throne was in hand, however, this period of attempting to shake off the Persian shackles ended, and Persia advanced on Egypt, following much the same route they had taken, with no success, years earlier. This time, however, they were successful, and two years later, Egypt fell once again and finally to Persian rule.

The Final Revival

During Dynasty 30, Egypt experienced a short-lived revival in both their native government and culture. Nectanebo I prompted a renaissance in nationalism and the arts, and participated in all the religious cults of the time, including that of the Apis bull at Memphis. Evidence of his building activities, largely centered on temple additions, can be found throughout Egypt, from the island of Philae, south of the first Nile cataract at Aswan, to the eastern Delta sites of Per-Sopdu and Tanis. At religious sites in between—Heliopolis, Memphis, Elkab, and Karnak—indications of Nectanebo I's presence can be seen in the temples and other structures. The widespread signs of this architectural piety appear to be a royal program of reconstruction and new creations, begun during the early years of his reign, and carried on by his dynastic successors. The indications are that this was a calculated and methodical plan on the part of the king in an attempt to reinstill a sense of pride and autonomy in Egypt.

Nectanebo I's great-grandson, Nectanebo II, followed his ancestor's example, and the evidence of his building activities can be found in even more sites than those of Nectanebo I; approximately one hundred different sites provide proof of Nectanebo II's continuing program of restoration and building.

Both Nectanebos shared the problem of a powerful priestly elite comprised of native Egyptians. In part to bolster the allegiance of the only native group wielding any kind of power in Egypt during this multicultural period, the rulers endowed several of the largest religious estates and joined in the ritual practices of cults throughout Egypt. Nectanebo II, for example, initiated his reign by officiating at a festival of the Apis bull in Memphis.

The arts and artists also seem to have benefited during this period. The artworks and relief from the Thirtieth Dynasty stand with earlier artistic endeavors as among some of the most accomplished in Egypt's long history. While the style may have changed, thanks to the introduction of foreign styles of representation, the execution remained of the highest quality, aiding in the lasting impression of this final native dynasty as one of nationalist pride and feeling.

Left **Religion and politics.** A painted limestone stela dedicated to the sacred Apis bull. Both Nectanebo I and II were careful to make the proper observance of popular Egyptian religions, primarily to appease the priestly elites.

Left **Honoring a former king.** This fourteenth-century CE Greek manuscript depicts Alexander honoring a statue of Nectanebo—who, it was suggested by the Greeks, may have been his father.

The Second Persian Conquest

With the defeat and flight of Nectanebo II to Nubia and the resubduing of the country by Artaxerxes III, native rule in Egypt came to an end. The Persians—who had previously ruled Egypt for almost two centuries—were again in control.

Below **An uncertain lineage.** In this fourteenth-century CE Greek manuscript, Alexander the Great is seen with his mother, Olympias, and father, Philip of Macedon. Yet it was suggested that Philip may not have been Alexander's real father.

This second period of Persian rule was to last but a short time, however, due to regicide in Persia and the appearance of Philip II of Macedon on the horizon.

A Time of Harsh Rule

The new conqueror of Egypt committed heinous acts upon re-establishing Persian rule, which included the demolishing and plundering of the temples and defenses of the major cities in the Delta. The cult treasures of the temples were then sold back to the priests at exorbitant rates. A Persian satrap, Pherendates, was installed and foreign rule resumed. The evidence for this period comes primarily from Greek and Egyptian sources, and for the most part indicates a harsh, incompetent, and vicious rule.

The Persians made use of Egyptian administrators, such as Somtutefnakht, for whom records exist. He was a priest of Sakhmet, the Egyptian lion-goddess, who left an autobiographical inscription describing the Persian takeover of Egypt, an action he ascribed to the abandonment of Egypt by the gods. Together with Harsiese, another Egyptian administrator, possibly a vizier, the evidence points to the use of natives in some of the highest offices in the land. In turn, this may indicate the difficulty that Persia encountered in attempting to rule a restless Egyptian population from afar.

This renaissance, of a sort, of Persian rule in Egypt was short-lived, despite what must have seemed at the time to be a permanent situation. The Achaemenid Empire lasted for less than a decade. The rule of Artaxerxes III was cut short by his murder by poison and the similar murders of his family by the general Bagoas. The general put Arses on the throne, who faced a similar fate within a few years, and the throne was then filled by Darius III. Two years into his reign, in 334 BCE, he was deposed by Alexander the Great. The then-satrap of Egypt, Mazaces, handed the country over to Alexander and, for the final time, Egypt was no longer politically autonomous.

Alexander and Nectanebo: A Greek Perspective

According to a late literary Greek text, the father of Alexander was not Philip of Macedon but rather Nectanebo, the last king of Egypt—whether I or II is not mentioned. In this tale, Nectanebo was a mighty sorceror, as well as the Egyptian ruler. When Egypt fell to the Persians, Nectanebo escaped to Macedonia to live in the capital city, where he prospered as a magician and soothsayer. Olympias, the future Alexander's

Left **Final stand**. Darius III, the last of the Persian kings of Egypt, takes on Alexander the Great at the Battle of Issus in 333 BCE.

mother, had been told by her husband, Philip of Macedon, that, should she not conceive a son when he came back from war, he would have nothing further to do with her. Concerned, Olympias consulted Nectanebo, whose reputation as a great magician preceded him. Nectanebo fell in lust with the beauty of Olympias and he determined to father her son himself. Coming to

KHABABASH

During the second Persian occupation of Egypt, a rebel by the name of Khababash was successful in ruling Egypt, although this was for a very short period of time (c. 338–336 BCE) and, most likely, in name only. From his very un-Egyptian name, it seems probable that he was either Libyan or Nubian, although nothing is known of his origins. He seemed to have been operating in the Delta, in particular the northeastern Delta, but the only three sources for his existence are a stela from a later period, mentioning the donation by him of a piece of land to the gods of Buto, a legal document that is dated using his first regnal year, and a sarcophagus of a sacred Apis bull that mentions the second regnal year

Olympias in the guise of the god Amun, he sired Alexander. Using magic, Nectanebo convinced an unwilling Philip that Alexander was indeed the son of a deity, not of an interloper in his marital bed, though Philip maintained reservations regarding Alexander's true parentage. The Nectanebo portion of the tale, a romance in the tradition of late antiquity, ends with Nectanebo's death at the hands of Alexander, who, upon realizing that he has committed patricide, buries his father with full honors.

The use of Nectanebo as the antagonist in such a story, according him magical powers and the cunning of a snake (in this case, literally), is an indication of the perhaps wary esteem in which Egypt was held by the cultures in the ancient Near East. The ancient lineage of Egypt's culture and the memory of its once-great military and political power kept a certain amount of international respect for Egypt alive in its dying years, when, in reality, it no longer held even a vestige of that power.

Below **Crouching lion**. A Late Period statue of a lion goddess, possibly Sakhmet. An Egyptian priest at the time explained the loss of Egypt to Persia as due to abandonment by the gods.

TEMPLES AND PTOLEMIES
Alexander the Great in Egypt

Just 11 years after Artaxerxes III recaptured Egypt for the Persian Empire, Alexander the Great came to power. As a young man of 20, Alexander had taken over as King Alexander III of Macedon in 336 BCE. In 334 BCE he led his army into Asia to attack the Persians.

Above **Alexander the Egyptian.** This statue of the Macedonian leader portrays him very much in the style of the pharaohs.

Right **Amun's man.** This stela belonged to Ousirour, a priest of Amun. Alexander well knew the value of honoring Egyptian gods.

In 332 BCE Alexander captured Tyre, on the Phoenician coast, in an eight-month siege. He moved south through Sinai with his Macedonian and Greek army, and reached the northeastern fortress of Pelusium. His fleet was offshore. The Persian satrap (provincial governor) of Egypt, Mazaces, knew that Alexander had defeated Darius III in battle, and taken control of Syria. Knowing there was no hope of Persian reinforcements, Mazaces decided on prompt surrender. There was to be no new struggle for control of Egypt.

Alexander and his army marched south on the east side of the Nile, while his fleet sailed up river to Memphis. Once he had taken over the capital, he moved to show his gratitude to the gods—both Greek and Egyptian.

Celebrations in Two Cultures

Athletic and musical contests, a kind of mini-Olympic Games, were a familiar celebration for his Greek and Macedonian followers. The top performers in sports and music were shipped in from Greece to give Alexander's Greek celebration the sheen of a top-quality event.

But, unlike Artaxerxes III before him, Alexander decided to show respect for Egyptian religion by sacrificing to the Apis bull—the god of the most popular cult in fourth-century BCE Egypt. After the celebrations Alexander moved down river to the western edge of the Nile Delta. There he gave orders for the foundation of a city to be named Alexandria—after himself.

Alexandria

Alexandria is strategically sited. The Nile flood made it impossible to sail into the mouths of the river for several months of the year. This impeded trade and contact with the world outside Egypt. Alexandria,

which is clear to the west of the Nile mouths, has a fine natural harbor, and to the south of the city is Lake Mariout, which links up via canals to the Nile. Goods that came into Alexandria by sea could be transferred to Nile boats and taken inland for distribution throughout Egypt. Egyptian produce could easily come down river into Alexandria, and be shipped abroad.

Alexander personally decided where the marketplace of Alexandria should be, and the city walls, and the temples. He said what gods were to have temples: Greek gods, but also the Egyptian goddess Isis. According to one legend, the builders used flour to mark out the line where Alexander told them the perimeter of the city was to be. Birds came down, ate the flour, and flew away. When Alexander sent for prophets to interpret the incident, they said the new city would feed the whole inhabited world, and those who were born in it would reach all parts of the world.

The Oracle

In no hurry to leave Egypt and go on conquering the Persian Empire, Alexander moved on to the Western Desert, where he took his followers on a journey to the temple of Amun (known to Greeks as Zeus Ammon) in the oasis of Siwa,

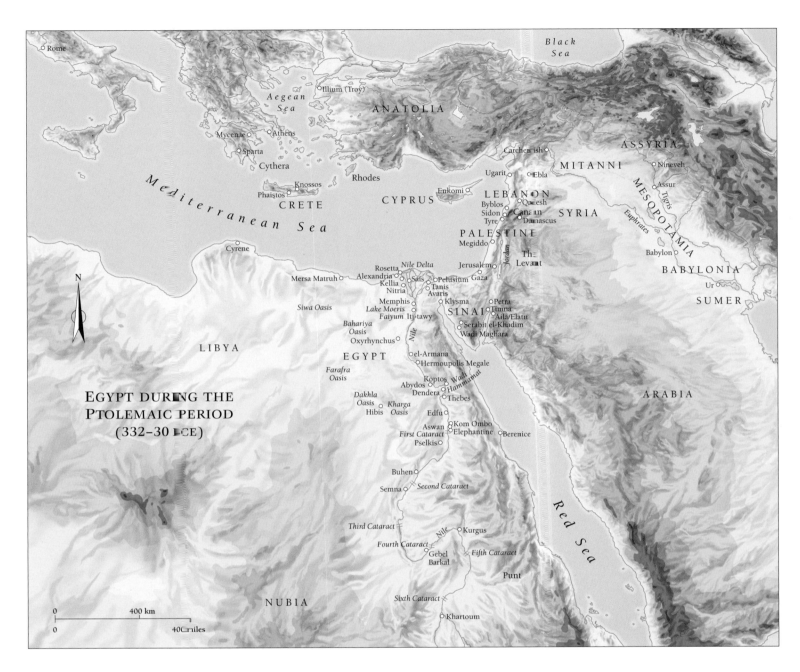

EGYPT DURING THE PTOLEMAIC PERIOD (332–30 BCE)

which is today just 30 miles (50 kilometres) inside the Libyan border. Located in a depression below sea level on the edge of the Great Sand Sea, Siwa has lakes and palm trees. On the way there, as recorded by Alexander's biographer Plutarch, there was rain (an almost unheard-of event), meaning that Alexander's men did not suffer the hardship of thirst while going across the desert; and then, when the guides got confused about the route, ravens appeared in the sky and led the way to Siwa.

In another version of the story, Ptolemy, who was the son of Lagos, later to be Alexander's successor as king of Egypt, wrote that the party was led out of the desert to the oasis by snakes which hissed until the Greeks and Macedonians started following them.

But he had a motive for telling the story that way: snakes were a symbol of royal power and pharaohship in Egypt. The uraeus (sacred serpent) formed part of the crown. So, by saying the snakes led Alexander to the Amun temple, he implied that the snakes recognized Alexander (his own predecessor) as the rightful pharaoh.

At Siwa, Alexander went to the Twenty-Sixth Dynasty temple of Amun, built by Amasis, the last Egyptian pharaoh before Cambyses' Persian conquest. The priests came to greet him and addressed him as the son of the god. This was, from their viewpoint, normal: Alexander had become king of Egypt (there was no coronation ceremony, but he took royal titles in the proper Egyptian form), and the standard belief was that the pharaoh was the son of Amun.

Above **The lion god Aker.** A papyrus from the *Book of the Dead*. Such gods maintained a following throughout Egyptian history.

The incident made an impression on Alexander, especially because he went on and asked the prophet for an oracle from the god, inquiring whether any of the murderers of his father (meaning Philip II of Macedon, who had been assassinated four years before) had gone unpunished. The prophet told Alexander he must not speak ill-omened words, because his was not a mortal father. Some of the writers about Alexander connect Alexander's later wish to be recognized as a god with this moment.

Egypt in Alexander's Empire

Back in Memphis, before marching on to Mesopotamia and Persia, Alexander appointed deputies to rule Egypt in his stead. He wisely chose two Egyptians as civil rulers. This was consistent with the messages for the Egyptian people which were implied in his worship of Apis and his visit to Amasis' temple at Siwa: He had been telling them that Persian overlordship was in the past and things were going to be different in Egypt.

At the same time he was taking no chances about possible rebellions. He left six of his

A BULL GOD

The Apis bull lived in a special enclosure in his temple in Memphis, and was treated as a living god. Worshippers could go to a special viewing window to see him. When an old Apis bull died the priests and all of Memphis would go into mourning, and preparations would be made to mummify the body.

Then the priests would journey out from Memphis and begin to search for the newborn calf that was the next incarnation

of the god. He had to have exactly the right markings—they were the sign of his divinity. When a possible calf was found the priests would consult, and, once it was agreed that the correct calf had been identified, he would be brought back to the Apis temple in joyful procession.

Left **Apis bull, Ptolomeic era.** This statue, made of diorite, shows the bull god with two significant features above its head: The sun disc and the sacred serpent.

Macedonian and Greek officers, three of them Companions (officers of the elite Macedonian cavalry force), in command of his garrisons and mercenary forces in Egypt, and two Greeks (Apollonius and Kleomenes) as governors of "Libya" and "Arabia" (that is, the Western and Eastern Deserts of Egypt).

These plans did not work out very well. Doloaspis, one of the Egyptian rulers Alexander appointed, refused to take the job. Initially Petisis, the other appointee, was left alone as ruler of Egypt, though with no powers over the military forces. But somehow, before Alexander died, Kleomenes, who had originally been in charge of the Eastern Desert, came to be the overall ruler of Egypt.

Corruption

Kleomenes had the reputation of being a sharp financier—or rather, a completely ruthless profiteer. When there was a famine in Greece in 329 BCE, for example, he banned the export of corn, and then, when there were complaints, he let up and allowed the exports but with an extortionate level of duty.

He did not share his king's positive attitude to Egyptian religion. He called together all the priests and told them that religion was costing the country as a whole too much, so the funding of temples would have to be reduced. Lands and revenues would be taken away from the priests and handed over to the crown. Priests, not surprisingly, began to scheme to stop this plan impacting on their own temples—let someone else's lands get expropriated, they figured. They started to go quietly to Kleomenes to offer him secret payoffs if he would allow them to preserve their temples and priesthoods. He was glad to accept.

Kleomenes had Egypt under his control for nearly ten years. The Egyptians, however, were not the only targets of his profiteering. His own boss was not exempt. After Alexander's best friend, Hephaestion, died in 324 BCE, Alexander sent a large amount of money to Kleomenes with instructions to build a huge temple in memory of Hephaestion on the island of Pharos, off the coast of Alexandria. Kleomenes took the money, but building did not commence.

The fact that Alexander died at Babylon in 323 BCE and never came back to Egypt was not enough to save Kleomenes. Ptolemy, after he reached Egypt with instructions to take it over, had Kleomenes put to death.

Left **Alexander as a young man**. Alexander was only 20 when he became king of Macedon, and he wasted no time in conquering other lands, including Egypt.

Below **A neglected friend**. Alexander (left) goes hunting with his friend Hephaestion, who, when he died, was denied a proper burial by the corrupt actions of Egypt's governor, Kleomenes.

The First Ptolemies

When Alexander the Great died in Nebuchadnezzar's palace at Babylon on June 10, 323 BCE, the contest between his generals that he predicted would be his "Funeral Games" began.

Above right **Ptolemy I, satrap of Alexandria 323–285 BCE, silver coin.**

H e had given his ring to Perdiccas on his deathbed. When the generals had declared Alexander's older brother Philip Arrhidaeus king, together with his unborn son (who became Alexander IV of Macedon), they reassigned the provinces of his vast empire to new governors—called "satraps." Ptolemy, son of Lagos, one of Alexander's bodyguards, was made satrap of Egypt. He traveled there immediately and took over.

Above **Cartouche of Alexander the Great, relief, fragment of temple wall.** The cartouche (or *shenu*) records Egyptian royal names.

A Sacred Relic

Meanwhile, Alexander's body was laid in a golden coffin packed with spices and put in a carriage which had been built with a barrel-vaulted roof, pillars, and friezes decorated with scenes summing up Alexander's character. The wondrous carriage, pulled by sixty-four mules and escorted by a crowd of mechanics and road-menders, was sent off towards Macedon, where Alexander's ancestors were buried.

Somewhere on the road the funeral procession was intercepted by Ptolemy's men. Without a fight, they diverted the carriage to Egypt.

Alexander may have wanted to be buried at Siwa, but that was not to be. For a few years his remains were probably kept at Memphis, where Ptolemy based his government. Then a shrine called the Sema ("Memorial"), or the Soma ("Body"), was built in the centre of Alexandria, and Alexander rested there for the next five hundred years and more.

Food for the Crocodiles

Perdiccas could not tolerate the independent line Ptolemy was taking. In 322 BCE he attempted to reassert his position as Alexander's most important successor by taking Egypt from Ptolemy. Marching his army to Egypt, he went up river and prepared to cross and attack.

Things looked desperate for Ptolemy. His forces were small. He and his successors did not

Right **Detail of sanctuary of Philip Arrhidaeus at Karnak.** The carved relief shows barques of the sun and has retained some of the original color.

trust Egyptians to fight for them until more than a hundred years later, and there had not been time to build up a strong immigrant army.

Perdiccas' men found a place where they thought they could ford the river, and began to cross. At first it went well, but the sandy bottom started to wash away, and a strong current began to sweep soldiers and horses off their feet. As they were carried floundering down the river, crocodiles moved in and began to feed.

The retreat was sounded. That evening in camp, some of his own officers killed Perdiccas. One of them was Seleucus, later to be king of Syria. Ptolemy was left in undisputed possession of the kingdom, which he and his descendants would keep for nearly three hundred years.

Wedding Bells

With the defeat of Perdiccas, Ptolemy secured his border from external threats. To maintain his

Right **Xerxes I, King of Persia, followed by two servants and fly-swats, relief, Persepolis, Iran.** According to a fourth century BCE inscription, Xerxes had confiscated land in the Nile Delta, and "had not giving anything of his to the gods of Pe Tep."

position as ruler of Egypt, however, he would need the security of a son and heir. Fortunately, Antipater, the trusted officer whom Alexander had left in charge of Macedon while he was away conquering, wanted husbands for his daughters in 322. He chose Craterus, an officer of Alexander's, who married Phila. His other new son-in-law was Ptolemy, who married Eurydice.

Ptolemy was already married, to Artacama, daughter of Artabazus, a member of the Persian royal family. But Macedonian kings practised polygamy, so an existing wife was no problem.

When Eurydice came to Egypt her retinue included a lady-in-waiting called Berenice. In time, it turned out that Ptolemy preferred Berenice to Eurydice, and indeed to any other lady who was involved in his life. Her son Ptolemy, born in 308, became Ptolemy II, the second Macedonian king of Egypt.

Assets for the Temples

Like Alexander (and unlike Kleomenes), Ptolemy thought it best to recognize and support Egyptian religion. In 311 BCE he made a grant restoring land in the Nile Delta, confiscated in Persian times, to the priests. The inscription recording the grant blames Xerxes, the old Persian king, for withholding the land from the gods: "...it is the property of the gods of Pe Tep from earlier time. The enemy Xerxes reversed it..."

Self-promotion

For some years Ptolemy kept the title of satrap, although Philip Arrhidaeus and Alexander IV, the kings whose governor Ptolemy supposedly was, were murdered in 317 and 310 BCE respectively. At last in 306 or 305 Ptolemy formalized the independence and sovereign status he had really had for years, and took the title of King.

By the turn of the fourth and third centuries, Ptolemy was safe on the throne, and powerful in the politics of Greece and the Near East. He decided he now needed something that would show to Greeks the intellectual achievement of his kingdom, as well as its worldly power.

The Library of Alexandria

Ptolemy I decided to collect every Greek book and house them in a building next to the Mouseion, the temple of the Muses, in Alexandria. He enlisted the help of Demetrius of Phaleron to plan the project. Ptolemy sent agents everywhere with money to buy books.

Right **Seventh century BCE gold "buttons" from Stilpo's home town of Megara, in Greece.**

Below **Ruins of the library at Alexandria (published 1801).** When drawing this view Luigi Mayer believed that the remains at the seafront in Alexandria were part of the Ptolemies' library. Certainly they are in the correct area.

The agents had orders to get books Ptolemy did not already own. He did not need multiple copies of common titles. This brief caused a rash of counterfeiting: The price was better for a book by a well-known author, so people who had a rare book by an obscure author would tell the buyers it was an unknown title by a big name.

Meanwhile any ship that came into Alexandria was searched for books. If any were found which the king did not yet have in the library, they were copied, and the copies (not the originals) returned to the owner.

An Intellectual Metropolis

The plan to collect all these books was only part of a project which Ptolemies I and II had to make Alexandria into a city which could rival Athens as the capital of Greek culture.

They brought as many representatives of Greek high culture to Alexandria as they could. Perhaps the one who made the greatest impact was Euclid (c.325–c.265 BCE), whose textbook *Elements* was the basis of mathematical education until the nineteenth century.

Questioned by Ptolemy I about his work, Euclid famously said, "There is no Royal Road to

geometry." Ptolemy, following Alexander, had gone to Persia on the Royal Road, and so found his way to success in life; Euclid meant that his own kind of distinction was not gained by walking along a road already traveled.

Callimachus, considered the best Greek poet of his generation, came from Cyrene to live and work in Alexandria. He was entrusted with organizing the library, and the catalogue he produced was a pioneering work.

In the field of anatomy, Herophilus, who wrote the book *On Dissections*, was another of the brilliant men the Ptolemies attracted to Alexandria. He dissected human bodies, which Greek doctors before him had shrunk from doing. It is not clear how far he was influenced in deciding to do this by the way Egyptians would process human bodies for mummification.

Not all the intellectuals the Ptolemies wanted to attract to Alexandria would agree to come. When Ptolemy I captured the city of Megara, in Greece, he went to see Stilpo, the philosopher, gave him generous presents, and asked him to come to Egypt. Stilpo returned most of the gifts, and went away to the island of Aegina until Ptolemy had left town.

The Bible in Greek

The first Ptolemies ruled Israel–Palestine as well as Egypt. Many Jews came and lived in Egypt. Someone suggested to Ptolemy II that the holy book of the Jews was a valuable work and ought to be added to the Alexandrian Library.

So Ptolemy II, the story goes, wrote to the High Priest of Jerusalem, sent gifts and asked him to provide scholars who could translate the scriptures into Greek. Seventy-two were sent, six from each of the twelve tribes of Israel. They were entertained royally in Alexandria, then did the job of translating the Bible into Greek.

Their translation, called the Septuagint or "Seventy", was used by Greek-speaking Jews in Egypt and beyond. It is the source of most quotations from earlier scriptures which are included in the New Testament. To Orthodox and other eastern Christians, the Septuagint is the authoritative text of the Old Testament, though western Christians view the Hebrew text as more official.

Above **Euclid, fourth to third century BCE, Greek mathemetician, whose books formed part of the Alexandria Library.** This mid-thirteenth century manuscript tract on fortune telling shows Euclid (seated on the left), with the natural philosopher Herman Dalmatin.

BOOKS AND BOOK STORAGE

Handwritten on papyrus, a light brown writing material made from reeds that grew in the Nile, books consisted of rolls which were read as the reader unrolled them side to side.

In the Library of Alexandria these books were not stored on bookshelves as in the modern world, but in boxes or bins.

One of the many fragments of papyrus that have been discovered contains part of a poem from Callimachus' *Aetia* (a poem written in about 270 BCE). Callimachus, the first librarian of Ptolemy's Alexandrian Library, was the brilliant small-scale poet who said "big book, big bad".

Right **Working in the fields of the afterlife, chapter 10, Book of the Dead of priest Hornedjitef, papyrus, first century BCE.** Note the papyrus reeds being harvested in the middle register of this illustration.

Royal Rivalry

The Ptolemies did their best to make Egypt as Greek as they could, but there was competition. King Seleucus of Syria, and his son Antiochus, built new cities in Syria and brought Greeks to live in them, offering land and privileged status.

Syria gained as many as half a million new Greek immigrants in the half-century after Alexander the Great died in 323 BCE. Egypt, despite everything the kings did to make Alexandria an attractive city, brought in fewer Greek migrants. As well as Greeks, the Ptolemies brought in as many Jewish migrants as they could. Jews were particularly useful in the armed forces. The first three Ptolemies felt they could not trust Egyptians to fight for them: The first time Egyptians were allowed in the Ptolemaic army was in 217 BCE, in a time of great emergency.

A New Development

In the 250s BCE, Ptolemy II decided to strengthen his kingdom by encouraging settlers in the Faiyum, an area to the west of the Nile irrigated by canals and dykes which brought water from the Nile. Watercourses were put in order and allotments of land were made to soldiers who had retired from the army.

The lake at the north end of the Faiyum traditionally belonged to the queen. Arsinoe II, Ptolemy II's wife (and sister), had died a decade or so previously and been declared a goddess.

On her behalf, rights to fish and other resources of the lake were waived. Egyptians lived in the Faiyum along with immigrants and descendants of immigrants, but for the most part the development of the Faiyum benefited Greeks and Jews.

Religion for All

In an empire that worked mostly in the interests of non-Egyptians, the kings were disposed to want to meet the needs of Egyptians and promote social cohesion. Ptolemy I, who had made land grants to temples (thus claiming to be a more righteous pharaoh than his Persian predecessors), made other moves in relation to religion. He claimed that a god appeared to him in a dream and revealed himself as Sarapis, commanding Ptolemy to get a statue of him and set it up in its own temple in Alexandria.

Sarapis was an equivalent of the Greek god Hades, the god of the dead and the underworld. Getting a statue of Hades was no easy task, since Hades was not usually given temples by the Greeks, and not many statues of him existed. But someone told Ptolemy that the statue in his dream was one which existed at Sinope, a Greek city on the Black Sea. He sent officials to tell the

Ptolemy	English
ΠΤΟΛΕΜΑΙΟΣ	Greek
P T O L E M A I O S	
PTOLMYS	Demotic
▪ ◖ ᴁ 🐦 ═ ‖ ᑭ	Hieroglyphic
◢🐦∫ ᴁ ▪ 🦅 ⟿ ⬭ 🦅	Hieroglyphic
	Demotic
KLEOPATRA	Demotic
Cleopatra	English

CRACKING THE CODE

The Rosetta Stone has the same message written in hieroglyphics, demotic, and Greek script, so the unknown hieroglyphs could be related to a known language, classical Greek. The name of Ptolemy, in a cartouche, could be identified and compared to other royal names such as Cleopatra. These examples show the same hieroglyphs representing the 'p', 'o' and 'l' sounds in both names. A pattern soon emerged.

Sinopeans that the god had commanded him to bring the statue to Alexandria. They were reluctant to let their god go. Tacitus, a Roman historian, says that, because the Ptolemaic officials' request had made no progress for a long time, eventually the statue got up, walked down to the harbor, and boarded King Ptolemy's ship to go to Egypt. Plutarch, less fancifully, says the Ptolemaic officials stole it. Either way, it reached Alexandria and was housed in its own temple.

Sarapis' name comes from the Egyptian *Osir-hapi*, the god who was conceived as being the Osiris (that is, the version in the land of the dead) of Apis, the bull god. But when Ptolemy I made Sarapis into a Greek god, Sarapis was pictured in human form, as middle-aged with luxuriant hair and beard—and often with a corn-measure on his head, symbolizing the land's fertility.

The Struggle for Israel-Palestine-Jordan

While the attention of Seleucus I, King of Syria, was distracted by another war in 301 BCE, Ptolemy I had moved in and stolen Israel–Palestine from him, together with some of what is now Jordan. At what is now Acre, a fortress town called Ptolemais was built, and Amman was the site of a Ptolemaic city called Philadelphia, after Ptolemy II.

Throughout the third century BCE, the rivalry of the kings of Syria and Egypt was played out in a series of wars. The advantage shifted from side to side. In 217 BCE, Ptolemy IV seemed to be a weak ruler who would be easy prey for Antiochus III (the Great), an aggressive king who had ruled Syria for six years. Antiochus overran Israel–Palestine before the Egyptian army could be organized. But Ptolemy's government took a risk that the first three Ptolemies had never dared to take—namely that Egyptians were recruited to the army and trained in the winter months. In the battle of Raphia (Rafaa, at the southern end of the Gaza Strip), Ptolemy's Egyptian phalanx defeated the main body of Antiochus' army and regained the lost territory for Egypt.

Above **Temple ruins**. These ruins attest to the once-thriving life of the Faiyum, an area in which Ptolemy II encouraged renewed settlement in order to strengthen his hold over Egypt.

Left **Painted mummy**. A gilded mask sets off this decorated mummy, found in the Faiyum region.

Antiochus Takes Over

But the setback for the Syrians was only temporary. In 200 BCE the Seleucids won the battle of Panium and took Israel–Palestine from the Ptolemies—and they were never to regain it.

But there seemed to be potential for diplomacy to achieve what military might could not. Ptolemy IV had died in 205 BCE at the age of 41, leaving his five-year-old son Ptolemy V as king of Egypt. The boy-king would need to marry. After careful maneuvering, it was agreed that his bride should be Cleopatra, Antiochus the Great's daughter—Cleopatra I, as she became. Her dowry would be "Hollow Syria," as Israel–Palestine–Jordan was called. The marriage took place in 192 BCE, but Antiochus' guards continued to hold the border posts. Probably the net revenue of the territory, after governmental expenses had been deducted, was brought to Cleopatra year by year.

Egyptian Priests and Macedonian Kings

The Rosetta Stone is a record of a meeting of all the priests in Egypt, held at Memphis in connection with the coronation of Ptolemy V (by then 13 years old) in 197 BCE. The priests recognize the king for confirming their privileges and forgiving "those...of the warrior caste, and of the rest, who went astray in their allegiance in the days of confusion"—Egyptian rebellions, which the royal forces had finally got under control. They agree to increase the honors they pay to the king, and "to set up an image of the ever living King Ptolemy in the most holy place of every temple, which shall be called 'The Image of Ptolemy the Avenger of Egypt,' beside which shall stand the leading god of the temple, handing him the emblem of victory, which shall be fashioned [in the Egyptian] fashion, and the priests shall pay homage to the images three times a day." So in

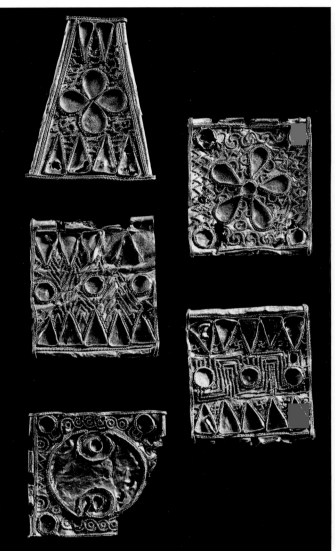

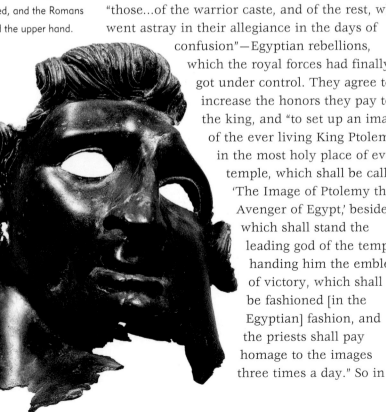

every temple in Egypt, the king was worshipped by the priests, alongside the god of the temple.

The Rosetta Stone was found by Napoleon's soldiers in 1799 in the seashore town of Rosetta in the Nile Delta. It proved to be the golden key that allowed scholars finally to figure out how to read Egyptian hieroglyphics. Previously, scholars in Europe had been unable to read hieroglyphics, and had to make guesses based on books in which Greek and Latin writers at a late date had said what they knew about Egypt. The guesses that resulted were sometimes fanciful.

The Rosetta Stone has the same decree written on it three times, once in hieroglyphics, once in demotic (the everyday form of Egyptian script), and once in Greek. Thomas Young, an Englishman, was the first to observe that the cartouches in the hieroglyphic text must represent the name of the king. In 1824, Jean-François Champollion, professor of history and geography at Granola, published a decipherment of the Egyptian version. His work made the study of hieroglyphics, and translation of Egyptian writing, possible. (Much earlier studies of the Rosetta Stone—by Arab scholars in the ninth century CE—were not known in Europe at this time.)

Syria Keeps Up the Pressure

King Antiochus III was succeeded in 187 BCE by his son Seleucus IV, who was king of Syria for a period of 12 years. After Seleucus died in 175 BCE, Antiochus IV Epiphanes took over.

Egypt in the 170s BCE looked weaker than ever. Ptolemy V had died in 180 BCE, at the age of only 29, and his son Ptolemy VI was another boy-king. Antiochus Epiphanes, spying a good opportunity, brought his army south and invaded Egypt. He captured the king and advanced to the suburbs of Alexandria.

The Romans had just won the Third Macedonian War. Their army was at this time, therefore, hundreds of miles away in Europe. Needing to at least take some action, however, they sent Gaius Popillius Laenas to convey to Antiochus that they did not want him to take over in Egypt.

Antiochus Blinks First

With a small retinue, Laenas went to Eleusis, on the outskirts of Alexandria, and held a meeting with king Antiochus. He said the Syrians must withdraw their army from Egypt. Antiochus played for time. The answer he gave them was that he must discuss the matter with his advisers, but he would get back to Laenas with an answer in due course.

Laenas—so the story goes—used his walking stick to draw a circle around Antiochus in the sand. He said he would not allow time for debate on whether there would be a withdrawal: Antiochus had to answer yes or no before he stepped out of the circle. Under this direct

pressure, Antiochus said, yes, he would withdraw his army as the Romans wanted him to.

Why did Antiochus crumble, when the Roman army was so far away and Laenas had no force to back him up? Antiochus must have been afraid not only of losing Egypt, if he took it, but actually of losing Syria as well, if he got into a war against the Romans. So Rome kept Egypt "free," but increasingly dependent on the Romans for support ever afterwards.

Below **Protector of Eleusis.** Triptoleme, a former prince of Eleusis, is initiated into the Eleusian Mystery by the goddesses Demeter and Persephone. Antiochus Epiphanes could have done with some of his protection.

Queens and Kings

The family of Ptolemy, son of Lagos, ruled Egypt for nearly three hundred years. And yet before they rode to glory on the back of Alexander the Great's conquests, their ancestors were people of no great distinction.

Above **Lysimachos, Macedonian general of Alexander the Great, marble bust.** Lysimachos later became king of Thrace, and father-in-law and brother-in-law of Ptolemy II Philadelphus.

When Ptolemy I was on a military campaign in Greece, soon before taking the title of king, he met a famous expert on poetry and mythology. He asked him a question about a disputed point of Greek mythology: "Who was the father of Pelops?"

"I'll tell you," said the learned grammarian, "if you'll tell me who was the father of Lagos." The conversation ended.

The woman in Ptolemy I's life who meant the most to him was Berenice, who came to Egypt as a lady-in-waiting to Eurydice, the daughter of Antipater whom Ptolemy married in 322 BCE. In 308 BCE, Berenice gave birth to Ptolemy I's last son, the boy who was to be Ptolemy II.

Ptolemy II Philadelphus

Within a year or two of becoming king of Egypt in 282 BCE, Ptolemy II married Arsinoe, the daughter of Lysimachos, the king of Thrace. The match linked the families of two of Alexander's most prosperous successors. In the short term it was a successful marriage, and Arsinoe bore Ptolemy at least three children: Ptolemy III, Lysimachos and Berenice.

But in the 270s BCE something happened. It may have been suspected that Arsinoe was plotting against her husband. In any case, she was sent into exile at Koptos, up the Nile.

Arsinoe II

Ptolemy had a sister, also named Arsinoe. As a very young woman she had been married to Lysimachos, and had three of his children. In 281 BCE he was killed in battle. Afterwards Arsinoe married Ptolemy Ceraunus ("Ptolemy the Thunderbolt"), her half-brother, the son of Ptolemy I and Eurydice. The marriage was part of Ceraunus' attempt to make himself seem like the true king of Thrace, which

Right **Ptolemy II and his wife Arsinoe I.** This gold coin, called an octodrachm, was struck in Alexandria in 263 BCE.

he had succeeded in taking over after Lysimachos' death. However, fate was also rather unkind to Ceraunus. In 279 BCE he was captured and killed by invading Gauls.

Later in the 270s BCE, Ptolemy II, having exiled Arsinoe I, replaced her as queen of Egypt by marrying his sister, who became Arsinoe II.

Egyptian pharaohs had married their sisters in earlier centuries. Were Ptolemy and Arsinoe copying them, in order to look like true Egyptian sovereigns? Or was it more to do with Greek ideas about the gods—since Zeus was married to his sister Hera?

The marriage was controversial. "In Athens you can go half way," people grumbled, "in Alexandria you can go all the way." In Athens it was legal to marry a half-sister.

The Dangers of Poetry

The poet Sotades went further than most mutterers, with a direct and rather rude attack on the king, which labeled the marriage "unholy". He was thrown into prison. Later he escaped and journeyed by sea to Caunus. Ptolemy's admiral Patroclus recaptured him, but he did not live to be brought back to Alexandria. He was shut up in a lead chest and thrown into the sea.

Arsinoe and Ptolemy almost certainly never had a child together—they already had three children each before they married each other. Observers gleefully counted up how many mistresses Ptolemy had—he had not remarried because he was short of girlfriends.

A Great Career Move

From the late 270s BCE Ptolemy and Arsinoe were worshipped as the "Brother-and-Sister Gods." But Arsinoe was not destined for long life. She died, aged about 45, on July 9, 270 BCE.

After death, Arsinoe was built up by the Ptolemaic propaganda machine into a symbol *par excellence* of the dynasty's greatness. Fifteen or twenty cities—new or redeveloped—were named after her. Enclosures dedicated to her were built at holy sites across the Greek world. Statues were everywhere.

To this day, opinions remain divided about just how powerful Arsinoe herself was as queen. Was she the power behind her brother's throne, orchestrating the greatness of Egypt? Or was she simply another weapon in Ptolemy's propaganda arsenal, kept tucked away in a quiet corner of the palace until the end of her life?

Above **Zeus and Hera, part of a mid-fifth century BCE frieze.** Like Ptolemy and Arsinoe, Zeus and Hera were brother and sister who were married to each other.

Ptolemy III

Probably aged about 35 when he came to the throne in 246 BCE, Ptolemy III married Berenice, who was the daughter of Magas the ruler of Cyrene, a son of Berenice I by her previous husband (before she married Ptolemy I). Both grandchildren of Berenice I, this royal couple were cousins.

The great project of Ptolemy III's reign was his invasion of the Seleucid kingdom, which held sway through Syria and on into Mesopotamia and beyond. He had been on Egypt's throne for a year when he set out with his army to conquer.

Poets made the most of Ptolemy's sad parting from his bride Berenice when he went to war. She had been married before, but Callimachus the poet passed over that fact in silence when he described some marks a wedding-night tussle had left on Ptolemy, (supposedly) visible as he led out his army.

Berenice cut off a lock of her hair and dedicated it as an offering in the temple of Aphrodite, praying for Ptolemy's safe return.

The hair disappeared mysteriously. Conon, an astronomer, played along by claiming to have seen a new constellation. It had been taken by the gods to shine forever in heaven! And there it remains: Berenice's lock can be seen between the hunting dogs (*Canes Venatici*) and Virgo in the northern winter sky.

Powerful Queens?

That the wives of the Ptolemies were important and influential is clear. Did it go further than that? Were they in fact powerful? In the third century, seemingly not. Arsinoe II's great achievements were ascribed to her after her death. Berenice II was perhaps a "queen of hearts", but not concerned with politics.

A change came about after 200 BCE. Cleopatra I became the ruler of Egypt in 180 BCE when Ptolemy V died, because Ptolemy VI was only six years of age. However, by 178 BCE, two years before Cleopatra's death, Eulaeus and Lenaeus, who were palace eunuchs, were made regents and took power.

Two Rival Brothers

In the next generation, things got more complicated and it was less clear who was

going to be able to gain and maintain control. Ptolemy VI had a setback when he was captured by Antiochus Epiphanes, and the Alexandrians set his brother Ptolemy VIII on the throne.

Afterwards, Ptolemy VI and Cleopatra II, his sister (and wife) regained power and put Ptolemy VIII in charge of Cyrene. They were safe until Ptolemy VI died in 145 BCE, and Ptolemy VIII made a comeback by murdering the short-lived Ptolemy VII.

Married to his sister (Cleopatra II) and his niece (Cleopatra III), Ptolemy VIII Euergetes II held on as king until 116 BCE. Known popularly as Kakergetes ("Malefactor"), instead of Euergetes ("Benefactor"), or simply as Physcon ("Fatboy"), Ptolemy VIII, like King John, "was not a good king."

Cleopatra III Takes Over

When her two co-rulers died in 116, Cleopatra III was only 40 or 45 years old. She seemed to have her best days ahead of her.

She had two sons, Ptolemy IX (Soter II, also known as Lathyrus ["Chick-pea"]), and Ptolemy X (Alexander). In 107 BCE she ousted Lathyrus and brought Alexander in as co-ruler. But in the long term this was unwise: Alexander murdered her in 101 BCE, and took power without a mother to look over his shoulder.

In 105 BCE Lathyrus had gained control of Cyprus, which was still a Ptolemaic possession. In 88 BCE he made his bid to retake Alexandria, and succeeded, holding on until 81 BCE. His successor was his daughter Berenice III.

Rome Puts a Man in Charge

The next year, the most powerful man in the world, Cornelius Sulla, came to Alexandria. He planned to arrange the politics of the eastern Mediterranean to suit the Romans.

Sulla caused Berenice to marry Ptolemy XI, a son of Ptolemy X—apparently in order to have Egypt ruled by a man instead of a woman.

But the plan misfired. Ruthlessly, Ptolemy XI murdered his cousin and bride. But his hopes of having the throne to himself came to nothing. Berenice had been popular in Alexandria, and the Alexandrian mob soon killed Ptolemy XI. His reign lasted only eighteen days.

The next king was Ptolemy XII Neos Dionysus ("the Young Dionysus"), a son of Ptolemy IX. Some called him Nothos ("Bastard") others mocked his musical skills by calling him Auletes ("Piper"). However, he was a shrewd king who held on for three decades. He had two sons, who he might have thought would make the succession secure; but he also had daughters—one of whom, crucially, was Cleopatra VII.

A GRUESOME BIRTHDAY PRESENT

The struggle between Ptolemy VIII (Physcon or "Fatboy") and his sister and wife Cleopatra II went on for decades. They married in 145 BCE after the death of their big brother Ptolemy VI Philometor. About 140 BCE, Fatboy also married Cleopatra II's daughter, his niece, Cleopatra III. He got on better with her than with Cleopatra II.

In 132 BCE Cleopatra II was forced out of Alexandria and went to upper Egypt. In exile, she claimed to be the only queen. The people of Alexandria, who hated Fatboy, burnt down his palace in 131 BCE, and he fled to Cyprus, taking relatives with him. Cleopatra returned to the city of Alexandria in triumph.

In 130 BCE Fatboy murdered Ptolemy Memphites, his own son by Cleopatra II, and sent the head, hands, and feet to Alexandria in a box, to be given to the boy's mother on her birthday.

Below **Ptolemy VIII and Cleopatra II making offerings to the gods, stone raised relief.** Ptolemy is wearing the white crown of Upper Egypt.

Temples and Palaces

Like their Egyptian forebears, the Ptolemies were great builders of monuments—above all, to themselves. Today if you travel up the Nile many of the best and most impressive things you will see were built, or rebuilt, in the Ptolemaic period.

Right **Wonder of the world.** A Roman bronze coin showing the Pharos—the wondrous Lighthouse of Alexandria.

Alexander the Great and Ptolemy I set the trend of paying attention both to the Greek heritage, belonging to the royal family and Greek immigrants, and the Egyptian heritage. Later Ptolemaic pharaohs followed.

Alexandria and the Royal Palaces

The greatest monument of the Ptolemies was their city of Alexandria, which was perpetually being developed. The Egyptian name for the city was *ra-ked*. Greeks came to believe that a village called Rhakotis was one of the places Alexander had incorporated into his city in the beginning. But it was not so: *ra-ked* means "building-site." Over the generations, more and more was added to the royal buildings in the center of Alexandria. The museum and library formed part of what became a vast complex, and the Alexander monument, too, was there—perhaps at or near what is now the Latin cemetery.

The palace could be very confusing, even to people who spent their whole lives there. About

Below **Ruins of the gymnasium near the Canopic Gate.** One of many spectacular structures built in Alexandria during the Ptolemaic Period.

a hundred years after Ptolemy I had declared himself king, his great grandson Ptolemy IV had died and there was a power struggle between Agathocles, who was Ptolemy IV's minister and favorite, and Tlepolemus, a highly placed army officer. Tlepolemus was out of town and Agathocles was based in the palace. He began to suspect that Moeragenes, a bodyguard, was spying for Tlepolemus. He told Nicostratus, the secretary of state, to have Moeragenes arrested.

When Nicostratus' men came for Moeragenes, they dragged him to a remote part of the palace, stripped off his clothes, and began showing him the instruments of torture. Then a slave came in and whispered in Nicostratus' ear. He went off with the slave, leaving everyone else behind. The torturers waited. When their boss had been gone an embarrassingly long time, they began to sidle away. Finally the victim was left alone. He wandered naked through echoing halls, until at last he came to a guard-post. He told the guards what had happened. They found it difficult to

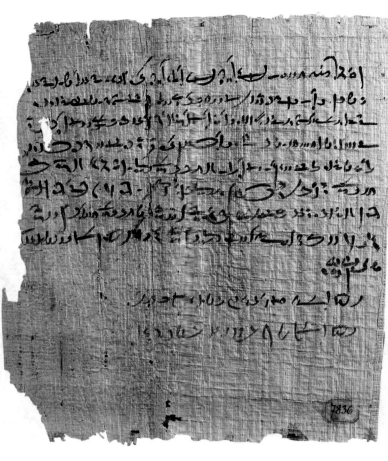

DEMOTIC SCRIPT

Egyptian hieroglyphics formed an elegant writing system that looked splendid when the pictograms, ideograms, and phonograms were carved on stone or painted on a temple or tomb. But the complexity of this script made writing slow.

The hieratic script existed almost as early as the hieroglyphic script, and represented a slightly quicker and more economical method of writing. It was, therefore, considerably more convenient to use.

Probably in the eighth century BCE, a more compressed writing system, which we call demotic, was first used. It was the regular method of writing documents in Egyptian (except the most ornate texts) throughout the Ptolemaic period, and until the second century CE.

Despite their differences, though, hieroglyphic, hieratic, and demotic scripts were all methods of writing down the same language.

Right **Time to pay up.** A fragment of a papyrus in demotic, from the eight century BCE. It concerns a farmer's payment of rent.

believe, but, faced with their naked informant, they could not ignore him. They gave him the help he asked for.

Almost none of Alexander's extraordinary palace complex survives today. However, in 364 CE an earthquake shifted the shoreline of Alexandria and left a slice of the royal quarters under the waters of the eastern harbor, making possible an intriguing modern discovery. Between 1996 and 2003, a team of underwater archeologists under the leadership of Franck Goddio explored this area and found many fascinating relics, including the site of Mark Antony's Timonium, a temple that had been built in the last years of his life.

The Lighthouse

The palaces were very impressive, but the most distinctive building in the harbor area was the lighthouse, the Pharos, one of the seven wonders of the world. Built to guide sailors into port, it also helped to put Alexandria on the map in other ways. Parts of the foundations of the lighthouse were identified in underwater explorations in 1994. Still standing in the tenth century CE, it was a lasting advertizement for the importance of Alexandria. With three stages, each on top of another, it must have been an impressive sight.

Ptolemy II's Pavilion

Something can be learnt about how Egypt looked at this time from descriptions of the things the

Ptolemies built and events they sponsored. In (probably) 262 BCE, Ptolemy II put on a great procession in Alexandria to impress foreign delegates; it was a mix of religious extravaganza and May Day military parade. One float in the procession had a statue on it that, as the float went forward, stood up, moved its hand to pour a drink offering, then sat down again. This impressive mechanism of wheels and levers showed what the king's clever scientists were able to come up with. Furthermore, a *symposion* (drinking party) for guests at the event was held in a tent 85 feet (26 meters) high which had room for a hundred guests in its main hall.

Traveling in Style

Another impressive project that is known from written descriptions of Alexandria in this period is Ptolemy IV's riverboat. This craft was built for the king to use to travel up the Nile. It had an audience hall and a banqueting room, a separate set of apartments for the queen, bedrooms for men and women, and rooms for yet more drinking parties. In a kind of chapel lined with stone there were statues of the royal family

The theme of extravagant use of space is in evidence in the remains of the palaces of governors here

Below **Demotic stela.** Over the demotic text of this stela is a black-winged sun representing the night.

Above **Egyptian zodiac.**
This papyrus depicts an
ancient calendar. It is
divided into four cardinal
points (the women in
white) and 36 decans
(10-day divisions, making
360 days in a year).

the gods—just as if he were an Egyptian pharaoh.

The great temple of Edfu, situated between Aswan and Luxor, was the largest Ptolemaic construction project outside Alexandria. Dedicated to Horus, it was built—little by little and with many additions and embellishments—over 180 years, between 237 BCE and 57 BCE. Its purpose was to inscribe Ptolemaic power and patronage on the land-scape of Upper Egypt. In 142 BCE Ptolemy VIII and Cleopatra II performed a dedication ceremony at the temple.

The Edfu temple, which remains today the best preserved temple in all of Egypt, with its ancient roof still in place in parts, was buried for centuries under desert sand. Hieroglyphics covering all the surfaces of the building document when each part of it was built, and show martial achievements (real or imagined) of the Ptolemaic kings. On the Pylon (entrance gate), for example, Ptolemy VIII is portrayed smiting his enemies and presenting captives to Horus. These inscriptions provide a wealth of valuable information to scholars.

At Kom Ombo, 28 miles (45 kilometers) north of Aswan, Ptolemy VI in the second century BCE started building a temple complex with one temple dedicated to Sobek, the crocodile god, and another dedicated to Haroeris (Horus the Elder). Construction continued under Ptolemy XIII in the first century BCE, and additions were made under Augustus, after the Roman takeover of Egypt. Less well preserved than Edfu, Kom Ombo still has impressive remains on view.

and there in the Ptolemaic dominions. At Ptolemais in Cyrenaica (a smallish seaside city) the governor in the first century BCE lived in a large complex of buildings with both official and residential functions. Just as in Alexandria, the message portrayed was the might and glory of the ruling power.

Egyptian Temples

While the palaces and lighthouse of Alexandria were built in a Greek style and encoded their messages in a Greek idiom, the Ptolemies certainly did not neglect the temples of the Egyptian gods. At the temple of Karnak (near Luxor), Ptolemy I developed the peristyle (pillared) court of Tuthmose III by adding a granite *naos* (sanctuary) in the name of Philip Arrhidaeus, Alexander the Great's brother, who had succeeded him and reigned as king until 316 BCE—though he never visited Egypt. Philip Arrhidaeus is shown in a relief on the *naos* wearing the Atef crown, dedicating offerings to

Hathor: the Last Hurrah

With interruptions when there were revolts in Upper Egypt, the Ptolemies added steadily to the long-established religious sites up and down the Nile. Their last great building project was begun by Ptolemy XII Auletes, who started redevelopment of the temple of the cow goddess Hathor at Dendera. Building went on at Dendera into the first century CE, so that the iconography of Roman emperors is mixed in with that of the Ptolemies of the final generation. Cleopatra VII and Caesarion are shown on the corner of the south wall making offerings.

Although he was a shrewd man who rode the storms of Alexandrian politics for three decades, Ptolemy XII Auletes was not always a popular king. In 58 BCE he was deposed by the Alexandrian mob and forced to flee for help to Rome. He needed an army—a Roman army—to put him back in power. But how to negotiate the politics of getting the Romans to back him with force? Somehow Auletes talked Pompey the Great, the most powerful politician in Rome (while Julius Caesar was away fighting the Gallic war), into getting behind him and instructing Aulus Gabinius, Roman governor of Syria and one of Pompey's foremost supporters, to use his Roman troops to put Auletes back on the throne.

But this assistance came at a price. Auletes had to hire the Roman army for cash—cash that he did not have. Pompey, and Gabinius, knew that he could get the money once he was back as king of Egypt. It was arranged that he should borrow what he needed from one Rabirius Postumus. Once Auletes was back in power in Alexandria in 55 BCE, Rabirius became his finance minister. This ought to have secured Rabirius' prospects of repayment, but—not

surprisingly—all did not go smoothly and Auletes ended up imprisoning him. When Rabirius escaped to Rome, he was put on trial on a charge of lending money to Auletes for unlawful purposes. The charge was a political move by Pompey's enemies. But Cicero, ex-consul and the greatest lawyer in Rome, took Rabirius' case and secured an acquittal.

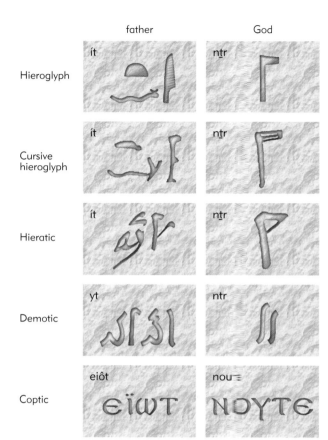

	father	God
Hieroglyph	it	ntr
Cursive hieroglyph	it	ntr
Hieratic	it	ntr
Demotic	yt	ntr
Coptic	eiôt eïⲰⲦ	nou ⲚⲞⲨⲦⲈ

Left **Hieroglyphs and later forms of writing**. The development of writing in ancient Egypt can be seen in these hieroglyphs for "father" and "God." The hieroglyph could also be produced in cursive forms, such as hieratic or demotic, a kind of shorthand version of the word. Coptic is the final stage of the ancient Egyptian language and it used letters of the Greek alphabet and a few demotic characters. A spoken form of Coptic has survived in the liturgy of the Christian Coptic Church.

Left **Sacred cow**. The cow goddess Hathor, from a column in the Temple of Hathor at Dendera, the redevelopment of which would be the Ptolemies' last great achievement.

Cleopatra VII

The death of Ptolemy XII Auletes in 51 BCE marked the beginning of the final act of Egypt's history as an independent kingdom. His eldest daughter was the last and most famous of the reigning Ptolemies, the princess Cleopatra VII.

Below **A legendary beauty.**
A sculpture of Cleopatra
by the English artist
Henry Weekes.

Cleopatra began her career as joint-ruler and wife of her brother Ptolemy XIII in 51 BCE, when she was aged 18 and he was only 12 years old. Cleopatra immediately began to show her ambitious and independent spirit by moving to exclude her brother from power, and within a year the siblings were at war. However, this was merely a petty power struggle compared to the great conflict that was about to engulf the Mediterranean world.

Cleopatra and Julius Caesar

In 49 BCE, civil war broke out between Julius Caesar and his rival Pompey, and both men sought to enlist the kingdoms of the East on their side. Cleopatra, already a shrewd diplomat, saw in the conflict an opportunity to restore Egypt's declining fortunes and secure power for herself alone. Legend has it that Cleopatra hedged her bets at first, seducing Pompey's son when he came to Alexandria in 49 BCE. But the Pompeians proved no match for Caesar on the battlefield, and a year later Pompey himself fled to Egypt, where the courtiers of Ptolemy XIII assassinated him.

Caesar met a cool reception at the court of Ptolemy XIII when he arrived in Alexandria a short time later. He began to wonder if the king's exiled sister Cleopatra might not prove to be a more suitable ruler for Egypt. The Ptolemaic princess and the Roman general met in secret, and began the affair that would change the course of Egyptian history.

Ascension and Assassination

Cleopatra's romantic conquest paid off in political power. When Caesar left Egypt after defeating Ptolemy XIII in the Alexandrian War, he established Cleopatra on the Egyptian throne with a far more amenable husband, her 11-year-old brother Ptolemy XIV. One other consequence of their union was a son born in June of 47 BCE, a boy called Caesarion.

With Caesar firmly installed as Dictator, Cleopatra visited Rome with her child-husband in tow, and set up court in the luxury of Caesar's villa on the Tiber River. The extravagance and arrogance of Egypt's queen offended some Roman aristocrats, who did not know what to make of this powerful, educated oriental woman. "I can't stand the queen," the Roman statesman Cicero wrote to his friend Atticus. "And I cannot recall her insolence without pain."

Some Romans also worried about Cleopatra's influence over Caesar, who was now acting more and more like a monarch himself. But whatever Cleopatra's place in Caesar's plans, his assassination by a group of Roman senators on the Ides of March in 44 BCE changed everything. Caesar's will, not surprisingly, ignored the illegitimate Caesarion and bestowed his estate upon his great-nephew, an obscure youth by the name of Octavian. Cleopatra fled Rome, perhaps fearing for her life—but she soon found her position in Egypt no less dangerous.

In Cleopatra's absence there had been serious famine and plague in Egypt, and the people were restless. Worse, the Mediterranean was now plunged into yet another civil war—between the Republicans led by Brutus and Cassius, the assassins of Caesar, and the surviving Caesarians led by Octavian and Mark Antony.

Cleopatra showed her greatest resourcefulness in adversity once again. She forestalled another palace revolution by murdering her brother Ptolemy XIV, and marrying her four-year-old son Caesarion. Although a storm prevented Egypt's fleet from aiding the Caesarians at the decisive battle of Philippi in 42 BCE, Cleopatra took advantage of the general confusion to expel her younger sister Arsinoe from Cyprus, the island she had been given in 44 BCE by Mark Antony.

CAESAR AND CLEOPATRA

The first meeting of Cleopatra and Caesar is one of the most theatrical moments in Egyptian history. The young queen risked her life to cross enemy lines in a small boat, and was secretly smuggled into Caesar's quarters rolled up in a carpet. There she used her considerable charm and intelligence to win Caesar's confidence, and the two became lovers. It is difficult to say whether their affair stemmed more from personal attraction or mutual advantage, for both Caesar and Cleopatra were ambitious leaders with much to gain from an alliance.

Right **Julius Caesar as a young man.** When Caesar came to know Cleopatra he was, at 51, much older than portrayed in this bust. Cleopatra herself was not averse to younger men, though, having married her son, Caesarion, when he was only four years of age.

Above **The baths of Cleopatra.** This nineteenth century engraving by Hector Horeau depicts a ruined Alexandrian bath complex, romantically imagined as the baths of Cleopatra.

unpopularity. Mark Antony's power was unchallenged, and he had no need or desire for closer relations with the Egyptian queen.

Antony's greed for the wealth of Cleopatra's kingdom, however, was another matter, which Cleopatra naturally exploited. When Antony summoned her to the city of Tarsus on the southern coast of Cilicia (in modern Turkey) she arrived on her royal barge in a spectacle of opulence worthy of the greatest of Egypt's pharaohs. The costly display, combined with Cleopatra's charisma and intelligence, had the desired effect on the Roman general. Antony accompanied the queen back to Alexandria for the winter of 41–40 BCE, and a year later she bore him twins. Cleopatra's troublesome sister Arsinoe was now executed at Antony's order.

The ancient writers tell us that Antony completely lost his head over Cleopatra. This image of Antony as pathetically lovesick is largely the creation of his enemies. It is clear at this stage that Antony still put politics before pleasure. He did not see Cleopatra for another four years, and in 39 BCE he patched up his alliance with Octavian by marrying his beautiful sister Octavia, who soon bore him a daughter. Octavia was now crucial to Antony's political position in Rome. Cleopatra could not compete.

Above Cleopatra makes her entrance. This painting by seventeenth-century Flemish painter Frans Francken II depicts the Egyptian queen meeting Mark Antony at Tarsus in 41 BCE. It was here, according to legend, that she began her seduction of the Roman general.

Antony and Cleopatra

The charismatic Antony (Marcus Antonius) had been Caesar's right-hand man in Rome. He was also a celebrated drunkard and womanizer, and very popular with his troops. The fame of Antony's tragic affair with Cleopatra has reflected back on history, leading to much romantic speculation. Did sparks fly when the future lovers first met during Caesar's Alexandrian War, or later in Caesar's villa in Rome?

Probably neither. Throughout her life, Cleopatra's romantic alliances so clearly suited her political ambitions, it seems inconceivable that she would have been attracted to a mere lieutenant of Caesar. Meanwhile Antony, for his part, showed by his elevation of Arsinoe to the throne of Cyprus that he was not averse to using Cleopatra's rival as a guarantee of her own good behavior.

By 42 BCE Brutus and Cassius were dead, and Caesar's heir Octavian seemed likely to succumb to a debilitating illness, if not to his own general

Right Mark Antony. His love of women and wine was legendary—the writer Pliny the Elder even named him "Rome's greatest drinker."

The Final Conflict

The alliance between Mark Antony and Octavian took a turn for the worse after 37 BCE, and it seemed as if a final showdown between the two Roman warlords was inevitable. With Octavian firmly established in Italy and the West, Antony decided to secure his power in the East with a glorious campaign against Rome's old Middle Eastern enemies, the Parthians Egypt now assumed a new logistical importance for Antony.

Antony summoned Cleopatra to meet him in the Syrian city of Antioch. When she arrived he flattered her by acknowledging their two children, Alexander Helios and Cleopatra Selene, and restored to Egypt the island of Cyprus. In fact he promised her much more: Vast territories in Cilicia, Phoenicia, Arabia, and Judaea, which he had no legal authority to give. Cleopatra in turn gave Antony the logistical support he needed for his invasion of Parthia, and another son. Their rekindled affair was as much about war, politics, and ambition as it had ever been.

Antony's Parthian campaign was a military catastrophe. He returned to Egypt in 35 BCE with his army and reputation devastated. He was now completely dependent on Cleopatra. Meanwhile, Octavian cleverly exploited Antony's insulting treatment of his loyal Roman wife Octavia. Further public relations disasters followed. Antony's behavior in Alexandria led many Romans to believe he was trying to set himself up as a Hellenistic monarch over Rome's Eastern Empire, a good chunk of which he had already signed over to Cleopatra and her children. These so-called "Donations of Alexandria" caused much outrage in Rome.

In 32 BCE Antony finally confirmed his break with Octavian by divorcing Octavia, and both sides prepared for war. In Rome the propaganda against Cleopatra had reached fever pitch. The Roman poets accused Cleopatra of being drunken, debauched, and ambitious to rule over Rome itself. Antony's crimes included betrayal of Rome and losing himself in decadent oriental luxury—he was even charged with the unforgivable extravagance of using a golden chamber pot!

The last stand of Ptolemaic Egypt as an independent kingdom was on September 2, 31 BCE. The fleets of Octavian and Antony clashed off the coast of Actium in Greece, and Antony's forces were routed. Antony and Cleopatra fled back to Alexandria, but within a year Octavian's armies were at the gates, and Antony committed suicide. Cleopatra would not give up so easily. Moving the contents of her treasury into a large tomb filled with firewood, Cleopatra let Octavian believe she was ready to destroy Egypt's wealth rather than let it fall into his hands. She shut herself in the tomb and awaited her conqueror.

WAS CLEOPATRA BEAUTIFUL?

This intriguing question has many answers—depending on whom one asks. The answer is no according to the ancient Greek writer Plutarch, who tells us that her beauty was nothing special. However, it seems that Cleopatra's charm and charisma were irresistible. Her voice was said to be like a beautiful instrument of many strings, allowing her to dance from language to language and cast a spell over everyone she met. Plutarch also tells us that Cleopatra was the first of her dynasty to learn the speech of the native Egyptians. She mastered at least seven languages fluently—and, we are told, a thousand kinds of flattery.

Left **Cleopatra as the Egyptian goddess Hathor.** In this relief from the temple of Hathor at Dendera, Cleopatra is depicted with the traditional accoutrements of a native Egyptian queen: The crown of Hathor, staff, vulture headdress, and ankh.

Egypt Captured

When Octavian marched into Alexandria at the head of his victorious legions, the ancient writers tell us that Cleopatra—ever the political, and romantic, opportunist—tried one last gambit to preserve her kingdom and her life.

Below **Marble statue of Octavian (Augustus).** Octavian was 32 when he conquered Egypt, and 76 when he died. Yet throughout his long life the portraits of Rome's first emperor hardly aged a day.

She put on a pitiful display of weeping before Caesar's adopted son, showed him her tear-stained love letters from the dictator, and—we are told—attempted to seduce him.

The story reads like an all-too-familiar attempt by the Romans to make Cleopatra look like a conniving seductress, while Octavian virtuously resists her advances. But Cleopatra was desperate, and her charms had never failed her yet. Unfortunately for the queen, Octavian was more interested in her money than her love. Cleopatra was left alone, whereupon she committed suicide with the bite of an asp, a fitting death for ancient Egypt's last independent ruler. In doing so Cleopatra cheated her enemy of the chance to display her in his triumph in Rome, but her suicide may have suited Octavian as well. Even in defeat, Cleopatra was still a dangerous adversary, and Octavian did not want the unpleasant task of killing a woman. He was less squeamish about getting rid of Caesarion and Alexander Helios, Cleopatra's sons by Caesar and Mark Antony respectively. The queen's younger children were not perceived as a threat, and were permitted to grow up safely in Rome.

Victor Takes All

Octavian set about establishing Roman rule in Egypt. The Ptolemaic and local Egyptian administrative structures were left largely intact, with Roman officials now taking the top positions. Roman forts and soldiers became a common sight throughout the country. The regulations for this new province were unlike any other in the Roman Empire. For a start,

most Roman provinces were governed for a year by a senator chosen by lot. Octavian reserved the right to choose the prefect of Egypt himself for an unspecified period, and this official was normally chosen from the order of equestrians (knights), the social class ranked below the senators. No Roman senator was even allowed to set foot in Egypt without Octavian's permission.

Egypt Under Augustus

Octavian now took the name by which he is best known to history: Augustus, first of the Roman emperors. In Egypt he took the place of the Egyptian pharaoh, and was depicted in the traditional way on Egyptian temples, even though he was never officially crowned. Augustus also put the native temples and their lands under tighter imperial control, not as an attack on Egyptian religion but with a view to keeping priestly loyalties in line with his own agenda.

Augustus would allow no challenges to his power in the new province. One of Augustus' first governors of Egypt, a celebrated general and poet called Cornelius Gallus, was the last man to make this mistake. Shortly after being placed in charge of Egypt after the death of Cleopatra, he started lording it over the Egyptians like a great conqueror. He even set up a trilingual inscription on the Great Pyramid to boast about his achievements. Gallus' recklessness cost him his friendship with Augustus, and soon afterwards he was forced to commit suicide.

There were many good reasons why the Roman emperors were concerned to prevent Egypt and its wealth and military resources

Egypt and its wealth and military resources falling into the hands of potential rivals. Egypt was a very fertile and strategic province that came to supply much of Rome's imported grain and a good deal of other revenue, and several Roman legions were stationed there. This explains why Augustus and his successors did not want any important senators controlling or even visiting Egypt without their permission.

The Nile was also the gateway to the African kingdoms of Ethiopia and the Sudan, and the Red Sea trade routes to southern Arabia and India. Augustus boasted that he had sent Roman armies deeper into Africa than any Roman before him—all the way to Napata in the kingdom of Kush. He omitted to mention that the African kingdoms, too, had launched successful raids into Roman Egypt, on one occasion carrying off over fifty of the emperor's statues. Archeologists recently discovered a head from one of these statues under the Nubian King's doorstep, where it had been placed so that he could walk on it every day.

The ancient geographer Strabo tells us that commerce between the Roman Empire and India and the Far East increased dramatically under Augustus, who developed Egyptian ports such as Quseir and Myos Hormos for that purpose, as well as improving the transport routes that

AEGYPTO CAPTA

While he was in Alexandria, Octavian visited the tomb of Alexander but refused to see the tombs of the Ptolemies. This gesture showed that he identified with Alexander as a world conqueror, rather than with the Ptolemaic "pharaohs" who had followed a traditional Egypto-centric model of leadership. Octavian cultivated Egyptian loyalties where he could, but at the same time left his new subjects in no doubt that he was establishing a new order in which Egypt was no longer the center of the cosmos. Egypt was now just another subject territory of the Roman Empire: *Aegypto Capta* (Egypt Captured).

linked the Red Sea with the Nile. "Now one hundred and twenty ships sail from Myos Hormos to India," Strabo tells us. "Before, under the Ptolemaic Kings, only a few vessels undertook to sail there and carry back Indian products." The capture of Egypt brought these eastern luxuries flooding into Rome.

At the confluence of all this trade between East and West, North and South, the city of Alexandria soon became the most vibrant market in the Mediterranean, rivaled only by Rome itself. And just as Egyptian grain and goods flowed into Rome, so too some Roman ideas now flowed into Egypt.

Facing page **First-century BCE Roman relief of three doctors.** In the Roman tradition of portraiture unflattering features are not glossed over (though perhaps they were for Augustus, opposite). The faces of these doctors command respect for their life experience rather than admiration for their beauty.

Below *The death of Cleopatra* by Juan Luna Novicio. Some scholars believe that the sensational accounts of her suicide were spread by Octavian to cover the fact that he murdered her himself. The truth of her death will probably never be known.

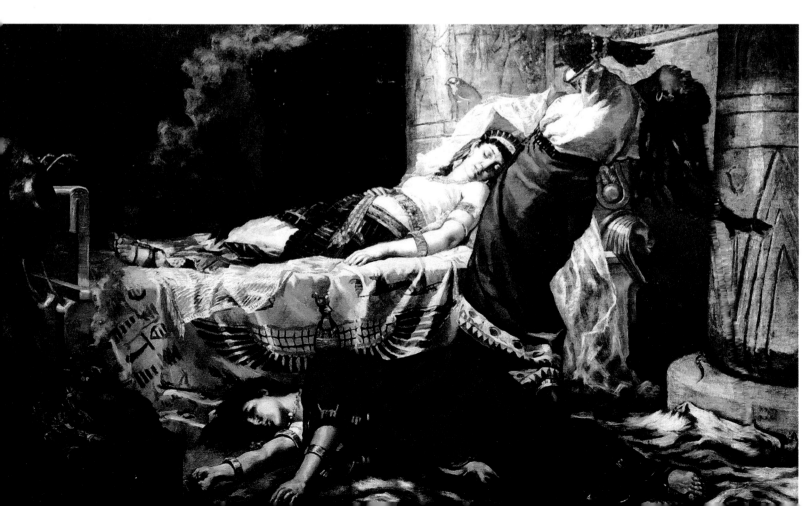

Left **Funerary portrait of an Egyptian woman.** Dating from the second century CE, this portrait in a style so different from earlier Egyptian practice shows how much Egypt was to change under Roman rule.

Faces of the Faiyum

When a Roman of wealth or importance died, his portrait might be depicted on his tomb, or it could be preserved and displayed by his family on special occasions. One of the interesting things about these portraits, and what distinguished them from traditional Egyptian funerary busts, is that they were usually far from idealized; they showed faces as they really were, even with signs of old age. This Roman tradition of veristic funerary portraiture had a huge impact all over the empire, and appears in Egypt from the first century CE onwards.

In Egypt at the Faiyum oasis, the unique environmental conditions have preserved a very large group of realistic funerary portraits of the local inhabitants. These Faiyum mummy portraits are the only substantial group of painted representations of individuals to survive from Classical antiquity.

The portraits were painted on wooden panels and set over the faces of the deceased, whose bodies were embalmed and encased in cartonnage (linen wrappings) and placed in wooden sarcophagi. Sometimes the whole body was represented. From the hairstyles and clothing fashions of the painted figures, we know that the practice really took off around the middle of the first century CE.

The first-century inhabitants of the Faiyum are thought to have been descended from the original Greek military colonists who came to

DEAD MAN'S PARTY

Describing different burial customs, the second-century CE writer Lucian once wrote that "the Greek burns, the Persian buries, the Indian encases in glass, the Scythian eats, the Egyptian salts. And the latter—I've seen what I say—after drying the dead man's corpse, they make him a guest at dinner!" Not much was made of this strange comment until archeologists observed that some of the Faiyum portrait mummies appeared to have become quite worn before they were finally interred in makeshift burials. Were these mummies once used in the rituals of household cults, or even invited to dinner parties? Archeological evidence to date is inconclusive.

Egypt with Alexander the Great, but later inter-married with the local population. It is interesting to see on the local papyri that, even while Greek personal names predominated in the Roman Faiyum, a significant number of these were Hellenized versions of native Egyptian names. Therefore it is not surprising that although they continued to assert their Hellenic identity, these Faiyum *Hellenes* were regarded as lower status than their Greek counterparts in proper Hellenic cities such as Alexandria, Ptolemais, and Naucratis, and not markedly different from the *Aigyptioi* (Egyptians).

The faces in these mummy portraits were the cultural and economic elite of the Faiyum. The males were probably educated in the traditional Greek gymnasium, and happy to assume local administrative responsibilities for the benefit of Rome. It is likely that some of them even had Roman citizenship. Perhaps they thought of themselves as Greek, Roman, and Egyptian, for in death they combined the latest Greco-Roman fashions with a fully Egyptian funerary context.

Life and Death in Roman Egypt

The record of wills and letters on papyri, and the remnants of ancient tombs and funerary rites, show us that the people of Roman Egypt—Egyptians and others—remained as concerned about their mortal fate as they had ever been. We know that elaborate funerals followed the deaths of important persons in both town and

countryside, and that many people took care to specify in their wills that their bodies should be preserved "in the Egyptian fashion."

That said, it is not surprising that the hybrid population of Roman Egypt seems to have followed an equally hybrid variety of mortuary practices. Some mummies from this time are perfectly embalmed or preserved by desiccation. Others, such as a young boy now in the British Museum, received exquisite wrappings and a portrait mask, but the rotting confusion encased within indicates that his body was probably kept on display for grieving relatives until it reached an advanced state of decomposition.

The survival of ancient Egyptian traditions of preserving and venerating the dead and their gradual adoption by non-Egyptians in the Roman period was to have at least one far-reaching effect. It is likely that the Christian tradition of preserving and venerating the bodies of saints had its origins in the beliefs and practices of the early Christian communities of Egypt.

Left **Bound in death.** This detail from a gilded mummy case of the Greco-Roman Period is illustrated with the traditional Egyptian motif of bound foreign prisoners.

Below **A gentle smile?** This painted stucco mummy from the Greco-Roman Period allows a certain character to come through in the face.

From Caligula to Caracalla

The history of Egypt during the first two centuries of Roman rule is marked by few dramatic turning points, but it has yielded a great wealth of information about the everyday lives and hardships of the local population.

Long before the beginning of the reign of Caracalla in 198 CE, Egyptian papyri record many signs of growing economic and social unrest, problems that reached their height in an empire-wide deterioration of order and prosperity that has come to be known as the third-century crisis.

The First Century

There are a few incidents and stories that stand out in the otherwise passive and domesticated existence of the province in the first century CE. One event which occurred with depressing regularity was the outbreak of violence between the Jewish and Greek populations of Alexandria, leading to a flurry of embassies between Egypt and Rome as each side tried to enlist the emperor's sympathy for their cause. The best recorded of these embassies was led by a Jewish intellectual called Philo in 38 CE. But when Philo and his fellow ambassadors tried to present their case to the Roman authorities, they were forced into an impromptu game of hide-and-seek with the eccentric cross-dressing emperor Caligula, who not surprisingly had no coherent response for Alexandria's problems.

The next emperor, Caligula's uncle Claudius (41–54 CE), took a firm line with the Alexandrians. A long edict survives in which the emperor scolds both the Greeks and the Jews for their destructive feuding. Claudius also appears to have cracked down on another endemic problem in the provinces: Illegal requisitioning by Roman soldiers. A papyrus from 42 CE promises the highest penalty for anyone who exploited Egypt's hapless peasantry with illegal demands for goods and services.

It is impossible to tell how much effect such imperial proclamations had in practise, for the voices of the oppressed for the most part do not survive. And Rome, too, had her own problems to deal with. When the reign of Claudius' successor Nero ended in chaos and rebellion, Egypt became one of the most important theaters in the ensuing civil war. It was in Alexandria that the Roman general Vespasian first proclaimed himself emperor on July 1, 69 CE, proving the wisdom of Augustus' fear that Egypt was the perfect place from which to launch a successful rebellion against Rome.

The Second Century

The reign of Vespasian and the Flavian and Antonine dynasties that followed saw Egypt revert to business as usual. Peace continued until 115–117 CE, when a Jewish revolt sparked by the appearance of a "messiah" in Cyrene took hold in Cyprus and Egypt as well. The many

Right **Sarcophagus of the child Petamenophis, 123 CE**. Despite high mortality rates, children from important families sometimes received burials as costly as those of their parents.

descriptions of this revolt that survive describe massacres of unparalleled scale and ferocity, during which the Jewish population of Egypt was virtually annihilated.

The revolt was put down and had in fact largely burned itself out by the succession of the emperor Hadrian in 117 CE, but resentment against Roman rule remained among Egyptian Greeks as well as Jews, as recorded on papyrus in the form of imagined trials of prominent Alexandrian Greeks before the Roman authorities, the so-called *Acts of the Pagan Martyrs*.

The emperor Hadrian (117–138 CE) was one of the only Roman rulers of this period to spend a significant amount of time in Egypt, which he visited with the empress Sabina in 130 CE. Hadrian's interests were those of a scholar and tourist as much as a monarch, and accounts of his journey record a visit to the famous singing colossus of Memnon, a carefully staged lion hunt, and a luxurious cruise on the Nile. Here, tragedy struck with the drowning of Hadrian's handsome young companion Antinous. Hadrian founded a cult for the worship of Antinous and established the Greek city of Antinoopolis east of the Nile to commemorate his beloved favorite.

Egypt became a stage for further imperial drama in 175 CE, when false rumors about the death of Marcus Aurelius prompted one of his former friends, the Egyptian-born Avidius Cassius, to declare himself emperor. He was assassinated only three months later, but until then he was recognized as emperor in Egypt, where he had previously gained fame by putting down an obscure local uprising by a group known only as "the herdsmen."

Egypt's next imperial visitor was the first emperor of the Severan dynasty, Septimius Severus (193–211 CE). The records of his visit in 199–200 CE consist only of mundane accounts of administrative reforms and legal judgments, though he did take the revolutionary step of granting every city in Egypt a town council.

The scattered details we have on native revolts and attempts at administrative reform in the second century attest to a growing level of economic hardship, political restlessness, and perhaps also religious resistance in the Egyptian

DEATH ON THE NILE

The Roman writer Aurelius Victor tells us that Hadrian was extremely fond of luxurious living, and suspicion about his sexual proclivities was probably well founded. There were plenty of rumors about Hadrian's passion for Antinous, who was awarded the most extravagant honors after he drowned in the Nile. Aurelius also records a story in which Egyptian magicians informed Hadrian that he could prolong his own life if someone else could be found to sacrifice themselves in his place. "They say that Antinous offered himself while everyone drew back, and this explains Hadrian's obligations to him," Aurelius writes, but adds that he still finds it suspicious that a person of Hadrian's age should take so much interest in the company of a much younger man.

countryside. In the major cities, too, resentment against Roman rule intensified. Severus' son Caracalla (198–217 CE) did not help matters when he responded to a slight offence by expelling all "Egyptians" from Alexandria and conducting a massacre among the rest of the population.

Roman Alexandria

Severus' grant of town councils to all Egyptian cities, with Caracalla's empire-wide grant of Roman citizenship in 212 CE, reduced the political primacy of Alexandria within Egypt (previously Alexandrians had been the only people in Egypt eligible to apply for Roman citizenship). Economically, however, the city retained its position as the most important market in the eastern Mediterranean. It retained, too, all the great monuments and institutions of its Hellenistic heyday: The Pharos, the museum and library, two magnificent artificial harbors, and the gigantic Serapeum.

The population of Roman Alexandria also clung to another more unfortunate tradition from ages past, an excitable temper and

willingness to mobilize in mass violence at the slightest provocation. It is hard to say whether the many vibrant festivals and sporting events the city was famous for in Roman times served to fan or channel off these energies. Certainly, for all their spirit of resistance, the Alexandrians adopted the spectacles and trappings of the cult of the Roman emperors with exceptional fervor, to the extent that official edicts were sometimes needed to keep their enthusiasm within the bounds of Roman taste.

Religion Under Rome

The Romans had something of a love-hate relationship with the strange gods and hybrid Hellenistic-Egyptian cults of the Nile. The cult of Isis flourished in Rome and throughout the Mediterranean world, where she became amalgamated with other great goddesses. Even before Egypt became a province, Egyptian subjects and motifs began to proliferate in Roman art. Some Romans built tombs shaped like pyramids, or decorated their houses with Nilotic scenes. This fascination with the land of the pharaohs did not, however, extend to any kind of empathy for the Egyptians themselves.

As for the Egyptians, they resisted the globalizing pressures of Greco-Roman polytheism and held on to their part-animal gods and ancient

DOGS AS GODS

The second-century CE writer Lucian has a character in one of his dialogues launch into a mocking tirade against Egypt's barking dog-headed deities, not to mention the painted oracle-pronouncing bulls, and the various apes and goats and "even more ludicrous creatures" that had somehow been smuggled out of Egypt into heaven. "How can you bear it, when they even put horns on YOU?" he asks the Greek god Zeus. Surprisingly, Zeus replies that the rites of the Egyptians have a mystical significance that a non-initiate should not presume to mock.

Left **Sarcophagus from Kom al-Shawqafah, Alexandria.** Anubis, Horus, and Thoth team up to embalm a mummy. Other inhabitants of the empire might have been scornful of Egypt's animal gods, but Egyptian magic and mysticism continued to be regarded with fear and respect.

traditions with a stubbornness that put other eastern Mediterranean cultures to shame. For this, at least, they earned some grudging respect from other inhabitants of the Roman Empire.

The native Egyptian priesthood remained a privileged class, but declined to a mere shadow of its former political and economic power in the first two centuries of Roman rule. This process was hastened by the diminishment of priestly revenues, and Hadrian's centralization of all their activities under a "high priest of Alexandria and Egypt'"—who was in fact nothing more than an equestrian bureaucrat.

The decline of organized native religion in Egypt was paralleled by an apparent rise in the number of independent practitioners of magic during the later Ptolemaic and Early Roman periods, as evidenced by a large number of papyri that survive from this time. In all, it is perhaps appropriate to call the early centuries of Roman rule in Egypt a time of growing mystical experimentation and religious freedom. The land of the Nile would soon provide a fertile ground for the growth of Christianity.

Above **View of modern Alexandria**. During Roman times Alexandria was a leading cultural and economic city.

Left **Anubis, the jackal-headed god**. A painted linen shroud from Roman Saqqara attests to the endurance of the native Egyptian gods and views of death and the afterlife.

Christianity in Egypt

The traditions of the church of Egypt, the Coptic Church, tell us that the apostle Mark brought Christianity to Egypt. He wrote his Gospel in Alexandria, became its first bishop, and was martyred there. In later centuries Christians could visit his tomb.

Right **This pair of leather sandals date back to the third century CE.** At this time Christianity was growing in popularity in Egypt.

Below **Ivory relief of the seventh century.** This Coptic era relief shows Christ holding a bible and blessing the faithful.

However, it is only in later centuries that this was first reported. No Egyptian writer cites this tradition before the fourth century BCE. It is first mentioned by Eusebius, Bishop of Caesarea, in modern Israel.

Christian Missionaries Target Alexandria

From the time of the New Testament little is known. St Paul wrote no letter to the Alexandrians, and although Alexandrian Jews who knew of Jesus appear in the New Testament, their understanding of his message was held to be suspect by Christians from other countries. But the city would have made a

tempting target for Christian missionaries. First century CE Alexandria was one of the largest, most cosmopolitan cities in the world. It had a reputation both as a center of philosophy and scholarship, and a place where the population started riots easily. Egyptians and Greeks lived alongside a large Jewish community.

However it arrived, Christianity grew in Alexandria, and by the early second century CE Christian teachers were traveling from the city to preach in Rome. But just as Apollos the Alexandrian Jew in the New Testament did not preach an orthodox view of Christianity, neither did Valentinus and Basilides. They found unwelcome fame as two of the first Christian Gnostics, and they were condemned as heretics by many other Christians.

Later in the second century, Clement of Alexandria led the city's famed center of Christian education, the Catechetical school. Clement was curious about other religions, dedicated to instructing Christians and converting those who had not yet heard the Gospel. He was also mindful of his training in Greek philosophy, and was not afraid to identify himself as a philosopher.

This engagement with other forms of wisdom was continued by Origen, who dominated Alexandrian Christianity in the first half of the third century. Immensely learned and a prolific writer, Origen drew on Christian, Hebrew, and Philosophical traditions to develop a Christian Neo-Platonism that was widely influential. In all their works, these early Alexandrian Christians pushed the boundaries of Christian theology, and continued the proud academic traditions of Alexandria. Along the way they made profound contributions to Christian thought and life. Origen's writings, for instance, laid the theoretical groundwork for the ascetic practises that were later to lead to monasticism.

Right **A portrait of a woman from the Faiyum from the second century CE.** Such portraits of the dead were frequently painted on the front of coffins. Many have been found in the Faiyum, a region that resisted being told how to interpret their Christian faith.

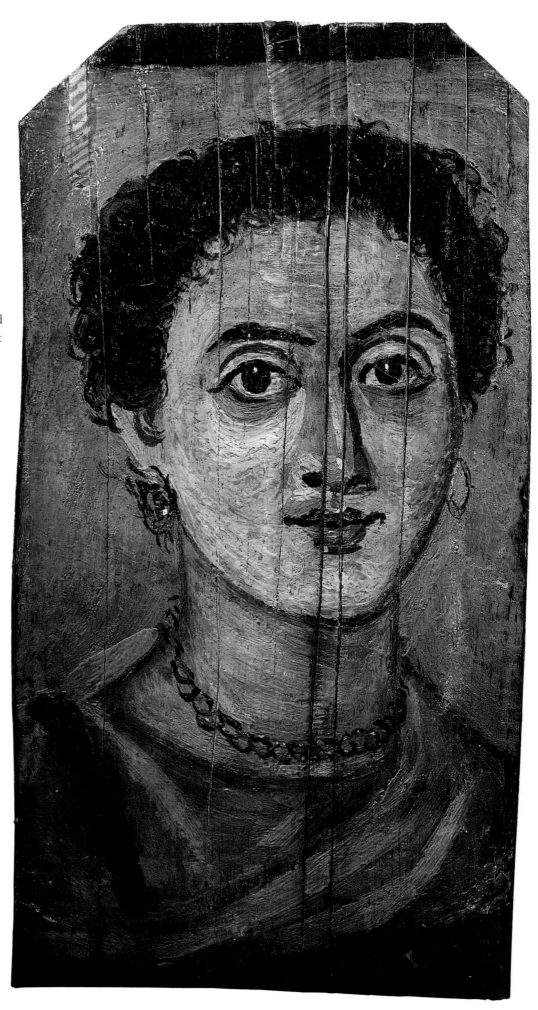

Christianity Spreads Down the Nile Valley

By the early third century, Alexandria was one of the world's most important and influential centers of Christianity. But the religion was still little known in the capital. In the Nile Valley, the older gods still held sway, and priests tended the temples, still the centers of town and village life. Copies of the New Testament dating from the second and early third century have been found on papyrus in Nile Valley cities such as Oxyrhynchus, Hermopolis, and Antinoopolis. But we know no stories of who used them or how they came to be there.

In the third century Christianity reached out decisively down the Nile. Whether or not this was always the initiative of the Church in Alexandria is not certain, because some of the new communities followed their own interpretations of the faith. At one such community in the Faiyum, the Bishop of Alexandria, Dionysius (Bishop 247–264 CE) had to argue with the locals for several straight days to persuade them to accept the beliefs of the Alexandrian Church.

From an unexpected source, we know of one man who may have been at this meeting. Around the same time, an unnamed local official drew up a list of nominations for the office of safeguarding the local water supply. This list has been preserved on a piece of papyrus, now in the National Library in Vienna. After each name, one of his colleagues later wrote a brief description of the nominee; where they worked, or an identifiable characteristic. Below the name of Dioscorus, an Alexandrian citizen now living in the Faiyum, the second official wrote: "Dioscorus is a Christian."

Above **A sarcophagus lid from the third or fourth century.** It depicts the Emperor Constantine, with Christian symbols in hand, receiving supplication.

issued a new edict to his provincial governors aimed specifically at Christian leaders. Christians had always resisted orders to sacrifice to the gods of Rome, and those who did so now suffered the ultimate punishment.

Yet persecution passed; Valerian too did not long survive, captured by the Persians during an ill-fated expedition against the old enemy of Rome. For the remainder of the third century, Christianity was able to spread unhindered throughout the towns, villages, and country-side of the Nile Valley.

The Bible in Egyptian

It was almost certainly in the early stages of the mission to spread Christianity outside Alexandria city that a crucial problem was exposed. Christianity had flour-ished in all its brilliant, typically Alexandrian, non-conformity in the capital since the early days of the religion. But, appropriately for this heartland of Hellenic civilisation and culture, it was articulated entirely in Greek, the language in which the New Testament was written. But much of the popula-tion knew only Egyptian: They could neither read the Scriptures, nor hear them explained.

To expand through the villages of the Nile hinterland, and the suburbs of the towns along the river, Christianity needed to be able to present its sacred text in the local language. Hieroglyphics were by this time used only for

Persecution and Resistance

In the mid-third century came the first organized persecutions of Christians. Under the emperor Decius, every occupant of the Roman Empire was required to sacrifice. Only then were they issued a certificate confirming this by specially appointed commissioners. Egypt's dry climate preserved these certificates on papyrus; we have forty-six of them, mostly from the Faiyum. Decius died not long after issuing these orders, but only a few years later, the Emperor Valerian

ceremonial purposes. Even demotic script was little known, and even less frequently used; only the Egyptian priests still knew how to read and write it. We do not know if Christians ever con-sidered translating the Bible into demotic, but they would probably have considered it futile: The people who would have been able to read such a translation of the New Testament would have been the least likely to accept its message.

A new phase of the Egyptian language, Coptic, provided the medium by which Christianity was finally able to spread throughout Egypt. The Old Testament, and then the New, was translated into Coptic. Hymns were written down, the Coptic script began to be taught in schools, and scholars wrote lists of Greek words, and their Coptic equivalents. Christian texts in the local language were copied and distributed among the residents of the Egyptian countryside. By the reign of the first Christian emperor, Constantine I (reigned 306–337 CE), the Bible was being read in various dialects of the native language throughout Egypt.

The Nag Hammadi Library

The most famous cache of early Coptic texts is the Nag Hammadi Library. In 1945 Egyptian farmers found a buried earthenware jar as they worked their land. In this jar were thirteen codices, a primitive form of the book. The handwriting and the type of book production showed that these codices were written in the middle of the fourth century CE, making them some of the oldest complete Coptic books. Among the texts were Gospels that had been left out of the New Testament, such as those of Thomas and Phillip. Other texts told stories of Jesus' infancy. There are the Acts of the Apostles, Revelations made to the Apostles, and letters between a number of Apostles. Others are not Christian works, and reveal other knowledge about the powers which created and ruled the universe.

Although these texts have many perspectives many reflect a Gnostic worldview. Gnostics believed that true salvation lay in the gaining of secret knowledge, and that the world had been created by an evil god whose power was potentially as great as the good god. In all there are fifty-two texts, including more than one copy of several works. Although the hoard is often referred to as a "Gnostic library," not all of the texts are explicitly Gnostic in their outlook. Gnosticism was not one religion, rather it was a wide variety of sects and religions which shared particular characteristics.

It is not certain who owned these books and what they used them for. They may not be the devotional library of a sect, but rather the private collection of an individual with exotic interests. They were found near the site of one of the monasteries of Pachomius. One theory is that they may once have formed part of the monastery's library until their unorthodox nature forced the monks to dispose of them, but this cannot be proven.

COPTIC SCRIPT

Few people could read any of the Egyptian scripts by the second century CE, but many could read the Greek alphabet. Already in the Ptolemaic period Egyptians had experimented with using the Greek alphabet to write their own language. In the Roman period various scribes had used this method to write down requests to the gods, or instructions on how to contact and control them. To control the divine world, it was crucial to pronounce the names of the powers correctly, and the Greek alphabet in which (unlike Egyptian) the vowels were written, provided a better way of ensuring this.

In the third century CE, under the impulse of translating the Bible into Egyptian,

Christians took this to a new level. They standardized spelling, and decided which signs were to be taken from demotic to represent sounds that the Greek alphabet did not have. The result was the birth of the last phase of the Egyptian script, Coptic, which remained in use until superseded as an everyday language by Arabic a millennium later, and gave its name to the Egyptian Church, known as the Coptic Church.

Right **A leaf from a Coptic copy of the Gospel according to Luke.** The parchment comes from the library of an Upper Egyptian monastery. Marks on the left indicate places where people speak.

Athanasius and Antony

During the first centuries of the Christian church, Egyptian pre-Christian religions were weakened by the way the Roman high priest of Alexandria and All Egypt managed the assets the Romans had taken from the temples when they assumed the reins of power.

This management structure delivered a net diversion of funds to the government—however, it reduced the income, and in the long term the prestige, of Egyptian cults. Egyptian priests continued to be ritual experts rooted in their communities. However, when the Christian churches grew in numbers they began to provide methods of access to supernatural power which people in Egypt found more effective than those that the priests controlled. The Egyptian gods, however, lived on in magical texts.

Above **Saint Catherine, a noble Alexandrian convert to Christianity, argues with the Emperor Maximinus Daia during the great persecution.** Although she was a very popular saint in later times, there is no proof she really existed, and the episode illustrated here is historically implausible.

From Peace to Persecution

By the beginning of the fourth century CE, the Roman Empire had changed. Where a single emperor had once ruled the Roman world, now four men shared the burden. This "tetrarchy" was instituted by the emperor Diocletian, who initiated an overhaul of the administration and economy of the empire when he came to power in 284. Egypt fell under the control of one of the two junior emperors, Galerius.

Christianity advanced throughout the land. By the close of the third century the Christian community in the town of Oxyrhynchus had built two churches. In Alexandria, where Peter I ascended the episcopal throne in 300, there were at least ten churches in which the now large Christian community gathered. Christians in different parts of Egypt wrote

Right **A porphyry statue of the four Tetrarchs (Diocletian, Maximian, Constantius I, and Galerius), now in the Basilica San Marco, Venice.** Their equal height, dress, and largely identical features symbolize the equality Diocletian intended them to have.

letters to one another, and sent those still learning the faith around the country to offer further instruction, carrying specially written letters of introduction. Christians lived in peace in Egypt, as in the rest of the Roman world.

This was not to last. Diocletian now turned his attention to organizing the religious world of the Roman Empire. In 303 he published an edict ordering Christian churches and books to be destroyed, and Christian meetings forbidden. Then clergy were ordered arrested, and finally Christians were again asked to sacrifice to the gods, and swear an oath to the emperors and the gods before they undertook public business.

In some parts of the Roman world these edicts were loosely applied, or not at all. Christians in Egypt were not so lucky. Those who refused to renounce their god were killed or sent to the mines in Wadi Faynan in modern Jordan. The suffering of the Egyptians was legendary throughout the Christian world, and many became martyrs. The lector in a small village near Oxyrhynchus turned over his church to the authorities, testifying that it now possessed nothing; we still have his declaration, although another man signed for him because this Christian "reader" was illiterate.

However, the government could not reach all Christians in Egypt; some interpreted their duty to god in a way which let them to live. In the early days of the persecution, a Christian man came to court in Alexandria

to find that sacrifice was required before the day's business began. Rather than being alarmed, he simply asked his brother to sacrifice for him, and continued to prepare for his trial. Other Christians tasted the sacrificial meat and praised the gods to avoid death. In later years this was to divide the Egyptian Church, with some claiming that those who refused to die for their religion, whom they called "the lapsed," should not be allowed to rejoin it after the danger had passed.

The Egyptian Church Divides a Christian Empire

Off and on, over the next decade, Christians remained in danger, the more so because of new emperor Maximinus Daia's enthusiasm for the persecution. In 311 Peter, who had survived in exile during most of the persecution, was finally beheaded after his return to his city. Only in 313, after the elevation of a new emperor in the West, Constantine I, did persecution finally cease, with the issue of the famous "Edict of Toleration."

Constantine had become the first Christian emperor, but his beliefs were not shared by the new emperor in the East (including Egypt), Licinius. By the end of the 320s Christians were again threatened. Either to save Christians or to acquire more power, Constantine crushed his rival, and united the Roman Empire under one man, and, he hoped, one god.

Above **The ill Emperor Constantine is advised in a dream by St Peter and Paul to seek the advice of the Roman Pope, Sylvester**. This thirteenth century fresco is part of series in the Saint Sylvester Chapel of Rome's Santi Quattro Coronati Church, intending to demonstrate the superior authority of the pope over the emperor to thirteenth century contemporaries.

S · ANTONIVS ·

Left **St Antony the Great, the first famous monk.** Detail from a medieval painting in San Alberto di Butrio Abbey, Ponte Nizza.

Constantine soon discovered the Church was anything but a harmonious body. The most serious disagreement arose in Egypt, and resulted in Constantine directing the bishops to meet at Nicaea in 325 to solve the problems. There the beliefs of the Alexandrian priest Arius were condemned. Melitius, Bishop of Lycopolis, who led those who opposed forgiveness for the lapsed (the "Melitians"), was ordered to return to communion with the Bishop of Alexandria, Alexander.

The disagreements only got worse. When Alexander died in 328 the election of the new pope of Alexandria was anything but unanimous. His enemies would later claim that, away from the arguments, and in the early hours of the morning, a select few bishops met secretly to consecrate the new bishop, Athanasius.

Father of Orthodoxy, Friend to Monks

Athanasius had been a young deacon to Bishop Alexander. He supported the theology of his predecessor against the belief of Arius, and was openly hostile to the Melitians. Throughout his long reign as bishop, Athanasius frequently fell foul of bishops in other countries who had the ear of the emperor. No less than five times he was exiled from his city, and stripped of the title of bishop. Sometimes he went overseas, to supporters in Italy and elsewhere. Other times he hid in the villages and deserts of Egypt, and the monasteries that were now there.

Athanasius' enemies were powerful, and his life was in danger a few times. But by the end of his reign, he was again secure on the throne of St Mark in Alexandria. His theology had carried the day internationally and with the emperors. Within Egypt, he had forged a much closer bond between the head of the Church on the shores of the Mediterranean, and Christians of the Nile Valley and distant Upper Egypt. The Bible, and Athanasius' yearly Easter letters, were read in Coptic throughout the province. By the time of his death in 373, more than half of Egypt's population were Christian. Most importantly, throughout his reign Athanasius had engaged with, and brought into the orbit of the Church, the most visible new Christian institution to appear in the fourth century, monasticism.

MAGIC

Egyptians had always used spells and invocations to plead for help from their gods. Under the Romans, their priests continued to copy their grimoires, containing all the information needed to contact the gods, and lists of spells to request (or demand) favors from the divine world. When asked—and paid—they would copy invocations on small pieces of papyrus for people who faced problems. Spells requesting help with love, health, or revenge are common, but magic was the answer for many problems, as the following papyrus text shows.

"I beg, I invoke you, lord, our God almighty, that you send to me from heaven Michael your archangel, that he might gather together the people of this village into the shop of [so-and-so] son of [so-and-so]."

The Books of Magic were written in demotic, Greek, and an early form of Coptic. They preserved native traditions, but also incorporated any divinity which it was thought might be helpful. The Hebrew god and the angels of the Bible were appealed to alongside the Egyptian gods, and as Christianity spread though Egypt, Jesus Christ was assimilated into this system. When paganism was finally overcome in the fifth century, its gods continued to be invoked in magical papyri, and monastic scribes now took over this ritual responsibility from the Egyptian priests.

Prayers in the Desert

One of the keys to the conversion of Egypt to Christianity was the popularity and effectiveness of the ascetic movement. It is hardly possible to say when this movement began; although its most famous "first-generation" leaders were Antony, who lived a solitary life, and Pachomius, who started a monastery and gave his followers a rule to live by. Neither man was doing something completely new.

When Antony heard the call to sell everything he had and come and follow Jesus, he began to live a solitary life; but he took advice from an older man called Paul who lived nearby and who had followed a solitary lifestyle and sought holiness for many years. And when Antony needed to make arrangements for his sister because he was going to live alone

and not be there to provide for her, he left her with a community of Christian women.

Early in his reign, in the 330s, Athanasius had undertaken a journey south to the Thebaid, to meet the monks of Pachomius (although not the great monastic leader himself, who hid when the bishop's ship passed by). In the same decade the most famous anchorite Antony visited Alexandria, and enlisted himself in the bishop's fight against heresy. After Antony's death in 356, Athanasius wrote the monk's biography for the nascent monastic communities in other parts of the world who wished to follow the example of the monks in Egypt's desert. *The Life of Antony* inaugurated a new genre of literature, and once again made Egypt famous throughout the world.

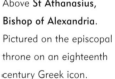

Above **St Athanasius, Bishop of Alexandria.** Pictured on the episcopal throne on an eighteenth century Greek icon.

Left **The first two monks:** Antony (on the left) with his legendary teacher St Paul, whom some styled "the first Hermit". This eighteenth century icon comes from the Church of Saint Mercurius in Old Cairo.

Desert Fathers and Mothers

In the fourth century CE thousands of Egyptian Christians followed the example of Antony and Pachomius, and sought perfection in an ascetic life. Their communities, often near the edges of the desert, left their mark on the landscape.

Nitria: From Desert to City

Nitria, just 25 miles (40 kilometres) from Alexandria, became a busy center, in a way almost like a regular town. An anonymous writer in the fourth century wrote of it having five thousand residents, all monks.

Below **Hermit life, from The Thebaid.** This fifteenth century painting by Fra Angelico depicts the hermits of Egypt at one with the animals and a benign landscape.

Father Amoun started Nitria about 315 CE. In the collection of sayings of the Desert Fathers, it says that he asked Antony why Antony got better publicity: "Abba Amoun of Nitria came to see Abba Antony and said to him, 'Since my rule is stricter than yours, how is it that your name is better known among men than mine is?' Abba Antony answered, 'It is because I love God more than you'."

Kellia ("The Cells")

A little further into the desert from Nitria a large area of ruins of monastic settlements called Kellia ("the Cells") begins. There are traces of sixteen hundred monastic settlements in an area of about 40 square miles (100 square kilometres).

These places were inhabited from the fourth century to about the seventh century. The

monks lived a religious life, praying and singing the Psalms. Their love of the Bible was real, but when asked whether Jesus' advice to sell everything one had included one's copy of the Bible, they tended to think the best answer was yes.

Houses in the Desert

Excavations at Kellia have shown a good deal about what kinds of buildings the monks used. Some monks lived right out in the wild under a simple shelter of rock, but more lived at the edge of the desert, where trade and business with the ordinary world could carry on.

Egyptian monks came out to the desert to get away from the world, and the world (as they saw it) consisted not just of the secular world but also of the Church. Their aim was to come close to God, and they believed that being a priest or a bishop would not help them to do that—quite the reverse, if anything.

Anti-clericalism

The monks' determination not to be priests could cause difficulties. A parish priest once found he was spending all Sunday walking, because he took a service at the village in the early morning, then had to go many miles into the desert to take the sacrament to the monks. When one week during the flood season the priest was delayed by crocodiles in a watercourse he wanted to cross, he complained to the bishop. The bishop called in the monks' leader, ignored his complaints, and ordained him priest. Then he told him to celebrate communion for the monks, and not trouble the parish priest by making him come out into the desert every week.

Purity of Heart

Mostly the monks were hostile to non-Christian Egyptian religion and its representatives. But there were some moments when communication was possible. Father Olympios told the story of a pagan priest who came and slept at his cell one time.

"Since you live like this," the priest asked Olympios, "do you not receive any visions from your God?"

"No," replied Olympios.

"When we make a sacrifice to our god," said

the priest, "he hides nothing from us, but discloses his mysteries...Truly, if you see nothing, it is because you have impure thoughts in your hearts."

Olympios went and reported this to the other monks. They were filled with admiration and agreed that impure thoughts separate God from man.

Men went into the desert to avoid all manner of temptations, including sexual temptation. When Antony fought the demons for two decades in an abandoned fort in the desert, they would appear to him in the form of women trying to seduce him. Since monks felt that their flight from the world was to an important degree a flight from sex, they might often be hostile to women and scornful of women's commitment to ascetic ideals.

Yet there were Desert Mothers as well as Desert Fathers. Mother Sarah rejected the idea that she ought to be apologetic to men about her calling: "If I prayed God that all men should approve of my conduct," she said, "I should find myself a penitent at the door of each one, but I shall rather pray that my heart may be pure towards all."

Mother Sarah had an eye for evidence of the inner life. She lived alone by the Nile for sixty years, and said that for the first thirteen she struggled against the temptations of sex. One time she and some nuns were going along a road, and a group of monks came from the other direction. The monks discreetly crossed the road, to avoid a face-to-face meeting with the nuns. Mother Sarah said, "If you were true monks, you would not have noticed that we are women."

Sometimes a woman would avoid completely the anxieties men had about women pursuing the solitary life. Father Bessarion and his disciple, on a journey, came to a cave in the

Above **Christ and Abbot Mena, paint on wood panel, late sixth century.** Jesus (right) places a supportive hand on an abbot's shoulder.

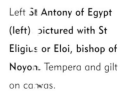

Left **St Antony of Egypt (left) pictured with St Eligius or Eloi, bishop of Noyon. Tempera and gilt on canvas.**

Right **Manuscript of sermons preached by Abbot Shenoute**. Coptic script on parchment.

desert where a monk was sitting plaiting a rope. He did not greet them, or even look up: they went on. On the way back Father Bessarion said to his disciple: "Let's go in and speak to him; perhaps God has told him to speak to us." So they went into the cave, but found him dead. When they took the body to bury it, they found it was a woman. "See how the women triumph over Satan," Bessarion said, "while we still behave badly in the towns."

Thaïs was a prostitute until Father Paphnutius came to her house. He paid her, but instead of having sex with her he asked if she knew there was a God. She admitted, yes, she knew about God and the Last Judgement. "Well then," Paphnutius said, "you'd better stop living this way." She repented and asked him to impose a penance on her.

Paphnutius took Thaïs to live alone in a cell at a nunnery, with nothing but a small opening in the door where the sisters could pass her bread and water. She had to face east and repeat, "You who made me, have mercy on me."

Three years later, Paphnutius wanted to know if God had forgiven her sins yet. So he went to Father Antony, who asked his disciples to pray for an answer to the question to be revealed. They went to their cells to pray. One of them had a splendid vision of a bed, in the sky, covered with precious cloths and guarded by

Below Christ the Saviour, between angels of the Lord. Seventh century Coptic fresco from the monastery of St Apollon.

three virgins whose faces shone with brightness. The disciple said to the virgins, "Surely so great a glory can only be for my father Antony?"

"This is not for your father Antony," the virgins replied, "but for Thaïs the prostitute."

The disciple reported back to Paphnutius, who then went to the nunnery to see Thaïs. "Come out," he said, "for God has forgiven your sins."

The Desert Versus the City

Monasticism as an institution never represented any sort of unity of opinion. In the early fourth century, Melitians had their own monasteries, and their monks and the partisans of Athanasius fought street battles in the capital. Under the Bishop of Alexandria Theophilus (385–412 CE) influential monks from Kellia, in particular the so-called "Tall Brothers," led delegations to the imperial capital of Constantinople, to argue against the Archbishop of Egypt, as the Bishop of Alexandria now indisputably was.

The theology of Origen, which had given the ascetic movement much of its vocabulary, was now causing dispute. The teachings of the great Alexandrian Church father were now abandoned by the Bishop of Alexandria, and a substantial section of Egyptian and world Christendom, as Theophilus both imposed his will on the Egyptian Church, and continued his involvement in international disputes.

Shenoute and the White Monastery

Around the time that Theophilus became bishop, a young monk near Panopolis (modern Achmim) was inheriting leadership of his uncle's monastery. This monk, Shenoute, lived until 466, and became the most famous monk in Egypt. At the White Monastery where he lived, governors and philosophers came to hear his sermons. Throughout his district, he drove paganism into submission, burning temples and criticizing pagans in his sermons. The White Monastery scriptorium became the premier scribal house in Egypt. Yet for all of this, no one

Right **Madonna and child, an enduring image of Christianity around the world**. Sixth century Coptic painted niche from the monastery of St Apollon.

outside Egypt paid any attention to Shenoute. None of the famous Lives or Sayings of monks written in Greek or Latin mention him, and it was not until French and English scholars and explorers discovered the lost library of the White Monastery in the nineteenth century that his importance and influence became known.

One Nature or Two?

Throughout the first half of the fifth century, theological dispute again divided the "Universal Church" (Greek: *katholike ekklesia*). Theophilus, and his successors Cyril (412–444 CE) and Dioscorus (444–454 CE), remained in the thick of the arguments. Many other bishops and their flocks from other countries agreed with the Egyptians that Christ had only one indivisible essence (Greek: *physis*), in which his divine and human natures were combined; they became known for this reason as Monophysites. Yet in Rome, Constantinople, and elsewhere, many more Christians believed that Christ had two natures. At the Council of Chalcedon in 451 CE the "Diphysites" finally won the day, and the Egyptian Church went into schism with most of the rest of the Christian world. Even today, the dispute has not been settled.

WHERE DO DEMONS LIVE?

The Desert Fathers and Mothers demonstrated the victory of Jesus by living in the Egyptian desert.

The desert was where demons were believed, by Christians and others, to live. Jesus explained (Matthew 12.43) that "When an unclean spirit comes out of a man, it wanders over the deserts seeking a resting-place..."

In the apocryphal/deuterocanonical book of Tobit a demon called Asmodeus is routed when Tobias and Sarah, on their wedding night in Media, following the angel's instructions, burn the heart and liver of a fish, making smoke. "When the demon smelled the odor," the story continues (Tobit 8.3), "he fled to the remotest parts of Egypt, and the angel bound him."

So by living in the Egyptian desert and not dying of hunger and thirst, or being driven crazy by demons, the Desert Fathers and Mothers showed that their religion was powerful even in places people were afraid of.

The Arab Conquest of Egypt

The reign of Constantine the Great (306–337 CE) as Roman emperor brought about many changes in the Mediterranean world. His "Edict of Milan" (313 CE) legalized Christianity, which became the most important force in Egyptian life for centuries.

But Constantine's decision to build a capital city named after himself (Constantinople), which was to be "New Rome," made almost as much difference to Egyptians.

Byzantine Egypt

Renamed in the 320s CE, Constantinople (previously Byzantium, now Istanbul) was dedicated in 330. As the greatest city of the Roman East, it eclipsed Alexandria, which had previously had an unassailable claim to being regarded as the second city of the Roman Empire.

As Constantinople's political importance grew, so did its population and its need for supplies. For more than five hundred years, Egypt, and especially Alexandria, had been vital as a provider of food for Rome. At the time of Hannibal, the Ptolemies were not strictly Rome's allies in

the war, but they earned long-lasting gratitude by continuing to sell food to the Romans while Hannibal was in Italy cutting Rome off from the allies it would normally have traded with.

Through the imperial years, a poor harvest in Egypt could lead to food riots in Rome. The yearly fleets of corn ships were indispensable. From 330, however, the destination of exports from Alexandria steadily moved away from Rome to New Rome, Constantinople. As connections between West and East in the Roman Empire weakened in the fourth and fifth centuries, Alexandria became a vital cog in the machine of the East Roman (Byzantine) Empire.

Christianity's development inside and outside Egypt was a complicating factor in the otherwise seemingly organic relations between the central government and the Egyptian provinces (since

Below **Christian offerings.** In this late tenth-century CE mosaic, Justinian offers the Church of Santa Sophia and Constantine offers the city of Constantinople to the Virgin with Child.

the late third century CE, Egypt had been divided into a number of mini-provinces, to strengthen the effectiveness of Roman rule).

The *Notitia Dignitatum*, a book recording the responsibilities of Roman government officials at the turn of the fourth and fifth centuries, shows the fortresses and features of Egypt and the Nile Delta. The division between Chalcedonian and Monophysite in Egypt from the middle of the fifth century was problematic for the imperial

government, which (usually) put its weight behind the Chalcedonian doctrine. Constantine introduced the idea that church and government should walk hand in hand. Once the majority church in Egypt no longer accepted this, it was only a matter of time until Egypt as a whole would be separated from that same government.

Justinian

And yet if the eventual separation of Egypt from the Roman Empire was made inevitable by the religious division, it was also delayed for decades by the remarkable reign of Justinian (527–65 CE).

The energetic Justinian tried to reverse the loss of the West, where Romulus Augustulus, the last western Roman emperor, had had to abdicate in 476 CE. Having cut a deal with the Persian King Khusro, in the so-called "Endless Peace" (532), he attacked the Vandals in Africa, regaining the African Roman provinces, then pushed on and attacked first Sicily (ruled by the Ostrogoths), then Italy. In 540 his general Belisarius entered Ravenna, which had been the capital of the last western emperors. The Endless Peace had effectively come to an end by 540, but the renewed effectiveness of the Roman military limited the inroads the Persians could make into Roman territory. Egypt remained in Roman hands throughout the sixth century.

Left **Justinian the victor.** An early sixth-century CE ivory relief, made in Constantinople, shows the emperor in triumph.

CROWN OF MOSQUES

In 642 CE, the twenty-first year after the *hijra* (Mohammed's move to Medina), and the year before completing his conquest of Egypt by taking Alexandria, the Arab general 'Amr ibn al-As started the building of the Taj al-jawamie, "Crown of Mosques," at Fustat, which was his base in Cairo.

A simple enclosure for prayer that overlooked the Nile, it had two doors on the north side, and two doors facing 'Amr's house. At first there was no *mihrab* (niche indicating the direction of Mecca) or minaret, and the ground was not covered. Thirty years later, walls and ceilings were decorated, and four compartments were added at the corners, from which the call to prayer could be made. The ground was covered with straw mats.

In 698 the mosque was demolished and rebuilt in a larger size, then in 827 its size was doubled. As "the Ancient Mosque," it has a special place in Egyptian Islam.

Right **Arabs in Egypt.** This fresco at Fustat dates from the Fatimid Dynasty (976–1171 CE). The town had come under Arabic rule centuries earlier, in 'Amr's time.

Persian Conquests

For a long time, the Persian kingdom looked like the Romans' most dangerous antagonist. In 225 CE the Sassanid family had overthrown the Parthians and reasserted the position of the Persians as the most powerful nation in western Asia. From 590 to 628 CE Khusro II the Victorious was their King of Kings. In 616 Khusro's armies completed the conquest of Syria, after six years of campaigning, by capturing Jerusalem. By autumn 617 they were ready to move on against Egypt, and when they moved in they took the fortress of Pelusium, on the east side of the Nile Delta, without a fight.

Alexandria was laid under siege in 618. The city gateways were strongly guarded, and the Persians were kept out. The Romans were unthreatened at sea, and there lay an opportunity that was spotted by an opportunistic foreign student named Peter of Bahrain. On his advice, the Persians obtained fishing boats and sailed into the harbor at night disguised as fishermen. Challenged, they gave the correct password, having been forewarned. Once ashore, they made their way to the Moon Gate, killed the guards, and let the rest of the Persians in.

The Persians spread up the Nile and took over all of Egypt, but the capture of Alexandria and Egypt—and, at the same time, their advance to Chalcedon in the west—was to be the high point of their advance. The Roman emperor Heraclius planned a campaign to split their recent conquests in half, attacking Asia Minor from the south in Cilicia and from the north at Trebizond (Trabzon). Under pressure from this, the Persians recalled their armies from Alexandria and Chalcedon. By early 628 the new conquerors had evacuated Egypt.

Mohammed

But events were to develop in a completely new direction, signaling the rise of Arabic influence in Egypt. In 622 CE Mohammed had led his followers on the Migration (*hijra*) from Mecca to Medina, the epochal event from which the years of the Islamic calendar are counted. Ten years later, shortly before his death, Mohammed declared a *jihad* (holy war) against the Roman/Byzantine Empire. His successors scarcely hesitated before taking the war forward. Damascus was surrendered to Khalid in 635, and in 636 the Emperor Heraclius set sail from Antioch to Constantinople, famously saying, "Farewell, a long farewell to Syria!"

The invasion of Egypt followed soon after, beginning in 639. As the Arabic sources see it, the divisions existing between the Christians at this time were crucial to the prompt success of the Arab cause. Cyrus, the Chalcedonian Patriarch of Alexandria, who is known in the Arabic sources as *al-Mukaukas*, had spent several years doing all he could to persecute the Monophysite Copts, and when he had the chance it was he who turned Egypt over to the Muslims.

'Amr ibn al-As

'Amr ibn al-As was a general who served in the Arab invasion of Syria, and took part in the siege of Caesarea while the Caliph Omar was at Damascus. Mohammed himself, in his lifetime, had described 'Amr as "the best Moslem and the most trustworthy of men." It was 'Amr who suggested the conquest of Egypt to Omar, saying it would be easy to conquer and well worth the effort. Omar agreed, but after 'Amr had set out with his army he discussed the matter with Othman, who reminded him of 'Amr's rashness and advised caution. Omar wrote again, telling 'Amr to turn back, if he were still in Palestine when the letter arrived; but if he were already in Egypt he had better not bring dishonor on the name of Islam by giving up the invasion.

The story goes that when the letter reached 'Amr he was careful not to read it until he had crossed the bed of a little watercourse. Then, after reading the letter, he asked, "Is this place in Syria or in Egypt?" "In Egypt," his officers told him. Then he read the letter aloud to them, and added, "The army will advance in accordance with the Caliph's orders."

'Amr captured Pelusium, then engaged the Roman forces in the eastern Delta. In 640 CE he transferred the point of attack to the Faiyum, then won a large battle at Heliopolis, which he attacked with 15,000 men when it was defended by 20,000. The storming of Trajan's fortress at Babylon, near Memphis, on April 6, 641, was the vital moment. In September of that year Cyrus, who had left Egypt before, was back with imperial authority to make a deal with 'Amr. On November 8 he signed a treaty agreeing that the Romans would evacuate Egypt and leave it in the hands of the Muslims: There would be an armistice of 11 months while the treaty was ratified by the Emperor and the Caliph.

In December 641 the Roman fleet sailed out of the harbor of Alexandria to be redeployed to Cyprus, Rhodes, and Constantinople. The last payment of tribute to Rome, and all the gold the Roman government could recover, were dispatched in the same month, and in the following year the Caliphate assumed the reins of government. Nothing in Egypt would ever be as it was before.

THE REDISCOVERY OF ANCIENT EGYPT

Introduction

In considering the events that turned Egyptology from a treasure hunt into a science, we commence with a lone Greek traveler, Herodotus, in the mid-fifth century BCE, and end with modern mass tourism at the beginning of the twenty-first century CE.

But before we begin, let us interweave the links between past and present, and dwell for a moment on the issues of euro-centrism, gender, and ethics.

Below Scientists measuring the Sphinx (Charles-Louis Balzac, 1798). Napoleon's Egyptian campaign of 1798–99 was a disaster militarily, but the works brought back by artists and scientists accompanying the campaign inspired a craze in Europe for all things Egyptian.

Egyptians Discover Themselves
It was indeed the Egyptians themselves who first discovered their own history, long before Herodotus. The first archeologist was Prince Khaemwaset, fourth son of Rameses II, who was high priest of Ptah at Memphis. He left inscriptions on some of the pyramids and tombs at Giza and Saqqara, stating that he had restored them. While doubtless only referring to minor restorations, it is significant that his purpose was to keep the ancient names of his ancestors alive.

A hundred years before the visit of our lone Greek tourist, there was a general harking back to the glories of the Old and Middle Kingdoms. Restorations were made to earlier monuments such as the wooden coffin and stone sarcophagus of Mycerinus, builder of the third pyramid at Giza.

The wheel has now turned full circle in the person of Professor Zahi Hawass, who, as Secretary General of the Supreme Council of Antiquities—or the modern-day Prince Khaemwaset—is the chief exponent of his country's past in a digital world.

The Female Perspective
The pages that follow sadly lack the female perspective, although we will later consider the contributions of Bertha Porter and Rosalind Moss, Amelia Edwards, and Barbara Mertz.

For women wishing to pursue an academic study of Egyptology in the nineteenth century,

the prospects were daunting. In 1888, since there was as yet no Chair of Egyptology in Britain, Mary Brodrick (1858–1933) had to go to Paris. She was to become the first woman to study Egyptology under Gaston Maspero at the Sorbonne and Hebrew and Semitic Archeology under Ernest Renan at the Collège de France. Initially, however, she had to resist Maspero's "But we don't take little girls here" and Renan's "I have never taught a woman in my life, and I never will." After the issue was eventually raised at a council meeting, Brodrick was accepted as a Sorbonne student, Maspero begrudgingly saying that she could come but "would probably have a very bad time." This was indeed the case. Her fellow students—some of the great names of French Egyptology—teased her mercilessly, even pouring ink down her back. But the indefatigable Brodrick succeeded in laughing it off and, in the end, became lifelong friends with many of her tormentors.

In 2003, exactly 125 years after Mary Brodrick began her studies in Paris, a permanent Chair of Biomedical Egyptology (the first of its kind in the world) was established at the University of Manchester. Professor Rosalie David—already the first female holder of a Professorship in Egyptology in the United Kingdom—fittingly became its first incumbent. In addition, she was that year awarded an OBE in the New Year's Honours List "for services to Egyptology."

Respecting Human Remains

Egyptian mummies have always fascinated humankind. In this chapter we encounter the mummy trade, and we find mummies in drawing rooms, books, and museums. In particular we discuss the examinations carried out on the mummy of Tutankhamun. Yet, as Zahi Hawass announced to the world's press after his recent extensive CT scanning of Tutankhamun's body: "The case is closed. We should not disturb the King anymore." Thus, as far as such research is concerned,

there now seems to be growing awareness that enough is simply enough.

Many people also now believe that it is problematic to exhibit bodies in a museum as it is disrespectful to the dead. In 2000 the Petrie Museum, University College London, sought to tackle this issue head on when designing its traveling exhibition "Digging for Dreams."

In the exhibition the mummified material was sensitively covered and screened from view, with visitors being given a choice whether to draw the screen or not. The screen itself was decorated with an image of an Egyptian shroud to provide magical protection for the dead residing in the case behind. Moreover, a translation of the traditional prayer for offerings in the afterlife was provided, with people being invited to read it aloud. Finally, the public was encouraged to record its immediate impressions in a book lying alongside.

Ever conscious of eurocentrism, gender, and ethical issues, we now start our own journey of discovery, commencing with Herodotus, the Greek historian, who, among many other legacies, happens to give us our first graphic account of the mummification procedure.

Left **Painting of a wall of the Tomb of Kings (Giovanni Battista Belzoni, 1822).** The spectacular tombs of Egypt inspired many visiting Europeans, such as Belzoni, whose painting here depicts the god Horus.

Below **A room in the Egyptian Museum, Turin (Lorenzo Delleani, 1881).** Due to an extensive acquisitions program in the nineteenth century, the small northern Italian town of Turin retains to this day one of the most impressive Egyptian collections outside of Cairo.

TRAVELERS TO AN ANTIQUE LAND
Classical Tourists

In "Ozymandius," the poet Shelley (1792–1822) is inspired by "a traveler from an antique land." Let us turn Shelley on his head and follow the many early tourists, scholars and travelers who—over two thousand years—went *to* the antique land of Egypt.

Above **Tourists visiting the Sphinx at Giza, 1895.** Egyptian artefacts in museums, and enticing written accounts of travels, made Egypt a desirable destination for adventurous Victorians.

Judging by the abundant Greek and Latin graffiti that can still be seen on the pharaonic monuments, Egypt was a great lure for tourists in the Classical Period. It is fitting therefore that we start with the very first visitor, who explored Egypt in the mid-fifth century BCE.

The "Father of History"
Dubbed by the Roman senator Cicero as the "Father of History," the Greek historian Herodotus has been conversely referred to by some Egyptologists as the "Father of Lies." The material in Book II of his *Histories*, vividly recounting his travels as far as Aswan, is indeed a mixture of fact and fiction. For instance, he tells of the daughter of Khufu (whom he named Cheops) who, pressed into prostitution by her hard-up father, was able to finance her own pyramid out of her ill-gotten gains. This aside, he correctly identifies the pyramids as royal burial grounds.

Right **The mummy of Rameses II (Egyptian Museum, Cairo).** Rameses II (called Ozymandius by the Greeks) was buried in the Valley of the Kings. His body was moved in the tenth century CE to Deir el-Bahri, where it was discovered in 1881 CE.

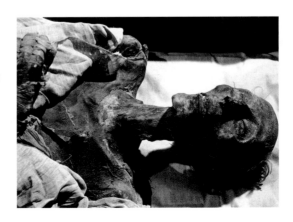

Continuing on the same theme, a number of Herodotus' more credible stories have been vindicated by archeology, for instance his description of the temple of the cat goddess Bastet at Bubastis in the Delta. Others, such as the prohibition of wool in Egyptian tombs due to a sense of its uncleanliness, have been proved to be totally unsubstantiated.

Having said this, it must be acknowledged that Herodotus has left us our best account of mummification, and is rather reliable when writing about contemporary events. Furthermore, he is still very much consulted today.

Greek and Roman Writers
Herodotus was extensively plagiarized by later Classical writers. However, the Greek historian Diodorus Siculus, who visited Egypt in c. 60 BCE, provides his own important description of mummification in his *Bibliotheca*, with details not found in Herodotus' work.

Diodorus also provides a strikingly accurate account of the Ramesseum in Western Thebes, where he correctly identified the name on one of the temple's colossal statues as that of Ozymandius, the Greek equivalent of Rameses II. He quotes this as reading: "My name is Ozymandius, King of kings." Inspired by his reading of Diodorus, Shelley reproduced these words in their entirety in his 1817 sonnet, where he also makes reference to "two vast and trunkless legs of stone" and the "shattered visage" of the monarch.

The Ozymandius statues at the Ramesseum were similarly admired by the Greek geographer Strabo in c. 25 BCE. The seventeenth book of his *Geography* has proved a valuable source. For instance, Strabo's account of the Serapeum at Saqqara was used by the French Egyptologist

Auguste Mariette when he rediscovered this structure two thousand years later. A subsequent Roman geographer, Pliny the Elder (24–79 CE), produced an encyclopedic *Natural History* which also includes much of interest on Egypt.

Looting the Obelisks

Pliny the Elder devotes an entire book to obelisks, noting that it was the Roman Emperor Augustus (27 BCE–14 CE) who removed the first obelisk from Egypt to Rome. Pliny describes "the most difficult enterprise of all"—their transportation by sea to Rome. He further relates how Augustus consecrated the vessel that had brought over the first example "as a lasting memorial of this marvelous undertaking." Very appropriately, considering the original function of these structures, the emperor dedicated it to the Roman sun god Sol, and it naturally served to epitomize his own conquest of Egypt.

The Romans seemed to have been obsessed with Egyptian obelisks because of their slender proportions and tantalizing hieroglyphic inscriptions. They even tried, rather unsuccessfully, to emulate their architectural form in their own cruder versions. Today, an amazing total of 13 obelisks stand in Rome.

With the fall of Rome in the fifth century CE, all of its obelisks, bar the Vatican example, similarly fell. They began to be rediscovered in the sixteenth century, at which time they were conveniently turned into Christian symbols. This was mainly due to the interest of a long line of popes, most notably Sixtus V (1585–1590), who has been dubbed "the Obelisk Pope."

Scholars and travelers to Rome admired the obelisks and attempted to read the royal names on them. But before we consider the Renaissance, we need to establish how ancient Egypt was being discovered by Arab scholars during the intervening one thousand years.

Arab Scholars

The modern discipline of Egyptology has been largely conducted from a Eurocentric viewpoint, ignoring any reference to the contribution of Egyptian and other Muslim scholars from the seventh to sixteenth centuries CE.

Below **Islamic quarter, Cairo (Louis Claude Mouchot, 1865).** The building shown is the Diplomatic Club—to which the locals depicted would certainly have been denied admittance.

Thanks to the painstaking work of a modern Egyptian scholar, it is now known that there was a keen and serious interest in the study of ancient Egypt during this period. Doctor Okasha El Daly, of University College London, recently spent seven years tracking down and deciphering handwritten manuscripts in collections all over the world, discovering fresh evidence of what he refers to as this "missing millennium."

Like-minded Scholars

A prime interest among these Arab scholars was discovering ancient Egyptian scientific knowledge, since many of them were alchemists. It is significant that they were by no means working in isolation, but met regularly to exchange ideas. Several manuscripts reveal that seminars were held by like-minded colleagues to discuss Egyptian materials and inscriptions. An example is a description of a meeting held as early as the tenth century to discuss a stela from a temple. Showing a figure with a sword in one hand and the head of a prisoner about to be decapitated in the other, the stela was thought to hold lost alchemical knowledge. Moreover, we learn that an even earlier group of astronomers described the same images as depicting planets.

By contrast, the first evidence of similar collaborative meetings among Western antiquarians is the Egyptian Society, founded in London in 1741 CE. Intended to promote "Egyptian and other learning," it died an early death after only a few meetings.

Describing Monuments

Arab writers provided accurate and detailed accounts of monuments that have now disappeared. A notable example is the Lighthouse of Alexandria, one of the Seven Wonders of the Ancient World. It was a favorite destination due to widespread interest in its technology. There is even a surviving early twelfth-century drawing with a description giving some measurements. It shows the three-tiered structure of the Lighthouse, with the famous mirror clearly visible at the top, correctly identified as being "of Chinese

DECONSTRUCTING CLEOPATRA

The Arab writers were responsible for keeping the names of the long-dead pharaohs, such as Djoser and other pyramid builders, alive. They had a particular fascination with Queen Cleopatra, whom they viewed as "the Virtuous Scholar," the writer of many definitive scientific works. Included among them, according to Ibn Wahshiya, was one on toxicology, and she was also believed to have written a treatise on mathematics. In El Daly's "missing millennium," Cleopatra was viewed as an alchemist, physician, and philosopher.

Furthermore, all the scholars praise her great building projects—she was even erroneously credited with constructing the Lighthouse of Alexandria. They also admired her considerable political and administrative skills.

This is an image far removed from that afforded her by Classical and modern Western writers, who envisage Cleopatra as a hedonistic, seductive beauty, a wily and deceptive queen. Judging by the monarch's unattractive portraiture on her coinage, the Arab scholars may indeed have been much closer to the real truth.

iron of seven cubits wide [364 cm]"; the mirror reputedly had the power to burn enemy ships.

A second favorite destination was the Sphinx at Giza, referred to by the writers as "The Father of Terror." Its impressive size and handsome smiling face, with fresh red paint still adhering, were much admired, not least by many of Egypt's rulers. We even have a description of a statue standing in front of the Sphinx.

It is significant that modern reconstructions of the Lighthouse strongly resemble the medieval drawing, and that modern archeology has confirmed the presence of a royal figure—representing the later Pharaoh Amenhotep II—standing below the head of the Sphinx.

Deciphering Hieroglyphs

It is now known that several Arab scholars recognized the fundamental principle that Egyptian hieroglyphs were phonetic a thousand years before Jean-François Champollion used the newly discovered Rosetta Stone in 1822 CE. Foremost among them was Ibn Wahshiya, a ninth-century alchemist who was born in Iraq

but spent many years in Egypt debating with fellow alchemists. He succeeded in deciphering at least half of the signs in the Egyptian alphabet and, crucially, distinguished these from signs that were purely ideographic. These he labeled "determinatives," the same word used today.

Ibn Wahshiya's work, which covered more than 80 different ancient scripts, was translated into English in 1806. It is in accordance with the eurocentric viewpoint that, as recently as 2001, French Egyptologists referred to this translation as the "English contribution" to the race for the hieroglyphic decipherment.

It is clear that much more work is needed before the vast potential and enormous contribution of Arab scholars can be fully appreciated.

Left **The Lighthouse at Alexandria, an 1804 engraving by Luigi Mayer.** The Lighthouse's technology fascinated many Arab scholars.

Below **A drawing depicting the anatomy of the eye, from a thirteenth-century Arabic manuscript.** This detailed illustration shows the sophistication of medieval Arabic learning, ignored to this day by Western scholars.

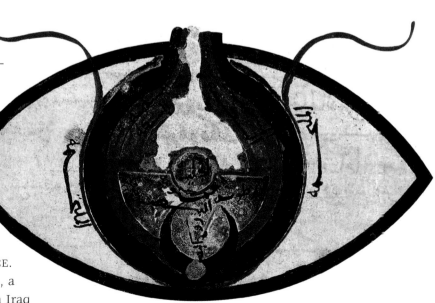

The Mummy Trade

Arab scholars, writing as early as 1000 CE, praised powdered "mummy" or "mumia" as a drug able to heal wounds and bruises. In 1203 the Baghdadi doctor Abd el Latif saw mummy taken from the skulls and stomachs of mummies on sale.

Abd el Latif himself "bought three heads filled with the substance." Originally referring to the bituminous substances in embalmed bodies, the term "mummy" was quickly extended to encompass the actual dried flesh, and its desirability grew equally quickly.

"Mummy" as a Western Drug
It is believed that a Jew from Alexandria treated both the twelfth-century crusaders and their Muslim adversaries with mummy, and thus ensured that knowledge of its properties spread to the East and West. By the Renaissance, powdered mummy flesh had become a standard drug in apothecaries throughout Europe, as attested by the great philosopher Sir Thomas Browne, writing in 1658: "Mummy is become merchandise, Mizraim cures wounds, and Pharaoh is sold for balsams."

Mummy could be taken internally, and various levels of quality were recognized, the best being dark brown to black in appearance and having a bitter taste and strong smell. The French preferred that it was taken from a "virgin girl." Indeed, nowhere was the substance more popular than in France, where François I habitually carried a packet that contained mummy mixed with powdered rhubarb for immediate treatment in case of injury.

To supply this insatiable trade, Egyptian peasants ransacked tombs, transporting the mummies they had dug up to Cairo or Alexandria, from whence they were packaged—either as entire bodies or fragments—and exported all over Western Europe. The Egyptian government levied heavy taxes on the traders—the Jews of Alexandria—and banned the shipping of corpses out of Egypt. This had little effect, for the potential profits were enormous.

Europeans in Egypt could also make great sums from the trade. In 1585 a certain John Sanderson, an agent for the Turkey Company, visited the famous mummy pits near Memphis. They were filled with ancient enbalmed bodies,

Below **Safe from the flesh trade.** This nineteenth-century French engraving depicts rows of mummies in their wrappings, found during excavations at Antinoe. Had they been found a few hundred years earlier they may well have been powdered and sold as medicinal "mummy."

covered with cloth. Sanderson shipped 600 pounds of this flesh in the form of one complete corpse and "diverse heads, hands, arms and feet" to be sold in England.

False Mummies

It is not surprising that with businessmen like Sanderson around, supplies of mummies diminished as early as the sixteenth century. The Jews of Alexandria then supplemented their supplies with another organized industry: Obtaining the bodies of executed criminals, beggars, and the dead from hospitals. They sun-dried the corpses to re-create the appearance of the ancient Egyptian bodies. Meanwhile, in Europe, mummies were made from bodies taken from the gallows and coated in resin in order to "authenticate" them.

Apparently, there was some demand for "white mummy"—the remains of travelers who had perished in desert sandstorms or been drowned in the Nile or off the Egyptian coast. Mummy prepared from the corpse of a red-haired person or a witch was said to be exceptionally potent.

Uses of Mummy

Opinions on the effectiveness of mummy were divided. While Sir Francis Bacon (1561–1626) claimed, "mummy hath great power in staunching blood," the physician Ambrose Paré, writing in 1634, stated that, "this wicked kind of drugge does nothing [to] help the diseased." It was indeed prescribed for almost every ailment, from nausea, heart murmurs, and epilepsy to poisoning and paralysis.

It is clear that mummy had myriad other non-medicinal uses—as bait for fish, as a condition powder for falcons, as an addition to oil paints, and even as a condiment at banquets. It even is mentioned in Shakespeare's *Othello*: In reference to Desdemona's infamous handkerchief, Othello comments that it was given to his mother by an Egyptian and "dyed in mummy."

In another piece of literature, this time from the nineteenth century, we should not take Mark Twain's words too seriously in his *Innocents Abroad* when he recalls, "the fuel they use for the locomotive is composed of mummies three thousand years old, purchased by the ton or by the graveyard for that purpose."

In their 1973 publication called *X-Raying the Pharaohs*, Harris and Weeks surprisingly note, "even today there is a regular, though admittedly not very heavy, demand at a New York pharmacy catering to witches for genuine powdered Egyptian mummy. The cost is forty dollars an ounce." The mummy trade therefore survived for a remarkable nine hundred years. Even more notable is that, given the wish of the ancient Egyptians, in their funeral ceremonies, to "live again" and "become young again," no one seems to have suggested that mummy had the power to lengthen life or lessen the effects of ageing.

Above **Truly gruesome!** The lower portion of a female mummy presented in the contracted position typical of earlier graves.

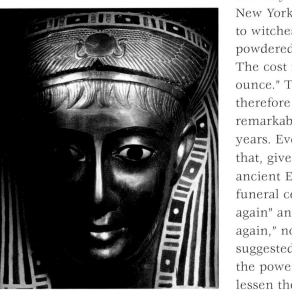

Left **Golden mummy mask from the Roman period, c. 25–30 CE.** Elaborate masks such as this were not the only treasures to be found in tombs—the mummies themselves were exceptionally valuable on the international market.

European Travelers

Two of the Seven Wonders of the Ancient World were located in Egypt: The Lighthouse of Alexandria and the Pyramids of Giza. By the Renaissance, only the pyramids remained, representing a constant lure to the intrepid adventurer.

For a verdict as to the pyramids' purpose, adventurers could have consulted a popular guidebook for pilgrims to the Holy Land: *The Voiage and Travaile of Sir John Mandeville, Knight*. Here Mandeville states, "that they be the garners [granaries] of Joseph." Little would our potential travelers have known that this work was a literary fraud. Sir John Mandeville never existed, and the author, a certain Jean d'Outremeuse, had never set foot on Egyptian soil.

The Founder of Modern Egyptology

By exploding the commonly held belief that the pyramids were granaries built by captive Hebrew slaves, John Greaves (1602–1652) can claim to be the founder of modern Egyptology. Greaves, who was professor of astronomy and mathematics at Oxford University, visited the Giza plateau where he took careful measurements of both the interior and the exterior of the Great Pyramid using scientific instruments. In 1646 he published his *Pyramidographia*, the first scientific

Below **Sunrise over Egypt**. This idyllic desert scene captures the romantic image of Egypt—an image that spurred many a would-be traveler to visit this ancient land during the eighteenth and nineteenth centuries.

study of the Egyptian pyramids. This sensible and solid work, which owed much to the work of the Arab astronomers, was to stand the test of time until the nineteenth century.

Two Men of the Cloth

A number of important eighteenth-century travelers, among them a Frenchman and an Englishman, were clerics. Father Claude Sicard (1677–1726), a French Jesuit missionary, made many journeys from his base in Cairo in an attempt to convert the Copts. He discovered ancient Thebes, visiting the Valley of the Kings, and became the first European traveler in modern times to penetrate as far as Aswan, and to describe Philae, Elephantine, and Kom Ombo. Regrettably, the bulk of his papers was lost.

Richard Pococke (1704–1765) was an English clergyman who subsequently became a bishop in Ireland. He visited Egypt on two occasions, traveling, like Sicard, as far as Philae. His two-folio volumes are especially valuable because he presents a detailed description of a large number of sites and monuments that had disappeared within a century.

A Danish Captain and a Scottish Laird

In 1738 Frederik Lewis Norden (1708–1742), a Danish naval captain, was sent by Christian VI as leader of a special expedition to Egypt. The first European to sail beyond Aswan into Nubia, he made accurate plans and drawings of monuments, including the Nubian temples, that were published in his *Travels in Egypt and Nubia* of 1751. In what represents a new departure, Norden's account shows his interest in the minutiae of ancient Egyptian life. He was clearly also concerned with the dangers of contemporary Egypt, advising the potential traveler to steer clear of prostitutes, for they will give him a memento "indelible by time, place, or mercury."

James Bruce (1730–1794), from Kinniard in Scotland, was the most celebrated African explorer of the eighteenth century, undertaking a five-year expedition starting in Egypt in 1768. He eventually reached the source of the Blue Nile in Abyssinia, an epic undertaking since that

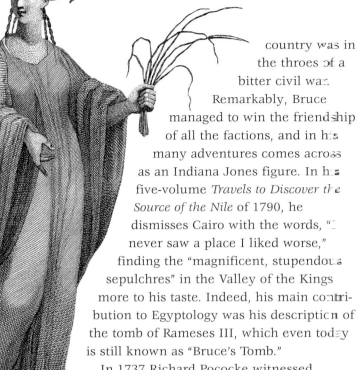

country was in the throes of a bitter civil war. Remarkably, Bruce managed to win the friendship of all the factions, and in his many adventures comes across as an Indiana Jones figure. In his five-volume *Travels to Discover the Source of the Nile* of 1790, he dismisses Cairo with the words, "I never saw a place I liked worse," finding the "magnificent, stupendous sepulchres" in the Valley of the Kings more to his taste. Indeed, his main contribution to Egyptology was his description of the tomb of Rameses III, which even today is still known as "Bruce's Tomb."

In 1737 Richard Pococke witnessed for himself the local destruction of temples and pyramids for building stone: "They are every day destroying these fine morsels of Egyptian Antiquity; and I saw some of the pillars being hewn into millstones." The daily pressure on the monuments would relentlessly increase during the remainder of the eighteenth century, spurred on by the growing foreign demand for Egyptian antiquities among private collectors and the first national museums. A ruthless treasure hunt had now begun in earnest, to be given an even greater impetus by French interest in the Nile.

Left **Arabian woman of the Beni Koresh tribe.** This engraving is from one of several books by intrepid traveler James Bruce detailing his travels to the African continent.

Below **Turtle from the Red Sea.** James Bruce's curiosity extended well beyond the study of monuments—as this engraving from one of his books shows.

AN EGYPTOLOGICAL FRIENDSHIP

Then, as now, there were some scholars who, for whatever reason, never became travelers to Shelley's "antique land." One such was the German priest Athanasius Kircher (1602–1680), who was highly influential in the emergence of Egyptology as a science. Following his appointment as professor of mathematics in Rome, Kircher made abortive attempts to read the names on the rediscovered obelisks.

This armchair scholar also made friends with the inveterate Italian traveler Pietro della Valle (1586–1650). Della Valle brought back a Coptic-Arabic vocabulary from Egypt for the young Jesuit priest to translate, and Kircher's subsequent books on Coptic proved of immense value to the hieroglyphic code crackers of the nineteenth century.

Writing a quarter of a century later, Kircher recalled the long and interesting discussions the two men had enjoyed, revolving around Pietro's travels, mummies, and hieroglyphs. No doubt Pietro often told his friend the bizarre story of how, for a five-year period following his wife's death, he had constantly traveled with a large wooden coffin housing her mortal remains.

NAPOLEON, NELSON...AND THOMAS COOK

The "Liberator of Egypt"

In 1798 the British, under Admiral Nelson, routed Napoleon's expeditionary force at the Battle of the Nile. Just a few days earlier, the young French general had entered Cairo following victory over Egypt's Marmeluke rulers.

Above **Napoleon at the Battle of the Pyramids, 1798.** In his memoirs, Napoleon mentions one overriding justification for his ambitious and ultimately failed Egyptian campaign: "Glory."

Addressing his troops before the conflict with the Egyptians, known as the Battle of the Pyramids, took place, Napoleon had uttered the famous and, as it turned out, remarkably correct words: "Soldiers, from the height of these pyramids, forty centuries look down on you."

Although the British continued to block the Egyptian coast, it was not until 1801 that they finally landed in Alexandria. This left the French ample opportunity to be vastly productive in the country. Meanwhile, Napoleon himself had fled Egypt in 1799 and, back in France, was hailed as the "Liberator of Egypt."

The Savants

Emulating Alexander the Great before him, Napoleon arrived in Egypt with a group of savants. Some of the 167 scholars of the Commission on the Sciences and Arts were to carry out an extremely thorough survey of Egypt—both ancient and modern—as part of the emperor's grandiose plans for the colonization of the Nile Valley.

On Napoleon's orders, the savants published the results of their efforts in the *Description de l'Égypte*, a magisterial twelve volumes that appeared between 1809 and 1822. Graced with more than 3,000 illustrations, the *Description* shows the antiquities—mainly the remains of ancient temples from Aswan to Alexandria—and also the villages and cities of that time, as well as the animals, plants, and minerals of the country.

However, the *Description* was pre-empted in 1802 by the *Voyage dans la Basse et la Haute Égypte*, the best-seller of the savants' leader, Baron Dominique Vivant Denon (1747–1825). The publication contained sketches of the ancient monuments, drawn rapidly by Denon while in the company of the French forces who were pursuing the fleeing Marmelukes into Upper Egypt. Denon relates: "Most of my drawings were made on my knees. Soon, I had to make them standing up, then on horse-back."

The Decipherers

The single most lasting result of Napoleon's expedition was the discovery in 1799 of a granitic slab at Rosetta in the Delta, bearing a trilingual inscription in hieroglyphic, demotic (a late cursive form of hieroglyphic) and Greek. Ceded to the British expeditionary force by the Treaty of Alexandria in 1801, the Rosetta Stone reached

the British Museum a year later. Meanwhile, the French had to be content with sending their casts and copies to the Louvre.

A frantic twenty-year race to decipher the hieroglyphic text then ensued, involving a Frenchman and an Englishman. Given the circumstances surrounding the discovery of the stone, it is fitting that the Frenchman was to win by a narrow margin.

The Englishman, Thomas Young (1773–1829), first realized that hieroglyphs contained both phonetic and ideographic signs, although, as we have seen, the Arab scholars had got there first in the ninth century. He also correctly identified the Greek names on the Rosetta Stone.

The Frenchman, Jean-François Champollion (1790–1832), had studied and become fluent in several languages, including Coptic, in order to achieve his boyhood aim of deciphering the Egyptian script. In 1822, after fifteen years of hard work, he discovered the largely alphabetic nature of the hieroglyphs by successfully reading the names of the Pharaohs Tuthmosis and Rameses on the Rosetta Stone. Uttering the cry "I've got it!", he promptly collapsed for three days. Later, he published his results in his famous *Lettre à M. Dacier*.

"The Egyptian Mania"

Napoleon regarded Pharaonic Egypt as the "cradle of the science and art of all humanity," and his expedition gave rise to a fad for decora-

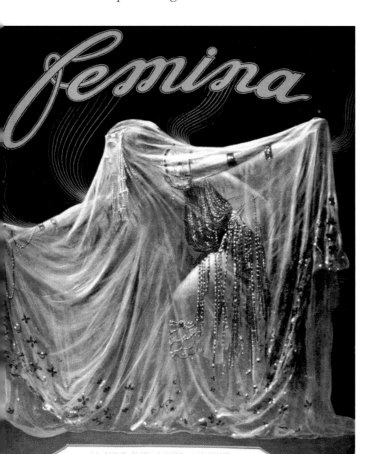

tive fashion—referred to by contemporary writers as "the Egyptian Mania"—in the first decade of the nineteenth century. According to the English poet Robert Southey, "everything now must be Egyptian: The ladies wear crocodile ornaments, and you sit upon a sphinx in a room hung around with mummies."

The mention of the crocodile is appropriate, for, on hearing of Nelson's victory at the Battle of the Nile, Lady Hamilton declared that, were she King of England, she would give him a series of titles so that "posterity might have you in all forms." She went on to have an affair with Nelson that scandalised the nation but enhanced his romantic image. One suggested title was "Baron Crocodile." Instead, he was named simply Viscount Nelson of the Nile. Fittingly, crocodiles were often mentioned in reference to his victory, thereby achieving Lady Hamilton's dream.

The remarkable work of Napoleon's savants had provided the impetus for the decipherment of hieroglyphs and for the first phase of a long process of Egyptomania, which has lasted to the present day. Conversely, it also initiated a ruthless race for Egyptian antiquities and accelerated the birth of the modern package tour, as we shall see.

Above **Jean-François Champollion (seated) in Egypt.** Several years after being the first European to decipher hieroglyphics, in 1822, Champollion joined an expedition to Egypt. In this painting by the expedition's artist he is seen with fellow traveler Ippolito Rosellini (left), both in local dress.

Left **French magazine cover, 1909.** The ballet *Cleopatra*, by Rimsky-Korsakov and Glazunov, was performed at this time in Paris by Les Ballets Russes. This cover captures perfectly the exotic appeal of Egypt in the European imagination.

Carving Up the Nile

The early nineteenth century is characterized by the stripping of literally thousands of antiquities from Egyptian soil. Their size and bulk proved no deterrent to the ruthless and ingenious men who transported them.

Right **Giovanni Battista Belzoni, c. 1818**. A rare moment of calm repose for this former strongman turned Egyptian adventurer. Belzoni successfully negotiated the transferral to Europe of some of Egypt's most valuable—and collosal—treasures.

Below **The tombs at Beni Hasan**. These were first recorded by John Gardner Wilkinson in his seminal work *The Manners and Customs of the Ancient Egyptians*.

The story of the acquisition and arrival of such objects in the great European collections will enable us to encounter some of the giants of this era: Two diplomats, two adventurers, an early Egyptologist, and an aristocrat.

Two Diplomats

Early diplomats in Cairo made it their business to collect antiquities. Among these were the Italian-born French consul-general Bernardino Drovetti (1776–1852), and his British counterpart, Henry Salt (1780–1827). Salt had been urged by his superiors to collect antiquities for the British Museum. The two rivals even silently agreed to carve up the Nile Valley into "spheres of influence." The Pasha of Egypt, Mohammed Ali, was too busy establishing his power base at this time to attend to the monuments.

The two protagonists both amassed enormous collections. While Drovetti's antiquities are now in Turin, the Louvre, and Berlin, those of Salt reside in the Louvre and the British Museum.

Thus these diplomats played a central part in the formation of four of Europe's major collections.

The Sheikh and the Strongman

In 1815 a meeting took place in Cairo between two adventurers who struck up an instant rapport. Johann Ludwig Burkhardt (1784–1817), a Swiss explorer, had been in Egypt for two years. Traveling as an Arab with the name "Sheikh Ibrahim," he had managed to enter Mecca. The first European to view the buried Abu Simbel, he remarked: "Could the sand be cleared away, a vast temple would be discovered."

Giovanni Battista Belzoni (1778–1823), a native of Padua, was an imposing 6 feet 7 inches (over 2 meters) in height, and had previously appeared in a strongman act in London. He listened avidly to Burkhardt's tales of Abu Simbel and of a colossal granite head lying at the Ramesseum Temple.

Burkhardt recommended Belzoni to Salt, and removing the head—at which Drovetti's agents had previously failed—became Belzoni's first task. At Thebes, he successfully located the so-called "Young Memnon"—"Its face upwards, and apparently smiling on me, at the thought of being taken to England." However, it was to require all his great strength, knowledge of hydraulics, and sheer ingenuity to achieve its removal to the British Museum.

The remainder of Belzoni's feats are equally spectacular: Fulfilling Burkhardt's words by opening the Great Temple at Abu Simbel; discovering the tomb of Seti I and five others in the Valley of the Kings; finding the entrance to the Pyramid of Chephren at Giza; and locating the site of the Ptolemaic Red Sea port of Berenice.

Ever restless for further adventures, the strongman died of dysentery in Benin while trying to trace the source of the Niger. A few years earlier, Burkhardt, "the Sheikh," had died of the same disease in Cairo.

The Public Schoolboy

In his *The Manners and Customs of the Ancient Egyptians*, Harrow-educated Sir John Gardner Wilkinson (1797–1875) recorded that: "The beauty of the texture and peculiarity in the structure of a mummy cloth given to me by Mr. Belzoni were striking." Published in three volumes in 1837, this book is still the most comprehensive view of Egyptian life to date.

Gardner spent 12 years in the Nile Valley from 1821, undertaking some of the earliest surveys and scientific excavations. The first person to record Beni Hasan and el-Amarna, he produced the earliest comprehensive map of the Theban necropolis, and excavated at Berenice, recently discovered by Belzoni. He was a pioneer in decipherment, reaching similar conclusions independently of Champollion. A benefactor of the British Museum, Wilkinson gave his own collection of antiquities to Harrow in order to inspire future public schoolboys.

In 1844 George Gliddon, the former American vice-consul in Egypt, recorded that: "In a very few years, travelers may save themselves the trouble of a journey beyond the precincts of the British and Continental museums." However, the tide was now about to turn with the spread of concern for protecting Egypt's national treasures.

Above **Transporting the head of "Young Memnon," 1822**. A feat both of staggering engineering achievement and reckless cultural plunder.

A SCOTTISH MUMMY

In 1837, the same year that Wilkinson's *Manners and Customs* appeared with its inevitable section on mummies and sarcophagi, Alexander, the tenth Duke of Hamilton, paid £600 for a sarcophagus that had been shipped to France. The Duke later commissioned a vast mausoleum in the grounds of his family seat, Hamilton Palace in Scotland, which was still incomplete on his death in 1852. According to *The Times*, the mausoleum "is believed to be the most costly and magnificent temple for the reception of the dead in the world—always excepting the Pyramids."

The Duke had left instructions that his body be embalmed by Thomas Joseph Pettigrew, first professor of anatomy at London's Charing Cross Hospital, and author of *A History of Egyptian Mummies* (1834). Pettigrew acted as Egyptian embalmer and chief ritualist, following which the Duke was transported to Scotland, where it had been necessary to chisel out the sarcophagus to fit his corpse. Made of basalt, covered with "the most exquisitely carved" hieroglyphs and bearing "a most beautifully chaste female face" on its enormously heavy lid, the sarcophagus, according to *The Times*, "originally contained the body of an Egyptian Queen." This is incorrect: It is Ptolemaic, derives from Memphis, and belonged to a lady with the Greek name of Ithoros.

Emerging Egyptology

From its adventurous and Eurocentric origins, Egyptian archeology was to be transformed in the second half of the nineteenth century by the creation of both an Egyptian national antiquities service and a national museum at Cairo.

Below **Descent into the pyramid**. Exploration of Egyptian sites in the nineteenth century was a dangerous but highly rewarding activity.

For this transformation we have two Frenchmen to thank, but it is to a German—or more accurately a Prussian—contribution that we initially turn, and in particular to the efforts of a brilliant young linguist called Karl Richard Lepsius (1810–1884).

The Prussian Expedition

Backed by the King of Prussia and headed by Lepsius, the Prussian Expedition worked in Egypt and Nubia from 1842 to 1845. Shortly after their arrival in Egypt, the expedition's members celebrated the king's birthday on top of the Great Pyramid. Lepsius describes the occasion: "Our flag floated from the top of the oldest and highest of all the works of man with which we are acquainted, and we saluted the Prussian eagle with three cheers for our king."

Other expeditions had gone to Egypt before—such as the first systematic survey conducted by Champollion in 1828–1829. But the Prussian Expedition was the best equipped, including skilled draftsmen among the team. It also traveled extensively—as far as Khartoum, and also to Sinai, even excavating at the site of the Labyrinth at Hawara.

The result was the largest Egyptological publication ever produced: *Denkmäler aus Aegypten und Aethiopien*, edited in Berlin in twelve volumes with 894 folio plates (1849–59). The five text volumes appeared after Lepsius' death, from 1897 to 1913.

The expedition shipped over 15,000 antiquities and casts back to Berlin, where Lepsius later directed the building of the Egyptian Museum.

The Antiquities Service

The French Egyptologist Auguste Mariette (1821–1881) arrived in Egypt in 1850, seeking Coptic manuscripts for the Louvre. Since these were unavailable, he turned to excavation instead. Seeing the head of a sphinx poking out of the sand at Saqqara, Mariette recalled a passage from the Greek geographer Strabo describing an avenue of sphinxes leading up to the Serapeum. Thus, Mariette had made his greatest discovery: The vast underground burial vaults of the Apis bulls. Following four years of excavation, the 7,000 finds and Mariette's copious notes ended up in the Louvre.

Concerned about the rapid destruction of the standing Egyptian monuments, and believing that his own discoveries should be kept in Egypt, Mariette lobbied Said Pasha, the new ruler of Egypt, for an organization and a museum in Cairo. The result was his appointment in 1858 as director of the Antiquities Service. Holding a monopoly on excavation eventually allowed Mariette to work at 35 sites simultaneously, employing over 7,000 workers. While site supervision was of course impossible, and led to much criticism from later archeologists, it is to Mariette's credit that in many centers he established workshops for conserving antiquities.

In 1863 Mariette was able to open the temporary Museum of Egyptian Antiquities at Bulaq, a quarter of Cairo, to house many of his finds. This enormously active man even had time to take a hand in composing the libretto of Verdi's *Aida*, first performed in Cairo in 1871. On his death, the Egyptians gave him a state funeral and interred him in a sarcophagus, now standing in the forecourt of the modern Cairo Museum.

The Cairo Museum

Another Frenchman, Gaston Maspero (1846–1916), succeeded Mariette as director of both the Bulaq Museum and the Antiquities Service in 1881. He was subsequently to catalogue the enormous collections in the new Cairo Museum, editing the giant *Cairo Catalogue*. This stood at fifty volumes by the time of his death.

As museum director, Maspero was involved in the removal to the Cairo Museum of the royal

mummies found in the Deir el-Bahri cache in 1881. He dramatically describes his feelings: "And what Pharaohs! Perhaps the most illustrious in the history of Egypt, Thutmose III and Seti I, Ahmose the Liberator and Rameses II the Conqueror...I still wonder if I am not dreaming when I see and touch what were the bodies of so many personages of whom we never expected to know more than the names." It is fitting to record that Ahmose's mummy has recently been returned to his place of burial, to reside in the new extension to the Luxor Museum.

Maspero built up the Antiquities Service by creating five inspectorates for different areas. He relaxed his predecessor's monopoly on archeological sites, allowing some foreign excavations. He himself organized a systematic clearance and preservation program at Karnak.

We leave the last words to Mariette, who did so much to protect and conserve antiquities, even freeing whole temples from the sand: "It behoves us to preserve Egypt's monuments with care. Five hundred years hence, Egypt should still be able to show to the scholars who shall visit her the same monuments that we are now describing." Mariette's use of the word "scholars" rather than "tourists" is significant. We are about to discover the reason why.

Above **A treasure safe in the Cairo Museum.** Frenchman Gaston Maspero made sure this mummy, of Rameses II, was moved to the Museum from Deir el-Bahri where it was found in 1881. Many similar finds had previously found their way to collections in Europe.

Left **Ruins of the temple at Karnak.** The survival of so much of this site is due to the careful and systematic approach of Gaston Maspero in his role as director of the national Antiquities Service, established before him by Auguste Mariette.

Notable Nile Visitors

One tourist who visited Upper Egypt in 1870 is recorded as having "a pot of tar in one hand and a brush in the other, leaving on all the temples the indelible and truly disgraceful record of his passage."

Right **The Nile steamer Egypt**. Thomas Cook & Co. began its rise to dominance of the tourist market with luxury steamers such as this, offering tours of the Nile for the very wealthy.

Below **The obelisk at Luxor, c. 1840**. One of the spectacular sites awaiting visitors to Egypt in Victorian times, when tourism began to grow.

Such was the comment of Auguste Mariette, who, as we have seen, was instrumental in preserving Egyptian treasures for scientific study. He was truly distressed at the influx of artists with their pots of paint and tourists with their knives, hobnobbing with European royalty as they made their way across Egypt.

Painting the Sphinx

Like the medieval Arabic writers, many Victorian artists were fascinated by the Sphinx. Scottish artist David Roberts (1796–1864), the first professional painter to work in Egypt, is arguably the best known and the most prolific. He was concerned to represent both the scenery and the monuments as accurately as possible. However, in his splendid composition *Approach of the Simoon* [dust cloud], *Desert of Gizeh*, he got carried away: His Sphinx faces in the wrong direction in relation to the sun.

The Pre-Raphaelite English landscape painter William Holman Hunt (1827–1910) was horrified at this lack of accuracy. Camped at Giza in 1854, he drew the Sphinx from the rear. Contemptuous of the "cockney visitors" to the site, he thereby showed his scorn for the conventional viewpoint of these tourists.

Dismissing the pyramids as "extremely ugly blocks," the artist regarded the people rather than the antiquities as the symbol of Egypt's former glory. He therefore drew some of the hundred or so children employed by Mariette, who was clearing the sand from around the Sphinx, and even persuaded one of his workers to sit for him, being much hampered by the sand which was blown onto his wet paint.

Royal Visitors

Many royal visitors attended the opening of the Suez Canal in 1869, by the Empress Eugénie of France. Among them were the Emperor of Austria, Franz Joseph, who was hauled to the top of the Great Pyramid, the Crown Princes of both Prussia and Denmark, and the Prince and Princess of Wales (later King Edward VII and Queen Alexandria). The latter subsequently traveled by river on their luxury dahabiya as far as Philae. Several barges carried their provisions, including "3,000 bottles of champagne, 20,000 bottles of soda water, 4,000 bottles of claret."

This was in fact the second visit for the Prince of Wales. Eight years earlier, Queen Victoria had dispatched "Bertie" off to Egypt and the Near East following the death of his father, Prince Albert in 1861, an event she partly blamed on "her chinless son." The Prince was instructed to travel incognito, avoid all society except royalty and people of a superior character, listen to a sermon every Sunday, read serious books, and visit ancient monuments. During his five-month absence Bertie grew a beard to hide his lack of chin, delighted in shooting crocodiles, quails, and vultures, and tried hard *not* to visit the Theban monuments. He said: "Why should we

TRAVELERS' GRAFFITI

In 1888 an American traveler, a certain Carter Henry Harrison from Chicago, stood on top of the Great Pyramid searching for two sets of initials he and a sweetheart had cut in the stone 36 years previously. He states that: "They are lost among masses of others. It is well. She is fat, and nearly 60; I am fat, and over 60…She did not even wait to learn from me if I had fulfilled my promise to grave our names upon the pyramid's highest stone." Carter and two traveling companions—his son William and a family friend called John—subsequently visited the Ramesseum where each of them left his mark on a column in the hypostyle hall.

While Ancient Egyptian and Greek and Latin graffiti have long been seriously studied, the potential of such modern instances is only just being realized. They can, for example, indicate how much of a temple was sanded up at the time such marks were inscribed near the column capitals.

An extensive collection of modern graffiti is now accessible on the internet, indicating that yesterday's vandalism has become today's research.

Right **"Because it was there"**. A tourist climbs the Great Pyramid of Khufu with assistance from no less than four native guides. This photograph was taken in the 1890s.

go and see the tumbledown old Temple? There will be nothing to see when we get there."

Thomas Cook Tours

Thomas Cook (1808–1892) was another honoured guest at the opening of the Suez Canal. In 1870 his son, John Mason Cook (1834–1899), took his first party up the Nile in a government-owned steamer. By 1880 the company had been granted exclusive control of passenger steamers. This monopoly meant that, four years later, John Mason Cook was called upon to provide the enormous transport for the British expedition to rescue General Gordon in Khartoum. As history recalls, the relief force arrived too late, but Cook fulfilled his contract by the date agreed.

In 1870 Thomas Cook & Co. published *A Tourists' Help-Book to the East*, followed in 1890 by its own specially commissioned guidebook. Every cruise passenger was presented with a copy of *The Nile. Notes for Travelers in Egypt* by the famous Egyptologist Sir E. Wallis Budge of the British Museum. Organized tourist travel had now begun in earnest.

Below **Festivities at the opening of the Suez Canal**. This impressive watercolour comes from the album of Empress Eugenie of France, who opened the canal in 1869.

SCIENTIFIC EGYPTOLOGY
Great Projects

Mention has been made of the *Description* and the *Denkmäler*—those two great endeavors of nineteenth-century Egyptology. Here, we review three twentieth-century projects that have produced standard working tools for today's Egyptologist.

All were the product of dedicated European scholarship: The *Description* was of French authorship and the *Denkmäler* Prussian, while the three more recent works were German, British, and Dutch respectively.

The *Wörterbuch*

In 1897 a congress of Orientalists took place in Paris, at which it was decided to compile a dictionary of all known ancient Egyptian words.

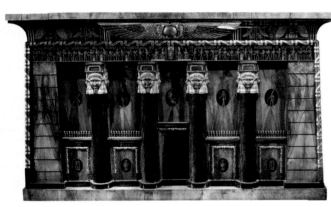

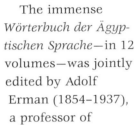

It was estimated to take 14 years, but in fact the final volume appeared over 50 years later.

The immense *Wörterbuch der Ägyptischen Sprache*—in 12 volumes—was jointly edited by Adolf Erman (1854–1937), a professor of Egyptology in Berlin, and his student Hermann Grapow (1885–1967). Because of his beautiful handwriting, Danish Egyptologist Wolja Erichsen (1890–1966) was employed to write out the five initial corpus volumes, comprising 2,786 pages. These were based on over one-and-a-half million paper slips of every word in every known text. Yet, the number of texts has almost doubled since work on the corpus stopped in 1947.

Since 1999 the slip-archive of the *Wörterbuch* has been available as a digital corpus. There is also a database listing words in alphabetical order. It is estimated there will be around five million words once the project is completed. This *Thesaurus Linguae Aegyptiae* was launched on the internet in 2004 to mark the one-hundred-and-fiftieth anniversary of Erman's birth.

The *Topographical Bibliography*

Bertha Porter (1852–1941), who had studied Egyptology in Oxford and Göttingen, spent over 25 years painstakingly collecting material. In 1924 she was joined in Oxford by Rosalind Moss

Above **Bookcase for a masterwork.** This ornate bookcase was built specifically to hold the 12-volume *Description de l'Égypte*, produced by the scholars who accompanied Napoleon on his Egyptian campaign of 1798–1799.

(1890–1990), where they established the *Topographical Bibliography of Ancient Egyptian Hieroglyphic Texts, Reliefs and Paintings.* The first volume, on the Theban necropolis, appeared in 1927, and the seventh in 1951, by which time revisions were needed. The meticulous volumes, covering the whole of Egypt and areas outside, are known universally as "*Porter and Moss*," "*PM*," "*Top. Bibl.*," or simply "*The Bibliography*."

In 1928, with Porter's retirement, Ethel Burney (1891–1984) started to work with Moss. The partnership was to last until the two retired as octogenarians in 1970. They were known as "The Two Ladies," after the tutelary goddesses of Upper and Lower Egypt. From their base at the Griffith Institute, Oxford, the two women would regularly sally forth on expeditions throughout Egypt and the Sudan, Europe and North America to track down material. There are legendary stories of The Two Ladies traveling at great speed in their old Morris Minor, and charmingly talking their way across closed European borders in order to view Egyptian objects housed in the vaults of Iron Curtain museums or the depths of Bavarian castles.

It is therefore fitting that a final volume of the *Topographical Bibliography*, which began appearing in 1999, records monuments of unknown provenance, including those in museums and private collections. This five-part volume is being brought to fruition by Doctor Jaromir Malek, their successor.

At the same time, a simplified version has been

made available on the internet, allowing regular updates and giving Egyptologists the chance to point out mistakes, omissions, or suggested additions.

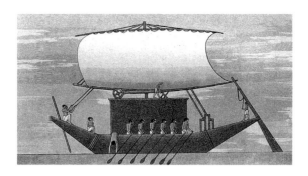

The *Annual Egyptological Bibliography*

The *Annual Egyptological Bibliography*, or *AEB*, was born in 1947 when a group of some twenty Egyptologists met at a conference in Copenhagen and founded the International Association of Egyptologists. The participants agreed that an annual bibliography, with titles and summaries, was urgently needed.

The Dutch Egyptologist Jozef Janssen (1907–1963) took on the task and almost single-handedly produced 16 volumes. During that time the number of entries for a given year had doubled, so that by the end he had summarized approximately 9,000 books and articles. In 1970 his successor handed the task to Jac Janssen of Leiden University, who has sometimes been mistaken for the son of Josef. Josef, however, had been a Catholic priest! Toward the end of the decade, the number of publications to be included began to grow at an unprecedented pace.

A project was initiated to construct a database to publish the revised contents of all previous volumes in digital form, resulting in a CD-ROM that appeared in 2001. Work is now apace to enhance the database in order to make the *AEB* accessible as an online bibliography. This will allow weekly updates of new entries and, eventually, direct input by authors themselves.

It is significant that each of these authoritative resources is ongoing today, thanks to modern computer technology. We are furthermore seeing the creation of a new interactive relationship between these great projects and their users, thereby taking Egyptology into the twenty-first century.

Left **Reliefs from Elkab (Elethia)**. This engraving was made in 1809, but it was not until over 120 years later that a comprehensive bibliography of such works was to appear.

Below **Cairo, 1839**. This evocative lithograph, by English artist David Roberts, presents a view of Cairo from the east, with the pyramids of Giza in the background.

Great Discoveries

In the hundred-year period from 1892 to 1989, some of the greatest of all Egyptological discoveries were made. Most of them were of course made in Egypt itself, but one was achieved simply by opening a book.

Fittingly, we start with the founding father of Egyptian archeology, Sir William Matthew Flinders Petrie (1853–1942), who, during his long career, made more major discoveries than any other excavator. His is a story of meticulous work and, in one case, heartbreaking frustration as he saw a precious site all but destroyed.

THE LUXOR CACHE

A turning point in the history of scientific excavation came in 1925 when Egypt changed its antiquities law, placing a ban on material from Tutankhamun's tomb or anywhere else leaving the country.

More than half a century later, during cleaning operations in the courtyard of the Luxor Temple in 1989, the Egyptian Antiquities Service made the surprise discovery of a cache of 24 exquisitely carved stone statues. All had been buried at the same time, perhaps by temple priests when Roman legions were present in the area sometime around 300 CE.

A spectacular redesigned gallery in the Luxor Museum houses 17 of the best statues. Each is in its own niche, forming a processional way leading to the masterpiece—a unique pink quartzite standing statue of Amenhotep III, wearing the double crown and represented as a cult statue on a sledge.

President Mubarak was present to witness the unearthing of the first five statues, while, later, the cache was fully published by Mohammed al-Saghir, then director of antiquities for the Luxor area. Egypt has now taken responsibility for its national treasures.

Below **Entrance to the temple at Luxor.** This engraving by English artist David Roberts was made almost one hundred and fifty years before the startling discovery of the statues in the temple courtyard.

Petrie's Pavement

In 1892 Petrie uncovered a large painted pavement from the North Harim at el-Amarna. He pronounced it to be "the most important discovery artistically that there has been since the Old Kingdom statues of Mariette." Its naturalistic designs comprised "tanks of fish, birds, and lotus; groups of calves, plants, birds, and insects; and a border of bouquets and dishes." There were also illustrations of bound captives—to be trodden underfoot by all who passed.

Petrie painstakingly covered the whole surface—250 square feet (20 square meters)—of the plaster with a coating of tapioca water, gently applied with his forefinger. He then single-handedly erected a walkway to allow visitors to view the paintings without damaging the surface.

For the next twenty years this masterpiece became a major tourist attraction for the Thomas Cook steamers. But the authorities never built a path to the exhibition shed through the surrounding fields, and one night the enraged owner of the trampled fields hacked the pavement to pieces with a hammer.

However, Petrie had recorded parts of the scenes in both color and black and white. Others could also describe the pavement, among them Petrie's 17-year-old assistant, of whom Petrie wrote, "it is of no use to me to work him up as an excavator." His name was Howard Carter.

"The Greatest Find"

On November 26, 1922, Howard Carter and his patron, the Earl of Carnarvon, had their first glimpse of the Aladdin's cave contents of Tutankhamun's tomb. The following evening Carnarvon wrote to the Egyptologist Alan Gardiner, saying, "I imagine it is the greatest find ever made." He was proved correct. The boy-king and his tomb caught the public's imagination, and "Tutmania" has continued thanks to traveling exhibitions of his treasures.

While the untimely death of Lord Carnarvon just six weeks after the tomb's discovery fueled rumors of "The Curse," it has been suggested

A second visit saw a search of bookshelves by the library fireplace. Edwards relates in his memoirs how, "Finally we reached the bottom shelf, where there were large folio volumes...We worked along the shelf until we had reached the third book from the end. It was either an eighteenth or an early nineteenth century atlas of Athens. On opening it we could see the papyri...[which] may well have been concealed in that atlas for nearly 150 years."

In 1982 Edwards finally published the papyri, which are now in the British Museum. They turned out to have nothing to do with tomb robberies. Such are the vagaries of an excavation.

Left **Howard Carter in Tut's tomb**. Carter (holding the crowbar) unseals the doorway to the sepulchral chamber. He is accompanied by Arthur Mace of the Metropolitan Museum.

Below **Tutankhamun's golden mask**. This spectacular mask was beaten from thick gold plate, and the details were created in inlaid glass and decorative stones such as lapis lazuli.

that the real Curse of the Pharaohs is that Carter, who died exhausted and disillusioned in 1939, did not live long enough to complete his definitive publication of the tomb.

In 2004 the archival material, housed in the Griffith Institute, Oxford, was made available online in order to "help bring the knowledge and love of Ancient Egypt to everyone." It includes Carter's meticulous diaries, the superb photographs taken by Harry Burton, and every one of the 5,398 finds.

Excavating in a Library

Not all great discoveries take place in the sands of Egypt. Many others are the result of excavations in museum basements and suchlike, as the following example illustrates.

When the British traveler William John Bankes was in Egypt from 1815 to 1819 he assembled a collection of antiquities, now displayed at his stately home, Kingston Lacy in Dorset.

Included among them were reputedly two tomb robbery papyri, for which Rosalind Moss searched in vain. Liddon Edwards (1909–1996) of the British Museum continued the hunt in 1952. Remembering that some famous missing papyri had recently been located in the late Professor Maspero's books in the Sorbonne, it occurred to him that Bankes might have put his papyri between the pages of a volume.

Approaching the Past

We here consider three ways in which both the general public and dedicated students of Egyptology can approach the past. In so doing we also discover how one can become an Egyptologist.

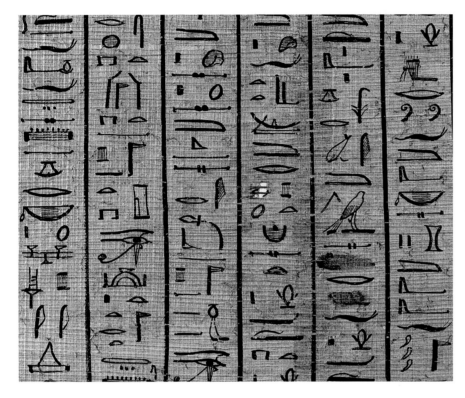

Above **Papyrus, first century BCE**. This papyrus shows the use of cursive hieroglyphics, a later development on the more pictorial style. A familiarity with scripts of various types is useful in Egyptological study.

Egypt has been a source of popular fascination since Napoleon's campaign at the beginning of the nineteenth century. It has inspired novels and travel diaries, and put many enthusiasts on the path to a career in Egyptology.

Writing Novels

An American obituary of Amelia Edwards (1831–1892) referred to her as "The Queen of Egyptology." This extraordinary Englishwoman was a prolific Victorian romantic novelist. But she stopped writing fiction completely following her visit to Egypt in 1873–1874. So concerned was she with the neglect and vandalism of the monuments that she began to write popular articles urging scientific excavation instead. Her best known book, *A Thousand Miles up the Nile* (1877), recounts her voyage.

As one of the co-founders of the Egypt Exploration Fund, by terms of her will, she

Right **Greek inscription found on Egyptian remains**. A knowledge of Greek is also invaluable to the study of ancient Egyptian life.

established The Edwards Professorship of Egyptian Archeology and Philology in 1882 at University College London. Her protégé, Flinders Petrie, became her first Edwards Professor, holding the first such chair at any British university for 40 years.

There had long been Egyptology chairs at German universities such as that held at Leipzig by Georg Ebers (1837–1898). Ebers wrote a series of popular historical novels with ancient Egyptian themes. The most famous was *An Egyptian Princess* (1864), translated into 16 languages and selling more than 400,000 copies by 1928. Its heroine is a Princess Diana figure: "Royal purple added to her beauty, the high flashing tiara made her slender, perfect figure seem taller than it really was."

We come full circle with the "Queen of Egyptological Fiction," a designation given to Barbara Mertz, a one-time doctoral student at Chicago's famous Oriental Institute. Writing under the pen-name Elizabeth Peters, she is the author of, among others, the *Amelia Peabody* series. Some famous Egyptologists of the time, such as Petrie, crop up in the novels.

Learning Egyptian

In 1894, aged just 15 and his first article already under his belt, Alan Gardiner (1879–1963) was kindly received by the real Professor Petrie when he became one of the first students to attend Egyptian language classes. The following year saw him in Paris, learning French and attending Maspero's courses. He spent the next year being tutored in Latin and Greek in preparation for Oxford. Leaving Oxford with a first in his finals in Hebrew and Arabic, he learned German at a parsonage in the Rhineland.

Visiting Egypt for the first time in 1901 on his honeymoon, Gardiner left his bride in Luxor while he went to Middle Egypt for three days to copy inscriptions. From 1902 to 1912 the couple

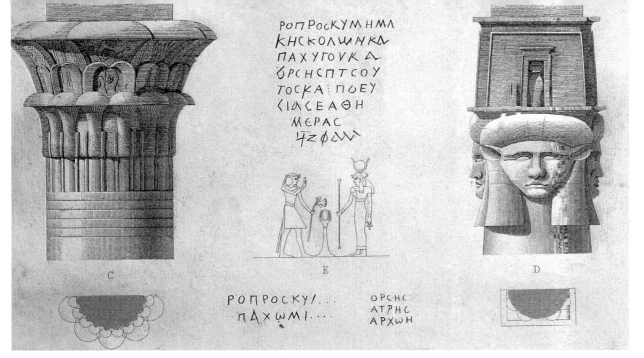

ΡΟΠΡΟϹΚΥΜΗΜΛ
ΚΗϹΚΟΛϢΗΚΛ
ΠΑΧΥΓΟΥΚΛ
ΌΡϹΗϹΠΤϹΟΥ
ΤΟϹΚΑ:ΠΟΕΥ
ϹΙΛϹΕΑΘΗ
ΜΕΡΑϹ

C   E   D

ΡΟΠΡΟϹΚΥ/...   ΟΡϹΗϹ
ΠΛΧϢΜΙ....   ΑΤΡΗϹ
             ΑΡΧϢΗ

Left **Greek and Egyptian side by side.** This elegant nineteenth-century engraving shows Egyptian capitals (tops of columns) with accompanyng Greek inscriptions.

Below **Excavation of the tomb of Tutankhamun in 1923.** Largely undisturbed by robbers over the centuries, this tomb was to yield some of the best-preserved Egyptian treasures ever found, and spur renewed public interest in Egypt.

resided in Berlin, where he worked as part of Erman's team on the great *Wörterbuch*.

Thus Gardiner set out to become the foremost philologist of his generation. Thanks to his financial independence, he could devote all his time to Egyptology. Indeed, he only lectured for two years, giving it up because the journeys to Manchester took too much of his time.

However, he contributed an immense legacy to students of the subject. This was his famous *Egyptian Grammar*, published in 1972, which put the teaching of Middle Egyptian on an entirely new basis, and is still the most influential book on the subject. It is divided into 33 lessons, each ending with a set of exercises for translating Egyptian sentences into English and vice versa. A list of hieroglyphic signs follows, now universally referred to as "Gardiner's Sign List."

The large tome was heavily subsidized—Gardiner's father funded the cost of the hieroglyphic fount. It went into three editions, and second-hand copies were hard to come by. Gardiner had a simple explanation: "Visiting a friend's family he was surprised to find his *Grammar* there. He was told that the book was nicely bound and looked well on the piano."

Becoming an Egyptologist

What words of advice are offered to potential Egyptologists today? The website of the Theban Mapping Project has a page devoted to the general requirements for a career in Egyptology, followed by a list of links to relevant universities around the globe. The need to learn French, German, and Arabic is stressed, plus "Greek or another Near Eastern language." (Gardiner had indeed prepared himself very thoroughly.) Advice is given to the potential archeologist in

Egypt to "consider learning surveying, photography, or drawing" in order to "increase your marketability."

As we are about to see, these are exactly the skills—with the addition of conservation—that are needed in order to contribute to the rescuing of Egyptian monuments today.

Rescuing the Past

Visiting Luxor in 1894, James Henry Breasted was shocked at the damage that had occurred since Napoleon's time. Using Luxor as a case study, we here highlight the attempts of Breasted and others to rescue the Theban monuments and remains.

Right Temple at Philae, 1840s. Missing stones and broken pillars in this finely detailed engraving, by German Egyptologist Karl Richard Lepsius, are evidence of a decay that would only get worse as time proceeded.

Breasted (1865–1935), an American Egyptologist, was in fact on his honeymoon, yet despite this he relates that: "For three days, from dawn till dark, I never lost a moment copying inscriptions—and on one night at Karnak I copied by moonlight." A subsequent visit to Egypt years later, in 1920, made him even more aware of "the dire need of epigraphic work to save from destruction the fast-perishing written records."

Recording Inscriptions

By the time of his second visit, Breasted was 15 years at his post as Professor of Egyptology and Oriental History at the University of Chicago, the first such American chair. In 1924, as first director of the University's Oriental Institute, his dream became a reality. Thanks to financial support from John D. Rockefeller, Jnr., Breasted founded the Epigraphic Survey in Luxor, known worldwide as Chicago House.

Breasted's mission was the rescue of the past by non-destructive means: Documentation so precise that it can stand as a replacement should the original monument be destroyed. The process of recording involves tracing from photographs and reconstructing on paper. Using the skills of photographers, artists, and Egyptologists (epigraphers), it has become known as "the Chicago House Method." Volume after volume of drawings of the inscriptions and reliefs on the Theban monuments stand as testimony to these unrivalled standards in recording techniques.

Conserving the Stones

We have already talked of Petrie at el-Amarna, his forefinger dipped in tapioca water to treat his newly dis-

Below Mummy with enbalming equipment. Pots, knives, potions, and oils were used in ancient Egyptian times to preserve the dead. Today the challenge is to preserve Egyptian treasures from decaying, and to accurately document them as well.

covered paintings. We ended with his pavements wantonly and irretrievably smashed. What can be done a century later in such situations?

The weathering noted by Breasted has increased dramatically, the steady rise of salt-laden groundwater being a major problem. The Epigraphic Survey therefore began a consolidation program at the Luxor Temple in 1995, aiming at on-site conservation and protection of 2,000 sandstone wall fragments, some of which had disintegrated into piles of yellow sand.

The blocks were firstly placed on special platforms to isolate them from the wet ground. The conservator then singled out stones for treatment and preventive conservation, using a consolidant (Wacker OH) drip-fed into the deteriorating surface of the stone. The application is as time-consuming a method as Petrie's tapioca water, although easier on the skin.

EXAMINING MUMMIES

The three examinations carried out on Tutankhamun's mummy, over a period of 80 years, demonstrate the progression in scientific studies on human remains, thanks to the development of non-invasive techniques. Each took place within the confines of the Valley of the Kings.

In 1925 an autopsy on the mummy was carried out by Douglas Derry, professor of anatomy at Cairo University. The autopsy involved the systematic unwrapping of the body. The boy-king was so poorly preserved that the mummy disintegrated and had to be reassembled on a tray. Carter was greatly disappointed that Derry was unable to offer a suggestion as to the possible cause of Tutankhamun's death.

In 1968 portable X-ray equipment was used by a team of anatomists, led by Professor Ronald Harrison from the University of Liverpool. The X-rays of Tutankhamun's vertebrae proved that he had not died of tuberculosis, as had been speculated. Moreover, the presence of two small fragments of bone within the skull led to the idea that the king was murdered.

Then in 2005 an Egyptian team, led by Professor Zahi Hawass, secretary general of the Supreme Council of Antiquities, used portable scanning equipment. This computed topography scanning—in all 1,700 scans were taken—shows a three-dimensional image. It now seems that Tutankhamun may have died after a leg fracture, rather than a blow to the head.

Taking another approach to a similar problem, Polish archeologists at the Temple of Tuthmosis III at Deir el-Bahri have found a way to restore thousands of painted limestone reliefs smashed into fragments. They devised a method of reassembling whereby the fragments are fitted onto a construction of stainless steel and the missing background reconstructed graphically.

Mapping the Past

The first systematic recording of the Theban necropolis was undertaken by Alan Gardiner and Arthur Weigall (1880–1934). Their *Topographical Catalogue of the Private Tombs at Thebes*, published in 1913, lists 252 tombs, their positions, names and titles of the owners, date, and conservation.

In 1979 the Theban Mapping Project (TMP) was established in order to prepare a detailed archeological map and database of the Theban necropolis, a designated World Monument Site. In 1987 the TMP rediscovered the largest tomb ever found in Egypt. Now known to be the burial place of the sons of Rameses II, this had been designated as "KV 5" by John Gardner Wilkinson in 1827, and at the last count has an amazing total of over 125 chambers and corridors.

Working under the directorship of Professor Kent Weeks of the American University in Cairo, the project is currently preparing master plans for site management in the Valley of the Kings, and at the many West Bank memorial temples. Field surveys are conducted using the latest scientific techniques: Extensive underground geophysical surveys, and aerial photography from satellites and balloons.

Rising ground water and flooding, expanding villages and fields, vandalism and mass tourism all present dire threats. A single rainstorm can age a monument centuries in a few hours. Never has the rediscovery of ancient Egypt been so urgent.

Below **Tutankhamun before the god Osiris.** The king, dressed as a priest and wearing a blue crown, is holding the *pesesh-kef*, a ceremonial knife. This image is painted on limestone in a tomb in the Valley of the Kings.

Chronology

The further back we go in Egyptian history the less precise we can be about dating. As a consequence you may encounter a range of dates in other works. We can be almost certain of the accuracy of the dates of the "Late" and subsequent periods; in the New Kingdom the margin of error is probably about ten years; in the Old Kingdom, about fifty; and before the Old Kingdom it could be up to 150 years—hence the use of c. (= "*circa*," "about") in this chronology.

A third-century BCE Heliopolitan priest, Manetho, is responsible for the dynasty divisions as we know them today, from Dynasty 1 to Dynasty 30. The ancient Egyptians themselves believed that all record-keeping was the work of the goddess Seshat. Seshat had a sacred tree at Heliopolis where "she" wrote down the names, reigns, and deeds of the rulers; as a priest Manetho had access to these sacred records, which were denied to the general public.

Manetho's works on Egyptian history and religion were intended as a refutation of Herodotus' accounts and were thus aimed at educating foreigners about Egypt. His writings, therefore, would be extremely useful in reducing the margin of era for the dynastic periods. Unfortunately, we only know his writings from fragmentary and frequently distorted quotations. Furthermore, many accounts of the early dynasties are dated by events and achievements of the pharaoh rather than years of his reign. This, in part, accounts for the imprecision of early dynastic chronology.

What we know from Manetho has been supplemented by other ancient king-lists, dated inscriptions, and astronomical records. These have helped keep the margin of error relatively low. Where the dates of dynasties overlap, particularly during the Intermediate periods, the dynasties were accepted in different regions. For the Predynastic Period the dates must be approximated from archeological evidence, in particular radiocarbon dating. This restriction of evidence is the reason for the vagueness of these dates. For the Late Dynastic Period onwards, precise dates can be taken from the Classical records.

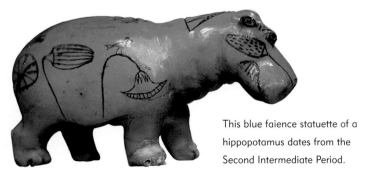

This blue faience statuette of a hippopotamus dates from the Second Intermediate Period.

Predynastic Period

Neolithic	c. 5300–4000 BCE (Lower Egypt)
Maadi Cultural Complex	c. 4000–3200 BCE (Lower Egypt)
Badarian Period	c. 4400–4000 BCE (Upper Egypt)
Naqada I	c. 4000–3500 BCE (Upper Egypt)
Naqada II	c. 3500–3200 BCE (Upper Egypt)
Naqada III/Dynasty 0	c. 3200–3000 BCE

Early Dynastic Period

Dynasty 1	c. 3000–2890 BCE
Dynasty 2	2890–2686 BCE

Old Kingdom

Dynasty 3	2686–2613 BCE
Dynasty 4	2613–2494 BCE
Dynasty 5	2494–2345 BCE
Dynasty 6	2345–2181 BCE
Dynasty 7 and 8	2181–2160 BCE

First Intermediate Period

Dynasty 9 and 10	2160–2025 BCE
Dynasty 11	2125–2055 BCE (Thebes only)

Middle Kingdom

Dynasty 11	2055–1985 BCE (all Egypt)
Dynasty 12	1985–1773 BCE
Dynasty 13	1773–after 1650 BCE
Dynasty 14	1773–1650 BCE

Second Intermediate Period

Dynasty 15	1650–1550 BCE
Dynasty 16	1650–1580 BCE
Dynasty 17	c. 1580–1550 BCE

New Kingdom

Dynasty 18	1550–1295 BCE

Ramessid Period

Dynasty 19	1295–1186 BCE
Dynasty 20	1186–1069 BCE

Third Intermediate Period

Dynasty 21	1069–945 BCE
Dynasty 22	945–715 BCE
Dynasty 23	818–715 BCE
Dynasty 24	727–715 BCE
Dynasty 25	747–656 BCE

Late Period

Dynasty 26	664–525 BCE
Dynasty 27 (= First Persian Period)	525–404 BCE
Dynasty 28	404–399 BCE
Dynasty 29	399–380 BCE
Dynasty 30	380–343 BCE
Second Persian Period	343–332 BCE

Ptolemaic Period

Macedonian Dynasty	332–305 BCE
Ptolemaic Dynasty	305–30 BCE

Roman Period	30 BCE–394 CE
Coptic/Christian Period	394–642 CE
Arab conquest of Egypt	642 CE

Index

Page numbers in plain text indicate references in text. *Italicized* numbers indicate references in image captions or maps. **Bold** numbers indicate references in break-out boxes.

Credits

Global Book Publishing would like to thank Gordon Cheers and Margaret Olds for their invaluable contribution to the production of this title.

The Publisher would like to thank the following photo libraries and other copyright owners for permission to reproduce their images. Every attempt has been made to obtain permission for use of all images from the copyright holder, however, if errors or omissions have occurred Global Book Publishing would be pleased to hear from copyright owners.

The publishers would especially like to thank Picture Desk for their assistance in sourcing images for this book.

Key: (t) top of page, (b) bottom of page, (c) center of page, (l) left side of page, (r) right side of page

The Art Archive: 115 b, 140 t, 368–369, 418 b, 435, 463 t, 475, 477 b

The Art Archive / Abbey of Novacella or Neustift / Dagli Orti: 124, 448 t

The Art Archive / Abbey of Saint Peter Salzburg / Dagli Orti: 480 l

The Art Archive / Archaeological Museum Djemila Algeria / Dagli Orti: 442 t

The Art Archive / Archaeological Museum Florence / Dagli Orti: 189 b, 295 t, 352 c, 473 t

The Art Archive / Archaeological Museum Naples / Dagli Orti: 150 t, 191 b, 411 t, 424 t

The Art Archive / Archaeological Museum Palermo / Dagli Orti: 425

The Art Archive / Archaeological Museum Spalato / Dagli Orti (A): 446

The Art Archive / Archaeological Museum Teheran / Dagli Orti: 422 b

The Art Archive / Archaeological Museum Venice / Dagli Orti (A): 426 b

The Art Archive / Ashmolean Museum Oxford: 51 b

The Art Archive / Biblioteca Nazionale Marciana Venice / Dagli Orti: 471 cr, 471 t

The Art Archive / Bibliothèque des Arts Décoratifs Paris / Dagli Orti: 63 t, 106, 118 b, 127 t, 128 t, 129 t, 129 t, 131 t, 248 t, 248–249, 257 t, 272 t, 277 t, 288–289, 314, 321 t, 332 t, 363, 376, 372, 428 b, 467 t, 468, 470–471, 474 t, 476, 478 t, 484 b, 485 t

The Art Archive / Bibliothèque Municipale Valenciennes / Dagli Orti: 367 b, 380-381, 478 b, 481 t, 482

The Art Archive / Bodleian Library Oxford: 419 t

The Art Archive / British Library: 374 t

The Art Archive / British Museum: 118 t, 261 t, 428 t

The Art Archive / British Museum / Dagli Orti: 91 t, 255, 358 b, 400

The Art Archive / British Museum / Jacqueline Hyde: 290 t, 324, 368 t

The Art Archive / Chateau de Compiegne / Dagli Orti: 479 b

The Art Archive / Collection Antonovich / Dagli Orti: 258 b, 258 t, 373 b, 416 cl, 424 b

The Art Archive / Coptic Museum Cairo / Dagli Orti: 444 b, 451 b, 454 b, 455, 458 t

The Art Archive / Culver Pictures: 125 t, 141, 343 t, 464 t, 479 t, 483 t

The Art Archive / Dagli Orti: 13, 18, 19 b, 24 b, 27 t, 32 b, 70-71, 73 t, 75 b, 80 b, 81 b, 84 t, 86 bl, 87 b, 88–89, 93 t, 97 t, 98, 99 t, 100 t, 101, 102–103, 104, 105 b, 107 b, 108 t, 110-111, 111 b, 111 t, 112, 113, 114, 115 t, 117 t, 120-121, 121, 125 t, 126 t, 128 t, 130 b, 132 t, 136 b, 137, 138, 139 t, 140 b, 142-143, 143, 147 b, 148 t, 148–149, 149 t, 151, 153 b, 154, 155 b, 155 t, 156, 157 t,

157 b, 158 b, 159, 160, 161 b, 161 t, 162 b, 164, 165 b, 165 t, 171 t, 173 b, 173 t, 174 tr, 176 b, 177, 178-179, 179 b, 183 b, 184–185, 185 b, 185 t, 190, 191 t, 212, 215, 219, 218 b, 221 t, 222–223, 223 b, 230–231, 237 t, 238, 241 t, 256, 262 t, 266, 271 t, 275 t, 280 b, 282–283, 283 t, 284 b, 285 t, 286 b, 286 t, 287 t, 288 t, 290 t, 292 t, 293 t, 295 t, 297 b, 298 t, 299 b, 299 t, 300 b, 301 b, 301 t, 302 b, 304 b, 305 t, 307 b, 307 t, 309 t, 310 t, 311, 315 t, 318 b, 319 b, 320 t, 323 t, 325 t, 326 bl, 327 t, 327 b, 330 t, 332 b, 335 b, 335 t, 342 t, 342 t, 345 t, 345 b, 349, 350 b, 351, 352 b, 353, 354 b, 357 b, 357 t, 360, 362 t, 365 cr, 366–367, 369 t, 370 t, 371 b, 371 t, 377 b, 377 t, 378 b, 380 cl, 380 t, 382 b, 383, 384 b, 385 t, 386 b, 387 b, 387 t, 388 cl, 388–389, 389 t, 395 t, 396, 405 t, 407, 408, 416 br, 417, 421 t, 426–427, 427 b, 431 b, 442 b, 448 b, 449, 456, 458 b, 460-461, 485 b, 487, cover back flap

The Art Archive / Devizes Museum / Eileen Tweedy: 354 t

The Art Archive / Diplomatic Club Cairo / Dagli Orti: 466

The Art Archive / Duomo di San Gimignano / Dagli Orti: 374–375

The Art Archive / Egyptian Museum Cairo / Dagli Orti: 7 t, 7 c, 8-9, 16 b, 19 t, 24 t, 28 l, 35 b, 37 b, 37 b, 43 t, 50, 52 t, 57 b, 67, 68 b, 74, 75 t, 76 t, 85, 89 t, 89 b, 90, 96, 99 b, 100 b, 102 b, 103 b, 120 t, 120–121, 122, 123, 129 b, 135 t, 136 t, 142 t, 146, 152 b, 152 t, 153 t, 162 t, 163, 166, 168 b, 169, 172, 174 l, 175, 183 t, 186 b, 187, 207 t, 209, 210, 211 b, 213, 214 t, 216, 218 t, 220, 221 b, 222 t, 226, 227 t, 227 b, 228, 231 t, 234, 246, 245 b, 253 b, 253 t, 254 b, 257 b, 265 t, 271 b, 272 b, 273, 278, 279 t, 281 t, 289, 292-293, 297 t, 308–309, 312 t, 313 t, 320–321, 322 t, 325 b, 328 t, 331, 333 t, 333 b, 334 b, 334 t, 338 c, 340 t, 341, 344, 346 t, 346 b, 347 t,

348 b, 348 t, 355 t, 364–365, 364 t, 366 b, 378, 379, 388 t, 394, 397 b, 397 t, 398, 399 b, 412 tl, 439 b, 464 t, 467 b, 469 b, 477 t, 480–481

The Art Archive / Egyptian Museum Cairo / Dagli Orti (A)

The Art Archive / Egyptian Museum Turin / Dagli Orti: 5, 10-11, 16 t, 17 b, 27 b, 31 t, 41 t, 46 b, 46 t, 47, 77, 79 b, 92 t, 117 b, 119 b, 130 t, 145 b, 176 t, 180 b, 203 b, 202, 217 t, 224, 225 t, 233 b, 235 b, 236, 237 l, 240, 241 b, 243 t, 252–253, 267 b, 280 t, 282 l, 287 b, 288 c, 296 t, 306, 308 bl, 312 b, 313 b, 316 t, 316–317, 322 b, 323 b, 384 t, 441, 463 b

The Art Archive / Eileen Tweedy: 465 b

The Art Archive / Ferens Art Gallery Hull / Dagli Orti: 432

The Art Archive / Fine Art Museum Bilbao / Dagli Orti (A): 437

The Art Archive / Galleria degli Uffizi Florence / Dagli Orti: 452

The Art Archive / Geographical Society Paris / Dagli Orti: 146

The Art Archive / Hellenic Institute Venice / Dagli Orti: 410

The Art Archive / Heraklion Museum / Dagli Orti: 279 b

The Art Archive / Jacqueline Hyde: 81 t

The Art Archive / Jan Vinchon Numismatist Paris / Dagli Orti (A): 416 t, 440 t

The Art Archive / Khawam Collection Paris / Dagli Orti: 21 b, 97 b

The Art Archive / Luxor Museum, Egypt / Dagli Orti: 6 bl, 22 t, 194 t, 211 t, 215, 260, 264 t, 298 b, 302 c, 303, 318 t, 319 t, 330 b, 336, 350 t, 375 t, 401 b

The Art Archive / Marc Charmet: 139 b

The Art Archive / Mechitarista Congregation Venice / Dagli Orti (A): 409 b

The Art Archive / Musée Champollion Figeac / Dagli Orti: 6 c